The Prevention Method for Better Health

The Prevention Method for Better Health

BY

J. I. Rodale

AND STAFF

RODALE BOOKS, INC.

EMMAUS, PENNA. 18049

STANDARD BOOK NUMBER 87596-015-4

COPYRIGHT MCMLX BY J. I. RODALE

ALL RIGHTS RESERVED

PRINTED IN THE UNITED STATES

TENTH PRINTING—AUGUST, 1972

H-356

FOREWORD

PREVENTION is not a magazine in the ordinary sense of the word. Rather, it is a system, and to get the best results with it, it is best to follow it as a complete system, with only minor modifications due to personal allergies. We are still in search of new ideas that will be the means of improving the system, and every year our explorations in medical literature reward us with a few important discoveries that add value to it.

As you read this book, you will find some prohibitions, for there are many things in modern life that we have found to be harmful. We counsel you here to beware of them. Many things you have been doing for years may be censured here, and you may feel that it is hopeless to try to regulate your life without these things. But our recommendations will convince you, we hope, for we have tried in every instance to assemble a quantity of trustworthy scientific information to back them up.

The positive aspects of the *Prevention System* are many, too. We suggest what to substitute for the unhealthful things. We believe that, following this system, even the most inexperienced person can work out a diet and way of life that will not only prolong his years on earth, but will make them happy, satisfying, full years, untroubled, or practically untroubled, by disease and the minor symptoms of ill health—colds, headaches, bad temper, fatigue, depression and many more.

We invite you to join the hundreds of thousands of *Prevention* readers who follow our system. Some of them don't see eye-to-eye with us on everything. And these folks get along very well—far better than the average person who takes no interest at all in health.

But we believe that, for best results, you should try the full system, as it is presented here, for a few months at least. Notice the improvement in the way you feel. If, for practical reasons, there are parts of the program that you simply can't work out in your daily life, then follow at least as much of the program as you can.

A glance through this book may make you feel that there are a lot of things to do and to remember. All these can be worked out on a gradual basis. You cannot, of course, be expected to give up all the harmful things by tomorrow morning. Try omitting one at a time, and get accustomed to doing without one for a few weeks before you eliminate the next health-hazard.

In the same way, introduce healthful items gradually. Don't negate the new resolutions you and your family have taken, by serving nothing but unfamiliar food, beginning tomorrow morning. Introduce new foods gradually. As a sample, your family may be inordinately fond of cold, prepared breakfast cereals. We believe that these are foods no health-conscious person should eat. Begin by making servings smaller and adding a bit of wheat germ to every serving. Gradually increase the wheat germ and decrease the cold cereal until, at last, your family is eating no cereal but wheat germ. And loving it!

As far as foods are concerned, the Editor of *Prevention* has worked out a simple rule. He doesn't eat foods that are made or processed in a factory. This means no bread, cereals, milk, ice cream, sugar, canned goods, packaged goods and so forth. What does this leave? Meat, fish, eggs, fruit, nuts, seeds and vegetables. The one exception he makes is vitamin and mineral supplements. They are made and processed in factories. But you will see, in this book, that the supplements recommended by the *Prevention* System are indeed wholly natural substances, quite different from synthetic vitamin capsules.

The Editor of *Prevention* takes the following at each meal:

> Bone meal
>
> Lecithin
>
> Rutin
>
> Kelp
>
> Sunflower seeds
>
> Vitamins A and D—*halibut liver capsules*
>
> Vitamin B—*wheat germ oil capsules and wheat germ flakes, desiccated liver*
>
> Vitamin C—*Rose hips*
>
> Vitamin E—*mixed tocopherols*

J. I. Rodale, *Editor*

Ruth Adams ⎫
Charles Gerras ⎬ *Assistant Editors*
John Haberern ⎭

CONTENTS

1

SECTION 3: Drugs, Household Preparations, X-rays, Cosmetics

SECTION 4: White Sugar

SECTION 5: Bread

3

SECTION 9: Milk

SECTION 10: Fruits, Nuts and Vegetables

SECTION 11: Sunflower Seeds and Pumpkin Seeds

7

SECTION 28: The Flavonoids   PAGE

12

SECTION 1

CHEMICALLY FERTILIZED AND SPRAYED FOODS

As far as possible, make an attempt either to raise your own food organically, which means without chemical fertilizers or poison sprays, or to buy such food from advertisers in our magazine Organic Gardening and Farming. *In the organic method, compost fertilizers are used made of manure, grass clippings, weeds and other plant and animal residues. A small garden will be enough to raise all the vegetables for the average family.*

Foods raised with chemical fertilizers have fewer vitamins and minerals, as well as dangerous amounts of poisonous insecticide residues which are harmful to the health. But if you have to eat commercially produced food, our system of taking vitamins and food supplements will protect you.

CHAPTER 1

What Does Organic Mean?

by J. I. RODALE

What does the word "organic" mean as we organicultur-ists use it? What is the organic method? We shall try to explain it, as illustrated by an inspired statement once made by the great composer, Richard Wagner. He said, "Man will never be that which he can and should be until, by a conscious follow-ing of that inner natural necessity which is the only true neces-sity, he makes his life a mirror of nature and frees himself from his thraldom to outer artificial counterfeits. Then will he first become a living man, who now is a mere wheel in the mechanism of this or that Religion, Nationality, or State."

Past Blueprint Applies to Present

This was said a long time ago, but applies just as truly today. In fact, could anything more to the point have been said, as far as the organic method is concerned? Wagner has given us a veritable blueprint—a strong, simple guide that says everything that needs be said, in deciding what a good organic gardener or farmer ought to be. When he speaks of "that inner natural necessity," it is comparable to the fervor of an organi-culturist which is almost akin to fanaticism, but never quite reaching that stage.

The genuine organiculturist is not merely an organic gardener or farmer; he lives his whole life in the organic man-ner. The organic principles must be felt deep in one's heart, and in everything one does.

Follow the Golden-Rule

It is not organic to grow a carrot organically, and to always eat it in the cooked form, or cooked with the addition of white sugar. It is not organic to produce milk organically, and then to pasteurize it. What good would it be if a man eats a dinner grown completely by the organic method, and then arises from the table and does a cruel unkindness to a neighbor? The organic way is the golden-rule way. It means that we must be kind to the soil, to ourselves, and to our fellowman. Organic means goodness. A heart that is full of benevolence will create in the body a spirit of physical and mental well-being that will enable it to better absorb all the nutritional elements from organically grown food.

Make Each Life a Mirror of Nature

. . . Wagner said that man will never be that which he can and should be until, by a conscious following of that inner natural necessity, he makes his life a mirror of nature. He should follow the ways of nature not only in growing his plants, but in his entire way of life. In nature there is no sitting at desks. Everything is movement. Even the stalk of wheat sways in the breeze, the leaf flutters, the birds fly. Nature means movement. And so it should be with man. He should move about as much as possible—walk, hike, play, exercise. And in gardening, he finds a beneficial kind of movement which gives robust health to his glands and larger organs. Unless we conceive the organic way as being a complete organic whole, we are not truly organic.

Look to Nature for Guidance

Man must observe the animals in the field, the birds in the sky and see how they eat. They seem to be guided by a native intelligence. They have set rules in regard to their nutriment, and will not swerve from them. The horse will not eat meat. The lion will not touch green herbs or plants. The animals have evolved methods which shield them from sickness. The squirrel will bury nuts in the ground to tide it over the winter months, but it does not chemically preserve or adulterate them. The ant punctures every seed of grain it will bury so that it will not take root and grow. But man—what methods does he follow? He blows wherever the wind blows. He eats anything that is put before him. Man—misguided man, ruler over the animals, does not know what is the right thing to eat.

Man should observe a primitive simplicity in his daily regimen of food. He should eat to live—not live to eat. And he should grow his food in nature's manner, using the decayed leaf and weed, and the decomposed animal's ordure as the source of the compost which is its nutriment.

He should know that nature feeds the roots from the lower strata as well as from above; that the fine particles, representing the disintegration of the rock that underlays most soils, are brought up by the earthworms and thousands of other soil organisms, and are partaken of by the roots of plants. These fine rock particles are a nutritious mineral food that is natural and healthy for plant life. Bread and roses, thus, can come from stone. Man also can feed the soil by fine particles of rock that he may apply to the soil. There are available for such purpose rocks like basalt, lime, dolomite, phosphate, granite and others.

Man Should Preserve Nature's Balance

Man should preserve nature's balance in the way she rules her insect and animal world. Nature has predators to destroy the injurious insects, but in maintaining order she does not destroy the regulator along with the ones that are destructive to plants. Man should do likewise. He should devise methods that destroy the one while they preserve the other.

. . . According to Wagner, man should free himself from his thraldom to outer artificial counterfeits. Chemical fertilizers are a base counterfeit of the natural composts and mineral-bearing rocks which are nature's type of plant sustenance. They give the plant bulk at the expense of vitamins and minerals. They bring disease and destroy strength and health. They require the application of poisonous sprays to reduce the destructive insects and pests. But these poisons are killing off our birds. They are causing the insect-destroying frog and toad to disappear. They are killing off the soil's true friend—the earthworm. And, as the years go on, the artificial way is becoming more and more artificial and deathly, but is being dangerously accepted by the public and the general scientist.

Foods Are Devitalized

We must also not overlook the fact that our foods, nurtured in the chemical medium of the fields, are further chemicalized and devitalized in the factories. More than 600 dangerous chemical additives are at the elbow of the food processor. With their aid, food is emulsified, synthesized, hydrolized, stabilized, pasteurized, tenderized, textured, artificially flavor ized and colorized, besides being bleached, conditioned and now radiated without due process of prolonged testing. What will be the ultimate effect on man?

To be a true disciple of the organic doctrine, one should not eat foods made in factories, but should limit oneself to meats, fish, eggs, fruit, vegetables and nuts. One should not drink water that has been chlorinated or fluoridated. Purchased spring water is cheaper in the long run. One should speak up to the grocer and butcher and demand food that is fit for the human stomach—food that is grown and processed properly. We should reject those spurious and artificial methods and devices by which our food is being produced, and we should do everything in our power, either to produce, or see that others produce, healthful food.

We Must Be Articulate

Wagner says that if we mirror nature, and free ourselves from the thraldom of outer artificial counterfeits, then will we become living men, and not mere wheels in the mechanism of our religions, our nations and our States. We must become active, articulate churchgoers and citizens. We must not sit in fear of the self-appointed authorities who are, dog-in-the-manger fashion, standing in the way of improvement of the world's conception of good nutrition. We must speak up to our ministers, to our teachers, congressmen, judges, businessmen, scientists and statesmen. We must be organic on the soil, in our homes, in our offices, on the streets, in our churches, in the schools, in the voting booths, and in the vegetable and meat markets. We must be vocally and actively organic. We must live it day and night, making no exceptions, tolerating no loopholes or subterfuges.

We must rule our lives with the God-given intelligence that has been bestowed upon us. We must honor and cherish that intelligence. We must not degrade it! This is part of the organic system.

CHAPTER 2

Systemic Sprays

by J. I. RODALE

One excellent example of the devastating nature of insecticides is the systemic spray, the subject of this chapter.

Something sinister is occurring in American agricultural practice, far worse, in my opinion, than the imagination of anything agronomical science has conceived thus far, and which should be a cause for great alarm. It concerns a new method of preventing insect infestation in plants by means of poisonous insecticides, and involves such a dangerous mode of action that I wonder if, adopting it, financially hungry industry isn't going a bit too far, or, are the men who guide these concerns sick in the conscience? Is it possible also that the ignorance of these men in matters of diet plus the fact that they are consuming devitalized and poisoned food as a result of the products sold by their very own companies, is causing their mental powers to decline so that they cannot clearly see the effect of what they are doing? An English scientific organization has recently made a study in their country and America and has found that the mental ability of people has been declining 2 per cent per generation. Is this fact related to the quality of food produced by modern industrialized agriculture and the food processors?

Poison Spraying Born

About 75 years ago the poison spraying of apple trees was practically an unknown procedure in orcharding. Some insects came to plague the apples, but nature provided enemy insects that kept the trouble-makers in check. But, as is always the case in nature, it was not a 100 per cent effective arrangement and some fruit damage occurred. The public was used to seeing and even eating an apple here and there that exhibited an insect bite or two. However, a trend was developing in American life which demanded perfection of appearance. It was part of the movement that gave America automobiles with beautiful chromium fittings. The public began to demand white eggs, thinking they were "purer," and willingly paid a premium for them. Apples had to be large and perfect, without an insect bite or other disfiguring blemish. The citrus interests began to add color to oranges and the dairy people put the cancer-causing butter-yellow into butter (now banned). Industry scandalously pandered to the consumer's taste for beauty and added eye-appeal to all items of food regardless of how it damaged their nutritional values. This tendency encouraged the chemical interests to play a big part in the beautification of food products.

Upsetting Nature's Applecart

As the years went on, the problems in the orchards became more perplexing. The chemist mastered one insect, and another appeared from nowhere. In one season Chemical X destroyed insect Y, but the next year insect Y developed a tolerance to poison X. This led to the perfection of more and more powerful chemical compounds, and the need for increasing the number of applications to about 15 or 16 a season, disturbing the balance of nature to such an extent, that even the bees that were needed by the orchardist to pollinate the apple blossoms disappeared, so that the farmer had to hire additional people to hand-pollinate his trees. And when this insecticidal bludgeoning with poison sprays got beyond the physical capability of the farmer to handle, he took to the air, and in 1951 the farmers of the United States used 6,500 airplanes to shower upon the earth these expensive chemical poisons.

A New Approach—Feeding Plants Poison

The entomologists—those people who spend their lives trying to prove that man is superior to the insect—are having a tough time. They are frantically attempting to breed varieties of fruits and vegetables that are more resistant to disease and insects. They are working feverishly to discover magic formulas that will stop the insect dead in its tracks. But for a long time they have had a dangerous idea in the back of their heads. Why not feed some kind of poison to the plant instead of to the insect, so that every cell and bit of tissue becomes saturated with it. Thus, when an insect feeds upon the plant, it will be done for. This would be science with a vengeance. They thought of it so long that they actually did it.

Early in 1952 such a product, called Systox, was launched with powerful hullabaloo in the ballroom of New York's Waldorf Astoria hotel, by the Pittsburgh Coke and Chemical Company. The product, made from coal, has the chemical name of "Octamethyl Pyrophosphoramide." This pesticide is either put on the soil around the roots or is sprayed on to the plant itself. In either case it forces itself into every cell of the entire plant. One can judge the potency of such a chemical which has the power of forcing itself so thoroughly and saturating every part of a plant.

Poison in Edible Crops

Several years ago this idea was discussed in agricultural literature, and it was announced that soon such a product would be placed on the market. When I was called as a witness, a few years ago, in a hearing in Washington, conducted by the Pure Food and Drug Administration for the purpose of determining permissible residues of poison sprays on foods, I expressed alarm at the possibility that such a practice would be encouraged on food crops, that the public would be eating foods, every cell of which was tainted by these systemic chemicals. Up jumped a representative of one of the insecticide companies and stated that it was not the intention that this product be used on food crops. It was only thought of for ornamental plants. But in my mind I harbored misgivings. It was a dangerous trend. I was sure that it was bound eventually to be used on edible crops. And that is exactly what is happening.

A Promise Not Likely to be Upset

Professor R. W. Leiby, entomologist of Cornell University, in the June, 1952, *Country Gentleman*, speaks of experiments with Systox on potatoes and apples, and states, "Much more experimentation must be made with the systemic insecticides, before they will be approved for use on fruits, vegetables, or crops fed to livestock." But, in the demonstration at the Waldorf Astoria, mentioned above, Systox was applied to a garden plot of widely assorted plants, including green beans and tomatoes. I feel certain that, unless some powerful consumers' group files an injunction against a few hundred farmers who begin to use systemic poisons on food crops, in a short time every mouthful of food eaten by the public will carry a quota of poison distributed in every cell of it.

Will Our Government Permit Race Suicide?

The United States Department of Agriculture, at the time Systox was announced, advised that the systemic types of insect poisons were definitely not for use on edible crops, although it did state that some day these might be recommended for such crops. If that day ever comes, it will be the most formidable blow ever struck against the public interest and the health of our citizenry. It will be the biggest step yet taken towards race suicide through the sterilization of the reproductive functions of man, by the irritating effect of these harmful systemic chemicals upon them.

The experts say that systemic insecticides do not remain long inside a plant and that if you wait a few weeks after fruit and vegetables have been treated, they will be safe to eat. But in the same breath they state that the systemic insecticides last 3 to 4 times longer than ordinary poisons. I have seen so many of these sales talk statements prove to be false that I do not trust this one. I do not think that all of this poison will be excreted by the plant, and if it does, what effect will it produce on the plant's tissues while it is tarrying in its midst? And who is going to fence in all the orchards and farms to keep innocent wayfarers from this deadly produce before the poison is excreted?

Systox Doesn't Harm Bees—But!

The company that makes Systox states that its investigations have shown that bees tapping the nectar of plants treated with this systemic poison were not affected by it. Perhaps they were not affected outwardly or immediately, but careful study might indicate that they are less healthy. They might become lethargic and produce less honey. And did the Pittsburgh Coke and Chemical Company check on the quality of the honey produced by these bees? Does it contain a residue of these poisons?

Farm Chemicals magazine in its June, 1952, issue says that Systox is approximately as toxic to mammals as Parathion, and brother, Parathion is extremely toxic, having in only a few years' time killed many orchardists who were applying it to their trees.

A newspaper states that Systox will save the nation's farmers millions of dollars worth of crops a year, but I might add, it might cause the people who eat Systox-treated foods, tens of millions of medical and hospital costs. Business is in the form of a monetary equation and we must not fail to study that formula in its every aspect, paying attention to both sides. The agricultural press widely acclaims this new product, mouthing the prepared statements of the manufacturer, to the effect that the product is not dangerous to human beings in the quantity present in harvested crops. But if it is added to all the food preservatives, all the germ killers, the benzoates of soda, the chlorine and alum in water, the sodium nitrite in frankfurters, the chemicals in bread and in every item of food on the daily menu, what then would be the total cumulative effect? The Pittsburgh Coke and Chemical Company, I am sure, has not made such a test.

The Public Must Fight

This is a situation that calls for immediate action. The public must speak out boldly and at once. We must write to congressmen, senators, newspapers, agricultural colleges and the Pure Food and Drug Administration, asking that an unqualified ban be placed on this type of insecticide, even for ornamental plants. I say again that our readers must take immediate action to protect the public. It must be brought up for discussion in public forums and at parent-teacher meetings. The public has an inalienable right to eat unpoisoned food, and industry must learn to make profits without infringing upon that right.

I am horror stricken as I observe the activities of these conscienceless chemical companies—truly organizations without souls, coldly proceeding with their devious money-multiplying devices, regardless of the effect it has upon people's health; I am shocked, and never have I been so shocked before. Chemical fertilizers are bad, but the chemical fertilizer companies do not ask you to eat them! But Systox and now Pestox and a hundred other competitors are chafing at the bit, in order to force their share of this new poison down the public's gullet.

I cannot emphasize this warning sufficiently—we are in the greatest danger we have ever been. It is worse than military war. The public must become aroused and act at once to prevent this disaster from overtaking us.

Of late we have been leading the world in finance and to a certain extent in science. Many countries look to us for inspiration in regard to innovations in technology and culture. If we begin to use these systemic poisons, many nations will undoubtedly blindly follow in our footsteps. Are we ready to accept the responsibility for the possible ruinous effects of such false leadership? We must be careful what we do, not only for our own sake, but for the sake of the effect it has on the rest of the world. We must cast out this idea before it takes strong root!

CHAPTER 3

Arsenic Is Poisoning You Every Day

One of the insecticides in earliest use, and still in use today, is arsenic. It contaminates just about everything you eat.

Arsenic lay at the bottom of what was almost an international incident in July, 1956. Ambassador Clare Boothe Luce, looking tired and ill, had left her post in Italy in 1954, to come back to America for the diagnosis of a mysterious illness that had plagued her since she undertook her residence in Rome. After several months in New York, her complaint, diagnosed as serious anemia and nervous fatigue, disappeared and she felt well enough to return to Rome and resume her duties.

In a short time the symptoms of nervousness, nausea and tiredness returned as strong as ever, and were complicated by falling hair, brittle fingernails and loosening teeth. A hunch on the part of a doctor at the United States Naval Hospital in Naples led to a laboratory test for arsenic, and the report was eventually returned which confirmed that the patient was indeed suffering from severe arsenic poisoning.

The urgency of the situation, from a diplomatic viewpoint, cannot be exaggerated. The report that an official representative of the United States was actually being poisoned at her post, in a foreign country which was presumed to be friendly, created quite an international stir. Foul play on the part of the Communists and spies was, of course, suspected, but the culprit was eventually discovered to be the lady's bedroom ceiling.

Particles of Arsenic Found in Her Coffee Cup

Mrs. Luce's daily habit was to awaken quite early and ring for coffee and the daily papers, reading them and having her coffee for about an hour before arising. During this hour, the ceiling above was shedding dust particles from its paint into her coffee cup. These particles were found to contain arsenic. The ceiling was repainted at once and the problem ceased to exist.

But notice the extreme consequences brought on by the small dose of arsenic that Mrs. Luce ingested. The particles were not raining down from the ceiling in a blizzard—or even a fine mist—of paint. The amount dropping into her coffee cup each morning was so minute as to be invisible and odorless, making no apparent change in the atmosphere of the room. There wasn't even any kind of hint in the taste of the coffee! Yet even this amount of arsenic could have been deadly.

This was rather a celebrated case of arsenic poisoning, but the danger of being affected by this deadly element is ever present in modern living. It is possible that we are slowly being poisoned with arsenic and don't know it. It is in just about every food we buy—fruit, vegetables, meat. It is in cigarettes, in the air of industrial cities and even in medications.

Arsenic Still Used As Medicine

Arsenic is familiar to most people as the tool of the murderer in many a detective story. Ever since the Middle Ages its efficiency as a killer has been known. As time went on the theory developed that, while a large amount of arsenic might kill, a much smaller amount might kill only diseased parts of the body, thus clearing the way for good health. So for many years arsenic was used to treat psoriasis, general ill health and anemia (the very thing it has been found to cause!).

The most persistent use of all has been in a medication for asthma known as Fowler's solution (potassium arsenate). As recently as March 7, 1953, the *Journal of the American Medical Association* carried a letter which told of two cases of arsenic poisoning—an 11-year-old boy and a 9-year-old girl. Both were asthmatic and had been taking Fowler's solution as part of their medication. Their mothers noticed the appearance of discolored blotches of skin on their arms, legs and chests, and were prompted by these early symptoms to have the children examined before serious consequences could develop.

Not so fortunate was a 41-year-old woman whose case was described in the same journal in an earlier number, October, 1952. This lady used Fowler's solution to control her asthma for three years. She developed the classic symptoms, including nausea, diarrhea, stomach cramps, skin blotches and an enlarged liver. The physician who wrote this case history noted that he did so as a warning to physicians who expose patients to low concentration sources of arsenic for prolonged periods.

We can see no reason to countenance its use as a medication even for the shortest of periods. T. Sollman in the *Manual of Pharmacology* sums up the intelligent attitude on the use of arsenic in this manner: "Inorganic arsenic is capricious, unpredictable and uncontrollable, both as to good and harm; but the harm is more certain and generally more frequent than the good."

Everyone Gets Arsenic in His Daily Diet

Though some of us might encounter arsenic as part of a medication, there are other areas in which we are far more likely to encounter it—food, for example. The use of arsenical insecticides in agriculture has turned the value of fresh fruits and vegetables into a calculated risk! Lead arsenate, for example, is widely used as a spray for fruits, such as apples, pears, cherries and grapes, and for such vegetables as celery and cabbage.

When this spray is applied, the plan is that it will remain on the fruit or vegetable throughout the season, in spite of rain, wind or any other natural laundering. It's logical, else the grower would be forced to repeat the spraying chore after each rain. Knowing the spray stays on the fruit a full season, in spite of all weather, how can the housewife imagine that a few passes of the fruits under the faucet in the kitchen sink will decontaminate the fruit her family eats? But she does—and she is unaware that the shiny apple or pear her child takes from his lunch box can be anything but good for him. The outer skin of fruit, once an excellent source of vitamins and minerals, has become a possible source of arsenic poisoning. Unless one can be sure of a source of unsprayed fruit, peeling the skin off it before eating is by far the safest procedure.

Where vegetables are concerned, the problem is even more frustrating. Boiling the vegetables might—we say might— remove the arsenic, but boiling removes many of the nutrients, too. Aside from this, tomatoes, celery, lettuce, cabbage, peppers and the like just don't lend themselves to cooking if the flavor is to be preserved.

Arsenic Absorbed Through the Roots of Plants

And finally, all the boiling, peeling and washing we can do may be a waste of effort, if the ground of the orchard, garden or field has become saturated with sprays, for then the arsenic is likely to be absorbed into the pulp of the fruit or vegetable through the roots. The only way to protect yourself in such cases is to avoid eating the food.

It is a fantastic and frightening thing to know that even foods that have high nutritive value can be dangerous, even poisonous. And this alarming fact is due to short-sighted farmers and scientists who are more interested in having a beautiful product than they are in having healthy customers who will buy and eat it. The wise consumer will try to find a source for unsprayed foods, and when he is uncertain he will peel whatever he can before eating. Aside from this, one can only defend one's self from unsuspected dangers, by getting a good supply of vitamin C daily, for this vitamin is active in repairing hurts to the system and the tissues. Sufficient B vitamins are needed too, for they are essential in defending the liver from infection.

Even Meats Contain Arsenic

As if to block every arsenic-free supply of food available to the consumer, the poultry farmer is infecting his stock with the stuff, too. *Farmers Digest* (August-September, 1957) reported that most poultry growers insist on feed rations containing arsenic, for this poison is thought to increase the rate of growth. Why it works—if it does—we don't know. Anyway, the FDA has set a tolerance limit on the amount of arsenic permissible in chickens. Further, they have forbidden the use of arsenical feed for 5 days before the poultry is butchered. How effective such prohibitions are is something else again. Has the government checked the chicken *you* are eating for maximum arsenic content? Has the farmer who raised *your* chicken been careful to feed the bird non-arsenical food for five days before butchering? Does he maintain two separate feed bins? What about the arsenic that has accumulated (and it definitely does accumulate) in the bird's system from all the arsenic feedings—who is to say that that won't bother you?

So, reading this, you resolve to avoid poultry and determine to eat other meats untouched by arsenic—lamb, maybe. The situation looks hopeless—*The Journal of Animal Science* (13:668-76, 1954) tells us that arsenical supplements are being added to lamb-fattening rations.

Cigarettes and Arsenic

Arsenic is in food dyes, in boric acid and in papers sometimes used to wrap foods. It's even in cigarettes. *Consumers' Research Bulletin* (April, 1957) says that the arsenic content of various brands of United States cigarettes has increased from 12.6 micrograms per cigarette in 1933 to 42 micrograms per cigarette in 1951. This increase is attributed to the increased use of arsenical pesticides on tobacco plantations. Cigarette smoking has increased 300 per cent in the same twenty years. When considering the cause of the 200 per cent increase in lung cancer in women and the 600 per cent increase in men in the same twenty year period, their inhalation of arsenical smoke should not be dismissed lightly.

This dismal picture of yet another additive for Americans to deal with will raise the question: "How can we protect ourselves?" The answer is that we can only try. We can make every effort to raise as much of our own foods as possible, organically, of course. If that proves impractical, we can try to locate a reliable source for foods that have not been treated with arsenic—an organic farmer, or a grocer who sells such foods. Beyond this, we can and must use food supplements every day. We must give our bodies every chance to fight the ravages of arsenic, as well as other poisons being used in foods. Finally, you can bombard your congressmen with pleas and demands for a revaluation of our food laws. This additive business has got to stop somewhere!

CHAPTER 4

Poisonous Chemicals in Food

by DR. CLIVE MCCAY, *Cornell University*

In 1950, congressional hearings were held on chemicals in food. Some startling facts turned up. Here is part of the testimony given at these hearings, by Clive M. McCay, of the Department of Animal Nutrition at Cornell University.

Statement made before Congressional Committee investigating the use of chemicals in food. — September 19, 1950

Toxicology is described usually as that field of science concerning substances, which introduced in the living organism, tend to destroy the life or impair the health of that organism. Nutritionists who study the effects upon the body of foods eaten by man and animals are regularly faced by the problems that arise from the chemical compounds found in these foods that may be injurious to health. Since very early times, in the interests of making more profits, men have attempted to introduce chemicals into foods in order to make a cheaper product appear like a better one.

In England more than a century ago, when wheat crossing the Atlantic often moulded, it was common practice to mill this wheat and then treat it with alum or copper sulfate to make a flour that resembled that from sound wheat. In those early days flour was commonly diluted with white, ground gypsum which the chemist knows as calcium sulfate. Today we still allow alum as a conditioner for flour and most of us probably ate some ground calcium sulfate in our breakfast toast or roll. This latter was probably used by your baker under the name of yeast food and as a carrier for bromates which helped the baker get a larger loaf volume.

Toxicology and Public Health

A substantial fraction of the mail of many nutritionists originates from an anxious public that is regularly trying to learn if some specific chemical added to a foodstuff is liable to be harmful.

The entire subject of chemicals added to our foods is probably far more important in the health of our nation today than any of us dream. The survival of our nation and of democracy must certainly depend upon the health of our citizens. The shocking number of our young men who cannot meet the relatively modest physical requirements of our Armed Services and who must labor in our industry with only partial effectiveness must make every one of us ask the reasons for this reservoir of ill health. The mental hospitals of New York State care for 117,000 patients or about two-thirds of a person for every hundred citizens. How much of all this illness can we ascribe either to substances introduced into our foods or to essentials that are lacking from our diets?

The Toxic Effect of Chemicals

The experience of nutrition students in relation to the toxic effect of chemicals falls into 4 rough categories:

1. The first of these concerns the accidental introduction of some toxic chemical into a foodstuff. An example of this can be drawn from naval experience. At a beach picnic the boys made lemonade in a new clean garbage can. The lemon juice dissolved the zinc coating from the can and those who drank the zinc citrate were pretty sick although no one died. Such problems are rare and minor in importance because cause and effect are easily related and a remedy can be applied.

2. The second type of problem is more intricate. This concerns the ingestion of injurious materials at irregular intervals. An example of this type of problem is one that is arising today. As you are aware some producers of chickens are intro-

ducing under the skin into the neck of the chicken diethylstilbestrol. Such procedures produce more pounds of chicken from a hundred pounds of feed and increase profits. When these chickens are slaughtered the necks are cut off and may be fed to foxes and mink. Some of these farms have reported substantial failure in breeding. Now the question arises whether enough of this compound finds its way into the flesh to affect the person who consumes the chicken.

The same type of problem arises when meat producing animals are fed compounds to injure the thyroid so that the basal metabolism of the pig or steer will be lowered and more meat will result from each pound of feed. Does enough of the compound fed the animal remain in the meat so that the consumer will be injured?

Assembling sound evidence in these fields is very important and also very difficult.

A third interest of the nutrition worker concerns changes in the effect of chemicals upon the body in relation to age. There is substantial evidence that the living body may be more easily injured at one age than at another.

Our laboratory has given substantial attention to this problem in relation to oxalates which are commonly found in such foods as chocolate, spinach and rhubarb. If eaten in moderate amounts these foodstuffs are very wholesome and noninjurious at all ages. For centuries, rhubarb leaves have been eaten as a meat sauce in England. However, during World War I there were a number of deaths in England from the consumption of rhubarb leaves eaten as stewed greens.

Our own researches have indicated that oxalates are very useful chemicals in foodstuffs because they tend to protect teeth against acid erosion. However, oxalates may cause loss of body calcium and hence bone building powers if eaten during the first few months after weaning or during the later period of life. During middle life oxalates do not have this effect. During the last third of life such compounds as oxalates may be very detrimental, because most of us are already losing our body calcium in our bones. Hence we are heading for that broken hip at age 70. (*Arch. Biochem.* [1950] 27,48.)

This example is cited because it illustrated a basic factor in all evaluation of toxicity, namely that experiments must be continued for a long time and cover the whole span of life of animals. Seldom has this been done as was evident from the testimony in regard to softeners presented at the recent bread hearings.

The fourth and major problem of toxicology in relation to foods concerns the composition of foodstuffs and the chemicals introduced in the processing of basic foods and their constituents. Nutrition is not much concerned with toxic compounds that may be present in such foods that are eaten at rare intervals; it is greatly interested in foods that are eaten daily.

Thus, the dyes used on orange peelings or the spray residues on oranges may not be of much interest at present, because limited amounts of candied citrus peel or marmalade are eaten. However, we have discovered recently that the peel may be useful in the control of diarrhea. In such a use it might be ingested by babies for long time periods and the added chemical might be very important.

Philosophy of Nutritionists

The basic philosophy of nutrition specialists is first that no chemical should ever be added to a given foodstuff unless it has long been tested on many species of animals. Long testing means a period of 10 years or more. Testing of many animal species needs to cover the whole span of life of small species, such as rats and mice. Many species of animals means that monkeys, rats, chickens, dogs, guinea pigs and finally men should be used in such testing. We will not soon forget the experience during prohibition days when tricrosyl phosphate was allowed to be used as synthetic ginger until some men drank it for liquor and died. Several common species had been used in testing this compound but chickens and men were the most easily poisoned by it. Testing had been done on neither.

Long ago the eminent biochemistry professor Otto Folin of Harvard called our attention to the serious mistake we make in not allowing life-termers in prison to volunteer to be subjects for such tests after thorough preliminary testing with animals. Certainly such testing upon prisoners is better than that upon the American public.

Not only should compounds be well tested before use but nutrition never sanctions the use of even a compound in a foodstuff if the given product can be made just as well without it.

Thus in the Triple Rich Bread which was originally devised for mental hospitals in New York and which is now widely used in many places, we discourage the use of chemicals in both the flour and bread. In the bread baked and sold in Ithaca we use only unbleached flour. No bromates are used in the Ithaca bakery although we believe the evidence is sound that the amount of bromates employed in yeast food is harmless. No gypsum is added to our bread although much of the calcium in the bread of the whole nation is present as calcium sulfate. We doubt if such calcium is well utilized and much prefer that the calcium of bread be contributed by nonfat milk solids or some other more assimilable form.

Bread and baked goods must be watched with extreme care by all of us because the staff of life plays such an important part in the nutrition of most of our older people and all of our low income group. For this reason we need expend great efforts to see that bread is baked from high quality ingredients, that it has the best possible formulas and that it is free from injurious substances.

Substances that are used daily by vast numbers of people such as breads must be given continuous attention by nutritionists. This holds for most processed foods.

The Case Against "Soft Drinks"

In closing, brief discussion will be given to problems concerned with carbonated beverages which we commonly call "soft drinks." During the past half century the growth in the use of these beverages has been tremendous and the retail sale is now said to exceed the value of three-quarters of a billion dollars.

Since 1943, we have devoted substantial research to the study of the injurious effects of the class of soft drinks known as the cola beverages. During World War II while working with some of the food problems of a CB unit in Rhode Island, I made a study of food purchased by men at Ships Service. Much money was spent for "cokes." The cola industry was given sugar certificates for all the sugar sold to the Armed Services. While studying these certificates I was amazed to learn that the beverage contained substantial amounts of phosphoric acid. Later we analyzed many soft drinks in the

Washington, D. C., area. We found that the cola beverages had 0.055 per cent phosphoric acid. This was essentially the amount disclosed in the suit by Harvey Wiley in 1911.

Cola Drinks and Teeth

At the Naval Medical Research Institute we put human teeth in cola beverage and found they softened and started to dissolve within a short period. They became very soft within two days.

In the intervening years 1943-1950 we have made numerous studies of the effect of these cola beverages upon the teeth of rats, dogs and monkeys. One of our technicians became so expert in judging the conditions of the surface of the molar teeth of rats that she could tell those that had had one drink of cola beverage amounting to 2½ teaspoonfuls or 10 milliliters. We have published data indicating that the molar teeth of rats are dissolved down to the gum line, if the rats are well fed but given nothing to drink except cola beverage for a period of six months. (*Journal Nutrition*, 1949, Vol. 39, 313.)

Monkeys that drink in the same manner as man and can be trained to drink from a cup suffer erosion similar to that of rats. Dentists of the Mayo Clinic, Rochester, Minnesota, have published photographs of patients' teeth that were believed to have been eroded by cola beverage. We have published tables showing the rate at which human teeth dissolve when suspended in cola beverage.

Data have been published indicating that the cola beverages contain substantial amounts of caffeine. These cola beverages deserve careful consideration not only in relation to our national problem of poor teeth but in relation to our numerous cases of gastric ulcers, and welfare of our children.

The acidity of cola beverages, which the biochemist expresses as pH, is 2.6 or about the same as vinegar. The sugar content masks the acidity and children little realize they are drinking this strange mixture of phosphoric acid, sugar, caffeine, coloring and flavoring matter.

Several other acids are used in other carbonated beverages and these all deserve careful study since solutions even one-tenth as acid as the cola beverages are claimed to erode the enamel of teeth.

Since soft drinks are playing an increasingly important

part in the American diet and tend to displace good foods such as milk, they deserve very careful consideration.

As a constructive solution we believe that labels on all foods to which chemicals have been added should disclose the amounts whether we are concerned with bread softeners, yeast foods or the acids of cola and other carbonated beverages. We believe these beverages should also state their content of drugs such as caffeine.

CHAPTER 5

The Effect of Chemicals Added to Food

by JONATHAN FORMAN, M.D.

Jonathan Forman, M.D. is one of the country's leading allergists, former editor of the Ohio State Medical Journal, *a long-time crusader for conservation and president of Friends of the Land. This is what Dr. Forman has to say about the dangers of chemicalized food.*

Leonard Wickenden, a retired chemist who combines the critical precision of a scientist with a rare felicity of expression, describes in a new book the disastrous effects of man's arrogant assumption that he can solve the complex biological problems of agriculture and public health by dissemination of deadly poisons.

He discusses DDT and the newer sprays, the soils they poison, the case against the addition of fluorine to the public water supply, vaporizers and fumigators, dangers of being beautified with certain cosmetics, perils of hormones and the doctoring of our daily bread.

To understand these poisons, one must gain a new and more accurate concept of life's processes and maximum health.

The Cells

Each of us has a body composed of billions of tiny units called cells. Each is a living separate unit joined with other cells to make a human being. Through the process of evolution these cells have given up their independence in order to enter a cooperative state and become specialists in communication, transportation, food supply, locomotion and defense.

To carry on the life processes, each of these cells must digest food, excrete its wastes, repair itself and be ready in one-millionth part of a second to perform its specialized task.

. . . and the Enzyme System

Every reaction depends upon a chemical response triggered and controlled by a specific enzyme system. All life is merely a great number of these enzymes working together in coordination. In other words, life is the function of the protein of the cell joining with a particular vitamin and one of the mineral nutrients originally from the soil, to form an enzyme with a highly specialized function.

Every cell in the body must contain from 50,000 to 100,000 of these enzyme systems ready always to go to work in a millionth of a second. Some have been assigned the task of remembering when you had mumps or measles or diphtheria and being prepared to defend against specific germs for the rest of your life.

What most of us fail to appreciate is that each of the enzyme systems is affected by the merest trace of certain chemicals—often as little as one part in a million, or less.

The specific mineral and vitamin as well as the building stones for the proteins must be in the cell at the same time and in proper proportions if the enzyme system is to be in perfect working order. Then each cell is doing its assigned task with a minimum of wear and tear, and the body which these cells compose will live out its expectancy and fall apart of senility at about the same time.

Biologists say that under such ideal circumstances all

mammals, including man, would live about 5 times as long as they take to mature. With man, life expectancy would be from 90 to 125 years, compared with the 68 years the average new-born baby can expect today.

The Effect of Pesticides

According to the United States Department of Agriculture we of this country were using 5 years ago enough pesticides to kill 15,200,000 persons annually. Since that time their usage has been increased and several more deadly ones have been developed.

Before 1945 our country regularly produced crop surpluses without the use of these poisons. But now the experts in bug poisoning have convinced us that without these chemicals we cannot raise enough to eat, that millions will get sick and die from insect-borne diseases, that our flower gardens will become unsightly, our mattresses will become alive with bedbugs and our clothes full of holes.

Such is the plight, they would have us believe, of the country which eradicated insect-borne disease from the Panama Canal Zone (without these poisons), the country which produces so much new fiber every year that it produces one crisis after another for the textile industry, the country which first produced synthetic fibers which no insect would eat!

Here we are concerned with the widespread, careless and indiscriminate use of chemicals which are introduced into our foods to preserve them and improve their texture or appearance.

Today there are nearly 800 of these chemicals found in our food. In the case of nearly 500 of them no one knows whether or not they are harmful in an accumulated way.

Man has persisted on into the age of insects, where, but for his intelligence, he would have disappeared long ago, with other prehistoric animals. We know our agricultural practices have destroyed the fertility of our soil, and it may be that without these poisons we could not produce enough to fill our stomachs. So it may be better to die a slow death by poisoning than to starve to death this year. But do we have to?

Insects demand carbonaceous food (woody fibers), while man demands proteinaceous food. So in general it holds that insects like poor, woody crops, while man thrives on rich, succulent ones. Hence it would be possible to outwit the whole insect world by good farming practices and soil conservation.

Side Effects of Chemical Additives

In the case of many chemicals added to our foods, we know nothing about their long-time effects. However, since they are so universally used, it is impossible to single out any one and decide whether it affects the death rate or the age at which the people die.

We are just finding out that for every vitamin there is an anti-vitamin. For every amino acid, for every purine base, and for most hormones there is an anti-metabolite—a substance almost identical chemically, but producing opposite effects.

In addition to these anti-metabolites there are hundreds of chemicals now being used by our people which have an inhibiting effect on the work of other chemicals which are essential to the functioning of enzyme systems in our bodies.

Vitamin Killers

To illustrate this problem, let us consider some of the biologic antagonists to the vitamins. Three chemicals, which we take into our bodies every day, can produce a vitamin deficiency even though we may be eating a balanced diet.

Other than the anti-metabolites, these substances include all chemicals which destroy vitamins directly; inhibit activity of enzyme systems by interfering with other component proteins and minerals; enhance development of opposing enzymes, or cause excessive elimination of vitamins.

Damaging effects of these antagonists may not be complete, yet they can substantially interfere with the normal physiologic processes to the point where they produce a recognizable deficiency disease.

More often, however, the deficient person drags about half-sick, and no one, not even his physician, has any idea of the cause of his half-sickness. Occasionally excessively large doses of vitamins will turn the tide. Hence the introduction of the so-called therapeutic capsule in clinical medicine.

In some instances, where the offender may be fluorine in the drinking water, the use of distilled water for beverage and cooking purposes will bring the patient back to health. Too often these unfortunates are looked upon as pitiful neurotics and the cause of their ill health is sought in childhood experiences.

Now for a listing of the general biologic antagonists to essential vitamins:

1. Improper cooking, sterilization or pasteurization will destroy vitamins.

2. Many mineral drugs such as arsenic, mercury and bismuth have a double action, by displacing the mineral in the enzyme system and greatly increasing excretion of the vitamins.

3. Astringents, laxatives and solvents may deplete the tissues of their vitamin content.

4. Narcotics and analgesics such as nicotine, morphine, alcohol, barbiturates and aspirin are inhibitors to vitamin functioning.

5. Antibiotics kill vitamin-producing germs of the large bowel.

6. Infections with fevers burn up immense quantities of vitamins.

7. Bleaching agents, such as those used on white flour, destroy most vitamins.

8. Sulphuring of foods for preservation and the use of sulphides to "freshen" the appearance of meat are destructive to vitamins.

9. Insecticides and disinfectants often are absorbed and retained in the food, so washing and peeling are not enough to rid the food of the poison.

10. Alkaline phosphatases essential to the use of sugars and starches by our bodies are inhibited or destroyed by fluorine in the drinking water, as are the enzymes concerned with the conduction of nerve impulses. This is a fact which those who propose to add fluorine to the drinking water to protect some children's teeth overlook.

The modern American is living under conditions conducive to the prevalence of many antagonisms to health and longevity.

These are hazards which each of us must do something

about if we are to improve our health significantly now that infections are well on the way to being conquered.

This article is reprinted by permission from *The Columbus Dispatch* for February 12, 1956.

CHAPTER **6**

The Health Benefits of Organically Grown Foods

How do we know that organically-grown, unchemicalized food is better for you than factoryized food? Here are some facts to help you weigh the evidence and decide for yourself.

We have a letter from a *Prevention* reader who says, "All of us know that many organically raised products are good for us . . . but how about finding out if there are enough data anywhere in existence coming from legitimate formal professional men, and I am speaking both of medical doctors and scientists, to indicate beyond argument and without conditions that we have reached a stage where we can definitely say and advance conclusive proof that we are making progress in this field, and that persons whose diet consists largely of whole, fresh, natural foods, organically grown, are in better health than persons whose diets are not."

Difficulties Involved

Before we give you the data we have on this subject, we ask you to consider for a moment the difficulties you encounter when you set out to prove, by experiment, that eating a certain kind of food—organically raised or any other kind—will produce certain results. You might be able to work it out convincingly with rats in a laboratory, but then you'd meet with the objections of people who say that we human beings are not laboratory rats and that the fearful and troubled world we live in can certainly not be compared to the antiseptic calm of a laboratory.

So let's say you start with people. Where are you going to find a group of people to carry on such an experiment—over a period of several generations, of course, for that is what you need, with another group of people willing to act as "controls" —that is, willing to live exactly as the first group lives, except that this second group will eat food that has not been organically grown?

Do you see what difficulties immediately arise? People move to other locations; they get married to people whose ideas on diet are quite different; they go on vacations where they eat in hotels; their children go away to school and eat what's served there, and so forth. How could you possibly keep such an experiment going long enough to mean anything and observe the "scientific" regulations that absolute scientific accuracy demand? You couldn't, obviously.

Investigating the Hunzas

All right, you'll say, what about studying a country where organic gardening has been practiced for generations and "civilization" has not penetrated? The Hunzas, people living high in the Himalayas, were studied and written about by Sir William McCarrison, one of the greatest nutritionists of all times. He found them to be practically free from degenerative disease as we know it—cancer, heart trouble, appendicitis, colitis and so forth.

Yet a recent book about Hunza relates the devastating diseases found there several years ago. From correspondence with the ruler of Hunza, a great friend of his, Editor Rodale finds that the Hunzakuts no longer live in their isolated paradise. Foods from the outside are common there now; aluminum cooking utensils are used; "civilization" has come to the country; the inhabitants travel to other lands; they bring back new ideas on food and agriculture. So Hunza can no longer be studied as the proving ground for the organic method.

An excellent experiment on human health which could have meant much to the organic movement in terms of actual facts and figures on the healthfulness of eating organically grown food was the experiment at Pioneer Health Centre, Peckham, England. In this remarkable undertaking, 875 families—about 3000 individuals—gathered together to help in a study of health. Not disease, mark you, but health. Their doctors examined patients to discover not just what disease they had, but also what degree of health they had, what minor and seemingly unimportant ailments bothered them and how much right living could do to correct these ailments.

In the initial examination it was found that out of every 10 supposedly healthy and uncomplaining persons, 7 had not even the negative attributes of health—that is, freedom from diagnosable disorder. Still less had they the positive attributes—vitality, initiative and a competence and willingness to live. The list of diseases among the first 500 families examined ranged all the way from one case of claustrophobia and 86 cases of overweight to 284 cases of decayed teeth and 983 cases of iron deficiency.

The Peckham Diet

One of the most important considerations of the directors of Peckham was diet. They decided early in the history of the Centre that they could not depend on the excellence of the milk, meat, fruit, vegetables and so forth purchased at the local market. They must secure as much as possible of their food organically grown, or grow it themselves.

Research at Peckham was disrupted by the war; the Centre was closed and the buildings vacated. After the war it was re-established. Many of the original families returned and hundreds of other families clamored to join. However, the Centre was forced to close because of lack of financial support. Apparently none of the grants or public funds available for scientific projects could go to Peckham because such funds are earmarked for studies of disease and this was a study of health!

The story of this experiment is available, incidentally, in a book called *Biologists in Search of Material,* published by Faber and Faber, London.

Organic Gardening Abroad

Some classic examples of better health through organic gardening are given by Sir Albert Howard in his writings. In his book, *The Soil and Health* (published by the Devin-Adair

Company), one chapter is entitled "Soil Fertility and Human Health." In it he tells of the experience of the Chief Health Officer of Singapore who conducted an experiment in his department, giving out small allotments of land to all employees who would farm them according to organic principles using compost and who would guarantee to use all the produce for their own families.

"At the end of the first year," this officer wrote to Sir Albert, "it was obvious that the most potent stimulus to this endeavour was the surprising improvement in stamina and health acquired by those taking part in this cultivation. Debility and sickness had been swept away and my men were capable of, and gladly responded to, the heavier work demanded by the stress of war." Unfortunately, war put a stop to the experiment after the first year.

Organic Experiments in Northern Rhodesia

A second example quoted by Sir Albert involves a copper mine in Northern Rhodesia—an area formerly so devastated by tropical diseases that it was uninhabited. Through a program of organic gardening, the personnel who were brought in to mine copper were kept at a high degree of health. "The positive health of these people is based on food . . . They have beaten back disease and turned that part of Northern Rhodesia into what is a health resort."

Reference is made, also, to Prince Edward Island in the Gulf of St. Lawrence which, says Sir Albert, is a small community, cut off from the rest of the world. "There we have a high standard of health, an extraordinarily vigorous, active population and no fall whatever in the birth rate. It is the only social organization composed of western Europeans which has not shown in the past 50 years a really sharp fall in the birth rate." Few chemicals are used in farming. The land is kept fertile by composting with "muck" and seaweed.

. . . and in Sidmouth, England

A third example is provided by St. Martin's School, Sidmouth, England, where for many years the fruits and vegetables were raised from fertile soil. Says the headmaster in a letter to Sir Albert: "Our exceptional health record has been chiefly due to the school menu. I firmly believe that this would have proved impossible had not the soil been maintained in a superlative state of fertility by means of compost beds and farmyard manure. Epidemics were unknown during the last 15 years. We had many lads who came to us as weaklings and left hearty and robust."

. . . and in Dublin, Ireland

Another example in St. Columba's College, Rathfarnham, near Dublin, Ireland, where the boys who attend the college grow their food on about 50 acres, by means of compost made on the spot from animal and vegetable residues. Superlative health has resulted. A fifth example is the Co-operative Wholesale Society's bacon factory at Winsford in Cheshire. The wasteland around the factory was made into productive land by the use of compost; vegetables grown were used in meals at the factory canteen. "Already the health, efficiency and well-being of the labour force has markedly improved," says Sir Albert. "The output of work has increased; absenteeism has been notably reduced."

In a feeding experiment at Mt. Albert Grammar School in Auckland, New Zealand, garden produce grown by organic methods and fed to the students resulted in great improvement in health: a marked decline in colds and influenza, excellent physical growth and stamina, fewer accidents, resistance to fractures and sprains; constipation and stomach upsets are rare; skins are healthy and clear; dental conditions are greatly improved.

Health and diet ideas are being put into dynamic operation at Fairleigh-Dickinson College in New Jersey. And now the college has purchased a farm where they plan to raise food organically for the students' meals. We should have some revealing evidence within a few years from Fairleigh-Dickinson.

The Haughley Experiment

Organic Gardening and Farming reported in the July, 1957, issue on the Haughley Experiment made by the Soil Association in England. Here 3 separate farms have been farmed for 16 years to test organic methods. One of the farms is operated organically. The other two serve as controls. Chemicals are used on these. Crop yields on the organic farm have been up to or greater than yields on the other farms. Soil tests at the organic farm show that even though the yields are greater, the fertility of the soil is actually increasing, while on the other farms it is decreasing. Tests also show that the organically-raised produce contains more minerals. Vitamin analyses have not shown significant variations, but it appears that the animals on the organic farm are reacting better than those on the other farms. Cows produce more milk and the milk has a higher protein content. You can get full information about the experiment from The Soil Association, Ltd., New Bells Farm, Haughley-Stowmarket, Suffolk, England.

We think you can use facts like these to convince skeptics of the advantage of organically-grown food. What we have reported on are not scientifically controlled experiments in the strict sense of the word. We suggest that the best way to test the organic theory is to put yourself on organically-grown food for a few years and see what the difference is in your own health.

SECTION 2

PROCESSED AND CANNED FOODS

Processed and canned foods, almost without exception, contain preservatives, coloring matter, sugar or other sweetening, emulsifiers, softeners or some other chemical substance. The effect of these is cumulative. It isn't a question of whether or not your body can handle one or another of these chemicals safely. If you continually eat canned and processed food, you must be ingesting hundreds of them daily.

More than 700 chemicals are being used in foods regularly, of which only 428 are known to be safe. And of the ones "known to be safe," many may later prove to be unsafe as new methods of testing are developed.

Latest additives are hormones and antibiotics, used either in the treatment and feeding of food animals or applied to the meat itself. Dangers of these two substances alone cannot be estimated.

Frozen foods are in general more free from chemicals than canned foods. Of course, don't buy the prepared frozen foods—fried, baked or stewed. If you are freezing food at home, we recommend sticking to the rules for blanching vegetables. Freeze all fruits raw, and, of course, without sugar.

CHAPTER 7

A Surgeon Prescribes Natural Living

A surgeon in the Royal Navy of England believes that natural food and natural living is the answer for good health. Here are his very cogent, very reasonable arguments.

"The Neglect of Natural Principles in Current Medical Practice"—how's that for a title for a medical article? It appeared in the Spring, 1956, issue of the *Journal of the Royal Naval Medical Service* (pp. 55-83) and it was written by Surgeon Captain T. L. Cleave, Royal Navy. Dr. Cleave prefaces his article with this quote from Horace: "You may drive out Nature with a pitchfork, yet she will ever hurry back, to triumph in stealth over your foolish contempt."

Rely on Nature

Throughout the penetrating and reasonable 30-odd pages of this article, Dr. Cleave shows us step by step just how important it is for medical men to keep "natural principles" uppermost. He contends that "nature is never wrong," when she is acting in a natural environment—that is to say, the environment in which the organism has been evolved. For example, our sense of taste was provided partly to warn us against poisons. It cannot warn us against the poison arsenic, because this has never occurred in our natural environment, being dug up from the underground. Strychnine, on the contrary, has existed in our natural environment (in plants); hence the tongue can taste it and be warned by its bitter taste.

Nature and Our Diet

Applying this law to the subject of diet, it would seem that the only important recommendation is "eat exactly what you like." And this indeed would be true if all food were eaten in its natural state. But "unfortunately," says Dr. Cleave, "our food has been altered a great deal from its natural state, and so with such advice as this we may be far from safe." There are two procedures by which man alters the composition of food: cooking, and concentrating the food by means of machinery. Cooking has been a common habit of the human race so long that we have by now become partly adapted to it. Changes in the shape of our jaws bear testimony to this. Modern teeth in general are not meant for chewing the all-raw diet our ancestors had to eat. So, although we are not likely to run into great difficulty just by cooking our food, still there are pitfalls here, too. Overcooking may result in presenting our stomachs with highly-coagulated and even charred protein which is difficult for the digestive juices to penetrate and digest. Frying makes things still worse, for the coating of fat over the protein renders it harder to digest. This possibly has a great deal to do with the formation of ulcers, Dr. Cleave believes, for the stomach pours out excessive gastric juice in an effort to digest this undigestible mass.

Cooking carbohydrates may be responsible for damage to our teeth, he believes. Sweet sticky foods are known to cling around the teeth and cause fermentation. Why then do nations where dates are a staple food not have rampant tooth decay? The cells of the date are alive when they are eaten, so they are protected from bacterial attack. But cooked carbohydrates are dead foods, so they ferment around the teeth.

Concentration of Foods

Concentrating foods by the use of machinery is a far more dangerous procedure than cooking. Whereas cooking has been going on for 200,000 years, concentrating foods by machinery is of such recent date that our bodies cannot possibly adapt themselves to it. Carbohydrates are, of course, the foods generally treated thus. "Nearly all the harmful consequences that arise from this are due to the concentration leading to a definitely excessive consumption of the carbohydrates," says Dr. Cleave. Their taste (in concentrated form) is too highly geared for the tongue to be able to know when to stop. A bar of chocolate, for example, contains as much sugar as a dozen average apples. The tongue would know when to stop eating the apples, but not the chocolate bar. Dr. Cleave then notes that the consumption of refined (concentrated) sugar in England jumped from 15 pounds per head in 1915 to 104 pounds in 1954.

The Effect of Sugar Concentration

The concentration of sugar is thus the most damaging item in our modern diet. What are some of its results? Dental decay, peptic ulcer, diabetes, obesity, constipation and intestinal toxemia, says Dr. Cleave. Speaking of dental decay, he describes the classic example of the island Tristan da Cunha. In 1932 the population was living largely on fish and potatoes. Since then "civilization" has arrived and sugar, flour and sweets are available everywhere. As a result the decay rate in permanent teeth has jumped from 18 per thousand in 1932 to 91 per thousand in 1952. In deciduous teeth (baby teeth) the decay rate has jumped from one per thousand to 226 per thousand!

Peptic Ulcers

Speaking of peptic ulcers, Dr. Cleave tells us that protein is the natural substance for neutralizing the hydrochloric acid of the stomach. All foods except pure fats and refined sugar contain some protein. But when the food is concentrated, as in sugar refining, the protein is removed. Consider, he says, the amount of refined carbohydrates consumed at a movie. These produce a great flow of gastric juice, but, since they are almost entirely pure sugar, they have no neutralizing power of the hydrochloric acid they have called forth. So the tissues of the stomach are bathed for several hours in full strength acid. In 1900 duodenal ulcer was so uncommon in England that it was mentioned in no textbook. At present about 10 per cent of men and 3 to 4 per cent of women develop peptic ulcer at some time in their lives. In addition, it seems that peptic ulcer is practically unknown in nations where refined food is unknown, even though these people may eat a largely carbohydrate diet. "It is not protein foods that are protecting these races," says Dr. Cleave, "it is the protein in the carbohydrate foods." And, of course, this protein disappears when the carbohydrate is refined.

In the case of diabetes it seems to be obvious that the eating of carbohydrates does not cause the disease, provided they are natural, not concentrated carbohydrates. Irish peasants, for example, have lived for years on a diet of practically nothing but potatoes, and are seldom diabetic. In 1900 diabetes ranked as the twenty-seventh cause of death in American mortality statistics. Today it ranks third.

Obesity

Obesity is another widespread disease in civilized countries. It does not occur in primitive races living on primitive diets; it does not occur among wild animals, birds or fishes which have no access to refined foods. Says Dr. Cleave, "The writer feels that it is a tragic error ever to relate obesity to an excess of appetite. To see the truth here, we have only to notice that no rabbit ever ate too much grass, no rook ever pulled up too many worms, no herring ever caught too much plankton; that no creature in the wild state is ever overweight. They may vary in size, but never in shape."

Constipation, says Dr. Cleave, is well known to be due to the removal of the pulp of carbohydrate. In all probability hemorrhoids and varicose veins are also due to the weight of static bowel contents on the the veins involved.

Intestinal toxemia, according to Dr. Cleave, is partly caused by eating cooked food, since the living cells have been killed when the food is cooked. But, far more important than that—eating refined carbohydrates maintains "a vast horde" of bacteria in the bowel which should never be there.

Dr. Cleave's Answer to What Is "Natural"

There is another angle to this matter of what foods are "natural." Honey, for instance, is not "natural" according to Dr. Cleave, for under natural circumstances we could not get it from the bees in the quantity in which we eat it. Dates are not a natural food for people in northern countries. They contain far too much sugar—nearly 60 per cent, whereas bananas contain less than 20 per cent and are perfectly safe.

Taking up disease in terms of "natural principles," Dr. Cleave tells us that the infectious diseases are "natural" diseases and all others are "unnatural." By this he means that infectious diseases are caused by one animal organism (a germ) preying on another animal (the human being) just as animals prey on one another in nature. The unnatural group of diseases, however, does not occur in nature, but does occur in human beings and in animals which live a civilized or partly civilized life. Those animals which, like the dog, are eating diets almost completely unnatural for them, suffer from the same diseases as humanity.

Because the infectious diseases are "natural" diseases, we are perfectly justified in using drugs to cure them, is Dr. Cleaves' opinion. If we were attacked by a wild animal, we would feel justified in using a weapon against it, wouldn't we? So, therefore, we should use all the drugs at our command to fight and conquer the germs which are responsible for the infectious diseases.

"Unnatural" Diseases

But the "unnatural" diseases are a different story. "The treatment of this group in the early stages should be as *natural* as possible, and should lie in the replacement of the unnatural environment by the natural one in the particular factor concerned—which very often means the institution of a natural diet. . . . In this group (of diseases) it would seem, the (medical) profession substantially fails. Fundamental cures are seldom obtained and the doctors suffer from these diseases as much as their patients, because, it is submitted, antidotes are used instead of the restitution of natural conditions," says Dr. Cleave.

He goes on to say that, after diseases in this catagory have gone on for long enough to cause advanced irreversible consequences, it is usually too late to cure them by natural methods. *However, they could have been prevented.* "The writer believes that, if it led to a greater grasp of the natural law, the profession might derive considerable value from studying the methods of naturopathists and other related cults." (Why, Dr. Cleave, what kind of talk is that from a Surgeon in Her Majesty's Royal Navy?) He goes on to remind us that medical treatments are in vogue for 10 years or less. "Does any treatment of a century ago exist today?" he asks. "Yet the treatments that are based on natural principles remain the same from age to age."

Prevention of Unnatural Diseases by Diet

After describing some unnatural ways of treating disease and explaining just what is wrong with them, Dr. Cleave takes up the prevention of "unnatural" diseases by diet. Varicose veins, for instance, can be prevented or treated in their early stages by a natural diet. Late treatment, he believes, lies in an operation.

Stomach ulcers, he says, can be prevented by eating only natural foods, avoiding any overcooked or fried foods and never eating anything for which you are not hungry.

Diabetes? Reduce starchy foods to their original, unconcentrated form by the substitution of wholemeal flour for white flour and all its combinations and by the substitution of such natural sweets as raw or dried fruits for white sugar. If blood sugar fails to go down to normal on this kind of diet, then insulin must be taken as well. Obesity? The initial treatment is a period of partial starvation (a real "reducing diet," that is) to get off the existing fat. What should this diet consist of? Practically no carbohydrates or fats, but a fair amount of protein and fruits and vegetables in any quantity desired. Once the weight has gone down, the diet must include no refined carbohydrates from that time on. We have always advocated such a diet. "In one of the earliest editions of Price's textbook of medicine," says Dr. Cleave, "30 years ago, the contributor to the chapter on obesity suggested that the simplest way to effect the necessary reduction in weight was to let the patient eat any food he liked—as long as it was raw."

For intestinal toxemia, Dr. Cleave has this to say, "the substitution of a natural diet and the most careful attention to the appetite leave the causative organisms in the bowel nothing to live on and the result is the disappearance of the toxins they have been producing. . . In the urticaria (hives) and eczema cases the result of this approach has been often, and in the case of chronic boils almost invariably, successful."

Summary

Dr. Cleave's diet is really the essence of simplicity—omit processed foods and then eat anything you like or want. In conclusion, says Dr. Cleave, "many of the ills of today are due to a massive interference by machinery, progressively over the last century, with the carbohydrate components for our diet, leading to a great increase in their concentration, which in turn has led to a great increase in their consumption."

This article is undoubtedly one of the finest that has ever appeared in a medical journal, so far as the theory of natural living is concerned. It is the perfect answer to critics who tell us that no intelligent medical man will go along with our ideas. Dr. Cleave, a surgeon no less, says in essence, in this article, that all the degenerative diseases are caused by our modern diet.

CHAPTER 8

So You Think You Know What You're Eating!

If you doubt that the food you buy has been chemicalized, discover in this chapter just how many added chemicals you may eat in one day's meals.

Once upon a time . . . a glass of orange juice was simply juice from an orange; butter was churned milk, nothing more; a piece of meat had nothing in it but the spices *you* added in cooking it. If you wanted to take your chances on a piece of chocolate cake, a look at the recipe would tell you the whole story of how much sugar and white flour your body would have to contend with—there would be no unknown ingredient in the flour or the chocolate. Even with ice cream or candy you knew what you were up against, and if you wanted to eat such things . . . well, the risk was yours. Today, if you want to eat these things the risk is still yours, but with this difference: to understand just what you're up against, you'd have to be a chemical engineer!

There's Something in Everything!

Food additives have become a mighty part of the food industry in the past 30 years. It is almost impossible to purchase a commercially produced food product that has not been treated in some way to give it a characteristic the producer wants it to have, or one he's educated the consumer to want and expect. There are hardeners and softeners, foaming agents and anti-foaming agents, acidifiers and alkalizers, bleaches, coloring agents, thickeners and on and on—ad nauseum. These chemicals are dumped into the vat, one on top of the other, to create the perfect product that won't spoil, harden, change color, stick together nor fall apart. There are often 5, 10 or even more additives in a single food product. This food, in turn, is often combined with several other food products, each equally "enriched" with additives, to make a single dish.

The casual consumer usually has neither the training nor the interest that would prompt him to attempt an interpretation of the numerous ingredients listed on the label of the average food package. He buys a jar of olives and expects olives; he buys a pound of cold cuts and it never occurs to him to ask about the casing in which the meat is wrapped, nor about the stuff that's used to hold it together or to make it pink. He's thinking of a sandwich, not a course in chemical preservatives.

How Does the Body Cope With It All?

The question that presents itself to one who is concerned by profession, as we are, with what goes into foods is this: how can the body cope with the sheer volume of chemical substances which trickle into it from a hundred different food sources each day? How much of a strain is it on the body's organs to process and rid itself of so many useless and harmful substances which it cannot use? Do all of them leave the body? How do these chemicals react on one another while they are in the body? There are many related questions that come to mind and should have been asked by the food processors long before they incorporated these chemicals into the products they sell. If we find out later that the body can't handle them, it will be too late for a lot of us.

In 30 years the aspects of this question have become so complex that the Federal Food and Drug Administration, which is required to answer only a part of it (are the chemicals poisonous of themselves?), has thrown up its hands and admitted that it can never tell if all of the chemicals in food, even when used one at a time, are poisons or not. An estimate of the effect on the body of the ones being used, over long periods or in combination with other chemicals, has hardly ever been attempted.

How Could Such Small Amounts Hurt You?

Rather than tell the public that conclusive tests have never been made on the safety of the additives they use, the food processors pooh-pooh the suggestion that those teensy amounts of chemicals they add could possibly affect American consumers who have been told that they are among the healthiest people in the world. To impress us with the ridiculousness of the suggestion, they quote the additive in parts per million, or the microscopic micrograms per pound and dare us to imagine how we could be poisoned by such infinitesimal amounts. What they don't say is that these infinitesimal amounts accumulate in the body; that we ingest such infinitesimal amounts of chemicals dozens of times a day, for years on end.

A Menu Many Eat Throughout the Country

To dramatize a bit more graphically the menace of food additives that confronts us every day, we have made up a day's menu generally familiar to most persons in our country. As you will see, it is not a menu we would recommend, but we have included foods that many people eat every day and have been told are perfectly safe, even wonderful, for them. With each food item mentioned we have included the intentional additives used in its manufacture, as listed by the National Academy of Sciences, National Research Council, Washington 25, D. C., in their publication 398, *The Use of Chemical Additives in Food Processing*, February, 1956. (Price $2.00). These do not, of course, include any spray or other insecticides, nor any gases to which most fruits and vegetables are subjected before they are even eligible for additives. Nor are we mentioning more than one additive per food for each specific job; for example, in bread there can be several anti-oxidants (perhaps even in the same loaf) but we will list only one; in sodas there are many additives possible for each soda flavor, but again we will list only one. It should be understood, however, that the consumer who eats a slice from two different loaves of commercially baked bread is likely to get a different set of additives with each slice. The person who eats two kinds of processed cheese might well be eating two separate groups of preservatives. Recalling the number of different types of food one eats each day, and the different varieties and flavors in which they come, should give one an idea of the complex problem of additives in food which can only be hinted at in the menu below.

Are You Eating a Salt-Free Diet?

For the person on a salt-free diet who thinks he is avoiding salt simply by not adding it to his foods in cooking or at the table, the menu will be a sobering revelation. The sodium and chloride compounds he should avoid are present in almost every food he eats. It would be well for anyone restricted against a specific element commonly employed in foods to study the list of additives given below and carried in labels to be sure that such an element is not contained.

Even if you are careful in selecting the foods you eat, it is practically impossible to live in our civilization without unknowingly eating some food additives. For those who never read a label and try each new work-saving food product that is offered, the chemical intake must be staggering! The only protection you have is to eat as many fresh foods as possible whose origin you know and to fortify yourself with natural food supplements.

Non-Nutritive Sweeteners Are Not Included

The additives mentioned below do not include non-nutritive sweeteners which are used, as suggested by the National Academy of Sciences' booklet in: beverages, canned fruit products, canned vegetables, flavoring extracts, frozen desserts, gelatin, jellies, jams, marmalades, baked goods, salad dressings and frozen fruits. But remember, they could be added to the list of any or all of these foods' additives. The use of glycerols in each food is also not included, but they can be assumed to be present with any flavoring or coloring, for they act as solvents for these items. Isopropanol is another additive we've omitted, but it is contained as a solvent in foods which require synthetic flavoring agents.

When we came to colorings and flavoring agents, we included only a few representative ones, since items such as cake, pie, sodas or candy can have dozens of variations on these additives.

How many of these foods do you eat? How many can you be sure of?

Chemical Additives You Eat on an Average Day

BREAKFAST:

Juice—Benzoic Acid (preservative) dimethyl polysiloxane (anti-foaming agent).

Cereal—Butylated hydroxyanisole (antioxidant), Sodium acetate (buffer), F D & C Red #2 (dye), F D & C Yellow #5 (dye), Aluminum ammonium sulfate (acid).

Meat—(sausage, spiced ham, hash), Ascorbate (antioxidant), Calcium phosphate (anti-caking agent), Sodium or potassium nitrate (color fixative), Sodium chloride (preservative), guar gum (binder).

Toast or Bread—Sodium diacetate (mold inhibitor), monoglyceride (emulsifier), Potassium bromate (maturing agent), Aluminum phosphate (improver), Calcium phosphate monobasic (dough conditioner), Chloromine T (flour bleach), Aluminum Potassium sulfate (acid-baking powder ingredient).

Buns or Coffee Cake—Calcium propionate (mold inhibitor), Diglycerides (emulsifier), Sodium alginate (stabilizer), Potassium bromate (maturing agent), Aluminum phosphate (improver), Butyric acid (butter flavor), Cinnamaldehyde (cinnamon flavor), Aluminum Chloride (dough conditioner), Chloramine T (flour bleach), Aluminum potassium sulfate (acid- in baking powder).

Margarine—Sodium benzoate (preservative), Butylated hydroxyanisole (antioxidant), monoisopropyl citrate (sequestrant), F D & C yellow #3 (coloring), Diacetyl (butter flavoring), Stearyl citrate (metal scavenger), Synthetic vitamin A and D.

Butter—Hydrogen peroxide (bleach), F D & C yellow #3 (coloring), Nordihydroguaiaretic acid (antioxidant).

Milk—Hydrogen peroxide (bactericide), Oat gum (antioxidant).

Jelly or Jam—Sodium benzoate (preservative), Dimethyl polysiloxane (anti-foaming agent), Methyl cellulose (thickening agent), Malic acid (acid), Sodium potassium tartrate (buffer), F D & C green #3 (coloring for mint flavors), F D & C yellow #2 (coloring for mint flavors), F D & C yellow #5 (coloring for imitation strawberry flavor), Gum tragacanth (stabilizer).

LUNCH:

Soup—Butylated hydroxyanisole (antioxidant), Dimethyl polysiloxane (anti-foaming agent), Sodium phosphate dibasic (emulsion for tomato soup), Citric acid (dispersant in soup base).

Crackers—Butylated hydroxyanisole (antioxidant), Aluminum bicarbonate (leavening agent), Sodium bicarbonate (alkali), di-glyceride (emulsifying agent), Methylcellulose (bulking agent in low calorie crackers), Potassium bromate (maturing agent), Chloramine T (flour bleach).

Sandwich—Sodium diacetate (mold inhibitor), monoglyceride (emulsifier), Potassium bromate (maturing agent), Aluminum phosphate (improver), Calcium phosphate monobasic (dough conditioner), Chloramine T (flour bleach), Aluminum Potassium sulfate (acid-baking powder ingredient), Ascorbate (antioxidant), Sodium or potassium nitrate (color fixative), Sodium chloride (preservative), guar gum (binder), Hydrogen peroxide (bleach), F D & C Yellow #3 (coloring), Nordihydroguaiaretic acid (antioxidant).

Candy—Sorbic acid (fungistat), Butylated hydroxyanisole (antioxidant), Mono- and Di-glycerides (emulsifying agents), Polyoxyethylene (20) Sorbitan monolaurate (flavor dispersant), Sodium Alginate (stabilizer), Calcium carbonate (neutralizer), Cinnamaldehyde (cinnamon flavoring), Titanimoxide (white pigment), Mannitol (anti-sticking agent), Petrolatum (candy polish), Propyleneglycol (mold inhibitor), Calcium oxide (alkali), Sodium citrate (buffer), Sodium benzoate (preservative).

Soda—Sorbic acid (fungistat), Sodium benzoate (preservative), Polyoxyethylene (20) sorbitan monolaurate (flavor dispersant), Sodium alginate (stabilizer), F D & C blue #1 (brilliant blue coloring), F D & C yellow #5 (coloring),

Cinnamaldehyde (cinnamon flavoring), Caffeine (stimulant added to cola drinks), butyated hydroxyanisole (antioxidant).

Ice Cream—Mono- and Di-glycerides (emulsifier), Agar-agar (thickening agent), Calcium carbonate (neutralizer), Sodium citrate (buffer), Amylacetate (banana flavoring), Vanilldene Kectone (imitation vanilla flavoring), Hydrogen peroxide (bactericide), Oat gum (antioxidant).

DINNER:

Fruit Cup—Calcium hypochlorite (germacide wash), Sodium chloride (prevent browning), Sodium hydroxide (peeling agent), Calcium hydroxide (firming agent), Sodium metasalicate (peeling solution for peaches), Sorbic acid (fungistat), Sulfur dioxide (preservative), F D & C red #3 (coloring for cherries).

Meat—Alkanate (dye) Methylviolet (marking ink), Asafoetida (onion flavoring), Sodium nitrate (color fixative), Sodium chloride (preservative), Sodium ascorbate (antioxidant), Guar gum (binder), Sodium phosphate (buffer), Magnesium carbonate (drying agent).

Canned Peas—Magnesium carbonate (alkali), Magnesium chloride (color-retention and firming agent), Sodium chloride (preservative).

Fruit Pie—Sodium diacetate (mold inhibitor), Sorbic acid (fungistat), Butylated hydroxyanisole (antioxidant), Sodium sulfite (anti-browning), Mono- and di-glycerides (emulsifier), Aluminum ammonium sulfate (acid), F D & C red #3 (cherry coloring), Calcium chloride (apple pie mix firming agent), Sodium benzoate (mince meat preservative), Potassium bromate (maturing agent), Chloromine T (flour bleach).
(Pie will also contain additives found in shortening and white flour used in making the crust.)

Cottage Cheese—Annatto (vegetable dye), cochineal (dye), Diacetyl (butter flavoring), Sodium hypochlorite (curd washing), Hydrogen peroxide (preservative).

Cheese (Processed)—Calcium propionate (preservative), Calcium citrate (plasticiser), Sodium citrate (emulsifier), Sodium phosphate (texturizer), Sodium alginate (stabilizer), Chloromine T (deodorant), Acetic acid (acid), F D & C yellow 13 (coloring), Aluminum potassium sulfate (firming agent), Hydrogen peroxide (bactericide), Pyroligneous acid (smoke flavor).

Beer—Potassium bi-sulfite (preservative), Dextrim (foam stabilizer), Hydrochloric acid (Adjustment of pH), Calcium sufate (yeast food), Magnesium sulfate (water corrective), Polymixin B (antibiotic).

CHAPTER 9

Chemicals in Foods . . . a Practical Approach

by W. C. HUEPER

W. C. Hueper, Environmental Cancer Chief of the National Cancer Institute, states clearly and unequivocally just what the dangers are concerning chemicals in food. This chapter is part of a speech made by Dr. Hueper at the meeting of the International Union Against Cancer in Rome, August, 1956. This condensation of Dr. Hueper's remarks was made by John Lear, Science Editor of The Saturday Review.

A rapidly growing number and variety of non-nutritive substances have been introduced during recent decades into foodstuffs intended for general human consumption through the use of modern methods of food production and processing. Some of these chemicals are intentionally added to foods for various reasons, while others are employed for different purposes in the production of foodstuffs and remain unintentionally in them as residues. A disturbing aspect of this development is that there exists no mandatory provision for assuring, *a priori*, that biologic properties of each of these additives and contaminants, particularly long-term or delayed effects, have adequately been studied. The circumstances suggest the virtual certainty that many have not.

Carcinogenic Elements in Chemicals

It is especially important in this respect that observations made during recent years in men and experimental animals have demonstrated a not inconsiderable number of chemicals similar to, or identical with, those introduced into foodstuffs which possess carcinogenic [cancer-provoking] properties. The actual or possible existence of cancer hazards related to carcinogens in foodstuffs therefore poses a serious public-health problem. The daily and life-long exposure to such agents would represent one of the most important of the various potential sources of contact with environmental carcinogens for the population at large.

A List of Food Additives

The main groups of food additives and contaminants . . . include . . . natural and synthetic dyes, antioxidants of fats and lipoids and vegetable matter, thickeners, sweeteners, flavoring agents, surfactants (detergents, foaming agents), humectants (smoke agents), preservatives and chemical sterilizing agents, water conditioners (iodine, fluorides), antifoaming agents, salt substitutes, shortenings, softeners, bleaches, modifiers and improvers (meat tenderizers, etc.), oil and fat substitutes, organic solvents, emulsifiers and solidifiers, pesticide residues, anti-sprouting and antimaturition agents of fruits and vegetables, insect repellents, hormonal fattening agents, antibiotics (fed to food animals and added to foodstuffs), enzymes, antienzymatics, pan-glazes (silicones), pan-greases (mineral oils), water pollutants, chemical sterilizing agents, wrapping and coating materials (paraffin, waxes, resins, plastics), soot adherent to smoked foodstuffs and roasted and toasted products, household detergents and their coloring agents, non-ionizing radiation (ultraviolet) products, ionizing radiation (radioactive) products, and radioactive substances taken up by plants and food animals from air, soil, or water contaminated by radioactive fall-out.

The bulk of the still rather restricted pertinent information on potential cancer hazards from these additives and contaminants is of relatively recent date. Knowledge of such observations is often limited to parties mainly interested in scientific aspects of carcinogenesis and is sometimes not fully appreciated by those parties concerned with the practical aspects of potential human cancer hazards inferable from these experimental findings.

There is no necessary relation between toxicity [poisoning now effectively prevented by food and drug laws] and carcinogenicity of chemical agents. As a rule, the minimal carcinogenic dose is distinctly lower than the minimal chronic toxic dose. It is for this reason that not infrequently carcinogenic reactions may develop upon exposure to carcinogenic chemicals without a preceding or simultaneous appearance of any toxic symptoms.

Carcinogenic Screening

In a graduated scale of the relative significance of potential environmental carcinogenic agents from a public health viewpoint, the highest priority for carcinogenic screening should be extended to those agents with which large parts of the general population have frequent and prolonged contact, whose possible carcinogenic effects on man can least readily be ascertained, and which for this reason are most difficult to control by preventive methods. Chemicals included in this group are those which enter in general human environment of every home in the form of consumer goods, or as environmental contaminants. Agents of this type are the large group of chemical additives and contaminants of foodstuffs in addition to many environmental poisons, pollutants of water, air, and soil, household drugs, sanitary supplies, cleansing agents, polishes, paints, and cosmetics.

Seven Tips on the Carcinogens

If one adopts the principle that the protection of the health of the general public deserves foremost attention, the following considerations may profitably be used as guide lines in arriving at intelligent and rational decisions.

1. Carcinogens vary greatly in their relative potency. Coal tars of different derivations, for instance, vary greatly in their relative carcinogenic potency in man and experimental animals. Coal tars are in turn usually more potent than wood

tars or vegetable tars obtained in the fractionation of petroleum.

2. Dose observations made in experimental animals are not directly applicable to man. There exist marked differences in potency of a particular chemical for various species.

3. Repeated exposures to carcinogens produce a cumulative carcinogenic effect in the exposed tissues. Cells once exposed to a carcinogen seem to retain the entire or a considerable portion of the initial effect exerted by individual exposures, even if these by themselves may be insufficient for eliciting a neoplastic [malignant] response. Subeffectively exposed cells can be challenged into carcinogenic activity either by additional subminimal carcinogenic exposures or by contact with specific promoting chemicals.

4. Actual exposure to a dietary carcinogen does not always stop with the cessation of environmental contact. Some chemicals are not metabolically destroyed or excreted but are retained in active form in certain tissues from which they may gradually be mobilized long after the environmental exposure has ceased.

5. Exposure to a dietary carcinogen may be complicated by occupational, medicinal, cosmetic, sanitary, or environmental contact with the same chemical or some other chemical.

6. It is perhaps possible to enforce, to a reasonable degree, laws concerning the maximal content and adequate purity of food additives and contaminants in foodstuffs, merchandised by relatively large trade organizations dealing in large quantities in nationwide and interstate commerce and using standardized and well controlled methods of processing, handling, and shipping. Considerable difficulties in this respect may be encountered, on the other hand, regarding the proper supervision of foodstuffs produced and sold on a local level. The mere passage of laws establishing standards in such matters without providing adequate means to enforce them might produce in the population a deceptive impression of safety. The most effective method of control of health hazards of this type doubtlessly is found under such circumstances in a complete elimination of the dangerous agents from the human environment, wherever such a procedure is possible.

7. Since many foodstuffs containing artificial food additives and contaminants are not adequately labeled as to the amount and type of chemical added to the natural food products, the general consumer is relatively rarely able to make any intelligent selection between different products of the same type, particularly between "natural" foodstuffs and "artificially modified and contaminated" ones. Indeed, in many instances, he may have little choice in such matters, because all or nearly all foodstuffs of certain types which he is able to purchase are of the contaminated or modified variety. The consumer under such circumstances is a member of a "captive" population which may be subjected to potential, long delayed health hazards which he has neither consented to nor is able to avoid. For these reasons the general public is entitled to expect that all chemical additives and contaminants are subjected to comprehensive and thorough studies for toxic, carcinogenic, and cocarcinogenic properties before they are used or introduced in human foodstuffs.

Do All Additives Contain Carcinogens?

It is unlikely from an application of our present knowledge of environmental carcinogens that many of the presently used additives and contaminants of foodstuffs introduce any carcinogenic hazard into the general food supply and, therefore, deserve any immediate attention. The large number of additives as well as the complexity and costliness of the biologic testing for carcinogenic properties of any one of them, moreover, precludes for merely practical reasons any large-scale attack of the problem on the entire front at the present time. It is quite obvious that under the existing conditions a step-by-step procedure will have to be adopted and that investigative efforts would best be expended for the time being on those circumscribed groups of chemicals which from the already available information have furnished carcinogenic or cocarcinogenic agents, *i.e.,* synthetic dyes, chlorinated pesticides, animal and plant hormones, and detergents.

Carcinogens in Synthetic Food Dyes

Among the various formerly and presently used synthetic food dyes, carcinogenic properties were discovered during recent years in a surprisingly large number when tested in rats and mice. Rodent cancers have also been produced by chemical compounds of the same stilbene family which has recently been introduced as coloring matter in many household detergents used for the cleaning of kitchen utensils, dishes, and cooking equipment of homes and commercial eating places.

Carcinogenic Chemicals from Other Sources

Potential carcinogenic contaminants also may be introduced into foodstuffs if vegetables, fruits, fish, oysters, and livestock are grown on soil or in water polluted with known carcinogens, such as radioactive matter, arsenicals, selenium and polycyclic hydrocarbons contained in ship fuel oils. Consideration, moreover, must be given to the possibility that carcinogenic chemicals may be formed from noncarcinogenic ones under the influence of heat. Possible examples are (1) charred or tarry carbonaceous matter formed when bread or biscuits are excessively toasted or meats are grilled or roasted or (2) hydrocarbon constituents of mineral oils freed by cracking of the oil when it is used as a fat substitute and subjected to heat during grilling or baking.

There exists also the possibility that originally noncarcinogenic additives and contaminants may interreact with each other or with food constituents and form new compounds possessing carcinogenic properties in the foodstuffs. They may be produced under the influence of processing procedures or during the preparation of food in the kitchen. Plastics used as wrapping material, sausage skins and coating material of fruits, cheese, meat, butter, and can linings may carry a similar hazard.

Mention may finally be made of several experimental observations indicating that a dietary intake of certain spices or alkaloids which contaminate foodstuffs (chilies, alkaloids of senecio plants, crude ergot) may result in the development of liver tumors when given to rats.

Radiation May Produce Carcinogens

The use of various types of radiation energy in the processing of foodstuffs also deserves consideration from a carcinogenic viewpoint, since these agents (ultraviolet radiation, ionizing radiation) produce in the constituents of food, such as sterols and nucleo-proteins, definite chemical changes. No reliable information exists and no adequate experimental studies have been made for establishing the noncarcinogenic nature of the radiation products, although both types of radiation are eminently carcinogenic when acting on living tissues of both man and various species of animals.

A Cancer Warning

The great majority of the different cancerous reactions mentioned here were produced either by the administration of excessively high doses or followed upon their introduction through routes distinct from those encountered under ordinary alimentation. The cancers developed in animals differed in various metabolic respects from man. But the mere fact of the existence of such responses presents a definite warning deserving serious attention if possible endemic and epidemic cancerous manifestations among exposed population groups are to be avoided.

Reprinted by permission of *The Saturday Review* Research Section: Science and Humanity.

CHAPTER **10**

Cancer Is Traced to Food Additives

by ARNALDO CORTESI

Reports from cancer experts indicate that many of the substances used in our foods are unsafe and may be causes of cancer.

Rome, August 20, 1956—A number of food additives used in the United States and Europe as dyes, thickeners, sweeteners, preservatives and the like were labeled cancer-producing today by a symposium of the International Union Against Cancer.

Other food additives were put on a suspect list as unsafe until their properties had been more thoroughly tested.

The cancer experts meeting in Rome acknowledged that this created a "serious public health problem." They unanimously recognized the "urgent necessity of international collaboration for the protection of mankind" against such hazards as cancer-producing food additives.

The participants in the symposium also acknowledged that food additives were only one part of the vast problem of environmental cancer, which includes occupational and lung cancers.

The symposium was attended by 42 cancer experts from 21 countries, including 7 Americans and 4 Russians. It was called by the congress of the International Union Against Cancer held in Sao Paulo, Brazil, in 1954.

Report Subject to Review

The joint report unanimously adopted by the symposium is subject to review by the Executive Committee of the International Union Against Cancer. It is, therefore, possible that some of its conclusions may be modified.

The report laid down the basic principle that no food additives should be used unless specifically permitted by legislation based on lists of substances that have been proved innocuous after stringent laboratory tests.

It went on to give the first lists of food preservatives and dyes that were found either acceptable, dubious or definitely dangerous. Dubious preservatives requiring urgent retesting included ethyl and butyl esters, thiodiprionic acid and its derivatives and formic acid.

The dangerous preservatives condemned as "carcinogenous and to be avoided for human use" included thiourea, tioacetamide, 8-hydroxyquinoline and hydroquinone. Most and perhaps all of these are used in the United States and Europe.

The report said certain mineral oils and paraffines used for coating milk containers had produced cancer in man and experimental animals. It issued a warning against foodstuffs sterilized by radiation as potential cancer hazards and again-t the use of estrogens as fattening agents for poultry and meat animals.

It said that several detergents had "cocarcinogenous and prompting effects" and that their use for cleaning food containers therefore required caution.

Food Dyes Condemned

Food dyes came in for particularly severe condemnation from the symposium. Its report stated that no food dye at present met "agreed criteria of safety." Twenty-nine dyes were listed as "unsuitable" or "potentially dangerous" with the statement that they should on no account "be added to food or drink for men or animals."

Another list contained 23 dyes that might prove satisfactory after further tests.

Dr. Heuper's Report

The fundamental paper that formed the basis of the symposium's recommendations was read by Dr. Wilhelm C. Heuper, German-born member of the United States delegation. IIe is chief of the Environmental Cancer Section of the National Cancer Institute and is co-chairman of the symposium.

Dr. Heuper listed 20 groups of suspect food additives and 17 groups of suspect food contaminants. Many of these agents, he said, have not been adequately investigated for carcinogenic qualities. The food additives included dyes, thickeners, synthetic sweeteners and flavors, preservatives, shortening, bleaches, oils and fat substitutes. The food contaminants included antibiotics and estrogen for fattening animals, pesticide residues, soot, chemical sterilizers, antisprouting agents, wrapping materials, radiation.

At the end of their labors the symposium and Executive Committee of International Union Against Cancer were received in audience by the Pope at his summer residence of Castel Gandolfo. He delivered a brief address and imparted an apostolic blessing to them and their work. *(Reprinted by permission from the New York Times, August 21, 1956.)*

Newspaper articles following this one in American papers quoted our Food and Drug experts as saying that we in this country are "well protected" against any possible harm from food additives. Here is a sample of how well protected we really are.

Food and Drug Research for July, 1956, gives a chart of

food colors (that is, dyes used in foods) which are permitted in the United States along with their status in other countries.

A certain blue dye, allowed and declared as safe in food in this country, is not allowed in food in Argentina, Brazil, France, Germany, Great Britain, Italy, Sweden or Switzerland. The scientists of those countries are not exactly nitwits. Is it possible that a substance considered by them as too toxic for inclusion in food is perfectly safe for Americans to eat day after day, year after year?

A green coloring permitted in America is not permitted in 5 other countries surveyed. An orange dye we are permitted to use is banned in all the countries listed except Canada. This is the one recently "decertified" by our Food and Drug Administration as too toxic for use in food. We have been eating it all these years, until the experts made up their minds.

Another dye (red this time) is allowed only in Canada and two other countries. No other country permits its use. Yet in America, this dye, which is used to color Florida oranges, was recently declared unsafe for human consumption. The Florida citrus industry set up such a howl that Congress has passed special legislation permitting its use for 3 more years, *in spite of the fact that we know it is poisonous!*

Another red and another yellow dye are banned in practically every other country, but permitted in America! How much longer will this kind of thing go on? How much longer are you going to stand for it, especially in view of the Report from Rome?

Doubletalk from the FDA

One more note, showing how headlines and doubletalk can cancel out the powerful effect this startling Report might have on our national life. In *Food Field Reporter* for September 3, 1956 (the newspaper of the food and grocery industry), this headline appears: "No Food Additive is Cancer Cause, Says Dr. Lehman of FDA." A flat statement. Just like that. Dr. Lehman is head of the Food and Drug Division of Pharmacology, and he said to the gathering in Rome that no intentional food additive used at present in the United States is cancer-causing.

So, in one sentence, he demolished all the careful work, the thoughtful and courageous planning that went into the announcements of the scientists meeting in Rome. So far as the United States is concerned, he said, all chemical additives have met the "margin of safety" requirements. They cannot cause cancer. A flat statement, blazoned in headlines to allay the fears of anyone in the grocery trade who might begin to wonder about some of the things on his shelves.

But apparently some outraged reporter just couldn't let Dr. Lehman get away with it, so he checked back with the office of the Food and Drug Administration. Farther down in the article we read that what Dr. Lehman said was "an obvious inadvertence," according to Wallace F. Janssen, assistant to the commissioner of the FDA.

"What Dr. Lehman obviously intended to say was that all chemical additives which have received informal FDA clearance and approval have met the . . . margin of safety principle . . ." continued Janssen, "He certainly did not mean to say that all additives used in the United States have met the requirements, since Dr. Lehman himself has frequently pointed out there are many now in use which have not been studied sufficiently to establish their complete safety."

Chemical Week for September 1, 1956 carries more doubletalk from the National Cancer Institute Research Director, G. B. Mider. Why, says Mr. Mider, this report was talking about a lot of things that contaminate food—including bacteria that get into it in home kitchens. You certainly can't say that these are cancer causing!

The FDA and Industry

The *Chemical Week* quotes a spokesman of the Food and Drug Administration as saying what appears to us to be the most damaging admission made yet in this jungle of weasel-words and doubletalk. "Moreover, some dosages might take years to build up enough quantities to be dangerous." *This is what we food faddists have been saying right along! This is the crux of the matter!* Many poisons are cumulative. And it isn't the slice of baker's bread or the piece of pie you eat today that will bring you ill-health, be it cancer or some other degenerative disease. *It's all the poisons you take in every day and the terrible sum of them over the span of a life-time that are important!* And here is the spokesman of the FDA himself admitting that you really can't do tests to prove what all these poisons may do to you, for they accumulate year after year—all of them. How can you subject laboratory animals to all the poisons to which we human beings are subjected every day when we don't even know how many of these there may be, let alone how poisonous any given one of them is?

And the FDA uses this as an argument *against* the testing of food additives—it "would be too heavy a burden on industry" they say, and you can't tell how much of a dose you need over the years to run into danger. So, therefore, says the FDA (whose sole function supposedly is to protect the health of the American people), we'll just have to let them go on putting additives of unknown toxicity in food.

The final inane and meaningless statement was made, according to *Chemical Week* by an unidentified "research director" who said, "It's up to industry and the government to keep aware of the effects of such materials, and, as time provides the answers, take what steps are necessary."

A Program Against Additives

What can you do to protect yourself from the food additives listed in the Report from Rome? There seems to be no way you can continue to buy food and escape even a small part of these poisons. We believe the final solution must be food cooperatives established by health-minded folks in every community where only organically-raised foods can be purchased.

Until that day, how can you protect yourself and your family? First of all, do not buy processed foods, dyed foods, refined foods. Shun anything that contains any of the additives listed in the Report from Rome. Read labels. Ask questions of your grocer. Demand to know whether the fresh foods you buy have been exposed to any of these dangers. And protest if you find they have been.

Secondly, protest to everyone involved—your grocer, the people from whom he buys food, your congressman, your minister, your local newspaper. Third, keep yourself in the best possible health, for healthy folks can withstand poisons more readily. Follow the *Prevention* program for healthful living and get plenty of vitamins and minerals! Eat meat, fish, eggs, fruits and vegetables. Eat no food that has gone into a factory.

CHAPTER 11

What's Wrong With Soft Drinks?

A few facts about the ever-present carbonated beverages which have become an American diet habit.

Probably most of us Americans have by now a general idea that soft drinks are not especially to be recommended as part of one's diet. But did you ever get into a discussion of the subject with a friend or neighbor, or, what is worse, at your PTA or club meeting, and find that you can't actually state with clarity and conviction just why soft drinks are harmful? You won't find today many people who will give you an argument when you discuss the harmfulness of alcohol and tobacco. Even the most devoted addicts will admit that they are harming their health when they drink or smoke to excess. But have you ever tried to reason with someone who regularly consumes from 1 to 5 or 10 bottles of carbonated drinks per day?

Have you ever raised your voice at the meeting of the committee which is planning the Sunday School picnic, or the field day or the club outing to which the kids are invited? Pop, colas, ginger ale, birch beer and sodas are accepted as part of the day's fun, and you are nothing but a wet blanket if you enter any protests suggesting that other kinds of drinks might be more healthful, especially for the children.

Harmful Effects of Soft Drinks

Here is some ammunition that may be helpful to you in your next discussion over carbonated drinks. Written by George Blumer, M.D., the first article appeared originally in *Annals of Western Medicine and Surgery* for February, 1952. Dr. Blumer reminds us that the American Medical Association through all its outlets of literature for the layman has for a number of years been calling attention to the possible harm that the habitual consumption of soft drinks can bring about.

This harm falls under 3 heads: 1. some of the drinks contain harmful drugs, 2. most of them have a chemical reaction strong enough to injure certain parts of the body, especially the teeth and 3. their constant use is almost bound to have a deleterious effect on other aspects of diet.

Caffeine in the Cola Drinks

The cola beverages contain caffeine—about two-thirds of a grain of caffeine to 6 ounces of the beverage—that is, 3 bottles of "coke" contain about as much of the drug as one cup of coffee. We know many parents who will not permit their children to drink coffee, but, knowingly or unknowingly, permit them to drink, day after day, cola drinks whose total caffeine content may far exceed that of a cup or two of coffee. Most medical men today believe that the use of caffeine is harmful, especially for youngsters. We know that it is a drug which has a stimulating effect. There is evidence, says Dr. Blumer, that caffeine increases gastric secretion, making it undesirable for use by individuals with peptic ulcers. Ulcers have been produced in animals and in some human beings by the excessive use of caffeine. Some people, hypersensitive to caffeine, are unable to take it at all. Others develop dizziness from drinks containing caffeine.

The American cola beverage has a pH of approximately 2.6. This means that it is highly acid. Erosion of the enamel and dentine in rats' teeth has been brought about by habitual consumption of cola drinks. The relation of the consumption of carbonated drinks to the high incidence of tooth decay in America is undoubtedly being investigated right now by a number of highly qualified researchers. Meanwhile, does it not seem reasonable that a substance which can erode the calcium from the teeth of rats cannot help but harm human tooth enamel, when this same substance is in contact with the enamel day after day, year after year, summer and winter?

Carbonated Beverages Affect Dietary Habits

Perhaps their most dangerous aspect, especially for the health of our children, is the effect of carbonated drinks on dietary habits. As you will see in the chart below, these drinks contain absolutely no food value, except for calories, which produce quick energy and fat. So there is no way to compare the value of milk, or a fruit or vegetable drink with a cola drink.

The former contain in varying amounts proteins and fats, along with many, many vitamins and minerals. The cola drink contains nothing the body can use except the calories of its sugar.

When your children select a soft drink at the school lunch counter, at the drug store on the way home from school, or at home in the evening, they are consuming a disproportionate amount of sugar, which contributes nothing useful to their health and which satisfies their appetites so that they have no desire for the healthful foods, containing food elements their growing bodies must have. Then, too, it is surprising how rapidly one can get the habit of soft drinks on every occasion rather than herb teas, fruit or vegetable juices as the natural accompaniment of food. Of course, radio and television programs, billboards and magazine advertising presenting your favorite screen star or crooners swigging down soft drinks by the gallon—this is bound to have an effect on all of us, too, but especially on the young folks.

Erosive Power of Soft Drinks on Teeth

The experiments to which Dr. Blumer refers are those performed at Cornell University by Dr. Clive McCay and Lois Will. Four sets of rats were used. One group was given tomato juice to drink as their only beverage. The second group drank orange juice, the third distilled water and the fourth phosphoric acid and sucrose in the same percentages in which they are found in the cola drinks.

Distilled water was the only drink that did not erode the rats' teeth. Tomato juice caused the least erosion, phosphoric acid the most. In fact, at the end of six months the researchers could no longer estimate erosion of the teeth of those rats who drank the cola mixture, because their teeth had eroded right down to the gum line. Remember, conditions of the experiment were not exaggerated in any way. The rats ate a good diet, and all other circumstances of their existence were directed toward good health. But they drank the cola mixture every day. (How many folks in your family do the same?)

Its Action on Human Teeth

As further proof of the violent action of phosphoric acid on tooth enamel, the two Cornell experimenters suspended human teeth in a cola solution, then calculated the quantity of calcium in each tooth at intervals. In three hours, 1.4 milligrams of calcium per gram of tooth had been dissolved. In 336 hours, 14.6 milligrams of calcium had been dissolved. Now this doesn't mean that a human tooth, suspended in a cola solution will disintegrate before your eyes. It does mean, however, that over a period of time (two weeks, for instance) that tooth may lose its calcium, which is the most important constituent of tooth enamel.

What relation does this fact have, do you suppose, to the current rate of tooth decay in this country, especially among our young people?

Acid Content of Soft Drinks

Consumer Reports became greatly interested in Dr. McCay's experiments and did some investigating of their own, which they reported in their July, 1950, issue. Their laboratory purchased 13 common soft drinks and tested them for their acid content. The results follow. To interpret these results, one must understand the chemical term pH, which is the way of indicating acidity or alkalinity. A neutral liquid, like water, has a pH of 7. Numbers less than 7 indicate acidity, and the lower the pH number, the greater the acidity. In other words, according to an investigation, the cola drinks are much more acid; club soda less so.

	Brands	*Average pH*
Colas	6	2.4
Ginger ale	12	2.7
Lime, lemon, and lemon & lime	7	2.9
Grape	6	3.0
Raspberry	4	3.1
Cherry	7	3.1
Orange	11	3.2
Root beer	4	3.4
Cream soda	11	3.9
Sarsaparilla	5	4.0
Cocoa cream	3	4.3
Club soda	10	4.7

Consumer Reports counsels: "The safest procedure is to minimize the risk of acid erosion by going easy with the more acid beverages, drinking them in moderation and preferably with food (which dilutes the acid effect)."

A more recent experiment performed by Carey D. Miller of the Foods and Nutrition Department of the University of Hawaii is reported in the *Journal of the American Dietetic Association* for April, 1952. One hundred and twenty-nine rats were given carbonated drinks with their food—flavored sodas, root beer and other nationally advertised drinks. The lower molars of the rats were observed and rated respectively for the following five conditions: 1. high polish of enamel, 2. slight etching, 3, mild destruction, 4. moderate destruction and 5. severe destruction.

Results ranged from .8 for root beer to 3.4 for one kind of orange drink. This researcher discovered the interesting fact that the *p*H, or acidity, of the beverage apparently did not indicate always the amount of erosion that would occur. Some of the less acid drinks were found to be as erosive as the more acid ones. Three cola drinks produced 3 different degrees of enamel erosion; two ginger ales gave entirely different results and one orange soda produced almost twice as much erosion as the other, even though their degree of acidity was very similar.

Lithium in Soft Drinks

Miller brings up the use of lithium in soft drinks, indicating that lithium seems to reduce somewhat the erosive quality of the liquids. One lemon soda *without lithium* gave a score of 1.4 erosion. Another of the same brand *with lithium* gave a score of .9. Incidentally lithium is a substance "regarded unfavorably" by the Food and Drug Administration, which recommends that its use be discontinued. We reported on the use of lithium in certain salt substitutes. The action of the lithium was violent enough to cause several deaths, and the product was immediately withdrawn. However, when the Food and Drug Administration "recommends" that lithium be discontinued in soft drinks, this apparently remains a matter of choice to the manufacturer.

It is interesting to note, in Miller's report, the erosion scores resulting from the use of noncarbonated beverages—drinks made from synthetic beverage powders. Both of these noncarbonated drinks—orange and strawberry—brought about a higher rate of erosion than the carbonated drinks. Miller is careful to point out that no one has proved definitely that enamel erosion brings about cavities in human teeth. But we agree with him when he states that it seems reasonable to assume that overindulgence in such acid beverages as carbonated drinks and powdered fruit drinks must cause defects in the enamel of human teeth.

Nearsightedness and Cola Drinks

Several years ago we reported the point of view of Dr. Hunter H. Turner in an article in the *Pennsylvania Medical Journal* for May, 1944, on the subject of prevention of myopia or degenerative nearsightedness. Lamenting over the large numbers of Americans who are doomed to wear glasses, he suggests that incorrect diet undoubtedly plays an important role in producing myopia. Furthermore, he believes that carbonic acid is the eye's worst enemy, and he attributes the alarming increase in cases of myopia to "the pernicious guzzling of carbonated beverages by young children today." Carbonated beverages exposed to air break down into their basic ingredients of water and carbon dioxide, so that such drinks would be much less harmful if they were allowed to stand until they were "flat." But, of course, their most attractive characteristic is their "fizz." So they are taken into the stomach while they are still actively effervescing. There is no atmospheric pressure in the stomach, so a large amount of the acid is assimilated by the body.

Soft Drinks Worthless as Food

Dr. Michael J. Walsh, Instructor in Clinical Nutrition at the University of California and past president of the American Academy of Applied Nutrition, had this to say about soft drinks at a meeting of the California State Dental Association in 1950: "When it comes to the comparison of the fruit juices with some popular soft drinks, this table shows the actual difference in nutritive value:

	Lemon Juice	Orange Juice	Grape-fruit Juice	Cola	Ginger Ale
Protein, grams per 100 grams	1.0	.5	.5	—	—
Fat, grams per 100 grams	.7	.1	.1	—	—
Carbohydrates, grams per 100 grams.	8.5	11.4	9.8	10.5	9.0
Calories	48.	49.	42.	42.	36.
Calcium, milligrams per 100 grams	28.	26.	19.	—	—
Phosphorus, milligrams per 100 grams	7.	14.	18.	—	—
Iron, milligrams per 100 grams	.2	.1	.2	—	—
Vitamin A, I.U. per 100 grams	50.	270.	14.	—	—
Thiamin, milligrams per 100 grams.	.060	.080	.028	—	—
Riboflavin, milligrams per 100 grams	4.	80.	90.	—	—
Niacin, milligrams per 100 grams	.15	0.5	—	—	—
Vitamin C, milligrams per 100 grams.	45.	45.	30.	—	—

Now ask yourself, are these beverages comparable?

"Lemon juice, when consumed consistently and regularly is known to be a prominent factor in erosion (of tooth enamel). . . . The cola drinks are well known for their caries-producing effect, not only because of the sugar content but also because of their known content of free phosphoric acid which is a well-known solvent of tooth enamel. When Dr. Hockett asks 'is the orange juice better than the soft drinks for total health,' I refer him to the table and let the facts speak for themselves." We are opposed to the excessive use of citrus juice, because of its harmful effects on the teeth. But at least citrus fruit, taken in moderation, is *food!*

What Exactly Is in Soft Drinks?

Soft drinks contain carbon dioxide which makes them "fizz." The carbon dioxide used by soft drink manufacturers may be the by-product from some other manufacturing process, such as the brewing or coke industry, or it may be produced by reacting chalk, limestone or bicarbonate of soda with sulfuric acid.

As one of the earnest defenders of soft drinks points out, the only sugar used in making these beverages is "sugar of the highest degree of purity." This means, of course, sugar that has been refined until there is not a chance of even one iota of food value remaining in it. This means, too, that all of the other food factors in the sugar cane, beet or corn from which the sugar was made, are omitted in the refined sugar. These other food factors are important for a proper assimilation and metabolism of sugar in the body. But you don't get them in refined sugar. Sucrose made from cane or beet sugar and dextrose made from corn sugar are the most commonly used sweetening agents in soft drinks. Of course, in many states, saccharin or some other synthetic sweetening agent is used. The acids poured into the carbonated beverage may be citric, tartaric or phosphoric, depending on what the flavor of the final product is to be.

Coloring and Flavoring

The sparkling clear green of a lime drink does not mean that the product has been anywhere near a lime. If the luscious purple of a grape drink bears any resemblance to a grape, living or dead, it is purely coincidental, for this drink has probably never been near a grape. The coloring agents for soft drinks are almost without exception certified coal tar colors. This means that they are the coloring matters made from coal tar which the government has certified as safe for human consumption, in spite of the fact that other coal tar colorings are known to produce cancer.

The flavors of soft drinks may come from natural or synthetic sources or compound essences which are a combination of both. In other words, the orange drink reposing in your refrigerator may perhaps actually contain some orange juice, or it may contain merely an approximation of orange flavor produced from coal tar.

The Position of the Soft Drink Industry

When Dr. Clive McCay reported his rat experiments before the Delaney Committee investigating chemicals in foods, one lawmaker present reminded him that the soft drink industry has large proportions. (Indeed it does—it is a billion dollar industry!) He suggested soft-pedaling the facts Dr. McCay had reported, because they might disrupt this industry and have a serious effect on the economy as a whole. Dr. McCay agreed that they might, but added that he believed the health of the nation's children might be as important as the welfare of the soft drink industry. However, a conspiracy of silence seems to surround McCay's testimony. At any rate, it never made the headlines of our newspaper—did it in yours?

What Can We Do About Soft Drinks?

Dr. Miller's article makes no recommendations for solving the problem of excessive consumption of acid beverages, except to point out that it may play a part in promoting dental decay. Dr. McCay would, we strongly suspect, advise, nay insist upon, the complete elimination of soft drinks from the diet of any health-minded individual. Dr. Blumer has 3 positive suggestions to make.

First, further education of the public, especially parents, in regard to the possible dangers of excessive soft drink consumption. (Through the newspapers and magazines, Dr. Blumer, which also carry millions of dollars worth of soft drink advertising?) Second, requirement by law that the contents of such beverages be printed on the label and third, further search and investigation of the effects of carbonated drinks, so the presentations may be made intelligently to parent-teacher associations, medical societies and so forth with far more factual material than is now available.

It seems to us that enough research has already been done to incriminate carbonated drinks. We agree wholeheartedly that the contents of soft drinks should be listed on the label, just as the contents of all packaged, canned and bottled foods should be listed on the label. Furthermore, we insist that this labeling be made simple enough that it really means something to the average housewife who has not had a course in the higher intricacies of chemistry. Which of us shoppers in the super market would have any idea what was meant by the chemical names of coal tar flavorings and colorings? We believe, too, that all government agencies (state, national and local) that deal with general health should make available to interested persons all the facts reported above on the subject of soft drinks. You might try writing to your congressman, state legislature and local board of health about this.

Educate Children Away from Soft Drinks

We hope sincerely that any adult who has read this article will be wise enough to shun soft drinks in the future. And for the young folks, we have another suggestion to make. Children nowadays are scientifically-minded. They study and respect science. They are, in general, aware that good health must be earned and learned—it is not just a hit-and-miss proposition. They admire and respect good health. And—when they're teenagers at any rate—they admire good appearance. We think it's possible to educate the children of America away from carbonated drinks, beginning individually in our homes, if we do it on a scientific basis without resorting to blind unreasonable commandments.

We can say to our children, "We know you like to drink soft drinks They taste good. Everybody else drinks them. But here are the facts, the scientific facts, mind you, about soft drinks and the harm they may do to your good health and your appearance." Scientifically-minded as they are today, young folks will take heed, we believe, if you point out to them calmly and objectively just where the harm lies in soft drinks.

SECTION 3

DRUGS, HOUSEHOLD PREPARA-
TIONS, X-RAYS, COSMETICS

We are opposed to the indiscriminate use of drugs. A healthy body, completely nourished, withstands disease. Drugs that alleviate one disease may produce another. Modern wonder drugs (antibiotics, cortisone, sulfa preparations and so forth) all bring a train of misfortunes sooner or later.

We especially protest against medicine chest remedies such as aspirin, bicarb of soda, "nerve pills," sleeping pills, benzedrine, mineral oil and other laxatives. Hormones given during the menopause do nothing but postpone the day when the menopause finally arrives. And they can cause cancer in those who are especially susceptible.

Nose sprays are dangerous and should be avoided.

We believe radiation by X-ray should be resorted to only in dire necessity and then under supervision of trained experts. Many cosmetics, cleaning fluids and household preparations contain substances irritating or poisonous. If you must use them, obey instructions on the label, test cosmetics on a patch of skin for 48 hours to see if you are allergic to them. Use detergents, bleaches, cleaning fluids with extreme care. Keep all medicines and even preparations that may seem harmless out of reach of children. Do not use insecticides in your home. They are deadly poison.

CHAPTER **12**

Dangers of Aspirin

Aspirin is only one of the thousands of drugs Americans use. The greatest danger associated with its use is that it is generally accepted as being safe as rain—a medicine chest remedy that everybody takes all the time.

"An open foe may prove a curse, but a pretended friend is worse," wrote John Gay, 18th century English poet and author of *The Beggar's Opera*. Under the guise of being helpful and well-disposed, a so-called "home remedy" can steal from the storehouse of its host's health even more craftily than an open housebreaker, a common thief or an enemy of society. For his work goes on, undetected, night and day, steadily diminishing the goods of those who trust him. As an example, in this age of self-administered drug-store cures for everything from stomach ills to common colds, there are many persons who put their confidence in this type of "friendly" aid, but all such as resort to a "painkiller" instead of heeding Nature's well-intended "painful" way of showing them that all is not well within their bodily economy must eventually wake up to a day of reckoning, when the "pretended friend" has decamped and left them with a heavy inventory of serious damage.

The most trusted and seemingly beneficial of these fair-weather friends is *aspirin,* which by dictionary definition has practically come to be a synonym for "comfort" and "relief." Its true chemical composition thus hidden 'under a cloak of mis-understood origin, would be scrutinized more carefully perhaps if it were realized that this apparently inoffensive name is itself derived as follows: *A* for "acetyl—*SPIR* for "spiraeic acid," an old name for the more modern "salicylic acid"—plus IN, orig-inally used as a trademark suffix or termination to a word. The resultant compound, *acetylsalicylic acid* (aspirin), is one of a class of remedies known as "analgesics" (painkillers), and is today in universal use to relieve pains of varied origin, ranging from headache, rheumatism, gout, to sore throat, neuralgia and the like. Many readers will, of course, recognize that it is dangerous business to go about blindly suppressing bodily discomforts without inquiring into their origin and value as symptoms, thereafter treating the *cause* rather than the *effect*.

Aspirin Came from Germany

First introduced into this country from Germany some 43 years ago, the original "Bayer" patent expired in 1917, but continues even today to harvest rich financial rewards from a product that now is being manufactured by many other laboratories over fundamentally the same prescription. Nowadays, advertising of the chemical ingredients of most of these aspirin-content derivatives is given second place to their more easily pronounced trade names, and the basic compound is also contained in other products in which it is impossible for the nonscientist to identify it under its fancy name. Furthermore, doctors often prescribe it in a variety of forms without a patient's knowledge, acting on the assumption that in moderate and regulated dosage it can do no harm in its twofold general action of *fever-reducer* (antipyretic) *and pain-soother* (analgesic).

The Case Against Aspirin

However, because of the increasing stack of evidence supporting the dangers involved in frequent self-dosing with aspirin, it is time to publish all the truth about the drug. *The British Pharmaceutical Codex* (an official dictionary on medications published by the Council of the Pharmaceutical Society of Great Britain) has this to say about its action and uses: "Aspirin passes through the stomach unchanged, but is slowly decomposed by the alkali of the duodenum (first part of the small intestine), salicylic acid being liberated."

Reginald E. E. Austin, M.D., writing in *Health Culture* (June, 1948), adds that "concentrated solutions of the acid are caustic and are used as paints or plasters for the removal of corns or warts. Since it destroys tissues and does not build them up, obviously, then, salicylic acid is *not a food but a poison,* and should find no place in the body, even in minute doses. Yet it is often made use of in the preservation of foods and beverages."

Dr. Austin then warns his readers even more sternly of the potential damage to health that is contained in a single tablet of aspirin. Elaborating on its action, he quotes from Bruce's *Materia Medica,* an authoritative teaching manual recognized by leading American medical schools, as follows: "Salicylic acid is rapidly absorbed and circulates as sodium salicylate. . . . *A moderate dose* causes a more rapid heart beat, and rise in blood pressure, flushing and warmth of the surface, perspiration, fullness in the head, tinnitus (a ringing sound in the ears), deafness, impairment of vision, and possibly a slight fall of temperature. *Larger doses* may cause delirium, especially with visual hallucinations; respiration is disturbed; the heart is slowed and weakened; the vessels are relaxed, and the blood pressure falls; and perspiration is increased. . . . Occasionally it induces a morbilliform (measley) eruption. . . . Sometimes albuminuria and haematuria (albumin or blood, respectively, in the urine)."

Dr. Carey Eggleston, Professor of Pharmacology in Cornell University Medical School, is quoted by Dr. Austin as having said, "The worst charge I can bring against aspirin is that it is without a doubt indirectly responsible for thousands of deaths. . . . The way aspirin kills is by deadening pain. Make no mistake about pain. It is unpleasant, but it is beneficent. It is a flag set by Nature to warn us that something has gone wrong. Aspirin pulls down that flag and makes people think everything is all right—till often it is too late to make it right. Aspirin lulls them into a false sense of security. It conceals the symptoms; it waves aside the sore throat, the slight cough, the headache, as a thing of no consequence; and allows the disease to work under cover, till it gets a grip that no medical skill can break."

The Danger of Aspirin Known—But!

This being the grave state of affairs, why have we not been warned publicly against habitual self-dosing with this readily available drug that can be purchased by even a child? As long ago as October 5, 1940, an editorial in the *Journal of the American Medical Association* reasoned that the main safeguard against overdose lay in a ringing sensation (tinnitus) in the ears of aspirin users, "so that the drug may be discontinued before these persons become seriously poisoned." The editorial admitted that undoubtedly, considerable indirect harm has resulted from its indiscriminate use, since disturbances for which it was taken were not helped. The article pointed out the appearance of many reports on the *adverse effects* which may stem from its careless use. These, it said, have included habit formation, heart depression, miscarriage and allergic reactions which have caused such alarming symptoms as hives, itching, swelling of the skin due to blood vessel disorder (edema) and even ulceration and gangrene.

This same editorial then went on to discourage all use of aspirin on the part of drunkards, diabetics and persons with kidney inflammation (nephritis). It concluded by quoting figures from *The Lancet* on a wave of fatalities that occurred in England from the use of aspirin. This source indicated that 735 deaths due to poison in England and Wales in 1938 were reported. Of these 591 were suicides, 92 were accidental, and the remainder listed as doubtful. The cause of 43 of the suicides, 8 of the accidental fatalities and 14 of the uncertain number was determined to be aspirin, thereby making *aspirin responsible for 65 of the 735 fatal poisonings.*

This record was then compared with that for the year 1937, in which aspirin was noted as having been responsible for 61 deaths, which, when added to those for the preceeding year 1936 (about half of the number of 1938) made a grand total of approximately 150 *deaths from aspirin in a 3-year period* in England and Wales. Since *The Lancet* considered it "curious" that a drug that can cause such a high number of fatalities in so short a time is not classified as a poison, the editorial in the *Journal of the American Medical Association* came to the cautious conclusion that if aspirin is capable of causing so many deaths in Great Britain, perhaps further investigation should be given it.

How Aspirin Works

The recommendation that aspirin be investigated came in 1940 from a highly respected professional journal that added this sobering truth about the seriousness of the common drug: "The only country in the world that permitted a patent for acetylsalicylic acid (aspirin) was the United States." But even then its actual harmful workings on the human system were known through an ingenious invention called a *gastroscope* (stomach-observer). Made in Germany, this instrument through which stomach reactions of patients can be visibly seen by the trained eye of an examining doctor, consists of a flexible rubber tube lined with a series of 20 or more lenses. A British magazine, *Good Health,* for October, 1939, reported on the work of two English doctors, A. H. Douthwaite and G. A. M. Lintott (Guy's Hospital, London), who decided to use the gastroscope in the effort to determine why aspirin was likely to cause indigestion, usually in the form of heartburn, blood in the stool, or vomiting of blood in persons using it. After thoroughly emptying the stomachs of 16 patients, they gave them the drug, got them to swallow the gastroscope's tube and watched the results. "In 13 cases there was a positive reaction varying from slight redness to considerable congestion with minute hemorrhages beneath the stomach lining. Three persons were not affected. The inflammatory response was usually confined to the lesser curvature, that is, the right side of the stomach. Significantly, this area is particularly liable to ulceration. The doctors proved that beyond doubt the continuous use of aspirin may bring on a chronic gastritis, that is, a chronic inflammation of the stomach lining."

Its ill-effects are by no means limited to the stomach, however. *The Lancet* for August 5, 1950, observed that the action of aspirin also affects the colon: "Ten grams of aspirin stops (the) colon from contracting normally (a procedure necessary for bowel movement)," and, "The effect is the same whether the aspirin has been taken for lumbago or toothache or for the more usual headache."

Aspirin and Hemorrhage

Queried as to the hemorrhage-producing properties of aspirin when used locally in the throat to reduce inflammation and soreness after surgical removal of the tonsils, the "Answer" (in the "Questions and Answers" section of the *Journal of the American Medical Association* for February 3, 1951) advised as follows: Although experiments have been conducted for the purpose of determining whether such a use of aspirin materially affects supply of the factor in blood that enables it to coagulate and clot (prothrombin) and tends to bring about a deficiency of this anti-hemorrhaging factor to the point of producing unrestrained bleeding, "there is no convincing data" to prove this point. *However,* except for the drug's inability to affect this normal blood-clot rate, used locally, aspirin might contribute to hemorrhage following tonsillectomy by irritation in some other manner.

Thus, in spite of the fact that some aspirin preparations now contain a certain quantity of vitamin K (which bears a reputation for possessing anti-hemorrhagic qualities), the use of aspirin tablets, according to the medical testimony cited above, involves a serious and dangerous interference with the blood stream's usual ability to heal over incisions or wounds through the formation of clots. Practice prevention on this score too: don't go on treating yourself to self-doses of aspirin.

Other Irritations Caused by Aspirin

From evidence submitted so far in this article, aspirin is known to have an irritant effect on the stomach, kidneys, colon and throat. The *British Medical Journal* for December 23, 1950, now adds to this list a new series of aspirin-reactions observed by Cochran, Watson and Reid. Considering these reactions to be characteristic of the symptoms of Cushing's disease (a condition due to overgrowth of certain cells in the pituitary gland), the English doctors blame the effects they saw on the use of aspirin by patients suffering from rheumatic fever. These bad effects included rounding of the facial features, acne, abnormal amounts of sugar in the urine and a nervous mental state. They also cite other testimony concerning the appearance of facial puffiness and skin eruptions following the use of aspirin. That the drug was directly responsible was proven by the fact that the reactions appeared with its use and disappeared with its discontinuance.

Aspirin and Asthma

This list of undesirable aftereffects of aspirin also includes asthmatic attack, as related in an article entitled "Allergy to Aspirin," by C. H. A. Walton, M.D., and H. W. Bottomley, M.D., of Winnipeg, Manitoba (*The Canadian Medical Association Journal,* March, 1951). Stating that, "In relation to its very wide use the number of cases of aspirin sensitivity is small, but the effects are so striking and often dangerous that physicians should be familiar with its character," the authors include hives and skin puffiness from disordered blood vessels among these already known manifestations of allergy following small intake of the drug. But its relation to asthma is their special interest, and among such patients they cite estimates of from 2 to 10 per cent as demonstrating this type of sensitivity.

Reviewing 830 cases of asthma seen by them between January 1, 1946, and April 30, 1950, they found 22 cases of definite aspirin allergy (2.7 per cent of the whole). But since more than a quarter of their 830 cases were in children lacking this special sensitivity, they reckon the incidence in their adult group to be nearer to 3.5 per cent. Fifteen of the 22 sensitive cases were women, a ratio of two females to one male, which agrees with other estimates that find the asthmatic reaction to be twice as frequent in women as in men.

The 22 cases ranged in age from 20 to 60, and were graduated according to 4 degrees of severity. All 5 in the most severe grade died within the 4 years of the authors' study. "That is, 22.7 per cent of our aspirin-sensitive cases were dead within 4 years. Three of these cases were examined at autopsy and showed the characteristic findings of death from bronchial asthma."

"Frosst 217" Poisoning

One of the patients of the Winnipeg doctors was an asthmatic woman, aged 41, who had been in the habit of dosing herself with an aspirin-preparation known as "Frosst 217" in order to relieve chronically recurrent headaches for which she did not know the cause. Admitted to the hospital for asthma treatment, she was almost in the stage of being symptom-free when she complained of a severe headache, requested and was granted two of these headache tablets. Within a matter of minutes she was in a state of collapse, exhibited no sounds of breathing, had turned blue and recorded a blood pressure that could not be read. After reviving her with oxygen and adrenalin, the doctors discovered that "her normal cycle was headache, aspirin, asthma, adrenalin, and headache." Later found to have a similar allergy to certain foods and to dust as well, her nasal passages proved to be blocked by the presence of growths known as polyps, and she also showed evidence of sinus disease. She died within a year of her discharge from the hospital.

With other headache-victims as well as with this particular patient, the continued use of aspirin actually produces headache. A vicious circle of chain-reactions is thus established, so that the habitual user ultimately finds himself forced to take aspirin to soothe a new headache that was caused by aspirin taken for an old one. And so on *ad infinitum*.

A cure that is not a cure, aspirin and addiction to it, present a menace so serious in its implications that Drs. Walton and Bottomley are gravely concerned over the fact that such small quantities of this openly purchasable drug are still sufficient to produce such "tremendous reactions." The precautions they took to guard against the possibility of encouraging a patient's innocent addiction deserve to be quoted in full as a warning to all readers: "The intern and nurses on (the) ward (of the 41-year-old woman) never forgot this drastic and frightening experience and have since been cautious in their use of drugs on asthmatic patients without the full knowledge and written authority of the attendant physician. However, it is notoriously difficult to prevent nurses and interns from administering such customary analgesics as aspirin and its compounds, believing them to be innocuous. We have felt it important to try to emphasize to our nursing and intern staff the dangers of such medications in asthmatics and always write an order forbidding the use of any medication without express authority."

Conclusions

In the light of this incriminating evidence against the dangerous "playing-with-fire" consequences of the aspirin-habit, all products containing the drug should be avoided. A depressant and not a stimulant, aspirin disorders the nervous system, thereby lowering the functions of life and retarding the healing process. This means that, even in those cases where the drug does not actually kill, it merely prolongs the suffering and often produces chronic disease. Obviously, then, any temporary relief brought by this "pretended friend" may well prove in the course of time to have been purchased at too high a price to justify a purely passing comfort, one that is far worse in its aftereffects than the cause for which it was originally taken.

Note: So unaware are most people of the dangers of the

aspirin habit that a contributor to the *Market Bulletin of West Virginia* burst into print (Oct. 16, 1950) with the following recipe for preserving fresh apples:

"Peel, core and slice apples. Put in jars and completely cover with water . . . Add one aspirin tablet to each quart of apples (two tablets if using half-gallon jars). Seal and store anywhere other foodstuffs are stored. When you are ready to use, simply rinse and use same as fresh apples. *They will foam some when opened as the aspirin is canning acid.*" (The italics are the contribution of the author of this article on aspirin.)

We heard of the preservative virtues of adding an aspirin tablet to a dozen or two of fresh-cut roses—but, after all, one does not eat roses. As for eating one quart of apples enhanced with one tablet of acetylsalicylic acid, well, that is the height of ignorance.

Serious effects may result from the indiscriminate use of such salicylates as aspirin, according to a report in the current (Sept. 8, 1951) *Journal of the American Medical Association.*

Intestinal Bleeding from Overuse of Aspirin

The case of a 74-year-old man who experienced 8 years of continuous intestinal bleeding as the result of prolonged use of aspirin was reported by Drs. Walter Modell and Russel Patterson of the Department of Pharmacology and Surgery, Cornell University Medical College, New York.

The patient, according to the report, suffered from weakness, anemia and a decrease in the number of colorless blood corpuscles which are believed to aid in the clotting of the blood.

The symptoms disappeared with the discontinuance of the use of aspirin. However, the doctors pointed out, they were unable to determine positively the connection between the taking of the aspirin and the reduction of the number of colorless blood corpuscles.

Aspirin and Children

The *United States Armed Forces Medical Journal* for January, 1952, presents us with a shocking revelation of the harmful effects of aspirin on children. In an article by Arthur C. Dietrick, Captain, M.C., USA, Harold L. Guard, Major, M.C., USA, Leo J. Geppert, Lieutenant Colonel, M.C., USA, the authors describe 6 cases of salicylic poisoning of children, for two of whom the aspirin had been prescribed by physicians. In the first case, a 3-month-old boy who had a cold was given 0.3 grams of aspirin every hour by his doctor. Twelve hours after he was brought to the hospital, seriously ill, his condition was critical, with convulsions, high temperature, coma and other symptoms. Salicylates were present in his urine. This child was hospitalized for 7 days before he was well enough to go home.

In the second case the physician did not write his prescription plainly enough and the druggist made up 12 powders containing the total amount intended for 12 doses. After the 5-month-old child was given this mistaken dose for several days, he went into such a deep stupor that he could not be awakened. It took 3 days in the hospital to bring him back to normal.

Editor's Note: Prevention magazine recently had a long article attacking the use of aspirin, and a very interesting thing occurred which I think our readers would like to hear about. I recently visited an optometrist in the city of Allentown, who is a reader of *Prevention,* and he said: "Rodale, I think you will be interested in the following happening: A lady came to me to have eyeglasses prescribed and I noticed her eyes were bloodshot. Remembering your article on aspirin which I read in *Prevention* magazine, I immediately associated bloodshot eyes with the overuse of aspirin as you wrote about. So I asked the lady, "Do you use aspirin?" She answered: "Do I use aspirin? I live on the darn stuff."

Fatal Poisoning

A 5-month-old girl, with a cold, was being treated by a physician who prescribed several different medicines, including penicillin. It seems incredible, but the child's parents gave the baby, in addition to the prescribed medicine, .13 grams of aspirin every 4 hours! They did not consider this important enough even to mention to the physician when the child became so ill she was taken to the hospital. She died of salicylic poisoning 4 days later. In the other 3 cases older children had taken by accident considerable quantities of aspirin. Symptoms were serious and the children were not released from the hospital for from 1 to 5 days.

The symptoms of salicylate poisoning are difficult to diagnose, say the authors, because, unless some adult has seen the child accidentally taking large quantities of aspirin, no one thinks to tell the physician the child has had aspirin, since it is given so freely by parents and physicians alike.

Don't Use Salicylic Acid in Any Form

While this article was being written, the Allentown *Morning Call* carried an article about a 4-year-old girl who died in a hospital here from accidentally drinking a quantity of oil of wintergreen, which also contains large quantities of salicylic acid. In *The Lancet* for September 29, 1951, is the story of an adult who experienced oozing of blood from the sockets of his teeth following extraction during the previous week. Several years before he had had the same experience. Both times he had taken aspirin for toothache before the extractions. Whenever he had teeth extracted without having taken aspirin beforehand, he had no difficulty with bleeding.

The lesson seems to be clear: throw away the aspirin now in your medicine chest and don't buy any more. If an average dose of aspirin is enough to cause serious or even fatal poisoning in a child, is it not taking the most dangerous kind of a chance to give any aspirin at all to children? And if the drug is powerful enough to produce these symptoms in children, what might it do eventually to adults who take it regularly every time they have a pain? Finally, if you must have aspirin or other substances containing salicylic acid, such as oil of wintergreen, keep them under lock and key at all times, and out of reach of small, curious hands, if there are young children about.

CHAPTER **13**

Barbiturates–"Safe" Sleep?

Barbiturates, or sleeping pills, are used every night by millions of Americans. How safe are they?

The danger of barbiturates in large doses has been widely publicized. Hardly a week goes by without a notice in the newspaper of a death "from an overdose of sleeping pills." But, comments an editorial in the February 23, 1952, *Lancet,* "not so well recognized are the occasional ill effects of taking these drugs over long periods."

As early as 1927 and again in 1933 Sir William Willcox warned in British medical journals against the use of these drugs. He claimed that repeated doses could cause such symptoms as mental depression, drowsiness, hallucinations, dizziness, lack of muscle coordination, slurring of speech, double vision and muscular paralysis. He cited two patients who were sent to him with supposedly organic nervous disorders. They were suffering from chronic barbiturate intoxication. Whether or not a drug causes addiction depends on whether or not there is violent distress when the drug is withdrawn. In some cases, convulsions and delirium have been reported when the use of barbiturates was stopped. So they should be classed as addictive drugs.

How Many People Take Sleeping Pills?

In Great Britain, goes on the editorial, a report on one month, September, 1949, revealed that of 17,000 prescriptions filled, 9.4 per cent were for barbiturates. In England sleeping pills can be purchased only by prescription. In this country the 1948 production figure for barbiturates was 672,000 pounds, or enough for 24 sleeping pills a year for every American. Considering the millions of children and the many adults who never take barbiturates, imagine what the average yearly consumption must be for those who take them habitually!

Dr. Victor Vogel, in charge of the Federal Narcotics Hospital at Lexington, Kentucky, has said that in this country sleeping pill addiction is becoming a more serious problem than morphine and heroin, because the drugs are so easy to obtain and withdrawal of them causes such distress to the person using them. An international committee, meeting in Geneva in January, 1952, recommended that national measures to control the distribution of the drugs should be strengthened.

CHAPTER 14

Tranquilizers–Newest Wonder Drugs

The newest wonder drugs are causing just as many health problems as the old ones did. Doctors and psychiatrists are worried about the widespread use of tranquilizers.

The latest "wonder" drugs are the tranquilizers. Their history reads like the history of all the other wonder drugs of our wondrous age. They were discovered and tried out and found to suppress symptoms of certain disorders. The drug companies and the national magazines then began a campaign of selling the drugs to the medical profession and the public respectively. Articles containing ecstatic, hysterical paeans of praise appeared across the country. Literature from drug companies recommending the tranquilizers for almost any condition from nail biting to transient irritability to high blood pressure and senility poured into doctors' offices all over the country.

Doctors, besieged by troublesome patients who had nothing wrong with them but "nerves," started in desperation to write prescriptions for the new drugs. An estimated 30 million prescriptions were written for the tranquilizers during 1956—accounting for 40 per cent of the total increase in prescriptions during 1956. One estimate is that tranquilizers accounted for 3 out of every 10 prescriptions written. The cost? One hundred and fifty million dollars!

Now the headlines turn ominous: "Stiff Code Urged on Tranquilizers," "Two Experts Warn on Tranquilizers," "Tranquilizers' Relationship to Suicide Reported by Medic," "Three Government Agencies Plan Evaluation of Tranquilizers."

On all sides the air is full of denunciations and denials. Someone is responsible for this gigantic and terrifying mushroom of drug addiction, for that is what it has become. And doctors, drug companies, public and government alike say, "Who, me? I wasn't the one who started it."

Classifications of Tranquilizers

There are two general classifications of tranquilizers— the very powerful ones and those a little less potent. In the first category come chlorpromazine and its related compounds. These are used generally on patients in mental hospitals. *Public Health Monograph Number 14, Public Health and Social Problems in the Use of Tranquilizing Drugs,* says significantly, "the dosages of chlorpromazine used in man impinge closely upon dosages that have been found to be lethal in animals." It seems to us there is room for considerable concern here.

The second group of tranquilizers may, however, be even more dangerous, we believe. These are the rauwolfia compounds and they go by a variety of trade names—the so-called "milder tranquilizers" now being wolfed down by millions of people all over the country in the belief that by so doing they can find "peace of mind." It seems impossible, but we have medical reports indicating that people are taking these "happiness" pills to stop smoking, to stop drinking, to stop quarreling with members of their family. They are recommended by some drug companies for people who must make speeches, perform before audiences, attend "high pressure" sales meetings, give parties or entertain difficult guests. One clipping tells us it is fashionable to add to party invitations, these days the letters "B.Y.O.T."—"Bring Your Own Tranquilizers."

How safe are the tranquilizers? Everyone was assured at the beginning, as they always are, that the drugs presented no hazards at all. Then reports of side effects began to pour in. At present we know that the tranquilizers can produce such symptoms as: nasal stuffiness, drowsiness, too-low blood pressure, shaking palsy, miosis (a shrinking of some organ), swelling of the face, blood disorders of the most serious kind, jaundice, dermatitis, dry mouth, sensitivity to light, rapid heart beat and depression so serious that it may lead to suicide.

These are the known side effects of the drugs now being taken so casually and so widely. "Only by prescription" we are told. But we are also told that many people deal out their prescription pills to friends and family. (They bring you "peace of mind," why not?) Black markets have flourished in some locales. And, of course, no one knows how many prescriptions are being refilled continually.

Practically No Knowledge of Final Effects

We are horrified by the information in the Public Health Monograph referred to above which indicates that we have practically no information at all as to the safety of the drugs, their toxicity, their effects over a long-range period, their dosage as related to sex, age, condition and so forth or what their final effect may be on the mental state of the person taking them. We are horrified by casual medical reports indicating that, after shaking palsy has been brought on by giving one of the tranquilizers, it is customary to continue to give the drug and then give another drug to combat the palsy. In fact, throughout all the medical articles we find suggestions that, if the tranquilizers should "tranquilize" too much, you can always give a stimulant to counteract it.

The Results of Habit Formation

In a recent statement, reported in the *New York Times* for February 10, 1957, the American Psychiatric Association expressed concern that these drugs, helpful in the treatment of serious psychiatric disorders, were now being used in a manner medically unsound and dangerous "to treat common anxiety, emotional upsets, nervousness and the routine tensions of everyday living." Earlier reports that the tranquilizers were not "habit-forming" have recently been disproved.

Perhaps most frightening of all are the reports of people driven to suicide as a result of taking tranquilizers. Dr. Walter J. R. Camp, State Toxicologist at the University of Illinois

College of Medicine, is quoted in a clipping (sorry, we do not have the name of the paper or the date) that in the past 4 months he had investigated the deaths of 15 persons who had been taking tranquilizers. "Whether these victims ended their lives intentionally or perished through accident while under influence of the tranquilizers could not be established in each instance," he said. He also stated that in some instances the drugs might lead to addiction to alcohol or barbiturates.

He said he was also "terribly concerned" over the increasing number of automobile drivers found dead at the wheels of their cars. Are the tranquilizers adding to the already frightening hazards of alcohol on our highways, he asks?

Dr. Frederick Lemere, writing in the *Archives of Neurology and Psychiatry,* August, 1956, states that the tranquilizers are definitely habit-forming. He says that the widespread taking of these pills is "without parallel in the history of modern drugs." He has had 13 patients among 600 of whom he has given one of the tranquilizers who have shown evidence of addiction. And an article in *The Lancet* for December 1, 1956, recounts the story of 3 elderly patients suffering from dangerous and sudden lowering of blood pressure after an average dose of a tranquilizer. A report before the American Psychoanalytic Association revealed that the drugs affect a certain portion of the brain—the *globus pallidus.* This is the part of the brain that is disordered in cases of palsy.

A Typical Case History

A paper on "Mood Therapy in the Aged" read by Dr. Joseph O. Smigel before the Third Annual Meeting of the Academy of Psychosomatic Medicine, October 4, 1956, and reprinted in *Medical Times* for February, 1957, describes some interesting case histories. A 62-year-old man, manager of a factory, was given a tranquilizer because of his anxiety over business and a troubled home life. For several weeks he experienced calmness and tranquillity. Then there was a letdown, and the doctor discontinued the medicine. Three times this patient went through this same experience.

Then, "after the third renewal, he refused to take the medication again. He explained that he and his associates were aware of a change in him and his business. They agreed with him that his acuteness of judgment diminished during the course of medication." The man stated that the work he did while he was taking the tranquilizer was just plain no good. His mind had lost its sharpness. This case, says Dr. Smigel, does not stand alone.

His report goes on to describe side effects—skin irritation, drowsiness, gastric distress. He states, we think, the clearest explanation for why the tranquilizers are being used so widely —"one has to deal daily with patients complaining of varieties of symptomatic complexities, which need attention—now. These patients cannot await the ultimate determination of the causative agent."

So, we fill them with tranquilizers, give them more drugs to counteract whatever bad effects the mood pills had and keep our fingers crossed that they won't commit suicide in a moment of depression brought on by our treatment. Does that make sense?

Our Twentieth Century Diet

Editor Rodale has written a book, *"This Pace Is Not Killing Us,"* in which he shows clearly that the so-called feverish tempo of American life is not responsible for our mounting incidence of heart deaths. Our diet is responsible. This premise is just as true of our nervous complaints. Our nerves, like every other part of us, are made up only of what we put in our mouths. When, over a period of years we eat little or nothing to nourish our nerves, we are going to suffer from anxiety, irritability, depression and all the other personality disorders that baffle our doctors and psychiatrists.

Taking tranquilizers will not nourish our nerves. What will? Well, chief among nerve nutriments are calcium and the B vitamins. American diets are short on these. Could not our twentieth century case of jitters be largely due to a diet in which we are getting but a small fraction of the calcium and B vitamins which were plentiful in diets 200 years ago?

CHAPTER **15**

Antibiotics Are All Around You

*Though they have their place in emergencies, the wide-
spread use of antibiotics for colds and minor infections is playing havoc with our national health.*

According to an editorial in the *Lancet* for July
11, 1953, there are supposedly three general types of reaction to
penicillin—"the least toxic of the antibiotics." Most serious
of these is the anaphylactic shock which may result in death
within a matter of minutes. Six per cent of everyone who
receives penicillin develops a "serum-sickness-like" disease.

Dentistry in Relation to Antibiotics

Speaking before the Southern California State Dental
Association on April 21, 1953, Dr. Donald A. Kerr of the
University of Michigan told of a woman who lost all of her
skin, from head to foot—even the lining of her mouth, as a
result of sensitivity to penicillin which she took by mouth. He
said further that the incidence of gum disease is increasing
sharply all over the country, because of the habit of taking antibiotics, especially penicillin, by mouth. There has been a
notable increase in *thrush,* he said—an ulcerative infection of
the mouth which causes white patches there.

"The same type of sensitivity can result from taking
large doses of penicillin to curb pneumonia and other serious
diseases," said Dr. Kerr. "It's quite definite now that the indiscriminate use of antibiotics is a bad and dangerous thing. The
gum trouble it may produce is difficult for dentists to heal.
Metabolism difficulties such as those caused by diabetes and a
shortage of vitamin C also damage the gums."

Dentistry in relation to antibiotics comes up again in a
note in *Today's Health* for February 1954. Antibiotics are now
added to the dental cements and resins used in filling teeth,

because they apparently help to prevent decay from recurring under the fillings. What will be the effect of this additional use of antibiotics on those who are sensitive to them already?

Sensitization to Antibiotics

In an article in the Journal of the *American Medical Association* for September 12, 1953, Charles W. Fairlie and Ralph E. Kendall, M.D. write as follows: "Fatal staphylococcus enteritis (inflammation of the intestines) following antibiotic therapy is now a familiar entity." The article goes on to describe in detail 5 patients, 3 of whom died. The patients were all in hospitals for operations, some of them minor. They were given antibiotics as a routine thing. When they developed alarming symptoms, the antibiotics were increased, apparently with the notion that antibiotics will cure anything. The two patients whose dosages of antibiotics were stopped as soon as the symptoms began, lived.

A survey done in England in 1953 revealed the fact that, of the hospitals queried, between 1 and 5 per cent of the nurses using antibiotics became sensitized to them! Streptomycin and penicillin were the two drugs responsible for most of the sensitizing. In most cases skin sensitivity was involved—on the hands, arms, face and neck. This seems to point to local contact with the antibiotics—in handling sponges or bandages and swabs or in expelling the air from syringes before giving injections. An article in *The Lancet* for July 11, 1953, indicates that such sensitization may be permanent, especially if it is not caught in the early stages. In this case, of course, the nurse cannot continue in her profession.

Must Antibiotics Be Used?

The editorial in *The Lancet* goes on to say, "Too often it seems not to be recognized that uncomplicated recovery is the rule after minor surgical operations done with proper regard for asepsis; even before antibiotics were used it was exceptional for clean operation wounds to show signs of infection... In process of evolution microorganisms generally have proved their power to adapt themselves to many changes in their environment; and it is improbable that we shall fundamentally improve our position by affording them uncalled-for opportunities to grow accustomed to our antibiotics. Uncritical use of antibiotic 'umbrellas' is likely to lead to an increase in both resistant bacteria and sensitized patients."

This was written in 1953. Have you heard of any decrease in the use of antibiotics during the past years? *Chemical Week,* October 9, 1954, states that production of penicillin increased from 318,622 billion units in 1951 to 371,589 billion units in 1953.

Sudden Fatalities from Penicillin

Perhaps most disturbing of all are the stories of penicillin (given for colds) causing sudden death. Penicillin has no beneficial effect whatsoever on colds. Says Dr. Sheppard Siegal writing in *The New York State Journal of Medicine* for April 15, 1955, "In viral respiratory illness there exists no indication for penicillin apart from patient pressure for the 'magic shot.'" In other words the doctor, giving his patient penicillin for a cold or "flu," knows perfectly well that it will do no good. Why does he not give plain water, if the patient insists on a shot? Dr Siegal tells us that reaction to penicillin has been reported after a penicillin lozenge, after an instillation of the drug in the antrums (for sinus trouble, we suppose) and even after the use of an eye ointment containing the antibiotic.

Listen to the account of a couple of cases of individuals who became suddenly sensitive to penicillin without knowing it. A 67-year-old woman with chronic asthma, sinus disease and aspirin allergy had received penicillin many times for "colds." On her last visit to the doctor's office, she was given the antibiotic, and within 30 seconds had collapsed and died. A 27-year-old physician had had penicillin frequently without any ill effects. One day he reacted with a rash. Some months later he had trouble breathing after an injection. Two months later he was given penicillin again, went into collapse within 30 seconds, fell unconscious and would undoubtedly have died had a powerful drug and oxygen not been administered immediately. This was a physician, mind you, who had a family history of allergy.

Penicillin and Respiratory Disorder

A woman of 35 had had penicillin often for respiratory illnesses. On the last occasion she complained of itching in the palms of her hands 15 minutes after the injection had been given. This patient's physician was a sensible man. He sought advice from an allergist, who gave the patient skin tests for allergy to penicillin. Up to a dose of 6000 units she was fine. But at that dosage she had an immediate reaction. If her physician had paid no attention to her first mild reaction but had gone on giving her penicillin at the usual dosage, she would undoubtedly have died in shock.

You Can Become Allergic to Penicillin

One thing to keep in mind about reaction to penicillin —the fact that you have never been sensitive to it is no indication that you will not be—THE NEXT TIME. Says Dr. Siegal, "The majority of patients with penicillin shock have given a negative history as to previous penicillin allergy." A reaction need scarcely be feared in patients never before exposed to the drug, says he. The most hazardous injection is the first given after an interval since previous administration of the drug. You should watch for immediate reactions such as itching or rash, faintness, generalized tingling, chokiness or difficulty in breathing, asthma or pain or constriction across the chest.

"Allergic reactions to the antibiotics . . . constitute a major problem in current medical practice," says Dr. Siegal.

Avoid Antibiotics if You Can

Our conclusion in regard to taking the antibiotics—any of them, but penicillin in particular—is, don't. Don't let your doctor give you any of the antibiotics if there is any possible way to avoid it. It has been known for a long time that using the antibiotics off and on for minor illnesses and infections will make them completely ineffective for major illnesses. But we have not had, until fairly recently, the rash of sudden fatalities from the antibiotics. If, for an extreme emergency, you must take one of the antibiotics, by all means give your doctor a full history of how much of it you have had in the past, and also what your past history as to allergy has been. If you have or ever have had asthma, it would be especially important to tell him that.

But suppose you know you are sensitive to antibiotics and must avoid them at all costs—how are you going to do it? That's a harder question to answer, for antibiotics are becoming almost as common as DDT in almost everything we eat. Says the *Drug Trade News* for August 3, 1953: "The Food and Drug Administration is faced with a serious problem as a result of use of drugs to treat animals, subsequently slaughtered for human consumption." Antibiotics are, of course, given to treat diseased animals. And, in addition, they are now being added to the feed of healthy animals, because it appears that the animals grow faster if a little antibiotic is added to their food. How much of the antibiotic is left in the meat? Your guess is as good as ours. We do know that antibiotics in milk (coming, of course, from those that have been fed to the cow) have caused trouble in the cheese industry, for so much remains in the milk that the bacteria responsible for making the cheese are killed and cannot perform their function.

Even vegetarians have cause to worry. An undated article from a Madison, Wisconsin, paper tells us that the "wonder drugs" are now being used to fight fruit diseases. Streptomycin and terramycin are used to treat apple and pear orchards.

Can We Put an End to Antibiotic Use?

In an article in the British Journal called *Nutrition,* J. S. Willcox, Senior Lecturer in Agricultural Chemistry at the University of Leeds, says that the value of the sale of antibiotics for animal feeds exceeds the value of all the antibiotics used for medical purposes in the United States!

On the basis of such a report as this, how much chance do you think there is of getting the antibiotic-makers to stop selling their products for use in food? What can you do about antibiotics in food? Raise your own food if it's humanly possible. Or get a farmer friend to raise it for you, organically. If you must eat food bought at the local market, check as closely as you can with the people who produce it. Buy food that has not been treated in any way with antibiotics if you can get it. And protest! Protest to your grocer, your doctor, your congressman, your board of health!

CHAPTER **16**

Cosmetics Can Be Troublesome

Once in a while the experience of a friend will prove startlingly to us that cosmetic preparations—lipsticks, hair dye, wave set lotions, and so on—can leave permanent scars or kill. Do you know enough about the ingredients in the cosmetics you and your family use to consider them harmless?

An article in the *Eye, Ear, Nose and Throat Monthly* for June, 1952, deals with the subject of the dangers of careless and indiscriminate use of cosmetics. It was written by a woman physician, Dorothy Niederman Bogdanow of Chicago, who has apparently specialized in treating the kind of disorder that may arise from using cosmetics.

Dr. Bogdanow tells us that the skin disorders caused by cosmetics are, generally speaking, not brought about by something that irritates when it is first applied, but by something that sensitizes the skin. A sensitizing agent is some substance in a cosmetic that does no harm when it is first applied. But after several days, weeks or months it may bring about skin trouble. The difficulty in diagnosing the trouble lies in the fact that most of us use cosmetics all the time without thinking very much about them, so when we break out in an unexpected rash we would never think of blaming it on the lipstick we have been using for years or the shampoo we bought from a salesman several months ago.

Skin Reactions Caused by Cosmetics

Freckle creams, bleaching creams and cleansing creams are the worst offenders for producing unpleasant reactions on the skin, says Dr. Bogdanow. Acids and oxidizing agents such as perborates, hydrogen peroxide, and zinc peroxide are the ingredients most likely to cause trouble. Vanishing creams may produce reactions due to the stearic acid, the alcohol, fats, lanolin or synthetic preparations they contain. In addition, vanishing creams leave the skin alkaline, whereas the natural condition of the skin is acid. Then, too, she says, the perfume in the vanishing cream may be responsible for skin trouble.

Cleansing creams contain mineral oil, petrolatum, paraffin, beeswax, borax, lanolin or vegetable oils. The substances that cause the most trouble are the petroleum oils, the detergents and the perfume they contain. Don't forget for a moment, when the names of these ingredients hit your consciousness, that practically all of them are made from coal tar—most specifically the petroleum oils, detergents and perfumes. We believe that coal tar preparations are suspect—whether you take them inside or outside. Many of them have been shown to be cancer-causing. We have no proof to offer showing that the coal tar products in cosmetics produce cancer—but why take a chance, when we know that certain other coal tar products are regularly used in laboratory experiments to produce cancer?

Astringent creams contain salts of zinc sulfate, aluminum sulfate or bismuth sulfate, resorcinol or salicylic acid (which is also used in aspirin). None of these should ever be applied to the skin in our opinion. And Dr. Bogdanow indicates that they quite frequently produce dermatitis (or skin trouble). Depilatories may contain sulfides or sulfhydrates, carboxylic acid or calcium thioglycolate. All of such preparations should be strictly avoided by the health-conscious person, we believe.

Hair Preparations Most Dangerous

The cosmetics that most often cause dermatitis are those used as hair preparations—dyes, bleaches, lacquers, tonics, straighteners or wave lotions. The complicated names of the substances in these preparations are not important. It *is* important to know that numerous eye injuries have been caused by their use, including extremely serious disorders, which in some cases have proved to be fatal. One of these substances is forbidden today in eye make-up, but is apparently still being used in preparations for the hair. Beauticians are required today to make a patch test of any dye they use—that is, they must paint some of it on a skin surface, cover it and examine it 24 hours later for evidence of irritation. Such a test is good, but not nearly conclusive enough, for the sensitivity to the substance may not develop for several days, and the surface painted with the dye is very small indeed compared to the whole scalp which is exposed to the dye when the hair is dyed.

Listen to the list of substances that may be in the hair lotion some honey-tongued salesman has talked you into buying—resorcinol, arsenic, tar, sulfonamides, glycerine and quinine! Any or all of these substances can cause dermatitis. Permanent wave solutions—many readers have written us inquiring about one or another of these! Skin disorders may result, says Dr. Bogdanow, from either the reducing agents used with cold wave permanents, or from the gums that are added to hold the curl. Wave setting solutions, used for finger waves, very rarely cause dermatitis. According to *United States Public Health Reports, Reprint No. 2523,* there has been a recent outbreak of skin trouble from hair lacquers in which a resin of maleic anhydrid was used. Bleaching preparations made from chlorine or oxalic acid can cause dermatitis. Those containing hydrogen peroxide or sodium carbonate seldom do.

Lipstick and Nail Polish

The perfumes, dyes, oils, waxes, fats and flavors of lipsticks—chiefly the indelible lipsticks—can cause serious trouble mostly about the corners of the mouth. Nail polish dermatitis may mislead the person searching for the source of the trouble, for the eruptions may occur around the eyes, ears, face, or chest where the fingers have touched. Several years ago a member of the Rodale Press staff was miserable for a couple of weeks with a dermatitis about her eyes and eyelids which proved to be the result of the nail polish she was wearing. Nonallergic nail polishes are available in many drug stores—but why not avoid the problem once and for all by doing without nail polish entirely? A fine set of nails, well-trimmed and well-cared for, with the cuticle carefully pushed back to avoid harming it, is every bit as handsome as a set of blood red ones.

Perfume and Powders

Do you know what perfumes are made from? Alcohol, a natural flower oil and a fixative such as musk or ambergris are the main ingredients, and these may cause not only dermatitis but sinusitis and "runny nose" as well. Sensitivity to perfumes is common and it is extremely hard to locate which ingredient of the complex perfume recipe is responsible. Liquid, cream or cake face powders may be responsible for dermatitis—regular face powder rarely is. Soap, as readers know, is very hard on one's skin, because, in order to remove dirt, it must contain alkalis and the normal condition of the skin is acid. So next time you read a magazine ad which counsels you to scrub your face well with such-and-such a soap as a "beauty treatment," take it with a grain of salt. Scrub your face *without* the soap, if you would have beautiful skin. It's perfectly possible for other ingredients of soap, aside from the alkalis, to cause skin reactions—the dyes, perfumes, solvents, fatty acids and so forth. Shaving soaps, shampoos and after-shave lotions are just as likely to cause dermatitis as soap.

The Patch and Usage Test

Now how are you to know whether that annoying, itching, burning or runny blotch on your face is the result of some cosmetic you have been using? Says Dr. Bogdanow, it's hard for even a professional dermatologist to find out. The time-honored method is the patch test. A small amount of the suspected substance is put on a piece of muslin, covered with cellophane and taped to the upper part of the back or the arms—cellophane side out, of course. After 48 hours, take off the patch and examine the spot of skin. If no redness or irritation is present, you may feel pretty safe; although, of course, there is such a thing as a delayed reaction. If you find your skin irritated, you must go through the long and often costly process of having a doctor break down the cosmetic into its various ingredients and then test each of these to find out which you are sensitive to. In some instances you may fail, for, in the case of lipstick, for instance, the kind of skin on which you use lipstick is different in texture from the skin where you have the patch test. If you cannot solve the problem with a patch test, perhaps you can with a usage test. Stop using all cosmetics until the eruption has cleared. Then begin using just one at a time until one or another of them brings the dermatitis back again. From then on, that is the cosmetic to avoid assiduously.

How to Avoid Dermatitis From Cosmetics

We think there are two far better solutions than either of these for avoiding reactions from cosmetics. First, stop using them, if you can. Secondly, if you must use them, make certain that you are in such a robust state of health that they won't cause you any trouble. Most of us have certain cosmetics we are slaves to. Suppose you simply can't get along without lipstick. Wear it, then, but eliminate those 60 other cosmetics that clutter up the top of your dressing table. Perhaps you don't feel well-dressed without face powder. Use it, then, but eliminate as many as possible of the rest. Did you honestly ever try cleansing your face with plain water—soft water, even if you have to put out a bucket and catch it as it falls from the sky? Try it sometime for a month and see if your skin is not just as attractive and soft as it was when you were using a dozen different kinds of creams and lotions. Remember, too, that the largest part of the price you pay for cosmetics goes for the perfume, the color, and the advertising that surround this so-called dainty and alluring product which may bring you nothing but grief.

Of course, there are available in health stores cosmetics made from vegetable and herb substances with none of the possibly damaging ingredients. Many of them have been especially designed to be really good for your skin. Use them if you feel you just aren't properly turned out without cosmetics.

Incidentally, we can't advise you whether or not the cosmetics you, individually, are using may be dangerous. Aside from information such as appears in this article, we do not know any more about what may be contained in any product than you do. If you have pretty definite evidence that one or another of your cosmetics is causing you trouble, stop using it at once. Then write to the manufacturer to find out (if he will tell you) what this particular cosmetic contains. This will be a great help to your doctor when he attempts to treat you.

CHAPTER **17**

Detergents Rebound to Home Owners

by DAVE HARRIS

Detergents are used by almost everybody these days, instead of soap. Their dangers to skin are well known. But there are other, farther-reaching perils, too, associated with using detergents.

Detergents—those miracle cleansers that make water wetter, washes brighter and housewives happier—have been making a lot of home owners unhappy recently.

Persons in some areas depending on wells for drinking water and cesspools and septic tanks for sewage disposal have found detergents, unlike old-fashioned soap, refuse to stay put in sewage pits once they are flushed down the drain. Even worse, detergents have been showing up in wells with the result that water drawn from such a well winds up with a head as foamy as tappings from a beer keg.

What's Happening to This Water

As far as local health authorities have determined, no one has been made ill by drinking water from a detergent-shot well. The thought of what might be riding along with detergent from cesspool to well, however, has been the basis for some serious thought by William J. Young, Board of Health officer.

The cause of Young's thoughtful frown has been reports he's received from Martin E. Alpers, a water analyst, who tests water regularly for Dover and a number of other municipalities, private water systems, well drillers and individual home owners in his laboratory on George Street.

Alpers has been testing water in the West Morris area since 1913. About a year ago—shortly after detergents came into general home use—he began finding sewage bacteria in wells that had been pure for more than 8 years in some cases.

The same condition began to show up in wells drilled as recently as 6 months prior to testing. He found the unexplained bacteria where none had existed before in all types of wells, driven, dug and point.

Tests Show Detergent

A methodical man by nature, Alpers began a series of tests. He found detergent in one polluted water sample. He turned it up in a lot more when he tested further. Alpers also found in water containing detergent, typical sewage bacteria, coliform bacteria that comes from a variety of rotten organic matter—including human excrement.

The explanation for this, Alpers reasons, lies in the fact that detergents break the surface' tension of water, actually making it wetter. Detergent in a septic tank or cesspool is not stopped by earth as is other sewage. Instead it opens a path through the porous soil, pushing down and out from the cesspool, refusing to be absorbed.

Soap and other fat or grease base cleansers did not do this. Instead they actually formed a greasy coating inside cesspools that prevented other sewage from getting out.

This is Alpers' explanation and so far it's the only one for why detergents and bacteria show up in wells where pollution was not previously present. He's tried to get the soap companies who have millions invested in detergents to explain what has been showing up in his tests. They tell him he's wrong, but they don't say why. One promised last March to send an expert to investigate his findings. Alpers is still waiting.

Explanation Lacking

"I'm not saying detergents have bacteria in them," Alpers said. "All I'm asking someone to explain is my belief that the detergent opens a path from cesspool to well and takes some of the sewage along for the ride. Some sandy soils such as that around Succasunna filter out the bacteria but can't hold the detergent. Other soils let it all go through. Sooner or later the stuff shows up in wells and then I have to tell a man that's spent a thousand dollars to sink a well that his water's no good."

Alpers has been advising such cases to write the soap companies and ask them what to do. "Maybe they'll have better luck than I did," he says with a shrug.

He's hoping to be proved wrong, because if he's right a lot of persons who depend on wells for water—and that's the case in just about all the rural and semi-rural areas of the county—are in for a peck of trouble.

"It's all right when the well can be located several hundred feet from the septic tank," Alpers said, "But most of these people building homes on lots of one-third acre or less around here put a house, a cesspool and a well mighty close together.

"I had one fellow say the well should be higher than the septic tank. That's easy to say but hard to do when you build on a level piece of ground. Besides, I've found detergent in one case in a well 165 feet away from a cesspool and I've found it in others with less distance between them where pollution was never a question when the folks used soap.

"There's one way I know of to get clean water and that's to install a small sewage system for each of these housing developments going up around here. Every drop of water we take out of the ground is passed through some household appliance or our bodies and then goes right back into the ground. You can see the day coming when all ground water, even big municipal supplies like Dover's deep wells, will be polluted."

Here's a Simple Test for Detergents

Here's a simple test for detergents in well water devised by Martin E. Alpers, Dover water analyst, that any home owner can perform in his own kitchen.

Take a clean quart jar and fill it half full with tap water. Shake vigorously. If foam and bubbles persist once the water stops sloshing around, it's time to have your water analyzed by an expert—and probably too late to save your well.

—Reprinted by permission from the *Morristown Jerseyman* (New Jersey), August 8, 1957.

SECTION 4

WHITE SUGAR

Refined white sugar is not only worthless as food, but extremely dangerous to health in the quantities in which we consume it. It is a very soluble food and rushes through the stomach wall without being digested, creating imbalances in the blood which permit viruses, etc., to get a stronger foothold.

Sugar, besides being fattening, has been found to be dangerous for heart cases as it distorts the calcium-phosphorous relationship in the blood, and strange as it may seem, if consumed in large amounts, it creates low blood sugar which could lead to mental and other troubles. There should be no candy, cake, pie, ice cream, soft drinks, chewing gum, etc., in the diet. The best form is the natural sugar found in fruits and some vegetables. Honey in moderation. We do not favor brown sugar either, nor do we recommend saccharin, sucaryl or any of the other synthetic chemical sweeteners.

CHAPTER **18**

The Story of Sugar

The story of sugar seems to be one of the finest examples of man's inability to let well enough alone. Considering all the splendid and worth-while improvements man has brought to his environment, it seems almost incredible that this same being, man, could also have invented and perpetrated one of the most serious and stupid mistakes in history—a mistake which, as one doctor of our acquaintance prophesies, may very well end our civilization within a few generations.

The story of sugar is a story of stupidity, greed and ignorance. It is the final devastating removal of man from his natural environment. We are talking now of white sugar—the sugar you buy at the grocery store—white, crystal, delicious, "pure." Throughout this chapter this is the sugar we mean when we say sugar. When we are speaking of *natural* sugars— from fruits, vegetables, honey and so forth, we will qualify them as natural sugars.

Difference Between Carbohydrates and Proteins

The chemistry of sugar is complex and we will not trouble you with it. There are many different kinds of sugars, chemically—fructose, glucose, sucrose, dextrose, lactose and so forth. They differ from one another in the chemical structure of their molecules. They are all carbohydrates. In other words, when you read or hear the word carbohydrate, as different from protein and fat, you will know that what is meant is sugars and starches.

The carbohydrates are the energy-giving foods, as separate from the proteins, which are the body building and repairing foods. We are told that 68 per cent of the food we eat is changed by the body into sugars to produce energy. The other 32 per cent is used for building and repairing the body.

Not only sugars and starches but also fats and proteins can be changed by the body's marvelous mechanism into the kind of sugar that the body needs to produce energy. So it appears that we need sugar! Why, therefore, did we say that the story of sugar is the story of man's most colossal mistake? We do need sugar, yes, but the important thing is the *kind* of sugar we need.

Why Do We Like Sugar?

We have developed a taste for sweet things. Sweet things are delightful to eat. Melvin Page, D.D.S., in his splendid book, *Degeneration and Regeneration* (published by the Biochemical Research Foundation, 2810 First Street, North, St. Petersburg, Florida), tells us we were given a desire for sweet-tasting foods because, in natural foods, a number of very necessary food elements exist in combination with a sweet taste—vitamins and minerals, to be exact. Now a vitamin in the quantities in which it appears in food has no taste, so wise Mother Nature teams up a sweet taste with a number of vitamins. We need vitamin C if we are to live in good health for even one day. But we cannot pick vitamin C off a vine or tree and no amount of persuasion will get us to eat vitamin C if it has a disagreeable taste.

So vitamin C comes ready-packaged in cantaloupes, strawberries, guavas, oranges and so forth and we eat them actually because we have a need for the vitamins they contain. But we *think* we eat them because of the sweet taste. One-half cup of carrots is a compact little bundle of 4500 units of vitamin A, but nobody would eat them if they tasted bitter. So our taste for sweets is a reliable guide to foods that are good for us. But this guide is reliable only so long as the foods we have to choose from are natural foods that man, in his matchless inability to let well enough alone, has not tampered with.

What We Mean By "Refining"

Most of us are not familiar with sugar cane, so let's take as a sample grapes, which are rich in sugar. What could be more enjoyable than pitching in to a big dish of luscious Concords, purple and dewy and fresh from the vines! And healthy, too, for grapes come equipped with vitamins A, B and C, calcium, phosphorus, iron and many more food elements that are good for you, as well as all the substances your body needs to digest them.

Now suppose somebody—a chemist or scientist with a

lot of degrees behind his name—came over to your dewy grape arbor and told you he was going to "improve" your grapes. He was going to put them through a process that would guarantee that they would keep practically forever, so that you could have them, in condensed form, on your table. You could flavor all your foods with their sweet taste, summer and winter. In addition, he would "purify" your grapes. This purification process wouldn't mean much to you, except that you have come to believe that "purified" foods are somehow better, because they have no dirt in them, no germs, nothing extraneous. But, on second thought, what needs to be "purified" about your grapes as they come from the vine? Nevertheless, your scientist proceeds with his terribly complicated and expensive process, which somehow, due to our technological genius, results in a product that is much less expensive than grapes, keeps indefinitely, tastes sweet and can be bought at any grocery store the year 'round.

A Synthetic Product Produced

Now we've solved all our problems. But have we? Let's look a little more closely at this very practical, sweet, inexpensive, pretty-looking product you can use to your heart's content in cakes, candies, cookies, lemonade and coffee. Any vitamin B in it? Not an atom. Any vitamin A or C, any iron, phosphorus, calcium? Not a sliver. What then is left? Nothing at all is left but the sweet taste and the pure carbohydrate which will give you calories and nothing else, for your clever scientist has stripped the grapes of every vestige of food value and has left you only the sweet taste which, remember, was put there by nature to guide you to the healthful food elements that were in the original grapes. Would you say that the scientist was clever or would you say he had made a colossal mistake?

Nobody has yet discovered how to make a satisfactory, practical table sugar out of grapes. But the story above is precisely what happens in the manufacture of table sugar from sugar cane or beets. From the point of view of commerce, the refining of sugar is a stroke of genius, but from the point of view of human welfare it is one of the world's greatest tragedies.

History of Sugar

"Since we have no satisfactory knowledge of the beginnings of the culture of sugar cane, we can only infer that it was cultivated in northeastern India long before the Christian era. The earliest reference to sugar is contained in the comments made by several officers of Alexander the Great during his Indian campaign in 327 B. C.," says Andrew Van Hook in his book, *Sugar,* published by the Ronald Press, New York City. He goes on to say, "It was still to be almost 1000 years before the consumption and cultivation of sugar began to spread beyond the borders of India. During this time, however, its sweet and honey-like nature became known and was mentioned by such writers as Theophrastus, Herodotus, Discorides and Pliny." So we see that human beings have arrived at eating sugar from sugar cane in recent times, in terms of man's life on earth. The Arabs and ancient Egyptians used sugar. The Chinese were using sugar when Marco Polo visited them in 1270-75. As history moved forward and the medieval crusades brought knowledge of eastern ways to western Europe, the use of sugar spread and eventually, of course, got to America. Among those early Europeans only the very wealthy could have sugar on their tables, because it was expensive to import. In the western hemisphere sugar cane planting and slavery went hand in hand. In North and South America the tall sugar cane with its waving tassels was soon a familiar sight. "The sugar in those days was a highly impure and dark product which was shipped to the refining cities of the motherland countries for further processing," says Van Hook.

What exactly does he mean by that? He means that, to collect and ship the sugar, certain things had to be done to it, but in those days men didn't know how to remove all the dark colored substance (containing the vitamins and minerals). So their sugar was dark and sticky and difficult to handle—but much more nutritious than the white sugar we have today. It doesn't seem far-fetched to guess that none of us in the western world would be alive today if those old-timers had had the technical skill we have for "refining" foods.

The Birth of the Refining Industry

As scientific knowledge developed, ways and means were discovered to refine the sugar still further. Refining processes grew more general, and sugar became cheaper and more popular. In America the first refining plant was established in New York in 1689. By the middle of the nineteenth century sugar refining as we know it today had developed. Meanwhile someone had discovered that sugar might be made from beets which will grow in climates where sugar cane will not grow. And gradually the sugar beet refining industry began to grow. By 1940 the United States was producing well over two million tons of sugar per year *and consuming more than 7 million tons!* A recent estimated value of the world production of sugar was two billion dollars, only a little less than the value of all the iron and steel produced in the United States. (Incidentally, it is also interesting to note that the cigar and cigarette industry of this country was valued at one billion, two hundred million dollars in 1939.)

In 1939-1940 the people of the United States consumed 106.5 pounds of sugar per person—that means almost one pound every three days, *per person!* Taking into account all the babies and the sick people who dare not eat sugar, what kind of an average does that leave for the rest of us?

The Refining Process

There is no need to follow a piece of sugar cane through all the various complications of the refining process, but here are some of the substances used to produce those sparkling white crystals: lime, phosphoric acid, special clays known as diatomaceous earth, bone char, boneblack or animal charcoal. To powdered or confectioner's sugar, cornstarch or calcium phosphate is added to keep the sugars from caking. In producing lactose or milk sugar which is used mainly in infant foods, "the whey is first clarified with lime, decolorized with carbon and then concentrated and crystallized," says Mr. Van Hook. In refining beet sugar, lime, carbon dioxide and sulfur dioxide are involved in the "purification" process.

In harvesting sugar beets, the tops are carefully cut off while the beets are still in the field. The sugar beet industry has had some difficulty in disposing of its "wastes" which ferment easily. We put that word in quotations, for, of course, the "wastes" in sugar beet refining consist of everything that is worth while as food in the beet and beet top. But just as we finally learned that the germ and bran from refined wheat makes good food for cattle, so we discovered that cattle thrive on the "wastes" from beet sugar manufacture. Why shouldn't they thrive? In the wastes are concentrated all of the vitamins and minerals from the beets. Out of the whole procedure, the human beings involved—and this means you and me—get once again only the pure carbohydrate, stripped of all food value except calories.

The Food Value of Sugar

Following through on this whole senseless waste of good, healthful, wholesome food in a two billion dollar industry, do you get some idea what we mean when we use harsh and violent language in speaking of white, refined sugar? In the most sweeping evasion it has ever been our misfortune to meet in modern literature, Mr. Van Hook in his book, *Sugar*, has this to say about the food value of the product he is writing about: "In spite of its prominent place in the diet all over the world, the role of sugar as food has never been completely ascertained." Obviously, Mr. Van Hook, because it has no role as food. Applying even the most lax and generous interpretation to the words "food" and "nutrition," no one can show that white refined sugar has any place at all in the diet of any living thing. In speaking of the fashions in sugar all over the world, Mr. Van Hook says, "In the United States a hard, white sugar of high purity is usually demanded, but in Europe considerable tolerance is allowed in respect to color. Native sugars (this means the sugars of those backward savages who are not as civilized as we) are soft, dark colored and impure, and the purity (that is, the per cent of sucrose in total dry product) is often as low as 60 or 70 per cent. *Whether or not American standards mean a superior product in nutritional value is questionable.*" We italicized that last sentence to emphasize it, for it seems to us a masterpiece of understatement. Certainly, any literate person with any nutrition chart before his eyes can readily see that American white refined sugar has absolutely no nutritional value whatsoever, so why do we need the half-hearted word "questionable?" So the uncivilized world which does not have our technical excellence has to be content with dark sugar which includes at least some (perhaps 30 to 40 per cent) of the original food elements of the beets and cane, while we civilized people deliberately choose to eat the pure, white worthless chemical left after refining.

Or do we "deliberately choose" to eat white sugar? Throughout all our research on sugar we found again and again the suggestion that the American public just won't have a dark sugar. No sir, they tell us, it must be "pure" and white as snow or Mrs. America will reject it scornfully. Mrs. America is a refined and cultured lady, they tell us, and her angel cakes must be white as moonlight, her boiled frosting pearly as Mt. Everest on a clear day, even the sugar she dumps into her morning coffee must glisten with silvery lights in her sugar bowl. Somehow we feel that this assumption is a libel on the good sense and practicability of Americans. We are absolutely certain that, if the gentlemen of the sugar industry would go to Mrs. America through the pages of her favorite magazines and in the commercials of her favorite radio and television programs, and would tell her the full story of sugar cane and beet sugar, would show her exactly what is subtracted from the cane and beet in the process of refining and would explain to her what is left in the pure white sugar she uses every day, Mrs. America would not only change her mind practically overnight about white sugar, but would march in a body to Washington and fight for legislation to make white sugar illegal!

And oh, what changes we'd have at the county fair and the mother's club bake sale! The darkest angel cake would win the blue ribbon, and the cupcakes with the deep brown icing would sell best. To say nothing of the wonderful new opportunity for home economic experts to dream up new recipes requiring raw sugar, blackstrap molasses and honey!

Blackstrap Molasses As Food

What about blackstrap molasses anyway? Is it really the fountain of youth, guaranteed to banish any and all ailments and put hair on the chest of the scrawniest boy scout? No, we don't think so. But we know—because we read nutrition charts —that blackstrap molasses is a food, and a good food. Sugar is not. See for yourself. Here are the vitamins and minerals in one hundred grams of sugar and one hundred grams of blackstrap:

	Molasses	*Sugar*
Calories	220	400
(All these are B vitamins)		
Thiamin	245 micrograms ...	0
Riboflavin ...	240 micrograms ...	0
Niacin	4 milligrams	0
Pyridoxine ..	270 micrograms ...	0
Pantothenic		
acid	260 micrograms ...	0
Biotin	16 micrograms	0

(These are minerals)

	Molasses	Sugar
Calcium	258 milligrams	1 milligram
Phosphorus ..	30 milligrams	trace
Iron	7.97 milligrams ...	.04 milligram
Copper	1.93 milligrams ...	.02 milligram
Magnesium ..	.04 milligram	0
Chlorine	317 milligrams	trace
Sodium	90 milligrams	.3 milligram
Potassium ...	1500 milligrams ...	.5 milligram

Source of Vitamins and Minerals

Where does molasses get all these vitamins and minerals? Obviously these are what is left when the sugar cane is refined. These are the vitamins and minerals Nature put in the original sugar cane to nourish you after you had discovered that the sweet taste is pleasant. But blackstrap molasses is "impure" scream the writers in the big popular magazines! That's right, folks, it is "impure." And the "impurities" are vitamin B, calcium, phosphorus, iron and other minerals which are completely essential to human nutrition. Blackstrap molasses doesn't taste as good as sugar until you get used to it. It doesn't look pretty in your sugar bowl. And blackstrap molasses that has been prepared for use in cattle food is not for human consumption, of course. But blackstrap molasses for human beings (and most grocery stores carry it these days) is every bit as free from germs and dirt as any other food that must pass federal inspection.

In the following pages we will show you what harm white sugar does to your body. It's not just something you can go right on eating, you know, so long as you eat good foods, too! Anything you put into your body that does not belong there is harmful, you may be sure. White sugar is a drug to which we Americans have become addicted. You will see in the following pages what devastating inroads on American health have been made by this particular drug. As you read, keep in mind that the average American (adult and child alike) consumes in toto about a pound of this drug every 3 days. Keep in mind, too, that white sugar and white flour (another completely worthless food) make up well over 50 per cent of the average American diet.

After you have read, dump the contents of your sugar bowl and sugar canister into the garbage can and start a new life!

CHAPTER 19

The Disadvantages of Sugar

Some of the disadvantages, healthwise, of using sugar, are clearly pointed out in this chapter.

"You shouldn't eat so much candy, dear. It's not good for you. Well, just one more piece." And Mama hands Junior another piece of candy. Where did we pick up this idea that sugar is not good for us? Even those folks who stuff themselves on sweet things all day will mention, meanwhile, that they know it's bad for them. Have you ever talked to anyone who believes that eating sugar is good for him? "Oh I just can't get along without my dessert," he will tell you. But he won't add that the dessert is good for him.

So in your campaign to get friends and relatives to stop eating sugar, everyone you talk to will know in a sort of indefinite and reluctant way that sugar is not good for one's health. But, before you can get him to delete sugar from his daily meals, you will need a lot more definite and persuasive information than this. We hope that this article will provide you with the further information you need. We also suggest that the content of this article would make good material for a speech before the Parent-Teachers Association or Mothers' Club, or for a term paper in high school.

Isaac Schour, D.D.S., Ph.D., and Maury Massler, D.D.S., M.S., of Chicago have a lot to say about sugar and dental decay in an article in the *Journal of the American Dental Association* for July 1, 1947. These two investigators have contributed much to the literature on dental decay including a brilliant article in which they showed that fluoridated water is quite likely to be harmful to the teeth of badly nourished children, although it seems to postpone decay in children who are well nourished.

Refined Sugar and Dental Decay

In this particular article mentioned above, they discuss the situation in post-war Italy when 3,905 children were examined for dental decay and the figures were compared with dental decay in our country. In the Italian age group, 11 to 15 years, there was an average of 1.05 decayed, missing or filled tooth per child. In the same age group in the United States the average was 4.66 per child. On the other hand in 4 Italian cities examined, 53.4 per cent of the children between 11 to 15 years had no dental decay. In the United States only 9.5 per cent of the children in this age group had no dental decay. Figures on older age groups showed a similar story.

Discussing the reasons for this astonishing difference in tooth decay between Italy, a country which suffered greatly during the war, and the United States, where deprivation was certainly at a minimum, the authors point out that the amount of refined sugar available for Italian children was very limited. The Italian children were not especially well nourished, so apparently good nutrition is not the only essential for dental health. These Italian children lacked in their diets many of the healthful foods they should have had. But—and this is the crux of the matter—they also lacked refined white sugar, or at any rate did not have it in anything like the quantity in which it was available to American children. During the years 1930-34 the per capita consumption of sugar in Italy was 18 pounds, as compared to 103 pounds in America.

The Influence of Dietary Habits

The investigators tell us that Clapp reported a remarkably low incidence of caries in young adult Italians who were born in Italy and who were living in Bridgeport, Connecticut. They had grown up on the Italian diet with a particularly low intake of sugar—about one-seventh that of American boys. On the other hand, Day and Sedwick examined the teeth of 500 children 13 years of age and of Italian descent (whose diet, presumably was now Americanized and high in sugar) and found no great difference between the prevalence of caries in this group and American children. This might lead to the supposition that dietary habits have a greater effect on the incidence of caries than does one's heredity, although the latter cannot be discounted.

The authors also remind us that the average Italian diet is high in carbohydrates. Spaghetti, bread and so forth make up a large part of it. Some experimenters have shown that carbohydrates produce the mouth acid that leads to tooth decay. But apparently in the case of the Italian children the carbohydrates made no difference. Even though they were badly nourished and their diet lacked many necessary foods, even though they ate a large proportion of carbohydrates in comparison to the amount of protein they had, still their teeth were infinitely better than those of American children who had been living on good diets—but had been eating large quantities of sugar.

One of the most complete discussions of refined sugar in relation to dental health comes to us in a symposium conducted by the California State Dental Association, April 24, 1950, and printed in the journal of that organization . . . *Sugar and Dental Caries.* In this 95-page booklet the speech most interesting to us was that of Dr. Robert C. Hockett of the Sugar Research Foundation, Incorporated, and the answer to his speech given by Michael H. Walsh, M.Sc., F.R.I.C., Instructor in Clinical Nutrition at the University of California.

Why Sugar Is Not Economical

Here are some excerpts from Dr. Walsh's brilliant rebuttal to the arguments that sugar is an economical food. . . . "If, as he (Dr. Hockett) asserts, sugar is the most efficiently produced food, why do not the commercial hog feeders, beef producers and poultry raisers feed their animals sugar in large quantities? . . . Surely if sugar were the most efficiently produced food, these scientists who are experts in animal nutrition would have advocated long ago the consumption of sugar in large quantities for the feeding of farm animals. . . . By efficiency (Dr. Hockett) means the ability to produce calories, and calories are identified as the only index of nutritive needs of man, without any regard for the need for nutrients such as essential amino acids, essential fatty acids, the many minerals and vitamins without which all the calories of sugar in the world are not only utterly useless as food but are physiologically harmful. What does it profit a man to have a million calories a year in the form of sugar if he does not have the essential nutrients to enable the sugars to be utilized?

" . . . When it comes to animal metabolism, every type of nutrient must be ingested—prefabricated, so to speak, and in that metabolism of animals—including humans—protein assumes primary importance because it is the essential raw material from which tissues are built. The most favorable development is obtained when proteins, fats, carbohydrates, minerals and vitamins are furnished to the animal organism simultaneously in amounts and proportions which we now know to be desirable; if there are to be limitations on the supply of these necessary foods, sugar cannot substitute for protein, fat cannot substitute for protein, but on the other hand, both fats and sugars can be and are derived from the metabolism of protein.

Sugar Destroys Essential Nutrients

"Hence when it comes to human diets, there is no object in furnishing sugar unless appropriate amounts of proteins, fats, minerals, and vitamins are also furnished. Refined sugar, because of its highly concentrated form, and being completely devoid of essential proteins, vitamins and minerals, is now regarded nutritionally as a diluting agent of the modern diet. It is a displacer of other factors far more essential than sugar. Thus, the more sugar consumed, the less opportunity for getting essential nutrients into the diet. If sugar is furnished as a replacement of proteins, fats, minerals and vitamins, then serious physiological consequences follow. This is the essence and the crux of the physiological problem we have to deal with not only in dentistry but also in medicine.

"At this meeting the emphasis is on sugar and caries. To me there are far more serious disease problems to be dealt with than tooth decay. Far more teeth are lost today through periodontal (gum) disease than from tooth decay. There is growing and accumulating evidence that the patterns of food habits —including excessive sugar consumption—which are associated with dental decay in childhood, adolescence and early adult life are similar in structure to those of periodontal patients in later life. There is also coming to light, evidence of a dietary relationship between high sugar consumption and polio, rheumatic fever, arthritis and many degenerative diseases."

The Important Matter of Low Blood Sugar

What is some of this evidence Dr. Walsh refers to? First there is Dr. Sandler's fight against polio in North Carolina several years ago, when he brought to a standstill a polio epidemic that had frightened the residents so badly that many of them were willing to try out the diet he recommended. It is in the book, *Diet Prevents Polio,* available from the Lee Foundation for Nutritional Research, 2023 West Wisconsin Avenue, Milwaukee, Wisconsin. The essence of the diet is a reduction of sugar.

Dr. Sandler forbids all forms of refined sugars (desserts, soft drinks, candies and so forth) and even limits sharply the amount of fruit to be eaten. His theory (and we are entirely in agreement with it) is that low blood sugar makes individuals susceptible to polio. Low blood sugar is brought about by eating sugar, paradoxical as this may sound. Eating sugar brings up the blood sugar level for a short time, but then it plunges down far below normal. This makes you feel uncomfortable and you need something sweet again, so you have a soda, a piece of candy or a doughnut, and the blood sugar rockets up again, only to fall much too low a little later. As you can see, the net result is a vicious cycle of eating more and more sweets all the time, just to keep going.

Polio is not the only disease related to low blood sugar. Dr. E. M. Abrahamson in his excellent book, *Body, Mind and Sugar* (published by Henry Holt and Company, New York), tells us that low blood sugar is far, far more prevalent in this country than its opposite—high blood sugar, which is diabetes. Recommending a diet very similar to that of Dr. Sandler, Dr. Abrahamson relates spectacular cures for asthma, alcoholism, neuroses, fatigue, rheumatic fever, ulcers, epilepsy, depression and so forth—the list is encouraging.

What About Mosquito Bites?

Insect bites are probably not a very serious menace to health, except in countries where malaria is prevalent. But insect bites can spoil a vacation, cause loss of sleep, ruin one's appearance and otherwise be a pesky nuisance, especially when one is dedicated to avoiding insecticides. Over the years we have accumulated an amazing file of information on the relation of sugar-eating to susceptibility to insect bites. The only possible conclusion we can draw is that insects simply do not bite people who eat no sugar, we suppose because of the excellence of their blood chemistry. Here is a letter that came in the other day from a reader—a sample of many in our files: "A friend of mine was working in northern Canada where there was a settlement of Indians. It was during the black fly season and it was quite evident that the flies were concentrating on jabbing me, while the Indian chief who sat nearby was entirely free of them. My astonished friend asked why. The chief's reply was 'One month before the black fly season all Indians naturally know enough to leave all sugars from their diet.'" We civilized Americans, with all our knowledge of chemistry, have not figured out a number of basic facts about nutrition that are well known to primitive people.

A Personal Experience

Editor Rodale confirms this story with an observation from his own experience. He visited Dr. Page in Florida and discussed his work on minerals and sugar. "When that was explained to me," he says, "I immediately realized that I wanted to have my blood as healthy as possible, and began to severely eliminate all these artificial sugars. It meant, however, that I could eat fruits and such things as honey and molasses in moderation.

"That summer I noticed that I was practically immune to mosquitoes. When all others were complaining about being bitten, I was not. And when I discussed this matter with an aunt of mine who has diabetes and who also has to forego artificial sugars, she said she has had the same experience. She does not get bitten by mosquitoes."

Disorders Related to Sugar Consumption

Here is a quick review of several other articles on other aspects of sugar consumption. J. W. S. Lindahl, M.Chir., F.R.C.S., writing in the December, 1951, issue of *The Practitioner,* says, "It has been suggested that one predisposing factor (in tonsilitis) is an unbalanced diet with too much sugar and starch in relation to protein and green vegetables and I believe there is much to be said for this theory."

Dr. Sidney A. Portis of the University of Chicago believes that a diet *low in sugar* will reduce fatigue, according to the *Journal of the American Medical Association*, Vol. 142, 1950. Dr. Portis, a nervous and mental disease specialist, says that an excess of emotion stimulates the pancreas, resulting in low blood sugar.

Sugar and Vitamin B Deficiency

In the December, 1951, issue of *Prevention* Editor Rodale says, "I had a very interesting experience in meeting with a former aviation pilot who was active in World War II. He related to me an experience. He suffered from blackouts which lasted only a few seconds. But in a plane that would be very serious and dangerous. The doctors cured him by giving him vitamin B1. This would seem to indicate that airplane pilots should not eat the sweet foods such as ice cream, pies, pastries and others that contain artificial sugars, including cola drinks, because the chances are, if this pilot had been on a diet that did not take in these artificial sugars, he probably would not have suffered from these blackouts which were caused by vitamin B1 deficiency and cured by taking vitamin B1."

White Sugar Robs You of Vitamin B

Natural sugars, as they occur in fruits and sugar cane, have with them the full assortment of B vitamins that are necessary for the assimilation of the sugars, and its use by the body. As we have seen, none of these B vitamins is present in white sugar. But, if the sugar is to be used by the body they must be present. So they are drafted—from nerves, muscles, liver, kidneys, stomach, heart, skin, eyes, blood. Needless to say, this leaves these organs of the body deficient in B vitamins. Unless a tremendous amount of vitamin B-rich food is taken, this deficiency will become worse and worse. As more sugar is eaten, more B vitamins are stolen.

Look around you. We are a nation of sufferers from "nerves," digestive disorders, tiredness, poor eyesight, anemia, heart trouble, muscular diseases and a hundred assorted skin diseases. How much of this suffering is due to lack of the

B vitamins caused by the amount of sugar we eat every year? No one will ever be able to answer that question precisely, but we are willing to hazard a guess that nine-tenths of these troubles would disappear within a year of the time that white sugar was banned from our tables and from our food.

Try It Without Sugar

Do you suffer from any of the above complaints? Are you "nervous" and tired, do you have any kind of digestive disorder or skin disease? Are you willing to try an experiment to see just how much the eating of white sugar has to do with your complaints? For 6 months drop sugar from your menu. No halfway measures are permitted. You may eat *nothing* that contains refined sugar. This means no bakery products, no candy, soft drinks or chewing gum, no ice cream, canned fruit (unless it is packed without sugar), no sugar in your beverages or on your cereal. You may and should eat lots of fruit and vegetables, meat, eggs, nuts and fish. In addition, you should certainly take brewer's yeast or desiccated liver which contain all the B vitamins, for, if you have been in the habit of eating white refined sugar, you are almost bound to have a serious vitamin B shortage.

For the first week or so you'll probably suffer gnawing hunger for sweets. Satisfy your hunger with something else. Eat an apple, a handful of sunflower seeds or nuts, a raw carrot. When you stop with friends at the soda fountain, order fruit juice or tea (with no sugar). Fresh fruit and yogurt is a wonderful dessert and once you have become accustomed to ending a meal with fruit and yogurt you'll wonder why you ever wanted all those gooey pastries and sticky pies and cakes.

CHAPTER **20**

What's Wrong With Sugar?

But, you may say, everybody knows we need sugar for energy. And besides, a food so widely used surely can't be harmful. Can't it? Read on and see.

We had a letter from a reader who enclosed an ad cut from her local paper. It was a full page ad glorifying white sugar, filled with brilliant half-truths and carefully shaded statements. "Why do you say sugar is harmful," asked this lady, gently, "if it were harmful surely they would not be allowed to advertise it."

Does Advertising Convince You?

First, let us say to the reader above that the fact that something is advertised does not mean that it is good for you. The sugar industry is Big Business. They spend hundreds of thousands of dollars every year to convince you that sugar is good for you. They cannot say just that in so many words, because they know as well as we do about the volumes of medical research which prove the opposite. But the sugar industry hires advertising geniuses whose business it is to convince you that you should go on eating sugar in any quantities. And they do it with one of the greatest collection of half-truths and evasions now current in the advertising industry which is famous for generalities and evasions. Here is a review of material on sugar we have presented earlier:

Why Do We Call White Sugar a "Drug"?

We call white sugar a "drug" because in the refining process everything of food value has been removed except the carbohydrates—pure calories, without vitamins, minerals, proteins, fats, enzymes or any of the other elements that make up food. Pure carbohydrates do not exist in nature, so it is our belief and that of many nutrition experts that white sugar is extremely harmful, as harmful as a drug, especially in the quantities in which we present-day Americans consume it.

Why Is It Harmful?

Each cell in the human body is equipped to deal with natural foodstuffs. Certain vitamins and minerals are necessary for the body's use of fats, certain others for protein, certain others for carbohydrates. Natural foods (fruits and vegetables, honey, sugar cane and maple syrup for instance) come equipped with all the things necessary for their metabolism—the calcium, the B vitamins, the enzymes, the phosphorus and so forth. In the case of the sugar beet and the sugar cane, we have unhappily discovered, how to remove all these parts of what started out as perfectly good food and leave nothing but the sweet taste, and the calories. Our cells, accustomed over hundreds of thousands of years to dealing with natural foods, cannot handle such a substance.

What happens is slow starvation of the cells, starving for all the natural good food value that should be present in foods. Can such starvation bring cancer? We have no direct proof that just the eating of white sugar by itself will cause cancer. But we know that animals kept on diets of refined foods, as white sugar is, have far more cancer than animals eating natural foods. Obesity, diabetes, arthritis, tooth decay, pyorrhea, asthma—is it not possible that diseases like these are related to our enormous intake of white sugar? Why not? Doesn't it seem probable that cells, so deranged and sidetracked from their natural kind of nutrition, will eventually become diseased?

Raisers of livestock have to feed their animals on the best possible diets, because billions of dollars are at stake in the health of these animals. Did you ever hear of a cattle or pig grower feeding his stock on white sugar? He knows well what the consequences would be. Yet he'll feed his children and himself on a food so deadly he knows his stock could not survive on it.

Don't We Need to Get Energy From Our Food?

Sure we do and practically any sound nutritive menu you can devise will give you enough energy and far more than you need without using a single grain of the "white drug." For thousands of years before human beings knew how to refine sugar, man worked from sun to sun at jobs requiring infinitely more energy than present-day work requires. He never knew there could be such a thing as white sugar. Where did he get his energy?

Why Do We Like Sugar, if It's So Bad for Us?

It's a peculiar thing about "liking" the taste of sugar. One theory is that we were given a taste for sweet things to guide us to foods rich in minerals and other valuable food elements. Grapes, carrots, apples, figs, dates, plums—would primitive man have eaten these unless they tasted sweet?

When we eat these natural sweets, we are completely nourished and we do not want more. But when everything is removed from these foods except the sweet taste, our body can no longer gauge its needs. We eat the sweet sugar and we are not satisfied. We are craving the minerals that should go along with it. So we eat more sugar and get even hungrier. A vicious cycle. We have the testimony of many, many readers who have eliminated sugar from their diets. They are amazed at friends and relatives who continue to crave this unwholesome sweet, for they can honestly say that they have no desire, absolutely no desire, for anything sweeter than an apple or a grape.

What Harm Is Done by White Sugar?

1. Tooth decay. Even the most conservative dental associations are passing resolutions these days condemning white sugar as the tooth's worst enemy. We have volumes of scientific evidence on this score.

2. The calcium-phosphorus balance. We know what the balance between these two important minerals should be in the blood—two and one-half to one. We know, too, that eating foods containing white sugar throws this balance off decidedly. What might this cause? We don't know all of the answer, but it seems quite likely that arthritis, polio, cancer, and all the other degenerative diseases of our time are certainly related to such a serious bodily condition as an imbalance of calcium and phosphorus.

3. Mental illness and "nerves." One of the surest results of eating white sugar is a deficiency in the B vitamins, for these vitamins must be present in the digestive tract if sugar is to be digested. The B vitamins which naturally occur in sugar

have been removed, so the digestive apparatus must steal the necessary B vitamins from other parts of the body. This results in certain deficiency—and the nerves may be the first to suffer. A diet of soft drinks, candy, sodas, pastries, chewing gum, pies and so forth leads to the nervous breakdown and the mental hospital, just as surely as does a diet of alcohol—which, incidentally, is another "pure carbohydrate." Pretty shocking, isn't it, to think of today's children as drunkards? But so far as destruction of healthy tissue is concerned, white sugar is every bit as harmful as alcohol.

4. Low blood sugar is at present more prevalent in our country than its opposite, high blood sugar or diabetes. Low blood sugar is the result of a derangement of glands brought about by a diet high in carbohydrates—chiefly refined carbohydrates. We say this because it is impossible to eat enough of natural sweets (fruits and vegetables) to bring about low blood sugar. But foods consisting of little but sugar slide down easily and—bingo—down goes the blood sugar level!

During digestion, sugar and starch are broken down into simple sugars in the intestine from which they go to the liver. In the liver they are changed to glycogen and released gradually into the blood stream or stored for future use. After a meal high in refined sugar or starch, the level of glycogen in the blood rises rapidly—much too rapidly. Then it falls, just as rapidly, rather than remaining at a reasonable level. People who eat lots of refined sugars do not have enough glycogen in their livers to keep the blood sugar level normal for long.

Result? Fatigue, nervousness, hunger, restlessness, dizziness, and eventually such disorders as migraine, epilepsy, polio, alcoholism, asthma and so on and on. Correcting low blood sugar begins with saying goodbye to refined sweets and concentrating on a diet high in good quality protein. It's just that simple.

5. The vitamin B deficiency produced by eating refined sweets can contribute to many other disorders—beriberi and pellagra are two extreme examples. But vitamin B deficiency leads to heart trouble, also to constipation, colitis, many skin diseases, mouth disorders like Vincent's disease, and so on.

6. The most important elements of our diet are foods which are high in protein, vitamins and minerals. The more

refined sugar we eat, the less of these good foods we have room for. So sugar-eating leads indirectly to all the diseases that result from lack of protein as well as lack of minerals and vitamins. Anemia, goiter and other diseases like these are related to sugar consumption.

7. We do not know as yet all the possible harm that white sugar can do. We may not know for many years, and by then it may be too late.

How Can You Get Along Without Sugar?

We think the best answer to this question came from a reader who wrote us that she was trying to do without sugar, and found that she made out very successfully; but surely, she asked, *no one could be expected to eat lettuce without sugar!* We have never heard of anyone eating lettuce *with* sugar. The story shows clearly that eating sugar is purely and simply a matter of what you are accustomed to—just as eating salt is.

Get used to doing without sugar. It will help if you add quantities of protein to your diet—meat, fish, eggs, nuts, legumes—and large amounts of fresh raw fruits and vegetables. Food supplements will help, too, for they supply the missing minerals and vitamins you are really craving, when you think you crave sugar. Sugar is a drug. You will have to go through a period of difficulty, as all drug addicts do when their drug is removed. But you will be amazed how soon the smell of a bakery shop or a candy store becomes disgusting to you. You will be happily surprised how soon you will be looking forward to a dessert of fruit, dried fruit, nuts, sunflower seeds or something equally healthful.

What About Raw Sugar, Brown Sugar, Etc.?

We think it is best to do without any sweetening at all. The longer you dabble with excessively sweet things, the longer it will take you to get on that wonderful, happy, level plane where you won't crave anything sweet. If you do feel you must have sweetening, use honey or real maple syrup, both of which are completely natural foods, well fortified with vitamins and minerals. But use no more than a couple of teaspoonfuls a day even of these good sweets. Blackstrap molasses contains the minerals and vitamins that have been refined out of the sugar cane. So it contains more of some minerals than most foods.

Use it if you must, but in extreme moderation. Raw sugar and brown sugar have both been subjected to processing and refining. We think they are just about as bad as white sugar and we urge you not to use them.

Where Can You Get More Information?

The best source, we think, is a booklet called, *Sugar, the Curse of Civilization,* available from Rodale Press, Emmaus, Pennsylvania. Price fifty cents.

The book, *Degeneration and Regeneration,* by Melvin Page, D.D.S. contains much information about the harm sugar does in the body. It is available from Dr. Page at 2810 First Street, North., St. Petersburg, Florida.

What About Artificial Sweeteners?

These are the greatest fraud of all, for they are sold with the proud boast that they contribute absolutely no nutritive value whatsoever to your body. Anything you eat must be digested by your body. How can your poor digestive tract handle something like this? Artificial sweeteners are made of coal tar. Several have been forbidden because they were found to be harmful—one of them after we had been assured for many years that it was completely harmless. Shun the artificial sweeteners—saccharin, sucaryl and all others.

Here are a few more facts on sugar-eating. Surgeon Captain T. L. Cleave, writing in the Spring, 1956, issue of the *Journal of the Royal Naval Medical Service* says that concentrating foods by machinery is a dangerous procedure. It is of such recent date that our bodies cannot possibly adapt themselves to it. Carbohydrates are, of course, the foods generally treated thus. Nearly all the harmful consequences that arise from this are due to the excessive consumption of the carbohydrates. Their taste is too highly geared for the tongue to be able to know when to stop. A bar of chocolate, for example, contains as much sugar as a dozen apples. The tongue would know when to stop eating the apples, but not the chocolate bar. The concentration of sugar is the most damaging item in our modern diet. Dr. Cleave blames sugar directly, for such diseases as dental decay, peptic ulcer, diabetes, obesity, constipation and intestinal toxemia.

One more story—told by Editor Rodale. We started this chapter with the innocent query of why anyone is allowed to

advertise sugar if it's harmful. It's a free country. Almost any-
thing can be advertised with almost any kind of superlatives.
And what happens to the people who try to warn against sugar?
Read this experience quoted from the *Dental Digest* for
December, 1956.

Says the writer: "I know at first hand something about
the power of the sugar interests and how adroitly they operate.
My wife and I prepared a cookbook *Sweet Without Sugar* that
gives recipes for desserts and other dishes that may be prepared
without the use of refined sugar. The foreword was written
by our family friend, Barbara Eisenhower, the President's
daughter-in-law.

"Two of the largest book publishers in the United States
were eager to publish it until they talked with their front
offices where subjects of dollars and business are discussed. In
both cases they turned away from publication. In one case the
managing editor stated honestly that he did not wish to offend
the sugar-candy-soft drink-ice cream-bakery interests. Nowhere
along the line were there questions of bribery or coercion
involved, no threats of boycott, no strong-arm tactics. It was
a matter of business judgment not to offend industries that
operate in billions of dollars a year.

"I doubt if the sugar-using industries were even asked
their opinions of such a cookbook and I am quite sure that the
publishers did not show them the manuscript. I am not accusing
the sugar interests of exercising any form of direct censorship,
restraint of freedom of publication, or pressure. Subtle forces
are always more effective!

"The only reason for pushing this personal experience
into the light is to show that the $350,000 annual advertising
campaign of the candy makers will be smooth and subtle. No
controversy, no direct attack, no taking issue with scientific
statements, no offense intended!"

CHAPTER **21**

Some Plain Talk About Sugars

There are different kinds of sugar, of course. This chapter describes these in some detail.

What do we mean when we say dextrose, fructose, sucrose, glucose or lactose? Are these names for foods you can buy in cans or bags? Should we seek them out or shun them? If we throw away our sugar bowls and stop eating desserts and sweetened fruits, how can we be sure we are getting enough sugar for the body's needs? What about sweeteners that are advertised as having little caloric value?

Some Answers

Sugar is a carbohydrate, which means that it is made from carbon, hydrogen and oxygen. The way these elements are combined in different formulas makes the chief difference in sugars. There are single sugars, double sugars and multiple sugars—a fact which need not concern you in any way, except that it shows you how complex the subject of sugars is bound to be, when you are dealing with three separate groups of substances and many subdivisions in each group.

We should be concerned chiefly with sugars which occur naturally in foods along with all the substances that accompany them, as opposed to white sugar and similar products, which are nothing but pure carbohydrate without a single particle of mineral, vitamin, enzyme or anything else that makes them food.

Glucose, also known as *dextrose,* is grape sugar or blood sugar. It occurs in our blood and it also occurs in almost all fruits and vegetables. It is more than half the entire solid matter of honey and grapes.

Fructose is found in most fruits and many vegetables.

Lactose is a sugar which occurs only in milk. It is less sweet than other sugars, digests less readily and hence is not so fattening. As it is digested in the body it changes into *glucose* and *galactose*. Lactose is food for the intestinal bacteria which change it into lactic acid. This, we believe, is one of the reasons why yogurt is such a valuable food and has such a reputation for restoring valuable intestinal bacteria. It contains lactose, of course.

Sucrose is the chemical name for white sugar. This sugar also occurs in fruits and vegetables. It makes up about half the solid matter of a carrot. During digestion it is changed into *glucose* and *fructose*.

Maltose is a sugar found in malt (germinated grains).

Cellulose is that part of vegetables and fruits that is almost completely indigestible by human beings—the skins of fruits, the "core" of vegetables, the husk of grains. The ruminant animals can digest cellulose. Since we cannot, why bother to eat it? It's good for us because it forms the bulk which is so important for our good digestion. People who do not eat enough foods containing cellulose are bound to suffer from constipation.

Inulin is the other sugar which we only partly digest. This occurs in onions, garlic and Jerusalem artichokes. For this reason there has been lots of rather unwarranted enthusiasm about these artichokes. The mere fact that their sugar is largely undigested and hence is not fattening is surely no reason why anyone should decide that they are a "wonder" food.

Should You Eat Sugar?

Now, how are you going to know which of these sugars you should eat and which you should not eat? As you can see, if you look back over our list, you can get lots and lots of all these different kinds of sugar if you eat plenty of fruits and vegetables. Let's say you have crossed white sugar off your list entirely, never have any of it in the house and never eat anything away from home that contains it. Isn't it possible that you may suffer from lack of sugar? After all, sugar in your food is the main source of energy for your body. True. Sugar does not keep you healthy, does not rebuild broken down tissue, does not take part, as proteins and fats do, in many of the intricate and necessary body processes. But sugar does give you energy. How then can you be sure you are getting enough?

Do you have any idea how much sugar you get in a well-planned diet which does not include a single grain of white sugar? Eating fruits, whole grains, cereals, vegetables, eggs, meat, nuts and milk, you would get close to two cups of sugar as a total for the day! Impossible, you will say. But it's so. Do you think you could possibly need more than two cups a day?

Carbohydrates in Food

Here is a list of fruits and vegetables along with their carbohydrate content. We use the word "carbohydrate" here rather than "sugar," for in some of these foods the carbohydrate is in the form of starch rather than sugar. But the starch is changed into sugar almost as soon as you eat it, so in considering the total of your sugar intake, you should count this starch as sugar. *Foods very low in carbohydrate content* (the ones you think of first in connection with a reducing diet): These contain about 5 per cent carbohydrate: carrots, cauliflower, okra, onions, peppers, pumpkin, radishes, string beans, watercress. *These foods contain about 7 per cent carbohydrate:* avocado and olives (quite high in fat), grapefruit, lemons, strawberries, watermelon.

These foods contain about 10 per cent carbohydrate: parsnips, peas, Hubbard squash, turnips, berries, cantaloupe, muskmelon, oranges, peaches, pineapple, raspberries.

These foods contain about 15 per cent carbohydrate: apples, apricots, cherries, currants, grapes, huckleberries, nectarines, pears.

These foods contain about 20 per cent carbohydrate: corn, lima beans, navy beans, sweet and white potatoes, rice, bananas, fresh figs, plums and prunes. Dried fruits may contain as much as 75 per cent carbohydrate.

What Do We Have Against Sugar?

Since so many of our foods are so rich in sugar, why then do we, along with all responsible nutritionists, argue against the use of white sugar? There are two reasons. First of all, the very fact that so many of the foods which we should be eating every day contain so much sugar is certainly the best possible indication that we do not need to add any more sugar to our diets. It seems perfectly obvious that this is the way Nature intended for us to get our sugar, as all her other creatures do—from natural foods.

Secondly, all the sugar that occurs naturally in fruits and vegetables, no matter which kind of sugar it is—sucrose, fructose, glucose or whatever—occurs in the food combined with all the enzymes, vitamins and minerals that belong with it. Your body needs all of these things if you are going to use the sugar as it is meant to be used. Now, suppose you concentrate the sugar, throwing away everything else. Of course, you manufacture sucrose or glucose this way. But you will have only a "pure" substance left—like a drug, just as white sugar is. None of the natural accompanying substances will be left with it. And therein lies the terrible danger from the use of white sugar— its unnatural concentration.

Unnatural Sugar—a Drug

Concentrated, pure sugar is a drug, unrelated to anything that occurs naturally. For this reason it makes terrible demands on your body. First, it throws off the calcium-phosphorus balance and disrupts this entire, important phase of your body machinery. Secondly, because refined sugar has been robbed of the B vitamins that are necessary for its assimilation by the body, it latches on to these wherever it finds them— namely in your digestive tract, so that the person who eats refined sugar is bound to be short on the B vitamins. Result? Nervousness, skin troubles, digestive trouble and a host of other disorders which lead to much more serious trouble later on.

Other Concentrated Sweets

What about honey, real maple syrup and blackstrap molasses? They contain minerals and vitamins that are natural to them, so for this reason they are the only sweets we can approve. But don't forget they, too, are highly concentrated— maple syrup is the boiled-down sap of the tree, molasses is prepared from sugar cane. And honey is, let's face it, not a "natural" food for human beings. We steal it from the bees, and when we eat it we should take into account the fact that the metabolism and furious activity of a bee are quite different from those of a human being. Honey is a highly concentrated food. Don't eat too much of it.

You sometimes meet with the words we've defined above on labels of foods. Should you buy foods that contain glucose, or dextrose or sucrose? No, because you can be certain that they are "purified" sugars, hence harmful from our point of view.

Some Other Sugars and What They Do

Pure glucose, for instance, is made from cornstarch and is sold as corn sugar. Health-conscious people shouldn't use it for it is "pure." Some of the sugars we mentioned are used in foods for various reasons. Lactose is used to preserve many foods. It is a coating agent for olives, preserved fruits and sugared almonds and a flavoring agent for chocolate products.

It is used in many bakery products and confectionery products. It is an ingredient of baking and biscuit mixes, of some cheese, of dry coloring matter for edible fats, of infant and invalid foods and it is sometimes used as a substitute for other sugars in jams. It is used as a preservative in meat products.

Maltose is used in beer and malt production, in making beverages and soft drinks, in bread doughs, in confectionery products, in jams, in milk and coffee substitutes, in tea extracts, in corn syrup.

This will give you some idea of the many many ways sugars are hidden in food. Apparently it is almost impossible to eat any processed food that does not contain "hidden" sugars, in addition to all the many chemicals that may be there.

The Starchy Foods

Now we must take into account the fact that starchy foods (also carbohydrates) are changed into sugar during digestion. So when you are figuring how much sugar you get in a day's rations, figure as well on the purely starchy foods that don't even taste sweet. There are 35 to 40 grams of carbohydrate in the serving of macaroni, which will be pure sugar within a few minutes from the time you eat it. Wouldn't it be better to eat a piece of meat or an egg instead?

Here is a quote from three well-known authorities on what your body does with carbohydrates. Say Jolliffe, Tisdall and Cannon, the authors of *Clinical Nutrition* (B. Hoeber, Inc.): "Factors which influence the amount of carbohydrate absorbed in a given individual at a particular time are: 1. the normality of the mucous membrane of the small intestine and the length of time during which the carbohydrate is in contact with it; 2.

endocrine (gland) function, particularly that of the anterior pituitary, the thyroid and the adrenal cortex and 3. the adequacy of vitamin intake, especially that of the B complex." In other words, your digestive tract must be in good shape (watch your intake of B vitamins and vitamin A), your glands must be in good shape (all the vitamins and minerals are important for this and don't forget iodine for the thyroid) and, finally, you must get enough of the B vitamins along with the sugar or starch.

You fail entirely to fulfill these 3 essentials every time you eat processed sugar or starches, for they contain no vitamins or minerals. Nowhere in a natural food can you find starch or sugar without some of the vitamins or minerals accompanying them. Fruits, vegetables, whole grain cereals—all are rich in the elements you need to use the carbohydrates properly. But the minute you begin to tamper with the natural food, the whole delicately balanced machinery is thrown out of gear. And therein lies the horrible menace of the refined carbohydrates—chiefly white sugar, with white flour products running a close second. Don't forget, too, all the worthless and dangerous "hidden sugars" lurking in prepared foods—bottled, packaged or canned.

CHAPTER **22**

What About Saccharin and Sucaryl?

The artificial sweeteners are not to be recommended, as their use, over a lifetime, may be dangerous.

We say a positive and unequivocal "no" to any and all sugar substitutes—that is, the various chemicals you can buy labeled saccharin, sucaryl, dulcin, sodium cyclamate and so forth. All these are many times sweeter than sugar. A small tablet of one of these chemicals dropped into your coffee or dissolved in your pudding gives you no calories, hence no energy, and absolutely nothing else, either, except a sweet taste.

They are all products made from coal tar. Applying to them our rules of what we should and should not eat, we discover that these chemicals give us nothing that is needed nutritionally, and do much that is harmful. So we cannot possibly recommend that you use them even for a short period of time to tide you over the uncomfortable few days when you are learning to get along without sugar.

Saccharin and Others

We have done considerable research on saccharin, which we will review here rather than going into an individual discussion on each of the sweeteners. New sweeteners are being discovered all the time, out of the busy test tubes of our chemists, in a nation where the largest portion of the population suffers from overweight. These sweeteners are announced with great fanfare as they appear. We are told we can eat them with safety while we are reducing; we can give them to children and sick people; we can feed them to diabetics. What we have to say about saccharin applies with equal force to all these synthetic sweeteners. *Leave them alone if you would be healthy.*

Since its discovery about 75 years ago, saccharin has been the subject of endless investigation, because, apparently, most researchers have had serious doubts as to its harmlessness in the human body. In our file on saccharin, we cannot find a single article that does not caution that we should use saccharin "with care." Its use should not be abused, they say. To us this means only one thing. If it were harmless, we could eat all of it that we happen to want and suffer no ill consequences. In Europe, country after country has forbidden its use in food and drink. In 1912 our Food and Drug Administration forbade its use in foods because, they said, it would constitute an adulteration. People might think they were getting sugar which, as we know, has a certain value in calories which saccharin does not.

Its Food Value and Relation to Cancer

Early in our medical history physicians advised the use of saccharin because it has no food value, which seems to us just as idiotic as if a coal dealer should advise us to fill up our

winter furnace with steel because it will not burn! Why in the
world should we take anything into our bodies *because* it has
no food value? And what is our body supposed to do with something that scientists agree cannot possibly be called food?

Here is a quote from an article on saccharin: "In the
British Medical Journal of October 9, 1915, H. C. Ross, M.D.,
whose address given at the end of the article is 'Lister Institute'
tells us that 'recent research at the McFadden Laboratory at the
Lister Institute has shown that saccharin is a powerful auxetic,
like several other constituents and derivatives of coal tar; and
there is now strong evidence that it is these auxetics in tar and
pitch that give rise to the predisposition to the cancer known as
pitch and sweepers' cancer.' The next reference we find to it
appears in Dr. B. M. Gupta's article published 20 years
later in the *Indian Medical Gazette* (September, 1935): 'Although this statement (of Ross') does not seem to have been
contradicted in any medical journal, it appears from a private
communciation that the suggestion that saccharin may predispose to cancer is not accepted by the present authorities of the
Lister Institute.' Who lost the evidence in a file somewhere?
What became of the records of the experiment proving the
association of saccharin and cancer? Is it possible that they have
just been overlooked all these years?"

Effect of Saccharin on Plants and Animals

We discovered several experiments revealing the deadly
effect of saccharin on plants and one-celled animals. E. Verschaffelt, M.D., writing in the Dutch Medical Journal, *Pharma-
ceutisch Weekblad,* Vol. LIX, 1915, describes an experiment in
which he soaked dry seed peas in 4 different solutions: plain
water, salt, sugar, and saccharin. Two days later 94 per cent of
the peas treated with water had sprouted; 87 per cent of the
peas treated with sugar had sprouted; 44 per cent of those
soaked in salt water germinated and none of the peas soaked in
saccharin solution sprouted. Using a saccharin solution only half
as strong as the salt solution, Dr. Verschaffelt once again found
that the salt-treated peas germinated twice as fast as those
soaked in saccharin. His conclusions are that saccharin is a
protoplasmic poison, that is, regardless of how long the process
may take, saccharin eventually poisons protoplasm, which is

nothing more or less than the substance of which plants and animals are made.

Dr. W. A. Uglow, M.D., tested saccharin on one-celled animals, and his experiments are reported in the German medical magazine, *Archiv fur Hygiene,* Vol. XCII, 1924. Testing saccharin solutions and phenol (carbolic acid) solutions of varying strength, Dr. Uglow found that saccharin is 12 times as deadly to bacteria as carbolic acid, which is another coal tar derivative and a deadly poison. In a further test, he found that a solution of one part of saccharin to 500 parts of distilled water almost corresponds in its toxicity to a .05 solution of sulfuric acid—another violent poison.

In a solution of one part of saccharin to 400 parts of water Dr. Uglow placed some cyclops quadricornis (a microscopic one-celled animal). They died within 40 minutes. In a solution of one to 800 parts of water, they died within an hour and so on until he found that it took a solution of one part of saccharin to 8000 parts of water just 24 hours to kill all the cyclops. Incidentally one part of saccharin to 10,000 parts of water is approximately the solution we get when we slip a saccharin tablet into a cup of tea or coffee.

A one-celled animal is made up of one tiny cell of protoplasm—the same protoplasm that makes up all the many tiny cells of your body. Cancer research deals largely with what goes on in cells. Certain coal tar products are known to produce cancer through their effect on the cells of the body. Saccharin is a coal tar product. Saccharin means certain death to a one-celled animal. Do you need further proof of the harmfulness of saccharin and all other synthetic sweeteners?

Incidentally, although saccharin is illegal in food and drink so far as interstate commerce is concerned, there is nothing to prevent local food processors from using it in all their sweet products, unless your state has a law which forbids it. Why not write to your state department of health and check?

Must We Sweeten Our Foods?

Only one word more on saccharin. We receive many letters from healthy people who are getting along happily and serenely without ever using sugar or any other kind of sweetener except fruits and vegetables. We have also shown that saccharin is a poison. What possible excuse can there be to continue to prepare foods for diabetics (desperately sick people) using saccharin? Why do we continue to propagate the fable that Americans simply can't get along without a sweet taste in their mouths at every meal and most of the time between meals? In many parts of the world, whole nations have never tasted sugar or sugar substitutes. In our own country, thousands of people have not eaten sugar or sugar substitutes for years. Why must we continue to feed the poisonous sweet-tasting sugar substitutes to sick people?

SECTION 5

BREAD

Bread is not the staff of life and in the Prevention *system there is no place for it, even though it be made of whole wheat. It is fattening, constipating, ferments in the stomach, causes heart symptoms in many heart patients, celiac disease in children, rickets if there is not sufficient vitamin D, is a factor in causing colds, stuffed noses, and many other conditions too numerous to mention here. Try a breadless and grainless diet for a month and see what it will do for you. This means cutting out also cakes, spaghetti, noodles, gravy, etc. By cutting out this form of starch you will have to fill up on more vegetables.*

You can eat bread, and still not eat it, by taking it in the form of wheat germ flakes and vitamin E. Everything in the wheat grain but the bran and the wheat germ is worthless starch out of which paste can be made.

147

CHAPTER **23**

The Story of a Loaf of Bread

The making of a loaf of bread, from the time the seed of wheat goes into the ground until the wrapped loaf issues from the bakery, lends itself beautifully to demonstrate the extent of chemicalization that goes on in the manufacture of the average food product that the public eats. If you will follow me, step by step, you will be amazed at the recklessness of American manufacturers, at their lack of consideration for the health of the bread-consuming public, and at the incredible apathy of that public and its medical advisers, in not electing to power public officials who will see to it that toxic chemicals are banned from use in food products.

The average person eats bread but never stops to look behind the loaf. To him or her, bread is bread. Man has eaten bread since caveman days, and some think it sacrilegious to utter a word against it. However, I intend to utter quite a few words against it. I will tell you my story of a loaf of bread. Hear me out and then *you* be the judge.

Good Soil Is Important for Good Bread

First, we must consider the soil in which the wheat crop is going to grow. Soil erosion has removed some of the finest topsoils of our country. It has been stated that over 61 per cent of the topsoil of American agricultural land has been lost in the last hundred years of farming, most of it probably in the last 20 or 30 years. Consider the fearful loss of topsoil in the recent Kansas flood, which cost 800,000,000 dollars of damage. This is in the wheat-growing section of our country. A great part of the wheat produced in the United States comes from the Dust Bowl. That name itself indicates what can be expected insofar as quality of soil is concerned. It has been stated, that people are merely an expression of the soil from which their food is produced. Poor soil, poor people.

Our suicidal agricultural policy of using chemical fertilizers takes from the soil without putting back, kills bacteria,
and deposits caustic, corrosive chemicals in the soil, which
destroy the natural antibiotic organisms such as penicillium.
The wheat seed is planted in a soil in which we are spraying
poisons, such as 2, 4-D and other insecticides to kill weeds. In
many cases, previous crops grown on the land have required
highly poisonous insecticides, which have killed off many of the
necessary bacteria and earthworms. The earthworm is such an
important ally of the farmer. He burrows into and aerates the
soil, and deposits his own manure in it to enrich it.

All of this is the introduction for the little wheat seed
that goes into the ground. He starts life in a dirty, devitalized
medium. The cards are stacked against him right from the
beginning.

Wheat Seed Must Be Healthy

Secondly, we must see what is done to the seed and what
it has become from years of abusive practices in agriculture. Dr.
William Albrecht, of the University of Missouri, has recently
said that the protein-content of the grains grown in the middle
west has gone down 10 per cent in the last 10 years. This is due
to the commercial type of farming with its over-use of chemical
fertilizers, especially potash, which increases the carbohydrates
and reduces protein.

In medical literature in the last 20 years, the value of
protein has been stressed. It is not only concerned about the
diminishing quantity of protein that is left, but of late there
have been researches showing that the quality, too, has been
degenerating. Protein, for example, consists of amino acids, of
which there are about 20. One of them, as a typical example,
is arginine. A medical research has recently shown that cancerous tumors in animals could be cured by the use of arginine. On
the other hand, Dr. William Albrecht himself has also recently
shown that the more fertile the soil, the more arginine would
be reflected in the crop. At any rate, we are now placing our
little seed into the ground with less protein and with less
arginine. But that is not all. In our agriculture in the last twenty
or thirty years, disease has been on the increase, and the organisms of such disease are carried in the seeds. The average wheat
seed is full of the smut and rust organism. The seed then is sub-

jected to a treatment with a substance called *ceresan,* which is a mercury poison and which kills the smut and rust disease organisms, but unfortunately it has been known that the poison penetrates into the seed and some of it will show up in the seed of the new crop which will be used to make bread. Today, when you purchase wheat seed at the feed dealers, it has probably already been treated with the mercury poison, and the bags are marked "caution," with prohibiting instructions so that the seed will not be fed to chickens or other farm animals. Occasionally, however, a farmer is careless or forgets, and kills animals with such feed. In veterinary laboratories, mercury poisoning is seen each year on specimens of swine and chickens, which have been submitted to them for testing.

The Harm of Chemical Fertilizers

Now we come to the third step, the farmer saturates the soil with a chemical fertilizer. When the plant is growing and at a certain point, if it is infested with weeds, a spray of 2, 4-D will be given from the air. Very little research has been done as to the effect of these weed-killers on the soil and the bacterial life of that soil, as well as on the crops and the health of people consuming such crops. We do know that some of these weed-killers kill other crops. For example, grapevines can be hurt badly, if the wind goes the wrong way and brings some of the 2, 4-D to it. The same thing would apply to a crop of soybeans. These weed-killers are chemicals that are used because the farmer is at his wit's end as the result of poor farming practices, and it seems to him to be the simplest thing to do. On our own experimental farm, on the other hand, where the organic method is practiced and where no chemical fertilizers are used, the soil is in such fine shape that at the proper time we can cultivate out the weed seeds and kill them. Our soil's sponge-like quality and the ease with which it can be worked by farm implements are due to the structure that is given to it by the organic matter that we use. Our farm is a wonderful example of the control of weeds by natural biological methods rather than by chemicals.

Must Wheat Be Fumigated?

We now come to the fourth step. The farmer harvests the wheat. In the old days, when there were not the automatic combines which took the wheat in and threshed it at the same time, the farmer shocked the crop and let it season in the field. The heads of the seeds ripen slowly in this manner and give the flour mill a much easier seed to work with. Today, I have been told by a flour mill manufacturer that he has all kinds of trouble because of the fact that the wheat is taken in somewhat green, and is not seasoned or ripened in the field. Various treatments are given, therefore, to prevent spoilage or to make it easier to handle, but very little is known about such treatments and of what they consist. The farmer himself takes in the wheat, stores it in his bin in the barn, and now treats it with cyanogen gas, which is such a dangerous poison that he has to wear a gas mask while applying it. Cyanogen is used to kill grain weevils. On my own farm we do not spray any gas, and we have very little trouble. It is possible that wheat grown by the organic method, that is, with use of organic matter and rock fertilizers ground up without the use of acids, has a better keeping ability. At any rate, I would rather have the few grain weevils, than saturate the whole mass of a food product with something as violently poisonous as cyanogen.

Stone Grinding Is Best

We now come to the fifth step. The wheat is ground up fine in the steel roller process. In the old days, grain was ground in stone mills which revolved slowly and kept the flour at a low temperature. But a new process was discovered by a Hungarian, about 80 years ago, in which rapidly revolving steel rollers were used. This heated the flour and removed a large amount of the valuable nutrients it contained. It is rather strange that the first known cases of polio came about just a little after the steel roller mill process began about 80 years ago. Several physicians have remarked about the coincidence. The flour that came out of the old-fashioned mill, 75 and 100 years ago, contained about 75 per cent of the vitamin B1 of the wheat. Your white flour of today probably retains only 10 per cent of it. The difference is what is destroyed in our modern milling and refining process.

Since the beginning of steel rolling, many physicians believe that we have more digestive disturbances, poorer teeth, more constipation and more widely spread nervous diseases. It is a known fact that the steel rolling process produces a poorer

gluten in the flour, which makes it difficult to work with in
the mill. Add to this the fact that the wheat itself is poorer
today, because of the deterioration of soil fertility, brought
about by its over stimulation with chemical fertilizers.

There's Profit in Removing the Bran

We now come to the sixth step. In the milling process,
the bran or outer coat is removed. This is a very important part
of the wheat seed, and contains large amounts of vitamins and
minerals, especially iron which is so necessary to make good
red blood, and phosphorus for nerves and bones. The outer
bran contains proteins of very good quality. But because the
bran is so good, it is set aside and sold to farmers who feed
it to pigs. In this way the flour mill makes more money. What
is left is the inner part of the seed kernel containing, outside of
the wheat germ which we will discuss in the next step, practically no vitamins or minerals. It is mostly starch and gluten
and is good for making paste.

It would certainly be fairer to the public if it was placed
at least on the same level with the pig. Actually, the separation
of the two elements of the grain creates nothing. The pig gets
the bran, and man gets the white stuff. Why not give both
the man and the pig their proper share of the whole grain?
Let each one get some of the white and some of the brown.
Why should pigs become healthy at the expense of the ill-health
of man?

The Germ is Removed, Too

We now come to step number seven. The wheat germ
is removed from the wheat. In the human being this would be
equivalent to removing his heart. The wheat germ is the very
heart and life of the seed, rich in vitamins and minerals, and
when that is gone, the seed certainly will never grow into a
plant. It is one of the richest sources of vitamins B and E and
contains valuable proteins and fat. The vitamin E is usually
sold to farmers to make their horses more fertile, and some
people buy it for themselves. The drug industry makes millions
out of this wheat germ. The public, therefore, must take
vitamin E to replace the lost wheat germ from the bread that
it is eating. It is our suggestion that the public be sure to take
wheat germ, brewer's yeast and bone meal to replace the valu-

able vitamins and minerals that have been lost in the removal of the bran and the germ from the wheat. We are now left with a really dead substance.

Why Bleach Flour?

The eighth step is the bleaching of the flour, which Dr. Carlson of the University of Chicago called "social custom and biological stupidity." When in Germany and England last summer, I found that all the bread and rolls there were of a grey color, which indicates that the wheat is not bleached. I also noted that the span of life is higher, especially in Germany. In bleaching, various chemicals are used, such as alum, ammonia, gypsum (which is plaster of Paris) and others, which are known to be toxic to human beings, in spite of some in high authority, who say they are not. All bleaches are poisonous. It cannot be otherwise. The amount, however, is small, but when you consider the cumulative effect of the various preservatives that the public gets in all of its foods, and the chlorine in its drinking water, that cumulative amount then becomes a serious factor in the equation of health. Gypsum is used partly for its bleaching effect and also because it absorbs water, thus cutting down more expensive ingredients needed in the bread. Bleaching enables the miller to use inferior flours—flours that are also of undesirable grades. One of the most common bleaches is nitrogen trichloride or agene. A few years ago, Sir Edward Mellanby in England discovered that the use of this chemical gave fits to dogs. The government of England became aroused and began to hold hearings on the question of discontinuing the use of nitrogen trichloride. There is a controversy raging in this country also between the Food and Drug Administration and the baking industry regarding its use. The bakers say that dogs are not people. Personally, it doesn't make any difference whether it is dogs or even flies, if it will give fits to anything that lives. I want none of it. Nitrogen trichloride ages the flour at once instead of waiting two or three weeks for natural aging to take place. That is why it is called agene. It enables the miller to work without skill. Bleaching increases the acidity of the flour. It is done also to deceive and it takes the strength from the flour. It is a reproach to the milling trade and an insult to the customer. It certainly does not make us think of the miller as the "merry miller of old" with his friendly, jolly face, a man in whom we had the utmost confidence and who was really turning out what is the staff of life. This reminds me of a little jingle that I once heard: "The whiter the bread, the sooner you're dead."

As we have seen in the fifth step, the rolling mill process, the nitrogen trichloride that was used did something to the gluten in the flour, which made it difficult to work. Therefore, other things have to be added at a later stage of manufacture, in order to make the flour easier to work with.

Is Bleaching Dangerous?

A great deal of work has been done in England to find out whether the use of nitrogen trichloride is dangerous. Dr. Barnet Stross, in the December 1, 1951, issue of *The Lancet*, stated that this chemical had been tried on more than just one species of animals, namely, dogs. It has already been tried on 6 animal species, and in every case it has caused the symptoms that were found originally, which gave running fits to dogs. Sir Edward Mellanby himself stated that the nitrogen trichloride causes part of the wheat protein to be converted into a substance that is poisonous to all species of animals. Actually, this bleaching agent converts the yellow carotenoide pigment to colorless compounds. By taking the color portion out of the flour, vitamins are removed. Sir Edward Mellanby also stated that "some of the increase in the common disorders of the alimentary tract—appendicitis, cholecystitis and peptic ulcer—might possibly be attributed to this large-scale tampering with natural foodstuffs." Dr. H. Pollak, physician in charge of the allergy clinic of the Central Middlesex Hospital of London, stated in the issue of July 5, 1950, of the *Medical Press,* that "Since then in the course of the last 3 to 4 years, we have encountered many food-allergic patients whose symptoms were partly or entirely controlled, on a restricted diet containing non-agenized, but excluding 'bleached' (agenized) wheat products, in whom symptoms could frequently, or invariably, be reproduced by ingestion of agene-bleached 'white' bread. In numerous subjects, such symptoms have followed from as little as a slice of 'white' bread. In a few patients, usually with dyspeptic symptoms, the 'white' bread was better tolerated than the 'brown' (non-agenized) one."

Dr. Anton J. Carlson, Professor Emeritus of the University of Chicago, and world renowned physiologist, in the United Press dispatch of December 29, 1950, called nitrogen trichloride (agene) a nerve poison and asserted that it might be a contributing cause of alcoholism. Dr. Carlson says that this chemical changes a good protein into a bad one, which causes nervous instability, very frequently, and which instability causes a person to become an alcoholic addict.

Mental Diseases Related to Bleached Flour

Dr. William Brady, M.D., in his newspaper column has stated that "dogs fed mainly on entirely white bread or white flour products, may develop what is mistaken for rabies—shunning food, losing weight, avoiding light, trembling, cringing when patted, climbing walls, falling backwards, howling piteously, falling into their pans if they try to eat, and running around madly."

Psychiatrists claim that bleached flour may contribute to mental diseases. Dr. Ethel Mae Shaull, of the Stanford Medical School and former staff psychiatrist at Agnew State Hospital, has suspected that the tremendous increase of mental diseases among Americans is due in part to eating of bread and other foodstuffs made of bleached or agenized flour.

Bakers Return to Chlorine Dioxide

In spite of all this evidence, the baking industry still claims that nitrogen trichloride is not dangerous to human beings. However, they have decided not to use it in this country, and now they have gone back to chlorine dioxide which was used a long time ago for this purpose. It is hard to believe that they would rush right in to substitute another chemical which might perhaps be not quite as harmful as nitrogen trichloride, but might still be toxic. But I read in an article that chlorine dioxide is definitely toxic to laboratory animals, although tests on humans so far have shown no injurious effect. However, the tests have not been carried on long enough in the opinion of such distinguished food scientists as Dr. McCay of Cornell and Dr. Carlson.

Here is something, however, that is very incriminating to chlorine dioxide. It is taken from Lockwood's *Flour Milling*, 1948 edition (Northern Publishing Company). It says: "Chlorine dioxide is more powerful than nitrogen trichloride; the quantities used are one-third to one-half those of nitrogen trichloride.

Chlorine dioxide not only oxidizes the flour pigment, but also has a valuable bleaching effect on the coloring matter of bran, which makes it particularly valuable for bleaching very low grade flours." This has not received any publicity. Everybody just takes for granted that since bakers are changing over, they would naturally change over to something that is not dangerous, but really I believe that something very fast is being pulled on the public and on the government officials and scientists who are passing on this matter. Let's look into this chlorine dioxide.

Trying To Put Back What Has Been Removed

We now come to the ninth step, the enriching of the bread with synthetically manufactured vitamins and some iron. After the heart is removed, the conscience of the miller is disturbed and he rushes to enrich the bread with vitamins made from coal tar. Twenty-eight states have laws that require bread to be thus enriched. It is sad to think of states passing such laws without making the thorough researches that would show up definitely whether this has any harmful effect on the people eating the bread. Yet, some 20 odd natural vitamin and mineral elements are removed from the wheat by an expensive process and then only 4 or 5 are put back, including a little iron. It reminds me of the way orange juice is being sold to the public today. In the Florida factories the water is first removed from the orange juice. The resulting product is sold to the public who then put ordinary tap water that has been treated with chlorine back into the concoction. In this case the orange product is "enriched" with tap water. In the bakery, enriching is a very simple process. All the baker does is to add a few cheap vitamin tablets to his batches.

Natural Products vs. Synthetics

There is a question whether substances such as vitamins or medicines made from synthetic chemicals are worse than the same vitamins made from natural substances such as food. There are experiments which have been done on an optical instrument which throws a beam of light, and it seems to show that when a certain element made synthetically is placed in this instrument, the light will be thrown on one side. When the same element made from a natural source is placed in the machine for test, it will usually throw its rays on the opposite side. I do not know what the significance is but evidently there *is* a difference. There are also researches which show that vitamins produced from natural foods are better than those made synthetically. For example, I know of one that was done within the last 10 years in Russia and which was reported in the Russian medical publication called *The Vitamin News.* Two groups of mice were taken and each was given a diet that was supposed to produce scurvy. But one group was given synthetically made vitamin C, while the other was given vitamin C made from a natural food product. The group of mice that got the synthetic vitamin C still had their scurvy after the experiment was completed, but those that obtained the vitamin C from natural food were cured. It would seem, therefore, that when synthetic vitamin tablets are thrown into the flour mix, there is a question in my mind how good it is.

Vitamin B₁ and Sterility

There are also researches that indicate that an excess of vitamin B1 can produce sterility in humans. I do not think any comparative research was made in these experiments of vitamin B1 produced from natural sources, as against those produced synthetically, but I *do* know that vitamin B1 by itself cannot be made or isolated from natural food sources. In such a product, it must be the whole vitamin B complex, such as is obtained from brewer's yeast, or nothing. It is, therefore, dangerous to take the synthetic vitamin B1 over long periods of time. I wonder what happens to drunkards who are given tremendous doses of vitamin B1 in order to cure their alcoholism? They must all become sterile, I imagine, which in itself is not such a bad thing either, in their case. It is a form of poetic justice.

The Baker Embalms the Bread

We now come to step ten, or the disinfecting process. The flour finally goes to the baker, and brother, what he does to it is just plain murder. He looks at the flour. He is not satisfied with it, because it is not completely dead. The success of commercially manufactured bread is to make it completely dead, so it does not pose any problems to the baker as he works it, and as it goes through the various processes in the bakery. The flour must be completely embalmed. That is the only word I can find that would fit it. The baker takes another look at the flour and scratches his head. It seems to him that

the flour still has a little life. Its toes are wiggling, so to speak.
A bug might want to take a little nibble on it. You know that
when something becomes sterile and lacks the spark of life, a
bug has sense enough not to want to touch it, but it is different,
of course, with man. The baker wants the bread so dead that a
bug won't touch it with a 15-foot pole. So he calls in the
experts, and whom does he call? The same firm that made the
mercury poison that we started off with, way at the beginning,
when the seed was doused with mercury in order to kill the smut
and rust organism. This company obliges the baker with a
product which kills the fungi and the remaining bacteria. It
saturates itself into every atom or molecule of the bread.
Naturally, it would have to do that so that no bacteria or fungi
would work in the minutest part of the bread. It is more or
less of a disinfectant, you might say. The bread is thoroughly
disinfected. The baker would not use CN or Lysol, but he
does use Mycobahn. Mycobahn is calcium propionate, which
was discovered by the Dupont Company. They had noticed
the fact that Swiss cheese did not mold the same as other cheese,
and found that the presence of calcium propionate retarded
mold's growth. Anything that would retard growth of a living
thing is dangerous to people and to our intestinal flora. Only
a pinch of Mycobahn is put into the bread mixture, mind you,
but it is a powerful enough pinch that spreads itself into every
atom of the dough mixture. It is a known fact that Mycobahn
destroys the enzyme that makes it possible for the body to
assimilate the limited amount of calcium left in the flour,
after all this *Farben-izing* and *ersatzing* to which the staff of
life is subjected.

Then More Chemicals Are Added

The next step, eleven, is the conditioning of the dough.
This is accomplished by chemicals which are known as emulsifiers, extenders and improvers, and were developed as a
result of war conditions when milk, fat and eggs were scarce.
By the use of these emulsifiers, some foods such as milk, fat and
eggs are not put into the bread, and instead chemicals are substituted. Some of these chemicals, I am told, are used in the
antifreeze of auto radiators. The general name of this kind of
chemical is surface-active compounds, which are added during
the processing of the flour to make the bread retain its fresh-

ness longer and to give it a smoother texture and more attractive appearance.

The baker has a problem of staleness of the bread on his hands. He wants to bake a loaf that will stay in the stores for extra days and feel soft to the touch. The chemical accomplishes this by making the flour absorb much more water, in some cases 6 times its weight, which makes it retain its softness and fresh-looking appearance. It is a game of fooling the customer. The lady buyer feels it and thinks it is fresh, but really it is not fresh. The bakery trade has given a name to the way a woman customer feels the bread to see if it is fresh. The way she touches and pinches it is called "playing the piano on the bread." There are doctors who claim that it is healthier to eat stale bread. Probably one of the reasons is that you have to chew stale bread more and thoroughly salivate it, whereas with the soft, chemicalized loaf, the tendency would be to gulp it down.

Polyoxyethylene Monostearate

One of the most common emulsifiers is polyoxyethylene monostearate. Note the ethylene. The bakers use nothing but the best. I have before me an article from the December, 1951, issue of *Industrial Medicine and Surgery,* entitled "Clinical Experiences with Exposures to Ethylene Amines." It seems that workers in factories where ethylene is used develop various kinds of trouble, mostly skin rashes. In one case, asthma was developed. In another, a man stepped into some ethylene amine compound which had been spilled on the concrete and some of the chemical splashed on his leg. Five days later he reported to the medical department with a very bad rash all over his feet. It was found that he always developed a rash after each contact with these liquids or the vapors of this compound. Surely, even though small quantities are placed in the bread, this substance should be looked upon with suspicion. Dr. Pollak, mentioned above, has suggested that these bread "improvers" could be a cause of cumulative adverse effects and cause some persons to easily develop allergies.

Is the Addition of Chemicals Lawful?

On May 20, 1950, Dr. William J. Darby of Vanderbilt University, representing the American Medical Association Council on Food and Nutrition, said the following in the government Food and Drug bread hearings:

"Available knowledge of the possible toxicity of these substances," he said, "is fragmentary. Particularly is evidence lacking as to chronic toxicity. . . . Unless the complete harmlessness of these agents can be demonstrated beyond a reasonable doubt, they should not, in the Council's opinion, be used in basic foods." And, he added, the reduction of natural food products in bread that might be entailed by the use of these extenders "is not desirable from a nutritional standpoint."

Dr. James R. Wilson, secretary of the American Medical Association Council on Nutrition, also made a statement in the *American Medical Journal* of July 2, 1949, in which he viewed with alarm the use of these surface-active compounds, because he said that little is known of the poisonous effects of these substances being added to food, or about their possible lowering of its nutritive value. But Joseph Callaway, secretary of the Foods Standards Committee of the Food and Drug Administration, said, "It seems pretty clear that these substances are not poisonous in the ordinary sense." Mr. Callaway, can you please tell us in what sense they *are* poisonous? He does say that there is a possibility that over-use of the materials might be injurious, and "the use of these substances may be ruled out later on the possibility that they might be dangerous, but so far there is no evidence that any individual has been injured by eating these agents." This is a very unscientific type of allusion, trying to find one individual instead of conducting experiments on groups of people, possibly persons in jails. What Mr. Callaway overlooks is that perhaps small amounts of chemicals in bread may not be directly toxic to the individual who eats a loaf containing it, but what is the effect of a diet which all day long includes items which have chemicals in them. The total cumulative effect may be highly toxic and highly dangerous. That is the type of testing that must be done in connection with the use of chemicals in foods.

Is Money or Health More Important?

It seems that the use of these surface-active compounds has practically replaced one-third of the soybean crops raised in this country. When the soybean association came to be heard in the Food and Drug Administration, their representatives did not attack the use of these surface-active compounds from the point of view of health. They merely stated that it threatened their industry. They were worrying about economics and not health. This is true of so much in industry today.

Polyoxyethylene monostearate is also being used in the making of peanut butter, ice cream, candy, salad dressings and many other foods. In our opinion, one is safest to eat as much of natural, primitive, earthy sorts of food as possible and to stay away from anything that becomes processed in factories. I do not trust the food processors. Either they are deliberate in their means of going about making a dollar, or "they know not what they do."

Food Manufacturers Defy the Supreme Court

And they do all of this in spite of a ruling of the Supreme Court in 1918 that flour must not be tampered with by adding any poisonous substances, and that such an inclusion is a violation of the Pure Food law, but evidently this Supreme Court ruling has been forgotten, just as the dangers of chlorine dioxide have been forgotten, when now the bakers are going to substitute it for nitrogen trichloride.

In his book, *A History of a Crime Against the Food Law*, Dr. Harvey A. Wiley, who originated the food and drug legislation in this country wrote, stating what he would do if he could really enforce the Food and Drug Act:

"No food product in our country would have any trace of benzoic acid, sulfurous acid or sulfites, or any alum or saccharin, save for medical purposes. No soft drink would contain caffeine, or theobromine. No bleached flour would enter interstate commerce. Our foods and drugs would be wholly without any form of adulteration and misbranding. The health of our people would be vastly improved and their life greatly extended. The manufacturers of our food supply, and especially the millers, would devote their energies to improving the public health and promoting happiness in every home, by the production of whole ground, unbolted cereal flours and meals."

The Baker Does Other Things

Other things that the baker does may make your hair stand on end. But not all of his doings are known to the public or possibly to government officials, who are too busy coping with the high spots, so that the low spots may become very dangerous. For example, the baker uses artificial colorings and flavorings. Some of these are coal tar products which are certified by the government as safe, but which many scientists look upon as cancer-causing. Many fancy breads and cakes have had nitric acid applied to the mixtures, in very small quantities, true. This is done to give the cake a deep yellow coloring as if eggs were used. Only a pinch is used, but a pinch here and a pinch there, add up to a handful. Gold and silver decorations on cake icings have been found to be very harmful by the California Bureau of Food and Drug Inspection in reference to the California Pure Food Act. In one case they found a sample of cake icing that contained aluminum and brass. The county health officer banned the use of metallic decorations by county bakers. The amount of copper present in the brass was considered very dangerous for human beings, particularly children. In some cases ammonium bicarbonate is used, in old-fashioned cookies, and God knows what else. All over the country, health inspectors are at their wits' end in trying to regulate bakeries, and as soon as they clamp down on them regarding the use of one item, the baker will pop up with something else.

One of the purposes of bread is to furnish the teeth with a hard food to chew upon. Trying to masticate or break down the hard crust in former times gave the teeth much exercise and was probably exceedingly good for their well-being. Today you would have to chew on a piece of wood or leather to get the same prophylactic benefit.

What the Public Gets

We now come to the last step, twelve, where the bread is pre-sliced, made moisture- and air-proof in a waxed paper jacket, and as one writer said, "It is given to you as white as Kleenex." In other words, when the bread has been so disinfected and embalmed that a bug will not go near it with a 15-foot pole, you, the public, get it. And when I say get it, I mean it. Some writers have spoken disparagingly of the taste of such bread. They refer to it as a tasteless mass, probably with the flavor of a brim of a straw hat, but I do not want to tell a fib. These darn bakers are so clever that they have given us a loaf of bread that really does not taste bad at all. The only trouble is that there is a joker in the deck, in the form of the chemicals I have spoken about, which are tasteless, like carbon monoxide gas, but which poison nevertheless.

As you can readily see, that little seed that we started with, way back at the beginning of this story, never had a chance.

Whole Wheat Bread

Now for this part of the article you had better hold on to your seats. You would imagine that it would be safer to eat whole wheat bread rather than the white kind, made as described herein. That would be true if you made it yourself or if you bought it from the few companies that really make it with a conscience. But it has been found by scientific experiment that the average whole wheat bread on the market is even worse than the white bread, for a peculiar reason. I am talking about whole wheat bread that contains the wheat germ in it. There are many so-called whole wheat breads today which are called whole wheat but which do not have the wheat germ. The whole wheat flour must be treated with the poisonous preservative chemicals in much higher quantities than the white flour which does not have the wheat germ, and it has been found, therefore, that this type of whole wheat bread is terribly deadly to test animals that were fed with it.

Research on Mice

A few years ago, the Wellcome Research Laboratories at Tuckahoe, New York, made an experiment with mice in which they fed 50 with whole wheat bread diet and 50 with white bread diet. Then all were injected with pneumonia germs. The mice receiving the whole wheat diet died in an average of 1.7 days, while those receiving white bread survived more than twice as long, namely, 3.8 days. Another experiment was done by Riggs and Beaty, which was written up in the *American Journal of Dairy Science,* Vol. 29, pp. 821 to 829, 1946. Six groups of female laboratory mice, each subsisting on one of six types of bread, were observed on the same diets until they had produced and weaned their third litters. Where on ordinary nonfat milk white bread, the mice were able to wean 54.8 per cent of their litters into the third generation, in the case of those that were fed whole wheat bread, none were able to live into the third generation.

In other words, in order to put such a type of whole

wheat bread on the market without any danger of its turning rancid, the amounts of preservative chemicals that have to be used in it are toxic, sometimes 400 per cent more of such chemicals being used in the whole wheat than in the white. Now it is interesting to see that if ordinary tests are made with a group of mice in one generation, probably nothing would show up. But in this type of scientific test where it was worked into the third generation, the dangers *did* develop. Is it possible that in the case of many chemicals being absorbed into our bodies through our foods, some of the dangers may not show up until a later generation? Is it possible that 4 or 5 generations from now, sterility in women will be so common that the race may have difficulty perpetuating itself because of the chemicals that the present generation is eating? This is something that we owe to future generations to study now.

You Must Take Food Supplements

The consideration of the way in which bread is made and the public robbed of important ingredients of the wheat seed is an indication of why the public must take such things as vitamins (made from natural foods and not the synthetic variety) and bone meal containing minerals. Bread is only one of the examples, but for every item of food that we eat, there is always something that is taken out of it. We are usually getting only a fragment. That is why, unless everyone takes the right kind of natural vitamins plus bone meal and such things as brewer's yeast, he is not getting a whole diet. When you consider the way foods are refined, pasteurized, sterilized, homogenized, fortified and enriched with coal tar derivatives, and chemicalized in so many different ways, it is a wonder that diseases are not worse than they really are. This is a tribute to the strength of the body that God gave us.

Is Bread Really the Staff of Life?

This whole thing about the importance of bread as the staff of life leaves me cold. I think the average person is better off to severely restrict the use of bread until he can be sure that it is produced in a manner that will nourish him and not kill him. About eight or nine years ago, our family made an experiment in which we absolutely cut out not only bread, but all the grain food such as rice, corn and such foods as spaghetti, etc., for a whole year. The results were extremely interesting. There were less colds in the family. But one thing we observed was startling. My son Robert used to get poison ivy attacks every summer, even if he never went into the ivy, but the year that we didn't eat bread, he never had a touch of it. The following year when we went back to eating bread, back came the poison ivy. The way we figured it out was that when he did not eat bread, he had to satisfy his hunger by eating more vegetables and fruit. (With children there is always a tendency to give them a few slices of bread and stuff them up. Thus, when it comes to eating the other important foods of the diet, they just won't.) Evidently, my son was suffering from what might be called a sub-clinical case of scurvy in the skin, caused by a lack of the vitamins and minerals contained in vegetables. In other words, contact with the burning poison ivy substance, when the skin is afflicted with a scurvy condition, caused it to burn much easier. By being better nourished, the skin probably became more "thick-skinned," and resisted the burning effect of the ivy leaf. Persons who have begun taking bone meal and vitamins have written to me that suddenly they have found themselves immune to poison ivy. In fact, this occurred in my own case, and when I realized what had happened, I went out one day and actually took poison ivy, rubbing it on my skin, and nothing happened, whereas I used to get it any time I had contact with poison ivy.

CHAPTER **24**

Bread Again

by J. I. RODALE

The mere fact that a loaf of bread is made from whole grain flour does not recommend it to the health-conscious person. We believe that all bread and cereals should be avoided, if you would be healthy.

I am definitely against any wheat or rye product for human consumption, and am not afraid to express my attitude, which, as a rule, brings down a shower of verbal brick-bats and dressing-downs from the whole-wheat school of health, and especially from those who make their own bread from organically raised wheat. To them it has become a sacred ritual—a symbol. To me it is a matter of searching for the truth. What is the best program for a person who wishes to live to 120? I say, don't eat bread. It is the worst form of starch. I put bananas at the head of the starch list, and somewhat further down . . . potatoes, but bread? I wouldn't even give it any place in the list. It is not edible starch. It is for paste. I eat the wheat germ and perhaps the bran portion . . . but not the paste portion of the wheat.

The Danger in Wheat

What is wrong with wheat? First of all, it is one of the most fattening of foods. The *Esquire* reducing diet which consists of merely cutting out wheat and rye, guarantees a loss of about 20 pounds in two months. Bread is one of the most common causes of colds, a fact proven by medical researches which we have cited time and time again. If you suffer from a stuffed-up nose or head, cut out bread and see what an improvement will come about at once. Bread fills people up, it gives them a false feeling of hunger satisfaction. Thus they eat less of fruit, vegetables and other important foods. Bread is difficult to digest by the human stomach. Dr. Alvarez of the Mayo Clinic showed that bread can pass through the whole of the small intestine without becoming digested at all. Bread requires a large production of digestive juices for its complete solution. The protein of the bread especially is defectively absorbed by the intestine. A significant medically proven fact is that whole wheat bread interferes with the absorption of other foods. I have found this to be so in my case.

Bread is fine for cows who have four stomachs and keep chewing their cud. But in the human digestive system, because it is not completely digested, it ferments or rots.

Many Disorders Caused by Wheat

It is one of the most common causes of constipation. Wheat causes rickets in children where there is an overconsumption of this type of food. It is the underlying factor in a disease of children called celiac disease, which is increasing alarmingly. The abdomen becomes distended, there is fat in the stools. The doctor orders an immediate elimination of all wheat products. Wheat has been found to be one of the causes of tooth cavities. Wheat products are one of the common causes of asthma.

One physician discovered that bread was one of the causes of conjunctivitis (an eye involvement) under certain conditions. In a study of two African tribes, the Masai and the Akikuyu, it was found that the latter eat a great deal of the grain foods. Deaths from bronchitis and pneumonia in that tribe were 10 times as great as in the Masai. The Akikuyu also had bone deformities, dental caries, lung conditions, anemia and tropical ulcer.

Many persons suffer from gastric irritation due to the large amounts of bran in whole wheat bread. Wheat is the greatest culprit among foods in connection with the causing of allergic effects. Dr. Albert H. Rowe checked on 500 persons with allergies. He found that at least one-third of these allergies were caused by wheat. Bread is a common cause of hives, eczema and migraines. Dr. Alvarez of the Mayo Clinic recently said, "that according to allergists the commonest cause of migraine is wheat."

I could go on and on . . . and I haven't mentioned the 7 or 8 harmful chemicals used in the milling and baking of bread, nor the recent work that indicts bread and other starches as a cause of heart attacks.

In my own case (I have a heart condition) wheat has an immediate effect, and I am sure this is not an allergy. After a meal that is heavy with bread or cake, I experience severe angina symptoms on my chest. I will eat such food perhaps on my birthday when the pressure from "well-meaning" relatives is too great to resist, but ordinarily I go for months without a slice of bread or a piece of cake.

Overweight and Overconsumption of Bread

I want to stress the weight-producing aspect of eating bread. It seems not only to add the weight of the bread consumed but, because it prevents the complete digestion of other foods in the stomach, it adds some of their weight also.

Every once in a while someone will complain of a stomachache, and would never think it could come from the overconsumption of bread, cake or pie at a meal. How could it be? Bread is the staff of life. It can be tolerated by very healthy people—by persons who have wide arteries, perfectly operating glands, who lead an active outdoor life—and they will write in and tell me how wrong I am about my attitude on eating bread, not realizing that if they avoided this food they could live to 100 instead of a mere 80 or 90. Some of these oldsters are old, but they suffer from various chronic conditions, including the various phases of senility. Who knows? Without bread, they might free themselves of all these things.

Try a Wheatless Diet

If you never have gone on a completely wheatless diet it is worth a trial, regardless of whether you are over- or underweight. Cut out all bread, cakes, pies, gravies in which there is flour, spaghetti, breaded foods, etc. Try it for a month and see what it does to you. But include wheat germ flakes or wheat germ oil perles, or both, in your diet. And increase your fruit and vegetable intake, especially bananas. It will give you a volume type of food and a type of carbohydrate which will be a delight to your system and a great help to it.

SECTION 6

PROTEIN

We are in favor of a low-carbohydrate, high-protein diet, including meat, fish and eggs. The latest medical researches show that a diet high in carbohydrate can lead to a heart attack. Carbohydrates are also very fattening. Bananas are a very fine carbohydrate food, far more easily handled by the body than potatoes or bread. They are not as fattening as has been assumed. Eggs are one of the finest foods in our dietary, and at least one should be eaten every day, even if you are a heart case, so long as you cut out the other animal fats such as milk, butter, etc. The egg yolk contains lecithin, which is an emulsifier of the cholesterol it contains.

CHAPTER **25**

Protein

A contractor builds houses out of many different materials, but if he is a man who deals mostly in brick houses, we might say that the most important single material necessary for his houses is bricks. If the design of each of his houses is different, the arrangement of the bricks will be different. Some houses will have brick chimneys, others brick porches, in still other houses the bricks will be arranged in designs to form railings or terraces. Some houses have brick floors, brick fireplaces or brick walls in the garden. There is a wide variety of color and kinds of bricks for the contractor to choose from.

If you buy the house and do not like the design, you can take apart the bricks and put them together again to form an entirely different house, out of the same bricks. If you were to number each brick in the house and then rebuild the house, putting each brick in a different place, you would be able to continue for thousands of years, combining and recombining the different bricks and never getting quite the same house as the original one, for each time you would make some slight change in the arrangement of the bricks.

As your house grows older some bricks would have to be replaced, and after a certain length of time you would probably have replaced all of the original bricks at one time or another. Now regardless of what plumbing, insulation, roofing or wallpaper you use in the house, the bricks are still the most important part, for you must have them or there simply will be no house.

Your Body Similar to a House

Just like a house, the human body is made up of building blocks or bricks, if you want to call them that. These bricks are the amino acids which go to make up the protein of which the human house is made. Although they can be arranged and rearranged in thousands and thousands of different combinations, they are still protein and they are still the essential part of your human house. Without them life could not go on. No living thing survives without protein. When it comes to building a fire to keep your house warm, you use materials that are largely carbohydrate. But the house itself must be made largely of protein.

What exactly does this mean in terms of body physiology. Your blood is protein, your tissues, organs, skin, hair, nails are protein. Your bones are made of protein, which supports all the various minerals that give them strength. The fluids your body secretes are protein—hormones, and. enzymes. Your nerves and brain are made of protein. Obviously when you were an infant, then later through childhood and adolescence, you needed large amounts of protein, for then you were building the house and every day you needed more and more bricks for the bricklayers to use. But as a house grows older, bricks crumble and must be replaced. Human protein—marvelous substance that it is—does not have the hardness and durability of bricks. It is subject to terrific stress and strain, and some of it wears out a little each day. So there is no reason to believe that, as you grow older, you require less protein. Quite the opposite is true.

Now, taking a look at your human body, it is difficult to believe that fingernails are made of the same substance as blood or nerves. They don't look the same. Well, neither does a brick chimney look like a brick floor, but both are made of bricks. The difference in your body lies in the various combinations in which the amino acids, or bricks, are put together. And if you can have many different designs of houses, all made of brick, just think for a moment of all the different kinds of protein you can have by re-arranging the various amino acids. Of course, you can't actually imagine such a number, for it is bound to be astronomical.

What Is Protein?

In 1839 a chemist first isolated a substance containing nitrogen, which he announced was the basis of life. He named it protein, meaning "primary substance." It was not until 1906 that other chemists first demonstrated an essential amino acid— a building block of the substance protein. The carbohydrates that we eat are made of carbon, hydrogen and oxygen. Proteins are made of carbon, hydrogen, oxygen and nitrogen. It is this nitrogen apparently that makes all the difference between proteins and carbohydrates—building blocks and fuel. After the first amino acid was discovered, a great deal of research was devoted to this branch of biological chemistry and many more amino acids have been discovered. We do not have any idea of how many there may be. We have so far discovered about 21 in protein food products.

The study of protein is extremely complex, as you can imagine, for it deals with all the different combinations of these amino acids, which may be put together by nature in different quantities and different arrangements to make up any given kind of food product. Then, of course, in most foods the protein amino acids are combined with fat and carbohydrate as well. When we speak of protein, we are not talking about something like vitamins which exists in infinitesimally small quantities and which are necessary just to cause certain processes to take place inside the body. *You can see protein.* The white of an egg is almost pure protein, composed of a series of different amino acids. So the *bulk* of protein food you eat is quite important—for this is the substance from which the body makes or replaces actual body structure.

After you have eaten protein, the digestive juices of the stomach and intestines go to work on it and break it down into its amino acids. This is because the actual cells of a human body are put together differently from the white of an egg, for instance. So the digestive juices, the enzymes and the body hormones are all involved in putting these amino acids together once again in a different combination, so that they can form part of the body. One re-constituted protein substance will go to make up red blood cells. Another will be rushed to the fingernails which are constantly growing, therefore needing new protein constantly. Another will be sent to the brain where a lot of thinking has worn out a number of cells. Still another protein will be transferred to a gland where it helps to form a gland secretion or hormone. You can easily see why we must have protein every day, and must have it in quantity.

But it appears, from later research work, that the most important thing about protein is not quantity, but quality. What do we mean by "high quality" protein? We mean protein containing all the essential amino acids in the proper proportion. If one of them is missing, the protein will not sustain life in laboratory animals. If one of the essential amino acids is present in too small a quantity, this protein will not maintain health. It is as if you were building your brick wall and trying to use a brick that is smaller than the other bricks. In a wall, you might fill up the gaping space with mortar, but there is no mortar that will replace protein in body structure. So your wall, with several bricks too small, will sag and be out of line.

Practically, in selecting food, how does this amino acid set-up work out? You should try to eat as much "complete" or "high quality" protein as you need. Foods containing an incomplete quantity or proportion of one or another of the essential amino acids will not sustain health. Complete proteins appear in foods from animal sources—meat, fish, milk, cheese and eggs are complete proteins. In the vegetable kingdom these are the protein foods that most nearly approach completeness: nuts, sesame seed, soybeans, wheat germ. You can see that a completely vegetarian diet presents hazards. In order to maintain good health a vegetarian must know the amino acid content of all the vegetables and fruits. If he is going to eat a vegetable that is short or completely lacking in one of the essential amino acids, he must eat something that contains this amino acid, even though it may be short on another. So a constant vigilance and a great deal of knowledge about the quality of the protein in the various vegetables and fruits is necessary.

The Essential and Unessential Amino Acids

The names of the essential amino acids are complicated and not especially meaningful to those of us who are not chemists. But it is well to be familiar with them, for you often run across them in articles dealing with food or health, and if you do not know what they are you may become confused and think they are vitamins or enzymes or something else. The essential amino acids are those that have been found to be absolutely necessary in the diet of human beings. Nothing can substitute for them. They are: Arginine, histidine, isoleucine, leucine, lysine, methionine, phenylalanine, threonine, tryptophan, valine. The amino acids that at present are listed as unessential are: alanine, aspartic acid, cirrulline, systine, glu-

tamic acid, glycine, hydroxyproline, hydroxyglutamic acid, nor-
leucine, proline, serine and tyrosine.

As researchers progress in their study of the proteins, it
is quite possible that they may discover that one or more of the
unessential amino acids also have important functions in the
body and should be considered essential. However, it seems that
we may be able to manufacture within our bodies some of these
unessential ones. We cannot manufacture the essential ones,
so they must be supplied in food. However, just as in the case
of the vitamins, the amino acids work together and, if you are
getting a lot of the unessential ones, it seems that this makes up
somewhat for a slight deficiency in the essential ones. But keep
in mind that you can get amino acids—essential or unessential—
only from protein. They do not exist in carbohydrate foods.
White sugar is the one outstanding example of a so-called food
that is pure carbohydrate, without any protein whatsoever. This
is one of the main reasons why white sugar is worthless as food.
Your body cannot use it to build or replace any cells. And the
more sugar you eat, the less you can eat of the protein foods
that have so much value for your good health. Vegetables and
fruits contain, in general, far more carbohydrate than protein.

You can make a quick check on all the foods you eat, so
far as protein content is concerned, by sending to the Superintendent of Documents in Washington, D. C., for a copy of
the Agricultural Handbook, Number 8 which lists all the common foods, along with their protein, carbohydrate and fat
content.

What Results From Protein Deficiency?

The list of diseases resulting from protein deficiency is
almost endless. Just stop and think for a moment of all the
things that would go wrong with the house you tried to build of
bricks if there were few or no bricks available. The hemoglobin
of blood is 95 per cent protein. Lack of protein will produce
anemia. The antibodies your blood manufactures to fight germs
are made of protein. Lack of protein leaves one an easy prey
to all kinds of infections. Proteins protect the liver against
poisonous chemicals to which we are all exposed all the time.
Protein regulates the amount of water in body tissues. The
unhealthy swelling or dropsy that accompanies so many diseases
(especially of the heart or kidneys) may be simply an indication

of too little high quality protein in the food. And speaking of kidney disease, researchers used to think that people with kidney disease should not eat protein. The kidneys were already excreting a great deal of nitrogen (one of the main constituents of protein). Therefore, reasoned these physicians, the nitrogen is irritating the kidneys, so we will eliminate nitrogen (protein) from the diet. But patients died; for, of course, all the diseased tissues of their bodies needed the nitrogen desperately to rebuild themselves. Nowadays kidney disease patients are placed on a high protein diet. And the protein replaces the nitrogen lost through the kidneys.

If you have a wound, cut or burn, protein is lost in the fluid and blood that escape. Furthermore, to remake healthy tissue over the site of the injury, the body must have protein, for this is what the cells are made of. So ample protein in the diet helps hasten the healing process. Muscles are made of protein. Lack of protein breaks down these muscles faster than they can be replaced, resulting in fatigue and lack of stamina. The poor posture of adolescents may often be the result of lack of protein, for flabby muscles simply cannot hold the body erect. The health of your skin, hair and nails depends on protein supply—they are made of protein and cannot grow or replace dead tissues, unless they are supplied with the necessary substance, protein. Constipation may be the result of flabby muscles in the stomach and intestines, that cannot contract and expand as they should, to move the food along our digestive tracts. Protein in the diet will form and strengthen these muscles. Finally, we know that vitamins and minerals will not be used in the body unless the proper hormones and enzymes are there to combine with them. Hormones and enzymes are made of protein. So all the vitamin and mineral preparations in the world will not make you healthy unless you also provide protein so that these substances can be used.

Absorption of Proteins

The subject of absorption of proteins is an important topic in itself. People who suffer from diarrheal conditions do not absorb protein properly, so whatever protein they eat may be partly wasted. Bacteria in the intestines can make the amino acids of protein unabsorbable. Protein must be digested in an acid medium, so if hydrochloric acid is lacking in the stomach, protein food will be wasted. Then, too, those folks who follow every meal with a dose of bicarbonate of soda, or one of the other so-called "alkalizers" will produce a condition in the stomach where the protein simply will not be digested. It has been found that the proteins of some foods are more thoroughly digested than those of others. Ninety-seven per cent of the meat you eat is completely digested (in a healthy person), only 85 per cent of the protein of cereal is digested, only 83 per cent of vegetable protein, 78 per cent of legume protein and only 85 per cent of the protein that appears in fruits.

How To Get High Quality Protein

How are you going to know how much protein you need every day and which proteins contain the essential amino acids? And, perhaps just as important, how are you going to pay your grocery bill once you start living on T-bone steak? First of all, there is no necessity for living on T-bone steak, pleasant though the prospect sounds. In general, all meats contain the same amounts of the essential amino acids. Liver, heart, kidneys and brain actually are a little higher in amino acid content. And hamburger may be even more acceptable to the youngsters and oldsters in your family because it is easier to chew. Whole wheat bread contains far more protein than white bread and is no more expensive. Can you substitute beans or soybeans for meat? Sometimes, but remember no vegetable food is as rich in all the essential amino acids, as food of animal origin, so don't depend on beans day after day for protein. Can you substitute macaroni or spaghetti for meat? No, you cannot, despite all the attractive recipes offered in the women's magazines during Lent. Cereal foods (especially refined ones) are largely carbohydrate foods and cannot be used as building blocks for a healthy body. Fish is cheap and an excellent source of high quality protein.

Gelatin as a Source of Protein

What about gelatin as a source of protein? Often we hear recommendations for taking one or two packets of gelatin every day for a good supply of protein. It's cheap, certainly, but we must report that gelatin is the one animal protein that is not complete. In other words, it does not contain all of the essential amino acids. It will not sustain life in laboratory animals when it is used as the sole source of protein. Now, of course, if you were living under extraordinary circumstances where you could not obtain any protein except gelatin, it would be best to eat the gelatin, because it will sustain life longer than a diet completely lacking in protein. And, of course, if you are hesitating between a dessert made of white sugar, cornstarch or corn syrup, and another dessert made of gelatin, you should choose the gelatin dessert, for it does have protein value and the others do not. But don't depend on gelatin, cheap as it is, for protein, for it simply cannot fill the bill.

How Much and What Kind of Protein?

How much protein do you need? As you know our pioneer ancestors lived chiefly on high quality protein in the days when they hunted game, before they had gardens or farms. Many people believe this is the reason they were able to endure such hardship and perform such prodigious feats of work. Arctic explorers have lived healthfully for as long as two years on meat, lean and fat—nothing else. No carbohydrates at all. So there is no chance of your getting too much protein. There is every chance of your getting too little. Recent surveys have indicated that as many as 60 to 80 per cent of Americans get far too little protein in their diets. The official recommendation of the National Research Council is 40 to 100 grams of protein every day for children, depending on age, and 60 to 70 grams of protein for adults. It is generally agreed among nutritionists that these allowances are far too low, and actually may only be enough to keep from suffering some kind of deficiency disease.

When you are planning menus, your Agricultural Handbook, Number 8 will indicate in grams the amount of protein in any given food. For instance, 5 tablespoonfuls of dried skim milk give you 34 grams of protein. Four ounces (one-fourth pound) of lean beef give you 22 grams of protein. One cube of cheese, two by one by one inches, gives you 12 grams of protein.

Synthetic Amino Acids

One final word about amino acids. Scientists have learned how to synthetize them. We say it with regret. Our information comes from an article in the *Herald-Tribune* for December 27, 1952, in which it was announced: "Four cheap factory-made chemicals can double the protein value of the world's food supply, a chemist said here today." The synthetic amino acids, made from coal tar, are to be added to foods like wheat, corn and so forth to double their protein value. However, the scientific journals are full of warnings about the possible harmful effects of tampering with proteins. Says *Borden's Review of Nutritional Research,* "Recent investigations, however, indicate that indiscriminate supplementation with amino acids may precipitate a dietary imbalance having dangerous consequences." The articles goes on to tell of an experiment where, by adding synthetic amino acids, the proper balance of the protein was thrown completely out of line and the experimental rats developed a serious nervous condition very shortly. Protein is the fabric from which living tissue is made. Isn't it obvious to even the most unenlightened of us, that you cannot make something out of coal tar and substitute it for living tissue? Be on your guard against any food to which synthetic amino acids have been added. Shun it as you would shun synthetic vitamins.

However, do not confuse synthetic amino acids with natural amino acid preparations made from food. Food supplements exceptionally rich in all the essential amino acids have been made from food substances such as meat, yeast and so forth. These are no more artificial than are dried milk or powdered eggs. And the amino acids are so concentrated in them, as to provide a wealth of these valuable food elements in the proper proportions as they occur in nature. If you are in doubt about the source of any amino acid preparation or any individual amino acid, such as methionine, that your doctor may have prescribed for you, check on whether the amino acids came from a food source or whether they are synthetic. The synthetics are not for you.

CHAPTER **26**

Eggs and Rheumatic Fever

Probably our best protein food is the egg. The following chapter relates some scientific observations that seem to show how valuable eggs are, especially in the diet of children.

Is it possible that eating or not eating eggs may have something to do with the occurrence of rheumatic fever? An editorial in the April 17, 1954, issue of the *British Medical Journal* discusses this theory at some length. It seems that one researcher, Wallis, first began to study the question of eggs in the diet of rheumatic fever patients. May G. Wilson, in her book, *Rheumatic Fever* (published by Oxford University Press, 1940), theorizes on the fact that cases of rheumatic fever reach their height in April and then decline during the summer months. Could this be because eggs are plentiful during the spring and summer and not so plentiful (hence more expensive) during fall and winter months?

The scientific argument goes like this: Eggs contain choline, a B vitamin, which is essential for the health of the liver. Further facts about choline—it is necessary for all animals, especially the young. It must be present in the diet for the normal nutrition of baby chicks and for egg production in the hen. Choline is necessary for the manufacture of a certain substance in the blood—phospholipid. This substance, phospholipid, is one of the elements in normal blood that fights against streptococcus infection. Rheumatic fever is associated with streptococcal infection. Therefore, the reasoning goes, rheumatic fever might be conditioned partly by egg intake.

Argument Put to a Test

The editor of the *Journal* states that this is a long and tenuous chain of reasoning, but it can be tested to a certain extent. Wallis, writing in the *American Journal of Medical*

Science, Vol. 227, p. 167, 1954, relates how he did a survey among 184 adult and adolescent patients with rheumatic heart disease and a group of normal subjects. Forty-one per cent of the rheumatic heart patients said they thought they ate few eggs in childhood. Only 16 per cent of the normal people claimed they did not eat eggs. Ten per cent of the rheumatic heart patients declared they did not like eggs, as compared to 5 per cent of the other group.

How dependable can such figures be, since they are based on the patients' memories of their childhood? Perhaps we cannot call them infallible, but all precautions were taken during the survey to eliminate bias from the answers. Two other researchers, Coburn and Moore, reporting in the *American Journal of the Diseases of Children,* Vol. 65, p. 744, 1943, state that the former diet of rheumatic heart children appeared to be lacking in eggs as well as other valuable nutritional elements. So they supplemented the diet of 30 convalescent children with the equivalent of 4 egg yolks a day. (The yolk of the egg is the part highest in choline.) The rheumatic fever recurred in only 7 per cent of these children compared with a recurrence of 38 per cent in children whose diets were not so supplemented. Later in 1950 Coburn reported in the *Journal of the American Dietetic Association,* Vol. 26, p. 345, that 8 to 10 egg yolks daily given to children who had previously had rheumatic fever prevented relapses when the children were later subjected to streptococcal infection.

What Does This Theory Mean to Us?

The editor of the *British Medical Journal* frankly admits that this whole theory about egg yolks is only a theory, but, says he, "we should welcome theories if they are founded on fact and lead to the discovery of more facts. The egg theory might be described as 'good in parts.'"

By telling our readers this story from one of the leading medical journals of our day, we do not mean to imply that stuffing children with egg yolks to the exclusion of other foods will positively prevent or cure rheumatic fever. We think the theory is interesting from an entirely different point of view. What if a close examination of the diet of children who contract rheumatic fever should indicate that, through some quirk of circumstance or appetite, their diets were completely lacking in choline—the B vitamin that is apparently so important for preventing the disease? This would certainly mean that other B vitamins were lacking as well, for they appear in most of the same foods as choline. The lesson to be learned,. we believe, is simply that the rules of good diet cannot be disregarded by any conscientious mother. And how and where are mothers expected to learn these vitally important facts about the proper foods for their children? Certainly not from the women's magazines.

Every mouthful of candy, soda pop, white bread, cake or dessert robs a child of a mouthful of good wholesome nutritious food, which will protect him from many diseases, not just rheumatic fever. Every egg, piece of fruit, meat or fish, every vegetable, every salad, every serving of real honest-to-goodness whole grain cereal means just so much more protection from the menace of poor health. And for the mother whose child refuses to eat foods that contain choline and the other B vitamins, the answer is just as simple as buying a package of powdered brewer's yeast (higher than any other food in most of the B vitamins) and using it liberally in preparing food in the kitchen. For suggestions on using brewer's yeast every day in your kitchen, we recommend our favorite general cookbook, *Let's Cook It Right,* by Adelle Davis, available from Rodale Books Incorporated, Emmaus, Pennsylvania.

CHAPTER **27**

The Place of Meat in Your Diet

Meat is, of course, the other best protein food available. We should eat it at least twice a day. Here are some of the reasons why.

Historians and nutritionists have theorized that the American pioneers who settled our continent were able to endure the many hardships, the cold, the hard work, the lone-

liness, the fear, because their diet consisted almost entirely
of meat. Today we know that they lacked, in wintertime
especially, many of the food elements needed for good health—
vitamin C, for example. But in general their meals were high
in the complete protein of meat and it seems fairly obvious that
this was one reason, at least, why they survived and triumphed.
Of course, we must not forget, too, that none of their food was
refined or processed, as we think of processing.

Is Meat a Good Food?

Why exactly is meat such a good food? Or is it, for
modern man? Perhaps the outstanding reason for the superiority of meat as food is the fact that it is a complete protein,
as are all other animal proteins except gelatin. By "complete
protein" we mean that meat contains all the amino acids which
we human beings cannot manufacture inside our bodies. These
are called the "essential amino acids"—for it is essential that
they be present in our food since our bodies do not synthetize
them.

Some vegetables contain some of these amino acids; other
vegetables contain others. Soybeans and sesame seed have been
found to be the only nonanimal sources of complete proteins.
If you are skilled enough in nutrition, it is possible to arrange
entirely vegetable meals to include all the essential amino acids—
but this requires infinite knowledge, patience and attention to
the planning of each meal, for you cannot make up at lunchtime
the essential amino acids that were lacking at breakfast. You
must eat them all at the same time to achieve best results, nutritionally speaking.

Our bodies are made of protein and to be healthy we
must provide them with sufficient protein to keep cells and tissues in good repair. These are constantly breaking down and
wearing out. If good complete protein is not available, how can
they be repaired? Vegetarians believe that we are able to
manufacture protein from vegetables and fruits, as horses and
cows do. It is our belief that, since our digestive tracts are not
made like those of the vegetarian animals, we need to get our
protein from animal sources, rather than from vegetable
sources exclusively.

The second valuable food element in meat is its vitamin
content. All meats, but especially the organ meats, are high in

B vitamins. The different kinds of meat vary in their B content, but, as you can see in the chart following, all rank extremely high. For a country like America where refined carbohydrates make up so much of the diet, meat thus becomes doubly important. The B vitamins that have been removed from these starches (white flour and white sugar) during their processing must be supplied somewhere in the diet, for they are necessary for the proper digestion of the carbohydrates. There is a chemical laboratory in each body cell where certain substances must be put into the test tube before other necessary substances can be manufactured. The B vitamins and carbohydrates are linked. One cannot benefit the body without the other. And the B vitamins that have been removed from refined foods are present in meat in large quantity.

We sometimes hear of folks who have broken many of the rules of good health. They drink, they smoke, they eat starchy desserts and soda fountain food, and still they are healthy. Probably no one will ever solve this mystery. It may have to do with the glands, arteries and other physical equipment they were born with. It may be that they are just naturally able to resist much of the nutritional degeneration that should affect them. But we have a strong suspicion that, if you look closely into their diets, you will find they eat lots of meat, fruits and vegetables. And perhaps this alone protects them from the results of their other bad habits.

Meat for Infants and Young Children

Meat is now a recommended food for babies. We uncovered a very revealing article on meat diets for infants in which milk was not given at all. Mildred R. Ziegler, Ph.D., of the University of Minnesota, writes in the *Journal of the American Dietetic Association* for July, 1953, of the successful results obtained. She tells us that many infants cannot drink milk for one reason or another. (We rather suspect it may be the quality of the milk these days.) These children must have lots of protein, of course, and meat seems to be the answer. She tells us that the American Indians used to feed their infants meat—pounded dried meat mixed with pounded dried choke cherries and the fat skimmed from boiled bones of the buffalo.

Dr. Ziegler also tells us that animal proteins have a much higher digestibility than vegetable proteins—up to 98 or 100

per cent. Meat, which is very rich in iron (needed after the
infant is a year or so old) and the B vitamins, is not rich in
calcium. Milk is, of course, very rich in calcium. So in preparing the diet Dr. Ziegler had to add calcium and trace minerals
to the meat. She used the ash from veal bones. This contained
not only calcium and phosphorus in their proper physiological
proportions, but also all the various trace elements whose possible importance to nutrition we do not know as yet. The
meat was cooked and strained.

Case Histories Prove Value of Meat

All the children on the enriched meat diet throve. Dr.
Ziegler describes the cases of two children—one with an allergy
to milk, the other with a disorder called *galactosemia* which is
an inability to use properly the galactose—a sugar occurring
in milk.

The two-and-a-half-month old boy who was allergic to
milk had had diarrhea almost since birth. He was in an
extremely serious condition, with a distended abdomen, bad
color, feeble cry, and no gain in weight. He was put on the
enriched meat formula and began to improve almost at once.
At the end of 5 months he had gained normally and there
was no diarrhea. He continued on the meat formula with added
fruits and vegetables as he grew older.

The second infant had jaundice, indicating possibly that
some liver disorder had brought on the *galactosemia.* "The
child showed marked clinical improvement with an amazing
change in her activity and in her disposition, after the mineral-
enriched meat formula was substituted for the previous milk
diet," says Dr. Ziegler.

In an earlier experiment, reported in *Pediatrics* for
October, 1952, we learn that the only illnesses that occurred
among the healthy children eating the meat and milk diet were
respiratory and digestive disorders. Those on the meat diet had
considerably fewer of these and they were much less severe.
Drs. Jacobs and George who wrote the article, estimate that
the disease rate for the meat-fed children was about 40 per cent
less than that of the milk-fed children. Dr. Ruth Leverton and
associates, writing in the *Journal of Pediatrics* for June, 1952,
·tell us of another group of children part of whom were fed milk,
the others meat. The hemoglobin and red blood cell count were

better in the infants who got the meat. She also says, "The infants receiving a dietary supplement of meat had approximately one-half as many colds as the control subjects and the duration of the colds was reduced. All infants were reported to have slept better and appeared more satisfied when they received the meat supplement."

Today's Meat Is Chemicalized

We must consider for a moment all the various things that happen to meat before it reaches our tables to make it unhealthful. Cattle and other meat animals are not always fed the most nutritious diet, just as gardens and farms are not always fertilized properly. However, in general, it is well known among breeders that healthy animals are profitable. So there is much less than there used to be of selling diseased or half-starved animals for meat.

Antibiotics and Hormones in Meat

However, scientists have recently discovered that animals grow faster when they are fed antibiotics along with their meals. So many farmers use feeds spiked with antibiotics. For years poultry raisers have used a hormone preparation to fatten poultry. By injecting a pellet of stilbestrol into the neck of the chicken, they produced an artificial castration which made the chicken grow fat and big much earlier than previously. During the Congressional Hearings on Chemicals in Foods, there was a lot of discussion of stilbestrol and the possibility that it might be harmful to individuals eating the poultry. It was felt generally among the experts that carelessly injected pellets could easily be eaten by poultry buyers with resulting harm. In fact, there was one government cancer expert who believed there was serious harm, perhaps even the possibility of cancer, to be feared as a result of the use of stilbestrol.

Now we read that stilbestrol is being used to fatten cattle. The aim, of course, is to save the cattleman money, by causing the cattle to grow much more rapidly so that they can be taken to market much sooner, hence a lot of feed will be saved. But the question, of course, is—what will be the effect of the stilbestrol on the person who eats the meat? And how much nutrition does one get from meat produced to some extent by the action of stilbestrol?

We do not have the answer to any of these questions as

yet. We can only assume that any and all unnatural tinkering with animals meant for food is not good. The only way to avoid chemicalized meat is to buy your meat from someone you know, preferably an organic farmer.

Talk to your butcher about the kind of meat he sells you. If you buy from a large supermarket, find out where their meat comes from and write to the source. Inquire what treatments their animals are given—do they get antibiotics, do they get stilbestrol and so forth? Indicate that you do not want to buy meat from animals that have been treated with any of these substances. One letter will do little good, of course. You will probably get an answer assuring you that there is no harm in any of these things. But if many people write—if you, your friends and neighbors, relatives and health club members write, perhaps the meat producers of this country will wake up to the fact that doping their animals is not really economical.

Should You Stop Eating Meat?

We have merely scratched the surface of all the things that are done to meat, for, of course, other processes are involved before the meat reaches your grocery store. You may well ask if it is really healthful to eat meat, considering all these outrages. Don't forget that similar things have been done to plants, too. Vegetables and fruits are subjected to hormone treatments, poison sprays, artificial fertilizers, various methods of breeding and forcing, that are just as unnatural as the processes the meat goes through. So do not make the mistake of turning from chemicalized meat in disgust and eating nothing but chemicalized vegetables and fruits. The meat contains much that will keep your body strong against the unhealthful things in your diet—the proteins and B vitamins of meat are necessary to protect you against the possible harm you may suffer from any or all of our modern chemicalized food.

Vitamins and Minerals in Meat

Glance at the table below, which shows the vitamin and mineral content of the various meats. Note that the organ meats contain far, far more nutriments than the muscle meats. Make certain that you serve an organ meat at least once a week—oftener if possible. Get accustomed to using the less popular ones—kidneys, brains, sweetbreads, heart. There are many appetizing ways in which these can be served. They are economical and nutritious.

B Vitamins in Poultry and Meat

Milligrams per 100 grams (In general 100 grams equals an average serving)

	Thiamin	Riboflavin	Niacin	Pyridoxine	Pantothenic Acid	Biotin
Chicken	.90 - .150	.070-.260	8.6	.100	.550	.005-.009
Goose	.150	Good	3	?	?	?
Turkey	.120- .150	.190-.240	7.9	?	?	?
Duck	.360	.230	3	?	?	?
Beef	.100- .220	.120-.270	4.5	.077	.490	.002
Lamb	.80 - .210	.230-.266	5.9	.081	.600	.002
Pork	.90 -1.040	.040-.240	.9-4.4	.086-.270	?	?
Veal	.170- .180	.140-.280	3.1-6.5	.056-.130	.110-.260	.001

Mineral Content of Organ Meats

Milligrams per 100 grams

	Calcium	Phosphorus	Iron	Copper
Brains	8	380	2.3	0
Heart	10	236	6.2	0
Kidney	14	262	15.0	.11
Liver, beef	8	373	12.1	2.15
Liver, calf	11	205	5.4	4.41
Sweetbreads	14	596	1.6	0
Tongue	31	229	3.0	0

Vitamin Content of Organ Meats

Milligrams per 100 grams

	A	Thiamin	Riboflavin	Niacin	Inositol	Pyridoxine	Pantothenic Acid
Brains	0	.25	.26	6.0	200	?	
Heart	0	.54	.90	6.8	260	.120	1.8-3.6
Kidney (I.U.)	750	.45	1.95	7.4	0	4.0	2.0
Liver (I.U.)	19,200-53,000	.27	2.80	16.1	55	.170-.730	37.0
Pancreas	0	.320	.590	.584	?	?	4.4-7.6
Sweetbreads	0	.150	.550	3.3			?
Tongue	0	.15	.23	4.0		1.25	10.6
Tripe	0	.006	.12	.003			

	Biotin	Folic acid	Choline	Vit. C	Vit. D
Brains	.0074	.052	?	14	0
Heart	.0049	.130	?	14	0
Kidney (I.U.)	.92				
Liver (I.U.)	.096-.112	3.25-3.80	.380	31	15-45
Pancreas					
Sweetbreads				20	
Tongue	.003				

CHAPTER **28**

The Nutritional Value of Different Meats

Here is some help in choosing which meats to eat to best serve your nutritional needs and stay within your budget.

A survey by the Department of Agriculture showed that 9 out of every 10 Americans suffer from protein deficiency. Meat is our best source of protein.

You have been warned to stay away from animal fats? Then how can you eat meat, of which a certain portion is bound to be fatty? There is, of course, some fat in most meat. It's a good idea, therefore, to study the different kinds of meat and make certain you are not favoring the fatty kinds day after day. In fact, it would be best to avoid the very fatty ones.

Vitamin and Mineral Differences in Meats

How do the different cuts and kinds of meat compare as far as vitamin and mineral content goes—for you want to get as much of these substances as possible while you are consuming the good meat protein? In general, the organ meats are much richer in vitamins, so you should plan to include them often in family meals. In the case of vitamin B_{12}—so necessary, so valuable and so scarce in foods—liver contains from 20 to 50 times as much of this vitamin as the muscle meats. Kidney contains up to 10 times as much. If your family refuses to eat organ meats, it's a near certainty that they're short on vitamin B_{12}.

Table 1 shows the protein, fat and mineral content of the various cuts of meat. Notice the wide variety in fat content. Breast of lamb contains about twice as much fat as leg or loin. You would expect, then, that breast of lamb would contain less protein and sure enough, it does. Notice the quite high content of fat in pork products and the low fat content of veal.

The mineral content of meats is not extremely important in your meal planning, except for iron and phosphorus. In this country, we get, generally speaking, plenty of phosphorus, since meat and cereals, both rich in this mineral, form quite a large part of our diets. But many of us, especially children, young people and women, are short on iron which tends to make us anemic. Meat is valuable for its iron content. One hundred grams is about one-fourth pound, or the average serving.

Table 1. Proximate Composition, Mineral and Caloric Content of Fresh Muscle Cuts

Muscle Cuts Medium Grade	Protein	Fat	Calcium mg/100g	Phos- phorus mg/100g	Iron mg/100g	Calories 100g
BEEF						
Chuck	18.6	16	11	167	2.8	224
Flank	19.0	18	12	186	3.0	247
Loin	16.7	25	10	182	2.5	293
Rib	17.4	23	10	149	2.6	282
Round	19.5	11	11	180	2.9	182
Rump	16.2	28	9	131	2.4	322
VEAL						
Cutlet	19.0	5	6	343	10.6	141
Leg	19.1	12	11	206	2.9	186
Shoulder	19.4	10	11	199	2.9	173
PORK						
Ham	15.2	31	9	168	2.3	344
Loin	16.4	25	10	186	2.5	296
Shoulder	13.5	37				387
Spareribs	14.6	32	8	157	2.2	346
LAMB						
Breast	12.8	37				384
Leg	18.0	18	10	213	2.7	235
Loin	18.6	16				217
Rib chops	14.9	32	9	138	2.2	356
Shoulder	15.6	25	9	155	2.3	295
POULTRY						
Chicken	20.2	12.6	14	200	1.5	200
Turkey	20.1	20.2	23	320	3.8	268
Duck	16.1	28.6	9	172	2.4	322

One more fact of importance in selecting meats. There is considerable difference in the amount of fat and protein any given cut of meat may have. For instance, a chuck roast of beef which contains very little fat may have as much as 19 per cent protein content and 9 per cent fat. A very fatty piece of chuck may have only 15 per cent protein and as much as 32 per cent fat. The same is true generally of other cuts.

Table 2 shows the protein, fat and mineral content of the organ meats. Observe the generally low figures for fat content and the high content of iron. Since there is less fat in organ meats, there are, too, fewer calories, which should be of great importance to reducers.

Table 2. Proximate Composition, Mineral and Caloric Content of Fresh Organ Meats

Organ Meats	Protein %	Fat %	Calcium mg/100g	Phos-phorus mg/100g	Iron mg/100g	Calories 100g
Beef						
Brain	10.5	9	8	380	2.3	127
Heart	16.9	4	9	203	4.6	108
Kidney	15.0	8	9	221	7.9	141
Liver	19.7	3	7	358	6.6	136
Lung	18.3	2				89
Pancreas	13.5	25				279
Spleen	18.1	3			8.9	99
Thymus	11.8	33	14	596	1.6	344
Tongue	16.4	15	9	187	2.8	207
Calf liver	19.0	5	6	343	10.6	141
Calf pancreas	19.2	9				156
Calf thymus	19.6	3				106
Pork						
Brain	10.6	9				126
Heart	16.9	5	35	132	2.7	117
Kidney	16.3	5	11	246	8.0	114
Liver	19.7	5	10	362	18.0	134
Lung	12.9	2				71
Pancreas	14.5	24				272
Spleen	17.1	4				103
Tongue	16.8	16				210
Lamb						
Brain	11.8	8				121
Heart	16.8	10				158
Kidney	16.6	3	13	237	9.2	105
Liver	21.0	4	8	364	12.6	136
Lung	17.9	2				85
Spleen	18.8	4				110
Thymus	14.1	4				91
Tongue	13.9	15				189

Experience has shown that the B vitamins and mineral contents of muscle meats correlate well with the protein content of the cut. If you have a high-protein cut, chances are the vitamin, mineral and amino acid content will be high, too. If you have a fatty cut of meat, lower in protein, the content of vitamins, minerals and amino acids will almost certainly be lower.

Table 3 shows the vitamin content of meats. As you will notice, meat is valuable chiefly for its vitamin B content. With the exception of liver (rich in vitamins A and C), there is little in the way of other vitamins in meat. However, since vitamin B is one element we Americans are deficient in, meat once again shows itself as one of our most valuable foods. And, of course, the organ meats assume an even greater importance here, as seen in Table 4.

For instance, riboflavin is one of the least plentiful of vitamins. But it is extremely important and hundreds of thousands of us are deficient in it. It occurs in quantity only in eggs, milk and meat and, of course, food supplements like brewer's yeast. If you don't use milk and eat few eggs, you are almost certainly not getting enough riboflavin every day. And it is a water soluble vitamin which must be supplied every day. The smallest possible amount you can get along on, without showing symptoms of deficiency, has been estimated as 1.2 milligrams daily for adults. You surely can't get that much from two servings of ordinary meat a day! An egg contains about 1.06 milligrams. But see how rich liver is in riboflavin!

One final word on cooking meats. Cooking at a low temperature saves vitamins and protein. Extremely high temperatures used in frying or pressure cooking are particularly destructive to the protein. Soaking or cooking meat in liquids (water, vinegar or wine) causes loss of many vitamins if the liquid is discarded, for vitamins and minerals have soaked into this liquid.

Table 3. Vitamin Content of Muscle Cuts

Muscle Cuts Medium Grade	Thiamin mg/100g	Riboflavin mg/100g	Niacin mg/100g	B6 mg/100g	Pantothenic Acid mg/100g	Biotin mcg/100g	Choline mg/100g	B12 mcg/100g	Folic acid mg/100g
BEEF									
Chuck	.08	.17	4.5	.38					.013
Loin	.10	.13	4.6						
Rib	.07	.15	4.2		.41	3.4			.014
Round	.08	.17	4.7	.37	1.0	4.6	68	2.0	.026
Rump	.07	.14	3.9						
VEAL									
Leg	.18	.30	7.5	.37			102		.023
Shoulder	.14	.40	6.1	.14			93		.018
Sirloin	.19	.31	7.1	.41			96		.020
PORK									
Ham	.74	.18	4.0	.33	.72	5.3	120	0.9	.009
Loin or Loin Chops	.80	.19	4.3	.50	2.0	77	77		.007
Picnic	.94	.18	4.0						
Spareribs	.92	.18	3.9						
LAMB									
Breast						2.1			
Leg	.16	.22	5.2	.29	.59	5.9	84	2.5	.009
Rib Chop	.13	.18	4.3						
Shoulder	.14	.19	4.5						.007

Organ Meats	Thiamin mg/100g	Riboflavin mg/100g	Niacin mg/100g	B6 mg/100g	Pantothenic Acid mg/100g	Biotin mcg/100g	Choline mg/100g	B12 mcg/100g	Vitamin A IU/100g	Vit. C mg/100g	Folic Acid mg/100g
BEEF											
Brain	.12	.22	3.6	.16	2.5	6.1	410	4.7		18	.012
Heart	.24	.84	6.6	.29	2.3	7.3	170	9.7	30	6	.110
Kidney	.28	1.9	5.3	.39	3.4	92.3	262	28.0	1,150	13	.041
Liver	.23	3.3	13.5	.71	7.3	101.3	510	65.0	43,900	31	.081
Lung	.11	.36	4.0	.07	1.0	5.9		3.3			
Pancreas	.14	.34	3.1	.20	3.8	13.7		4.8		11	
Spleen	.13	.28	4.2	.12	1.2	5.7		5.1		6	
Tongue	.16	.28	3.9	.13	2.0	3.3	108				
Calf liver	.21	3.1	16.1	.30					22,500	36	.046
Veal liver	.52	3.3	16.5	.30	6.0	75.2					
PORK											
Brain	.16	.28	4.3		2.8		375	2.8		18	
Heart	.31	.81	7.3	.35	2.5	18.2	231	2.4	30	6	
Kidney	.26	1.9	8.6	.55	3.1	128.8	286	6.6	130	13	
Liver	.25	3.0	13.9	.33	6.6	84.7	552	23.0	14,200	23	.074
Lung	.09	.27	3.4		0.9						
Pancreas	.11	.46	3.5		4.6		329	6.5			
Spleen	.13	.30	4.3		1.1		208	4.1			
Tongue							137				
LAMB											
Brain	.15	.26	3.7		2.6			7.3		18	
Heart	.31	.86	4.6		3.0			5.2			
Kidney	.38	2.2	6.8		4.3		360	26.0	1,150	13	
Liver	.29	3.9	12.1	.37	8.1	127.0		35.0	50,500	33	
Lung	.11	.47	4.7		1.2			5.0			
Pancreas	.13	.50	3.9		3.5			19.0			
Spleen	.09	.27	4.7		1.5			6.7			

CHAPTER **29**

Carbohydrate, the Villain

by J. I. RODALE

The value of protein in the diet is shown clearly in the work of a noted doctor who believes that carbohydrate-high diets are responsible for many serious disorders. Here are the findings of this physician.

There is a book called *How to Prevent Heart Attacks,* by Benjamin P. Sandler, M.D. (Lee Foundation for Nutritional Research, 2023 West Wisconsin Avenue, Milwaukee, Wisconsin), which is so revolutionary and startling that it may completely revise our conception of heart disease. Dr. Sandler's book, *Diet Prevents Polio,* is based on the same theory for polio as that given for heart disease, namely, that low sugar in the blood is the cause of both diseases. Dr. Sandler is connected with the Veterans' Hospital at Oteen, North Carolina.

Dr. Sandler does not believe that the fat content of the diet is responsible for the recent increase in heart disease. This sounds incredible, based on the huge amount of research that has been done on cholesterol and fat, but perhaps eventually it may be found that Dr. Sandler's low carbohydrate diet will be more effective in curing heart disease than the low fat diet. Probably a combination of both will be found to be the answer.

United States and Italy Compared

There is a tendency to jump to conclusions. For example, doctors who are working on the fat theory will ascribe the low incidence of heart disease in Italy to the low fat consumption in that country, which is about one-half of what it is in the United States. But they overlook other important factors, such as that in Italy people get far more exercise than people do in the United States. In Italy they walk much more and there is quite a bit of riding on bicycles. Such activities give a person physical fitness, they take the fat out of the heart muscle, they reduce the pulse and the blood pressure, all of which are important considerations in the health of the heart.

They also ignore overconsumption of sugar in the United States, which was 103 lbs. per year per person in 1940, whereas in Italy it was only about 21 lbs. It is probably a combination of the 3 factors—low sugar consumption, low fat consumption and increased exercise in Italy which keeps their heart disease rate down.

The Real Enemy, Sugar

The proof of the pudding is in the eating, says Dr. Sandler, because the low carbohydrate diet he devised has been successful in many cases in giving relief from attacks of heart pain, and in preventing their occurrence. One of the clues that convinced Dr. Sandler of the dangers of carbohydrates and sugar to heart cases was the fact that in diabetics, heart disease is more serious, occurs at an earlier age and is more common.

Dr. Sandler does not believe that arteriosclerosis (hardening of the arteries) is a precipitating factor in a heart attack, because, he says, "Many victims of heart attacks, especially those between 20 and 40 years, show no evidence of arteriosclerosis at necropsy (autopsy)." In other words, one may be the victim of a heart attack with entirely normal coronary arteries . . . also, he says, many individuals reach old age with advanced arteriosclerosis, usually generalized, and die from some non-cardiac cause without ever having suffered with symptoms of impaired cardiac function.

The Cholesterol Theory

Regarding the cholesterol theory, he says that the researchers have overlooked the fact that the body can make cholesterol from sugar and starch as well as from fat. But Dr. Sandler does not believe that cholesterol has anything to do with the heart attack caused by arteriosclerosis, because, he says, many persons with arteriosclerosis do not show elevation of the blood cholesterol level.

"Another argument against the fatty theory," says Dr. Sandler, "is the fact that the Eskimo living within the Arctic circle is notoriously free of arteriosclerosis and heart attacks, and yet consumes an extremely high fat diet compared with the

average diet of Americans in the United States. The Eskimo . . .
lives entirely on protein and fat in the form of meat, fish and
blubber."

Low Sugar Level in the Blood

Dr. Sandler draws attention to the fact that 100 per cent
of the carbohydrate food (sugar and starch) one eats, turns to
sugar. Such food items as potatoes, bread, macaroni, rice,
spaghetti and cereals are typical starchy foods. So, in order to
keep the sugar consumption low, we must be extremely cautious
with respect to the carbohydrate content of our diets. A high
consumption of sugar and starch will lead to a low level of sugar
in the blood, and that is what leads to heart symptoms.

How does a high sugar diet lead to a low level of sugar in
the blood? When one ingests sugar, or starch that turns to sugar,
insulin is secreted in the pancreatic gland in order to prevent it
from raising the level of sugar in the blood. The function of the
insulin is to keep the sugar down. But if too much insulin is
secreted, as occurs where large amounts of sugar are ingested,
then the sugar in the blood declines considerably. The liver,
certain glands and part of the nervous system also enter into the
process, but it is the insulin directly that lowers the blood sugar.

In actual practice, since 1937, Dr. Sandler has seen hundreds of cases in which he made sugar tests of the blood of
people, and in more than half of them he saw evidence of low
blood sugar due to a high carbohydrate intake. Clinically it is a
definitely proven fact that too much sugar and starch in the diet
produce a low sugar status in the blood.

The heart muscle requires a steady supply of sugar
(glucose) in order to function. If there isn't enough, this muscle
will stop beating and death will ensue. Quoting Dr. Sandler, "I
also wish to emphasize the fact that the blood sugar supply to
the central nervous system is particularly important, because
abnormal fluctuations in the blood sugar level affect not only
the function of the heart but also the function of the central
nervous system. Many of the symptoms experienced by heart
patients are due directly to the effects of the fall in blood sugar
on the cells of the brain and the spinal cord. The blood sugar
must not only be supplied continuously, but must also be maintained at optimum level, around 80 mg. per 100 cc. When the
blood sugar falls below 80 mg. certain organs, especially the
central nervous system, will be embarrassed and sign and symp-

toms of disturbance in function make their appearance. The severity of the signs and symptoms will depend on how low and at what rate the blood sugar falls."

Physical Strain and the Heart

In some cases, says Dr. Sandler, excessive physical exertion has caused fatal heart attacks. But such exertion, he says, causes a fall in the blood sugar to abnormal levels. He goes into quite some detail to explain this.

Dr. Sandler states that the pressure chest pains of angina in a heart condition are caused by a rapid and sharp fall in blood sugar level. Dr. Sandler cured such conditions by a diet capable of preventing the abnormal fluctuation in blood sugar level, said diet being effective in all age groups.

In order to understand how this theory works, we must know the effect of sugar on the heart's action. "The heart muscle is made up of innumerable muscle cells," says Dr. Sandler. "Like all muscle tissue, it needs certain nutrients to perform its work of contraction and relaxation. The chief nutrients are sugar and oxygen, both of which are brought to the muscle by the blood. . . In the muscle cells, the sugar and oxygen react chemically to yield the necessary energy needed for the work of contraction. . . Among the many varied and complicated chemical reactions that occur during (heart) muscle contraction, is the production of lactic acid. . . Under certain conditions, lactic acid may accumulate in abnormal quantities in a muscle, including the heart, and it is believed that this accumulation of lactic acid along with a few other acid metabolites produced during muscle contraction is responsible for the heart pain. One of the conditions that may cause this abnormal accumulation of metabolites is the . . . abnormally low sugar utilization by the heart muscle. . . Any significant interference with the supply of sugar or oxygen will embarrass heart action, and the degree of interference will determine the degree of embarrassment—from a mild fleeting chest pain to the severe crushing pain of the fatal heart attack."

Fluctuations in the Blood Sugar

But it isn't merely the low blood sugar that does the harm. Dr. Sandler has found from experience that it is the violent fluctuations in the blood sugar that create trouble. Eating a meal rich in carbohydrates will do that because first it raises the blood sugar, then it lowers it. "The rapid rate of change in the downward direction results in a severe environmental change for the heart muscle, to which it fails to accommodate readily and so the muscle is embarrassed and the symptoms of pain are felt by the patient."

Nicotine and caffeine cause a rise in the blood sugar. That's why, when the blood sugar is low, between meals, a pick-me-up cigarette or cup of coffee is taken. This raises the blood sugar and contributes to the violent fluctuations that are so dangerous.

The Influence of Oxygen on the Heart

In addition to sugar, as has already been said, oxygen is important to the healthful operation of the heart muscle. Quoting Dr. Sandler, "It has been shown that a cell utilizes oxygen in proportion as it utilizes sugar. But oxygen is useful to the cell only if there is some fuel to burn (oxidize) for the production of energy. The blood may be normally saturated with oxygen but if the blood sugar level is half of what it should be, the body will consume less than normal oxygen. . . It has been accepted by many that the immediate cause of heart pain is an acute oxygen lack on the part of the heart muscle."

Diet and the Prevention of Heart Pains

Dr. Sandler, in great detail, describes 15 cases in which the correction of the diet, reducing the carbohydrate and increasing the protein, but not reducing the fat, resulted in the prevention of heart pains.

Here is a typical case: "E. C., a white boy, 13 years old, was brought in by his mother because of two recent attacks of unconsciousness without convulsions. The first seizure occurred in school about an hour after lunch, lasted about 20 minutes and was followed by spontaneous recovery . . . He had frequent attacks of smothering sensations and tightness across the chest on exertion such as running . . . He responded readily to the low carbohydrate, high protein diet with between-meal feedings. He became less nervous, had better color, and gained weight. The attacks of chest pains gradually became infrequent, and stopped altogether after several weeks."

Case No. 2: "A white boy, 14 years old, came into the clinic with his mother because of attacks of pain in the upper abdomen and lower chest, which came on during exertion

. . . The mother volunteered that he was 'cranky', easily angered, and that he always wanted to eat, preferably something sweet. . . . He responded readily to a low carbohydrate diet and was soon free of the attacks of chest and abdominal pain. There was marked improvement in general health with loss of his nervousness."

Case No. 12 was that of a white man aged 69, who was first seen on August 17, 1937. "His general health had always been good until the summer of 1936, when he began to get bouts of pain on exertion and during excitement. . . The attacks gradually increased in severity and frequency, so that by the summer of 1937 they occurred almost daily after walking one to two blocks. The pain was described as severe and 'sticking' . . . attacks of dizziness came on almost any time and sometimes made him walk as though drunk. . . He was given sedatives and dilator drugs without relief." He did not go on the low carbohydrate diet until early January, 1938. "He returned on January 13, 1938, stating that he was unable to follow the diet because he could not afford the more expensive proteins. Arrangements were made with the relief bureau to give him extra money to buy these foods. With this help he was able to follow the diet, though not completely.

"He showed improvement within two weeks. The precordial pain became milder and occurred less often. He was able to walk greater distances. The epigastric pain disappeared after 3 weeks. Headaches and dizziness gradually disappeared. On April 12 he reported practically complete freedom from these symptoms. . . On May 3, 1938, he reported occasional headache and said he had 'no more pain at all.' He felt so well during 1939 that it was necessary for him to come to the clinic only twice. During 1940 he came only once. When last seen on January 21, 1941, he reported occasional mild pain which came on while walking. He said he could walk up to 8 blocks and return before feeling any pain. He also got mild pain during excitement. Questioning revealed that he was eating some bread, sugar, and now and then potatoes. He said that since he was feeling so well, he thought he could be more liberal with these foods." This patient had very high blood pressure to begin with and the diet reduced it from 250/110 to 156/90.

There are many more cases, and to me they are amazing!

In every one of them, a very low carbohydrate diet cured the condition of angina pains.

The book is full of remarkable statements. For example, in some cases the low blood sugar causes subnormal body temperatures, with an inability to tolerate cold weather. In some cases due to low blood sugar, "the fall in oxygen absorption may be so great and so prolonged as to cause a marked lowering of the body's ability to resist an acute infection, such as polio and pneumonia." I wish to remind the reader that vitamin E is a conserver of oxygen in the body, and therefore, together with a high protein diet, and plenty of exercise, a condition can be created that will really prevent a heart attack.

Dr. Sandler's Diet

The following is Dr. Sandler's recommendation as to diet. The following foods should be avoided: sugar, soft drinks, ice cream, ices, sherbets, cakes, candies, cookies, wafers, pastries, pies, fruit juices, canned and preserved fruits, jams, jellies, marmalades, puddings, custards, syrups.

Coffee, tea, cocoa, lemonade, etc., may be sweetened with saccharin or other artificial sweetener. So-called "diabetic foods and desserts" and food preparations may be used. Nuts may be eaten in unlimited quantity except the starchy ones such as peanuts, cashews, chestnuts. These may be eaten sparingly.

The following foods should be eaten in reduced quantity because they contain starch: beans, dried; beans, lima; tapioca; macaroni; rolls; crackers; corn; peas, dried, split; potatoes, white or sweet; yams; lentils; rice; spaghetti; vermicelli; noodles; breads; buns; biscuits; cereals: oat preparations, rice preparations, rye preparations, corn preparations, wheat preparations.

The following fresh fruits should be eaten only in limited quantity because of their sugar content: oranges, grapefruit, peaches, honeydew melons, cantaloupe, watermelon, apples, pears, pineapple, strawberries, blueberries, raspberries, grapes, cherries, plums.

Fresh fruits are allowed, but only one portion should be taken with a meal, that is, one apple or one orange. The sugar in fruits may cause low blood sugar if they are eaten in excess. Fruit juices, canned fruits, dried fruits, preserved fruits should be avoided. Fruits may be stewed without sugar. Apples may be baked without sugar. Tomato juice is allowed since it contains no natural sugar.

The following carbohydrate foods contain little or no starch and may be eaten in unlimited quantity: artichokes; asparagus; avocados; bamboo shoots; beans, string; beans, wax; beans, soy; beets, red; broccoli; brussels sprouts; cabbage; carrots; cauliflower; celery; chard, swiss; collards; cucumbers; eggplant; endive, leaves; greens, beet; greens, dandelion; greens, turnip; kale; kohlrabi; leeks; lettuce; mushrooms; okra; onions; parsley; parsnips; peas, fresh; peppers; pumpkins; radishes; rhubarb; rutabagas; sorrel; spinach; squash, summer; tomatoes; turnips; watercress; pickles; horseradish; mustard; vinegar; olives; capers; mayonnaise.

All animal foods may be eaten in unlimited quantity. Such foods are: beef, pork, lamb, mutton, veal, poultry, fish. These may be purchased fresh, canned, smoked, dried, etc. Eggs can be used freely whether fresh or dried. All dairy products may be eaten in unlimited quantity; milk, buttermilk, fermented milk, butter, sweet and sour cream and all cheeses. Milk may be fresh, evaporated, or powdered.

In this section he doesn't mention bananas, but later on states that they contain chiefly sugar and starch.

Examination of His Diet

In connection with this low carbohydrate diet I would like to say that I have always been sensitive to an overindulgence in wheat and sugar, as far as my heart condition is concerned, but I used to eat enormous amounts of bananas and sweet potatoes without experiencing the slightest angina pains. For years I have eaten practically no wheat or rye products—no bread, cereals, cake, gravies, noodles, etc., but should I make an exception then invariably the chest pains would occur soon after, upon exertion.

Dr. Sandler threw all the carbohydrates into one group. He didn't attempt to evaluate one group of them clinically against another. I feel that it was the bread, cereals, cake, and sugar of his patients' meals that brought on the angina. He didn't attempt to get his patients to eat one kind of carbohydrate and then another to see if the effect was uniform. It would be interesting if he would go into the subject more thoroughly.

I am reminded of the old lady who had a mixture of various herbs that kept a heart condition in check, but when the medical profession investigated they found that only one of her herbs was responsible—the foxglove. And this is how digitalis was discovered. In connection with Dr. Sandler's carbohydrate theory, the same probably is true.

My Own Diet

I received Dr. Sandler's book several months ago and read it immediately with great excitement. I then decided to cut out bananas and sweet potatoes and to go easy on all the other starches. I had already cut out sugar and wheat products. My experience was not good. First, I found it difficult to reduce weight. There is something about bananas and sweet potatoes that make me lose weight. Isn't that strange? But it's true as far as I am concerned. Secondly, without my bananas and sweet potatoes, I lost my usual cheerfulness. Thirdly, and most serious of all, I soon began to experience my chest pains upon walking uphill. I, therefore, resumed the eating of these two products and the 3 symptoms disappeared. I became cheerful. I began to lose weight, and could walk uphill without experiencing angina. I am glad to be eating bananas and sweet potatoes because they put sparkle and zest into my diet. They are very satisfying.

A Critical Look at Bananas, Bread and Potatoes

Now a word of comparison between bananas and bread. Wheat is a substance that in my opinion is resistant to digestion. It ferments easily in the stomach and can cause bloating. It is extremely fattening. It requires the 4 stomachs of a cow to digest it and to turn it into meat. But bananas are so easy to digest that they are fed to babies and to old people. I can't picture a cow having to digest bananas as she does the grains.

I would like to mention another comparison between bananas, sweet potatoes and bread. When I eat bread, I not only put on some extra weight, but it seems that it is more than the weight of the bread eaten. It seems that the wheat exerts some kind of effect on the other food in the stomach and causes some of it to turn into fat. The reverse holds true for bananas and sweet potatoes. They cause a loss of weight more than their own weight. They must contain some mysterious factor that works on other foods to prevent them from going in to fat. Of course, this is my own experience, and is not scientific, but it is worthwhile checking.

One more thing: Normally, upon exertion, if something about my daily life is off the beam, I may experience slight angina pains—but always while in the throes of the exertion—never in bed at night. But should I overindulge in bread and cake at an evening banquet, I will feel it in bed some time thereafter. This is a note of warning about the danger of wheat and rye products to a heart case.

Banquets and Heart Attacks

One often reads of a man having a heart attack later in the evening on which he participated in a banquet. On such an occasion, due to the exhilaration of being with other people, one throws caution to the winds and commits excesses in connection with bread, cakes, ice cream, etc. One takes in too much wheat and sugar.

By way of example, Roy H. Glover, chairman of the board of the Anaconda Company, died shortly after attending a dinner given by the State Department for visiting representatives of the Chilean Congress. He was only 67 years old. Did he eat a lot of bread, gravy (containing flour), cake and perhaps other wheat and sugar products? I am sure that wheat and sugar are very dangerous for a heart case. Possibly he overindulged in the fat category, too. I can't go along with Dr. Sandler who says you can eat all the fat you want. After many years of concentrated experimentation and study I came up with researches which showed that within a short time after a meal that was heavy with fat, the blood tends to coagulate much more quickly than normal. In such case a fatal thrombosis (blood clot) could occur.

Dr. Abrahamson's Theory

In connection with the theory of low blood sugar, I would like to mention the work of E. M. Abrahamson, M.D., whose book, *Body, Mind and Sugar* (Henry Holt and Company, 1951), created a sensation in the popular health field. He showed that low blood sugar is far more common than high blood sugar (or diabetes) and how it can cause such conditions as asthma, epilepsy, hay fever, rheumatic fever, alcoholism, fatigue, neuroses, depression, ulcers, headaches and multiple sclerosis. But he did not incriminate it as a factor in heart disease.

Dr. Abrahamson builds a convincing case against coffee. A person who suffers from low blood sugar, he contends, will drink several cups of coffee for breakfast, which will raise the sugar, but it will wear off in an hour or so, and he will find his efficiency decreasing. His head may begin to ache, he may get grumpy and irritable, and have an "all gone" feeling in the pit of his stomach. Obviously, then, he has another cup of coffee for a pick-up, and the cycle begins all over again. This happens 3 or 4 times a day between meals and his blood sugar level, therefore, must be zigging and zagging all day long. These fluctuations, Dr. Sandler claims, are extremely dangerous to a person's well-being.

To the islands of Langerhans in the pancreatic gland, sugar is sugar. These glands go to work by producing insulin, to force the blood sugar back to its normal level. In the course of time, because of continuous attempts to bring down the sugar level, the islands lose their sensitivity and overrespond to a normal stimulus. This is what brings about the low blood sugar.

The Importance of This Theory

Here is a letter written by a man who read about Dr. Abrahamson's book in Mary Haworth's column in the New York *Journal American*. The letter appeared in the April 5, 1957, issue of this paper. "Dear Mary Haworth: I would like to take this opportunity to congratulate you for the wonderful work you are doing—particularly in calling attention to such timely books as *Body, Mind and Sugar* by Abrahamson and Pezet . . . The editors of a national magazine are interested in a story about my wife, who was a so-called mental patient for some months, and had been regarded as a hopeless case; and then was healed by the diet outlined in *Body, Mind and Sugar,* that counteracts hyper-insulinism (blood sugar starvation)." Miss Haworth printed several other letters from readers who have been helped by Dr. Abrahamson's low sugar and starch diet.

There seems to be evidence that the teenage problem could be ameliorated by this diet. The youth of today is confused by an imbalanced blood stream created by cokes, ice cream, candy, cake, etc. This idea would be worthwhile experimenting with.

The work of Drs. Sandler and Abrahamson should be brought out into the open. The various medical funds should make it the subject of extensive researches and investigations. This may even be the long sought for answer to the cancer problem. But, as far as heart disease is concerned, it seems to me that this diet should become standard practice in medical practice.

SECTION 7

SALT

It is common medical practice to limit salt consumption, in cases of kidney disease, dropsy or high blood pressure. We have found evidence indicating that excessive table salt may be an important factor in cancer, heart disease, deafness, sinus trouble, obesity, hives—to mention just a few disorders. A salt-free diet in pregnancy means an easier delivery. Cases of cancer have been reported which improved within two weeks on a salt-poor diet. Completely deaf persons have regained their hearing just by giving up salt. We believe that most of us eat far, far too much salt and would do well to eliminate it entirely from our tables and cooking. You obtain ample salt (sodium chloride) in the natural foods of a good diet.

In recent researches it has been shown that salt-taking may be a cause of baldness.

CHAPTER 30

Why Use Salt?

How many diseases could be prevented if our bodies could cry out "Too much salt" as our taste senses can when food is too highly seasoned. With the evidence we have against salt and its effects, how much wiser we would be to break ourselves of the salt "habit"—for it is a habit like tobacco and liquor—than to wait for the sword to strike and then run for the cure.

Enough salt can be obtained from most foods in their natural form. R. Ackerly, M.D., in *Proceedings of the Royal Society of Medicine,* 1910, states that the body requires only from 2 to 3 grams of salt a day, and that "western nations eat, on an average, 7 to 10 times as much salt as is necessary, and frequently more." Dr. Egon V. Ullmann in his book, *Diet, Infections and Colds* (Macmillan, 1933), shows how 5 grams of salt a day may be obtained from food without added table salt, and gives a list of everyday foods and their sodium chloride (salt) content. Dr. L. Duncan Bulkley, editor of the medical journal, *Cancer,* believes that one-quarter of an ounce of added salt per week "is ample to supply the body with the actual needs in the replacing of chloride of sodium lost in modern methods of cooking and the preparation of food."

Why Is Excess Salt Bad?

(1) *Excess Salt Causes Hyperacidity.* The formation of hydrochloric acid in the stomach depends on the salt intake. The chlorine of the sodium chloride goes to make up part of this hydrochloric acid. So if too much salt is taken, too much of this acid will be produced (hyperacidity). Too much hydrochloric acid is generally accepted as one predisposing cause of stomach ulcers.

(2) *Excess Salt May Prevent Proper Use of Calcium in the Body.* Much of the sodium of the sodium chloride will be

held in the tissues and will reduce the effect of calcium, which is so badly needed in the body. Where salt is reduced, calcium action will prevail and will counteract inflammations. These two points are made by Dr. Ullmann in his book mentioned previously.

(3) *Excess Salt Stimulates the Body and Nerve Cells.* We know how salt irritates an open wound, or salt water stings the eyes. In the same way it irritates delicate membranes throughout the body. Dr. Henry C. Sherman in his book, *Chemistry of Food and Nutrition* (published by Macmillan, 1952), states that "through overstimulating the digestive tract, salt may interfere with the absorption and utilization of the food." He also states that an excess of salt may disturb the osmotic pressure of tissues, involving almost every portion of the body. Although some salt is needed to keep the tension of the body fluids at a normal level, we get enough in our foods in their natural content to serve the purpose.

(4) *Excess Salt Causes the Retention of Fluid.* Every gram of salt binds and holds 70 grams of water. The bad effects of this accumulated fluid may be seen as the cause of many diseases.

(5) *Table Salt Contains Chemicals.* Most of us are wary of ordering just any old chemical from the druggist's shelf without competent advice, but how many of us have looked into the effect of the chemicals that have been added to packaged table salt? One box of salt listed the following added items: .01 per cent potassium iodide, .05 per cent sodium bicarbonate, and .90 per cent tri-calcium phosphate. Sometimes hyposulphite of soda is added. Though the individual chemical added may not be harmful in itself, the combination of all of them may well be.

(6) *Chemicals Must Be Used To Combat Bad Effects of Salt in the Body.* There are research findings that may eventually prove the prescription of salt-free diets unnecessary. Work along this line was described in *Science News Letter* for September 16, 1950. In brief, the researchers found that certain chemicals called "ion exchange resins" can combat the accumulation of fluid and the inability of the body to get rid of too much sodium, such as is contained in common table salt. These resins, they found, can remove the salt from the body, and "in

order to avoid robbing the body of potassium as the sodium is being removed, a combination of ammonium and potassium forms of the resin was adopted." However, as we have said before many times, why put something irritating into the body that needs something else to undo the harm? And who knows the effect of these added chemicals over a long period of time?

(7) *Salt Contains Bacteria.* "Refined salt from various sources was found to contain up to 8,300 bacteria and 400 mould (spores) . . . and toxic cultures were obtained in some cases. Brines of various sources and ages were badly contaminated," according to the *Analyst,* June, 1926. Commenting on this, Frederick L. Hoffman, M.D., a member of the American Association of Cancer Research, in his book, *Cancer and Diet* (Williams and Wilkins), stated: "If this should be substantiated, it might be a clue to the injurious effects of common salt in introducing irritating bacteria into the human body, directly operating as causative factors in tumor growth."

Diseases and Salt

Cancer. Because cancer is still baffling medical science, we have come to assume that its cause must be tremendously complex and mysterious. But there is evidence that the seemingly harmless substance, common table salt, is held in positive suspicion by medical authorities.

One of the earliest writers on cancer, Dr. James Braithwaite, of Leeds, England, tells of the increase in diameter of a tumor from $2\frac{3}{8}$ inches to $3\frac{1}{4}$ inches when one of his patients resumed daily use of salt, even in small quantities. He says that salt, being an inorganic chemical and not a food, is dangerous in oversupply. It harms the body tissue as it is a powerful stimulant to cell metabolism. This information is from his book, *Excess of Salt in the Diet and Three Other Factors, the Probable Causes of Cancer.*

Frederick T. Marwood, a layman, made the interesting observation that in Denmark, where the consumption of salted fish is the highest in Europe, the cancer rate is also the highest in Europe *(What Is the Root Cause of Cancer—Is It the Excessive Consumption of Common Salt, Salted Foods and Salt Compounds? 1910).*

In contrast, Dr. L. Duncan Bulkley tells us of the low incidence of cancer in Mexico and among the Indians, where the use of salt is relatively small. He describes how "chloride of sodium, or common salt, in any excess with the food may disturb the balance of mineral ingredients of the blood, replacing the tissue of the cells when worn out, instead of a potassium salt, thus starting them on their riotous malignant action, in response to local irritation, and ending in fully developed cancer." This statement appeared in the publication, *Cancer*, July, 1927.

As salt has the property of holding fluid about it, a diet rich in water again favors cancer cell growth. The tissue of the tumor contains a larger amount of fluid proportionately than any tissue in the body according to Frederick L. Hoffmann, M.D., in *Cancer and Diet,* quoting Dr. Bernhard Fischer-Wasels, Director of the Pathological Institute of the University of Frankfort.

High Blood Pressure and Kidney Disease. Dr. Frederick Allen, who introduced the low-salt diet for this disease into this country in 1922 has had consistently good results from the restriction of salt. He also conducted animal experiments which proved that with the feeding of salt, blood pressure increased, causing hypertension. This research is reported in the *Journal of the American Medical Association* for June 4, 1949.

"Twenty-one patients treated with low-salt diet were observed by Svith for 1 to 5 months. In all cases the blood pressure was reduced from 20 to 75 mm., usually in 2 to 4 weeks, "and the patients' other symptoms disappeared, too," according to an article in *Ugeskrift For Laeger*, Copenhagen, March 30, 1950.

Dropsy. Doctors now believe that the cause of dropsy is not too much water, but too much sodium, which prompts the body to hoard water in abnormal amounts, usually as a result of a heart or kidney ailment. Dr. Ferdinand Ripley Schemm's salt-free diet has won wide acceptance and his tireless work on the disease resulted in the establishment in 1947 of the Western Foundation for Clinical Research. Dr. Schemm believed that if the sodium taken in with food were cut down, the body itself could in dropsy cases regulate the sodium already in the body and give the kidneys enough water so that they could work properly and flush out the sodium salts through the urine. The "restriction of water is harmful and a cause of suffering," he said in cases of dropsy.

Heart Disease. Though a low salt diet is not infallible, there is definite evidence of its beneficial effects in many cases. Wheeler, Bridges and White in *The Journal of the American Medical Association* for January, 1947, describe the treatment of 50 cases of congested heart failure with a diet low in salt, containing about five-eighths of a gram of sodium per day. Patients were chosen for whom all other treatments had failed. Of the 50, only 35 followed the diet honestly, and out of this number, 22 received definite benefit, while 13 did not.

Pregnancy. Seventy patients, put on a salt-free diet in the latter weeks of pregnancy, showed a definite reduction in the length of labor and, as far as could be measured, in the severity of the pains. It is believed that the decreased sodium and chloride (from salt) resulted in removal of water from the maternal tissues, bringing about a lessening in excitability of the nerve centers and a definite sedative effect, according to an article in *Hospital Topics,* 1940.

Deafness and Sinusitis. Here is a beautiful "believe-it-or-not," the more beautiful because it is backed up by scientific medical knowledge. Dr. Frank Graham Murphy, of Mason City, Iowa, had as a patient a woman who had been deaf for years and according to the specialists was apparently incurable. Questioning her eating habits Dr. Murphy found she was a heavy consumer of salt, and advised that she drop it completely. After three weeks she returned—her hearing restored, as good as ever!

Dr. Murphy says that the ears and sinuses are affected when there is an excess of salt in the body tissues. When free perspiration does not help get rid of the excess, the kidneys force the salt into other organs or tissues. As salt collects water about it, a waterlogged condition may result in the ears and sinuses. Other fluid-retention foods, with a high number of calories, such as bread and sugar, when eaten in excess, may also play a role, he says in *Clinical Medicine* for August, 1944.

Obesity. A drastic reduction of salt is advised because of its water-holding properties. Fluid adds to the weight. Salt also excites thirst, making for a greater intake of water, and excites appetite by increasing the flow of saliva.

Headaches. Migraine and other headaches are attributed by Dr. Max Goldzieher to pressure caused by an increased flow of water to the tiny blood vessels in the head, because of abnormal retention of salt in the tissues.

Other Diseases. Hives, epilepsy, insomnia, nervous tension states, and rheumatic swelling also respond to the restriction of salt intake, says the magazine, *Good Health.*

Forbidden Food on the Salt-Free Diet

The following is a list of foods commonly forbidden by physicians to patients on a low-salt diet: Processed meats: salted, smoked, canned, spiced, and pickled foods, bacon, ham, sausages, bologna, frankfurters, liverwurst, salami; shell fish: clams, oysters, lobster, shrimp; processed fish; canned vegetables (unless specially packed without salt); beets, celery, endive, spinach, kale, sauerkraut; broths, meat soups; regular commercial bread and rolls, salted crackers, pretzels; peanuts; all salted cheeses, salted butter; commercial ice cream. Also forbidden are olives, raisins, catsup, mayonnaise, pickles, relish, salted meat gravy and salted meat sauce.

This list is for sick people who have to be extremely strict. An ordinary healthy person may use his judgment as to how far he wishes to go. Remember that in their raw state fruits, vegetables, meat and cereals naturally provide all the vital food salts we need for our well-being and preservation. If a person will go to a little pains to figure out an appetizing diet, the saltless features of it won't be hard to take.

Salt Substitutes

There are two kinds of salt substitutes, if substitute you must. First there are the nonchemical substitutes like Vege-Sal which is sold in health food stores This contains some sodium chloride (which is what you are trying to avoid), soybean extract, sea salt and vegetable powders. This is far safer than the chemical salt substitutes such as Diasal, Gustamate, Neocurtasal and so forth. But it is our opinion that no salt substitutes should be used. By omitting salt in cooking and not adding any at the table, you will find, after a matter of several weeks, that you do not miss the taste of it. As a matter of fact, you will begin for the first time to appreciate the actual taste of many foods whose flavors you have up to now been drowning out with salt. Honestly, you'll soon begin to enjoy food more without salt! There are many primitive nations in the world whose people have never tasted salt and many other people, such as the Eskimos, who will not eat food that has been salted!

There are diseases such as Addison's disease where the body mechanism is so badly disordered that salt is necessary. If you are suffering from any of these diseases, of course, follow your doctor's direction about the amount of salt you need. Otherwise you are perfectly safe in cutting down on the salt you add to food in cooking and at the table, for you are already getting all the sodium you need in food.

Heat and Salt Tablets

Many people believe they should take salt tablets during the summer months. Taking salt tablets to prevent heat shock or prostration started with steel workers, who stand before searing furnaces all their working day, losing a large amount of salt and water in perspiration. In our usual haste to take up anything new, many employers provided salt tablets even in cool offices where employees were not being especially active physically. Recently the tendency has been to swing away from taking salt tablets. The National Research Council, official authority on matters of nutrition and health, has concluded that the average American gets from 10 to 15 grams of salt a day, which is easily enough to make up for loss in perspiration. In addition, it has been found that one soon becomes accustomed to hot weather, and one's perspiration becomes less salty. So it now appears that, for the average person, exerting himself in an average way, there is no need for extra salt during the summertime.

If you eat a purely vegetarian diet, you may feel the need of a little more salt than those of us who eat meats, butter and eggs, for the fruits and vegetables do not contain as much natural sodium as the animal products. Our final word on salt—and we believe the facts we have presented prove our case—throw away your salt shaker, gradually begin to use less and less salt in cooking, and enjoy the increased health and good flavor of natural foods that will be your reward!

CHAPTER 31

Salt and Colds

The possible relation of too much salt and respiratory disorders is shown in the work of a famous physician.

In his excellent book, *Diet in Sinus Infections and Colds* (Macmillan Company, 1942 out of print), Egon V. Ullman, M.D., advises among other things the use of a salt-poor diet for chronic cold sufferers. We have long recommended giving up the use of salt in cooking or at the table, regardless of whether or not one is suffering from any disease. Dr. Ullmann is very emphatic about not using salt, if you would be free from colds.

Part of his explanation is this: The chemical content of table salt is sodium and chloride. The chloride serves no purpose in our bodies except that it may go to form hydrochloric acid in the stomach, a certain amount of which is necessary for digestion of proteins. An excess of salt in the diet can result in too much hydrochloric acid in the stomach, which will surely produce stomach ulcers.

The sodium part of table salt is the part most of us have been warned against. It seems that, to a certain extent, sodium cancels out the excellent and necessary functions of calcium. "If large amount of sodium chloride are taken," says Dr. Ullmann, "a good deal of it will be stored in the skin, mucous membrane and other tissues, and calcium will be liberated. Therefore each sodium molecule retained in the tissues will diminish the calcium effect. . . . On the other hand, with a reduction of sodium chloride in the diet the calcium action will prevail and lead up toward an anti-inflammatory effect. . . . To sum it up, it can be said that the secret of calcium action lies in the relation of calcium taken with food to the other minerals, especially sodium, magnesium and phosphorus. If any of those are taken in too large amounts the calcium effect may be impaired."

We want to point out here the importance of calcium in relation to cold susceptibility. Sir Robert McCarrison in *The Journal of the Royal Society of Arts* for September 4, 1936, shows how malnutrition can contribute to a condition in the nose that might create susceptibility to cold catching. He says:

"Let me draw your attention to the kind of change that is brought about in epithelium (skin or mucous membrane) by the lack of this vitamin (vitamin A). This membrane is covered by tall epithelial cells, each of which has a fringe of cilia. A function of these cells is to secrete mucous, which not only traps bacteria, but permits the cilia to perform their movements— this they can only do when the membrane they fringe is moist *and the moisture contains calcium* (italics ours). The function of the cilia is, by their rapid movements in waves, to propel bacteria or foreign particles, as of dust, towards the exterior of the body, whence, in normal circumstances, they are ejected. It has been estimated that the cilia move at the rate of about 600 times a minute. Now when the food is deficient in vitamin A the cilia slough off and the cells themselves lose their secretory character, becoming horney or keratinised, as it is called. Figure to yourself what this means: no longer is this trapping, this propelling of harmful particles, whether of dust or bacteria or both, possible in the areas so affected. For, unless the deficiency be very grave, it is only at certain places that these changes occur. Where they do occur the local defenses are broken down and bacteria are free to implant themselves in the soil thus made ready for them and to invade the tissues."

Why Use Salt?

In the diet Dr. Ullmann outlines for chronic cold patients, he specifically recommends that no salt be added either in cooking the food or at the table. He suggests ways of making food tasty with herbs and seasonings other than salt. He also advises against the use of non-sodium salt substitutes. They are generally not liked by patients, he has found, they may leave an aftertaste, are hard to get used to and are expensive. He advises instead, and we agree completely, that the best way to learn to get along without salt is simply to stop using it. Within a few weeks you will be used to the taste of food without salt and will, in fact, for the first time in years begin to appreciate the real taste of food, for you will be tasting the food itself rather than the salt you used to douse it with.

Do We Need to Salt Our Food?

He covers in his chapter on salt all the old arguments offered against the practice of doing without it. People will tell you, "But animals have to have salt. Human beings cannot get along without salt. Throughout history salt has been a valuable commodity and wars have been fought for possession of it." Spices have also been a valuable commodity down through the ages—so valuable that the voyages of explorers like Columbus were undertaken to find new sources of spices or shorter ways of reaching the old sources. But surely no one would claim that man cannot live without spices! There are whole nations of people whose languages do not contain a word for salt. There are many parts of the world where salt has never been eaten and where just the taste of it sickens the people. Animals who do not get enough sodium chloride in their food frequent salt "licks" because they have a need for the sodium and the chloride. But we human beings get plenty of both in our daily food. The only reason why we add more salt is the same reason why we add sugar—we like the taste of it.

It is generally agreed among authorities that we do not need more than 5 grams of sodium chloride per day. Adding up the sodium chloride in the foods eaten by the average American for a week, Dr. Ullmann lists the sodium chloride content of meat, milk, eggs, rice, wheat, peas, cream, bread, potatoes, fruits and vegetables and finds that we get, from a diet like this, without salting the food, 5 grams of salt per day. "The trouble is," he says "that most of us consume about 15 grams or more per day, an amount which is in excess of what the body really requires. There is hardly a dish to which the cook does not add just 'a pinch of salt,' and at the table salt is frequently added in amounts which remind one of the salt licks of the animals."

Sodium Chloride Contained in Foods

Here is a chart showing the amount of sodium chloride in a number of common foods. Study it and you will agree with us that you do not need any more salt than your food naturally contains:

Food	Usual Portion and Weight	Milligrams of Sodium Chloride Per Ounce (A milligram is 1/1000 of a gram)
Almonds	20=1 ounce	7.4
Apples	1=1⅓ ounces	2.8 to 4.2
Asparagus	6=2½ ounces	.5 to 4.5
Bananas	1=5 ounces	.02 to 12
Barley, pearl	3T=1 ounce	.7 to 16
Beans, butter	¾ cup=2½ ounces	17.4
Beans, green lima	½ cup=2½ ounces	.28 to 25.4
Beans, dried lima	½ cup=2½ ounces	47.7 to 80.5
Beef, lean	½ pound	15 to 24
Beets	⅔ cup=3⅓ ounces	15.1 to 31.4
Bluefish	½ pound	19.4
Cabbage, red	½ cup=⅚ ounce	1.4 to 10.8
Cantaloupe	¼=3⅓ ounces	3.4 to 13.7
Carrots, raw	½ cup=2⅔ ounces	8.8 to 27
Celery stalks	2=1⅓ ounces	28.8 to 38.9
Cheese, American Swiss	⅛ inch=1 ounce	120.0
Cheese, Cheddar	⅚ ounce	154.2
Chicken, breast	½ pound	15.4 to 26.0
Chicken, leg	½ pound	15.4 to 31.4
Coconut, fresh	1 inch=⅓ ounce	4.7 to 11.4
Cream	1T=½ ounce	8.8 to 11.4
Dandelion greens	½ cup=1⅔ ounces	21.7 to 48
Duck, leg	½ pound	27.4
Eggs	1 average=1⅔ ounces	31.7 to 40
Flounder, steamed	¼ pound	32.6
Goose, roasted	¼ pound	41.2
Haddock, steamed	¼ pound	34.4
Halibut, steamed	¼ pound	31.5
Kale	1¾ cup=6 ounces	14.2 to 31.4
Kidney, beef	5 ounces	60 to 69.5
Kohlrabi	½ cup=1⅔ ounces	14.2
Lamb, without fat	1 chop=3⅛ ounces	14 to 31.4
Lentils	¼ cup=2 ounces	16.2
Liver, beef	½ pound	6 to 24.8
Liver, calf	½ pound	24.8 to 31.4
Mackerel	½ pound	43.7
Milk, fresh whole	1 cup=8 ounces	13.4 to 14.5
Oatmeal	¼ cup=1 ounce	.5 to 20.5
Pork, without fat	½ pound	16.5 to 23.1
Radishes	6 med.=1⅔ ounces	2.3 to 23.7
Spinach, boiled	½ cup=3⅓ ounces	34.9

(*Table continued page 219*)

Food	Usual Portion and Weight	Milligrams of Sodium Chloride Per Ounce (A milligram is 1/1000 of a gram)
Trout, steamed	4 ounces	25
Turkey, breast	8 ounces	11.4 to 37.1
Turkey, leg	8 ounces	26.2 to 37.1
Turnips, white	¾ cup=4 ounces	10.5 to 29.7
Turnip greens	1 cup=3⅓ ounces	2.8 to 74.2

CHAPTER 32

What About Iodized Salt?

We have been told that iodized salt is necessary to prevent thyroid disorders. But it seems to us that there are other, and better ways, to get the minerals one needs.

Years ago when it first became apparent that lack of iodine in diet and water might render inhabitants of certain parts of the world susceptible to thyroid disorders, it was suggested that we solve this nutritional problem by adding iodine (as potassium iodide) to common table salt. In this way, it was argued, we could be sure that everyone got enough iodine to prevent any thyroid difficulties.

So in many sections of the world today iodized salt is available and in some countries its use is mandatory. However, a booklet entitled *Iodine in Drinking Waters, Vegetables, etc.,* by G. S. Fraps and J. F. Fudge published by the Agricultural and Mechanical College of Texas, tells us that potassium iodide added to the rations of various animals "rarely gave any beneficial results and sometimes gave detrimental ones." The surveys and experiments were done in areas where it was known that iodine was low in food and where goiter was prevalent. Nevertheless among sheep fed a daily ration of iodine, reproduction was abnormal; in the case of hogs, no beneficial results were found and there was some indication that the animals' use of calcium was disordered. Calves that had the iodine ate less hay and made considerably less gains in weight than those which did not. The conclusion of researchers Fraps and Fudge is, "The use of iodized table salt for human consumption in Texas is not recommended, except under the supervision of a competent physician. The use of iodized mineral mixtures for livestock in Texas is not recommended."

The Results of Iodized Salt Consumption

In a book called *Trace Elements in Food* (published by John Wiley and Sons, New York City), G. W. Monier-Williams, formerly of the Ministry of Health in England, has a great deal to say about the results of using iodized table salt. He says that it is pretty well agreed that the thyroid gland is of importance primarily in childhood and that treatment with iodine has not the same effects later on in life, except during pregnancy with the object of preventing goiter in the unborn child. Children tolerate iodine much better than adults, he says, and their iodine requirements are three times as great. It is alleged, he says, that adults constantly receiving small doses of iodine are likely to develop toxic symptoms.

One researcher in 1936, for instance, found that there was a marked increase in cases of hyperthyroidism (overactivity of the thyroid gland) in adults after iodized salt was introduced, which could be ascribed only to the action of the iodine in the salt. She believes that sensitivity to iodine is apparently quite common among adults, especially in goitrous regions. Other authorities have argued that the dose of iodine from table salt is very small indeed—far less than that given in medical treatment and that any excess of iodine over that required to maintain the thyroid gland in good health is promptly excreted in the urine.

Iodine and Fluorine Related

However, Monier-Williams reminds us that iodine belongs to the same chemical family as bromine (and fluorine, too, we might add). Bromides are excreted very slowly indeed from the body. "It may be that occasional massive doses of iodides cannot be considered in the same light as daily small doses continued for many years, and that the habitual use of iodized salt, while beneficial and even essential to children, is not altogether without risk to a certain small proportion of adults," he says. "Hyper-sensitiveness to iodine may be commoner in some districts than in others, but even if it affected only 2 per cent of the population, this would seem to be sufficient reason for objecting to the compulsory iodization of all household, or even all table salt." We go along with Dr. Monier-Williams 100 per cent in this opinion.

Move Against Iodized Salt

There are a number of other reasons why we object to iodized salt. One of them is that the potassium iodide is lost very rapidly from salt in cardboard containers. We are told that salt containing 5 parts per million of potassium iodide may lose as much as one-third of that within 6 weeks depending on the atmospheric conditions. So one never knows how much iodine may actually be in the box of salt he purchases. If he depends on the iodine to protect him from iodine deficiency, perhaps he will be cruelly deceived.

If, on the other hand, he is sensitive to iodine, the very small amount that may remain in that salt carton may be just enough to start trouble for him, taken day after day, and year after year. Consider for a moment—if 2 per cent of our population suffer from iodine sensitivity—that is more people than suffer from most of our great chronic diseases, so, of course, it is important to consider the reactions of these 2 per cent before we arbitrarily decree that everyone everywhere should take iodized salt.

"Doctored" Foods and Iodine Sensitivity

Our principal reason for avoiding iodized salt stems from another reason, however. We do not like "doctored" foods. The potassium iodide placed in table salt was not placed there by nature. So it is not accompanied by all the other substances that go along with iodine in foods. And it is not in what we call "organic combination" with the other ingredients of salt. This makes it a drug, from our point of view.

We know that potassium iodide is used extensively in medicine. In fact, one of the principal ingredients of several very famous cancer treatments is potassium iodide. But this, mark you, is treatment, given under the strict supervision of doctors, to very, very sick people. This is surely no indication that we should all be taking potassium iodide every day of our lives along with food!

What Is Iodine Sensitivity?

Iodine sensitivity is nothing to joke about. We have an article from the *Journal of the American Medical Association* for July 2, 1955, in which two Buffalo, New York, doctors discuss the case of a young patient who was suffering from a horrible dermatitis involving ulcers, eyelids swollen shut and so forth. He had been taking potassium iodide as an expectorant. It was believed that taking iodized table salt had sensitized the patient over a period of years so that when he got medicine that contained potassium iodide he reacted immediately, with a serious allergic response. The authors go on to tell us that fatalities have resulted even from the application of iodine *to the skin of sensitive persons.*

Now, of course, this does not mean that we should all stop getting any iodine at all in our diets. We must have iodine —a certain very small amount of it—or we will perish. But doesn't it seem that nature is trying to warn us not to take iodine in the concentrated, nonorganic form in which it appears in iodized salt? We have never heard of anyone reacting negatively to iodine in food—sea food or seaweed or mushrooms, because here the iodine is part of the food and combined with it in nature's proper way.

Should You Get Your Iodine from Salt?

Of course, it may have occurred to many readers to ask why we should mention iodized salt at all, since we do not think any of us should salt food, either in cooking or at the table—a highly pertinent comment to make. Of course, those of us who have stopped using salt or have cut down drastically will not need to worry about iodized salt. Yet, from letters, we know that these are the very people who worry most, for they write us in great concern. "Since I am not taking salt I am not getting any iodine—how shall I make up the loss?" Of course, our answer is, "Go right on skipping the salt and get your iodine from some organic source—sea food, kelp or seaweed." In fact, it seems to us that powdered kelp would be the best possible salt substitute for those readers who are trying desperately to cut down on salt, but haven't yet conquered that all-American gesture of reaching for the salt shaker before eating anything. Fill the salt shaker with powdered kelp—far, far richer in iodine than iodized salt, and with a pleasant taste, too.

We Shouldn't Salt Our Food Anyway

We have a new story about salt restriction which we think is extremely important. It is generally widely known these days that doctors prescribe salt-poor diets for heart patients. Now we find in a lead article in the *Journal of the American Medical Association* for November 26, 1955, that salt restriction helps greatly in cases of cirrhosis of the liver, too. The treatment was given to 30 patients in Bellevue Hospital by Dr. Charles S. Davidson. All of them suffered also from *ascites,* which means an accumulation of fluid in the abdomen. Of the 30 patients, 28 were known alcoholics, but two clearly were not, although the cause of their disease was not known. Four of the patients were considered well nourished. In 16 undernutrition was moderate and 10 of the patients were definitely severely undernourished.

These patients were put on a good nourishing diet rich in vitamins and minerals and their salt intake was restricted to 200 milligrams per day—that is about one-fifth of a gram.

The results were uniformly excellent. All of the patients improved. It took longer in some cases than in others—as long as 16 months in some cases, until the patient was free from the terrible swelling that deformed him and, of course, distorted all his body functions immeasurably. At the same time the nutritional status of all the patients improved, too, and the liver began to function much more normally. The doctors believe that the livers of the patients were actually regenerated. Improvement in a feeling of well being, return of appetite and successful readjustment of many body functions went along with the salt-poor diet.

Summary

Many disorders may be related to the consumption of too much salt. We have told of deafness, sinusitis, miscarriages, headaches, insomnia, hives, kidney diseases, Meniere's Syndrome, dropsy, pregnancy toxemia, epilepsy, migraine, high blood pressure and heart conditions relieved when a low-salt diet was taken.

There is no medical or physiological evidence that the

human body needs more sodium chloride (table salt) than is contained naturally in foods. Our continual daily overconsumption of salt (the only food we eat which has neither an animal nor vegetable source) may well be the cause of many more troubles than we know. Don't depend on iodized table salt for your iodine. Get it from a natural source like kelp or salt water fish, and cut down on salting your food until you arrive at that happy stage, where you will not miss the taste of salt at all and will, instead of tasting salt, be tasting the food you eat.

CHAPTER **33**

Is There a Need for Salt?

by J. I. RODALE

Many peoples in the world do not use salt at all, in fact, find it abhorrent. The same is true of animals and birds.

Civilized men are of the conviction that salt is one of the necessities of life, and the prospect of being forced to do without it for months would terrify most of us. However, the truth of the matter is that salt-using is as much a habit as is the use of tobacco with many individuals.

The Eskimos, far from civilized centers, have to get along without salt. They have no difficulty doing so. In fact, when a food tastes salty they won't eat it. They detest salt.

Vilhjalmur Stefansson, the famed Arctic explorer, in his book, *My Life with the Eskimo* (Macmillan), relates interestingly enough that when Eskimo visitors came too often to the expedition's encampment and brought with them voracious appetites which threatened to clean out the white man's larder, the Arctic adventurers would place a pinch of salt in the food—and the Eskimo would speedily depart for his own home where the fare was more tasty.

Stefansson tells of his experiences in giving up the use of salt. He says the longer you do without it, the less you want it. Of course, there is a certain period of time—about two weeks after one has stopped using it—that a great longing for salt seizes one. But this longing gradually passes away.

Stefansson says he has known white men who have claimed it more difficult to drop the salt habit than to cease using tobacco. However, adds the Arctic explorer, where the longing lasts more than a few weeks, the individual is suffering from a purely mental—or imaginary—desire for salt. Such an individual is quite likely to discover, when he starts using salt again, that it really doesn't taste pleasant to him after all. Stefansson asserts that he has known no person who enjoyed salt after being without it for half a year.

A white man without salt for a year is exactly like an Eskimo in his distaste for it—except that the white man knows that if he continues to use salt he will come to like it again, while the Eskimo is convinced that he will never acquire a liking for the substance.

However, Eskimos can and do acquire the salt habit when forced to eat salted foods. Eskimos who work on ships, where one must of necessity consume salt foods, learn the salt habit about as quickly as they do the tobacco habit.

Stefansson brings out the point that a necessary element of food cannot be dropped from the diet. For example, he tried to get along without fat. The longer he did without it, the more intense became his longing for it. In fact, this desire for fat became so powerful that it was more consuming than the hunger of a man who does without food altogether.

Salt, then, is not necessary to the diet where one eats meats. The Eskimos secure the amount of salt necessary to carry on life in the flesh of the animals they consume.

Other People Live Without Salt

The Islanders of Tristan da Cunha eat practically no salt and are extremely healthy, in fact, one of the healthiest races in the world. The Hunzas of Northern India, about whom I have written a book called *The Healthy Hunzas,* do not eat salt. They are in a valley cut off from the outside world and eat only what they raise themselves. Sir Robert McCarrison, a research medical scientist, who lived among them for 11 years did not see one case of cancer among them. They are one of the healthiest peoples in the world, with practically no disease of any kind. They, of course, grow their food by the organic method, using no chemical fertilizers.

True, salt has always been a popular part of the diet of most of mankind. The word *salary* comes from the word salt. The Roman soldiers were sometimes paid off in salt. Wars have been fought over salt deposits. The Bible mentions the salt of the covenant which denotes the communion which the Israelites had with God, salt being a symbol of friendship and incorruption. But the belief that man must add to his diet artificial salt, is based on a gross fallacy. It can be classed with the fallacy that you can catch a bird by sprinkling salt on its tail.

Ullmann, in the book referred to, says that there are races whose languages know no word for salt such as the East Finns, the Kamtchadales, the Tunguses and Kirgises, the Tudas, the shepherds of South American Pampas and Fire Islands, the natives of New Holland and the Fiji Islanders.

Dr. Dahlke, who visited the South Sea Islands in 1898, noted that the natives used absolutely no salt except what they got naturally in their foods. E. V. Ditmar noted the same thing in the wilds of Siberia.

Do Animals Need Salt?

There seems to be an idea that animals are aware of their need of salt and will travel miles to get it. This is nothing but a fallacy. We often hear this said about deer. But it is usually not the salt that these animals are after. It is other minerals in which the salt is contained that they crave. Let me give you a quotation which explains this. It was made by Dr. A. C. Morrow, in an article read at the convention of the American Pheasant Society in San Francisco recently. He said:

"Under feral conditions birds and animals migrate temporarily, seasonally or permanently to those places containing the minerals they need. The deer lick was utilized by many wild animals and by our range stock before they were fenced off. Deer licks often are soils containing more than the usual amount of potassium or magnesium sulphate, and not common salt as is usually supposed.

"At French Lick Springs, Indiana, I have observed birds, rabbits, squirrels and a raccoon drinking the overflow water from the famous Pluto spring, and drinking with an apparent gusto. Whether these birds and animals were natives or migrants I do not know. I do know that at the time I was unfamiliar with mineral requirements for birds and animals and was greatly puzzled as to why they drank a water I heartily disliked, while other sweet water was available.

"Later, observing cattle and sheep eating so-called alkali dirt to the exclusion of good stock salt, a chemist's report explained the seemingly depraved appetite was desire and a need for the magnesium and potassium sulphate in this soil."

The fact of the matter is that the animals need the minerals but not the salt and in some way their taste seems to guide them.

An Experiment on Salt Consumption by Animals

An experiment was made in the Department of Chemistry of the University of Pittsburgh, under grants from The Nutrition Foundation Incorporated and the Buhl Foundation, which was written up in the *Journal of Nutrition* of June 10, 1950. The experimenters, Scott, Verney and Morrissey, tried to determine whether rats would satisfy their need for salt if they were given a free choice to do so. In the experiment rats were first given a low sodium diet to make them sodium deficient. Then they were given opportunities to feed from two cups—one that contained a normal amount of sodium and the other a larger amount to see whether the animals would know enough to eat from the latter so as to correct their deficiency. The article pointed out the report's conclusion that it is difficult to determine whether preference for salt flavor is caused by a need for salt, is learned as a result of the beneficial effects of it or is only a flavor effect, actually unrelated to salt need. However, it further indicated that even when a change in salt need brings a change in salt appetite, then either the first or second causes must be in operation—but also that this does not mean the third explanation is without influence.

The experiment showed that sodium-deficient rats do not show a greater preference for sodium-containing diets than do control animals.

CHAPTER 34

Excessive Table Salt and Pregnancy

*Effects of salt in the diet show up plainly in the work of
a Dutch physician planning diets for expectant mothers.*

A Dutch gynecologist, Professor K. DeSnoo of Utrecht,
claims that excessive salt in the diet is mainly responsible for
eclampsia, a serious, often fatal, complication of pregnancy. Dr.
DeSnoo presents further evidence of the harmfulness of salt
during pregnancy in an article in the July 10, 1948, issue of the
Netherlands Medical Journal, a professional magazine corresponding in prestige to the *Journal of the American Medical
Association* in this country.

Dr. DeSnoo reminds us that civilized man has been salting his food for centuries, simply because food tastes better that
way, rather than because he needs the salt. He tells us that prehistoric man, living a nomadic life and eating plant and animal
foods as he found them in nature, did not know there was such
a thing as sodium chloride or table salt. There are still many
localities in the world where the use of salt is unknown and
some people who find the taste of salt extremely unpleasant.

There Is No Need for Additional Salt

These facts alone prove to us, says Dr. DeSnoo, that the
sodium chloride existing in its natural form in the food we eat
supplies us with quite enough of this substance, so that there
is no need for us to use additional salt. The sodium chloride
contained in the average unsalted daily diet would be about
one-half to one gram, whereas, salting food as we usually
do, we consume about 10 to 20 grams, surely an enormous overdose. Among the Dutch people, he says, the average sodium
content of the blood is 333 milligrams per 100 grams. In
an individual who does not salt his food, it may be as low as
320 milligrams. In cases of sickness it may fall as low as 300
milligrams or increase to 370 milligrams.

He grants that some salt may be necessary to replace that lost in food through cooking, but certainly we do not need 20 grams to replace a possible one gram that may be lost. It's astonishing, he marvels, that we can generally eat so much salt, year after year, without noticeable harm. Or is the harm being done, perhaps without our knowing it? Thirty milligrams of salt given to a healthy person will produce edema—a swollen condition in which water collects in the body tissues. This caused by the fact that salt attracts water, as anyone knows who has tried to use a salt shaker on a damp day. Drops of water are clustered even on the outside of the shaker, let alone all the additional moisture that has caked the salt inside.

During the last months of pregnancy, there is lessened tolerance for salt in the expectant mother's body, as evidenced by frequent cases of edema. When salt is omitted or even decreased in the diet, the edema disappears. For a long time, comments Dr. DeSnoo, this proof of salt as a cause of pregnancy complications was not recognized by physicians, for sometimes women on a "saltless" diet did fall prey to eclampsia. From his own experience Dr. DeSnoo says regretfully, he knows that prescribing a saltless diet to an apparently cooperative patient is not enough. By regular checking of the urine, the physician must find out whether or not this diet has been adhered to.

Effect of Saltless Diet on Miscarriages

There are many women whose unborn children die during successive pregnancies, who have had living children when their diet was saltless during pregnancy. Twelve women from Dr. DeSnoo's own clinic were used as examples in a medical article published back in 1917. These 12 women had had a total of 77 children, of whom 55 were born dead. Ten of the women succeeded in having healthy living children after they had been put on a saltless diet. Some of these 10 women started to use salt again and once again had interrupted pregnancies. Those who continued their saltless diets bore other healthy live children. No other therapy was used, no other conditions of the patients' lives were changed, so it cannot be doubted that the saltless diet produced results little short of miraculous.

During the last war when food was rationed in Holland, living conditions were not of the best and, one would suppose, all conditions making for health were at a low ebb. But later research has revealed that fewer children were born dead during the war years than either before or after the war. The same was true in England and Switzerland. In Holland 1700 fewer children died before or during birth while Holland was in the grip of the war. Other writers have attributed this tremendous decrease in miscarriages and other complications to various war conditions: there was a tendency to get more sleep and more exercise and to eat less food. What about salt consumption? Salt was not rationed and apparently as much salt was eaten as during the previous years. However, we'll have more to say about this later. Figures for miscarriages per 1000 births are given below. Note the drop of almost 7 per 1000 during two of the war years:

Miscarriages per 1000 births in Holland 1931-1946

1931-1935	25.1
1936-1939	24.9
1940	25.08
1941	21.26
1942	19.33
1943	18.47
1944	18.50
1945	19.38
1946	20.29

To arrive at an interpretation of these figures, Dr. DeSnoo studied the mortality figures of his own clinic from 1927 on. During those 21 years about 40,000 expectant mothers were cared for there. As methods of treatment at the clinic did not change, it seems logical that, at least among this representative group of the population, some valid conclusions may be drawn.

Decrease in Mortality Rates During War

The death rate for developmental disturbances (that is complications during pregnancy) is the same for the period before the war, during the war and after the war. The death rate for difficulties during birth decreased during the war. The death rate for diseases of the mother and "unknown causes" remained constant up to 1941, then *showed a decrease of 45 per cent during the war*. Hence the greatest saving of life among the children occurs in that group where the cause of death was either an illness of the mother or an unknown cause. This means that death because of hemorrhaging, venereal disease, diabetes, and so forth did not decrease. But death from eclampsia and various unknown kinds of poisoning did.

Of all possible factors involved, says Dr. DeSnoo, food is by far the most important. The fact remains that edematous conditions (waterlogging) decreased decidedly, and that healthy women do not become edematous on a low-salt diet. So the only possible conclusion is that less salt was consumed during the war.

How Less Salt Improved Health

According to national health statistics in Holland from 1937 to 1941 there was an average of 21.7 per cent of edematous patients. In 1942 it dropped to 16 per cent. From then on it dropped steadily every year until 1945 when it was 9 per cent. In 1946 it rose again to 20.5 per cent. In pregnancies where serious toxic states developed, the same was true. From 28 per cent in 1937-41, the percentage dropped steadily each year until 1945, when it was only 12 per cent. The next year it increased again to 29 per cent.

Dr. DeSnoo is convinced that this decrease is due to a decrease in the amount of salt actually consumed. The sales of salt did not decrease. But, in general, people were consuming less food and hence, in an age when food is as heavily salted as it is in our century, food rationing would produce this evident decrease in the amount of salt consumed. Bread, for instance, is apparently very heavily salted in Holland, and bread was rationed by 1941.

Less Salt Is Important for All of Us

We must study much more closely all the pertinent facts concerning the food of expectant mothers, says Dr. DeSnoo, and we must try our best to find the optimum food, which will be food that comes close to the natural food of our ancestors, before it had been changed by cooking or salting or the addition of all sorts of other ingredients. We must battle even more strongly against the salt-habit, not only for the sake of mothers and children, but for the population in general. In Indonesia, he tells us, salt is strictly rationed. No one receives more than 4 grams per person per day. Eclampsia is practically unknown, and the number of miscarriages is extremely small. There is, of course, recognition of the unhealthy role of salt in high blood pressure, for even in our country low-salt or saltless diets are commonly prescribed by physicians for these patients.

We have noticed among our letters from readers, an increasing number who are eating less salt and reporting improvement in health. We also get lots of letters from people marveling on how many of their friends are on salt-free or salt-poor diets. For those of you who feel that a diet lacking in salt would be extremely monotonous and dull, we recommend *The Salt-Free Diet Cook Book* by Emil G. Conason, M.D. and Ella Metz, published by Lear Publishers in New York City, 1949. This includes many recipes and menus for patients whose physicians have placed them on diets as low in sodium as possible. In the book the amount of sodium present in the average portion of every food is given, along with the calories that food contains. So if you do without salt and are afraid you may not be eating a normal amount of sodium, you may easily check your menus against the lists of food given in the book.

SECTION 8

CITRUS FRUIT

Evidence from medical and dental journals indicates that large quantities of citrus fruit juices may harm teeth and health in general. Individuals who are especially sensitive have found that by omitting citrus juice they have cleared up stubborn cases of bleeding gums, headaches, fatigue and so forth.

We suggest that not more than one or two oranges, grapefruit halves or tangerines be eaten every week—not juiced.

CHAPTER **35**

Reduction in Citrus Consumption Is Beneficial

Egon V. Ullmann, M.D., in his book, *Diet in Sinus Infections and Colds* (The Macmillan Company, 1933, out of print), says:

"A word may be said here about the abundant use of citrus fruits in relation to calcium. Like everywhere else, so here, too much may be as harmful as not enough. Years ago, Von Noorden showed that citric acid precipitates calcium and makes it ineffective. The enforcement of the calcium action against inflammation by natural ways is one of the main principles of our diet. If large amounts of citric acid are taken the effect of this principle will be lessened. It is in my opinion unnecessary to drink huge amounts of orange juice and grapefruit juice in order to provide the organism with vitamin C. For this purpose minute amounts are sufficient. In cases where calcium as a drug is given, citrus fruits should be left out for about 4 to 5 hours after the calcium is given. The second reason for which citrus juices are given is their alkaline effect on metabolism. This alkaline effect can be produced just as well with other fruit or vegetable juices. I, therefore, advise the reduction in the amount of orange and grapefruit juices to some extent. This should be remembered especially in cases suspected of calcium deficiency. The problem is different when quick action against acidosis is needed, as in very acute conditions or before and after an anesthetic."

Editorial Speaks Against Citrus

The following editorial appeared in the *Journal of Home Economics,* June, 1951, commenting on an editorial which appeared in the February 3, 1951, issue of the *Journal of the American Medical Association.*

"Erosion of the teeth by acids was recognized as the fundamental cause of dental caries a half century ago. Experimental evidence has supported this hypothesis repeatedly during the past 50 years, both in small animals and in man. The demonstration of a high acidophilus count in carious mouths suggested a mechanism for the production of acid from food residues in the mouth. In a group of caries-free children, the buffer capacity of the saliva was found to be strikingly higher than it was in those with active caries. That contact of food with the tooth surface is a prerequisite for caries production was demonstrated in an experiment with young rats in which a caries-producing ration was fed through a stomach tube without resulting in caries.

" 'Soft' drinks, which usually contain a considerable concentration of organic acid, and various acid-sugar combinations, as well as acid fruit juices were all found to produce etching of the enamel and dentine in the teeth of laboratory rats, hamsters, and dogs. The buffer action of the saliva tends to counteract the erosive action. Tomato and prune juice were found to have a less pronounced effect than apple, grape, pineapple, orange, and grapefruit juices. The fruits themselves were found to produce much less etching of the tooth substance than the juices from these fruits.

"Although there are doubtless nutritional and metabolic factors favoring the sound development and the integrity of the teeth, the presence of acids in the mouth appears to be a prominent factor in dental decay."

Citric Acid and Tooth Damage

Grapefruit juice has now been proven to have an effect many times more erosive on the teeth than grapefruit eaten in sections. An article in the *Journal of Nutrition* for January 10, 1951, describes the experiments of Ross A. Gortner, Jr., and Reuben K. Kenigsberg of Wesleyan University, who attempted to discover what it is about the juice that makes it so much more erosive.

They tell us that it has been known for many years that acid fruits and beverages can damage the teeth considerably. In tests done in 1950, it was shown that the juices of acid fruits were 3 to 10 times more erosive than the same amount of fruit eaten in sections. It was believed that the explanation might be some protective substance in the fruit itself which was not present in the juice, or some ingredient created in the juice after it has been removed from the fruit, or, possibly, a difference in the way in which the juice and the whole fruit come into contact with the teeth while the juice, or fruit, is in the mouth.

What Is the Real Cause of Tooth Erosion?

All these possible explanations were taken into account and tested in the experiments described by Gortner and Kenigsberg. First of all, two groups of laboratory animals were tested with the juice and the sections of grapefruit. It was found that the animals receiving juice developed about 3.5 times more erosion than those who ate sectional fruit. Then a simulated fruit was made using grapefruit juice mixed with a gelatin material. The animals eating this "fruit" showed no greater tooth erosion than those who ate the original grapefruit, so it seems that no destructive substance is present in the juice and no protective substance is present in the whole fruit.

Then the experimenters tested to see whether the effect of the salivary glands reacting on the juice or the fruit might make a difference. Rats whose salivary glands had been removed were tested along with normal rats. It was found that there was no noticeable difference in the amount of erosion resulting. Hence, the only possible explanation left, these experimenters believe, is that the difference in the manner of ingesting the juice and the whole fruit is responsible for the erosion.

A Dentist's Evidence on Citrus Fruit Consumption

Dr. Henry Hicks, D.D.S., is convinced that excessive citrus juice consumption is responsible for unpleasant symptoms in the mouth and health generally. The entire article from which this is taken appeared originally in the magazine *Oral Surgery, Oral Medicine and Oral Pathology* for July, 1951.

"My subject," says Dr. Hicks, "one of the most confused and abused of the past two decades, has been of special interest to me for the past 15 years. Excessive citrus juice consumption and its effect on the superficial and deep tissues of the oral cavity has been overlooked by professional and lay groups alike because citrus fruit juice has been oversold to the public. It has become the standard, highly nationalized, and most advertised health food in America, its vitamin C factor a cure-all! Citrus fruit and vitamin C have become synonymous in the minds of most people. While we cannot deny that citrus fruit is one of the best sources rich in vitamin C and that vitamin C is essential for normal connective tissue and bones and for normal metabolism, we overlook the fact that other substances which are also present in citrus fruits may do more harm than the good that is derived from the vitamin C when taken in excess."

It would be uncommon for one to consume 3 or 4 whole oranges at one time, Dr. Hicks believes, but it is common for one to consume the equivalent of this in the form of juice. Those who do this do not stop with that, but eat or drink some other similar fruit containing citric, tartaric, or malic acid during the day. So over a period of time, too much of these substances must be handled by the body and Dr. Hicks believes that this is the reason for the harmful effects his case histories show.

During the last two decades many professional and lay persons have written that large quantities of citrus fruit juices are healthy. For instance, says Dr. Hicks, a leading magazine recommends for prettier skin a large glass of fruit juice for breakfast, stewed fruit, and a large glass of fruit juice for lunch, with a fruit cup and stewed fruit or gelatin dessert for dinner. A standard obstetrical text recommends the daily consumption of about 10 ounces of orange juice daily and the use of one-half grapefruit twice daily, to take the place of rich desserts.

Citrus Juice Overemphasized in Average Diet

"These are only two examples of the numerous diets which contain quantities of citrus fruits and are being followed for other purposes such as weight reducing, treatment of hypertension, and treatment of common colds. These diets may or may not have merits. However, there is the question of whether in an attempt to meet adequately the requirements of vitamin C, citrus fruit juice, as the sole source, is not overemphasized. Many other fruits and vegetables are fairly good sources. Green peppers, for instance, are extremely rich in vitamin C, but no one would think of eating three or four peppers at a time."

I have discussed this aspect of the subject in detail, says Dr. Hicks, because it is not my purpose to disagree with the findings of investigators regarding the beneficial effects of moderate quantities of citrus fruits upon connective tissue, but the words "moderate quantities" should be strongly emphasized. We have learned to recognize the results of an overdose of drugs, food and drink. It is rather shortsighted on our part not to conceive that serious effects might result from this innocent food drink, the citrus juice.

Mouth Tissues Affected by Citrus Juice

After 15 years of the closest kind of observation and record-keeping, Dr. Hicks finds that there is an element of harm for the mouth tissues in the drinking of large quantities of citrus juice. These effects include easy and excessive bleeding, teeth that move about in their sockets, and tissues of the mouth that become hypersensitive. Other physical symptoms have included headaches, constant physical exhaustion, stomach pains, dizziness, prolonged colds and joint pains.

Starting in 1932, Dr. Hicks kept careful records of all patients, questioning them closely about their daily intake of citrus juices. All those whose gums bled easily and whose teeth were hypersensitive were instructed either to eliminate or decrease the amount of citrus juices they were taking and to substitute calcium, vitamin B, and ascorbic acid (50 milligrams daily), when it was found that these were deficient in their diets.

Case Histories from Dr. Hicks' File

Case 1. This patient, a school teacher 21 years old, habitually drank large quantities of citrus juices. When she came to Dr. Hicks in 1934 with an aching tooth, he found that she had a number of cavities, but her gums and the tissues of her mouth appeared to be fairly normal. He advised her to reduce the amount of citrus juice she was taking, but she refused to believe that this was wise. By 1937 she had a number of new cavities and by 1939 a great many more. She had also developed a severe case of sinusitis. By 1944 her teeth were loose in their sockets and were sensitive to air and touch. Her gums bled easily. She also suffered from exhaustion, nausea, stomach pains and loss of weight. Finally, convinced of their harmful effects, she stopped taking citrus juices on March 10, 1949, supplementing her diet with brewer's yeast, calcium gluconate and vitamin D. Two months later, her gums showed great improvement with less redness and bleeding. Her teeth were also firmer in their sockets. Up to 1951 the patient, avoiding citrus juices entirely, regained her health, showed no evidence of bleeding gums or loose teeth, had no new cavities and no fillings. Her sinusitis also disappeared.

Case 2. A woman of 28 came to Dr. Hicks in 1931 with many cavities, shrinking gums and redness of the gums. They also bled at the slightest touch. This patient had been drinking 6 to 8 ounces of citrus juice daily for 4 years. During the following 6 years she continued to drink citrus juices against Dr. Hicks' advice. Her cavities increased and her teeth began to loosen in their sockets. She also complained of anemia, stomach pains, acne and physical exhaustion by 1941. She was again advised to give up citrus juices and did so immediately. By August 1, 1942, her mouth appeared almost normal, her teeth were more firmly imbedded and her general health was much improved. Up to 1945 she had only two additional cavities and from 1945 to 1950 no new cavities. Today her teeth are firm, her gums do not bleed. Her acne disappeared along with the complaints of exhaustion and stomach pains. However, these pains recur when acid food is eaten.

Case 3. A woman aged 33 whose teeth and gums were in excellent condition came to Dr. Hicks for examination. She showed no signs of tooth movement or recession of gums. She ate 3 whole oranges per week, alternating them each day with other fruits. From 1925 to 1950 her mouth was completely normal, with no gum symptoms.

Case 4. A man aged 37 came to Dr. Hicks in 1936 with a great many cavities, red gums which bled when touched and symptoms of stomach and digestive disorders. He had been drinking from 6 to 8 ounces of orange juice daily. He was advised to take only 3 whole oranges per week and alternate them with other fruits. By 1938 only one additional cavity had developed. Since then there were no additional cavities, his gums returned to a normal and healthy state and his physical condition improved.

Case 5. A 35-year-old woman who had had diabetes all her life came to Dr. Hicks, believing that she should have all of her teeth extracted. Her gums were blue, bled profusely at the slightest touch and exuded pus. Her teeth were all loose. Her physical condition was poor and she was in a state of exhaustion. Her complexion was yellowish. She was able to do only a minimum of housework and, for this, she found it necessary to consume 5 oranges a day for quick energy. She used only standard diabetic foods and was on a regular schedule of insulin. Oral examination and X-ray revealed pyorrhea of all teeth.

With her physician's cooperation, her diet was changed as follows: rather than 5 oranges daily, she was told to eat only 3 oranges weekly, alternating with other unsweetened fruits. She was given calcium lactate, cod liver oil, vitamin C and brewer's yeast. Later her oranges were reduced to two a week. Thorough gum treatment was performed and rigid home care was instituted. In 3 months, from November, 1949, to February, 1950, all bleeding and pus disappeared and all teeth began to tighten. By the beginning of May all her mouth tissue appeared normal and her teeth were quite firm. Her physical condition improved until she was living a completely normal life, "with plenty of energy and vitality to carry on the same as any individual without her affliction. There had been no change in insulin requirement and no necessity for any quick energy food."

Conclusions After Fifteen Years of Observation

Dr. Hicks' conclusions are that during the 15 years in which he kept these records he found that 3 oranges or 3 grapefruit halves, or one orange and two grapefruit halves per week, interspaced with one normal helping daily of other fruits, together with good dental care and adequate diet, will maintain absolutely normal oral health.

He says that the following conditions are traceable to the habitual ingestion of large quantities of citrus fruits regardless of other diet factors: 1. Hyperemia (a condition in which the gums bleed easily). Between 1 and 3 years are required in the majority of cases with otherwise adequate diet. In occasional cases hyperemia may develop within 6 months. 2. Hypersensitivity of the teeth will usually occur in about 6 months to one year. 3. Mobility of the teeth will be apparent in from 3 to 7 years. 4. Resorption of the bone will begin in from 7 to 10 years.

The general quality of the diet influences the speed of change caused by the ingestion of excessive amounts of citrus juices, says Dr Hicks. Those taking diets deficient in vitamin B and minerals, together with excessive amounts of citrus juices are more easily susceptible to pyorrhea, while those with good adequate diets and excessive citrus juice intake had less serious symptoms at any given time. Those with poor diets who did not take excessive citrus juices did not develop symptoms. However, with good diets and an elimination of excess citrus juices, all mouth tissues of all patients returned to normal rapidly and remained so. The usual age at which mobility of the teeth and definite resorption of the bone becomes evident is about 32 to 35. Complaints such as exhaustion, headaches, digestive disorders and joint pains may occur from the age of 35 to 45.

Should We Totally Condemn Citrus Fruits?

In commenting on the vitamins B and D prescribed, Dr. Hicks mentions that, for controls, there were many cases in which the improvement was obtained by simply reducing the intake of juices alone, without supplementing the diet with vitamins B and D. However, with the addition of these vitamins, the recovery becomes more rapid.

"Again I wish to emphasize," says Dr. Hicks, "that citrus fruit is an excellent source of vitamin C which is necessary for connective tissue repair, but other substances present in this source seem to be the detrimental factor. In all cases where excessive juice was eliminated and pure vitamin C substituted, the patient improved both generally and orally. When calcium, vitamins D and B were added, the result appeared to be more rapid and the recovery positive. The current popular belief that ingestion of large quantities of citrus fruit juice is healthful should be carefully appraised. Citrus fruit in moderate amounts as a source of vitamin C in the diet is not to be condemned, it would seem that more than 2 or 3 oranges or one grapefruit per week is excessive in view of the fact that vitamin C is obtainable from other sources."

CHAPTER **36**

An Allergy to Citric Acid

Ample testimony from medical research shows that citric acid is probably the offending substance in citrus fruit that many people find unpleasant.

Allergy to foods manifests itself in different ways and can give rise to a host of clinical manifestations, according to an article in the November, 1956, *Journal of Allergy.* If, for instance, a child is allergic to eggs, he may develop a swelling of the mouth and an attack of asthma, when he eats eggs. The allergist can then give a skin test which will have a positive reaction. He will find, too, that there are "antibodies" circulating in the blood of the child. These are substances which appear in the blood to overcome the toxic effects of the allergenic substance.

Given a set of circumstances like these, it is easy enough for the allergy specialist to locate the offending food and remove it from the diet. But in many instances things are not quite this simple. The skin test does not "take"—that is, there is no reaction in the skin—no swelling, no redness, etc. There is then no way for the specialist to decide what is causing the allergy except to eliminate various foods one at a time, and see which is apparently causing the trouble.

Cause of Canker Sores Unknown

Dr. Louis Tuft and Dr. L. N. Ettelson of Philadelphia, writing on "Canker Sores from Allergy to Weak Organic Acids," in the *Journal of Allergy,* tell us that a patient who had been allergic for years had come to accept his almost continual canker sores as inevitable. Through various tests the doctors found that he was actually allergic only to citric acid and acetic acid. So long as he avoided foods in which these acids occurred, he was well.

The patient, a member of the Air Force, had been tested for allergies and had been found to be allergic to milk and a few other foods, dust, feathers, pyrethrum, and ragweed. He was given desensitizing treatments for more than a year because of "migraine" headaches and asthma. After this treatment he had less trouble with asthma, but he still got headaches when he ate chocolate or milk. The canker sores which he had had most of his life continued.

When the patient was discharged from the Air Force, he went to college in Philadelphia. Skin tests there revealed that he was allergic to house dust, ragweed, timothy, and plantain. His reactions to milk and chocolate were negative. While taking a course of desensitizing for these allergens, the patient continued to have canker sores and headaches. Also, frequent spells of lassitude, vague pains, irritability, and inability to concentrate.

When he came finally to see Drs. Tuft and Ettelson, he reported that he attributed the canker sores to eating sugar, sweets, "acid foods" or certain alcoholic drinks. He had found that taking alcoholic drinks alone did not bring on canker sores. But if he took them in fruit juice he invariably developed symptoms. The doctors found that the canker sores followed also the eating of grapes or anything made from grapes, chocolates and certain kinds of candy and carbonated beverages.

It seemed that the allergy might be due to citric acid— either the kind that appears in citrus and other fruits, or the kind that is added to many other products in the processing, such as soft drinks. The patient, who was now eating a restricted diet, began having spells of weakness so he took to eating candy. Chocolate bars gave him gas, headache, fatigue and brought on the canker sores. He took to eating Necco wafers.

Citric Acid Is Definitely the Cause

Then he began to notice that after he ate a yellow, green or orange wafer, he would notice a puckering or itching sensation in his mouth and discomfort in the stomach. The cinnamon, white or chocolate wafers gave him no trouble. To eliminate the possibility that sugar was to blame, he then ate pure cane sugar cubes and also rock candy without difficulty. Then he tried pure bitter chocolate that had not been processed into candy or candy bars. This caused no symptoms. But eating one of the regular candy bars brought on symptoms. (Candy bars contain citric acid.)

"This seemed to indicate that the patient was not allergic to chocolate itself but to substances combined with it. As a result of these experiences, the patient became quite adept at determining whether anything he ate or drank contained citric acid. Thus, for example, he found that he could not tolerate certain cough drops or troches (such as the red-colored Smith Brothers), whereas others were all right. This also was true of certain beverages; for example, he could drink unlimited amounts of Hires Root Beer (which, according to the label, does not contain citric acid) without symptoms, whereas one Coca Cola or even club soda (both of which contain citric acid) induced canker sores. As a result of experiences, the patient became label-conscious, inspecting all labels for citric acid and avoiding foods containing it. By strictly avoiding all substances containing citric acid, the patient could remain relatively free of canker sores for long periods and also could induce the sores at will by eating citric acid containing foods."

Proof Against Citric and Acetic Acids

The doctors then tested their patient with samples of citric acid and foods containing it, samples of which were placed on a certain spot within his mouth. Sure enough, every food containing citric acid produced an ulcer at that point. Other substances such as aspirin, bicarbonate of soda and so forth did not. Then other naturally occurring acids were tested in the same way. Tartaric acid, acetic acid, lactic acid, uric acid, ascorbic acid, a B vitamin and benzoic acid were tested. Of these acetic acid, occurring in vinegar, was strongly positive. Tartaric acid and lactic were mildly positive.

The reaction to acetic acid was surprising, but it appeared to explain why the patient got canker sores after eating foods like cole slaw, potato salad or beef cooked in vinegar. Vinegar is, of course, a source of acetic acid. The patient eliminated foods containing these two acids from his diet and suffered no more from canker sores except when he unknowingly ate some food that contained one of these acids.

Does this experience prove that these two acids are responsible for all canker sores? Not at all. Four researchers at Columbia University took up the challenge implied in the article we reported on above and tested 10 of their patients who suffered from chronic canker sores. They placed test swabs containing acetic acid, citric acid and ascorbic acid in the mouths of the patients and made careful checks for a period of a week. Not a single one of the patients showed any sensitivity to the tests. These researchers conclude, therefore, that the patient studied by Drs. Tuft and Ettelson was an isolated case and should be more or less ignored. This article called "Recurrent Ulcerative (Aphthous) Stomatitis: Intradermal Food Test Studies" appeared in *The Journal of Allergy*, September, 1958.

What About Other Food Additives?

Our conclusions are quite different. We are not allergists, of course. We are concerned chiefly with the troubles of the average modern American trying to find his way to good health in the complexity of today's food world. Citric acid is one food additive used in a great many different foods. In the book entitled *The Use of Chemical Additives in Food Processing*, published by National Academy of Science in Washington, D. C., we found listed some of the foods in which citric acid may be added during processing: buttermilk, mayonnaise, salad dressing, French dressing, cheese products, fruit butters, jams and jellies, canned vegetables, canned artichokes, cheese spreads, sherbets, candy, canned figs, dried egg whites, fruit juices, soft drinks, frozen fruits, frozen dairy products, margarine, lard, frozen peaches, wine, canned fish cakes, piecrust mix, prepared breakfast cereal, soup base and wine and beer.

This is one food additive to which an individual was found to be allergic only by the persistent efforts of two cooperative doctors. There are almost a thousand food additives being used in our food today and the number is increasing constantly. Where are you going to start to find out which of these food additives may be the one causing allergic trouble in yourself or some member of your family?

Beware of Citric Acid

Meanwhile, it is helpful, we think, to know that citric acid (even though it occurs quite naturally in many foods) can produce allergic symptoms such as the one patient described above suffered from. Possible citric acid may be at the heart of trouble you or some member of your family has with certain foods. It won't hurt to experiment. Try leaving the foods out of your meals for several weeks. See if your difficulty is relieved.

The best way, of course, to make certain you don't get any citric acid that has been added by processors for one reason or another to food is to shun like the plague any of the foods listed above. They are all processed, canned or frozen foods. They shouldn't be on your market list anyway. Eat fresh foods and prepare them at home, yourself, so that you know everything that goes into them.

CHAPTER **37**

Fruit Drinks and Tooth Erosion

Other kinds of fruit drinks, in addition to citrus, can prove disastrous to tooth health.

The child with a soda bottle in his hand has become almost as notorious a symbol of modern American civilization as the child with the toy gun. We know, in a general way, that soda is not good for us, for often you hear mothers protesting the second or even third bottle of soda. "It'll spoil your appetite for dinner," they say. And it does spoil your appetite for dinner. Unfortunately this is not all it spoils.

Our hesitancy in giving the children free rein with the soda bottles indicates that we have some inkling of possible harm in this quarter, but rare indeed is the mother who has any appreciation of the fact that fruit juices are likely to harm the teeth. On the contrary, most of us think of fruit juices as the most healthful of beverages.

Research Done on Fruit Drinks

We were interested to find in the May 6, 1958, issue of the *British Dental Journal* a piece of research done by 3 famous British scientists on this very subject. They (P. J. Holloway, May Mellanby and R. J. C. Stewart) tell us that reports of tooth erosion from fruit drinks have been studied for years. In 1907 W. D. Miller reported loss of calcium from tooth structure due to excessive fruit consumption, and Pickerill in 1912 noted that tooth enamel wasted away in persons who sucked lemons.

In recent years, there has been considerably more research on the subject, due to the fact that consumption of fruit juices (especially canned ones) has increased along with the tremendous increase in the drinking of soft drinks—cola or soda. Many research projects have shown that tooth erosion produced in laboratory animals by the consumption of fruit juices and acid beverages has its counterpart in man.

The Meaning of Erosion

What do we mean by erosion? It is quite different from tooth decay, although there seems to be considerable evidence that sweetened drinks produce tooth decay, too. But erosion is a loss of tooth substance leaving rounded outlines, increased sensitivity and dental fillings standing up from the general tooth surface.

In the tests which are the subject of this article, rats were given different substances as their only source of liquid. All of them were given the same diet. The drinks used were as follows: 20 different kinds of fruit squash (which, we assume, resembles our American fruit drinks like lemonade), cola and other carbonated beverages, canned and fresh fruit juices, iced lollipops (popsicles) and fruit candies.

In addition, another group of rats was given distilled water, another group citric acid and sugar combined, and a third group just sugar in water.

Some Conclusions

All the soft drinks brought about erosion of the teeth. The fruit drinks gave about the same amount of erosion as the mixture of citric acid and sugar. Rats which drank distilled water, whether or not the water contained sugar, did not show tooth erosion. The degree of erosion from cola and other carbonated drinks was not so great as that produced by the fruit-flavored drinks. This fact clearly incriminates the acid fruit in the beverage as the cause of the erosion. It was also found that the type and amount of the sweetening agent in any of the acid solutions made a difference in the amount of erosion. Sucrose, glucose or saccharin increased the erosion, but replacing these by an equivalent amount of fructose reduced the erosion by 20 per cent. Note that saccharin fruit mixtures (widely used in this country in the so-called noncalorie soft drinks) created as much erosion as the sugar-fruit drinks did.

Candies made from acid fruits and sugar, popsicles and freshly-made fruit juice were tested as well as black-currant juice and bottled rose hip syrup. The latter two are oustanding sources of vitamin C in England. The orange juice and the black-currant juice both produced considerable erosion. The rose hip syrup was less destructive. The rose hip syrup is, of course, sweetened to make it palatable. The popsicles caused less destruction of enamel than the candies.

Findings Indicate Saliva Resists Acid

Speculations on why the different concoctions should have the effects they do dwell mostly on the acidity of the foods and drinks tested. It is agreed that extremely acid foods or drinks cause erosion if they are held in the mouth. But there seems to be something in the saliva which protects against the corrosive strength of the acid. So the final amount of destruction depends not only on how much acid there is in the beverage, but also on the resistance of the saliva. It is generally agreed that sweetening the beverage makes it more corrosive, probably because sweetened beverages are held in the mouth longer. In a test on extracted teeth in either sweetened or unsweetened solutions, equally acid, the same amount of calcium was lost from each tooth.

Have the above results any bearing on human tooth disease, ask the authors. "The amounts of acid beverages normally drunk by adult human beings are probably too small to be of any great significance (remember, these authors live in England), but in the young and especially with certain methods of consumption, their influence is without doubt deleterious."

Sucking on anything that contains fruit syrup seems to result in tooth erosion. So eating popsicles which are held in the mouth for long periods of time would seem to be particularly undesirable. The same is true of fruit-and-sugar candy and especially lollipops or all-day suckers.

We are sure that readers will not be surprised at these findings in regard to sweet candies, frozen lollipops and soft drinks. All of us surely know that these things are harmful in other ways as well. The damage done by the sugar content of such foods is not limited to tooth erosion. Sugar in the digestive tract is absorbed much too quickly and goes immediately into the blood, shooting the blood sugar level up far too high and then plunging it down to dangerous depths. Sugar destroys the calcium-phosphorus ration in the blood, bringing about another dangerous condition. Sugar depletes the body's store of B vitamins—a rare enough vitamin in these days of refined foods.

Fruit Juice—An Unnatural Food

So we are hardly surprised to read of the harmfulness of soft drinks and candy. But the news that fruit juice can erode teeth must come as a shock to many readers. Yet we must caution against these beverages. In many fruit juices such as the canned varieties and especially in canned fruit nectars there is a great deal of added sugar. As we have seen in the testimony from the *British Dental Journal,* both the sugar and the acid in the juice cause trouble where teeth are concerned.

Freshly made fruit juice seems to be acid enough to erode teeth, too, even though not to the extent of the other foods tested. Does this mean we should avoid all fruit juices? What about freshly squeezed orange juice? What about frozen citrus juices? We say no to all of them.

Any way you look at it, fruit juice is an unnatural food. We were meant to eat fruit, not drink it. Dr. Melvin Page of Florida who is an authority on foods and the effect on the human body, has reminded us that we have a thirst center and a hunger center in our brains. When we drink something that was meant to be eaten we confuse this mechanism. Our hunger center would have told us we wanted only one orange. But it is not consulted when we drink the juice of 2 or 3 oranges. The thirst center is involved and we may not even be thirsty! So we give our digestive tracts something we don't actually want.

Our Biggest Mistake—Processing

Finally, the very worst thing of all that we do to orange juice is to strain it. And, of course, all frozen and canned juices have been strained. The bioflavonoids, fully as important as vitamin C in fruit juice, exist in the fibrous parts of the fruit. In citrus fruit they are present chiefly in the white inner lining of the skin, and in the white fibers that separate the segments. Juicing fruit means that you throw away all these valuable food elements. And whatever small bit of them might remain is finally lost when you strain the juice.

We strongly recommend eating fruit—not juicing it. And, because of its high content of citric acid which causes difficulty to many people, we believe you should not eat more than several oranges or grapefruits halves a week. Get your vitamin C and bioflavonoids from other fruits and from rose hips.

And, of course, watch your diet and take bone meal for good strong teeth!

CHAPTER **38**

Citrus Fruits or Rose Hips for Vitamin C?

We believe that rose hips are a far better source of vitamin C than citrus fruit. They are inexpensive, pleasant to eat and rich in many vitamins and minerals.

We think that perhaps the worst angle to the citrus juice question is the present-day consumption of quantities of frozen and canned citrus juices. We somehow seem to think that we don't have time to eat a piece of fruit properly, but must pour it from a container and drink it. And the frozen ones and canned ones are so handy! Many of them have added sugar, coloring matter and other serious drawbacks from the health standpoint, aside from which is the fact that they are not fresh! Canned fruit juice has been heated to high temperatures, destroying much of its food value. Frozen fruit juice, while it has not been heated, still does not have the health-giving qualities of fresh fruit.

Difference Between Citric and Ascorbic Acid

What is the erosive factor in citrus juice? Apparently the citric acid, for the higher the content of citric acid the more erosive the juice seems to be. We want to make certain that readers are clear in their minds about the difference between citric acid and ascorbic acid. Citric acid whose chemical formula is C6 H8 O7 occurs in free form in certain fruits—the citrus fruits, currants and others. It is responsible to a large extent for the acid taste of these fruits.

Ascorbic acid is vitamin C with a chemical formula C6 H8 O6. It is absolutely essential for human health and, since it is soluble in water, your body excretes it easily, so you must get some ascorbic acid every day. It occurs in fresh raw fruits and vegetables, is highly perishable and easily destroyed in foods exposed to moisture or heat. If you have trouble eating the citrus fruits (and many people do), it is not the ascorbic acid that is causing your trouble. It may be the citric acid. Try instead other foods that are rich in the vitamin and not so rich in the citric acid.

Foods Rich in Vitamin C

Green peppers are one such food. Parsley, green beans, raw sweet corn, tomatoes, brussels sprouts, kale, turnip greens, cantaloupe, guavas, are others.

And rose hips, of course.

Rose hips are the fruit of the rose bush, left after the flower withers, just as apples grow where the apple blossom has been. We do not know why nature planned this highly nutritious tidbit of food in connection with bushes and vines that we think of as being chiefly ornamental. We rather suspect that rose hips were meant originally as food for the birds. They love them, undoubtedly because of their sweet taste which goes along with an abundance of nourishment in the way of vitamins E, B, K, A and P, along with vitamin C.

Undoubtedly, nature painted the rose hip a bright ruby red at the time when its nutritive value is highest, to attract the birds to it. In answer to many questions many readers have asked us about rose hips, here are some facts. Yes, you can advantageously eat the hips of any rose so far as we know. Those grown in northern climates are richest in vitamin C. And some varieties are richer than others. *Rosa laxa, acicularis, cinnamomea, rugosa, Eddieii, Moyesii*—these are some of the varieties noted for their high vitamin C content.

Yes, you can pick and eat them right from the bushes as soon as they are ripe—a rosy red, before the fruit begins to turn dark or wrinkle. Yes you can preserve them for winter use by making a puree of them according to the following recipe:

Gather rose hips; chill. (This is to inactivate the enzymes which might otherwise cause a loss of vitamin C.) Remove blossom ends, stems and leaves; wash quickly. For each cup of rose hips bring to a boil one and one-half cups of water. Add one cup of rose hips. Cover utensil and simmer 15 minutes. Let stand in a pottery utensil for 24 hours. Strain off the extract, bring to a rolling boil, add two tablespoons lemon juice for each pint, pour into jars and seal. (Remember, don't make the mistake of using copper or aluminum utensils when you are cooking rose hips.)

The Effect of Heat on Rose Hips

Many readers question the directions given in this recipe. Doesn't all that heat destroy some vitamin C, they ask. It does, but we know that certain enzymes must be inactivated or the fruit will spoil within a few days. Heating inactivates the enzymes. Even though some vitamin C is lost, plenty is left if you follow directions carefully. It is impossible to preserve fruits without cooking, freezing or drying them. Drying rose hips by methods you can use at home is so slow that practically all the vitamin C is lost. Much less is lost in cooking.

Rose hip products are very carefully dried at body heat to preserve all possible vitamin C. Readers sometimes ask us how they can be sure the rose hip supplements they buy actually contain the number of milligrams of vitamin C indicated on the label. Of course, the processors do not test their rose hip preparations *before* they dry them and then take for granted that only a certain amount of the vitamin is lost in the process. They are constantly testing their products just as they appear in the bottle, because the laws are strict in regard to proper labeling.

Once you are convinced of the absolute necessity of taking a vitamin C supplement every day (and we hope you already are), why should you take a rose hip product rather than synthetic vitamin C or ascorbic acid which you can buy at the drugstore? The reason, of course, is the same reason why natural food supplements are always superior to synthetic ones. Scientists have recently discovered that the bioflavonoids are associated with vitamin C in fruits and vegetables. They are extremely valuable for good health. People who take synthetic vitamin C from the drugstore get no bioflavonoids. Those who take rose hips or other natural products do, of course.

Is Acerola Juice a Good Substitute for Rose Hips?

One final note. What about acerola juice which has received a lot of publicity as the best, the richest source of vitamin C? The acerola is a small red cherry which grows in Puerto Rico. So far as we know, the juice is not as yet available for general use. In some parts of the country you can buy apple juice canned for infants with added acerola juice. The acerola juice greatly increases the vitamin C content of the apple juice which is rather low in this vitamin.

From everything we can find on the subject, we believe that the acerola is not as rich in vitamin C as rose hips. When or if it becomes generally available for us to eat as a fresh fruit, we will say eat it by all means, for it will be a valuable addition to our diets. But at present it does not seem to offer any practical solution to our problem, for it is not available except in the very expensive unsatisfactory form of an addition to a canned juice.

SECTION 9

MILK

We are not in favor of adults drinking milk. For children it should be used in great moderation, for dairy food has been found to be a factor in making children grow too tall. There is medical evidence that very tall people are not as healthy as shorter ones. They have more high blood pressure, back and foot troubles, and don't live as long. But tall folks need not worry if they follow the Prevention *system. It will counteract the effect of the tallness.*

Modern milk, based on the artificial practices of agriculture and because of its pasteurization, is a far cry from old-fashioned raw milk. Its growth factor, which is supposed to help children, may be dangerous for adults. Excellent health can be maintained without milk.

CHAPTER **39**

The Case Against Milk

by J. I. RODALE

I don't drink milk, and am not ashamed to admit it. I have been away from milk-drinking now for over 5 years, and as yet there have been no signs of any deficiencies or repercussions of any kind. So far my body has taken no reprisals against me. At first there was a feeling of anxious uncertainty. Would lightning and thunder figuratively come and destroy me for such sacrilege? Not only has nothing of the kind happened, but I am going my merry way, thriving healthfully without milk, full of buoyant energy and with the confident feeling that (pardon the grammar) me and the cow (that is, its liquid white portion) have parted ways forever.

Now, from whence comes my calcium if I do not get it from milk? I have news for you. I now get it from *bone meal!* If there had been no bone meal substitute, there could have been trouble unless in expert fashion the rest of the diet had been tailored to make up for that calcium deficit.

I Hesitated to Speak Against Milk

For many years I would come across an item here and another there in health magazines, and in an occasional health book, disputing the value of milk as an item of diet, and I put them down as the unscientific talk of rabid physical-culturists. There were many of them, and I wish I had preserved them all. But one day, about 10 years ago, a man from Boston visited me and related the following story:

He had obtained a position with a mining company in an isolated section of Montana, and in a few months a very bad case of arthritis which had plagued him for over 10 years mysteriously cleared up; but completely! However, when he went back to Boston a few years later, his condition returned in full virulence. At first he put it down as being caused by living again in "civilization," but finally he recalled the fact that in the section of Montana where he had worked there had been no source of milk. For two years he had lived without it.

He decided to eliminate milk again and see what happened. Miracle upon miracles! In a few months his arthritis vanished. Again he began to drink milk and again his malady returned. No wonder he began to shout from the housetops what he had learned, and had to come all the way to Emmaus to tell me, first hand, what he had observed.

This made me think again about all those items I had read in the health literature, attacking milk as an item of our diet. Now arthritis is no mere result of an allergy. It goes deeper than that. I became thoroughly convinced that there were thousands of other persons suffering from this disease merely because they were drinking milk, and I was quite sure that the medics to whom they went were approaching their problem purely through palliation with drugs.

My Idea Finds Confirmation

I found confirmation of this idea in a booklet by C. Ward Crampton, M.D., formerly Associate Professor of Medicine of the New York Postgraduate Medical School and Hospital, and Chairman of the Subcommittee on Geriatrics and Gerontology, Public Health Committee, Medical Society of the County of New York. Dr. Crampton says, "The daily need of calcium is about one gram or 15 grains. A quart of milk daily will supply this. It is the natural food of the young. Cream, however, may be bad for the 'gouty and arthritic.' This is not as yet fully established but some arthritics seem to do better without any milk. Calcium is not harmful in arthritis even though there are some calcium deposits in and around the joints."

My Wife's Story

I recalled the case of my own wife who hasn't eaten any cheese or drunk milk since she was weaned from her mother's breast. For some mysterious reason or other she developed a deep-rooted aversion to milk and its whole family of related products. Yet, today, she is as hard as a rock. Where other women have already had an appendix removed and a hysterectomy performed, friend wife has a perfect record in keeping the surgeon's knife at a respectful distance. And how that woman hates milk and cheese! I have seen her in a restaurant returning a luscious-looking stuffed potato because her sharp nose detected that it had been surfaced with a microscopic amount of cheese. Which reminds me of her keen sense of smell—5 times better developed than my own. Can its sharpness have something to do with her no-milk diet? I would not rule the possibility out, yet I cannot submit this as a scientific affirmation. Oh, I forgot! My wife seems to have gotten along without milk and without having had the benefit of bone meal until about 5 years ago when we all began to take the latter. During all those former years she must have gotten her calcium from something else.

It is a strange thing, though, that although she got along so beautifully without milk, yet she tried to stuff it into our 3 children. Somehow or other she felt that it was wrong not to drink milk. She wanted to go along with the herd. On the other hand, for at least 15 years I had heard rumblings against milk and therefore was a considerable force in subduing this overpowering desire of hers to compel the children to drink milk. As a result, Nina, who is now over 18, merely takes a little milk with which to help her swallow her vitamin pills, and she has a practically perfect set of teeth.

Septic Sore Throat

In thinking back about milk, I recalled a visit I once made many years ago to a farming school where a herd of cows was kept. This was a school, mind you, not a private farm or dairy. When I went into the place where the cows were being milked, I immediately experienced a suffocating tightness. I will admit that the ventilation in the barn was poor. The next morning I had the most beautiful case of septic sore throat of my entire life. As you read the various articles about milk in this book, you will come across some statements about septic sore throat being transmitted through milk, in spite of pasteurization.

A few years ago while I was taking a summer course in geology, the students took a field trip to nearby quarries, and we took our lunches along. One of the teachers, after he finished his sandwiches, began a mad search for a grocery store.

Soon he returned with a whole quart of milk which he drank down with an avid fervor as if his life depended upon it. I am sure he felt that unless he drank at least two quarts of milk a day he was doomed to get cancer at the earliest possible moment.

I sized him up. I could see that his nose was a little on the stuffed side. When I questioned him I found that his nose gave him more torment than a human should ever endure —sinus, colds, catarrh and what have you. And when I told him that his overconsumption of milk could be at the bottom of his trouble, he laughed so loud that he must have scared some rabbits a mile away.

Still—Hesitation!

Looking back at all these facts I still hesitated to take up my cudgels in print against milk. For years, I thought and thought about it, debating whether or not we should tell our readers what we knew against milk drinking, but it seemed too revolutionary a thing to do. There had been built up such a sacred attitude towards milk, that it had become more than a fetish. Down through the ages it had become a powerful symbol. It had grown into a magic belief, a refuge, a sort of sacred fountain from which one drank and imbibed eternal youth. How could we snatch away this source of comfort from our friends?

But my conscience could not remain quiet. When I saw people breaking every rule of health, and then resorting to milk as if it would quench out all this error, I became aroused. When I realized how many persons are needlessly suffering through an overconsumption of milk, I came to a decision. I would do it regardless of consequences. I would cast the data I had upon the waters. If it comes as a shock to some, I hope that they will study the matter most thoroughly, possibly experimenting a little before they make up their mind.

I will say one thing most positively—if you think that milk, as it is produced under modern conditions, will be an appreciable factor in giving you health, I must tell you that you are not basing your belief on reality. Today's emasculated product is not fit for human consumption, not to mention the needs of the calf itself for whom the milk was intended. Poor thing! The modern calf is not growing up into a healthy cow.

This is proven by the increasing use of the antibiotic drugs given to cows. No one can tell me that this doesn't affect the cow's meat and its milk in some detrimental way. I have before me several strange circulars issued by the Tarkio Molasses Feed Company of Kansas City. In one of them dated March 22, 1955, and addressed to "Dear Cattle Feeder," the company says, regarding the stilbestrol drug that was approved about that time by the United States Food and Drug Administration, that it causes meat to go "soft" and not to age properly, and that their company did not intend to put any stilbestrol into its cattle feed. The other circular is a letter from the Williams Meat Company of Kansas City, one of the outstanding meat provisioners of our country today, who furnishes the best of meat for many large fancy restaurants. Here is what Mr. Williams of that company said in a letter to the Tarkio Molasses Feed Company on March 14, 1955: "As you know we specialize in prime quality meats, making Kansas City meats nationally famous. For some reason in recent months, the texture of the meat is exceptionally soft and not responding to proper aging. Are feeders experimenting too much with drugs?"

Much of this sort of wonder drug feeding is happening to cows and I wonder what it will do to the milk? At any rate, the whole thing is so unpredictable that one will never know at what moment Bossy will be given another "wonder" treatment, without waiting the necessary time in laboratory checking of dangers.

Propaganda

A great part of milk's popularity is due to the propaganda of the milk interests. They are powerfully organized. They send their tons of literature to the schools, the PTA's and to other places where it will do the most good. I recall an experience I had about 7 or 8 years ago which will throw some light on this activity. When we started the Soil and Health Foundation, I had some correspondence with a professor in a dental college, who wished to know whether I could run an experiment on our farm, feeding two groups of mice—one with food raised with chemical fertilizers, the other with food raised by the organic method. Then he came to the farm for further discussions. He advised that the experiment would be financed by a big milk foundation, but when he said that milk had to be one item of food for each group of mice, and when I expressed a few negative thoughts about milk, he left, never to return. I received no more letters from him.

Advertising

Much of our opinion regarding the healing quality of milk stems from this endless stream of propaganda—a torrent of advertising costing hundreds of millions of dollars. We are bombarded by it at every turn, through the newspapers, radio and television until milk has become crowned with a halo. But it is a halo purchased with dollars, and therefore I do not feel guilty when I tarnish it a little.

There is no question that milk has a delightful, satisfying taste, but so has strawberry shortcake and ice cream. However, one cannot live by taste alone if one wishes to live a long, healthy life, although there is nothing wrong with the taste of apples, carrots and roast beef.

How about those who do not drink coffee? If they also eliminate milk, they might complain of the loss of a hot or cold liquid with which to end the meal. But there are always the various kinds of mint and herb teas that one can come to enjoy highly. I occasionally drink an alfalfa mint tea and rose hip tea and find them satisfying from both a taste and a health standpoint.

My Diet

My own diet consists of meat, eggs, vegetables (mostly raw, some cooked) and a lot of fruit. I do not eat anything that has gone through a factory, and to me, milk is a highly factoryized thing—not only in the aspect of pasteurization, but also in the fact that a high production factory has been made out of the cow's udders. I eat no bread or cakes, and no soups, because I am on a reducing diet. But my diet is a very satisfying one, especially since I have stopped drinking coffee. I used to drink considerable amounts of coffee because it apparently helped a heart condition. I have discovered, however, that I am better off without it. Vitamin E and desiccated liver are good substitutes. I take a great many different natural vitamins, plus bone meal.

I am on a low salt, no sugar diet, and because of this

and my general diet, my blood pressure is like that of a new-born babe—120 over 65. Before I began all this I had a very high blood pressure.

It's Your Own Decision

Now a few words of advice. What you intend to do is entirely up to you. Read the articles that follow. Then make up your own mind. Some will cut milk out entirely. Others will merely reduce the amount they consume. But do not let nostalgia influence you, for nostalgia has filled too many a grave. You can point to some persons who are heavy milk drinkers and yet who are perfectly healthy, but it is possible that it is the way they are built. Perhaps they have wider arteries than the average person and a more tuned up set of glands. It is the way they were born, due to their heritage. Those are the people who smoke and drink and live to 80. But you and I may not be in that class.

It is too bad about the cow! If there were only a way that we could start to unbreed her—to breed her backwards so to speak, to progressively reduce the size of her udders so that one day again she could become a scrub cow. Then, and only then, would I consider taking a drink of her milk. On such a day perhaps ways could be found to keep her healthy and clean and by some other method, milder than pasteurization, to preserve her milk's nutritional qualities as well as kill its germs. Man has abused a good thing.

CHAPTER **40**

Further Arguments Against Milk

by J. I. RODALE

More of the hidden dangers in milk drinking by adults come to light as we probe farther.

I say to you who are really health-conscious, who want to live to 100 and over without the usual signs of crippling senility—don't drink milk, which means also, don't eat butter or cheese or any other dairy product. If you are satisfied to live to only 70 or 80, or even 85, and if you have been endowed since birth with a body structure that enables you to snap your fingers at the average health-producing procedures, and if you feel that you must drink milk, then drink it! But you will probably pay for it in some other way or another. You won't have that elastic step. You will dodder more. Your eyes may grow dimmer, your ears may lose their hearing edge.

After all, we are in search of something, and our search is not yet complete. We are looking for a program that will give us 100 active healthy years, and more. If we want that, then why take a chance? There is so much medical evidence against the drinking of milk, that where there is smoke there may be fire. Remember that half the world, the eastern half, does not drink milk. I was talking to a Chinese professor the other day and he confirmed this fact to me and more. He stated that the average Chinese student who comes to this country, and hears about the supposed health-giving qualities of milk, begins to drink it, and as a result, he gets gas on the stomach and many other digestive ills. But he does not get it from eating meat, fruits or vegetables!

A while ago I spoke of raw milk. Only the other day I was told of the case of the wife of an advertising executive, who visited her uncle's farm where there was a herd of 200 purebred cows. They kept one cow for themselves under unusually sanitary conditions and did not pasteurize its milk. The lady in question, who drank some of this milk on this visit, contracted a severe case of undulant fever which took 3 years to cure. But the people who were drinking this milk all along had become inured to it. Somewhere, years back, they may have experienced some kind of trouble, unless they may have had some natural immunity.

Heart Disease and Milk Drinking

I would like to speak about another phase of milk drinking—the heart disease question. In a recent study of this disease, the unusual amount of heart attacks in this country was attributed to the large amount of fat consumed in our diet, namely 40 per cent. The authors found that in Italy the consumption of fat is only 20 per cent of the total food consumed, and heart fatalities there are not one-third of what they are in this country. There can be no question that the total fat consumed is an important factor in bringing on heart attacks to vulnerable cases. This is brought out in hundreds of medical researches which I have gone over.

The usual practice is to tell the heart patient to cut down on eggs, but from what I have seen, as between eggs and dairy products, I would say to the average heart case, cut out all dairy products completely, but by all means eat eggs, for eggs are a seed from which a chick will come out. The egg contains terrific, living, nutritional elements. It is a complete package. There is sufficient food in it to feed the emerging chick for a few days and the poultryman does not have to do it. Anyone who passes up eggs is denying himself one of the finest foods that God made.

Of course, both eggs and dairy products contain fat. And the body needs some fat, to be sure. We cannot eliminate all fat from our diets.

And the government encourages the farmer to so feed his cows that more butterfat will be in the milk. That is the government standard as to how the farmer should be paid for his milk. It is based on its butterfat content. Less would be better. Of course, the physician will advise his heart patient to drink skimmed milk. Yet in restaurants he will put regular milk —even cream—in his coffee.

Another thing that militates against milk, as far as I am concerned, is the fact that practically all milk today contains traces of penicillin from shots given to the cow to prevent or cure disease. If we keep drinking such milk, the effect of this cumulative penicillin will be to kill all the body's protective bacteria, and already there is evidence that this will cause trouble when a real emergency arises. But now some research scientists are speaking of a new practice that they wish to see inaugurated with respect to milk—a practice which should be killed dead in its track by public outcry. It is based on researches conducted at the University of Minnesota, aided by the American Dairy Association of Chicago, which may set off such a dangerous trend in nutrition that anything that has gone before will pale into insignificance.

What is suggested now is that disease germs be injected into cows. They will then give milk containing large quantities of disease-fighting agents, or antibodies, which would protect people against certain diseases if they drink this milk. Already 10 years have been spent in these researches, all with animals, and the idea has worked, according to the research scientists.

Effects of Such Additives

However, two questionable thoughts arise in my mind. One—what will be the ultimate effect in the human body of 20 or 30 years' ingestion of such antibodies? Will it completely inactivate the body's own mechanism to produce the protective antibodies? Disuse encourages petrification. The day may arise when something will happen to the cow. She may become unable to pass on the antibodies. What will happen then, if the body has become so coddled and weakened that it has "unlearned" its ability to fight for itself? Modern practices tend to continually weaken the ability of the individual to assert the resistive qualities of his body. He has been called a machine, and is being treated purely as a machine in this case. But it is far safer to improve our primitive qualities in regard to the physical operation of our bodies, rather than to reduce them.

Number two—the dangerous trend set off by the fluoridation of drinking waters (namely, the concept of preventing something by doing something to that which we take into our bodies every day) is given another shot-in-the-arm. There is no telling where this idea will end up. What will the Christian

Scientists think of such milk? Nothing, I am sure. Such procedure is a threat to the liberty of the individual, who has a right to decide for himself whether he wishes to be "medicated" in such unorthodox ways.

A Complacent Attitude Results

Another hidden defect in this milk treatment is (and the same is true of fluoridation to reduce tooth cavities in children) that it lulls us into a false sense of security, preventing us from searching out the real causes of disease and rooting them out. If it were not for the prejudiced, money-tainted commercialism of the large-scale food-producing factories, the public would today know the simple basic causes of cancer, polio, heart disease and the host of other ailments that are bringing prosperity into the doctors' offices. Many readers already know their causes, but the problem is to get the general public to know them and to resist the fancy pseudo-scientific Salk vaccines, the water chemicalizations and the attempt to put a white coat on cows. That's what they are trying to do—to make doctors out of cows. This is really laughable, for if you knew the extent of disease that exists today in cows, you would see how badly *they* need the doctors themselves.

I, therefore, urge you to write to your congressmen, to your senators, both federal and state, and to other interested officials, write to the University of Minnesota and to the American Dairy Association of Chicago, telling them of the dangers involved which may cause many persons to stop drinking milk.

Milk looks innocent in its innocuous whiteness, in its wonderful taste, but still waters flow deep. There are 50 states and the dairy laws differ in each one. God alone knows what the dairyman already is doing to the cow and to the milk. There are far better, and more certain ways of getting the finest nutrition. And that's what you are entitled to—the finest.

CHAPTER 41

Milk from the Modern Cow

by J. I. RODALE

One of the chief disadvantages of modern milk is that it comes from an animal that has been made into a factory by modern agricultural methods.

The cow that went aboard Noah's Ark was a far different critter from what she is today. Noah's cow did not have heavy milk bags to carry around to plague her. Noah's and Father Abraham's cows had only small teats, like those of a horse. There was no dairy business in those days. Those who wanted milk kept their own sheep, goat or cow. But in the eastern part of the world, milk even today is generally not drunk.

Must a Cow Give Milk?

Now, why does a cow give milk? A cow gives milk for the same reason that a woman does—to provide food with which to nurse a newborn thing. As soon as a woman or a cow becomes pregnant, forces are set in motion in the body to build a milk supply. After a certain period goes by, and the calf gets to the age where it can forage for itself, the cow's supply of milk dries up. You can see, therefore, that in order for the cow to give more milk, she must have another calf. Thus, keeping a cow in milk involves maternity.

Most people are of the opinion that the cow has a set of spigots to be turned on and off when one needs milk, and that's what most city folks believe. Now, in the old days a family that kept a cow sometimes appropriated some of the milk for their own use, but the wise, all-seeing Creator foresaw this propensity of man's for taking things, without asking, and he gave the cow a bountiful extra reserve of milk. But as the centuries rolled on, man saw an opportunity of making money from the cow's milk supply, and with that devilish cunning he shows wherever money is concerned, he found a way to force the cow to give more milk.

Breeding Produced "Commercial" Milk Cow

He observed that some cows give more milk than others, and by closer study, discovered that such cows had larger teats than others. He found also that this ability to give more milk ran in families. So he mated cows from such families to bulls from similarly endowed families and that, still further, increased the capacity to give milk.

The result was that from generation to generation, cows gave more and more milk and their udders thus gradually became larger and larger. Now, by the time of George Washington, the cow's udders were at least 20 times the capacity of a cow in the days of King David. In Revolutionary War times you could already begin to call them milk bags, though they hung down only about 5 inches or so. But today, by further breeding, the cow's milk bags have been enlarged to 10 times the size they were when George Washington was president. Yes, sir! Today the milk bags of some cows are so huge that they pretty near drag the ground and you will find listed in Sears Roebuck's catalog girdles for cows to hold up their udders so that they won't drag or crack.

Man has made a factory—a milk machine out of the cow. Where in Noah's time, a cow gave about 200 pounds of milk in a year, today there are cows that give 15,000 pounds or 75 times as much milk. And this overproduction is causing more disease in cows. A lot of cows are getting leukemia today and many other diseases which they never used to get.

What Is Milk?

Now, getting back to what we moderns call milk—it is very diluted because of the large quantity the cow has to give. Milk is a very delicate thing, interrelated to almost every gland and organ of the cow's body. It is a part of the function of the animal in creating life. All of the best elements in its body must be assembled to make it, so that the calf can have a good start.

Our scientists do not seem to be aware of what they are doing. They are shallow fragmentists. All they are after is to secure increased volume of an opaque white liquid, with a reasonable amount of butter-fat content, but are they worried over the fact that its vitamins and hormones are below a safe level? No! Why, there were more vitamins in a thimbleful of milk at the time of King David than in a whole beer mug of today.

When we force a cow to give 75 times the amount of milk that God intended her to, it must be a kind of milk that is not up to snuff. That is point number one. No we come to point number two. Artificial insemination.

Scientists Are Making Artificial Animals

The dairymen seem to delight in making the cow a completely artificial animal. Formerly a bull mated with a cow in order to give her a calf, but that is too much trouble for dairymen today, so they have this artificial insemination. The bull is masturbated, and the amount of semen ejaculated is used to inject into 40 or 50 cows or even more. It is nothing but male prostitution. It is an irreligious, impious trick if I ever saw one. First they hang a hundred pound weight under the cow, then deprive her of her gentleman friend! What next? They are piling artificiality upon artificiality. Poor Bossy, with her big sad eyes waiting for the father of her children who never comes. One day she may realize that she has been let down, deceived, tricked, cheated out of the natural biological satisfaction which is her inherent right. Can the milk of such a cow be any good?

And the bull—what of him? There are going to be disastrous effects upon his character. Already bulls are refusing to work and are becoming obstreperous. Recently near Winchester, Indiana, a bull gored the auto of the county's artificial inseminator.

God does everything for a purpose. He makes fruit colorfully attractive and sweet so that the birds will seek it out and scatter the seed. Thus fruit trees spring forth all over creation. He has put glorious colors in the flowers so that the bee will be attracted to pollinate them and they will grow in profusion on the face of the earth. He has made the cow and the bull for each other but who is man to say, "I will change what God hath intended?"

When God promised the Land of Canaan to the children of Israel, describing it to Moses as a land flowing with milk and honey, did he mean milk from cows artificially inseminated and with oversized milk bags? According to Leviticus, the cow offered up for sacrifice in the temple was supposed to be absolutely pure and without a single blemish anywhere. Would a cow begotten in artificial insemination be an acceptable animal for the temple ritual? Would you consider her bloated milk bag a blemish? Should a good Christian drink milk produced in such a profane, ungodly way?

The End Result of Artificial Insemination

Now, since the practice of artificial insemination began there is much more disease in cows. They are dropping dead from unknown causes, and there are all kinds of reproductive diseases—mastitis of the udders for one. A cow's life is 20 per cent shorter than it was 30 years ago.

But God has methods of his own. In artificially inseminated births more male calves are being born than ordinarily, and this tendency will keep on increasing even with human artificial insemination births—we call them test-tube babies—60 per cent more boys than girls.

Do you realize what this means? If the percentage of males in births keeps on increasing and it will if these dairymen insist on continuing this suicidal insemination practice, God will see to it that eventually no females will be born at all. The species will die out.

Other Artificial Practices

You would think that scientists would be more careful. They should have tested artificial insemination for 50 years before letting it loose on the public. But science is running ahead of human wisdom and the public is not without blame, either. The public is lazy. It shirks its responsibilities. And that's not all about artificial practices and cows. Already there is a new and vicious thing that is being used. Instead of spraying insecticides in the barn and on the outside of the cow's skin, they are now injecting this chemical, right into the cow's blood stream, so that if a fly or mosquito bites her anywhere, it will automatically get a dose of the chemical and die.

This chemical that is powerful enough to kill a fly at one bite will be present in every cell of the cow's body, and will get into the milk. How brave these scientists are at the public's expense. Cato the Elder was right when he said, "There is a wide difference between true courage and a mere contempt of life." Nor have I mentioned the formaldehyde preservative that some dairies put into milk. Formaldehyde is a chemical used to embalm people.

There are many other artificial practices that are perpetrated against the cow, but it is all part of the processes of chemicalization and artificialization which have been thrust upon us—people as well as cows. The scientists are in the woods and cannot see the cows. And as far as I am concerned, I am through with milk. I have been through with it for many years now and feel as fit as a fiddle. Of course, I see to it that my diet is well balanced—the bone meal taking care of what was in the milk far more effectively than the milk did.

CHAPTER 42

Is Milk Drinking for You?

Some miscellaneous news items showing that we are not alone in pointing out that milk is not the perfect food. Contamination is a serious threat to our modern milk supply.

What causes cavities? Milk, says a Danish dentist. Cavities in children's teeth are caused by milk, according to a theory by Dr. E. A. Bruun, who practices on the dairy-farming island of Bornholm. He has invited further investigation of his observations that farm children have uniformly bad teeth, while children in fishermen's families, who drink less milk, have teeth much freer from cavities.

Dr. Bruun published his theory privately and circulated the paper to fellow dentists and the Danish Dental Association. He first hit on his theory some years ago when he was treating the staff of a large Swedish dairy. He was struck by the extreme decalcification of their teeth, which had gone beyond anything he had ever observed. Investigating further, he found that the dairy employees drank milk in large quantities. He asked some of them to stop drinking milk and claims that after about 6 months the teeth of the non-milk drinkers showed improvement, while those of the others were as bad as ever. (This information came from the New York *Herald Tribune,* August 10, 1957.)

A Similar Theory

A somewhat similar theory is put forth by a French dentist in an article in *Revue franҫois odontostomat* for June-July, 1956. Says Dr. R. Dubois-Prevost, milk must be pasteurized or boiled before given to children, because it contains microorganisms which are harmful to the teeth. These bacteria are added to those already present in the mouth. Research on the prevention of decay reveals, says our French dentist, that excessive milk consumption parallels an increase in decay. He then suggests something we cannot agree with—that after drinking milk, children should rinse their mouths with fluoridated water which will, he says, counteract the effects of the bacteria.

DDT Contaminates Milk

Reports William Longgood in the New York *World Telegram* for June 3, 1957: A DDT spraying plane recently sprayed by mistake the farm of an organic farmer who, of course, uses no insecticides. Previous laboratory tests have shown that milk from this farmer's cows contains absolutely no trace of DDT. But, within 24 hours after the farm was sprayed, milk from his 75-head herd was contaminated with the spray. A wire sent by the farmer to the Secretary of Agriculture said in part: "How can the Department of Agriculture justify its position when it contaminates dairy farms in a wholesale fashion not only in the 3 million acres under attack (for gypsy moth) but also outside the intended area where they are not even supposed to be sprayed. Since DDT is extremely persistent once deposited on pastures or elsewhere, many years must elapse before the milk from our dairy farm will again be free from contamination." What do you suppose the DDT content of milk is among dairy farmers who regularly use DDT on fields, garden, cattle feed and barns?

Upstate New York retail milk dealers reported their milk

supplies "contaminated" with penicillin, according to the *New York Times* for November 13, 1957. A spokesman of the health department of Binghamton stated that the amount of penicillin in the milk had reached the point where it "affects people who are allergic to penicillin—they are reacting to the milk itself."

According to *The Lancet,* famous British medical magazine, for February 23, 1957, dried milk, such as the government provides in England for infants and children, is relatively low in the essential fatty acids and rich in vitamin D. This might, according to Dr. Hugh Sinclair of Oxford University, lead to the wrong use of calcium in the bodies of infants. Such a consequence, goes on the *Lancet* editorialist, "might be regarded as a physiological penalty for our persistence in feeding babies with milk designed for the young of another species, and to which too much vitamin D has been added."

The Effects of Radioactive Iodine in Milk

A question to the editor of the *British Medical Journal* for December 28, 1957, asks what ill effects in infants, children and adults might result from the ingestion of milk contaminated by radioactive iodine. We do not know why such a question should be asked, but we suppose almost anything might be contaminated with radioactive substances in these enlightened and advanced times in which we live. And we know that several quite serious accidents at atomic installations in Britain have caused considerable alarm. Whether or not this question applies to such an emergency we do not know. The editor replies with a calculation which indicates that a child drinking about a quart of milk a day might get about one-tenth of the minimal toxic dose. He continues, "However such calculations are far from precise and hence the need for caution." We say amen.

Milk May Cause Goiter

An interesting piece from the *Medical Journal of Australia* for November 2, 1957, indicates that in districts where cows may be feeding on certain weeds, their milk can contain a "goiterogenic factor"—that is, something which may produce goiter. The weed is called *chou-moellier* in Australia. We could not find it in our garden encyclopedia. But it seems, according to the *Journal* that several other weeds—all of the *cruciferous* family—are also involved. The *crucifers,* incidentally, include those plants whose flowers have 4 petals placed opposite one another—cabbage, turnips and radishes are all in this family, as well as the weeds shepherd's purse, swine cress, crowsfoot and longstorkbill.

We know that eating a diet consisting almost exclusively of plants of this family will cause goiter in human beings. Conditions of war and famine have shown this. The Australian cows, during seasons when the weeds of this family are plentiful, eat large quantities of them and it is believed that this is responsible for the goiters which are caused in children who drink the milk.

It seems unlikely that milk from a dairy, coming as it does from many different farms, would be dangerous as a possible carrier of this goiter-causing factor. But on farms where weeds of this family grow and are widely eaten by milk cows, and where all the milk consumed comes from the farm herd, one can easily see that the goiter-causing factor would assume harmful proportions.

The Antibiotic Content of Milk

According to the *Journal of the American Medical Association* for March 9, 1957, the Food and Drug Administration has done surveys of the amount of antibiotics in milk. The first survey showed that 3.2 per cent of 94 samples tested contained penicillin. In the second survey 474 samples of milk were tested and 11.6 per cent were found to contain penicillin. In the third survey 1706 samples were examined. These were collected from all of the 48 states. There was penicillin in 5.9 per cent of the samples tested. In addition, one of the samples containing penicillin apparently contained streptomycin and 17 additional samples appeared to contain bactracin (another antibiotic). The article goes on to say that the experts who have been called together to determine what to do about penicillin have recommended that studies be made, to try to find out the quantity of penicillin in milk that would cause a reaction. Of course, penicillin gets into milk through treatments given to cows for mastitis.

This brings up the important question of why we should be drinking milk from sick cows.

Is milk a proper food for healthy adults? According to *Time* magazine for December 30, 1957, a change made in the dining halls at Yale University started a chain reaction that finally got as far as New York City's famous nutritionist, Norman Jolliffe. Instead of one big glass of milk per meal, dining room officials at Yale issued a smaller glass, but allowed the students as many refills as they wanted. Partly to protest against a fancied inconvenience, but largely out of orneriness (says *Time*) the undergraduates started on milk-drinking binges. Many went back for 4 or 5 glasses; some drank as many as 20.

This brought a warning from the director and assistant director of the University's public health department: "The normal, healthy individual can readily precipitate kidney stone formation by the simple ingestion of excessive mineral salts (in) ice cream, cheese, butter, and milk . . . a good rule of thumb to insure ample dilution: two glasses of water for each glass of milk."

We agree with *Time*'s comment that the formation of kidney stones is a complicated procedure involving much more than how much calcium one gets in his diet. However, the final authority on this matter was eventually consulted—Dr. Jolliffe, one of the leading nutritionists in our country today. Said Dr. Jolliffe: "With an adequate diet, milk is not necessary for an adult."

CHAPTER **43**

Mother's Milk Is Best

For infants, breast-feeding is infinitely preferable to formulas made from cow or goat milk. Aside from the fact that mother's milk contains protection from many different diseases, it supplies exactly those food elements needed by the human baby in exactly the right proportions. No formula can do this.

Not often in our research do we run across a subject on which medical opinion seems to be united, with no if's, and's and but's. The value of breast-feeding appears to be such a subject. We gather from our reading in some 45 medical journals and a number of lay magazines that the only members of the medical profession who do not whole-heartedly advocate breast-feeding are those who do not keep up with recent medical literature, those who think it is too much trouble to prepare and educate their maternity patients for breast-feeding, and a scattered few whose wives did not breast-feed *their* children, so the medico-husbands find it hard to accept the fact that breast-feeding may be desirable.

Scientific researchers are completely united in advising breast-feeding and for a number of very interesting reasons. First of all, from the baby's point of view, is the very obvious fact that breast-feeding is natural. The new mother of any species of animal is equipped to provide the best food for that particular species of newborn animal. Human beings are no exception. In spite of all the skill of modern nutritionists and scientists, no one has yet managed to reproduce human milk, containing all the substances known and unknown that are in it and yielding in experiments the same results that human milk yields.

It has been found, for instance, that some substance in human milk provides protection against polio. *Time* for May

29, 1950, reported on the research of Dr. Albert B. Sabin of the Children's Hospital Research Foundation of Cincinnati. According to Dr. Sabin, a polio epidemic in a Canadian Eskimo settlement resulted in 275 cases of the disease; 20 per cent of the victims were paralyzed and 14 per cent died. In no case, however, did any child under 3 years of age become paralyzed. Since the children were exposed to every other circumstance that surrounded the adults, the conclusion had to be that it was the infants' food that protected them. Eskimo children are nursed by their mothers up to and often beyond the age of 3. Working on this assumption, Dr. Sabin infected mice with the polio virus, giving some of the mice human milk in addition. Those who received the milk withstood the polio germ while the others got the disease and developed paralysis. An article in the *New York Times* reports that a team of scientists working at the University of Pennsylvania have isolated the health factor in human milk and discovered that cow's milk does not contain it. We don't know how this information strikes you, but it appears to us that any modern mother, knowing that breast-feeding may protect her child from polio, would willingly go to any trouble at all to make certain that she nurses her child.

Other Diseases Prevented by Human Milk

In addition, medical journals give us ample proof that other diseases, too, are prevented by mother's milk. F. Charlotte Naish, M.D., writing in the *British Medical Journal* for March 24, 1951, presents a chart showing the number of professional visits that were necessary for some ailment or other in babies she had delivered. Regardless of the social or economic status of the baby's family, those infants who had been breast-fed for less than 3 months required almost 5 times as many visits from the doctor, as those who had been breast-fed for longer than 3 months. Respiratory illness, infant diarrhea, contagious childhood diseases and eczema are much more common among children who are bottle-fed.

Mothers in other countries have always known that epidemics of diarrhea are likely to strike the child who is not breast-fed. In many countries this is because milk may be polluted. But in our country, too, where milk is uncontaminated, diarrhea develops often among formula-fed infants, seldom among those who are breast-fed. In fact, the only reference we found to a hospital epidemic among breast-fed children indicated that the only reasonable cause of the epidemic was probably the transmission of the germ in the boric acid, which was used for washing the mothers' breasts.

Constituents of Human Milk

Although all the constituents of human milk have not as yet been discovered, a great deal of research has been done on the subject. We know that human milk contains vitamin C, while cow's milk that has been pasteurized contains practically none. Cow's milk contains casein, whereas human milk contains lactalbumin, which is much more easily assimilated by the baby's digestive tract, because it forms soft, easily digested curds. This information is from a speech by Dr. Stuart Shelton Stevenson before the American Dietetic Association, reported in the *New York Times* for November 6, 1946. *The Lancet* for June 24, 1950, tells us that vitamin D is present in breast milk in very small quantities, so that both mother and infants should be given supplements in their diet. Vitamin A is likely to be low in breast milk, too, indicating that the mother who wishes to nurse her baby should get plenty of vitamin A in her diet and diet supplements. When the vitamin B complex is increased in the mother's diet, riboflavin and thiamin appear in larger quantity in the breast milk. It is significant, too, that thiamin is scarce in the milk of mothers whose supply of milk is scanty. (Can lack of thiamin in the refined foods of the average diet be responsible for the apparent inability of many modern mothers to nurse their babies?)

An article in *The Journal of Nutrition* for April 10, 1952, indicates that vitamin E is much more abundant in human milk, especially in the colostrum—the first milk after the birth of the baby—than in cow's milk. Of course, once we accept the premise that human milk is by far the best food for human infants, it seems useless to concern ourselves with why certain substances are lacking in other kinds of milk. Doesn't it seem obvious that nature would provide for the human child just what it needs in milk and would provide in the nursing mothers of other animals the substances those baby animals need?

The content of human milk, like the content of other

secretions of the body, certainly must depend on the mother's diet, for what else, aside from her own food, does she use to manufacture milk? We were disappointed that we cannot report greater understanding on the part of medical commentators for the important role played by nutrition in the question of whether or not modern mothers can breast-feed their infants. In the elaborate chemistry of the body the complicated process of pregnancy and lactation make much greater demands on the mother's body than are made at any other time in her life. Physicians seem to realize that at this time she needs more of all the vitamins and minerals. But only two writers on the subject (Dr. Pottenger and Dr. Krohn) indicated that the modern inability to breast-feed may quite possibly be due to actual malnutrition on the part of the mother.

In our grandmothers' day breast-feeding was taken for granted. Few and far between were the women who did not have sufficient milk for their babies. But these women ate whole grain cereals, unrefined foods and fresh vegetables and fruits from their own gardens. Today, how much of the failure in being able to nurse one's baby is due to psychological and economic reasons (the mother must return to her job, for instance) and how much is due to the fact that she actually cannot get in her devitalized daily food enough of the precious ingredients to make up human milk?

Nursing Develops the Child's Facial Contours

Perhaps most interesting of all the benefits the child receives from breast-feeding is the material presented in several articles on the subject of the facial characteristics of breast-fed children. Many pediatricians declare that they can tell by looking at a child whether or not it was breast-fed. Francis M. Pottenger, Jr., M.D. and Bernard Krohn, M.D., of Monrovia, California, open an article on this subject in the *Archives of Pediatrics* for October, 1950, with the startling statement that "Nursing in the first 6 months may control a person's facial contours for the rest of his life." They go on to describe experiments in which they measured the facial development of 327 patients and correlated their findings with a history of whether or not each patient was breast-fed.

Their conclusions are that certain bones of the face, head and jaws are important for esthetic, protective and functional reasons. Breast-feeding improves the growth of these bones. The authors explain this as follows: "A child gets more exercise from nursing at the breast than on a bottle, because it requires more effort to extract the milk. The nursing infant works his jaw forward and backward as well as up and down." The quality of the mother's milk is also important, say these authors. The well-nourished mother who is getting ample vitamins and minerals has not only a goodly supply of milk, but has milk that is rich in the food materials the baby needs.

Breathing and Nursing

A letter from an unnamed Doctor of Dental Surgery came to us in an advertisement. He says, "I have noticed that many bottle-fed babies did not breathe properly, that they had high, narrow vaults, small under-developed external nares (nostrils), that many developed sinus trouble as well as malocclusion . . . A vacuum must be created in the oral cavity by the firm gripping of the nipple by the lips, copious draughts of air must be taken in through the nose thereby forcing the vault downward into the oral cavity, widening the arch as well as developing a more adequate nasal area. The forced breathing of the act of nursing aerates the sinuses, developing and keeping them healthy; in fact it is a developing of the head and neck of the infant, preparing it to carry on with the acts of mastication and respiration in a proper manner by the time the normal nursing period is over."

Breast-Feeding Benefits Mother

We have been considering the advantages to the child of being breast-fed. Are there advantages to the mother? Two outstanding physical benefits are noted in medical literature, aside from the psychological ones. First, the mother who nurses her child regains much more quickly her good health, figure and physical condition after the birth of the child, because lactation is the natural conclusion of all the physiological functions created in the mother's body by the reproductive cycle. If her milk is cut off by the use of drugs, this cycle is interrupted and a feeling of depression may result, as her body gradually returns to its pre-pregnancy state.

A second excellent reason for breast-feeding is that the incidence of breast cancer is decidedly lower in women who have nursed their children. An article in *Science,* for August,

1946, indicates that apparently stagnation of milk in the breast plays a role in producing breast cancer in mice. This would seem to substantiate the observations that breast cancer occurs most frequently in women who have not had children, next most often in those who have not nursed their children and least of all among women who have successfully nursed a family.

For those who fear that breast-feeding may change the size of the breasts, the *Journal of the American Medical Association* for March 17, 1951, tells us that there is a temporary enlargement for only a few months in about 40 per cent of women, a temporary diminution in about 30 per cent and no change at all in about 30 per cent.

Psychological Benefits for Mother and Baby

Psychologically, too, breast-feeding appears to be by far the best plan for mother and baby alike. Although some writers emphasize it more than others, all are agreed that the baby's sense of security is enormously increased when he is breast-fed. He comes into the world from a warm quiet place where all his bodily functions were performed for him. Suddenly he is out in the cold world, faced with doing all these complicated things for himself. The nearness of his mother, her warmth, smell and tenderness make him feel loved and secure, which, it is agreed, safeguards him against later symptoms that are the result of insecurity, such as thumb-sucking, finger-chewing, bed-wetting, stammering and other nervous habits.

The child associates his mother's face with the pleasant feeling of satisfying his hunger, so in later years the breast-fed child does not suffer from all the signs of temperament over his food that bottle-fed babies often display. As Eleanor Lake expresses it, writing in the *Reader's Digest* for June, 1950, "Nursed and cuddled when he is hungry or upset, he begins to feel that the world is a pretty fine place after all. Soon he is quite ready to cooperate when family convenience says dinner at 6 or a nap at 2." Incidentally, this excellent article, entitled "Breast-fed is Best-fed," is available in reprint form (10 for .25) from The Reprint Editor, *Reader's Digest,* Pleasantville, New York.

In her book, *Male and Female,* Margaret Mead, outstanding anthropologist, goes so far as to say that bottle-feeding a baby is certain to lead to serious difficulties in sex relationships in later life. By giving the baby a bottle—a thing, an object—rather than a part of herself, the mother establishes in his mind the idea of material things having as much worth as successful human relationships. The bottle-fed baby, says Dr. Mead, will grow up to be the kind of man who arranges for his wife to have fur coats and jewels, but not a happy marriage. For those who must bottle-feed their infants, it is well to keep in mind that the baby should be held close to his mother while he is eating and the bottle should be held for him, so that he will experience as close an approximation as possible to breast nursing.

Mother's Benefits

Psychologically, nursing is also the best thing for the new mother, for she experiences not only a sense of well-being because the complex cycle of reproduction is thus biologically brought to a close, but also a satisfaction in having actually given of herself to her child, in the deepest possible meaning of the word. It seems to us that the lifetime relationship of a mother and child will be infinitely improved, if the mother actually wishes to nurse her child and does it successfully.

A Successful Breast-Feeding Program

Some writers believe that the mother's wish to nurse the child is of extreme importance in a successful breast-feeding program. Niles Rumely Newton and Michael Newton, M.D., report in *Pediatrics* for August 15, 1950, on a survey of 91 new mothers, some of whom said positively that they wished to nurse their babies, some of whom were indifferent and some of whom preferred bottle-feeding and did not want or like the plan of breast-feeding. Of the women who expressed a determination to nurse their children, 75 per cent were successful, of those who didn't care, only 35 per cent were, and of those who did not want to, only 26 per cent were successful. These authors feel that the reasons, which they call psychosomatic, may be as follows: 1. Since adequate sucking is necessary to encourage the flow of milk, perhaps those who opposed breast-feeding or were indifferent to it did not allow their babies a long enough time to get the flow of milk started. 2. The release of the milk inside the mother's breast may have been inhibited by the negative attitude or 3, the blood flow which is greatly influenced by emotion, may have prevented the proper functioning of the mammary glands in those whose emotions of repulsion or disgust were strong.

Family History Conditions Manner of Feeding

It seems that the mother's desire to nurse her baby depends to a large degree on her family history and on the attitude of those around her during pregnancy. If her mother and grandmother nursed their children, chances are good that the new mother will take for granted that she should, too. If, in addition, her family, husband, friends, doctor and nurse give lots of helpful encouragement, she is much more likely to nurse the baby successfully. Finally, her experience in nursing the baby is, we feel, bound to be successful if she has made a point of eating natural, unrefined foods and supplementing her diet with brewer's yeast and desiccated liver for the B vitamins, fish liver oil tablets for vitamin A and D, rose hips for vitamin C, wheat germ for vitamin E and bone meal for minerals.

SECTION 10

FRUITS, NUTS AND VEGETABLES

We believe you should eat lots of nuts, fruits and vegetables —as many raw as possible. If you can't possibly get organically-grown, unsprayed fruits, peel them before eating them. In this way you will avoid at least some of the insecticide that is there. Washing does little good. Most sprays are not soluble in water. Pineapples, bananas, coconuts and so forth are recommended because their skins are so thick the sprays cannot penetrate. Taking bone meal will make up for the loss of minerals when you peel fruit.

Eat some raw food at every meal. Enzymes, so important to good health, are destroyed by heat.

When you cook vegetables, use as little water as possible. Cook just until tender in a tightly covered utensil.

But don't think that everything should be consumed raw. Some people get "wind" from eating raw apples, pears, etc. In such a case they should eat applesauce or stewed pears (without sugar) plus wheat germ flakes.

Water is destructive of some vitamins, so do not ever soak fresh foods. Do not use baking soda in the cooking water, for it is an alkali and is destructive of vitamins. Cover foods when storing them in the refrigerator.

CHAPTER 44

Fruit and Vegetables

by J. I. RODALE

    I would just like to briefly discuss the question of fruits and vegetables from the point of view of the poison sprays that are used in the orchards and on the truck farms in order to keep down insects and disease in the growing of the respective products. Wherever possible, we would urge readers to grow their own fruit and vegetables by the organic method, namely, without chemical fertilizers and without poison sprays. But where this is not possible, try and purchase these products from organic growers. We have available *The Organic Food Directory* which lists people in various parts of the country who have such food for sale. This is available for 10 cents.

    In the event that you do not have your own source of supply that is safe, just a few words of caution about fruit and vegetables. With regard to such fruits as apples, pears, peaches, etc., the way they are sprayed is just plain murder. Every year the big chemical companies are producing more potent poisons, and these are absorbed into the fruit under the skin, and it is therefore necessary, in order to be safe, to cut off the skin. Do not worry about the minerals that you are losing by not eating this skin. You can make up for it by taking bone meal which is a far better source of the minerals. We do not recommend drinking ordinary commercial cider, as this has the spray residues in it, and also benzoate of soda, which is a poisonous preservative. I would not eat cherries because they are sprayed heavily, and I once traced back dizzy spells to eating them.

    Pineapple would be a good source of fruit because of its heavy skin protection. Very little poison could penetrate beyond that. For the same reason, bananas are a good source, but we would suggest that you buy bananas green and let them turn yellow in your own home because in some of the fruit markets, that is, at the source in the wholesale concerns, they use a gas to turn the bananas yellow. Oranges should be taken only in the whole form and not in the juice, and the same goes for grapefruit. It has recently been discovered that the orange contains a certain amount of citric acid which might harm the teeth of some susceptible people. Others might get away with it. Also, certain susceptible individuals may have stomach trouble on account of this citric acid. We recommend about two oranges and about one and one-half grapefruits a week, unless your teeth are made of steel.

Grapes are pretty badly sprayed and we, therefore, are awfully sorry that we cannot recommend them unless obtained from an organic source. Coconuts would be a good fruit, and, of course, all kinds of nuts in moderation, because they are fattening for those who are inclined toward obesity. If eaten before going to bed, they may cause insomnia. Nuts should always be very well chewed.

I believe that within this range there is sufficient fruit to satisfy a person's sweet tooth and also his or her needs for vitamins and minerals.

Vegetables

Here is a more difficult situation. The extent of chemicalization and poison spraying is unbelievable. If at all possible, get yourself a small piece of ground and grow your own vegetables. You would be surprised how much you can turn out for an average-sized family from a small plot. And there is a wonderful feeling of creation, as, year by year, you set into action the process of raising your own food. It is not difficult at all and many folks who just have a small patch in their back yard usually in lawn have dug it up and grown the finest vegetables by the organic method. It is very simple. Chemical fertilizers should not be used nor any kind of sprays. Usually you can purchase some compost or other organic matter, which will not only make your soil a pleasure to work with, but will cause the breakdown of minerals which will be absorbed into the plant.

I would recommend peas because the spray goes on the pod and the pod is not eaten. String beans, however, would not be in the same class because the spray goes right up against the string beans. Potatoes are not too bad, because, although the plants are sprayed, and some of the spray seeps into the ground, the potatoes, growing underground, do not have the amount that the average vegetable growing above ground would have. I would suggest, for the same reason as in the case of apples, that the potatoes be peeled, because the contact of the spray in the ground might go up against the skin, but probably not penetrate too much into the interior. Here again your bone meal will be the protector as far as minerals are concerned.

Corn is a good vegetable in the summer, because it is usually not sprayed, and you also have the protection of the husk.

In growing a vegetable garden, don't forget a little parsley bed. This plant is unusually rich in vitamin C and is very easy to grow. You can even grow it in a window box if you are an apartment dweller.

CHAPTER 45

Nuts Are Fine Food

Nuts are good for you. They are inexpensive, rich in protein and healthful fats, completely natural, and uncontaminated by any chemicals. You should eat more of them.

One pound of nuts is equal in calories to 2.3 pounds of bread, 3.7 pounds of steak, 12.3 pounds of potatoes or 15 pounds of oranges. One pound of oily nuts supplies all the calories needed for the day plus 40 per cent of the protein, 60 per cent of the phosphorus, 30 per cent of the calcium and iron and 4 times the daily requirement of fat.

What do you think of a food that has this kind of nutritive value, grows wild and free for the picking, needs little care while it is growing, is harvested by picking it up from the ground, needs no processing and no cooking, and keeps well with no refrigeration or preservatives? Doesn't this sound like the absolutely ideal food that we have been waiting for all these years? Well, its been here and waiting for us all these years. Why have we been so slow in recognizing nuts as one of our best and most practical foods?

Definition and Content of Nuts

Speaking generally, nuts are defined as hard-shelled seeds enclosing a single edible oily kernel. If you want to be technical about it, you will find that nuts are classified biologically as one seeded fruits, such as beechnut, chestnut, and so forth. But we have come to think of a lot of different products as nuts, including such varied edibles as cashews, peanuts, coconuts, and so forth. Most of these are high in protein and fat and low in carbohydrate. Some nuts contain as much as 60 per cent fat. Some kinds of pecans contain as much as 76 per cent fat.

This high fat content would seem to indicate the nuts are an excellent food for those who are trying to gain weight. They are a source of natural fat, delicious to pick up as a snack between meals. They are high in protein as well as fat, which means that they do a good job of helping to regulate blood sugar, which is so important to good health. Pound for pound they contain more calories than most foods.

In general, nuts are high in minerals and have peculiar affinities for certain kinds of minerals. The hickory tree, for instance, accumulates aluminum from the soil. The ash of hickory leaves is high in this trace mineral. Hickory trees also accumulate the rare earths—*scandium, yttrium, lanthanum, dys prosium, holium, erbium* and so forth—names we lay folks seldom hear.

The Brazil nut contains much barium, another trace mineral. In fact, some Brazil nuts have been found to cause distress if they are eaten in quantity because of the large content of barium. There is a deficiency of zinc in the pecan, English walnut and almond and a deficiency of boron in the English walnut. The European beechnut contains a toxic substance in its seed coat. The shell of the cashew contains liquids and oils which are toxic and irritating to the skin, much like poison ivy.

However, we need not concern ourselves with these analyses, for, of course, we do not ever eat those parts of the nuts which contain toxic material. And, since none of us lives exclusively on nuts, we need not worry about getting too much or too little of one of the minerals or trace minerals. Our other foods will balance this. Tannins, which most of us associate with nuts, are found only in the shells, wood and bark of the trees.

Vitamins and Minerals in Nuts

Most nuts contain a good supply of vitamin A and thiamin, one of the B vitamins. Some of them contain vitamin E. Immature English walnuts have been found to contain large amounts of vitamin C, which disappears as the nuts ripen. The walnut hulls are an excellent source of vitamin C, containing as high as 1550-3036 milligrams of this vitamin for every 100 grams. Of course, we can't eat the walnut hulls. In some parts of the world, we understand, efforts are being made to extract the vitamin C from the walnut hulls. The red skin of the peanut contains considerable thiamin, incidentally, so don't throw it away when you eat peanuts.

Nuts are not complete proteins, even though their protein content is high. We mean by this that they do not contain all of the amino acids, or kinds of protein essential for human health. Only foods of animal origin contain all these amino acids—they do not occur in any one vegetable food except soybeans. But, even so, nuts are a most important food if you want to increase your protein intake, and most of us should.

Are Nuts a Substitute for Meat?

The foods of animal origin that are high in protein such as meat and eggs have an acid reaction in the body, whereas most nuts have an alkaline reaction. Filberts, peanuts and walnuts are acid. All other are alkaline in their effect in the body. They are a highly concentrated food.

Nuts have the reputation of being hard to digest. But they were often eaten at the end of a heavy meal, by an individual who had stuffed himself on all kinds of indigestible desserts, and the nuts took the blame for his overindulgence. Nuts must be chewed carefully. Otherwise they will not be properly digested, for the digestive juices cannot break down the tough kernels.

Rich in protein, they do not present any problem of decay or spoilage such as occurs with meat and other animal products. True, nuts eventually become rancid but there is no question of refrigeration and threat of poisoning from spoilage. Nuts are free from uric acid and other substances produced in the body by eating meat. Do keep in mind, however, that they cannot be used as a complete substitute for meat unless you are highly skilled in balancing menus, for their protein is not complete. And they do not supply the same bulk that meat and other foods supply, which is important for propulsion in the digestive tract.

How Nuts Are Processed

Nuts, like other natural products, should be eaten in as nearly the natural state as possible. But we civilized twentieth century folks must always prove our superiority by processing nuts until we finally almost destroy their food value. The cashew nut is shelled in India from whence it comes. First it is heated in liquid to make the shells brittle and to extract the oily substance inside. The shell of the English walnut is sometimes loosened by exposure to ethylene gas. Almonds are bleached by dipping in chloride of lime. Pecans are sometimes bleached, sometimes dyed.

Blanching the nuts—that is, removing the inner skin, is accomplished by soaking in hot water. But pecans and English walnuts are dipped in hot lye, followed by an acid rinse. Another process is to pass the kernels through a heated solution of glycerin and sodium carbonate, then to remove the skins with a stream of water and dip in a citric acid solution.

Cooking the nuts in oil causes considerable loss of vitamin contents. We are told that in an experiment macadamia nuts were cooked in oil at 135 degrees centigrade for only 12 to 15 minutes and lost 16 per cent of their thiamin. Modern commercial methods of processing nuts bring about destruction of perhaps 70 to 80 per cent of the thiamin.

So what can you do to secure nuts whose food value has not been ruined before you get them? First of all, pass by the fancy, toasty-smelling nut and candy shops as if they weren't there. Never buy nuts that have been shelled or roasted. Buy them in the shells and shell them yourself. And then, whatever you do, don't roast all the goodness out of them before you eat them! If you have ever tasted an almond right out of the shell, you will agree with us that there is absolutely no excuse for roasting them. We do not know where you can get nuts that have not been bleached or dyed, except from organic growers who do not use chemicals of any kind. But the dye or the bleach is only on the outside of the nut which, of course, you do not eat.

Where and How We Get Our Nuts

The southern European and Mediterranean countries are the world's largest producers of nuts. Brazil nuts are grown in Brazil and Bolivia. Cashews come from India and Mozambique. United States is the largest producer of English (sometimes called Persian) walnuts and almost the sole producer of pecans. Although the total value of edible nuts produced in 1949 was 70 million dollars, the people of this country used only about one and a half pounds of nuts per person that same year. So you see we do not begin to appreciate the value of nuts as food. In spite of the fact that they are generally presented to us commercially in candies, pastries and so forth, we still eat only about a pound and a half per person per year, whereas we consume annually well over 100 pounds of sugar per person. And sugar has no food value whatsoever except calories.

Peanuts and Acorns

The peanut, which is of course not a nut at all but a plant whose nuts ripen in the ground, has recently come into its own as a food of surpassingly high quality from the standpoint of nutrition. Peanut flour contains over 4 times the amount of protein, 8 times the fat and 9 times the minerals that are in wheat flour. It can be used with great success in recipes. Adelle Davis in her excellent cookbook, *Let's Cook It Right* (Harcourt Brace and Company, New York), says she has never had a failure using peanut flour in baking recipes. For those who have difficulty of any kind with cereals and flours made from cereals, peanut flour would seem to be the perfect answer.

Acorn flour is used extensively in Europe and among the Indians of our Southwest. We are told that, in all probability, over the centuries, more human beings have eaten acorns than have eaten wheat. In Spain and Italy as much as 20 per cent of the food of the poor folks may be acorns. Some of them are edible as they grow. Others can only be eaten by first removing the tannins.

Nuts in their shells keep well. Shelled they become

rancid in 3 or 4 months, especially in the summer. They can be kept at refrigerator temperatures for a year. With the exception of black walnuts and hickory nuts, those which are available to us in this country are not so hard to shell, so there seems to be no reason for not keeping them right in the shell until you use them. They are an excellent and unusual dessert.

For those housewives who feel lost somehow now that they no longer serve cakes, pies, puddings or cookies for dessert, why not get yourself a big bowl of the family's favorite nuts, a couple of nutcrackers and picks and bring them to the table after each meal, along with fresh fruit as the best and most healthful kind of dessert! We often forget about nuts, if we keep them in a bag in the kitchen cupboard. So try to keep a bowl of them handy for everyone to dip into for snacks—on a table in the dining room or living room.

Mineral and Vitamin Content of Nuts

Here is the composition of a number of kinds of nuts. Note, please, that some of them are relatively high in starch content while others contain little starch. Some are as high in protein content as meat. Others contain less protein. Remember, too, that, although the protein of nuts is excellent protein, it does not contain all of the essential amino acids that are present in foods of animal origin.

	Carbohydrate	Percentage of Protein	Fat	Calories per pound
Acorn	57.10	6.65	5	1909
Almond	4.3	20.5	16	3030
Beechnut	13.2	21.9	57.4	2846
Brazil nut	4.1	13.8	61.5	3013
Butternut	3.5	27.9	61.2	3165
Cashew	29.4	21.6	39	2866
Chestnut	36.6	2.3	2.7	1806
Coconut	27.9	5.7	50.6	2760
Filbert	9.3	14.9	65.6	3288
Hickory nuts	11.4	15.4	67.4	3342
Lychee	78	2.9	.80	1539
Macadamia nuts	8.2	8.6	73.0	3507
Peanuts	8.6	28.1	49	2645
Pecans	3.9	9.4	73	3539
Pine nuts	6.9	33.9	49.4	3174
Pistachio	16.3	22.3	54.0	2996
Walnut, black	10.20	27.6	56.3	3180
Walnut, English	5.0	12.5	51.5	3326

The percentage of the mineral content of nuts is given in the following chart:

	Phosphorus	Potassium	Calcium	Magnesium	Sodium	Chlorine	Iron	Sulfur	Zinc	Manganese	Copper
Almond	.475	.759	.254	.252	.026	.020	.0044	.150	.0019	.0008	.0015
Brazil	.602	.601	.124	.225	.020	.081	.0028	.198	...	...	.0014
Butternut	...	...	...	...	...	...	.0068	...	...	...	.0012
Cashew	.480	...	.048	...	...	...	...	...	...	...	...
Chestnut	.093	.560	.034	.051	.065	.006	.0070	.068	.0004	.0031	.0078
Coconut	.191	.693	.043	.077	.053	.225	.0036	.076	.0010	...	...
Hazlenut	.354	.618	.287	.140	.019	.067	.0041	.198	.0010	...	.0012
Hickory nut	.370	...	...	.160	...	...	.0029	...	...	...	.0014
Macadamia	.240	...	.053	...	...	...	.0020	...	...	...	...
Peanut	.392	.614	.080	.167	.039	.041	.0019	.226	.0016	.0020	.0009
Pecan	.335	.332	.089	.152	...	.050	.0026	.113	...	.0043	.0010
Pistachio	...	...	...	...	...	...	.0079	...	...	.0007	.0012
Walnut, black ..	.091	.675	.071	.098	...	...	.0060	...	...	.0033	.0032
Walnut, English.	.308	.332	.089	.134	.023	.036	.0021	.146	.0020	.0018	.0011

Although they are not as rich in vitamins as some other foods, nuts provide some of the vitamins that exist in all natural food products that have not been refined. The B vitamins are scarce in modern American diets, for we have removed them from refined foods during the processing. So nuts, even in the small quantities in which we eat them, compared to other foods, are an excellent source of the B vitamins. Here is the vitamin content of some of the common nuts:

	Vitamin A	Vitamin B_1 Thiamin	Vitamin B_2 Riboflavin	Vitamin B Niacin
Almonds (¾ cup)	0	.25 mg.	.67 mg.	4.6 mg.
Brazil nuts (¾ cup)	trace	.86	....	....
Cashews (¾ cup)	....	.63	.19	2.1
Chestnuts (40)	0	.108	.24	1.0
Coconut (2 cups)	....	.30 .60	1.0	....
Peanuts (¾ cup)	0	.30	.13	16.2
Peanut butter (6 tbs.)	....	.12	.13	16.2
Pecans (1 cup)	50 I.U.	.72	.11	.9
Walnuts, Eng. (1 cup)	30 I.U.	.48	.13	1.2

In addition, peanuts are rich in pyridoxine, pantothenic acid and biotin, 3 other important members of the vitamin B family.

The almond includes both bitter and sweet among its relatives. The sweet almond is the one we eat. Both are closely related to the peach tree. As a matter of fact, the almond nut itself is almost identical with the peach stone. The bitter almond contains hydrocyanic acid, a toxic substance. Beechnuts, too, as they are grown in Europe contain a substance that can be harmful in quantity. But the American beechnut has no such ingredient.

Products Made from Nuts

We usually eat chestnuts cooked almost like a vegetable, but they are delicious raw, once you get used to them that way. In many parts of the world chestnuts are ground into flour which is used as cereal flour is here.

Peanut butter is made of peanuts that have been roasted and halved. Then their skins are removed and they are ground. Usually oils are added to keep them in a smooth, buttery condition. If you have access to it, we'd suggest buying raw peanut butter or grinding your own from raw peanuts. The famous scientist, Carver, produced 202 different products from peanuts —not all of them food products, of course.

Nonfood products are made from other nuts, too. A floor covering is made from nutshell flour mixed with pigment, resin. Loud speakers for radios are made from walnut shell flour. For some peculiar reason this substance seems to filter out vibrations more effectively than any other!

CHAPTER 46

Bananas

We believe that bananas are one of the finest foods imaginable—easily digested, seldom allergenic, rich in vitamins and minerals. Theirs is an especially healthful kind of carbohydrate, we believe, much preferable to that of bread or other cereals. Here is some further information about bananas.

Yes, we have bananas, today. We have them in all kinds of diets, for infants, adults—stout and thin—and old people who have trouble with their digestion. Not so many years ago it was fondly believed that bananas were hard to digest. This was probably because the bananas were eaten before they were fully ripe, and their raw starch caused considerable digestive trouble, just as that of green apples does. Faintly green bananas look attractive and feel firm to the touch. When dark specks begin to appear on their yellow surfaces, we are inclined to turn them down as rotten. But a banana is not fully ripe until its skin shows brown specks. By then its starch has been changed into completely digestible fruit sugar.

Their Usefulness and Content

They knew about bananas way back in history, for Alexander the Great found the people of India eating bananas in 327 B.C. Within the past few years bananas have been found to be a specific remedy for several infant diseases, such as celiac disease of which the outstanding symptom is diarrhea. It has also been discovered that bananas in the diet of infants result in better growth than is achieved with either apples or cereals. We have learned that people who are allergic to bananas can eat dehydrated bananas with no distress. Banana flour is sold as a substitute for wheat flour, tapioca, oatmeal, arrowroot and so forth. You can make bread from banana flour mixed with 5 per cent wheat flour.

Recently, an investigation was made of the suitability of bananas in the diet of elderly people. Even those who had never eaten bananas found that they felt well when eating a banana or two every day, had no trouble digesting them, enjoyed their flavor and were especially pleased with how easy they are to chew in comparison with other fruits.

The average-sized banana weighs about 100 grams, contains less than 100 calories, has an alkaline reaction in the body, as do most fruits, and in addition contains the following quantities of vitamins and minerals:

Calcium	8.	milligrams
Phosphorus	28.	milligrams
Iron	.6	milligrams
Copper	.21	milligrams
Manganese	640.	micrograms
Sodium	.5	milligrams
Vitamin A	430.	Internat. Units
Vitamin B		
Thiamin	.09	milligrams
Riboflavin	.06	milligrams
Niacin	.6	milligrams
Pyridoxine	300.	micrograms
Inositol	34.	milligrams
Biotin	4.	micrograms
Folic Acid	95.	micrograms
Vitamin C	10.	milligrams
Vitamin E	.40	milligrams
Protein	1.2	grams
Fat	.2	grams
Carbohydrates	23.0	grams

Eat Bananas Raw

You will find recipes in your cookbook for baking or frying bananas. It seems to us that there is actually less excuse for cooking a banana than for cooking any other fruit. So we would advise eating them raw. We have read a good many stories about gases used in ripening bananas commercially. So we would suggest that you buy them fairly green and ripen them yourself. The best way to do this is to keep them with little or no ventilation until they begin to color rapidly. Then keep them always at room temperature, until they show the brown mottling which means they are ready to eat. Like other tropical fruits, bananas should not be kept in the refrigerator.

CHAPTER 47

Enzymes

One reason why fruits, vegetables and nuts are so valuable is that they can and should be eaten raw. When foods are cooked, enzymes are destroyed. These are precious elements which we discuss in this chapter.

Physiology teaches us that man lives by the process of converting some of his food into building blocks of protein which replace his cells as they wear out, and by burning other food as energy which enables him to play, work and enjoy life. We all learned in school that the various substances of which food is made (carbohydrates, proteins and fats) are "changed" by the digestive process and in this "change" they become useful to our bodies. Now obviously considerable change must take place. Look at a plate of steak, potatoes, vegetables, salad and fruit. It certainly does not look like the flesh of a human being. Yet, that is what a large part of it becomes. It certainly does not seem possible that by burning that plateful of food in a fire, one could obtain enough energy to carry a working man through a day of strenuous ditch-digging or hard mental work. Yet the energy released by that plate of food does just that, once it has been exposed to the chemical magic of digestion and assimilation.

We know in a general sort of way that our body is equipped with digestive juices. We know that, during a meal, the saliva pours out a substance that partly digests starchy foods; the stomach pours out another substance that digests protein; the pancreas and the intestine exude some substance that finishes up the digestion of protein and starch. So right here—during and immediately after a meal—this process of "changing" food into human substance begins. But what is it in the digestive juices that works this magic? Finding the answer to this question leads us into the complex and largely unexplored, but very fascinating story of enzymes.

Scientists have known for many years that there are substances present in tiny quantities, in every living cell, that possess marvelous properties. It all began with a study of yeasts and fungi. The active living organism that causes fruit juices to ferment and bread to rise is yeast. As the tiny yeast plant grows, changes take place in the medium in which it is growing. The fruit juice becomes alcoholic; the bread dough rapidly expands to many times its former volume. But early scientists discovered that after the yeast plants had been killed, something remained that was not a living plant as is the yeast. This something was called a "ferment" because it brought about a state of fermentation. Not until many years later was it named an "enzyme."

What are enzymes and where do they exist? Are they alive? Are they necessary to life? How can they best be preserved and how are they destroyed? What do they do in the body? What do they do in plants? Can we make them synthetically in a laboratory? These are some of the questions that have occupied researchers in the intriguing study of enzymes. Out of all this study have come many observations that have greatly increased our knowledge of how human beings live and also what and how human beings should eat. We will try to answer these questions, so that you can understand the immense importance of enzymes. Some of the answers are not completely understood as yet even by the most learned scientists, for enzymes still involve much that cannot be answered, with our present means of exploration. Perhaps in the enzyme we have the secret of life itself.

Enzymes Cause Chemical Changes

As you know, many physical things take place in this world because of chemical changes. If you drop some sugar into a teacup of water, the sugar changes. It dissolves. During this process many chemical changes take place in the mixture you have in your teacup. If you let the teacup stand for several weeks, other changes will take place gradually and slowly. But if you heat the mixture, changes begin to take place right away. The sugar and water turn into syrup. Now, imagine that you have in your kitchen some substance which, if you dropped it into the cold cup of sugar-water, would immediately change it into syrup, without any cooking. Such a substance is called in chemistry a "catalyst." It brings about a chemical change immediately, without heat.

What Is a Catalyst?

A catalyst is further defined as a substance which will perform this job of bringing about a chemical change without itself becoming involved in the change. In other words, you could, with proper chemical procedure, remove all the catalyst from your syrup and it would still be syrup. The catalyst needs to be present in extremely small amounts—one part of a catalyst can act chemically to change substances whose volume is millions of times greater than its own. For instance, one part of catalyst to millions of parts of sugar-water would still produce the same effect. And the catalyst would remain unchanged in the middle of all this chemical activity.

An enzyme is a catalyst. So enzymes are present wherever chemical changes take place rapidly, without the added stimulus of heat. Since everything that takes place in physiology involves chemical change, enzymes must be present everywhere. They are. They are present in great abundance in every living cell—plant and animal. Are they alive? James S. McLester, M.D., in his book, *Nutrition and Diet in Health and Disease* (W. B. Saunders, 1949), says, "As crystalline organic compounds these materials are lifeless; as substances which have the property of increasing in the presence of living cells, they assume a property characteristic of living things."

The antiseptics that kill living organisms like germs and yeasts do not inactivate enzymes. You could drop formaldehyde or iodine or lysol into your teacup, destroying all germs that might be there, but the chemical process brought about by the enzyme you have in the cup would go right on, proving that the disinfectant has not disturbed it.

The Effect of Cold and Heat on Enzymes

However, there are two circumstances that disturb the activity of enzymes very much—cold and heat. Cold inactivates them. That is, if you put your teacup into the refrigerator, no chemical change would take place. The enzyme would stay there in the cup, but the sugar would remain sugar and the water would remain water. You would have no syrup. But when you take the cup out into the warm air again and the temperature of the mixture goes up to room temperature, the enzymes would become active again and would make syrup. So they haven't been destroyed. They have only ceased activity for a short time.

A small increase in heat causes the enzymes to work more rapidly. But more heat destroys them entirely and, even after the mixture has cooled down, they will not become active again. Between 32 degrees and 104 degrees Fahrenheit—that is, anywhere from freezing up to the temperature of a hot summer day —enzymes are very active. But when you heat them to a point above 122 degrees Fahrenheit, enzymes are permanently destroyed. The boiling point of water is 212 degrees Fahrenheit. So when you boil vegetables or fruit, all enzymes in the food are destroyed. When you roast meat at a temperature of 200 or 300 degrees, of course, all enzymes in the meat are destroyed.

What does this mean so far as preparing food and cooking are concerned? Well, it means first that refrigeration is one of the greatest inventions of modern times, for foods can be kept with their enzymes intact, but inactive, so long as you keep them in the refrigerator or freezer. While a plant is growing and ripening, the enzymes are busy inside forming vitamins and bringing about other changes that make the fruit or vegetable tasty and nutritious. But as soon as the food is picked it should be refrigerated, for otherwise the enzymes go right on working, and this time their activity is destructive. Lettuce and radishes wilt, and fruit skins wither when they are kept at room temperature, for the enzymes go on working. On the other hand, when you cook food at high temperatures, you destroy immediately all enzymes. Is this good or bad? Healthful or unhealthful? To have the answer we must know what enzymes do in the body.

How Enzymes Act in the Body

Actually, they must be present (in very small amounts) for any process that takes place in the body. They are present in every cell (and don't forget that your body contains many billions of cells), and they are the cell's only connection with the outer world. That steak on your plate is some day going to form part of a certain number of cells of your body, but it can't possibly do that unless there are the correct enzymes in the right places at every single moment during that transformation.

The salivary glands, the pancreas, the wall of the stomach and of the intestines contain the chief digestive enzymes (there are 9 of them). But even after the food has been changed by these enzymes into a form that can be transported to all the cells of the body, there must be other enzymes in those cells, that continue the process of changing this substance even more, according to what use the body will make of it.

The Vitamin-Enzyme System

We talk a lot about vitamins and we know that vitamins are essential for good health. But vitamins can do their work only in the presence of enzymes, for they form part of complicated "enzyme systems." For instance, thiamin, a B vitamin, is necessary to good health. Thiamin forms part of an enzyme system that digests sugar and starches. The thiamin must be present if these carbohydrates are to be converted into energy, but the enzymes must be present, too. Every vitamin whose use in the body is known has been discovered to be a part of an enzyme system. There are (so far discovered) 5 enzymes which contain riboflavin, a B vitamin. "It has been claimed for some time that vitamin C is also an essential constituent in enzymatic reactions in the cell," says Morris Jacobs in his book, *Food and Food Products*. (Interscience Publishers, 1951.)

Enzymes are named in accordance with the food substance they "work on" chemically. So an enzyme that brings about a chemical change in the presence of phosphorus is called phosphatase, an enzyme that works to break down sugar (sucrose) is called sucrase and so forth.

The Effect of Acids on the Enzymes

Now, of course, the temperature of the body will never rise high enough to destroy the body's enzymes. But there is another characteristic of enzymes that makes them subject to destruction in the body. They are fussy about the acidity of substances in which they are working. Some enzymes can work only in a quite acid medium. Others need to have more alkalinity. Pepsin, for instance, which is the enzyme that breaks down protein in the stomach, functions at a pH (or acidity) of about 1.2 to 1.8. Trypsin, the enzyme in pancreatic juice, must have much more alkaline surroundings—about 8.2. Now if, because of some condition of ill health, there is not enough hydrochloric acid in your stomach to keep the pepsin working properly, you will not be able to digest proteins. As people grow older the hydrochloric acid in their stomach tends to decrease, so they may have trouble digesting proteins, because their supply of the enzyme pepsin simply cannot function in an alkaline stomach. Taking bicarbonate of soda also makes your stomach alkaline and stops the activity of pepsin.

How does it happen, then, if the stomach is acid enough and there is plenty of pepsin, that the walls of the stomach are not digested? They are made of protein. There is disagreement among scientists as to why we do not digest our own stomachs. One school believes that there may be anti-enzymes secreted by the cells of the stomach wall which prevent the digestive enzymes from working on them. Others say that the thick mucous coating on the lining of the stomach protects it from coming into contact with the digestive enzymes. How does it happen that tapeworms can live in a human intestine? Apparently, say the scientists, there is something present in living cells that prevents the enzymes from breaking them down and digesting them.

Can We Obtain Enzymes from Food?

Where does the body get the material from which it manufactures enzymes? Just stop and think for a moment of the enormity of this chemical factory that is humming away inside you, day and night. Think of all the complicated processes in which these enzymes take part. While you are eating, all the digestive organs are pouring out juices rich in enzymes. In every tiny cell, from your brain right down to your little toe, enzymes are fermenting furiously, combining and recombining into the thousands of different enzyme systems that move your muscles, stimulate your nerves, keep you breathing, thinking and feeling. The body manufactures enzymes out of food, water and air —those are the only ingredients available. So what you eat becomes many times more important, when you consider it from the point of view of manufacturing enzymes.

Processing Destroys Enzymes

In the days before fire was invented, man ate his food raw, just as wild animals do. Raw food contains enzymes, as we know. Aside from other chemical changes that take place, cook-

ing food destroys enzymes. It seems logical that enzymes from
raw food could be transformed into useful enzymes for one body
system or another, after they have been eaten. They consist of
the same chemical substance—that is, a plant enzyme contains
the same elements in the same proportions as the enzymes of a
human body contains. Is it possible that the raw food our
ancestors ate, far back in history, contributed vast stores of
enzymes to their bodies, so that they themselves did not have to
manufacture so many enzymes? Might not such an arrangement
have a very beneficial effect on the body? After all, manufacturing enzymes is a difficult job, especially when the only materials
available are present-day denatured, diluted, processed foods.

Yet our bodies must go on manufacturing enzymes in
enormous quantity every day, if we are to go on living. After
an enzyme has completed its work, the next process that takes
place generally destroys the enzyme, so we must be replenishing
the supply all the time. For instance, salivary enzymes function
only in an alkaline medium. When we swallow our food, all the
salivary enzymes which are busy breaking down starch and
sugar are thrown into the stomach where the high acidity destroys them within a half hour or so. So our salivary glands must
immediately manufacture more.

Raw Food Best

Might it not be that this continual loss from the body of
enzymes that are not replaced in our food is one of the main
causes of aging and disease? In the Bible we read of men who
lived many times longer than we do today. The mythology of
other religions also contains stories of men who lived to a great
age. In those early days men lived on fruits, nuts, berries, raw
meat and unheated milk. What cooking was done was very
primitive, and the heat could not penetrate to the very interior
to destroy enzymes. Perhaps this kind of nourishment was so
full of enzymes that bodies were not worn out so soon by the
incessant need for producing more.

Wild animals, who have no contact with man, do not
become diseased in their wild state, unless, of course, they must
exist under conditions of starvation or drought. Wild animals
brought to the zoos of civilized cities used to show a high mortality from the diseases to which man is subject—pneumonia,
tuberculosis, cancer and so forth. Because these animals were so

very valuable, zoo keepers experimented and found that diets of completely raw food kept the zoo animals healthy. Morbidity rates have dropped almost to zero in zoos where all animals eat only raw food. We know, of course, that many of the chemical changes brought about by cooking destroy vitamins and otherwise decrease the nutritional value of the food. *But perhaps the destruction of enzymes is easily the most disastrous result of cooking.*

Advantages of a Raw Food Diet

We know that those primitive Eskimos who eat practically all their food raw do not suffer from the diseases of modern man; in fact, they have so little sickness that there is no tradition of medicinal remedies or medicine men among them. On the other hand, the American Indians, who cooked their food, have an enormous array of medicines and remedies, and their medicine men were the most important persons in the tribe.

Another interesting observation is that an herbivorous animal who lives entirely on uncooked plants, has a pancreas which is extremely small compared to man's. Apparently its pancreas does not need to produce nearly so many enzymes as a human pancreas, because a large part of the necessary enzymes are already present in its uncooked food. It is true too that Oriental peoples whose diet consists largely of cooked starch have pancreas glands much heavier than Americans. This seems to indicate that the amount of enzymes needed to deal with this cooked starch necessitates an overworked pancreas, which continually increases in size trying to become more efficient. Herbivorous animals have inactive salivary glands. The salivary glands do a big part of the job of digesting starches. But even so, the cow can get along with the small amount of starch-splitting enzymes turned out by a tiny pancreas, while man, with his efficient salivary glands, must have a large pancreas, and the more cooked starch he eats, the larger his pancreas becomes.

Kouchakoff found that the pathological condition present in the intestine after meals (with many white corpuscles present) did not take place when raw food was eaten. It does not seem possible that at our present stage of civilization, we could obtain almost all the necessary enzymes from our food as the cow apparently does. But we do believe that eating raw food day after day, in as great a quantity as possible will, over the years, greatly increase the body's store of enzymes and so will greatly benefit health, for these will be much less strain on enzyme producing organs if they do not have to work overtime supplying enzymes, which should logically be supplied by food.

Synthetic Enzymes

What about the possibility of taking synthetic enzymes? We know enough about the structure of enzymes that we can make them synthetically. Quite a number have been synthesized. Jacobs, in *Food and Food Products* says that our synthesis of enzymes has not contributed greatly to our knowledge of them. We know only that they are proteins, and we still have to solve the problem of protein structure. Jacobs also says, "In their normal environment, enzymes are partially protected against inactivation attributable to heat or other energy factors and to inhibition by metals. As they are progressively purified, these protective factors such as proteins, carbohydrates and the like are removed, leaving the enzymes open to attack by chemical and physical agents which inactivate them."

As you know, we do not recommend taking synthetic vitamins. It seems to us that a synthetic "pure" enzyme would be an even worse gamble, because there is not a chance that any of the natural substances protecting the activity of the enzyme would be present. And Dr. Jacobs substantiates this theory of ours. How, then, can you add to your enzyme supply, if you are interested in what we have said above and if you agree with us, that we moderns probably age earlier than we should and contract needless diseases simply from lack of enzymes?

How to Get Enough Enzymes

First of all, make it your business to eat as much raw food as possible and by this we mean that if half your diet is raw, that certainly won't be too much! Never cook fruits. There is no excuse nutritionally for destroying most of the food value of this excellent food, especially when fruits taste so much better raw! If your family and friends insist on serving stewed, baked or broiled fruits, simply refuse to eat them and ask for your portion raw. In the winter when fresh fruits are scarce, eat frozen rather than canned fruits. Having your own freezer is by far the best idea, for you can hurry the luscious beauties straight from the trees and bushes right into the freezer with a very minimum food value wasted. And remember, frozen food retains its enzymes! They disappear rapidly as the fruit thaws, however, so eat frozen fruit just as soon as it has thawed.

If you must eat often in restaurants, you probably suffer more than the rest of us from lack of enzymes, for the preparation and the wait before serving take just about all the food value from any restaurant food. But even here you can get fresh raw food, if you insist on it. A piece of fruit or a raw fruit or vegetable drink at the beginning of a meal, celery, salad, radishes during the meal and some other fresh fruit for dessert— these raw foods are available in most restaurants. And if you patronize one establishment, they will be glad to have raw foods on hand for you.

Eat as many vegetables raw as possible. Never cook carrots, cabbage, Swiss chard, spinach, broccoli stalks, onions, celery, turnips. Sure, it's rabbit food, but did you ever know a rabbit who died of heart disease or cancer?

Become an expert in fixing delicious raw vegetable dishes. Use a grater, a food mill, a blender, a chopping board. Use salad dressings for garnish if your family objects to plain raw vegetables. Try raisins, dates, fruit and nuts as "fixings." And remember, keep all raw foods chilled all the time.

Eat Only Organically Grown Foods

Then, too, it seems quite possible that organically-raised fruits and vegetables are richer in enzymes than commercially-raised produce. It has been shown time and time again that animals raised on organic food do not contract the diseases to which other animals are subject. Sir Albert Howard in his splendid book, *The Agricultural Testament* (Oxford University Press, 1949), recounts the story of his cattle raised on organic food, who were pastured alongside cattle with hoof and mouth disease. Even rubbing noses with these diseased animals, Sir Albert's cattle remained completely free from the epidemic malady. Now, undoubtedly, there is much more food value in food that has been raised organically—that is, without the use of chemical fertilizer and insecticide. Perhaps the most important of these food elements may turn out to be enzymes.

Our second recommendation is to buy and eat organically-raised food if you possibly can. Unless you live in an apartment, there is probably a small plot of ground somewhere near the house where you can put in a garden of your own, even if it means spading up lawn to do it. Or you can find through our *Organic Food Directory* (available from Rodale Press, for 10 cents) a list of farmers throughout the country who sell organically-raised produce. Perhaps there are some organic farmers who live near you. Or you can persuade some farmer (or gardener) friend or relative who lives nearby to begin gardening organically so that you can buy produce from him. It isn't really too difficult or expensive to make certain that at least a part of your food is organically grown. Perhaps a large measure of the increased good health you will experience will be due to the supply of enzymes in this most healthful kind of food.

CHAPTER **48**

The Harmfulness of Processed Foods

It was proved 20 years ago by a famous scientist that cooked foods create poisons in the digestive tract, apart from their destructive work in destroying enzymes. This is another reason for eating plenty of fresh, raw fruits and vegetables, whenever possible—at meals or between.

For a number of years articles have appeared at intervals in the medical journals on the experiments done by P. Kouchakoff, M.D., of the Institute of Clinical Chemistry of Lausanne, Switzerland. His theories are so challenging that the medical profession returns to them again and again, even though no one apparently has continued with the work he began.

His theory concerns leukocytes, the white blood corpuscles that fight infection and disease in the body. If you have an infected finger, for instance, the pus consists of leukocytes that have gathered at the point to resist the germs.

Our medical dictionary defines leukocytes as "the white blood corpuscles normally present in the intestine during the process of digestion." For many years doctors, chemists and physiologists have considered that white blood corpuscles are simply necessary in the intestinal tract when food is being digested, without questioning why this should be so, since the function of leukocytes is to fight poisons.

In 1930 during a meeting of the International Congress of Microbiology in Paris, Dr. Kouchakoff read a paper disclosing his observations of the "intestinal flora of man" by which is meant the bacteria that exist in the intestine. He had discovered the startling fact, that the leukocytes which appear in the intestine after meals appear *only when the food eaten has been prepared at high temperatures or by complicated manufacturing processes.* When an entire meal of raw, natural foods is eaten, no leukocytes appear. This is an indication, says Kouchakoff, that some unhealthy process is taking place in the body as a result of food that is not easily assimilated, hence the leukocytes appear in order to protect the body from harm.

Processed Foods Disturb Digestive Functions

Again in 1936 at the International Congress of Microbiology in London, Kouchakoff spoke, relating his studies of animals in the far north. He found that in some of the polar birds there were no bacteria at all present in the intestinal tract. In polar bears, of which he examined many hundreds, he found only one type of intestinal bacteria. However, when he took bear cubs and fed them for a period of two years on human diet, they developed many intestinal bacteria, and at the same time showed retarded development and stunted growth, compared to wild cubs of their age, in spite of the fact that they lived in complete freedom under identical polar conditions.

Leukocyte Formula Tests Correct Nutrition

"It is to be concluded," says Kouchakoff, "that the organs of digestion of the higher animals are capable of functioning properly in the absence of intestinal microbes provided the organism receives adequate nutrition in the form of natural foodstuffs. The consumption of food altered by high temperatures and by complicated manufacture causes a disturbance of the functions of the digestive organs and brings about the intervention of the microbes."

In the future, said Dr. Kouchakoff, it might be possible to create healthy human beings by correct nutrition alone, from the first days of life. The test of correct nutrition should be the leukocyte formula. All foodstuffs should be tested according to this formula for their nutritional value. He also announced that he had found by experiment that if the altered food products (that is, the processed, manufactured ones) are combined in our diet with food in its natural state, the leukocyte formula can be maintained at its proper level. However, if food is heated above 100 degrees Centigrade (212 degrees Fahrenheit) as in the case of canned food or food cooked by pressure cookers, no amount of added raw food will improve the state of affairs and prevent the leukocytes.

Why No Further Research?

Since 1936 we can find no mention of Dr. Kouchakoff in medical publications, except for a letter to the *British Medical Journal* of May 7, 1949, in which Dr. A. Orley criticizes an article on pressure cooking as the best way in which to preserve vitamins in cooked foods. Although pressure cooking destroys the least number of vitamins, says Dr. Orley, in the light of Kouchakoff's experiments on leukocytes, should we not condemn pressure cooking on account of the very high temperature required?

Apparently no further work has been done to advance Dr. Kouchakoff's theory, so what should be our attitude toward it? It seems to us that Kouchakoff performed a great service for the health of mankind in conducting and interpreting his experiments. He has added another link to the chain of evidence that is growing daily, to show that processing of food is harmful; that the closer all our food is to its natural state, the healthier we will be. So until we have further experiments to report on this subject, let's be guided by the following suggestions:

1. Avoid processed food as much as you can. By processed food we mean canned food, commercially prepared cereals, food "mixes," bakery products, white or commercial whole wheat flour, condensed milk and so forth.

2. Eat fresh foods. Buy your fruits and vegetables as newly-picked as you can get them and use them as soon after you buy them as possible.

3. Buy fresh meats—nothing that has been dried, rolled, canned, spiced, pickled or processed.

4. Always serve something in its raw, natural state at every meal, for instance, salad or nuts with a cooked dinner, raw fruit with breakfast, raw celery, carrots or lettuce with a cooked lunch.

SECTION 11

SUNFLOWER SEEDS AND PUMPKIN SEEDS

Sunflower seeds are extremely rich in vitamins and minerals, and have a factor that is very valuable for the health of the eyes. They should be eaten raw, never roasted or salted, and may be obtained, hulled; this makes them easy to eat—they are quite delicious. Their oil contains unsaturated fatty acids, reducing the cholesterol of the blood, thus aiding the heart. Eating them will enable one to be in glaring sunshine without sunglasses. All edible seeds are valuable food, especially if they are unheated and unprocessed.

CHAPTER 49

Sunflower Seeds

by J. I. RODALE

Deaf Smith County, Texas, in the latter part of 1941 gained national fame as the county whose inhabitants had teeth superior to anything known anywhere in the world. The people in and around Hereford displayed teeth so remarkably healthy that the incidence of dental caries was almost completely nil. To account for this amazing situation, it was found that the soil in and around Hereford was rich in lime and phosphorus and contained some fluorine. These 3 elements are basic to the formation of tooth and bone and since, through the food grown in this soil, the residents absorbed these elements, they developed this extraordinary incidence of healthy teeth and bones.

Dr. S. G. Harootian of the Worcester State Hospital in Massachusetts, after hearing about Deaf Smith County, immediately began investigations into the possibility of finding a food containing these 3 elements. After much research and experimentation, he found that the bones of beef cattle ground fine as flour would serve the intended purpose, for in an astounding 9-month experiment with 9 mental patients, the formation of cavities was absolutely arrested by the addition of bone meal to their diets.

I Check on the Food Value of Sunflower Seeds

As a spectator I was irresistibly fascinated by these momentous happenings. For several years on our farm we had been growing sunflowers and feeding the seeds of this plant to our chickens. Poultry authorities speak highly of this seed as a conditioner of barnyard fowl. Parrots live on them almost exclusively and seem to lead a contented existence. We had never thought of eating these seeds ourselves, but when I heard about Deaf Smith County and Dr. Harootian's ingenious experiment, the thought occurred to me to check on the food value analysis of sunflower seeds. To my amazement the ash of the seed showed a tremendous quantity of phosphorus (35 per cent), calcium (7.5 per cent) and a trace of fluorine.

My Health Improves

I started to eat the seeds, a couple of heaping handfuls every day, but did not adjust anything else in my diet. My dentist had found only one tiny tooth cavity in about 3 years, so I wasn't thinking in terms of dental improvement. But about 4 days later I noticed something that was truly startling. My gums had stopped bleeding. They say that 4 out of 5 suffer from pink tooth brush (actually the figures are more nearly one out of 5). If this condition is not checked, it may eventually lead to something far more serious than mere tooth cavities, namely, the dreaded *pyorrhea* and the loss of all teeth. When I used to eat an apple, I could sometimes see a slight bloody imprint on the white pulp. This embarrassing condition cleared up nicely, so I stuck faithfully to my sunflower seeds.

About a week later, a slight intermittent quiver in my left eye went away. I usually suffered from this only in the winter when there was little opportunity for exercise or sunshine. As this is written two winters later, I am glad to report that it has not returned, thanks to the fact that I still eat sunflower seeds practically every day.

My eyes are not my strongest point. In the winter I would have trouble in walking on snow-blanketed roads. Before I became aware of the value of eating sunflower seeds, I left the house on the farm one day for a walk but had to return after being out only a moment, as the excessive brightness of the snow interfered with my vision. In fact, it made the snow seem a pink color. After being on the sunflower diet for about a month, I noticed I could walk in the snow without distress. A little while later my car broke down, and I had to walk over a mile on a snowed-up highway in bright sunshine with no trouble at all for the first three-quarters of the way. On the last stretch the eyes smarted a little.

Vitamin A and B in the Seeds

The sunflower seed is loaded down with vitamin B. The oil found in sunflower seeds is very rich in vitamin A, which is known to be essential to robust eye health. I noticed also that my skin seemed to be getting smoother. This doesn't seem to be unreasonable because calcium and vitamin A are specifics for a good strong epidermis. Dr. Bogert in the book, *Nutrition and Physical Fitness,* says, "Hard, dry skin, which may be inflamed or show a peculiar eruption, has been noted in poor people of China, Ceylon and East Africa on diets low in vitamin A, and the skin returned to normal when cod-liver oil was given. Skin lesions in infantile eczema are also said to clear up after giving amounts of vitamin A." If the eating of sunflower seeds will give milady a smooth skin, there is a great future for them.

Recently Drs. H. C. Sherman and H. L. Campbell, of Columbia University, reported to the National Academy of Sciences that the proper amount of vitamin A intake is extremely important to the well-being of the individual. In fact, these doctors declare that it postpones aging and actually increases the length of life of the individual.

The Value of Sunflower Seeds for Others

I now decided to see if the eating of sunflower seeds would have the same effect on the bleeding gums of others. I, therefore, furnished these seeds to 4 girls employed in the shops of an electric manufacturing company of which I am president. Within 10 days two of them reported complete success; no more blood on toothbrushes. One girl claimed 50 per cent improvement. This girl stated her tongue did not seem to be coated any more. The fourth girl estimated a 75 per cent improvement. I have checked with 3 of these girls a year later and the improvements are holding.

I have gone over many books on nutrition, and nowhere have I seen reference made to the value of the sunflower seed in the diet. In lists giving the vitamin content of foods, the sunflower is usually left out. Evidently this is because it has always been a bird and chicken food. Thus it seems to be left completely out of the calculations of the best nutritionists. It is the forgotten food, if there ever was one.

Their Effect on Rheumatism

In a bulletin on sunflower seeds written by the late well-known nutritionist Harvey D. Wiley (United States Department of Agriculture Bulletin No. 60, published in 1901), he says that there was an old idea that the eating of sunflower seeds would cure rheumatism. However, Mr. Wiley stated further that there was no evidence that it would. Many of the so-called home remedies have proven unusually effective when checked by the medical profession. Digitalis for heart disease, for example, is a drug obtained from the foxglove flower. A physician discovered an old woman using it and on checking found it remarkably successful in his work. It is now a standard medical remedy. There are dozens of other similar cases. In fact, there is an entire field of botanical drugs used by many physicians. So perhaps, even as a specific for rheumatism, the sunflower cannot be waved away without some experimental testing. Our folklore is rich in cases of wholesome, simple cures by means of various plants.

Why Are Sunflower Seeds Valuable Food?

There are many reasons why the sunflower seed is a valuable food and should be included in everyone's daily diet. In the first place, nature protects it with a casing. It, therefore, stores well and loses very little vitamin value for long periods. When you remove the outer shell, you have a concentrated bit of healthy nourishment. It tastes almost as delicious a year after harvesting as on the day it was cut down. I have eaten with relish raw wheat seed on harvest day, but a month later it has already lost some of its palatability.

Secondly, you eat the sunflower seed raw. Nutritionists all agree that cooking, however skillfully done, destroys some of the vitamins. It is not factoryized or processed food. It comes to you in virgin form.

This plant is one of the easiest to grow. You have never heard of anyone spraying poisons on it because it is very hardy and is highly resistant to disease.

Now we come to a very remarkable fact about the sunflower. As soon as the head is formed, it always faces the sun. This is a phenomenon called *heliotropism*. In the morning the head faces the east. As the sun swings in its orbit across the heavens, the sunflower head turns with it gradually, until, late in the afternoon, it is facing due west to absorb the few last rays of the dying sun. Sometime before the sun comes up next morning the head turns completely back to start the process all over again. Every farmer boy knows this. In other words, it is just drenched with sun-vitality. Perhaps that is the reason it wards off the diseases which plague other plants. Another possible reason for the potency of this little seed is that from such a small speck, there comes in a few week's time quite a quantity of green material, much greater than that of any other of our food crop plants in proportion to size of seed. Nature, therefore, must pack this tiny kernel full of powerful stuff.

In the United States it is sometimes grown as a border to beautify a garden, and the seeds are later thrown away. A friend of mine admitted to this crime. He didn't know whether you eat the seed shelled or with its jackets. I have since discovered many other persons who were guilty of the same uncertainty. You throw away the shell, of course.

Sunflower Seeds Found Useful in the Past

The American Indian found copious use for the seed of the sunflower which he employed as food, hair oil and soap. Members of the Lewis and Clark expedition found much evidence of this. In their journal for July 17, 1805, when they were in Montana, there is recorded the following:

"Along the bottoms, which have a covering of high grass, we observe the *sunflower* blooming in great abundance. The Indians of the Missouri, more especially those who do not cultivate maize, make great use of the seed of this plant for bread, or in thickening their soup. They first parch and then pound it between two stones, until it is reduced to a fine meal. Sometimes they add a portion of water, and drink it thus diluted; at other times they add a sufficient proportion of marrow-grease to reduce it to the consistency of common dough, and eat it in that manner. This last composition we preferred to all the rest, and thought it at that time a very palatable dish."

Note the use of marrow-grease, a product made from bones. Columbus also noted how popular the sunflower was with the Indians and was instrumental in introducing it into Europe. Today, while this seed is so popular in many parts of Europe, it is practically unknown in this country as a food for human beings.

Sunflower Seeds and Bleeding Gums

As I stated before, the eating of sunflower seeds cleared up my case of bleeding gums. But I have a confession to make. A few months later the condition reappeared. I soon began to notice it on my morning toothbrush. That was indeed something to think about. I knew that there must be some reason for its returning and I felt confident that the cause would be discovered. In a few weeks I had a definite answer.

As a result of this new development, I want to state that the eating of sunflower seeds does good in 3 different ways. First and most important is its effect as a nutritious food containing much vitamin value which is absorbed by the body. Second, is the oil which it contains which is beneficial to the oral cavity in general. Many persons have irritations and inflammations of the inner cheeks. This becomes covered with the soothing sunflower oil which acts externally, and not through the blood stream in this particular situation, although in time, it would have acted in that way also.

The third advantage is the wonderful exercise the teeth get from eating the sunflower seed. It was the way I ate the seeds that gradually brought back my trouble, but in order to give you an understandable picture of this whole situation, I must go back about 18 years and describe the history of my teeth.

I have always had a fairly good set of teeth but have suffered somewhat from bleeding gums. I visited a schoolmate chum of mine in New York who had become a very prominent dentist. He was putting into very successful practice a method developed by Dr. R. G. Hutchinson of curing pyorrhea by a most revolutionary treatment.

The Hutchinson Method of the Even Bite

According to Dr. Hutchinson very few people have teeth which occlude properly, that is, they do not come together as they should. In a recent survey it was found that out of 35,000,000 school children, over 5,000,000 had malocclusion of the teeth. When the teeth do not come together properly, there is a congestion in the periodontal membrane which surrounds the roots. This affects the alveolar septum which separates one root from another, and eventually sets up a condition where the teeth get out of alignment. Then when the process of mastication begins, the tooth will rock in its socket.

Dr. Hutchinson worked out a method by which he ground the teeth so as to produce an even bite and to relieve the strain caused by teeth that were out of position. This seemed to work like a charm. I have seen photographs of patients, before and after the treatment, who showed a sensational improvement in the appearance of their teeth. I submitted to this grinding of my teeth and there was a great improvement effected. That was about 18 years ago. Four or 5 years ago my gums started to bleed again, and I have already related how the eating of sunflower seeds about a year ago cleared up the condition.

Don't Favor One Side When Chewing

One day, while eating some seeds, I noticed that I always ate them on the right side of my mouth. Thinking back about the way my "bite" was evened out, by the Hutchinson method, it occurred to me that favoring that side must have thrown my teeth out of alignment and thus created the condition as previously described. I then saw to it that I chewed only on the left side, in order to even out the bite, and after a week or so the bleeding stopped. After a month it started again. I have finally gotten it under control by seeing to it that I do not favor one side more than the other.

It is interesting to note that at the Baltimore Dental Centenary, recently, a Dr. Clyde H. Schuyler spoke about people who have an imperfect bite and said that they may "chew themselves deaf," or get sinus trouble, facial neuralgia and other conditions.

"Impaired hearing, stuffy sensation in the ears, tinnitus, snapping noises while chewing, dull pain within and about the ears, dizziness at times of prostrating severity, alleged sinus symptoms, headaches and burning sensation in the throat, tongue and side of nose," Dr. Schuyler said, "have been relieved by establishing the proper relation of jaws and opposing teeth." This condition can be overcome by grinding the teeth, said Dr. Schuyler.

Favoring One Side of the Body

Just as I favored the right side of my mouth more than the left, so do many people favor different sides of the body in many things that they do. In walking, a person stresses one side of the body more than the other. Usually, I believe the right side is favored. The right foot is put forward with more strength and tenseness, the left foot with a more relaxed feeling.

The Indians knew how to take advantage of this principle. When they went on a long journey on foot, they would walk for awhile stressing their right side, and then would change the stress to the other, in alternation. This prevented fatigue.

Carrying weights always on one side may cause a lateral curvature in the spine. For the same reason tennis is worse than rowing because it favors only one side of the body. Canoeing stresses one side more than the other. Many Indians had shoulders much more powerfully developed on one side than the other for this reason. Many coaches forbid swimmers to engage in track or other sports because they tend to favor or develop only one set of muscles, whereas in swimming, the entire body must be used.

This principle is very aptly explained in the following paragraph which appeared in a health magazine, the name of which I have apparently failed to make a record of:

"Using the right hand more than the left produces what is known as typical right handed distortion of the spinal column, which is caused by greater development and pull by the muscles on this side. This causes a distortion of every part of the body in a general way, and is more exaggerated in some people than others, according to the degree of the right handed habit. It is claimed by good authority, that even though one is left handed, whenever any task is before him which requires great strength, he always does more with the right side of the body on account of many generations of ancestors following the general rule of right handedness, and all having a tendency to do everything that requires strength more with the right side of the body. Our way of thinking and acting in using these voluntary muscles is greatly influenced by this hereditary tendency."

Good horsemen in trotting a horse know the value of not overstressing one side. They will "post" for a few minutes on the right "diagonal" and then change over to the left. When the horseman comes down in the saddle of a right diagonal, the horse's right foot is hitting the ground at the same time that the horseman is coming down with all his weight. Some "public livery" horses that have an overdeveloped right side due to being handled by poor riders, make poor material for good riders.

Coming back to sunflower seeds, because they are so small, they offer much more exercise to the teeth than most of our modern mushy food and it is this mechanical exercise that, I feel certain, brings about the stoppage of bleeding gums. It conditions the teeth. These short, choppy, masticatory motions have some effect in creating a healthy gum condition. In eating vitamin pills you get none of this advantage. Observe your regular eating motions in general and see whether you favor one side. If so, try and use both sides.

Food Value of Seed

Just about the same time I was experimenting with sunflower seeds as human food, two men in the Middle West were engaged in doing the very same thing. One of them was Ezra Levin, president of the Vio-Bin Corporation of Monticello, Illinois. His colleague in this research project was Professor Harry G. Day, of the Department of Chemistry of Indiana University. They discovered that a meal made from sunflower seed is superior in vitamin B to that of wheat germ, and we all know that the medical profession depends a great deal on the latter substance for use where there are deficiencies in this vitamin. Wheat germ is a specific for persons whose reproductive powers are below normal.

Regarding this experiment the Associated Press wrote at that time:

"Experiments with the yield from 100 acres of the flowers grown last summer, were so successful that the company is contracting with farmers for planting 500 acres this year, Levin said. If the next crop comes up to expectations, widespread cultivation will be sought, he indicated.

"Oil extracted from sunflower seeds by a low temperature solvent method which Levin said he developed is being shipped to a manufacturer for use in salad oil. Meal was sold to a processor making combination meat-protein foods. Levin said he believed these would be the first sunflowers used for human food.

"Last summer's experiments by about 12 Piatt farmers showed sunflowers can be raised for about the same production costs as soybeans, reported Levin, whose firm is engaged in various types of grain processing. Yields were slightly under

1,000 pounds of seed an acre, but Levin said this was because of late planting and that under normal conditions the flowers would produce 1,599 pounds an acre."

Products Enriched With Sunflower Seeds

As a result of their work, it is possible that, in the future, food products such as cake and bread may be enriched with sunflower seed meal. This is much superior to the use of vitamins for this purpose, produced synthetically. When my article appeared, it attracted the attention of a large Philadelphia candy and chewing-gum manufacturing company official, who wrote:

"Have read with considerable interest the article on sunflower seeds and marvel at what you have discovered. This manufacturer is seriously considering the addition of ground-up sunflower seed to his product and experimental work will be done."

CHAPTER **50**

What Do Sunflower Seeds Contain?

The worth of sunflower seeds is apparent when one studies the vitamin and mineral make-up of these foods. They are rich in many nutriments which are in short supply in our diets.

We have received a report compiled in a laboratory of the content of sunflower seeds so far as vitamins and minerals are concerned. We think this should be of great interest to readers.

MINERALS

		Percent of Official Daily Minimum
Iron	6.0 milligrams	60%
Phosphorus	860 "	115
Calcium	57 "	7.6
Iodine	.07 "	70
Magnesium	347 "	
Potassium	630 "	
Manganese	25 ppm	
Copper	20 ppm	
Sodium	.4 milligrams	
Fluorine	2.6 ppm	

VITAMINS

		Percent of Official Daily Minimum
Vitamin B		
Thiamin	2.2 milligrams	220%
Riboflavin	.28 "	24
Niacin	5.6 "	56
Pyridoxine	1.1 "	
Para-amino-benzoic acid	62 "	
Biotin	.067 "	
Choline	216 "	
Folic Acid	.1 "	
Inositol	147. "	
Pantothenic Acid	2.2 "	
Vitamin D	92 Units	23
Vitamin E	31 International Units	
Protein	25%	
Oil	48% (90% of this being the valuable) unsaturated fatty acids.)	
Carbohydrate	15.15%	

The figures arc given in terms of 100 grams, which is about one-fourth pound. In cases where a minimum daily requirement has been set for a vitamin or a mineral, we give the percentage of that requirement which is furnished by one-fourth pound of sunflower seeds. It is well to remember in this connection that those vitamins and minerals for which minimum requirements have not been set are necessary, too, and may be necessary in quite large amounts. But, officially, the research has not been done which shows exactly how much of each of these must be in the diet.

Then, too, you should keep in mind the caution we repeat so often—that getting far more than the recommended minimum, generally means increased good health.

A Comparison of Nutrition

Let's talk about these figures for a moment. How do sunflower seeds compare with other foods in the essential nutrients?

Some foods rich in iron are: wheat germ (8.1 milligrams), almonds (4.4 milligrams), liver (6 to 18 milligrams), egg yolk (7.2 milligrams). Sunflower seed compares very favorably with these. Of course, we would expect the seeds to be rich in phosphorus and low in calcium, as this is a characteristic of practically all seed foods.

The iodine content might differ with different locales. Seeds raised in parts of the country where there is plenty of iodine in the soil would probably contain more iodine. The potassium and magnesium content are very high. Compare the 630 milligrams of potassium with 720 milligrams in the same amount of raisins, 780 milligrams in wheat germ, 400 to 700 in various nuts, from 100 to 800 in vegetables of various kinds. These are foods that are, in general, higher in potassium than any others.

The magnesium content is even more abundant. The 347 milligrams of magnesium listed are more than we can find record of in any other food. Even such a nutritious food as soy flour contains only 223 milligrams. Almonds contain 252, Brazil nuts contain 225.

The fluorine content of sunflower seeds is not high. In fact, we were surprised to find that it is so low. Most foods contain fluorine. This is one of the reasons why we cannot understand the arguments for adding fluorides to the water supply. The average diet contains far more fluorine than anyone has suggested putting into the water supply. Potatoes, for instance, contain from .07 to 6.40 parts per million of fluorine. Fish contains 1.60 to 9.00 parts per million. An infusion of tea— that is, tea as you drink it—may contain 60 parts per million.

B Vitamins in the Seeds

So far as B vitamins are concerned, it is well to keep in mind that these are among the most important food elements for modern man, living in a world where refined foods are the rule of the day. All of the B vitamins have been removed from refined foods and only small fractions of one or two of them have been replaced, by the use of synthetic vitamins.

Important factors like choline, pyridoxine and inositol are missing from so-called "enriched" foods. These 3 B vitamins are absolutely essential for the health of heart and blood vessels. They are related to the way the body uses fat. Whether or not you are eventually going to get hardening of the arteries may have a great deal to do with how much of these 3 B vitamins you have in your diet today. Sunflower seeds are an important source.

Vitamin E, Proteins and Unsaturated Fat

Vitamin E is the essential vitamin for heart and blood vessel health. It enables the tissues of your body to get along with less oxygen. The vitamin E content of sunflower seed makes this food one of the best foods you can eat. Combined with the vitamin E is the valuable oil which makes up almost half the total volume of the seed. Practically all of this is the unsaturated fat that is so valuable a preventive of cholesterol deposits. This fat has also been mentioned in connection with skin and hair health and the prevention of prostate gland disorders. It is a part of food that can be obtained only in cereal and vegetable oils and unrefined foods like nuts, whole grains and seeds. Everyone needs it. Finally, sunflower seeds are 25 per cent protein—putting them on the same protein level as meat.

And you will find that children who are regularly given sunflower seeds rather than candy will come to prefer them to sweets.

Candy gives them nothing but empty calories. Sunflower seeds give them all the wealth of good, healthful eating listed above!

CHAPTER **51**

A New Theory on Prostate Gland Disorders

Most other seeds are healthful, too, along with sunflower seeds. The next chapter presents the theory of a German researcher who believes that the eating of pumpkin seeds has a beneficial effect on the health of the prostate gland.

We are told that most American men over the age of 50 have some difficulty with their prostate glands. This is a small gland in which sperm cells are stored. During and after middle age it may swell (hypertrophy, as the doctors say). Because of its position, close to the mouth of the urinary bladder, this swelling may cause great difficulty with urination. Because of pressure on the bladder, urination may eventually become almost impossible, with the result that urine accumulates in the bladder and may cause infection.

Operate—The Usual Answer

Operations and massage are the treatments most often suggested by doctors. In operations the entire gland is removed. This probably will not result in any change in sex life except for sterility, since the prostate is involved in storing sperm cells. Most men past middle age are not especially concerned with fathering children these days, so the operation does not seem too objectionable on this score. However, the prostate does grow back sometimes, as tonsils and adenoids do. And, of course, anyone who can avoid an operation should do so.

Sex Hormones As Related to Prostate Trouble

A German doctor has recently announced a new theory concerning pumpkin seeds in regard to prostate gland troubles. Dr. W. Devrient of Berlin in an article entitled *Androgen-Hormonal Curative Influence of a Neglected Plant,* tells us that enlargement of the prostate gland is caused by the functionally weakened organ trying to make up for the loss of the male sex hormones which, of course, decline with advancing age. Just as women experience menopause due to a lessening of their production of female sex hormones, so men go through a period during which production of male sex hormones slackens.

Says Dr. Devrient, "Its presence (enlarged prostate, that is) can be demonstrated in every fourth American once he has reached the age of 52. It is maintained that the number of impotent males in the United States amounts to some two million. This, too, is related to the hormone production of the prostate, although all these processes are centrally regulated. In Berlin two large specializing urological hospitals had to be founded, because the surgical divisions of the existing hospitals were not sufficient. The causes of this trouble are to be sought in false methods of living. The poisoning of the glands with tobacco plays the most important role among them."

Pumpkin Seeds the Answer

Giving hormone substances to make up for the deficiency in them does not meet with Dr. Devrient's approval. He says, "One gains the impression that artificial hormones favor the evolution of cancer rather than preventing it. We biological physicians, therefore, reject this treatment, basing our opinions on the conviction that an artificial hormone, though chemically identical, still does not for long have the same effect as a natural one.

"In view of the fact that, with the exception of operative urology (highly dangerous prostatectomy) and biophysical therapy, modern medicine has not been able to find any successful weapon against the early attrition and deterioration of the prostate gland, we have no other rescourse than to seek prevention in the realm of healing plants." He goes on to say that in certain countries where pumpkin seeds are eaten in great quantity throughout life, there is almost no incidence of enlarged prostate or other prostate disorders.

Dr. Devrient believes that the seeds contain materials which are the building stones for the male hormones. Thus they are actually supplying the body indirectly with the means of carrying on the work of the male hormones.

"Only the plain people knew the open secret of pumpkin seeds, a secret which was handed down from father to son for countless generations without any ado. No matter whether it was the Hungarian gypsy, the mountain-dwelling Bulgarian, the Anatolian Turk, the Ukranian or the Transylvanian German—they all knew that pumpkin seeds preserve the prostate gland and thereby also male potency. In these countries people eat pumpkin seeds the way they eat sunflower seeds in Russia: as an inexhaustible source of vigor offered by Nature.

"Investigations by G. Klein at the Vienna University revealed the noteworthy fact that in Transylvania prostatic hypertrophy is almost unknown. Painstaking researches result in the disclosure that the people there have a special liking for pumpkin seeds. A physician from the Szekler group in the Transylvanian mountains confirmed this connection as an ancient healing method among the people. Dr. Bela Pater, of Klausenburg, later published these associations and his own experiences in the Journal, *Healing and Seasoning Plants*.

"My assertion of the androgen-hormonal (the male hormone) influence of pumpkin seeds is based on the positive judgment of old-time doctors, but also no less on my own personal observations throughout the years. This plant has scientifically determined effects on intermediary metabolism and diuresis (urination), but these latter are of secondary importance in relation to its regenerative, invigorative and vitalizing influences. There is involved herein a native plant hormone which affects our own hormone production in part by substitution, in part by direct proliferation.

"Anyone who has studied this influence among peasant peoples has been again and again astonished over the effect of this plant in putting off the advent of old age. My own personal observations in the course of the last 8 years, however, have been decisive for me. At my own age of 70 years I am well able to be satisfied with the condition of my own prostate, on the basis of daily ingestion of pumpkin seeds, and with that of my health in general. This beneficial result can also be found among city patients who are prudent enough to eat pumpkin seeds every day and throughout their life. But one must continue proving this to the city-dweller. The peasants of the Balkans and of eastern Europe knew of the healing effect of these seeds already from their forefathers."

Dr. Devrient goes on to tell us that a number of different substances have been found to be contained in pumpkin seeds, but no one has ventured a guess as to which it may be that brings about the good results on the sex organs. We have been able to find out some facts about the make-up of pumpkin seeds. They are extremely high in phosphorus and low in calcium (as are most seeds). Their iron content appears to be higher than that of any other seed. The B vitamins are plentiful, as they are in other seeds, and there is a small vitamin A content. They contain about 30 per cent protein and about 40 per cent fat.

The fat is, of course, rich in unsaturated fatty acids, as are most vegetable fats. Experiments appear to show the unsaturated fatty acids to be essential for the health of the prostate gland. Perhaps these are the responsible agents in pumpkin seeds. We have come across information about the relationship of the mineral zinc to the health of the prostate gland. It seems that the healthy gland contains far more zinc than the swollen, sick one. Perhaps a deficiency of zinc in the diet may be partly to blame—and perhaps the pumpkin seed may supply much of this needed substance.

We also printed some time ago experiments that showed the effectiveness of a preparation made up of 3 of the amino acids or forms of protein. Protein, of course, is a most important part of one's diet. And it seems quite possible that the protein content of pumpkin seeds, along with the unsaturated fatty acid content, may be responsible for the seed's reputation as a regulator of sex organs.

Perhaps the best recommendation of all for the pumpkin seeds may at the same time be the explanation for the lack of prostate disorders in parts of the world where the seed is widely eaten. Pumpkin seeds are a completely natural food. Their fat and proteins are unchanged and untampered with. They provide in good measure all the rich nutriment that the plant needs to germinate and to grow.

Compare This With Average American Diet

The average American man's food for a day goes something like this: processed cereal (little nutriment—most protein and all the valuable unsaturated fatty acids have been removed); doughnuts and coffee at midmorning (the fats in fried foods have been ruined and made dangerous for human health);

lunch may involve a sandwich and a piece of pie (dangerous hydrogenated fats in the pastry); for dinner, unless he has a salad with plenty of dressing, there will once again be no un-processed fats. Protein will be limited to a serving of meat.

Doesn't it seem possible that the freedom from prostate trouble among the groups mentioned by Dr. Devrient may result from the fact that they are getting fresh unspoiled natural fats and proteins of the highest quality in their pumpkin seeds, and they are not getting all the unhealthful foods the average man in "advanced" countries is getting?

A Lesson We Can Learn

Why should folk lore and folk medicine prescribe the pumpkin seed as the specific prevention for prostate difficulty and the specific guarantee for male potency as Dr. Devrient states? Certainly the function of seeds in carrying the life spark from one generation to the next, approximates the function of the reproductive organs in human beings. There seems little doubt that the actual chemical substances that enable the seed to germinate and to produce another plant with the characteristics of the parent plant are present in reproductive organs of animals —the same hormones, the same enzymes, the same vitamins and minerals.

Primitive agricultural people observe, of course, how seeds reproduce, and without any knowledge of the chemistry of vitamins, hormones and all the rest, are able to apply the same natural laws to their own health. If you want to be the father of many children, they believe, eat that part of the plant that is responsible for producing more plants. Nothing could be simpler or more obvious.

We think pumpkin seeds would make an excellent addi-tion to your between-meal snacks. Eat some every day. They're delicious, crunchy, easy to eat and—best of all—completely satis-fying due to their high protein and fat content.

SECTION 12

FATS IN FOOD

The most valuable element in fats, aside from the fat soluble vitamins A, D and E which they contain, are the unsaturated fatty acids which are essential from the nutritional standpoint, because the body cannot manufacture them. They occur in unprocessed natural fats chiefly of vegetable origin, such as cereal and vegetable oils like salad oils, olive oil, corn oil, peanut oil. Also in avocados, nuts and, of course, sunflower seeds and other seeds. These are the fatty substances which are powerful to prevent cholesterol deposits in the blood vessels.

Animal fats contain little of these important fatty acids, and this is one reason why it is believed that a diet high in animal fats and low in vegetable fats causes cholesterol deposits. When vegetable fats are hydrogenated (that is, made solid), they are changed chemically, and the essential fatty acids are largely destroyed.

We advise keeping to a minimum the animal fat in the diet and shunning hydrogenated fats (solid ones like margarine and the canned shortenings). Salad oils and other sources of vegetable fats are good for you.

Never fry your food. Rather broil or bake. French-fried potatoes are your worst enemy. This kind of frying destroys a great part of their food value and creates conditions that are positively dangerous. Fats of any kind that are heated over and over again are known to be possible cancer-causers. The high heat needed for French-frying also destroys any value the original fat might have had and probably replaces it with harmful elements.

333

CHAPTER **52**

When You Use Fats and Oils . . .

What kind of fats shall we use? How about lard—isn't it as natural a fat as you can get? When vegetable fats are refined, isn't their food value largely destroyed just as the food value of other refined foods suffers? How does olive oil compare to corn oil from the nutritional point of view?

Meaning of "Fats"

First, let's talk about what we mean by "fats" in the diet. There are two kinds of fats—those that are solid at room temperature and those that are liquid. The liquid ones are generally spoken of as oils; the solid ones as fats. Of course, all of them will become liquids at some high temperature. (different in every case), and all liquid oils will become solids at low temperatures.

Fats and oils make up about 2 to 5 per cent of the average diet by weight. In many recent articles about fats we hear of the fat content of the American diet being as high as 40 per cent. We should keep in mind that this means that 40 per cent of the *calories* of the diet are from fat—not 40 per cent of the actual food eaten. Fat is high in calories, of course, so just a little fat adds considerably to this percentage.

Animal and Vegetable Fats

Animal fats—all of them, including milk, butter, fat meats, lard and so forth—contain cholesterol, the substance that apparently constitutes a grave danger to us since it appears to be responsible for hardening of the arteries, heart disease, gallstones, and so forth. Vegetable fats contain no cholesterol. To take its place they have sitosterols, which do not act the same way.

Vegetable fat contains, too, what we call unsaturated

fatty acids, as opposed to the saturated fatty acids that are contained in greater quantity in foods of animal origin. Although there is still considerable debate over the digestibility of fatty foods, we know for certain that the vegetable fats are more easily digested than the animal fats.

Lard

Lard, of course, comes from hog fat, hence contains cholesterol and lacks the useful fatty acids. As our readers know, we believe one should not eat pork products. But apart from our objection to lard as a pork product, we find that processors have, in recent years, been doing a lot of things to lard that make it even more objectionable as food. In an attempt to produce lard that compares with the vegetable shortenings, they have added chemicals to prevent the lard from becoming rancid; they have hydrogenated and deodorized it.

Margarine

Margarine is made from vegetable fats which have been hydrogenated, that is, hydrogen has been forced through them to produce a chemical change that makes the liquid oils solid, as margarine is. Such oils as cottonseed, soybean and, in Europe, whale oil, are used. Most margarine in this country is "fortified" with synthetic vitamin A. The reason is that the oils themselves contain very little vitamin A in comparison with butter. If margarine is to be used as a butter substitute, the additional vitamin A is supplied.

We do not recommend using margarine, mostly because of the many chemical substances used in it, of which the synthetic vitamin A is only one. Artificial coloring, preservatives and so forth are also used. But in addition, hydrogenation of the oils to make them solid destroys most of the essential fatty acids which are the chief reason for eating vegetable oils. So margarine is no better than butter as a spread, in spite of the fact that it is made from substances that do not contain cholesterol.

Linseed Oil

Linseed oil (made from flaxseed), sardine and other fish oils are generally considered to be inferior for eating purposes, because of taste, even though they contain large amounts of unsaturated fatty acids.

Soybean Oil

Soybean oil is another popular vegetable oil. We are told that it presents some difficulty, since it is subject to some slight "flavor reversion." We assume this means that its taste may suffer with age. Crude soybean oil is our best source of lecithin at present. Lecithin is the substance rich in unsaturated fatty acids which occurs in vegetable oils.

Sunflower Seed Oil

Sunflower seed oil, corn oil and poppyseed oil are all quite similar. Corn oil is a little darker in color than the others.

Cottonseed Oil

Cottonseed oil is the standard American "all-purpose edible oil" according to Jacobs in his book, *Food and Food Products, 1951.*

Peanut Oil

Peanut oil is suitable for all purposes for which cottonseed oil is used, except that it tends to cloud and thicken at low temperatures.

Rapeseed Oil

Rapeseed oil is difficult to deodorize and has an unpleasant reversion of flavor.

Olive Oil

Olive oil is the most popular oil of southern Europe and the Mediterranean. Its content of unsaturated fatty acids is not high, however. And we must see that we get plenty of unsaturated fatty acids. They are important.

Now what about the salad oils you find on grocery shelves? These are called "refined oils." It seems that most of the crude oils must be refined if they are to be edible. Cottonseed oil, for instance, is so strongly flavored that we are told we could not possibly enjoy eating it in the crude state. Peanut oil, sunflower seed oil, soybean and sesame oil are refined—which means deodorizing them so that they have practically no odor or taste.

Olive oil is not treated to remove its taste and odor. For this reason some folks feel that olive oil is far superior to other oils, "because it has such a marvelous taste," they say. Others, used to the bland salad oils that have been deodorized, cannot stand the taste or smell of olive oil. It is well to remember when you are deciding among vegetable and seed oils, that olive oil is low in the unsaturated fatty acids—those extremely valuable substances so powerful for good health in the way your body uses fat. On the other hand, it is unrefined which is a recommendation for it, we believe. We have been unable to discover any known disadvantages brought about by refining oils, but we are certain there must be some which simply haven't been discovered yet. We know that the unsaturated fatty acids are not destroyed in the refining process. Isn't it possible that other valuable nutriments may be, however? We think you should make up your own mind as to whether you want to eat olive oil.

Corn Oil

Corn oil has been used for extensive laboratory experiments. Much of what we know about the relation of cholesterol, lecithin, unsaturated fatty acids, vegetable and animal fats has been discovered in laboratories using corn oil as the source of unsaturated fatty acids in the diet of the laboratory animals.

An excellent book has been written by Dorothy M. Rathmann, Ph.D., entitled *Vegetable Oils in Nutrition, with special reference to unsaturated fatty acids.* The booklet is published by Corn Products Refining Company, 17 Battery Place, New York, New York. It is a technical book written for professional men— doctors, nutritionists and therapists. We advise all readers who are in this category to send for a copy. You will find a great deal of helpful information on fats in general and corn oil in particular.

Dr. Rathmann tells us, "The opinion is becoming more and more wide-spread that unsaturated vegetable oils, such as Mazola brand corn oil, possess distinct nutritional advantages. For example, the fact that diets containing corn oil result in lower serum cholesterol levels than do those containing more highly saturated fats has led to the hope that the incidence and course of atherosclerosis may be influenced favorably, in part at least, by dietary means.

Importance of Corn Oil

"This favorable effect of corn oil has been attributed to the presence of two different types of compounds capable of lowering serum cholesterol levels, namely sitosterols and essential fatty acids. In addition to a relationship to cholesterol metabolism, the essential fatty acids also appear to have important functions in the development of new cells and the maintenance of healthy body tissues, particularly the skin, liver and kidneys. Requirements for the essential fatty acids seem to be increased when food yields large amounts of saturated or isomeric fatty acids, as may be the case in American diets rich in animal and hydrogenated vegetable fats."

The book contains a great deal of detailed information about experiments involving corn oil in relation to cholesterol deposits. The further information is given that corn oil contains: 53 per cent linoleic acid (the most important of the unsaturated fatty acids), 1.5 per cent of sitosterols and, of course, no cholesterol. Compare this to other fats containing unsaturated fatty acids:

Linolenic acid per cent			
Linseed oil	20	Sesame	41
Sardine	15	Cottonseed	50
Safflower	70	Rice bran	34
Poppyseed	62	Peanut	25
Soybean	53	Olive	8
Sunflower	57	Wheat germ	50
		Corn	53

Avoid Animal Fats

Our final suggestions to you, then, are these: judging from the amount of information we have up to now (and remember, much more research will be done on fats in nutrition —the subject is new) we would counsel readers to avoid animal fats as much as possible, with the exception of eggs.

One cannot help getting some fat in meat, of course. But eliminate gravies and fatty sauces. Avoid butter and milk. Shun like poison the hydrogenated fats in which the important fatty acids have been largely destroyed. This means don't buy the solid, white shortenings. And don't buy prepared, processed foods, for you can be sure hydrogenated shortenings were used in them.

We Recommend Vegetable Fats

Do take wheat germ oil every day, because of its essential fatty acid content, vitamin E, and the many other factors that it contains. For fats in your meals use salad oils—olive oil if you like the taste (but remember it's low in unsaturated fatty acids) corn oil, cottonseed oil—any of the salad oils you find at your grocery store.

Although many of the experiments quoted in the newspapers and in this article concern corn oil, this is simply because that happened to be the oil used by researchers. It does not mean that other vegetable and cereal oils would be less effective in these same experiments.

We especially want to recommend sunflower seed oil. It is higher in linoleic acid than corn oil, and linoleic acid is generally credited as being the Good Fairy among the fatty acids which puts unwanted cholesterol to flight. We are told that in unsaturated fatty acids as a whole, sunflower seed oil is higher than any other. Its vitamin E content, too, is extremely high— 222 milligrams per 100 grams, compared to only 5 milligrams in sesame oil and 22 to 48 in peanut oil.

Sunflower Seed Oil and Cholesterol

One of the articles which sparked the recent investigation of fats and oils in the diet was published in *The Lancet* for April 28, 1956. In this article a now classic experiment was described by Dr. Bronte-Stewart and his associates in which sunflower seed oil was one of those used to bring about a rapid decrease in blood cholesterol.

And remember, it seems to be true that the more of the processed and animal fats you eat, the more you need of the vegetable fats, whose unsaturated fatty acids will counteract any cholesterol-forming tendency of the processed and animal fats low in unsaturated fatty acids.

CHAPTER **53**

The Fats and Oils in Your Diet

This chapter contains some questions and answers about fats that help to clarify this extremely complex and little-investigated subject.

We have been getting a lot of information during these years, to incriminate a high-fat diet as one, if not the main, cause of hardening of the arteries, and hence a multitude of heart and blood vessel disorders. A fatty substance, cholesterol, deposits on the inner walls of blood vessels, narrowing them so that blood cannot flow freely. Many researchers believed that a diet high in fat was responsible. Then other researchers declared that only animal fat was responsible. Vegetable fats were harmless in this respect.

Now in a book called *Unsaturated Fats and Serum Cholesterol* by Dorothy M. Rathmann, Ph.D. (Published by Corn Products Refining Company, Argo, Illinois) we have in one volume a comprehensive review of all the research that has been done on every aspect of this problem.

Here, in the form of questions and answers, is some of the information in the book:

1. Where is cholesterol found in the body?

It is estimated that our bodies manufacture about two grams of cholesterol per day and it is used chiefly by brain, muscle and fatty tissue. It also occurs in foods—chiefly fats of animal origin.

2. What is the "normal" amount of cholesterol one should have in his blood?

A summary of data on about 12,000 Americans shows

that their blood contained from 180 to 280 milligrams of cholesterol per 100 milliliters of blood. This is medical terminology and doesn't indicate much to a layman except when one compares it with figures from other countries. Inhabitants of India, eating a low fat diet, have a blood cholesterol of 144. The same is true of Japanese. Swedish individuals eating about the same amount of fat Americans eat show a cholesterol level of 235. Yugoslavians eating only about one-fourth as much fat as Americans still show 201 milligrams of cholesterol.

3. *What are some factors affecting blood cholesterol—diet and otherwise?*

Emotional stress, as evidenced in periods when pressure is on at work or family difficulties are pressing. Excess calories from either fats or carbohydrates, without a change in physical activity, cause a weight gain and a rise in blood cholesterol.

4. *Do all fats in the diet produce the same effect on blood cholesterol?*

It now seems probable, says Dr. Rathmann, that the more saturated fats (those in animal fat and hydrogenated fat) contain at least one component having a positive action in raising blood cholesterol levels. In experiments beef drippings, butter, chicken fat and lard (all containing saturated fats) caused a rise in the cholesterol level, whereas corn oil (rich in unsaturated fatty acids) brought about a drop in cholesterol. The level continued low so long as corn oil was taken.

5. *What about fat-free diets?*

In tests of fat-free diets cholesterol dropped sharply but began to rise again gradually. The addition of butter to the diet caused the cholesterol to rise sharply again. Adding corn oil sent the cholesterol level down, and this level hit its lowest mark when corn oil accounted for 60 per cent of the calories in the diet. That means that a considerable amount of corn oil was in the diet. Here are some actual cases: a woman 44 years old whose initial cholesterol level was 566. After a year on a diet high in corn oil—435. A man of 65 whose level of 490 decreased to 357 within a year. A man of 46 whose cholesterol level went from 472 to 283 in a year, and so forth.

6. What about diets containing both animal and vegetable fat?

It is believed that the important thing, so far as cholesterol deposits are concerned, is neither the amount of animal fat nor the amount of vegetable fat in the diet. The important thing seems to be the ratio of the two. In other words, animal fat does not appear to be harmful, *if the predominant fat in the diet is vegetable oil* which, of course, contains the unsaturated fatty acids.

In an experiment, one part corn oil to three parts of butter gave almost the same high blood cholesterol levels as did butter alone. Three parts of corn oil to one part of butter gave almost exactly the same low level as pure corn oil. The same is true of other vegetable oils.

7. How do experts explain the effect of vegetable oils in the diet?

"The way in which unsaturated vegetable oils act in achieving the decrease in serum cholesterol concentration is not yet clear," says Dr. Rathmann. "One possibility is that the highly unsaturated fatty acids from these oils aid in the transport of the cholesterol." Since there is no evidence that there is anything harmful in the diets high in vegetable oils, however, we do not need to concern ourselves with the why's and wherefore's. We do however, need to have some ideas as to how best to use these facts in working out a good diet for ourselves and our families.

8. How can you best arrange your diet to achieve the proper proportion between vegetable (unsaturated) and animal (saturated) fats?

In general, investigators believe that there is an optimum ratio, and that it may change with age. In healthy young adults the cholesterol can be maintained at relatively low levels on a much smaller proportion of the unsaturated fatty acids than older individuals require. In any case, it is not enough simply to add to your diet a couple of teaspoonfuls or tablespoonfuls of vegetable oil and expect results. You must learn to substitute one kind of oil for the other. The present average daily fat consumption of the American family, per person, breaks down into the following figures, available from the Department of Agriculture:

	Grams
Beef, veal and lamb	22.1
Pork (excluding bacon, salt pork)	15.1
Poultry, fish	4.4
Bacon, salt pork	13.4
Lard	9.2
Other shortening	9.0*
Oils, salad dressing	9.3
Margarine	10.4
Butter	10.6
Milk, cream, ice cream, cheese	28.0
Eggs	5.6
Other foods (purchased foods, nuts, fruits, vegetables)	18.0

* *We assume this means hydrogenated shortening—the solid, white kinds.*

(This is not a recommended amount of fat, as you will see. Rather this chart demonstrates how *not* to eat if you would avoid cholesterol deposits.)

The reader can at once see several places where he can eliminate animal fats the ordinary person is eating—pork products, lard, hydrogenated shortening, margarine, all the dairy products and baked goods. None of us should be eating any of these.

The fats and oils you can substitute for these are the highly unsaturated ones; the so-called salad oils (corn oil, cottonseed oil, soybean oil, safflower, and sunflower seed oil), the germ of cereals—wheat germ, rye germ and rice polishings. Walnuts, sunflower seeds, fish liver oil and wheat germ oil—all these are high in the fats you want to include in your diet and to substitute for the animal fats you should avoid.

Fats which contain *some* unsaturated fatty acids, but not as much as the group listed in the previous paragraph, are peanut and olive oils, most nuts and poultry fat.

Finally, the group you are trying to avoid includes: butter, margarine, hydrogenated shortenings (the solid white kind), coconut oil, fats in dairy products and fatty meats.

How to Plan Your Diet

In planning your diet, then, you have two objectives: to decrease the total amount of fat in the diet and increase the ratio between the healthful fats and unhealthful ones. Choose lean meats, poultry and fish rather than fatty ones. Skip dairy products, especially cream and, of course, ice cream. Use plenty of vegetable oi.s. Always use them for cooking and food preparation. Eat salad at least once a day, twice if you can manage it, with plenty of salad dressing containing oil. Instead of desserts and starchy snacks, eat nuts, sunflower seeds, squash seeds, wheat germ. These are the things you should be especially careful to avoid: all fried foods, all processed foods and anything that comes out of a bakery—for all of them are almost certain to contain a kind of fat you are trying to avoid.

So you see how, in these suggested changes, you have substituted vegetable fats for animal fats and, hence, improved the ratio of the two fats in the diet.

Concluding Remarks

Dr. Rathmann concludes her study with these words: "If only from the standpoint of avoiding obesity, even the most conservative authorities agree on the desirability of limiting dietary fat to something less than the 40 per cent level common in the United States."

She believes, and we agree, that a desired balance can be achieved easily by decreasing the amount of fat-rich food and planning the diet to contain plenty of protein (meat and fish) and plenty of vegetable oils. Dr. Rathmann does not take up the subject of eggs. We believe that they are one of our best foods and, in spite of the fact that they contain cholesterol, we should use them freely in meal-planning.

CHAPTER **54**

Experiments Show Heated Fats Can Cause Cancer

Beware the deep fat fryer, the frying pan and processed fat. New evidence shows they may be instrumental in causing cancer.

Have you ever passed the exhaust fan from the kitchen of a restaurant? When you do, it is easy to detect the dominating odor of frying fats. These fats bubble and spit in deep fryers for days on end, without even a slight decrease in temperatures, which are held at 350 to 400 degrees. When a customer orders fried chicken or fried shrimp or French-fried potatoes, with them he receives a free sample of the fat in which they were fried. This highly heated fat has been shown by some of our most prominent researchers to be a likely cause of cancer.

Are Fats Dangerous?

The distinction between highly processed or heated fats and natural ones is important. It would be wrong and dangerous to eliminate all fats from our diet. Our bodies need fats, and we number them among our most important foods. They are one of our best energy sources, offering 9 times as much energy per gram as sugar does. Fats carry the vitamin B, pyridoxine and the fat soluble vitamins A, D, E, and K, which make fats vital to cell formation, especially cells of the brain and nerve tissues. Finally, the body absolutely needs the unsaturated fatty acids contained in fats. These are indispensable in some processes of metabolism and cell structure. In high heats the vitamins A, E and K are utterly destroyed. This vitamin destruction is illustrated by an experiment conducted by Dr. Lane and reported in the publication, *Cancer*, Vol. 3, 1950. A group of rats were mated for 3 years into 7 generations. They were on a milk and white bread diet. After the second generation, a ration of lard heated to 350°, then cooled, was included in the rats' diet. From then on it was found necessary to feed the rats wheat germ oil and fresh vegetables prior to mating, because of the deficiencies in vitamins A and E caused by the pre-heated fats.

Use of Heated Fats Common

The use of heated fats by Americans is an insidious habit, so automatic that many health-conscious housewives include them in their menus without even being aware of it. For example, the lady who is so concerned about the health of her family that she wouldn't dream of serving deep-fried foods, can be found making a sauce from the drippings of a roast, quite unconscious that half of this liquor is fat that has been heated to 350° or more for several hours! Such fat has been made as hot as that used in the deep fryer—and it can be just as damaging.

Some Experiments with Heated Fats

In the periodical, *Cancer,* Vol. 3, No. 6, November, 1950, gastric (stomach) cancer is noted to be the leading cause of all cancer deaths, according to statistics. Further, Dr. Geoffrey Hadfield, Dean of the Institute of Basic Medical Sciences, Royal College of Surgeons, has stated that cancer of the gastro-intestinal tract appears to be associated with a high fat diet. If this is the case, and if the body needs unprocessed fats as seen before, it is entirely logical that the processed, heated fats are the culprits in the case.

It is especially so when one reads that experiments with local applications of heated fats have shown tumors to develop at the site of the application. *The British Journal of Experimental Pathology* (Vol. 22, 1941) published data on experiments that resulted in cancerous lesions at the site of the injection, in 2 out of 12 mice injected subcutaneously with cottonseed oil, which had been preheated to temperatures of 340-360° C. When highly heated fats are brought into close connection with part of the body, apparently a weakness and predisposition toward cancer is introduced to that same part. It should be noted, too, that in the same experiment cottonseed oil heated to a lesser degree (200-220° C.) did not produce any cancerous tumors in any of the experimental mice when injected in the same manner, leading to the conclusion that the dangers in fats vary in proportion to the heat applied.

In searching for clues to this highly heated fat and cancer relationship, a theory has been advanced by Dr. A. C. Ivy in *Gastroenterology* (March, 1955) which holds that hot fats reheated again and again, undoubtedly increase the chance of producing carcinogenic substances. Obviously Dr. Ivy feels that there is a dangerous change in the make-up of the fat each time it cools and is fired again, with the intensity of the heat of less importance. This should be a warning to housewives who save cooking fats for re-use.

A smiliar point of view shows up in the *Journal of Nutrition* (Vol. 55, 1955) in an article which discusses fats heated to relatively low temperatures (95° C.) and maintained at that heat for 200-300 hours. Refined cottonseed oil, heated thusly, was included to make up 15 to 20 per cent of the diet of experimental rats. It was observed that rats on such a diet rapidly lost weight and died within 3 weeks. The loss of weight was accompanied by diarrhea and the occurrence of enlarged livers, kidneys, and adrenals and by shrunken spleens and thalamuses.

Preheated Fats

In spite of varying theories the strongest suspicion for cancerous action of fats still seems to lie with fats that are preheated to a high degree, as witnessed by Lane and Associates and reported in the *Journal of the American Medical Association*, February 17, 1951. In an experiment, 54 rats were given regular rations of brown lard heated for 30 minutes at 350° C. Papillomas (tumors) of the forestomach and malignant tumors of the glandular stomach occurred in 37 per cent of the rats, while similar symptoms were observed in only 5.7 per cent of a control group which was fed unheated lard (though the fat was, of course, heated to make the lard in the first place).

For further data Dr. Lane injected 31 experimental rats with heated lard or vegetable oil. Three cancers developed in these rats, while none developed in a control group of 150.

A definite relationship between preheated fats and cancer showed up in a test discussed in *Modern Nutrition* for August, 1953, the official publication of the American Nutrition Society. A healthful, normal diet was fed to a group of rats. Then the rats were separated into two groups, and the normal diet continued, but for one addition: one of the groups was fed a daily ration of heated, hydrogenated fats, while the other group received a like amount of unprocessed fats.

After the eating pattern of this diet had been well established, a known cancer-producing substance, butter-yellow, was introduced into the diet of all the rats. Every one of the rats on the diet which included the preheated, hydrogenated fats developed tumorous growths, some of which proved to be malignant. The rats eating the unprocessed fats developed no tumors of any kind.

What Are Hydrogenated Fats?

Hydrogenated fats are everywhere. They come in cans and jars and cartons, looking as white and creamy as cold cream or yellow as the sun. They are guaranteed not to spoil, for there is nothing left in them that could spoil. And how did they get that way? They have been through about 18 different processes, including boiling, cooling and boiling again, agitation, straining, catalytic action, bleaching, coloring, etc. Every life-removing process imaginable is applied to these fats. Margarines are hydrogenated, too, and the false security bred by the idea that the margarines are not made from animal fats but from vegetable oils is banished in an instant by this fact. Hydrogenation is what makes them spreadable and unmelting in summer temperatures. They are as damaging to health as the frying and baking shortenings that are white and lardy-looking. Nor does the yellow color they are given, and the merchandising technique of presenting margarines in brick-shaped cartons make them as safe for you as "that other spread."

The Real Enemy—Heat

As seen by the various experiments noted here, it is still not generally agreed upon, which heated fats do the most damage. Some say the danger lies only in fats heated to very high temperatures, others say it lies in fats heated and reheated, still another impression has it that fats heated for very long periods, even at relatively low temperatures, are the ones to watch out for. But one thing on which all of the experts agree—preheated fats can and may cause cancer! The investigation of treated fats in this connection is still a largely unexplored area. The explanation as to why these fats are antagonistic to our system has yet to be discovered, but the evidence of danger is clear enough to act as a warning.

We are convinced that the body welcomes the vegetable fats much more readily than the fats from animals. If there were no other reason, it is undeniable that most animal fats go through some processing before we get them. This may consist of cooking them at high temperatures in a roasting pan or broiler.

Of course, the vegetable oils (especially those in unheated nuts, sunflower seeds and so forth) have not been thus exposed and they are able to give the body what it needs without the risk of cancer that is lurking in heated fats. But even vegetable and cereal fats, once they are heated, may be cancer-causing.

Some Practical Suggestions

How can you use this information practically, in your kitchen? Does it mean that you should stop using fats altogether? Not at all. Here are some rules to follow, if you want to be absolutely certain you are not exposing your family to this particular risk so far as cancer is concerned.

First, never buy anything that has been fried. This means no potato chips, no roasted nuts, no frozen foods that have been fried or breaded and fried. Steer clear of anything fried in restaurants—fried clams, fish fillets, French-fried potatoes, fried eggplant, etc. Check closely with the waitress on any food where there is the slightest doubt.

By the same token, don't fry foods at home. This means don't do any frying at all, either in deep fat or in a frying pan. Any meat you would fry can be broiled just as successfully. And we advise removing the fat before cooking the meat if you broil it and also discarding the fat from roasts. Let's say you want to sauté liver. A little vegetable oil—just enough to keep the meat from sticking to the pan—probably couldn't do harm if you keep the heat low at all times.

Finally, don't buy hydrogenated shortenings (the solid kind), and don't ever, ever use drippings or oils over and over again. There is the risk of such fats being rancid, and, of course, that they may be cancer-causing.

SECTION 13

ALUMINUM COOKING UTENSILS

Never use aluminum cooking utensils. It is a soft, toxic metal and some of it will get into the hot water of the cooked material and contaminate it. It causes digestive troubles in some people, and will usually raise the pulse. Pyrex glass, enamelware and stainless steel are better, in the order mentioned. There is a huge amount of evidence that cooking in aluminum utensils is dangerous.

CHAPTER **55**

Aluminum Cooking Utensils

by J. I. RODALE

The evidence is so conclusive against aluminum utensils that there is not the slightest question in my mind about it. One should ban them from the kitchen. I am fully aware that the American Medical Association, the United States Government, the Better Business Bureau, and Frederick Carleton believe that the use of aluminum utensils is not harmful to human health, but we have so much material that shows them to be wrong that it would be a grievous sin for us to remain quiet about it.

Canadian Rose Hip Experiment

In the *Canadian Journal of Research*, Vol. 21, Sec. C, is described an experiment in the cooking of rose hips in vessels of various materials. Quoting from this article we find that, "Dried, powdered flesh (of rose hips), 0.5 gram, was placed in the vessel being used in the experiment. This was covered with 20 ml. water and the mixture boiled for 15 minutes, then cooled, centrifuged, and acidified aliquots (equal parts) were titrated. . . . Tests with vessels of glass and enamel showed practically no loss of ascorbic acid (Vitamin C). The loss in the copper vessel is very marked, and in the aluminum less, but appreciable."

This would indicate that cooking in copper and aluminum would cause losses in vitamins, and that glass and enamelware are safest. The fact that glass and enamel are better than aluminum was shown in cases described by Arthur F. Coca, M.D., in his book, *Familial Nonreaginic Food Allergy*, published in 1945 by Charles C. Thomas, Springfield, Illinois. Coca quotes from the book, *Practice of Allergy*, p. 831, by

Vaughan, stating that the author mentions "the cure of cases of long-standing refractory colitis following change from aluminum cooking utensils to enamel or glass vessels."

Citric Acid's Effect on Aluminum

An experiment was performed at the University of Colorado which adds some additional light to this question of the effect on aluminum of contact with certain liquids. It was written up in the journal, *Food Technology,* of December, 1951. It showed that orange juice dissolved on the average 37 parts per million of the aluminum of the pot in which it was contained. In the case of grapefruit juice the average was about 23 parts. When we consider that in fluoridation of water great care is taken not to use more than one part per million, we can see how dangerous it is to use a substance as toxic as aluminum in as high as 37 parts. And bear in mind this is cold orange juice. There was no cooking involved.

Aluminum Poisoning

Another worker against aluminum is Dr. Leo Spira, who in 1933 published a monograph on the subject called *The Clinical Aspect of Chronic Poisoning by Aluminum and its Alloys,* which gives his experience with the subject over a period of 10 years.

Dr. Spira not only cured himself by discontinuing the use of aluminum cooking utensils, but also dozens of others. Symptoms of aluminum poisoning in various patients which were cleared up by not using aluminum utensils were constipation, flatulence, colicky pain, impairment of appetite, nausea, many forms of skin ailments, neuralgia, twitching of legs, giddiness, excessive perspiration, loss of energy, etc. Dr. Spira not only has his patients discontinue the use of aluminum utensils, but also has them stop using tap water, for in many cities alum (which is a form of aluminum) is placed in city water supplies to purify it. Dr. Spira has found also that many brands of aluminumware contain poisonous impurities such as copper, antimony, fluorine, zinc, lead, tin, etc.

When in 1935 Dr. Spira discussed the aluminum question in the columns of *The London Times,* many persons wrote in confirming Dr. Spira's experiences by describing their own cases of cure.

Dr. F. Von Halla, in "Aluminum und Darm," *Deutsche Aertze Zeitung,* pp. 195 and 201, describes 25 cases of patients with severe constipation who could not be cured by regular medical procedures but whose condition dramatically yielded when they gave up cooking in aluminum.

Dr. O. Putensen, in the *Deutsche Aertze Zeitung,* pp. 223, 231, 242, describes the case of a dog with rash sores and intense itching, who was cured only when the aluminum pans from which he was fed were thrown out. Dr. Putensen describes experiences with many patients showing cures of gastric and skin disturbances caused by cooking food in aluminum.

Dr. Coram James, writing in the *British Medical Journal* of April 9, 1932, in describing some cases of gastric disturbances which he was able to cure by substituting enamel or iron pots for aluminum, said, "It seems like riding coincidence too hard to suppose that a sequence of a score or more relieved could all have been hypersensitive to aluminum." What the doctor means is that the aluminum people and their medical friends believe that only *some* people are allergic to aluminum.

Dr. Alexander Francis, writing in the April 16, 1932, issue of the *British Medical Journal,* describes how he cured his own case of severe abdominal pain by discontinuing the use of aluminum. The pain had been so bad that at times it completely incapacitated him. Several times later, the pain returned, but in every case he found that he had eaten something cooked in aluminum. The abdominal pain caused by aluminum, says the doctor, is of such nature that it cannot be relieved by the usual sedatives. Dr. Francis, in this article, also reports 6 cases in which he cured abdominal pain by ordering the disuse of aluminum cooking utensils.

Dr. E. H. Rink, writing in the August 6, 1932, issue of the *British Medical Journal* describes how he treated two patients who were suffering respectively from abdominal pain, which was thought to be appendicitis, and a case of colitis. Following the method of Dr. Spira, he had them stop using aluminumware, and he gave them charcoal tablets to absorb some of the accumulated aluminum with striking cures in each case.

Dr. Eric Pritchard in the *British Medical Journal* of October 29, 1932, says, "I have had plenty of evidence of chronic aluminum poisoning among members of my own family and among my personal friends, and also in the case of a dog, and several large groups of infants in institutions under my charge. Except in the case of infants, who appear to be very susceptible to the acute effects of aluminum poisoning, symptoms do not usually arise in the case of adults until after prolonged exposure to its effects."

Aluminum Content of Foods

The following table shows the amount of aluminum taken up by foods cooked in aluminum utensils. Since food naturally contains some aluminum, a certain amount is present even when the food is cooked in a glass utensil. But notice the large increase in aluminum in the same food when it is cooked in an aluminum utensil. One can only conclude that the added aluminum comes from the utensil. The aluminum content is shown in parts per million.

Foodstuffs	Cooking Time in Minutes	Cooked in Glass	Cooked in Aluminum	Average Increase in Aluminum in Parts per Million
Boiled ham	120	.78	2.1	1.32
Creamed chicken	120	.95	2.43	1.48
Oatmeal	150	1.51	9.13	7.62
Stewed tomatoes (bright pan)	20	.12	4.36	4.24
Stewed tomatoes (dark pan)	20	.14	15.6	15.46
Creamed cabbage	45	.34	90.8	90.46
Cranberry sauce	10	.52	28.0	27.48
Rhubarb	5	.94	41.8	40.86
Apricots	40	24.6	73.3	48.7
Lemon pie filling	2	.31	118.0	117.69

What to Use

My suggestion as first choice for the cooking and storage of food is Pyrex glassware. It has the added advantage of cooking food evenly all through. It may be expensive because it is so expendable, but what is a little money compared to health, and you may stave off the undertaker's bill for many years. Think of the interest that can be earned on such a sum.

Next comes enamelware, but get only the best. Third in line is stainless steel. Porcelain ware is perfect for food storage. Keep lemons and other citrus and acid fruit juices only in glass, enamel or porcelain.

SECTION 14

PLASTIC UTENSILS

Plastic utensils should never be used for food or drink. They contain harmful chemical poisons, like formaldehyde, which get into the food. It is difficult to sterilize them, and in hospitals, for that reason, water in such containers has been found to contain harmful bacteria.

CHAPTER **56**

Plastics Are Not for You

by J. I. RODALE

A new danger has been insidiously creeping into our lives without anyone having said a word about it in print. I do not recall seeing anything about it in the popular health journals. This menace is the growing use of plastics as utensils. I was amazed the other day to see hot coffee served in plastic cups in a university dining room. I have seen it so used in restaurants. The reason for its growing use is the fact that it does not break as china does. But it is a dangerous material full of harmful chemicals. It is much softer than any metal. The worst offending element in it is formaldehyde.

Other Uses of Formaldehyde

In gardening, formaldehyde is used to kill organisms but, of course, a good organic gardener who does not use chemical fertilizers and poison sprays will never use it. In the *Wisconsin Medical Journal* of November, 1950, there is an article which describes a condition in the fingernails called *Base Coat nail disease* which is caused by the use of a liquid substance known as a base coat to the nails to preserve and protect coloring applied to them. This liquid substance contains formaldehyde. In medical research, in order to induce arthritis in mice and rats, formaldehyde is injected into their bodies. Canary bird's roosts are dipped in formaldehyde to kill lice. Formaldehyde is used in mushroom growing to sterilize the soil. Formaldehyde is a poisonous substance which definitely should not come in contact with food, not to mention hot coffee.

How the Formaldehyde Gets into Your Body

A circular issued by a company that makes plastic dishes admits that "staining of cups, when coffee is used, has been greatly reduced by proper cleaning techniques." It goes to show

how soft the plastic material is when an ordinary hot liquid can etch itself into its interior sufficiently to stain it. It is possible, then, that the plastic also stains the coffee and gives to it some of its poisonous formaldehyde. In another part of its circular there is the statement, "Any detergent or washing compound in ordinary use will have absolutely no ill effect, although chlorine compounds are not friendly to it. In time they will impair its fine surface." Do you realize the fearful implications of this? The average American drinking water that is used to make coffee contains chlorine. Chlorine is bad enough in itself. Now it comes in contact with formaldehyde and is not too friendly to it. Two wrongs do not make a right! Two chemicals at each other's throats with the public in between! How is such a thing permitted?

And yet, I understand that plastic dishes have been approved by the State of New Jersey as well as the United States Army. I find also that hundreds of hospitals, of all places, have plastic dishes as standard practice. It no doubt solves their problem of breakage, but how about breaking sick persons and invalids who should have nothing but the best. So far I have not found any evidence of tests on mice who have been submitted to hot foods served in plastic dishes. In such tests, however, we must bear in mind that the mice should be fed on such food into 3 or 4 generations, because toxic effects sometimes do not show up in the first generation.

Convenient—But!

The *Modern Hospital* for September, 1950, carries an article entitled *Will China Take a Back Seat?* which to me is extremely alarming. It shows how convenient these plastic dishes are for hospitals. The first year in a certain nurses' training school they saved 500 dollars because of no breakage. They admitted, however, that there was a tendency for the cups to stain. They were aware that there is such a thing as health, for they found that the bacteria count on plastic dishes was far less than on crockery ones. The article states, "Here where the health regulations are most stringent, the bacteria count surprised everyone; it was unusually low." Certainly! It should be low, because the formaldehyde, the well-known antiseptic, was killing the bacteria. But we don't drink antiseptics. The fact that there was a lower bacteria count on the dishes should have made the management suspicious. This is an easy test which any hospital can make, for they usually have the laboratory equipment to do so. They no doubt will find if they check it that the plastic surface will harbor less bacteria than china, which shows that the formaldehyde is right at the surface where it can come in contact with hot liquid.

Assurance from Plastic Manufacturers

In a letter received from the company that makes plastic dishes appeared the following:

"Please rest assured that we and the plastic dinnerware industry in all its phases have been fully aware of the implications involved in the fact that minute traces of formaldehyde can be found in a solution of water in which melamine dishware has been soaked for long periods of time. This concentration ranges from one-half to 5 parts in a million of the solution.

"Actually 5 parts per million of formaldehyde are permitted to exist in the air of industrial work places. This level represents at least a tenfold safety factor. No ill health results from breathing 5 parts per million, 8 hours a day throughout life. This limit has been established by the Annual Conference of Government Industrial Hygienists."

We must bear in mind that the test above was in a solution of water, but how about hot coffe? That might bring more of the formaldehyde into solution. But who wants even the slightest amount of it in our food?

An All-Out Campaign Against Plastic

We must fight this thing quickly before it becomes too strongly entrenched. Write to your hospital, to restaurants, to railroads in regard to their dining cars, to the army and the navy and if possible send them a copy of this editorial. If necessary a fund should be raised to make a grant to some hospital to conduct research on this question. Nothing should be too good for you as far as your health is concerned.

Now I read that they have developed a new plastic coating on dairy equipment to protect surfaces against erosion. It was written up in *The Milk Dealer* of August, 1950. A plastic called *corrosite* is used which combines chemically with the metal surface it covers. It is used as a coating for pasteurizing, bottle-washing and bottle-filling equipment. It is also being used on cement feed troughs on farms. I have not checked up on corrosite. Perhaps it does not contain a poison, but my little knowledge of chemistry tells me that something that has the ability of going into such a strong chemical action with a metal surface must carry "strong" elements. Will some of our chemically-trained readers go into this subject further and let me know what they find about corrosite?

There is a growing medical literature which shows that plastic materials which surgeons have been using as permanent plants at sites of operations seem to cause trouble as time goes on. It is possible that they will find safer plastics. It is possible that safer plastics will be found for utensils, but it is beyond me how our government does not see to it that such a product is checked before it is put into production. See for yourself. Try a cup of coffee served in one of these plastic cups. It definitely does not taste good.

China cup manufacturers—please get behind this movement to check into the dangers to our health of the use of plastic dishes.

CHAPTER **57**

Some Eminent Dangers from Plastics

Even the plastic manufacturers admit that chemicals penetrate into food stored in plastic. We believe that there is evidence enough to incriminate plastic utensils as dangerous contaminants of food.

We refer you to an article in *Industrial Medicine* for September, 1947, by C. Scott McKinley, M.D., who is the medical director of the Bakelite Corporation at Bound Brook, New Jersey. Dr. McKinley says that at the Bakelite plant about 1,000 raw materials are used in the manufacture of synthetic resins and the plastic which is made from them. During the manufacturing process, workers in the plant must be guarded against the toxicity of many of these materials. However, according to Dr. McKinley, once the actual operation has been completed and the plastic is made, there is no longer any danger.

Let's say a number of different toxic substances are being combined for one operation in the manufacturing process. Although each of these retains its poisonous quality during the process, "the finished plastic containing these materials is essentially inert," says Dr. McKinley—that is, it does not react chemically with other substances. When the resin is "reacted"as the manufacturers call it, the toxic properties of the individual materials are no longer present. "There will be other chemicals as new plastics are made or new modifying agents will be used, whose toxicity is unknown or little known," says Dr. McKinley, not very cheerfully, it seems to us.

The Toxic Effects of Formaldehyde

One of the substances used in making plastic is formaldehyde—a material made from menthyl alcohol. Frank Bamford, B.Sc., in his book, *Poisons* (published by Blakiston in 1951), says that of all the alipathic aldehydes, formaldehyde is the one most commonly responsible for toxic symptoms. Ordinarily a 40 per cent solution is strongly caustic, and diluted to even 3 or 4 per cent formaldehyde is a "powerful, irritant poison." He tells us that deaths have been reported from breathing air containing as little as ten parts per million of gaseous formaldehyde.

Alice Hamilton in her book, *Industrial Toxicology* (published by Harper and Brothers in 1934), tells us that "the danger limit (of formaldehyde) for man has never been determined." Concentrations of 4,900 parts per million in the air for 3 hours produce serious inflammation of the eyes and the air passages. Workers in industries where plastics are used show reactions to formaldehyde on their skin, eyelids, conjunctiva (tissue of the eyes) and cornea. Although individuals vary considerably in their sensitivity to formaldehyde intoxication, blondes have been found to be much more sensitive than brunettes. Cases of formaldehyde poisoning have increased rapidly with the great increase in the production of plastics. The manufacturing of phenol derivative resins (from which plastics are made) rose from 4 million pounds in 1920 to 33 million pounds in 1929. These same resins are also used in some kinds of varnish, and many other products as well as in the dishes, fabrics and so forth that we think of as plastic.

The Risk of Formaldehyde Poisoning

Miss Hamilton relates many stories of formaldehyde poisoning in industry—blisters, scaling and fissures on hands, chronic conjunctivitis, rhinitis (inflammation of the mucous membrane of the nose), pharyngitis and laryngitis, difficult breathing and nervous disorders, asthma attacks, coughs and tonsilitis. She also mentions a formaldehyde rash seen in women workers who apply caps to medicine bottles, thus constantly touching a material containing free formaldehyde. She tells us that acrolein, related chemically to formaldehyde, has been considered for use as a poisonous gas in trench warfare. Its action is similar to that of formaldehyde.

A booklet from the United States Public Health Service, *Formaldehyde—Its Toxicity and Potential Dangers*—describes this substance in its opening sentence: "Formaldehyde is an irritant gas and at the same time a protoplasmic poison." We discuss protoplasmic poisons in the article on saccharin in this book. Protoplasm is simply a collective name for living cells. The protoplasm of our bodies is composed of living cells. A protoplasmic poison is a substance which is poisonous to these cells.

The booklet goes on to describe an experiment in which volunteer subjects ate from 100 to 200 milligrams of formaldehyde along with their food for 15 days. There were no bad effects until the last 5 days of the experiment when the subjects began to suffer from headache, gastric and intestinal pain, cramps, nausea and vomiting. Quoting from an article by Warburg ("The Effect of Oxygen Respiration," *Zeitschrift fur Physiologischer Chemie,* Vol. 74: p. 479, 1911) the booklet tells us that formaldehyde inhibits the metabolism of oxygen in the cell, that is, oxygen, necessary to every function of our bodies, cannot be assimilated by the cell when formaldehyde is present.

In discussing poisoning from formaldehyde by exposure in industrial plants and also by drinking formaldehyde solutions, the Public Health pamphlet lists horrid symptoms of poisoning. Hardening of the upper digestive tract, larynx, pharynx and esophagus, hardening of the tissues in the stomach, degeneration of the kidneys, abscesses of the lungs, injury to the brain, and uremia resulting from injury to the kidneys are some of these symptoms. Formaldehyde in the air must be kept below 10 parts per million for safety, says the bulletin.

Plastic in Household Use and Medicine

What do we use plastic for, and why should we be concerned about its potential danger to health? Probably we are most familiar with plastic tableware—those beautiful, colorful and practical dishes which are now becoming increasingly popular and stylish. About 30 per cent of all hospitals in the country use plastic dishes, incidentally. We all know that shower curtains and fabrics, refrigerator bags and containers, watchbands, belts, braces, purses, luggage, table and sink tops and the covering of many food packages—an almost endless list of familiar things we use every day—are made of plastic. They're inexpensive, they're durable, they're pretty. Are they dangerous to health?

In addition to these many familiar things we know, the plastic industry is preparing more and more uses for their product. Dairies now have plastic-lined equipment for various operations concerned with milk, so that the metals from which these containers are made will not be exposed to daily washings, caustics, detergents and lactic acid. A new method of making bread pans is being tried out in which the pans are lined with a coat of plastic that makes greasing unnecessary. Plastic tubing is used regularly in hospitals for intravenous feeding where the tubing is inserted directly into the patient's vein, for catheters which are inserted into the patient's kidney, for prosthetic devices such as braces and pins for bones.

Plastics Used in the Medical Field

Several medical articles give us hints of the general attitude toward the use of plastics in medicine. An article in *New York Medicine* for 1949, Vol. 15, describes experiments of Dr. B. S. Oppenheimer of Columbia University, in which cellophane wrapped around the kidneys of white rats or embedded in the abdominal wall induced cancer in 35 per cent of the animals.

An editorial in the *British Medical Journal* for April 5, 1952, tells us that a number of different plastics are used in surgery, and it is sometimes difficult to know what kind of product is being used, for "the commercial name of the product does not necessarily indicate its chemical structure . . . Although a plastic may be pure chemical substance, other chemicals may be added to it during the course of manufacture and these latter substances may sweat out of the plastic and cause a severe tissue reaction." For instance, several investigators have discovered that pure polyethylene film is inert in the body, but that sometimes another chemical, dicetyl phosphate, is added during the course of manufacture, producing a film that is highly irritant and damaging to human tissues.

Lucite shavings implanted in the abdominal cavity resulted in a devastating inflammation. A polyethylene cup used as an artificial joint in a hip became roughened by friction and immediately set up an inflammatory reaction. Bakelite and "the casein" plastics also cause severe tissue damage so that they cannot be used. Attempts to use plastics in the lungs as part of tuberculosis therapy have failed miserably in many cases, producing infection and hemorrhage. In orthopedic surgery, says the editorial, artificial hip joints made of plastic have been successfully implanted in a number of individuals, but it is not known how they will wear and the assumption is that if they become rough from wear, they will immediately irritate the surrounding tissues.

The article concludes: "The use of plastics seems thus to be never completely without danger . . . and probably their use will consequently be restricted."

In the January 27, 1951, issue of the *Journal of the American Medical Association,* a letter to the editor inquires whether it is thoroughly ascertained that polyethylene or synthetic derivatives of that sort (that is, plastic) may be used for surgical purposes without danger of cancer. The answer given is that at present there is no clinical or laboratory evidence that the relatively inert tubing has any (cancer-causing) properties. How is such a conclusion possible with the evidence we have just cited available?

An article in the *Quarterly Bulletin of the Northwestern University Medical School* ("Complications from the Use of Plastic Intravenous Tubing," by Stanley W. Teull, M.D., Wayne B. Martin, M.D., and Harold Laufman, Ph.D., M.D., Vol. 22, 1948) describes a purely mechanical accident that occurred in an experiment with plastic tubing. Then the authors go on to say that different batches of plastic may have different properties depending on the temperature to which they were heated. They conclude: "Since it is possible therefore that various batches of tubing from the same manufacturer might result in tissue reaction (that is, bodily harm) while other batches might not, it has been suggested that spot checks be made for tissue reaction before the materials are released for use ... Until then, we feel it is unsafe to assume that *polyethylene* products in general are inert (harmless) to animal or human tissue."

Plastic Dishes

Consumer Reports, devoted to testing all kinds of objects and reporting to the consumer, has an article on plastic dishes in the January, 1951, issue. Their tests included many different brands, and they ranked them according to the results. In general, however, they found that plastic tableware is scratched rather easily and usually subject to staining by several common foods, including coffee, tea, ketchup and spaghetti sauce. They also advise against the use of plastic ware for storing foods, and that it should not remain uncleaned for long periods since it may stain or suffer severe loss of lustre.

A clipping from the *New York Times* of January 30, 1952, tells us that a small mining town in West Virginia is the first city in the country to use plastic pipes for a municipal water supply. Imagine the amount of formaldehyde in every cup of coffee and every bowl of soup in *that* town, especially if it is served in a plastic container! Imagine what the chlorine in the water will do to the inside of the pipes! Think of that day, not too far in the future, we suppose, when this small community may fluoridate its water. What is the effect of fluorine on plastic? Has anyone done research on this subject?

Manufacturers' Experiments With Plastic

We received letters from several manufacturers of plastics with whom we engaged in correspondence, asking them for information proving that their products are not harmful if they are used over a long period of time. We received a great deal of informative material, first-hand, from the plastic manufacturers. It related various scientific tests made for determining the amount of formaldehyde remaining in fluids contained in plastic dishes, and also experiments in which rats were fed ground-up plastic while the researchers watched them closely for any harmful consequences. We will not go into detail in describing these experiments. In general, they show that hot fluids placed in plastic dishes will contain from 0 to 28 parts per million of formaldehyde. If the fluid is left longer in the dishes (30 minutes) the percentage of formaldehyde will increase. We learn that rats whose diet includes ground-up plastic dishes will be healthy at the end of a 40-day experiment and will have excreted all of the plastic with no ill effects. It is not clear from the information we received just how long this experiment was conducted, and the researchers refer to it as "a long period." The chart accompanying the report seems to indicate that it was 40 days.

In the same literature from the plastic manufacturer certain specific cleansers are recommended for plastic dishes, we suppose because these cleansers contain no substance that will react with the materials in the plastic. We are also told that chlorine compounds "are not friendly to plastic. In time they will impair the fine surface." The letter from the manufacturer assures us that he is now quite certain we will be glad to withdraw what we said about plastic dishes and will print another article praising their merits and counseling our readers to have no fear of any harmful results from the use of plastic.

It happens that the evidence presented by the plastic manufacturer causes exactly the opposite reaction in us, although we certainly bear him no ill will and appreciate greatly the information he has given us. However, the sum total of the material in our files at present on the subject of plastic adds up to the same column of figures we've been studying all these years in our search for a healthful way of life in the twentieth century.

The Case Against Plastics

1. Doctor McKinley assures us in his article, quoted above, that all the various toxic ingredients used in plastic lose their individual characteristics during the process of manufacture. On the basis of this statement, we assume that free formaldehyde should *not* be extracted, no matter how hot a fluid is poured into a plastic dish and no matter how long it stands there. But by the evidence of the manufacturer's report itself, we find that up to 28 parts per million of formaldehyde are extracted from plastic by hot liquids.

2. Dr. McKinley tells us that new materials are constantly being used in plastic—most of them toxic, we assume. The article on plastic tubing tells us that, even in the same batch of plastic materials, the right results may not come about if the temperature should happen to be off a few degrees. How do we know which batch of plastic, heated to what temperature and containing what new poisons we are buying next time we shop?

3. We started our inquiry on plastics because we had lots of material on formaldehyde and were worried about its presence in plastic tableware. Our new research frightens us even more, for formaldehyde is apparently the least of our worries. What tests have been done on the toxicity of the other synthetic materials included in plastic—about 1000 of them, according to Dr. McKinley?

4. The plastic manufacturers advise that chlorine products "are not friendly" to plastics. They do not state why, but we assume that the chlorine combines with the plastic and effects it detrimentally. How many urban American housewives can wash their plastic dishes in water that does not contain chlorine? What effect will the chlorine have on the plastic and, therefore, on the person eating from the dishes? The report that various foods such as coffee and ketchup stain plastic dishes poses another question in our minds. Surely a substance that permanently stains a dish is combining with at least the surface of the dish, or you would be able to wash the stain away!

5. The rat experiment described above is exactly the kind of experiment we protest constantly. We are concerned with the possibility of formaldehyde and the other toxic substances in plastic accumulating in our bodies as a result of this long-time use. Of what significance is the experience of one group of rats over a period of 40 days? What about the rats when they grew old and tired and subject to degenerative diseases? Did their 40-day adventure with plastics affect them then? We are not told. What about their children and grandchildren? And *their* grandchildren? How many generations of human beings must we sacrifice to find out the answers to these questions? We note, too, that the rats in the experiment were fed a diet powerful enough in vitamins and minerals to withstand

almost any kind of poison. They got rations that included wonderfully potent grains, dry skim milk, blood meal, ground limestone, bone meal, cod liver oil and brewer's yeast. Now researchers know perfectly well that these very vitamins and minerals are protection against man-made poisons. The scientific journals are full of proof that this is so. How can they place animals on such a diet, expose them to poisons, note that they suffer no ill effects, then cheerfully assume that human beings are perfectly safe exposed to such poisons, when the researchers themselves know better than anyone else that relatively few human beings in this country are actually living day after day on a diet so well fortified with protective foods as those rats had in the experiment?

Plastic's Effect on Future Generations

We agree completely with the spirit of the experiment. We seriously doubt that anyone would drop dead as a result of eating from plastic dishes for 40 days. But we demand to know what will be the effect on human beings of daily ingestion of the plastic poisons over several generations. No one has answered that question for us. The United States Public Health Service tells us that formaldehyde is a protoplasmic poison. No one has yet managed to find out how much of a protoplasmic poison is required to destroy a piece of protoplasm over a period of years.

Protoplasm is a mighty complicated and mysterious substance. If scientists fully understood it, we could conquer disease. So far as our own piece of protoplasm is concerned, we're sentimentally attached to it, and we plan to keep it carefully shielded from formaldehyde and all the other toxic substances in plastics, by not buying or using plastic dishes or containers for any food material. And, because we sometimes "eat out," we'll guard against our friends' enthusiasm for plastic by eating a diet as rich in protective foods as the rats had in the experiment. No matter who calls us "food faddists" we'll go right on taking desiccated liver, brewer's yeast, bone meal, rose hips, sunflower seeds, fish oil capsules, and wheat germ. We'll spread them all out on the table before us at every meal—and they won't be in plastic dishes!

SECTION 15

DRINKING WATER

If you do not have your own well or spring, it is best to drink purchased spring water, for it does not contain any added chlorine or other chemicals. Chlorine uses up vitamin E in the body. As a rule also aluminum sulphate is used in public drinking water. No research has ever been done on the long-term effects of drinking chlorinated water.

CHAPTER **58**

The Water You Drink

Here are some news stories about water. (1) *The Canadian Journal of Public Health* for April, 1951, reviews a survey made by a joint United States-Canadian commission to study pollution of boundary waters. The report shows that a daily discharge of more than two billion gallons of waste material is poured into water being used for drinking water by four million persons.

(2) A clipping from a Seattle paper shows sewer pipes jutting out on a bathing beach and recites the grim story of a man who got paratyphoid fever from eating raw oysters he had gathered within 100 feet of a sewer opening.

(3) An article in *Time*, July 6, 1953, tells of 1490 Singer Manufacturing employees at South Bend, Indiana, threatened with amoebiasis, and 4 who died, as a result of drinking water from an old well whose cracked pipes were letting in sewage.

(4) The Detroit *Times* for September 15, 1953, displays a picture of millions of dead carp jamming a stream up to 5 feet deep leading into the Kalamazoo River. "River Pollution Killed These Fish" says the headline.

(5) The Oregon *Journal* for November 8, 1952, relates a tragedy that took place when some poisonous substance was dumped by an industrial firm—10,000 salmon headed up the Green River to spawn were killed. Investigators were trying to find out what firm was guilty.

Every week brings us new clippings, for water pollution is very much in the news at present. One reason for this is, of course, the fact that each day water pollution gets worse instead of better. In addition, the recent extensive droughts have forced us to realize anew that life simply can't go on without water—clean, pure water. A Public Affairs Pamphlet on water pollution, *Washing Our Water* by Helen Beal Woodward, (22 East 38th Street, New York 16, New York) says: "The unprecedented growth of industry, together with our expanding cities, has burdened many of our rivers beyond their capacity to flush away waste. The seriousness of this, as it affects the health and general welfare of people and industry alike is the subject of the pamphlet. . . . Pollution from human sewage and industrial waste increases in two ways as citizen and industries grow. Less water is available to carry waste away, because of increased water demands and at the same time the water flushed back into the common supply carries a heavier burden of waste. *Modern chemical industries have made the problem even more imperative, as ordinary methods of water treatment do not always affect the complex new chemicals.*" (Italics are ours.)

Now should we become concerned over the news above? Well, how do you feel about drinking water so poisonous that fish die in it by the millions? It seems to us there are two kinds of water poisoning we should discuss here—(1) the pollution that occurs in drinking water, either from natural sources or from industrial wastes, and (2) the chemicals that are added to water to remove the impurities.

Water Polluted by Human and Industrial Wastes

How dangerous can polluted water be? In the case of the Singer employees, they were drinking water from a well drilled 52 years ago when the plant was built. No one suspected drinking water as the cause of the 4 deaths until amoebae were found in stool sample. "A quick check of 138 Singer workers showed about half with amoebiasis." At present all workers who show evidence of amoebic infestation are being treated by the company at a cost 77,000 dollars. How much less expensive in money and lives it would have been to check the old well and drill a new one.

The Journal of the American Medical Association for May 5, 1951, tells us that during 1949 there was an increase of 951 reported cases of waterborne diseases over the previous year. Total figures for the years 1938-1949 are 130,524 cases of disease, 94 deaths. We wonder whether these figures include such incidents as that which occurred at Rochester, New York, several years ago when untreated water from the Genesee River was mistakenly pumped into the city water supply and in a short time there were 35,000 cases of gastroenteritis—a water-borne disease which inflames the stomach and intestines.

Polluted Water from Wells

A clipping from *Time,* September 16, 1949, discloses that infectious hepatitis (inflammation of the liver) was the main nuisance of World War II. Disabling 30,000 G.I.'s in the Mediterranean Theatre alone, it is caused by polluted drinking water. This was discovered in a summer camp for youngsters where 350 campers came down with the disease, and its cause was eventually traced to a camp well into which cesspools drained.

Much has been written about pure water for country-dwellers, and much literature is available from the government and in public libraries on how and where to drill wells, how to make certain that cesspools or privies will not contaminate the well, how to have the water tested for purity. Yet in spite of all this available information we are told that a large per-centage of wells on farms are unsafe. "Dug" wells are the worst offenders since surface water can drain into them easily. But the water from drilled wells should be tested for safeness, too, for it may be contaminated.

Action Against Pollution

What is being done about pollution? Up to now it seems that very little has been done, but now the problem has become so serious that steps are being taken in some parts of the country. For instance, the *New York Times,* for October 14, 1951, describes the arrangement made by 10 New Jersey cities to drain off and process all sewage in a jointly owned disposal plant. Seven of these cities had been under order from the state board of health to end pollution ever since 1934. The disposal plan cost 13 million dollars which is being paid off at the rate of 135 dollars per million gallons by each community.

State laws on pollution are tightening up, according to *Chemical Week* for July 4, 1953, so there is continual pressure on industry to solve their pollution problems, and constant urging by federal officials that plants that have solutions for their disposal problems should publicize them widely so that others can follow suit.

On the other hand, we find in many localities an attitude of indifference, or we hear people saying, "Why should we not throw our sewage into the river when all the other towns upriver do, so that the water is already filthy by the time it reaches us?" In cases where a water source crosses state boundary lines, the federal government can step in and, working with local authorities, can see to it that wastes from one state do not pollute the water of residents of another state.

What About Chemicals in Water?

It may be that your community solves—or tries to solve—its water pollution headaches by pouring more chemicals into the water. For instance, here is a sample of how water in swimming pools is treated. The 27 pools in New York City are "purified" each year by the addition of the following chemicals (according to *Chemical Week* July 4, 1953): Chlorine, 59,000 pounds; Anhydrous Ammonia, 5,000 pounds; Sodium hypochlorite, 12,000 gallons; Ammonium sulfate, 80,000 pounds; Soda ash powder, 140,000 pounds; Soda ash cake, 20,000 pounds; Copper sulfate, 8,500 pounds; ammonium alum, 20,000 pounds. Yes, folks, this is the chemical brew in which New York children swim. It's a wonder there is any room left in the swimming pools for water, isn't it?

We don't know how many of these same chemicals are in drinking water in New York City. We have the word of a reader that Columbus, Ohio, adds these chemicals to its drinking water each year: 500 tons of aluminum ore; 8,000 tons of lime; 3,000 tons of soda ash; 1,200 tons of sulphuric acid; 500 tons of coke and 8 tons of liquid chlorine. Now seems to be as good a time as any for all of us to get busy and do a survey on the water we are drinking. Why not find out, for your own information, just what chemicals are added to the water in your home town?

Chlorine Not the Only Chemical in City Water

Some time ago we quoted a question that appeared in the *Journal of the American Medical Association* for July 28, 1951, asking what research has been done on the effects of chlorinated water drunk over a period of years. The answer was that no official research has ever been done to determine the possible harm to human beings of drinking chlorinated water. And most of the urban water supplies are chlorinated! But now we see that chlorine is one of the least of the villains we have to contend with. Apparently city drinking water contains as well untold amounts of copper sulfate, aluminum, sulphuric acid, and who knows what else! A clipping from Canton, Ohio, December 4, 1951, indicates that a chemical was added to the water in that city for removing iron which, we suppose, was causing the housewives trouble, staining their washing and making rusty rings on their bathtubs. The treatment was sodium hexametaphosphate—170 pounds daily. Now if no one has ever done any research on the effects of chlorinated water, whose use is almost universal, what research has been done, do you suppose, on chemicals like this sodium hexametaphosphate and its effects on infants, sick people and pregnant women who drink the water?

We don't believe the fault lies with the waterworks officials who impress us as overworked and extremely conscientious public servants, more dismayed than anyone else at the pass to which we have come. It is up to us, Mr. and Mrs. Average Citizen, to take up the cudgels and announce once and for all that we simply will not put up with water pollution, nor with thousands of tons of chemicals of unknown toxicity being dumped into the drinking water to counteract the pollution.

A Program for Pure Drinking Water

Where do you begin on a program of this kind? We would suggest first of all that you write to the Superintendent of Documents in Washington, D.C., and ask for all the information available on water pollution particularly in your part of the country. An excellent pamphlet, *Clean Water is Everybody's Business,* is available as a starter for 20 cents. On the last page of this pamphlet you will find suggestions for how to investigate the condition of your own drinking water and what to do about it. Also send for the Public Affairs Pamphlet, *Washing Our Water,* 25 cents. Write or call on your city health department and gather information. Your poor, beleaguered water officials have probably been trying for a long time to get public support for a program for pure water. Give them all the help you can. After you have gathered information and know the point of view of your local officials, begin to write letters to the editor of the local paper. You might even ask the editor to assign a reporter to do a series of feature stories on the local water situation. In this way you can enlighten other citizens and enlist their support.

What Can You Do?

Meanwhile, are you going to go on drinking this filthy, polluted, chemicalized liquid that comes out of your water faucet? Are you going to go on giving it to your children to drink? We know, from scientific investigation, of the diseases that can result from polluted water—typhoid, amoebic dysentery, hepatitis, goiter, polio, gastroenteritis and many more.

So far as we know, no one has proved as yet, with a scientifically controlled experiment, that countless diseases of modern times may not be the result of the chemicals in the water we drink. Yet many cases are on record in medical journals of allergies, asthma, hives, and other conditions brought on by chlorinated water. So why should we not assume that chemicalized water is unhealthful until it has been proved otherwise?

If you live on a farm, by all means have your well or spring water tested. Your local county agent can tell you how to have this done. If the water shows any trace of pollution, stop drinking it. And don't wait until next month or next year to drill a new well.

If you live in a city, buy bottled spring water for drinking and cooking. This is not expensive and will pay for itself many times over in your own additional peace of mind. If there is no source of bottled spring water available, canvass every country dweller known to you or any of your friends and see whether you can obtain water from his well or spring, making certain, of course, that you have this water tested for purity. Your city waterworks will test the water for you.

All of us want good health for ourselves and our families. We spend a great deal of time and money buying and preparing the best and most nourishing food. But what does it avail us to have our own organic garden so that we won't be consuming for instance, copper sulfate insecticides, if we then drink water loaded with copper sulfate? What good does it do us to avoid the chlorinated hydrocarbon insecticides, if we then fill our poor bodies with heavily chlorinated water? Under ideal conditions of life, exposed to no poisonous substances, we might be able to resist both the pollution and the chemicals in our water supply. But, exposed as we are every day to countless poisons, the least we can do for the sake of our own health is to drink pure unpolluted and unchemicalized water.

CHAPTER **59**

Chlorine in Drinking Water

by J. I. RODALE

The almost universal contaminant of drinking water is chlorine. We suspect that this chemical may be the cause of a host of ailments of unknown origin.

In the excitement and unholy zeal to railroad through fluoridation of our drinking waters, people seem to have forgotten all about the fact that our water is being chlorinated. They take chlorine for granted. It is a *fait accompli,* and they believe that nothing can be done about it. Chlorination has been in use for so long that time has given it a sort of complacent acceptance. The sad part of it is, however, that in the eyes of some people it has a halo. The best people are for it, aren't they? The schools and doctors and congressmen recommend it, do they not? After all, we've been drinking chlorinated water all our lives, and we aren't all dead yet, so it couldn't possibly be harmful.

I have heard dentists, in public recommendations of the use of fluorine, practically predicate their entire case on the fact that since a city has the right to place chlorine in the water, it may also, therefore, put in fluorine. But fluorine is used to reduce cavities in the teeth of children—while chlorination is resorted to, to kill harmful bacteria that can cause diseases like typhoid. The latter has the barest semblance of justification, but the use of fluorine would set off a new dangerous trend. Where would municipalities stop? Would they eventually put aspirin in the water to prevent headaches?

Chlorine Is a Poison

Chlorine is a powerful disinfectant—a potent poison, highly irritative to the skin and the mucous membranes. In Clorox it is used for bleaching, and it has a great many industrial uses because of its active nature as a chemical element. If house plants are watered with chlorinated water, they will not thrive, nor will guppies live in such water. Many years ago, I was told by a man who conducted a market where fish were kept alive till sold, that the day the waterworks placed a charge of chlorine into the water, all his fish died. This is a point that has been completely overlooked. In the case of fluorine the machinery has been devised so that there is a constant change of fluorine into the water. An attempt is made to maintain a constancy of amount. But with chlorine there is an unscientific sledge-hammer treatment. Large amounts are dumped in at one time. How about sensitive people who drink water on such a day?

Here is a happening to illustrate what I mean. I will quote from the St. Petersburg (Florida) *Times* of September 25, 1954:

"A 25-year-old mother was almost totally blinded yesterday morning when she washed her eyes out with water and found too late the water supply at the trailer park where she resides had been treated with strong chemicals during the night, police reported.

"Les Grant, manager of the trailer park, said he and Chester Hamilton, the owner, had treated the court's water supply with chlorine at midnight. He said a health inspector told him the bacteriological count was off and the pipes needed flushing.

"Grant told the *Times* he posted a big sign warning about the water over the mail boxes at the court but it was too late to notify residents personally. He said no other residents made any complaints about the water."

A sad case, but it is only one of hundreds of deadly experiences with chlorine.

Clippings from a number of New England newspapers

tell us of a happening in a Cambridge (Massachusetts) swimming pool where a score or so of children became violently ill from chlorine poisoning. While the gasping, choking youngsters were given artificial respiration and taken to the hospital for oxygen administration, authorities were investigating the possible cause of the accident. It seems that a filter had backfired, causing an extra amount of the purifying powder to be released into the pool. It was surmised that some of the children had swallowed some of the water; others had simply been overcome by the fumes. At any rate, they turned blue and dizzy. They choked. True, it was a big overdose of chlorine that poisoned the children. But how much is an overdose for each individual cell of our bodies, when you and I drink chlorinated water daily, year after year?

Chlorine and Diarrhea

In the 1955 Pennsylvania floods many cases of diarrhea occurred in the city of Tamaqua, population 11,508, because of larger than usual amounts of chlorine used for fear of a typhoid epidemic. According to the Allentown *Morning Call* of August 30, 1955, "A state health department official has assured worried residents that an estimated 3,000 cases of diarrhea in the community are only 'seasonal' and the result of sensitivity to the increased amounts of chlorine added to the Tamaqua water supply since the flood." This sort of thing is only seasonal or incidental to a public health official, who overlooks the fact that such happenings occur many times a year when the chlorine charge is put into the water. How many are getting diarrhea under such conditions?

Is Chlorine an Allergy Causer?

Physicians do not seem to be aware, nor do they care much about the effect of chlorine on the human body. One rarely sees references to it in medical literature. In his book, *How to Help Your Doctor Help You* (Dell), Walter C. Alvarez, M.D., says: "It is hard to explain why many a highly sensitive person reacts strongly and in an allergic way to such simple chemical substances as aspirin or sugar or chlorine in the city water. These small molecules are very different from the huge and extremely complicated molecules of protein which were originally supposed to produce all allergic reactions."

The physicians are always ready to attribute something

that they do not understand to an allergy. Chlorine is about as much an allergy causer as the left front foot of my bed. I was going to say, "as my left shoe," but shoes are sometimes allergy causers. The doctors should learn more about chlorine, and they should seek for a substitute water purifier that is safer.

In the *Journal of Allergy* for November, 1944, appears an article in which M. J. Gutmann, M.D., of Jerusalem writes of a case of giant hives in an English officer. Skin tests showed no evidence of sensitivity; testing with over 40 different food substances showed no allergy, nor were there any indications of bacterial allergy.

Yet this officer's hives disappeared when he was transferred from Jerusalem to other stations. He could recollect no difference in his diet and way of life at these other stations except that he drank mineral waters. As soon as he returned to Jerusalem and once again drank the city water, he developed hives immediately. The water in Jerusalem is chlorinated. When chlorinated water is heated, for coffee, tea and so forth, the chlorine is given off into the air and can produce no symptoms. But, for those who drink the water cold, out of the faucet, a number of symptoms may arise.

Dr. Gutmann reviews an article in the *Journal of Allergy* for 1934 in which chlorine in water was found to be the cause of asthma and functional colitis. When the patient was put on distilled water exclusively for three days, he experienced no return of either disorder. Then when one drop of sodium hypochloride was placed in his drinking water, his asthma and colitis promptly returned. Dr. Gutmann tells us that he has had other patients who got hives from the addition of even the smallest amounts of chlorine to their drinking water. One was a woman of 28 who had hives from childhood. All her life she had tried the most extreme kinds of diet in an effort to locate the food which was causing the allergy. Eventually someone thought of changing her drinking water. The hives disappeared within a few days. As soon as she returned to chlorinated drinking water, the eruptions appeared within a short time.

What Research Has Been Done on Chlorine?

One day I was reading the *Journal of the American Medical Association* (July 28, 1951, issue) and I saw something that astounded me. In the section where the doctors ask questions, there appeared a question to the editor which asked whether studies had ever been made to determine the harmful effects of chlorinated water used for drinking purposes. The editor's answer said that a careful check of all the literature and all available information revealed the fact that no organized investigation had ever been made of the effect of chlorine on the human body. He admitted that there had been cases of allergic skin inflammation and many outbreaks of asthma that were traced to chlorine, but the editor refers to them as allergies.

Imagine, permitting hundreds of millions of persons to drink chlorinated water without ever having made a thorough investigation of its effect on the human system! At least there should have been a comprehensive study of the subject based on the fragments of existing facts which show up here and there in the medical literature. For example, in *Bridges' Dietetics for the Clinician* by Harry J. Johnson, M.D. (1949, Lea and Febiger) on page 91 appears the statement that chlorine destroys vitamin E. This is one of the most difficult vitamins to maintain a sufficiency of in the body, and it is one of the most important ones, for a lack of vitamin E will produce heart disease. Yet from the very first day of life one is given chlorinated water which slowly keeps undermining the body's dwindling store of this precious vitamin, a vitamin that is rarely included in the regular all-in-one vitamin capsules purchasable in drug stores.

Chlorine and Heart Trouble

Another medical bit of evidence incriminating chlorine in the causation of heart disease is contained in a book called *Poisoning* by W. F. von Oettingen, M.D., p. 72 (Paul Hoeber, Incorporated). The author says, "It has been claimed that injury of the mitral valve (of the heart) and cardiac (heart) insufficiency may result from severe exposure to chlorine, or carbon monoxide. Coronary thrombosis, characterized by palpitation, irregularities of the heart beat, and anxiety, has been reported in poisonings with chlorine, carbon monoxide and ferric chloride." The latter is a chlorine compound.

While this refers to severe exposures, we must not overlook the fact that taking in chlorine every day of one's life, beginning from the day of birth, will eventually accumulate into the equivalent of a severe exposure. In fact, the unborn child may already be suffering from the effects of chlorinated water its mother may be drinking during pregnancy, for why is it that 25,000 babies are born each year in the United States with heart trouble?

In connection with the relation between a lack of vitamin E and heart trouble, let us look into some sad mathematics. As we have seen, the main reason for chlorinating drinking water is to prevent typhoid. As we have also seen, the introduction into the human body of chlorine compounds results in a reduction of its vitamin E resources. So what do we have? The effect of chlorine is to reduce typhoid, and to increase heart disease.

In 1900 before chlorination was in very general use, there were 35,379 deaths from typhoid in the United States, or about 31 per 100,000 of population. In that same year, namely 1900, there were 68,439 deaths from heart disease, or 137 per 100,000 of population. Now, in 1950, as a result of the use of chlorine, plus a general improvement in the sanitation of the water supply, reduction of pollution, etc., there were only 90 deaths from typhoid in the United States, which means that it is down to practically zero. But what has happened with heart disease? By 1950 it had skyrocketed up to 535,920 deaths or at the rate of 355 per 100,000 of population.

So what have we done with our chlorine? We have traded 35,379 typhoid deaths for 535,920 heart disease deaths. Shown in table form here is how it looks.

1900	Typhoid	35,379	31.3 per 100,000
	Heart	68,439	137.4 per 100,000
1950	Typhoid	90	(zero)
	Heart	535,920	355.5 per 100,000

This does not look like a case of good management. Of course, the medical profession will say that the increase in heart disease deaths is due to the fast pace at which we are living, but if you will read my little book, *This Pace Is Not Killing Us* (Rodale Books $1.00), you will think differently.

Chlorine Is All Around Us

The case against chlorine is much worse than I have painted it. According to an article from a German magazine on this subject which we read, chlorine reduces vitamins A, B, C, E and H as well as destroying one of the amino acids of protein, namely tryptophane.

Water is not the only place where man comes in contact with chlorine in these modern times. He is breathing it in DDT, he is getting it in the chlorine dioxide that is applied to flour to bleach it. It is being used in processing potatoes to improve their dehydration qualities and to prevent them from turning brown in storage. It is contained in tobacco as a residue from insecticides. It is used in dozens of other applications throughout the present day system of industry, food processing, etc.

I am not considering table salt, which is a chloride namely, sodium chloride. In the body we know that its two elements break apart, the sodium wreaking fearful havoc in many susceptible persons, causing high blood pressure, heart and kidney involvements, etc. But what happens to the chlorine portion of table salt? No one seems to worry about it. As I say, I am not considering table salt, but am merely mentioning it. However, its effects on the human body, with regard to its chloride content should be thoroughly investigated. Until this is done, no health conscious person should use a grain of table salt.

A Variety of Chemicals in Our Drinking Water

In the meantime the problem of supplying drinking water is becoming more complicated, or is it the greed of the chemical companies who wish to sell their chemicals, for now there are available 48 different chemical compounds for processing drinking water. If you want to see what chemistry has done to our water, look at the list of chemicals reproduced herewith, 48 of them, that are used in public water treatment all over the country. We have in our possession the printed chart containing them, given to us by one of the engineers of a waterworks of a large city. Here is the list of 48 chemicals:

Activated Carbon	Chlorinated Copperas
Activated Silica	Chlorinated Lime
Alum. Ammonium Sulfate	Chlorine
Aluminum Chloride Soln.	Chlorine Dioxide
Alum. Potassium Sulfate	Copper Sulfate
Aluminum Sulfate	Disodium Phosphate
Bromine	Dolomitic Hydrated Lime
Calcium Carbonate	Dolomitic Lime
Calcium Hydroxide	Ferric Chloride
Calcium Hypochlorite	Ferric Sulfate
Calcium Oxide	Fluosilicic Acid
Carbon Dioxide	Hydrofluoric Acid

Alum, Liquid
Ammonia, Anhydrous
Ammonia, Aqua
Ammonium Silicofluoride
Ammonium Sulfate
Bentonite
Ozone
Sodium Aluminate
Sodium Bicarbonate
Sodium Bisulfite
Sodium Carbonate
Sodium Chloride

Sodium Chlorite (13)
Sodium Fluorid
Sod. Hexametaphosphate
Sodium Hydroxide
Sodium Hypochlorite
Sodium Silicate
Sodium Sulfite
Sodium Thiosulfate
Sulfur Dioxide
Sulfuric Acid
Tetra-Sod. Pyrophosphate
Tri-Sodium Phosphate

The same chart gives a list of purposes for which these chemicals are used. They are:

Algae Control
Boiler Water Treatment
Coagulation
Color Removal
Corrosion and Scale Control
Dechlorination
Disinfection
Fluoridation
Iron & Manganese Removal
pH Control
Softening

Taste and Odor Control
Miscellaneous
B. O. D. Removal
Condition-Dewater Sludge
Odor Control
Chlorination
Flotation
Neutralization—Acid
Neutralization—Alkali
Oxidation
Reduction

Think of the power put into the hands of the public waterworks engineer. He is given 48 chemicals and instructed to use them as he sees fit. If he has problems of flotation, or neutralization, or coagulation, he can use this or that chemical, but does he worry about its effect on the coagulation of the human blood of the people who drink this water? What does he know about its effect on human health? I see no doctor standing at his elbow to advise him in this regard. The United States Public Health Service is too busy trying to get more public waterworks managers to use fluorine to worry about chlorine. It should enlist the best engineering and medical brains of the land to develop methods to give us pure drinking water without benefit of dangerous chemicals.

Recently I was in the small town of Appledoorn in Holland and was amazed to discover that the people there drank the water without a single chemical being put into it for any purpose whatever. Upon investigation I found that the drinking water of this town of about 30,000 people is obtained from deep wells sunk for the purpose. This would seem to be an ideal solution for many American cities. The existing water lines could be maintained for nondrinking and industrial purposes, and a separate line could be used merely for drinking water.

A cheaper way would be for the city to deliver free non-chemicalized drinking water in bottles to every citizen of the city. The municipality already does certain things for the citizen such as to have a truck call at his home to take away the garbage, to clean the streets, to conduct a waterworks, etc. The city could acquire springs and make sure that its people drink only the purest water obtainable, because it is so basic to their health. It will save the city money in the end. I am not suggesting this for a large city like New York. Huge metropolises pose special problems. People should not live in them in the first place. There is far more cancer in such large aggregations of population.

As far as chlorination is concerned, have we re-evaluated the need for it based on the fact that the general conception of sanitation has improved so much today compared to the primitive conditions of 1900? We are treating our water based on a 1900 diagnosis. Is it not time for the medical profession to take another look?

The Hunza Drinking Water

An example of the proper attitude towards drinking water is found in the Hunza people of Northern India, a group of about 20,000 persons, one of the healthiest in the world. Let me quote from my own book, *The Healthy Hunzas* (Rodale Press, $3.00): "The Hunza drinking water is kept scrupulously clean in roofed tanks or closed cisterns placed down steep steps so that animals cannot come near them. The people do not wash their clothes in the running streams from which they obtain their drinking water, but draw off water which is used especially for this purpose. They are consummate in all matters pertaining to sanitation. They are singularly careful with regard to their privies which are operated by a system that makes it impossible to contaminate any nearby water supply."

The Hunzas are absolutely free of goiter but their neighbors, the Nagyri, who are careless with their water are wretchedly afflicted with it and its companion disease, cretinism. Sir Robert McCarrison, in his medical researches in that region, definitely connected polluted water supply with goiter. He was able to prove his point beyond any question of doubt in giving the disease to himself and fifteen others by drinking fouled water, and then calmly proceeding to cure it in every case, merely by drinking pure water.

How Can We Keep Our Water Clean?

We, on our side of the world, must keep our drinking water sources unpolluted. If we study methods to keep water as clean as possible, then chlorination, or any other chemicalization, would not be required. There must be safer means. The Romans used silver to purify their water—infinitesimal amounts of it, and I have heard that some city in this country is experimenting with it. Water can also be purified by ultraviolet light. Perhaps the cities could pasteurize the water as it goes into the mains, that is, to boil it in order to kill offensive organisms. Incidentally, this may be an excellent idea for the home. Boil all chlorinated water to be used for drinking, because boiling will eliminate all traces of chlorine from it. It will not, however, get rid of the fluorine. Distillation will do that. But cities might rig up automatic pasteurizing equipment that could work economically. Where are our vaunted engineering brains? You don't see them putting chlorine in milk to kill organisms. No! Milk is a commercial product that brings dollars. But water? What care the politicians if it reeks of chlorine!

Our trouble is that we put engineers to work mainly on commercial problems that mean immediate money. For example, a certain enterprising toilet tank-ball manufacturer has placed on the market a tank-ball, the tag on which reads, "The *Water Master* tank-ball is made of a special water resistant rubber which withstands chlorinated water," but who is taking pains to protect the sensitive cells and tissues of human beings who drink chlorinated water? They do not seem to be so important as a 50 cent tank-ball.

A Practical Example of Man's Foolishness

But sometimes it works in reverse from a commercial viewpoint. There's an ironic twist to the story about the calf that was to win the prize at the annual Houston (Texas) fair in 1954. Shell Oil Company, busy the year 'round making chemicals, sponsors a winning calf each year. This year they had a Hereford which, from all appearances, could win without half trying. But, according to *Chemical Week* for April 3, 1954, the Hereford had been drinking pure ranch water all his life and absolutely refused to drink the chlorinated city water when he was brought in for the fair. Result? The Hereford lost 40 precious pounds and the Shell Company lost the prize. You'd think somebody somewhere would learn the lesson which nature is trying so hard to teach us with an incident like this. But no, we go right ahead drinking chemicalized water that "dumb" animals know is not fit to drink.

What we need is pure water societies to spring up all over the United States, which could eventually grow into general health groups that could wield great power in moulding public and official opinion on health matters.

In the meantime, either boil your drinking water or buy bottled spring water, and watch carefully to observe the effects on the health of the family.

SECTION 16

FLUORIDES

We highly condemn the practice of adding fluorides to the water in order to reduce tooth decay in young children. From the research that has been done, any possible decrease in tooth decay is only temporary, and teeth become brittle and give more trouble later on. Fluorine is one of the most dangerous chemicals, and there is evidence that over a period of many, many years that the cumulative effect will endanger such organs as the heart, liver, kidney, etc.

CHAPTER **60**

One Part Per Million

by J. I. RODALE

In applying fluorides to drinking water in order to reduce the number of tooth cavities in children, only a very small amount of the chemical is used—an infinitesimal quantity—namely, only one part of fluorine to a million parts of water. But, to anyone who has even a rudimentary knowledge of chemistry, the fact that an amount is small is not the only factor to be guided by. The important thing is—how chemically *active* is that small amount?

It depends on the chemical with which you are dealing. For example, you can put a thousand times more calcium in the water than fluorine without any harm being done at all, because calcium is *not* too active chemically. But with fluorine, you are dealing with a powerful substance which is used as the base of many commercial poisons for destroying cockroaches, rats, and such ilk. A compound as death-dealing as that must be under strict, continuous control.

Can We Visualize One Part Per Million?

To the ordinary lay-mind, one part in a million parts seems like a negligible quantity. But when we realize that this tiny fraction can reduce the amount of cavities in some children's teeth, we must admit that, however infinitesimal it may be, *that* tiny amount has had an effect in the human body. Now —if only one part per million can accomplish one effect—there is no earthly reason why it could not accomplish another one, elsewhere in the body—an effect we did not bargain for—namely, a harmful one.

Sodium fluoride is an extremely powerful protoplasmic poison, and is very soluble. It is this factor of solubility that gives it the power to enter the blood stream, at once, and in full force—to stream through to every part of the body in a matter of moments, and to get into its every cell—teeth and all.

Solubility and Our Cells

The body contains billions of cells. Yet this practically invisible quantity of one part per million of fluorine has the property of being able to divide itself so that some of it is apportioned to every one of those cells of the body. We must strain our imagination to conceive a degree of smallness, a microscopic diminution—a transmutation that enables part of this one part per million to be portioned out to penetrate into the body's billions of cells. However, some of this fluorine penetrates into the cells of sensitive organs where its presence may become a cumulative detriment.

The ability of the body to reduce things to minuteness, is utterly fantastic. The cell, as microscopic as it is, is complete —self-contained—a microcosm—a world in miniature. Within it there are thousands of chemical compounds with their millions of molecules weaving in and out, exchanging atoms, and operating under scientific law. But man is only on a primitive threshold with regard to it. He is only first beginning to become aware of the merest elementals that make the cell an operating entity and much of what it does is a closed book to him. When, therefore, we intrude by force, a tiny amount of fluorine into that cell, however tiny that amount may be, we must be sure that we know exactly what it will do there, or take the consequences of a very unscientific action. The cell does not *want* this kind of forced fluorine. It does not *need* it. But it has to take it—willynilly.

Cells Affected by One Part in a Hundred Millions

To give you an idea of how effective smallness can be in connection with its effect on living matter, let us consider an announcement made by researchers from the University of Wisconsin, in connection with a cancer study that has been going on there. In that institution a team of botanists and biochemists have isolated a chemical called *kinetin* which has the power to make a cell divide into two parts. But the thing that should be interesting to us in this discussion of smallness is that it takes only one part in a *hundred million* to do it. This is only one one-hundredth of the amount, as compared with the quantity of fluorine used in water fluoridation. This extremely tiny amount of *kinetin,* when applied to plant tissue, causes it to multiply by division. In other words, it produces cancer of that tissue. When this small amount of *kinetin* is applied to plant tissues, cancerous tumors are formed. This unusual phenomenon was announced in *The Cancer News,* published by the American Cancer Society in April, 1955. Now, I do not say that fluorine will do this, but we do not know exactly what it *will do.*

An Example of Minuteness—Homeopathy

And if you think that one part in a hundred million is small, let us look at an example of the miniature that will really astonish you. Let us consider the science of homeopathy, a method of medical curing that resorts to such incalculable degrees of infinitesimality that the mind just cannot conceive or measure it. The word homeopathic itself has actually become an adjective in our language, meaning extreme smallness.

In homeopathy, substances are diluted to such an extent that they get down to next to nothing. The homeopaths use drugs in which the quantity of them have been so diluted that it can be measured by a fraction having one as the numerator, and *one* followed by 20,000 noughts as the denominator. This is more than a million billion times smaller quantity than the amount of fluorine used in water fluoridation. And yet homeopaths who are accredited M.D.'s achieve definite effects with such smallness. Otherwise there would not be the thousands of homeopathic physicians practicing their profession every day.

Bacteria and Virus

The idea of smallness is not a new concept in science, and if you wish an additional example, think of bacteria, millions of which can occupy the space of a pinhead. Yet, only one of them, if it is of the right species, can start an epidemic which could kill thousands of people.

But, if you think bacteria are small, then turn your attention to the virus, an example of smallness which baffles even the microscope, and defies all measurement. So you can see that it is *not* smallness of itself which is the prime factor in the consideration and evaluation of a substance, but what properties it hides within its interior.

In chemistry there are effects brought about by reduction of quantities which science cannot explain, but which are encountered time and time again. In a book called *Selective Toxicity*, written by Dr. Adrien Albert, there are related the interesting details of an experiment throwing further light on this principle. In this experiment a certain solution was applied to a culture of bacteria called *staphilococus,* and they were able to live with it. *But* when the amount of this self-same solution was reduced beyond a certain point, it acted as a poison and killed out all the bacteria. The experiment was carried out repeatedly, and the results were always the same. A passing below a certain point of smallness of the quantity caused it to become a killer.

Small Amounts in Agriculture

A most astounding example of the effects of smallness was shown in an unusual series of experiments performed in 1920 at the Biologic Institute at Stuttgart, Germany, which was part of a project to develop a remedy for hoof and mouth disease. At this institute they were working by the homeopathic method to potentize a substance, that is, to make it more powerful-acting. But they attempted to do it by reducing its quantity. They were not interested in mere matter as such, but in the force that lay behind it. In other words, they said, "What do we want in reality—the substance itself, or the inner quality of that substance?"

For example, they began to reason as follows: A farmer may feel that a certain field needs some calcium as a fertilizer. To supply this requirement he usually digs a large amount of lime into the soil. But at the Stuttgart Biologic Institute they felt differently. It was *their* opinion that it was merely the *effect* of the calcium that the soil needed and not its quantity. Their problem was to see to it that each molecule of soil and soil compounds should come in contact with *some* calcium, however small that amount might be; and not to approach it by the sledge-hammer method of putting in a huge quantity of calcium, figuring that only in that way would some calcium reach every molecule.

The Effect of the Smallest Entity

They studied the influence of smallest entities by using lime as the calcium-giving substance on the germination of wheat seed. They did this by a method of reducing the potency of a mixture of calcium hydroxide in water. They produced 8 successive dilutions, retaining some of each dilution down to the last or eighth one which was down to one part of calcium hydroxide to a hundred million parts of water. This is a hundred times smaller in amount than that of fluorides used by the water people. The results were nothing short of fantastic!

I wish you could see the pictures of each group of wheat seedlings, going from the first on down to the eighth, showing how they were influenced by the gradually reducing amounts of calcium. With the gradually lessening quantities, the size of the wheat seedlings increased, the eighth one being by far the biggest of them all—yet having had the least amount of calcium.

Other Experiments

This principle of the influence of smallest entities was repeated in growing hyacinths, measuring the effect of silver nitrate upon it—in growing *gladioli,* studying the effect of slaked lime upon it—on sunflower seeds and a solution of cow manure upon it, and dozens of other plants and substances that act upon them. In every case they established firmly the principle of the effect of smallness and did it, so thoroughly that no scientific mind that sees the German thoroughness of these experiments, the multiplicity of its charts and photographs, can doubt their validity.

Trace Mineral Research

In the growth of plants there are trace mineral elements such as zinc, manganese, copper, boron, molybdenum, etc., which, for optimum plant growth conditions, should be present in "trace" quantities only. For example, in the case of zinc, only up to one twentieth of one part per million in the soil is required for healthy plant growth. Larger quantities act as a poison, and will prevent the proper germination of the seed and growth of plant. The same holds true in the human body where certain minerals must be present in "trace" quantities only. Unfortunately, less is known about the effect of the trace minerals there, because not enough research has been done on that subject by the medical profession. This subject is a sleeper, a dark horse, and may very well become the white-haired boy of medicine of the coming decades. It may hold the solution to cancer and polio.

In agriculture the trace mineral research was done (and

there is a vast literature on the subject) because it is a matter of dollars and cents to the farmer. It involves economic values— a sort of industrial medical economics. But human beings are not valued at amounts in financial statements. They are not rushed off to market to be sold, so the heat is not on. The philosophy is, if we don't conquer cancer in this age, we will do it in the next one. The doctors are just about beginning to brush the edges of the subject of trace mineral elements. That is why so little is known about the effect of fluorine (a trace mineral) on the human body. But the United States Department of Agriculture by means of researches has found that fluoridated water is harmful to pregnant pigs, and has warned the farmer about it.

Can We Make Sea Water?

A curious example showing the disastrous effect of failure to take into consideration an element of minuteness, occurred at the London Aquarium a few years ago. A consignment of salt water fish had been brought in, but there was not enough sea water for them. It was decided therefore to make some sea water based on its known formula. The curators assembled the minerals and other compounds, and made the water, but when they placed a fish in it, it soon died. The process was repeated several times, but in each case the fish could not live in the artificially made sea water.

Then one curator at the aquarium had a bright idea. He said, "In the next batch of sea water we make, let us put in a tiny pinch of the real stuff. Perhaps it might contain a gleam of something which science has been unable to measure as yet, but which is essential to the life of a fish." And they did just that! In the next batch of sea water made, there was added the merest trace of real sea water—the slightest pinch of it—and lo and behold—miracle of miracles—the fish could live in it. It seems, therefore, that only God knows the whole formula of matter, and we are mere children playing in the complicated mazes of chemical science. But, and this is extremely significant, here is a microscopic gleam of something—a something which probably must be measured perhaps by the millionth millionth of a part, as far as fractions go, and yet that small millionth millionth of a part, or the lack of it, could mean life or death to a fish.

While we are on the subject of sea water, let us consider another aspect of smallness in the life of a fish. The sea itself contains all the elements found in the human body. But, says the *Encyclopedia Britannica*, "One can look on sea water as a mixture of very dilute solutions of particular salts (or minerals), each of which after the lapse of sufficient time fills the whole space as if the other constituents did not exist." (End of quotation.)

What this means is that the total of a certain space in the sea may be filled with an unusually small amount of some minerals, but when it is so diluted that some of it fills the whole space as if the other constituents did not exist, then it truly exists in fantastically small proportions. And in such small quantity it is a tonic to the fish. But should something happen to cause some of these minerals to accumulate in one spot to an extent that makes them poisonous, it could spell death to any fish that may come into that area. That this sometimes happens is evidenced by the millions of dead fish that are occasionally found floating on the water, with no satisfactory explanation for it.

Now the blood stream of the body is a sea, and the same thing could happen there with regard to fluorine taken in through drinking water. Should some emergency condition arise which distorts the body's chemical processes, it might accumulate fluorine in some weak organ which could begin a process of disease or pathology that could begin the death process. And there are millions of people today in hospitals whose body chemistry is distorted. Dare we give them fluorine?

Review

In review, we saw how the substance *kinetin* in a dilution of only one part in a hundred million, can cause cells to divide. This is a bad effect. On the other hand, we saw a good effect through smallness in homeopathy where their drug dilutions are as low as one part in a million billion. We saw how microscopic bacteria and viruses can kill thousands. We saw staphilococcus bacteria killed out by smaller amounts of a substance, where a larger amount permitted them to live. We reviewed the work at the Biologic Institute at Stuttgart where the smaller the amount of calcium applied, the larger the wheat seeds grew, and the London Aquarium experience where the overlooking of the need for a tiny gleam of substance caused death in fish. In other words, we have seen that smallness can be harnessed both ways—for good and for bad.

With all this evidence before us, we must not lull ourselves into a submissive attitude, favoring fluoridation, merely because the amount of fluorine used is only one part in a million. One cannot go by our everyday experience and attitudes with numbers and amounts. This is further illustrated by the case of the man who began to work for one cent the first day, with a doubling of the amount of pay every succeeding day, for 30 days. On the thirtieth day he was receiving a salary of over 5,000,000 dollars. Numbers and amounts are illusive things. So again we caution an antagonistic attitude towards this philosophy of there being no danger merely because the amount of fluoride used is only one part in a million parts of water. We must resist the attempt of the vested interests of medical science to browbeat an entire country into an untested, dangerous experiment where only a millionth part of a very potent poison might accomplish unforeseeable but hazardous consequences in the human body. As the old proverb goes—a small hatchet fells a great oak.

In closing may I cite a paragraph from a book called *The Failure of Technology,* written in 1939 by Dr. Frederich Georg Juenger: "We can reasonably assume, for example, that an apple contains a number of substances that so far have eluded the chemist and the biologist. It is likewise quite certain that even if all these substances *could* be synthetically reproduced in a pill, they could not replace the apple. For the apple embodies a principle that is higher than the sum of its parts. It is not a lifeless preparation, like the substances that have been, or could be extracted from it, but an expression of life that grows and smells and ripens and has fragrance."

It is the same thing with a child's teeth. They can retain their wholeness by feeding them wholeness, but it is our fragmented devitalized diet which is giving them holes. The basis for good teeth is not in fluoridation.

CHAPTER **61**

On the Fluoridation Front

Opponents of fluoridation who challenge the "author-
ities" are usually called "cranks" and "faddists." Here are some
scientific facts, with the references from whence they came,
which show positively that many learned and respected men of
science feel as we do about the foolishness and danger of fluor-
idating drinking water.

Many times fluoridation opponents are challenged by
members of local boards of health or dental or medical societies
to prove that there is any well-documented scientific case against
fluoridation. When you are faced with this kind of challenge,
it isn't enough to declare simply that you oppose fluoridation
on the grounds of its being mass medication, or unconstitutional
or illegal. You must produce well-documented proofs that
scientific researchers whose integrity is beyond question have
found evidence that fluoridation may be harmful.

This evidence is hard to find, because it involves going
through hundreds of scientific books and indexes of scientific
writings. We have therefore compiled below what we call a
"bibliography" of such articles, along with a sentence or two
on the general content of each article.

Explanation of a Bibliography

For those readers who are not familiar with the way such
bibliographies are written—the name of the magazine or book
in which information occurs appears first, then the volume
number, the date, the page and the author. After this, appears
our summary of what the author says. In cases where no
author's name is given, the article is probably an editorial.

In general, it is difficult to get copies of these articles
unless you have access to a medical library. Why not try the

medical library in your local hospital? Most hospitals have libraries which contain these and other sources of information concerning fluoridation.

Fluorine in Cattle

1. *The Cornell Veterinarian,* Vol. XLII, No. 2, April 1932. A Report on Fluorosis in Cattle in the Columbia River Valley, by D. H. Udall (New York State Veterinary College) and Keith P. Keller. Discusses source of fluorosis, fluorine poisoning, and symptoms noted in cattle who have disease.

Is Fluorine Mass Medication?

2. "Fluoridation is Mass Medication" (transcription of excerpt from Congressional Hearings on Fluoridation, February 28, 1952; p. 1654—Testimony of Bruce D. Forsyth, D.D.S., Assistant Surgeon General Chief Dental Officer, Public Health Service.) Offers excellent refutation to declaration that fluoridation is not mass medication.

Vitamin B Against Fluorine

3. *Experimental Medicine and Surgery,* Vol. VIII, 2, 3, 4, 1950. "Fluorine and Vitamin B" by Dr. Leo Spira. Reports effects of sodium fluoride in drinking water of rats—demonstrates that vitamin B offers some protection against effects of fluorine.

Varicose Veins and Fluorine

4. *The Medical Press,* Vol. CCXIX, 5674, February 4, 1948. Leo Spira, M.D. States and discusses author's belief that the frequent occurrence of varicose veins in United States population is associated with chronic fluorine poisoning.

Natural Fluoridation

5. *Journal A.A.A.N.,* Monthly Newsletter, February 1951. Robert Mick, D.D.S. "The Kisumu Story on Fluorine." Trip with Dr. Wm. Odom shows natives contracted fluorosis from highly fluoridated water occurring naturally. Also undiminished dental caries in natives drinking the water if they were also eating refined foods.

Chemical Effect on the Body

6. *The Bur,* April 1950. Gustav Wm. Rapp, Ph.D. "The Pharmacology of Fluoride." Chemical effects of fluorides

on various parts of the body are discussed with scientific detachment. Conclusion: fluorides and effects of same not fully known but caution is advised.

Dental Effects

7. *Archives of Pediatrics,* April, 1953, Dr. W. J. McCormick. "Domestic Water Fluoridation." Literature regarding fluorosis in man and animals is reviewed with reference to dental and overall effects on the body. Suggestions regarding preventive medicinal and dietary measures to counteract toxic effects of fluorine in drinking water.

Growth and Fluorine

8. *Journal of Biological Chemistry,* Vol. 109, p. 657, January 15, 1953. Paul H. Phillips and E. B. Hart. "Effect of Organic Dietary Constituents upon Chronic Fluorine Toxicosis in the Rat." Shows complete growth inhibition of rats by intake of 78 to 84 milligrams of sodium fluoride with natural grain ration. Changes in diet did not ameliorate effect of fluorine. Enzymes and fluorine are discussed.

Fluorine and the Mining Industry

9. *Information Circular 7687,* United States Department of Interior, S. I. Davenport and G. G. Morgis. "Review of Literature on Health Hazards of Fluorine and its Compounds in the Mining and Allied Industries." Physical and toxic properties of 3 fluoride compounds are charted. A history of fluoride poisoning from its discovery in 1670; how it affects plants, animals and man. Series of arguments for and against water fluoridation given.

Its Effect on Teeth

10. *Journal of Nutrition,* June 10, 1954, James H. Shaw and Reidar F. Sognnaes, Harvard School of Dental Medicine. Experiment in which fluorine was used in rats' diet to see if teeth were affected. Teeth shown not to be affected at all by fluorine in water.

Fluorine as it Occurs Naturally

11. *Journal of Dental Research,* Vol. 2, No. 5, October 1946. D. A. Greenwood, J. R. Blayney, O. K. Skinsnes and P. C. Hodges. "Comparative Studies of the Feeding of Fluorides as they Occur in Purified Bone Meal Powder, Defluorinated

Phosphate and Sodium Fluoride in Dogs." Experiment shows that fluorides occurring naturally in foods have no ill effect while added fluoride causes heavy fluoride deposits in the bones and makes no difference in teeth. Teeth of puppies fed sodium fluoride weaker than those receiving fluorine as it occurs naturally in bone meal powder.

Toxic Effect

12. *American Journal of Diseases of Children*, Vol. 78, pp. 72-76, July, 1949. Demarious C. Badger, M.D. "Toxic Level of Fluorine in Water Supplies." Discussion showing that more than .7 ppm of fluorine added to water supplies is dangerous to children under 6—damages calcification process of secondary teeth as they form in first 6 years. Arguments offered against safety of fluoridation.

Intoxication from It

13. *Physiological Reviews*, Vol. 20, pp. 382-616, 1940. D. A. Greenwood, Department of Pharmacology, University of Chicago. "Fluoride Intoxication." Fluorides in nature inhibit physiological functions. Discussion of known manifestations of intoxication. Discussion on feasible ways to remove (not add, but remove!) fluorides.

A Dentist's Opinion

14. *Journal of the New Jersey State Dental Society*, July 1954. A. Allen London, D.D.S. "Has the Dental Profession Been Misled on Artificial Fluoridation of Communal Water Supplies?" Presented at meeting of Tri-County Dental Society of New Jersey, April 21, 1954. A dentist asks fellow dentists to consider the possibility that fluoridation may be a mistake.

Nutrition and Fluoridation

15. *Oral Hygiene*, Sept. 1951. George A Swendiman, D.D.S. "The Argument Against Fluoridating City Water." Argues for better nutrition to preserve teeth rather than municipal intervention through fluoridated water supplies.

Move on Mass Medication

16. *Oral Hygiene*, January, 1953. Arthur B. MacWinnie, D.M.D. "Fluoridation Compulsory Medication." Fluoridation from the view of one opposed to the implications of mass medication, with suggested alternatives.

Spinal Compression

17. *Journal of American Medical Association,* Nov. 7, 1953. Article taken from *Journal of Indian Medical Association* (July, 1953) discussing a case of spinal compression due to skeletal fluorosis—drinking water in area contained high amounts of fluorine.

Its Effect on Cells

18. *Journal of Dental Research,* October, 1951. Experiment with rats shows that sodium fluoride affects serum-containing cells of the two kinds of salivary glands (paratoid and submaxillary) and makes definite modifications in them.

Expectant Mothers Affected

19. *Science News Letter,* March 15, 1952. Tells of findings by Drs. Dwight E. Gardner, Frank A. Smith, Harold C. Hodge, D. E. Overton and Reuben Feltman of University of Rochester School of Medicine and Dentistry. Article tells that fluoridated water might affect health of expectant mothers and newborn babies, because fluorine is known to concentrate in the placenta (the tissue-like sac which surrounds the unborn infant).

Absorption into Food

20. *Journal of Dental Research,* October, 1951. Dr. D. J. Martin. Details how fluorides from water are absorbed into vegetables while cooking.

Kidneys Damaged

21. *British Journal of Experimental Pathology,* April, 1952. Drs. A. M. Bond and M. M. Murray. Experiments with rats show fluorides affect kidneys as well as teeth.

Calcium-Phosphorus Balance Disturbed

22. *The Dental Practitioner,* November, 1952, Bristol, England. Charles Dillon, D.D.S., L.D.S. Points out that if fluoride ions reach blood stream in excess of calcium ions, the fluorine will react with bone and result in a serious disturbance of the calcium-phosphorus balance.

The Body Stores Fluorine

23. *Industrial Hygiene and Occupational Medicine,* July, 1952. Edward J. Largent. Tests prove the fluorides may be stored in human tissues for months or years.

A Campaign Against Fluoridation

24. *Maine Medical Association Journal,* March, 1954, p. 78. Adrian H. Scolten, M.D. Passionate plea for reversal of headlong endorsement of fluoridation.

Classical Objections

25. *Journal of the American Dietetic Association,* May, 1954, p. 463. A reminder of the classical objections to fluoridation.

How Much Fluorine Is Dangerous?

26. *Public Health Pamphlet,* Vol. 61, No. 11, March, 1946. "Drinking Water Standards." States on page 12 that fluorides in excess of 1.5 ppm. would make water unfit for consumption and constitute grounds for rejection.

New Mexico Fights Against It

27. *University of New Mexico Bulletin, Chemistry Series,* Vol. 2, No. 5, 1938. John D. Clark and Edward H. Mann, University of New Mexico. Chart of large natural content of fluorides in New Mexico water supplies—discussion of dangers of fluorides in water. Suggested means of removing fluorides from water.

The Need For Long-Range Research

28. *Dental Items of Interest,* Dec. 1953, p. 1135. Robert J. H. Mick, D.D.S. "Personal Findings and Ramblings on This Thing Called Fluoridation." Need for long-range experimentation stressed — fluorine in combination with other elements might make the difference.

Diet and Fluorine

29. *The Land, Spring,* 1953, p. 38. Jonathan Forman, M.D. "Fluorine and the Case Against It." Article lists many objections to fluoridation. Calls attention to danger in kidney, diabetes and pregnancy cases. States that little good can come from fluoridation without careful diet. Suggests yearly check-up on population to check improvement in teeth, if any, and general health checks to note any changes.

Cancer Causer in Fluorine

30. *Cancer Research,* June 1, 1953, p. 647. Alvin J. Cox, Jr., Robert H. Wilson, Ph.D., and Floyd DeEds, Ph.D. "Car-

cinogenic Activity of Two Acetaminofluorine Characteristics of
the Lesions in Albino Rats." Possible cancer causer in fluorine
united with other elements.

Toxicity Again

31. *Industrial and Medical Surgery,* November, 1950,
p. 535. Joseph Larner, "Toxicological and Metabolic Effects of
Fluorine-containing Compounds." Fluorosis is discussed
together with some effects of chronic fluoride toxicity.

Fluorides Postpone Decay

32. *Proceedings of the Royal Society of Medicine,* February 23, 1948. Robert Weaver, M.D., F.D.S. "The Inhibition
of Dental Caries by Fluorine." The short duration of the beneficial effects of fluorides on the teeth shows that fluorides only
postpone do not prevent decay in children.

Natural Fluorine in Water

33. *North Dakota Geological Survey,* Bulletin 9, 1937,
M. C. Smith, H. V. Smith and Lantz. "Study of St. David,
Arizona" where natural fluorine occurs in the water. Every
child living in the town during period of growth had mottled
teeth.

Fluorine in the Diet

34. *Journal of Nutrition,* Vol. 6, pp. 163-178, 1933. G.
K. Sharpless and E. V. McCollum. "Is Fluorine an Indispensable
Element in the Diet?" These two eminent researchers found
that it was not.

Help in Fighting Fluoridation

35. *Dental Items of Interest,* June, 1952, p. 19. V. O.
Hurme. Much helpful material on opposition to fluoridation.

A Poison

36. *Journal of the American Medical Association,* Vol.
139, p. 969, April 2, 1949. Sodium fluoride is a deadly poison
and toxic symptoms have been induced by doses as small as
60 milligrams.

Toxicity and Solubility

37. *Industrial and Engineering Chemistry,* 1934. M. C.
Smith and R. M. Leverton. "Comparative Toxicity of Fluorine
Compounds." Sodium fluoride is 85 times more toxic than cal-

cium fluoride as determined by lethal dosage. The authors attribute this to the varying solubility of the compounds.

How Much Fluorine Do We Get?

38. *Journal of the American Water Works Association,* Vol. 45, No. 4, p 376-386, April, 1953. J. E. McKee. "A Rational Approach to Fluoridation." The author states that the average total intake of fluorides per day should not exceed approximately 1.0 to 1.3 milligrams, including that eaten in food. This is a considerably lower recommended level than that recommended previously.

Fighting Fluoridation

39. *Harper's Magazine,* Vol. 206, No. 1233, p. 66-70, February, 1953. J. J. Rorty. "Go Slow on Fluoridation." Many excellent arguments against fluoridation.

Phosphatase Diminished

40. *American Chemical Society Monograph* Series No. 82. A. T. Stahl, "Mineral Metabolism." The author states that the important enzyme, phosphatase, is diminished in the condition of fluorosis.

What Affects Mottling?

41. *Journal of American Dental Association,* Vol. 44, p. 156, 165, February, 1952. M. Massler and I. Schour. The nutritional status of people especially the calcium intake, affects the prevalence and degree of mottling caused by fluorides.

Bone Meal for Calcium

42. *Journal of American Dental Association,* January, 1944. C. B. Branson. Calcium content of the diet must be ample to balance the effects of fluoride in the diet. Dr. Branson suggests bone meal as a source of calcium.

Calcium Retention

43. *American Journal of Physiology,* Vol. 109, pp. 645-654, October, 1934. M. C. Smith and E. M. Lantz. "The Effect on Calcium and Phosphorus Metabolism in Albino Rats." The rats who got fluorine excreted far more calcium and retained much less than those which got no fluorine.

· Iodine and Fluorine

44. *Abstract of Communications, International Physiological Congress, Montreal Canada,* August 31 to September 4, 1953. T. Gordonoff. There is an antagonism between iodine and fluorine. The thyroid gland takes up less iodine when there is too much fluorine present. He recommends that fluoridation be discouraged.

Goiter and Fluorine Related

45. *Some Aspects of Endemic Goiter,* 1937. R. P. Mathews and C. E. Perkins. Goiter exists to a larger extent in places where the water is high in fluorides.

Coagulation Slowed Up

46. *Biochem Zeitschr,* Vol. 212, p. 96, 1929. B. Stuber and K. Lang. A high fluorine content of the blood prolongs the time it takes for it to coagulate.

CHAPTER **62**

Fluorides and Fallout
A Deadly Combination

The theory presented in this chapter suggests that fluorides and strontium 90 combine in the body to magnify the worst effects of both.

Within recent years a second question has taken its place beside fluoridation as one which vitally concerns the future of human existence—the problem of atomic fallout. The purity of two of life's most basic needs, air and water, is at stake. We know that radioactive death floats calmly in the heart of the mushroom cloud, whether the bomb was detonated as an experiment or in war. We know, too, of the uncharted risk that lies in drinking fluoridated water. Continue either one of these short-sighted measures, even for those fine motives, world peace or healthy teeth, and know that in a generation the world can be paralyzed by sickness and mysterious disease. Continue both of them and know that it is a bid for self-annihilation, for together in the body, fluorides and strontium 90 (from nuclear fallout) interact upon one another and result in a combination that magnifies the worst features of both.

Why the Bombs Affect Us

As we know, the most devastating feature of a nuclear explosion lies not in the 10- or 20-mile radius of explosive destruction it can cause, but in the radioactive elements such a bomb releases to the atmosphere. A portion of these elements is sucked high into the sky when the bomb explodes, then in time the particles carried by stratospheric air currents rain down on the earth in a place far removed from the site of the blast, quite possibly in another corner of the world. These radioactive particles land on vegetation and in water, which we consume and which are consumed by the animals which supply us with milk and meat. In this way our food, and consequently, we ourselves, are contaminated by radioactive elements even though we might be thousands of miles from any nuclear explosions. There is not a bomb set off anywhere in the world that will not, in effect, sprinkle us with deadly radiation, either now or at some time within the next thirty years.

The Consequences of Radiation

Though the effects of radiation might not be obvious, they are insidious and destructive just the same. Here is the respected World Health Organization's opinion: "Generally speaking, the irradiation of living beings may produce radiobiological effects either on the irradiated individual himself, or through him on his descendants; the former being somatic and the latter genetic effects. Somatic effects vary according to the different organs or tissues affected, and range from slight and reversible disturbances such as cutaneous erythema (rash) to induction of leukemia, or of other malignant diseases."

These are the consequences brought on by strontium 90,

which is released at every atomic explosion. This substance has a strong affinity for calcium, hence it lodges in the bones when it enters the body. This accounts for the likelihood that it is a direct cause of leukemia, since its presence in the bones tends to pervert the process of blood manufacture which is carried on there. Though normal body processes eventually expel strontium 90 from the system, the relative insolubility of the element makes this process a slow one, too slow to avoid some damage.

A Similarity Between Strontium 90 and Fluorides

Here there is a similarity between fluorides and strontium 90. Fluorides are also attracted to the bones, and they are relatively insoluble, too. When they are in the body, fluorides are known to be powerful inhibitors of enzyme action. In other words, the poisonous fluorides prevent the changes in body chemistry brought about by enzymes. Many types of enzymes are affected, including some that are necesary for cellular oxidation (breathing). Interference with the function of an enzyme is interference with a link in the chain of chemical reactions that most body processes depend upon. Therefore, interference at any point is enuogh to disrupt the entire process. The wide variety of enzymes known to be poisoned by fluorides accounts for the different manifestations of fluorosis, that is, the different symptoms associated with fluoride poisoning.

When They Combine

It has been established in many journals, much more detailed than the few notes above, that either of these two elements, strontium 90 or fluorine, when existing separately in the body, is extremely dangerous. In an article in *Dental Digest,* February, 1958, James G. Kerwin, D.D.S. discusses the startling awesome theory that a combination of strontium 90 and fluorine in the body results in the formation of the compound, strontium fluoride. Together these two elements become even less soluble than they are separately. The body has infinitely more trouble in excreting them. As a result the irradiation of the bones due to strontium 90 is continued for a longer period, and the damage to the enzyme action of the body from fluorine also goes on for a greater time. What Dr. Kerwin has told us in his article is not a guess but an extreme and carefully investigated probability. It is not a case of "could happen," but a case of "most likely does happen."

The Facts Are Hidden

Until recently, the problems presented by adding fluorides to drinking water have been buried under the reams of publicity about fluoridation's so-called triumphs; the dangers of fallout have been minimized in discussions of the need for nuclear experiments to protect America's security. Neither of these forms of reasoning is valid any longer. Artificial water fluoridation has indeed made a miserable showing, with proof easily available that it is not effective in eliminating tooth decay, and that it is demonstrably dangerous to bodily health. As for the question of fallout, while the danger of war has lessened, the explosion of bombs has not, and the problems of radioactive particles in the air have increased literally by the hour. And even if war were dangerously imminent, it must be realized that detonating these nuclear devices is a form of self-annihilation that exceeds any but a war of complete and immediate universal oblivion.

We Can Avoid Artificial Fluoridation

There is, of course, nothing to be done about the fallout from bombs already exploded. According to the National Council of Research, there appears to be no way of preventing the accumulation of strontium 90 in bone tissue. Our only hope, therefore, is that the body will rid itself of it before any serious damage is done. But an intake of fluorides through our drinking water lessens the chances of our being so lucky. If there were no other arguments against fluoridation, if fluorides were even shown to be beneficial to teeth and general health, the fact that they detain the deadly strontium 90 in the bones would make their use completely impossible by all the rules of common sense.

We hope that this information will reach the authorities in New York City who are debating the fluoridation question. New York has been designated as the city in the United States that has been most heavily contaminated by fallout, according to the *New York Times,* April 4, 1958. As we have seen, fluoridation would multiply the threat imposed by fallout immeasurably. Can New York, or any city, take the chance of inviting such a disaster by instituting a program of artificial fluoridation of the public drinking water, a measure whose stated purpose is to effect a possible decrease or delay in tooth decay among children, a disease all of us, including the fluoridators, know well results chiefly from eating sticky refined carbohydrates?

A Course of Protective Action

Many of those who read this may already be victims of the fluoridation movement. What can one do if one's community is now adding fluorides to the public water supply? First of all, one can begin by using bottled spring water for drinking and cooking purposes. This measure, however, doesn't cover the many times one uses water away from one's home, so in general, we say, as we do when confronted with other health problems imposed by modern living, maintain a high level of nutrition. Eat as much fresh food as you can, and take food supplements until you feel secure in the knowledge that your body has all the ammunition it can use to fight the ravages of strontium 90 and fluorides.

Is Bone Meal Dangerous?

Our readers have asked if the hazard presented by strontium 90 and fluorides is increased by added intake of calcium through bone meal. They remind us of the affinity these elements have for calcium, and that the calves whose bones are used to make the bone meal are nursed by cows eating strontium 90 contaminated grasses and that the calves even eat the grasses themselves. Then, too, does not an intake of more calcium invite more strontium 90 and fluorides? In answer to the first question, there is no food which is not contaminated by strontium 90. It falls on everything; it is everywhere. If one does not get it in bone meal, it comes in vegetables, fruit or roast turkey.

As to the problem of excess calcium attracting fluorides and strontium 90, this probability works to our advantage. Two Canadian scientists of The University of British Columbia (*New York Times*, May 12, 1957) recommend a diet high in calcium to combat the effects of strontium 90. They explain that when the body gets more than enough calcium, the calcium is expelled, and because of its affinity for calcium, the strontium 90 is expelled, too. May we mention that fluorine is likewise attracted by calcium, and so the argument applies to both elements. The more calcium one gets, the more strontium 90 and fluorides one gets rid of. We say stay with a good diet as high in food value as possible, and bolster yourself with all the food supplements, especially bone meal for calcium. If you can't prevent fallout and fluorides, you can do your best to minimize their effects on yourself and your family.

SECTION 17

WATER SOFTENERS

If you use a water softener, have it connected to the hot water faucet only. To drink artificially softened water is extremely dangerous. The water softening process produces a chemical action in which calcium and magnesium are removed, and sodium is placed into the water. This is the equivalent of adding salt to the water. (See salt.) Calcium and magnesium are both of tremendous value to good health.

CHAPTER **63**

Are You Thinking of Buying a Water Softener?

The question of whether or not to install a water softener may arise in any average family on any average wash day about the time the Missus scrapes the last greasy curds of soap from the inside of the family washing machine and looks ruefully at her hands, rough and reddened from the quantities of soap or detergent she had to use to get the clothes even approximately clean. If she goes into the kitchen, then, and faces a stack of greasy dishes, she is quite likely to go on strike and issue a statement that no more housework will be done until she has soft water to work with.

The Terms, Hard and Soft Water

What do we mean by "hard" or "soft" water anyway, and what are the advantages or disadvantages of a water softener? We cannot, of course, discuss the water in your particular community, for all local water supplies differ in mineral content. But, in general, we can say that rain water is the ideal water for any cleaning work, because it comes straight from the sky and no minerals can possibly get into it.

Water falling from the clouds is free from minerals, although, especially in industrial areas, it may collect mineral substances from the air as it falls. Minerals in the soil are responsible for "hard" water. So the composition of your soil decides what minerals will be in your water supply, whether it comes from a deep or shallow well, from a city reservoir, a spring, river or lake. Calcium and magnesium in the chemical form of bicarbonates, carbonates and sulfates form the minerals most often present in water. This means simply that the calcium and magnesium have combined with carbon and sulfur in the water to form chemical compounds. These compounds make the water "hard."

Soap will not lather until you have used enough of it to precipitate the calcium and magnesium which then deposit themselves on the inside of the washing machine, the dishpan or the pockets of fine white blouses. In addition, the inside of your teakettle and plumbing pipes collect a lining of white flakes that are practically impossible to remove. Rain water is the answer, if you care to go to the trouble of installing a cistern or collecting water in buckets every time there is a shower. Few of us can spare the time.

How Do Water Softeners Work?

In water softeners a chemical process called "ion exchange" takes place. This is what manufacturers mean when they speak of a "zeolite" process. The material in the water softener which brings about this chemical change does not itself enter the water the manufacturers say. We ourselves are not at all sure what effect this may have on water which we are going to use for drinking and cooking. It causes the water to change and in this change the calcium and magnesium are removed and sodium is put in their place. After a time the sodium ions are used up, and you must replace them with ordinary salt which, as you know, is half sodium.

From *Consumers' Research Bulletin* for February, 1953, we learn that the term "zeolite," when strictly applied, refers only to naturally occurring minerals, but at present it is applied, also, to synthetic materials like the new ion exchange resins "which are becoming more popular for use in the home." This seems extremely important to us, for, as you know, we instantly become suspicious when we know that we are dealing with a synthetic substance, and it occurs to us that synthetic resins (made of coal tar, perhaps?) in a water softener are bound to release something in the water that would not be present if only natural minerals were used.

Advantages of a Water Softener—But!

However, whether or not the water softener you are considering contains synthetic resins, what are the advantages to having one installed? You will save on soaps and detergents and your skin will be healthier as a result, for these alkaline substances are very hard on your skin. Your clothes will be cleaner with less work on your part and less time for the clothes to be agitated in your washer, so the clothes will last longer. Bathing and washing dishes will be easier, for you will have no trouble with greasy or oily dirt, no rings around the bathtub or dishpan. Floors, woodwork and all the other things you wash in a house will be much easier to clean. The inside of your plumbing and teakettle will not collect scales.

But—and we think it's a pretty important but—you will be getting sodium instead of calcium in your drinking and cooking water and it won't be even that sodium you'd get from ordinary table salt or from those vegetables and fruits that naturally contain sodium. This sodium is the result of a chemical process in which synthetics are probably used.

A further warning about the use of water softeners comes to us from a book called *Trace Elements in Foods* (John Wiley and Sons, Incorporated) by G. W. Monier-Williams, O.B.E., M.A., Ph.D., F.R.I.C., formerly of the Ministry of Health in England. Discussing the use of aluminum cooking utensils, Dr. Monier-Williams says: "Aluminum is not attacked by distilled water, whether hot or cold, but hard water corrodes it slightly and may become cloudy with suspended aluminum hydroxide. London tap-water boiled in aluminum saucepans and allowed to stand overnight takes up from 8 to 20 parts per million of the metal. Water softened by base exchange processes, using zeolite regenerated with salt, may be extremely corrosive to aluminum, and kettles in which such water is used have a comparatively short life."

Don't Use Softened Water for Drinking

Consumers' Research Bulletin reminds us that the sodium content of softened water is high and that high-sodium water is very undesirable in many cases of heart trouble, especially in older people, where the sodium collects in the body, attracts water to itself and brings about overweight or edema (swelling), both of which increase the work of an already overloaded heart. In addition, the *Bulletin* says that scientific studies have established a relationship unfavorable to the use of soft water for drinking and cooking and have shown that when the drinking water is soft, there is a marked tendency toward increased deficiencies in tooth and bone formation and increased tooth decay.

We add: most of us get too much sodium, in the salted products we eat like salted nuts and potato chips, in addition to the salt we use for cooking and the salt we spread liberally over our food at the table. Practically none of us gets enough calcium to protect us from tooth decay and from soft bones in old age, as well as the many other disorders that can result from too little calcium. So drinking or cooking with water *from which calcium has been removed and to which sodium has been added* would seem to be the height of folly.

Where Can You Buy a Water Softener?

If you are interested in buying a water softener, you will find all the recommended leading brands listed in *Consumers' Research Bulletin* for February, 1953, along with the capacity of tanks they have for sale, the approximate flow per gallon per minute, the amount of salt needed for regeneration of the softener and the approximate price of the equipment. You can order a copy of this magazine from Conumers' Research, Washington, New Jersey. If you should buy a softener, we urge you to have an extra faucet installed for cold water to be used for drinking and cooking. If your community, like most American towns and cities, supplies you with water reeking of chlorine and has already added or is contemplating the addition of fluorine to this water, solve all your problems by installing the water softener without the extra faucet and buying bottled spring water for drinking and cooking. That way you're taking no chance at all.

SECTION 18

TOBACCO

We are against the use of tobacco in any form. It uses up vitamin C in the body. Not only is it a factor in causing cancer of the lungs, but it is bad for the heart, the functioning of the brain, the eyes, nervous system, blood pressure, pulse, lower extremities. Tobacco leaves have been sprayed with many poisonous chemicals, thus adding to the toxic effect of the nicotine.

CHAPTER **64**

Smoking . . . and Respiratory Involvements

The *Reader's Digest* for January, 1950, published an astounding article on smoking in which the following aspects of the tobacco habit were reviewed: the effect of smoking on the throat membranes, on lungs, on stomach and digestion, on the skill of athletes, on the heart, on the blood pressure and the blood vessels, on Buerger's Disease patients, on cancer incidence, on mortality figures, on colds. Author Roger William Riis came to the inevitable conclusion that smoking does nothing but harm. His own personal testimony is as follows: "When I began research for this article, I was smoking 40 cigarettes a day. As I got into the subject, I found that number dropping. As I finish the article, I am smoking 10 a day. I'd like to smoke more but my investigation of the subject has convinced me that smoking is dangerous, and worse—stupid."

Tobacco Tar More Harmful Than Nicotine

Mr. Riis tells us that if you smoke a pack of cigarettes a day you take in 840 cubic centimeters of tobacco tar in a year. That means, he says, that you have exposed your throat and lung tissues to 27 fluid ounces or 15 full cocktail glasses of tobacco tar containing benzo-pyrene. The ugly, greasy tar that is left in your ash tray, on your fingers or in the filter of your cigarette holder is not nicotine. It is instead the "soot" that is left from the incomplete combustion of the tobacco—just as disagreeable and dangerous as the soot from your chimney. Many physicians agree that, as an irritant, it is more dangerous to heavy smokers than nicotine is.

He tells us that of 100 smokers examined in one test, Dr. Frederick B. Flinn found 73 with congestion of the throat, 66 with coughs, 7 with irritation of the tongue. Dr. Emil Bogen reported on another 100 smokers, 30 of whom had mouth irritation and 30 of whom suffered from coughs. It appears that the way you smoke has something to do with how much injury you may encounter. The way you puff your cigarette, how long you hold the smoke when you inhale, how far down the butt you smoke your cigarette—all these have some bearing on how much irritation you are subjecting your throat tissues to. Rapid smoking, for instance, causes more irritation, because the smoke enters the mouth at a higher temperature.

What About Nicotine?

Most of the nicotine escapes into the air when you smoke. About a third of it gets into your mouth where some of it is absorbed. Perhaps a fifth of what gets to the lungs is absorbed. Smoking one cigar gives the same effect as smoking about 4 or 5 cigarettes. The nicotine effect from a pipe is a little more than that from a cigar. The smoke coming into your mouth reaches temperatures up to 135 degrees Fahrenheit. The hotter your smoke, the more nicotine you absorb.

Says Mr. Riis, "In pure form nicotine is a violent poison. One drop on a rabbit's skin throws the rabbit into instant shock. The nicotine content of a trifle more than two cigarettes, if injected into the blood stream, would kill a smoker quickly. If you smoke a pack a day, you inhale 400 milligrams of nicotine a week, which in a single injection would kill you as quick as a bullet."

Quoting *Risk Appraisal* published by the National Underwriters Company, Mr. Riis tells us that "Habitual smokers have 62 per cent higher incidence of gas on the stomach, 65 per cent higher incidence of colds, 76 per cent higher incidence of nervousness, 100 per cent higher incidence of heartburn, 140 per cent higher incidence of labored breathing after exertion, 167 per cent higher incidence of nose and throat irritation and 300 per cent higher incidence of cough." Insurance companies make it their business to do careful research; their business depends on it.

Colds and Smokers' Asthma

So smokers have a 65 higher percentage of colds, 167 higher percentage of nose and throat irritation and a 300 higher percentage of coughs! Surely this news should come as a surprise to no one. And we want to remind our readers, too, that "having a cold" is not the end of it. A cold, with its weakening effect on the body, may well predispose or lead directly to much more serious conditions.

An Associated Press News Release of April 17, 1953, quotes a Detroit physician, Dr. George L. Waldbott, as saying that there is a very definite disease known to medical science as "smokers' asthma." He told of a group of 58 cases of smokers' asthma, 28 of whom recovered immediately as soon as they stopped smoking, 24 others who recovered by discontinuing tobacco and taking other treatment as well, and the remainder of whom did not improve even after they gave up smoking.

He described smokers' asthma as "chronic inflammation of the Adam's apple area of the throat; wheezing, shortness of breath, a tendency to respiratory infections, constriction of the chest above the heart, and prolonged coughing in the morning, sometimes requiring several hours to clear the throat of mucus." He advised that other physicians should always make allowance for the possibility of "smokers' asthma" when they are diagnosing ailments.

Possible Effects of Tobacco Smoke on Your Family

Perhaps even more frightening is an article in the *Journal of the American Medical Association*, October 21, 1950, recounting the story of a one-year-old infant brought to the hospital with a history of watery eyes, nasal discharge and sneezing. At the age of 10 months she had had an asthmatic attack. When the baby's allergy tests showed that she was allergic to tobacco, her parents were questioned, and it was found that her mother had been an incessant smoker for many years, smoking even while she fed, nursed and diapered the baby. All smoking was stopped in the house and within a few days the baby's symptoms disappeared completely.

A year and a half later the baby developed a dry hacking cough, and it was found that the mother had started to smoke again. When she stopped, the baby's symptoms once again disappeared. Asthma is a very serious ailment, especially in the case of a baby. The extreme difficulty an asthmatic patient suffers in trying to breathe can result in death. Yet, from the story above, it seems quite possible that many of our asthmatic children today are the product of a household constantly blue with tobacco smoke. Perhaps much of the watery eyes, nasal discharge and sneezing that cause more absenteeism from school than any other reason, may be traced to a family which smokes and encourages visitors to smoke. Surely even if parents will not make an effort to stop smoking for their own sakes, they should take into account the possible harm being done to children and other susceptible people who must breathe in the tobacco smoke they exhale.

Tubercular and Post-Operative Patients

A question to the Editor of the *Journal of the American Medical Association,* September 30, 1950, asks whether or not smoking should be permitted in a tuberculosis hospital. The editor answers that tobacco smoke causes "hyperemia of the mucous membranes"—that is, excessive blood congesting the membrane. He states that some specialists in bronchial diseases can tell from the condition of the membranes whether the patient is a one, two or three pack-a-day smoker. In addition, he says, smoking causes coughing which is, of course, much more harmful for a tubercular patient than for a healthy individual.

In *The Lancet,* 1: 368, 1944 (a conservative British medical publication), H. J. V. Morton writes on the incidence of pulmonary complications in patients who have undergone operations. Patients were grouped into 3 categories: smokers, light smokers and non-smokers. The first category included anyone who smoked 10 or more cigarettes a day. The conclusions were that smoking definitely increases complications of many kinds in patients who are undergoing operations. There were 257 patients in the study, and results showed that the rate of complications for smokers was about 6 times greater than that of non-smokers. In addition, Dr. Morton says that smokers are more likely to develop complications associated with serious constitutional disturbance.

Undoubtedly a thorough search of medical literature would reveal much more evidence of this same nature. Since the respiratory membranes—nose, throat, larynx and lungs—are more directly exposed and hence more irritated by tobacco smoke than other parts of the body, it seems only reasonable to assume that all the most pesky nose and throat disorders (including colds) would be more common in smokers than in non-smokers. Once again, however, we must remember that families and friends are constantly exposed—though to a lesser extent—to the smoke of the tobacco user.

Smoking uses up vitamins that protect us against colds and other disorders—especially vitamin C and vitamin B. So the smoker, aside from irritating his nose and throat membranes, at the same time deprives them of food elements that might help to protect them against these poisons. Considering the fact that his respiratory membranes are pretty constantly in a state of irritation, is it any wonder that when the cold bugs attack, they find good pickings in these depleted, sick membranes? The weapons that might defeat them have already been used up, and the smoker becomes easy prey for the sniffles, the tears, the fevers, the chills, the coughs, the hoarseness and perhaps finally the pneumonia.

Our Research Based on Facts

When you show this chapter to some friend who may be a chain-smoker and who may have little regard for anything having to do with health, don't let him get away with sneering that we are cranks and crackpots. We didn't make up the figures on cold incidence among smokers just to frighten people. We don't have anything to sell in place of tobacco. The figures—65 per cent higher incidence of colds, 167 per cent higher incidence of nose and throat irritation and 300 per cent higher incidence of coughs—come from an insurance handbook put out by the National Underwriters Company.

We sent out some literature recently telling people about our series of articles on smoking. We were amazed to receive a reply—just one—doubting the quotes that we made, doubting that such an article as we quoted had ever appeared in a New York newspaper. So perhaps there really are people who are living wrapped up in a tight secure little cocoon of ignorance about what medical experimentation has shown in regard to the harmful effects of smoking. If you have a friend or relative like this, tell him to stop in at the local library and look through the *Reader's Guide to Periodical Literature.* All the magazine articles for the past 50 years or so are listed there. Ask him to look up smoking or tobacco or nicotine, and marvel, as we have, at the number of articles on the harmfulness of smoking that have appeared—and this in a country where many millions of dollars are paid out by tobacco companies for advertising in current periodicals! *Index Medicus* is a listing of all the articles in medical journals all over the world. Any one page of any one year of *Index Medicus* will yield enough information on the harmfulness of tobacco to cause the most hardened smoker to think a long, long time before he lights that next cigarette.

Why Do People Smoke?

"Plucky Strikes give you a lift," shrieks the billboard ad. "Scientific tests prove that Westerfields relieve fatigue," shouts the magazine ad. "Light up a Fall Mall and be the life of the party," croons the television announcer. And as the smoke curls up round his head, you can really almost see his eyes become brighter, his shoulders more erect, his smile more content.

We don't believe that Americans spend millions of dollars every year for cigarettes because they believe what the advertisements say about them. But actually what the advertisements say is true, in a distorted, back-handed kind of way. A cigarette *does* give you a lift. A cigarette *does* relieve fatigue in a pleasurable way. A cigarette *does* give you a spurt of energy you didn't have the moment before you put a match to that round, firm and fully-packed coffin-nail. Ever since the first European took his first draw on a pipeful of tobacco, scientists and medical men have searched for the secret of why tobacco should have a pleasant and relaxing effect. They have wondered, too, why the tobacco habit, once formed, should be so tragically hard to break.

Blood Sugar and Smoking

In our study of blood sugar, we were delighted to run across several articles dealing with blood sugar and smoking. In 1934 Dr. Howard W. Haggard and Dr. Leon A. Greenberg of Yale University noticed that they were getting very unusual results among a number of patients involved in an experiment they were conducting. They were trying to determine ideal mealtime hours for children and adults—that is, how often during the day you should eat for maximum health. Their article in *Science,* Vol. 79, 1934, tells how they recorded the blood sugar level for several hundred subjects under many different conditions—fasting, frequent meals, infrequent meals and

so forth. Some of the subjects showed wild fluctuations in blood
sugar level—ups and downs on their charts that could not possibly be related to any of their meals. These folks were not
suffering from any special emotional strain that might have
caused the difference, and they were all adults. The two
investigators thought of tobacco as a possible cause and found,
sure enough, that all those subjects whose blood level fluctu-
ated so noticeably had been smoking during the day.

Then they investigated the actual effect of smoking one
cigarette. They found that, when blood sugar level is low,
especially when it gets below the fasting level, a cigarette brings
about an almost instantaneous rise in blood sugar which does
not return to normal again for about 30 minutes. By further
tests they determined that it is the nicotine in the tobacco that
brings about this result. That explains why we smoke tobacco
rather than anything else—such as corn silk or the leaves of
some other plant. Why do we not smoke de-nicotinized products? Obviously because it is the nicotine in the cigarettes
that gives us the "lift," the feeling of relaxation and well-being
that comes from a rise in blood sugar. When the blood sugar
is fairly high, for an hour or so after a meal, a cigarette does
not produce this effect. However, it always speeds up the burning of sugar in our bodies and so reduces hunger pangs temporarily.

Why should nicotine have this effect on blood sugar? It
does not enter into the digestive tract; it is not assimilated by
the body as food is. Animal experiments have shown that
injections of nicotine stimulate the adrenal glands and these
glands react by releasing blood sugar. So the entrance of the
nicotine into the body sets off a chain reaction involving nerves,
glands and blood sugar.

Rise in Blood Sugar a Danger Sign

However, Dr. W. J. McCormick of Toronto explains
that this release of blood sugar and the feeling of well-being
that results do not mean at all that nicotine is good for you—
quite the contrary. In his article, "The Role of the Glycemic
Response to Nicotine," in *The American Journal of Hygiene*,
Vol. 22, 1935, he tells us that there are other states that raise
your blood sugar, too. A definite rise in blood sugar is noticed

following administration of morphine, strychnine, cocaine, chloral hydrate, carbon monoxide, bichloride of mercury, ether and chloroform. The sugar level goes up in infectious diseases such as diphtheria, tuberculosis, syphilis, influenza and typhoid, and in cases of burns, asphyxia, hemorrhage and cancer. Your blood sugar also rises when you are angry, fearful or in pain. It can increase as much as 20 to 30 per cent within 3 to 6 minutes after one of these emotions hits you. The reason for this rise in blood sugar is that the fear, anger or pain stimulates your adrenals which prepare your body to take immediate action. This reaction is protective. If your fear arises from rounding a corner on a quiet street and coming face-to-face with an escaped tiger, the sugar swiftly pouring into your blood stream gives you the inhuman energy you need for that desperate 20-foot leap that carries you out of reach of the tiger's claws. So extra blood sugar in an emotional emergency supplies extra energy. And during the course of infections, the extra sugar in your blood provides fuel for the added oxidation your tissues need to fight the infection.

Perhaps many of you have noticed that your tolerance for tobacco is greatly reduced or perhaps lost altogether after a serious, infectious fever, such as influenza. In other words, the first "drag" on a cigarette after you're well may even knock you out. This is because the infection has made such demands on your body's supply of adrenalin that there is none left to carry through the job of raising blood sugar. So you become dizzy and nauseated. Isn't it possible, asks Dr. McCormick, that constant smoking also exhausts the adrenalin, so that it is unable to provide protection against infection when the germs come along?

Blood Sugar Protects Body Against Nicotine Poison

Dr. McCormick tells us that blood sugar is raised by nicotine so as to protect the body from the poison of the nicotine. But it is brought about by a different mechanism from that which raises blood sugar after eating. When blood sugar is used to fight poison, it is withdrawn from its storage place in the liver, thus depleting the body's supply. After meals, the added sugar in the blood stream which produces the feeling of well-being, is on its way to this storage place.

It seems reasonable to us that the habitual smoker—the chain smoker, the individual who reaches for a cigarette the moment he is faced with a problem, the instant after he finishes a meal, the office worker who smokes constantly at his desk, and the housewife who carries her ashtray from room to room as she works—this individual gets along on an entirely artificial and dangerous kind of body chemistry. The vicious cycle set up goes something like this: the first cigarette in the morning stimulates the adrenals which release blood sugar from the liver. This means less blood sugar available for the body's use and within a half hour or so the effect of this first cigarette is gone. The smoker begins to feel a let-down. Nervously he reaches for another cigarette—another artificial rise in blood sugar with another "lag" later on. Unless something happens to intervene, such a pattern will probably go on all day with the result that this individual's body never gets a chance to catch up. All the nerves, glands and secretions involved in "operation blood sugar" are wearing themselves out all day long producing an artificial state of well-being, which nothing but another cigarette at definite intervals will prolong.

A Vicious Cycle Set Up

So the first puff on a cigarette (or pipe or cigar, of course) is, as Dr. McCormick says, "a burglar alarm" telling the sympathetic nervous system to release the blood sugar which will protect the body against this poison. If you could get enough nicotine in a given instant to paralyze this nervous system, so that the blood sugar would not be released, death would follow. Because of the small amount of nicotine entering our bodies when we smoke, the vicious cycle ensues—cigarette, blood sugar rise, "lag" another cigarette, another blood sugar rise and so forth.

As we have seen, a rise in blood sugar stills hunger pangs. So someone who is desperately trying to reduce is told to smoke, so that he will not be hungry. Dr. McCormick tells us that during famines in oriental countries, opium has been used for the same purpose, to decrease the craving for food when no food was available. But what a desperate gamble for any present-day American to take with his health! Says Dr. McCormick, "The 'lift' attributed to the cigarette is in reality a handicap which nature tries her best to counteract."

We have long believed that addiction to smoking is similar to addiction to any other drug. Its helpless victim, once started on the cycle nicotine produces in his body, can no more free himself than an opium smoker or a cocaine addict can. While smoking does not reduce one to a morbid or drugged state, still its effects on health are, of course, extremely harmful and, as we have shown, so subtly habit-forming that it is well nigh impossible for the inveterate smoker to "pull himself together" and stop smoking just by using his "will power." We all know the old joke about the man who thought it was easy to give up smoking—he'd already done it 75 times!

We do not believe that people smoke just to be ornery, or just to be in style. Not do we think people smoke because of an unsatisfied infantile urge to have something in their mouths, as psychologists have suggested. If this were true, why couldn't they chew a pencil and derive the same satisfaction? It has always seemed to us unfair and unkind to nag at the smoker and vilify him for his lack of will power, when perhaps it is a flaw in body mechanics that causes him to smoke. Nor does the habitual smoker seem to us any more degenerate a member of society than the sweet-tooth-hound who wolfs down candy, cokes and cupcakes all day long. He, too, is trying to make up for some lack in his daily nutrition and is probably doing himself about as much harm with his sugary tidbits as he would do by smoking.

One Reason Why People Smoke

So it seems that the nicotine-produced rise in blood sugar is at least part of the reason why some people smoke and find they can't stop smoking. If you are a smoker and want to experiment with the theory, we'd suggest that you concentrate for a couple of weeks on keeping your blood sugar level high and see if this has an effect on your desire to smoke. This means eating meals high in protein and cutting down sharply on starches and sugars. In fact, as you know, we advise eliminating all white sugar and white flour foods under any circumstances. You'll have to eat a breakfast high in protein. If you smoke at work, you'll have to carry along a supply of snacks, preferably protein foods—a bag of nuts, sunflower seeds, a couple of hard-boiled eggs. When you feel the "lag" that means you need a "drag," reach for a walnut instead. If you're seriously trying to reduce, better skip the experiment until sometime later when the extra calories won't throw off your schedule.

CHAPTER **65**

A Vitamin Deficiency *Plus Smoking* Equals Trouble

A serious eye disorder brought on by a shortage of B vitamins plus excessive smoking is discussed in this chapter.

A condition known as tobacco *amblyopia* has been known for many years. It is a dimness of vision or a loss of vision due to poisoning by tobacco. There are, incidentally, similar conditions caused by alcohol and other poisons. The one caused by smoking is seen only in people who smoke quite a lot.

The cure is, of course, to stop smoking. Blackouts, headache and inability to read, also premature farsightedness, cold fingertips in the morning after the first cigarette—all these are symptoms of tobacco damage. There is also a loss of the ability to see red and green colors. In every case the patient who was able to stop smoking soon regained full vision.

Vitamin B$_{12}$ Deficiency

An article in the British *Lancet* for August 9, 1958, relates another apparent symptom of tobacco amblyopia. Three physicians from the University of Bristol tell us that they found evidence of a deficiency in vitamin B$_{12}$ in patients suffering from the tobacco-caused disease.

They tell us that in their experience people who smoke

strong pipe tobacco are more likely to have the disease than are those who smoke cigarettes. Excessive drinking helps to increase the severity and incidence of the disease. One investigator found in 1954 that injections of vitamin B_{12} improved the condition whether or not the patient stopped smoking.

So our 3 investigators decided to find out by doing some research among their own patients. They laid out a set of rules to go by: the patient must be a smoker, he must display certain definite symptoms of amblyopia in the form of color blindness and blind spots in his eye. Of the 14 patients they studied, all of them who were given vitamin B_{12} recovered, whether or not they stopped smoking. Here are some typical cases.

Research With Vitamin B_{12} Therapy

One patient aged 62 was advised to stop smoking and was given thiamin (a B vitamin) by mouth. In spite of this his vision slowly deteriorated. When he came in at a later time, he was also complaining of a sore tongue, slurred speech and numbness in his legs. The level of vitamin B_{12} in his blood was low. He was given vitamin B_{12} by injection and within 6 months his eyes were normal.

Another patient, aged 75, who had been smoking for only a little over a year, was given vitamin B_{12} in injections and was allowed to continue smoking. Here again improvement was rapid.

A third patient, aged 81, had visible known symptoms of vitamin B_{12} deficiency. His tongue was red, smooth and sore. He had numbness and tingling in his hands and feet and weakness in his legs. He did not stop smoking, but he was given vitamin B_{12} and his poor sight and other symptoms disappeared within two months.

Hydrochloric Acid Loss Due to B_{12} Deficiency

Of the 9 patients who were given vitamin B_{12} all recovered more rapidly than would have been expected had they just stopped smoking. Three of them continued to smoke throughout. Our authors point out that a lack of hydrochloric acid in the stomach usually goes along with the anemia that is caused by lack of vitamin B_{12}. It is thought that this lack keeps the patient from absorbing the vitamin, even though he is getting it in his daily food. A considerable number of the patients treated had this hydrochloric acid deficiency.

A lack of hydrochloric acid in the stomach's digestive juices is quite common among older people and is one of the reasons they so often lack vitamins and minerals. If this important digestive juice is absent from the stomach, they simply cannot absorb vitamins and minerals.

Other Sources of Vitamin B_{12} Deficiency

Our authors say that vitamin B_{12} deficiency has been reported among "vegans," vegetarians who do not eat anything of animal origin. Diabetics, too, have a tendency to vitamin B_{12} deficiency, so, as might be expected, there is an increased incidence to tobacco amblyopia among diabetics. "A dietary deficiency of vitamin B_{12} may be present in some elderly men, particularly if they live alone," say our authors. We assume this is probably because of careless or improper preparation of balanced meals. This deficiency might be expected to predispose towards the development of tobacco amblyopia long before producing anemia and symptoms like numbness and tingling in arms and legs. The increased severity of amblyopia among prisoners of war could be explained in this way.

Lessons We Can Learn

What can we learn from these comments in *The Lancet?* The first lesson is, of course, to stop smoking, if you smoke. If you are over middle-age, it seems that smoking may be even more harmful. Whether or not you continue to smoke, make certain you are getting enough vitamin B_{12} in your diet. Liver is the best and most economical source. If you know that you lack hydrochloric acid in your stomach (doctors can test you for this), then you would do well to get injections of vitamin B_{12} from your doctor from time to time, for this is a mighty important vitamin that you cannot do without.

If you have symptoms of tobacco amblyopia, ask your doctor to give you injections of vitamin B_{12}, for, chances are, you are deficient in this vitamin. You can refer your doctor to the *Lancet* article which he can see at the nearest hospital library. It was written by Drs. J. M. Heaton, A. J. A. McCormick and A. G. Freeman.

CHAPTER 66

Lung Cancer and Tobacco

"That befogged, woolly sensation reaching from the forehead to the occiput, that haziness of memory, that cold, fish-like eye, that furred tongue and last week's taste in the mouth—too many of you know them—I know them—they come from too much tobacco." These words are from the renowned Dr. William Osler's address to Yale students, quoted in the March, 1952, issue of *The Medical Comment*. If you smoke, you are familiar with the sensations Dr. Osler describes. If you don't smoke, there is undoubtedly someone in your family or close circle of friends who does and who would also recognize these symptoms.

It has always seemed irrelevant to us to rail against smoking as a vice, an immorality. Probably each of us is addicted to some personal habit no more immoral than smoking. If I smoke 10 cigarettes a day and you drink 10 cups of coffee, which of us can call the other's habit a vice? If you puff constantly on a pipe and I carry with me a package of chewy candy for all-day munching, let's face the fact that we are both addicted to dangerous habits we'd do well to break. But let's not discuss them on a plane of righteousness or morality. Let's discuss them on the basis of health.

Most people who smoke realize that smoking is bad for them. They know it because of their own physical sensations while they are smoking, the aftereffects so graphically described by Dr. Osler, and the warnings they read constantly in newspapers and magazines. They know it in spite of the lilting jingles and the "scientific tests" of the cigarette ads. Most people who smoke regularly have tried once or many times to stop smoking, for social, health or economic reasons. Most of them have been appalled at how difficult it is to stop.

Physicans generally seem to regard smoking with a lenient eye; many of them smoke. Yet medical literature teems with evidence of the harmful effect of tobacco. For instance, *The American Heart Journal,* Vol. 42, 1951, shows the result of cigarette smoking on the action of the heart. The subjects in this experiment each smoked a single cigarette after not smoking for two hours. Out of 31 persons, 18 showed a difference in heart action after the cigarette. All of them had an increased range of pulse beat.

The British Medical Journal, Vol. 2, p. 1007, 1951, describes an experiment on the effect of smoking on blood flow through the hand. When smoke is inhaled every 20 seconds, there is a steady decrease in the flow of blood through the hand during the period of smoking. An article in *Modern Medicine* for March 1, 1952, reports on smoking and hyperthyroid (goiter) patients. The conclusion of the two authors, Elmer C. Bartels, M.D. and James J. Coll, M.D., is that smoking should be completely forbidden to the hyperthyroid patient because of the rise in rate of basal metabolism, blood pressure and pulse rate in the patients studied. *The Journal of the American Medical Association* has warned confirmed smokers of the danger of tumors of the vocal cords resulting from too much smoking. This warning issued from a study made of 143 persons suffering from injuries to the vocal cords due to oversmoking. The patients had smoked from 20 to 120 cigarettes daily.

Incidence of Lung Cancer

Most significant—and most frightening—of all the articles in our file on tobacco is a study of lung cancer in relation to smoking. This was an address delivered by Ernest L. Wynder, M.D. at a meeting of the Cancer Prevention Committee in New York on December 21, 1949, and reprinted in *Industrial Hygiene and Occupational Medicine* for March, 1952.

The author notes the fact that lung cancer has greatly increased in recent years. Although it affects a younger group than cancer of the stomach, yet the increase noted in lung cancer has not been paralleled by a similar increase in stomach cancer. In addition, lung cancer at present selects 12 men as victims for every one woman. While more and more women take up smoking as time goes on, still it is true that, historically, men as a group have been smoking longer than women.

Dr. Wynder's study was done mostly in a large city hospital whose patients were an average cross-section of American city people. In interviews he discovered whether or not patients smoked, how long they had smoked, whether they smoked pipes, cigars or cigarettes, and how many. Consistently, the lung cancer patients turned out to be those who smoked most and those who had smoked longest. Here are some of Dr. Wynder's statistics.

Among the non-cancer patients in the hospital, 14.6 per cent were non-smokers. Among the lung cancer patients, only 1.5 per cent were non-smokers. Eleven and one-half per cent of the regular patients were light smokers, while 2.6 per cent of the lung cancer patients were light smokers. Of moderately heavy smokers, there were 19.0 per cent among the regular patients, 10.3 among the lung cancer patients. You will notice that, as the figures of cigarette consumption go up, so do the percentages of lung cancer patients. Of heavy smokers, 35.6 per cent of the patients classified themselves in this bracket, while 35.2 per cent of the lung cancer patients were heavy smokers. Eleven and one-half per cent of the regular patients called themselves excessive smokers, while 30.3 per cent—almost 3 times as many—lung cancer patients fell in this group. There were only 7.6 per cent of chain smokers among the general patients, while 20.1 per cent of the lung cancer patients were in this category.

"This indicates," says Dr. Wynder, "that the greater the amount smoked, the greater the chance of incurring primary cancer of the lungs." In case you're worried about where your own smoking classifies you in this grim index, here is Dr. Wynder's interpretation: "light" smoking means 1-9 cigarettes daily; moderate—10-14; heavy—15-20; excessive—21-34; chain—more than 34 cigarettes per day. Pipe and cigar smokers are included by figuring one cigar as five cigarettes and one pipe as two and one-half cigarettes.

Which Tobaccos Are the Worst Offenders?

This is how the different kinds of tobacco stacked up. In the general hospital population, 7.8 per cent of the patients smoked cigars, while 3.6 per cent of the lung cancer patients smoked cigars. Twelve and four-tenths per cent of the general patients smoked pipes, and 4.0 per cent of the lung cancer patients smoked pipes. Now 65.2 per cent of the general patients used cigarettes, and—hold onto your seats!—90.9 per cent of the lung cancer patients smoked cigarettes. The percentage of cigarette smokers in the lung cancer group is greater than can be expected from the general use of cigarettes in the normal hospital population," says Dr. Wynder.

Cancer and How Long You Have Smoked

Here are more facts and figures, frightful enough to scare you out of even listening to cigarette commercials: more than 95 per cent of the lung cancer group had smoked for more than 20 years. About 85 per cent of them had smoked for more than 30 years. Among the regular patients, a number of men had smoked for about the same length of time, but had not smoked nearly so much each day. Among the women patients, there were very few in the non-cancer group who had smoked for as many years as this. "The difference in long-term smoking habits of the two sexes is believed to explain the present ratio in lung cancer," says Dr. Wynder.

Then he discusses surveys made by other scientists in which, for instance, two British researchers found (in 1950) only 2 non-smokers among 649 males with lung cancer. These two scientists concluded that "tobacco plays an important part in (causing) lung cancer and the risk of developing lung cancer increases with the amount of tobacco smoked."

Cancer Inducing Substances in Tobacco

Not nearly so much work has been done in studying the possible cancer-inducing substances in tobacco as has been done on coal tar products, Dr. Wynder believes, although there are two substances inhaled by smokers which should be studied in relation to lung cancer—the tobacco tars themselves and the arsenic residue present in tobacco. As Dr. Wynder points out, it is difficult to determine in animal experiments whether constant smoking produces cancer, since we obviously can't persuade animals to smoke. (And isn't it interesting that all animals intensely dislike the odor of tobacco smoke?) Also, it may be that animals are not susceptible to the same kinds of lung cancer that afflict mankind.

There may be a question in your mind about the 1.5 per cent of the lung cancer patients who were non-smokers and the 2.6 per cent who were light smokers. Dr. Wynder gives no further information about them. Evidence in our files makes us wish that a further investigation had been made into the occupations of these lung cancer patients who smoked not at all or very little. We're willing to wager that a large percentage of them work in plants where they must inhale the dust or fumes from such substances as silica, pitchblende, arsenic, asphalt, beryllium, asbestos, nickel or some of the many petroleum products. Although not all of these have been proven to produce cancer, yet all these and many more substances present a constant hazard to workers exposed to them day after day.

Conclusions

Some of Dr. Wynder's conclusions are:

1. The great increase in city living, though it may expose us to cancer-causing substances, cannot account for the recent increase in lung cancer.

2. Tobacco smoking and particularly cigarette smoking is believed to be the main cause for this increase.

3. Cigarette smoking is more prevalent than other kinds among all smokers. Cigarette smoke is more commonly inhaled than are pipe and cigar smoke, naturally exposing the lungs to more smoke.

4. Lung cancer is now one of the commonest cancers among men. Preventive measures, including a study of the possible cancer-inducing substances in tobacco, should be taken.

Arsenic in Tobacco

During the discussion that followed Dr. Wynder's remarks, Dr. Kanematsu Sugiura reported on tobacco tar and arsenic. Dr. Sugiura is the scientist who has conducted brilliant experiments in preventing cancer with brewer's yeast. He showed how he heated tobacco and collected the tar which the heat distilled from the tobacco. This material "induced tumors when painted on mice" said Dr. Sugiura. He added that, in addition to these tars, the other substance in tobacco is known to produce cancer. This is arsenic, residue from the insecticides used on the tobacco leaves. He referred to a table printed in the *American Journal of Public Health* and the *Journal of Industrial Hygiene and Toxicology* showing the arsenic content of tobacco.

	Milligrams per Pound	Mg. per Cu. M. of Puffed Smoke
Cigar tobaccos	5.3 to 12.1	0.6 to 1.9
Pipe tobaccos	14.1 to 20.5	1.7 to 3.3
Cigarette tobaccos	5.3 to 15.1	3.3 to 10.5
Maximum permissible in food	0.7	

It will be noted, said Dr. Sugiura, that the arsenic content of samples of tobacco products ranged up to 30 times the amount permissible by federal law in marketed foods!

How Can You Stop the Tobacco Habit?

How pleasant it would be if, in ending this chapter, we could propose a simple remedy that would forever "cure" tobacco addicts, one and all. It doesn't seem to be that simple. At present some of the most sensible suggestions we have found come from Dr. Gelolo McHugh, Psychologist of Duke University, reported in the *New York Times* for March 13, 1952. Dr. McHugh declares that swearing off cigarettes entirely is not to be advised, for if you fail, the next try will be harder. If you limit your cigarettes to 8 or 10 a day, chances are you'll spend much of that day thinking about the longed-for cigarette, wondering if it's time for another.

Instead, he suggests: set aside a certain time at the beginning of the day when you will not smoke at all. Do not take a chance on failure by deciding on too long a time. Perhaps two hours is long enough, perhaps you can hold out for 3. The rest of the day smoke as much as you wish. Based on research collected over 5 years and covering the smoking history of some 600 people, Dr. McHugh's idea is that you will at least *cut down* on smoking by this method, for, he claims, you will not smoke more than usual during the free part of the day. In fact, he says, you will find yourself lighting cigarettes less and less frequently after you have once accustomed yourself to not smoking at all during part of the day. This idea sounds reasonable to us. At any rate, considering the statistics on lung cancer, it seems eminently worth a try.

CHAPTER **67**

Lung Cancer Isn't All a Smoker Has to Worry About

Smokers who escape lung cancer are prey to numerous other physical hazards which can result in serious handicaps, and perhaps death.

Cigarette manufacturers are desperately busy these days trying to create the impression that the tobacco-lung cancer connection is a form of persecution completely unfounded in fact. It is hard to believe that anyone could be influenced by these protests when the evidence being presented by leading scientists to prove this relationship is so conclusive and so clinical.

But just for the sake of argument, suppose that what the industry claims were true. Suppose that tobacco smoking and lung cancer had no more relation than cigarette advertising and honesty, could the average steady smoker rest easy? Would the consequences of puffing a pack or two a day stop with stained fingers if lung cancer were out of the way? One might as well ask if, aside from a corroded stomach, there is any other consequence of drinking a cup of nitric acid than the stain it might leave on the lips. In the consumption of any poison, we know that the entire body suffers, even though the direct cause of death might be assigned to a specific organ.

Nicotine's Personal Reputation

The thing that makes tobacco what it is is nicotine. Without this element smoking a cigarette would be about as stimulating as smoking a shredded banana peel. It's the nicotine that swells the blood sugar reading, thereby giving one the "lift" a cigarette seems to promise.

Nicotine is classed, pharmacologically speaking, as one of the deadliest poisons known to man. The pure nicotine contained in a week's smoking at a pack per day would kill as suddenly as a bullet to the heart if the body were to get it in one concentrated dose. Further, to attest to the lethal qualities of nicotine, it is estimated that if the nicotine contained in a year's consumption of cigarettes were to be doled out with precision, it would be enough to kill 1,000 times the population of the United States. These facts are contained in an article on the subject in *Reader's Digest* for January, 1950.

The Effect of Small Amounts of Nicotine

You are wondering, quite logically, "Then why are there so many smokers still on their feet? The streets should be littered with dead smokers!" The answer lies in the fortunate fact that the smoker does not get all the nicotine a cigarette contains. Only about a third of it enters the mouth, and this amount is further dissipated when the smoke is inhaled. Some of what remains is sidetracked on its trip through the body until only about one-tenth of what nicotine the average puff contains is actually carried to the blood stream. Also, the body has some short time to recover between puffs, and the body elimination system gets rid of nicotine fast enough to keep a lethal dose from piling up in the system. Finally, the body of a smoker builds up a tolerance to expected quantities of nicotine, just as it can be forced to do with other poisons. These reasons are not advanced to accent the safe side of smoking for there is none, but rather to explain why regularly consuming a poison as deadly as nicotine doesn't kill the average smoker on the spot.

Acute Nicotine Poisoning

The tolerance factor is not to be lightly dismissed. It is probably more responsible than any other reason for the strong hold the cigarette habit can get on a person. How many smokers do you think there would be if each cigarette brought on the effects of acute nicotine poisoning that are experienced by the novice smoker? *The Ohio State Medical Journal* (December, 1950) describes these symptoms as nausea, vomiting, cramps, diarrhea, blurred vision and clammy perspiration. So characteristic of nicotine is this reaction that drugs with similar results are said to exert a "nicotine action." With increased use of tobacco, this reaction is toned down as the body adjusts to expecting this poisonous jolt. Still there are many regular smokers who experience one or more of these symptoms with the morning cigarette or after particularly heavy smoking. If any other poison were involved (with the possible exception of alcohol), such a reaction would be enough to warn the consumer against its further use. As it is, smokers smoke and drinkers drink no matter how sick it makes them feel.

Official Opinion on Smoking and the Heart

Cigarette companies spent much of their advertising budget, until recent years, trying to show that smoking is as healthful as eating an apple by picturing a "doctor" puffing a cigarette. The suggestion was, of course, that if a doctor smokes (and he's an expert on health) why shouldn't you? The answer to that question comes in dozens of articles printed in medical journals and secular magazines which show smoking tobacco to be a possible factor in the breakdown of almost every physiological function.

Doctors have warned heart patients for years against the effects of smoking. In March of 1955 the *Journal of the American Medical Association* ran an editorial which erased all doubt as to the official position of doctors on smoking and heart disease. "There seems now to be definite evidence that smoking, even though it may not directly affect the coronary arteries, can have a damaging effect on the myocardium (muscular wall of the heart) . . . No patient with coronary disease should incur the added risk to his heart imposed by smoking . . ."

Science News Letter (February 26, 1955) says, "Smoking affects your heart whether you are a normal person or one with heart disease." There is even a series of symptoms—chest pains, irregular beating, breathlessness and dizziness—brought on by what is known as "tobacco heart."

Science has long ago established a relationship between the number of fat molecules in the blood stream and difficulties with the heart. A report in *The New York Times* (April 6, 1955) gave proof that smoking had definitely been found to increase the number of these dangerous fat molecules.

The Journal of the American Medical Association editorial quoted above also lists the results of a test with 37 patients with heart disease (including 6 non-smokers). Of the 37, 30 showed an increased heart rate after smoking and 4 showed a decrease; 34 showed increased blood pressure. Add to these stresses the extra work the heart must do to force the blood through vessels which are narrowed with every puff of a cigarette, and you know that smoking is no better for the heart than a day at the races is for the rent money. Probably worse— at least at the races you have a chance to win.

A Disease Closely Related to Smoking

Another in the category of circulatory diseases is Buerger's Disease. Simply, this disease results from an impairment of circulation to the extremities. (Tobacco smoking constricts the blood vessels—the smaller the vessels the tighter the constriction. Fingernail blood vessels close entirely). The hands and feet tingle and feel numb as though "asleep." In time the affected areas show splotches of dead tissue that soon result in gangrene and eventually amputation must be resorted to.

A Cure—Stop Smoking

There are two outstanding facts about this affliction: its victims are almost exclusively male, and the disease is confined almost exclusively to smokers. The first characteristic does not seem to be sufficiently explained by the fact that there are more men smokers than women, though that is the only suggestion one finds in medical literature. The second point, however, is well documented by records such as a *Reader's Digest* article for January, 1950, which mentions that of 1400 cases of Buerger's Disease at New York's Mt. Sinai Hospital at the time, 1400 were smokers. A group of 100 Buerger's Disease patients was studied for 10 years, and in all cases the disease was arrested when smoking was stopped. In another study of 100 consecutive cases, it was recorded that 97 of the patients were able to avoid amputation. The 3 for whom amputation was necessary were the only ones who refused to stop smoking.

A similar record is found in the *Proceedings of Staff Meetings of the Mayo Clinic* (June 20, 1951) in which the history of a man 33 years old is told. He had Buerger's Disease and was, of course, a smoker. Doctors pleaded with him to give up his pack a day. He did not and was readmitted to the clinic twice more due to the same condition. After his last stay he gave up smoking, and after twelve tobacco-free years, returned to be pronounced completely cured.

While on the subject of Buerger's Disease, it seems

appropriate to mention a letter which appeared in the *British Medical Journal* for November 17, 1951. It was from a doctor who related his case of what he termed "dead hands" to a tobacco addiction of 40 years' duration. During this entire time he had smoked an average of one to one and one-half packages of cigarettes per day. For the 3 years before writing the letter, the doctor said, the numbness and tingling he experienced in his fingers on rising in the morning was so bad that he was unable to fasten his collar without pain. He stopped smoking and in two weeks his hands were back to normal. Unable to resist his yen for tobacco, the doctor went back to it, and with cigarettes came the symptoms once again, as strong and as definite as before.

How Smoking Affects the Respiratory System

The respiratory system takes an awful knocking around from prolonged use of tobacco. In this case it is not the nicotine so much as the accompanying tars which irritate these zones. It has been said by Dr. Mervin C. Meyerson, a laryngologist of Beverly Hills, California, that *all* smokers have post nasal drip. Dr. Meyerson maintains that "the mucous secretion of the nasal pharynx is affected by a single puff of the average cigarette. The larynx (of a regular smoker) shows anything from a mild infection to tumor formations."

The smoker's hack, well known to anyone who is often near a heavy smoker, is due to the irritation of the tars mentioned above. *The Practitioner* (March, 1952) says that smoking may irritate and cause inflammation of the mucous membranes of the entire respiratory system. Smokers have more colds that last longer, and sinusitis is more frequent and persistent in smokers.

The Effect on the Tubercular Patient

Of course, one of the greatest of respiratory diseases, tuberculosis, is aggravated beyond measure by the smoking habit. *The Journal of the American Medical Association* has a number of reasons listed in the September 30, 1950, issue which are intended to illustrate diastrous reactions of smoking on tubercular patients. Smoking is irritating to the lungs (whose texture tends to absorb any tars), causing inflammation. The smoker's cough (due to the strain it puts on the lungs) is another dangerous companion of the tubercular smoker.

Appetite is known to suffer when one smokes, and, for a tubercular patient, there are few things of greater importance than a steady intake of healthful foods.

In view of these obvious dangers for tubercular patients contained in cigarettes, we were confounded by a squib in *The New York State Medical Journal* (January 26, 1954) which remarked that out of 50 tuberculosis sanitoria canvassed, only 16 per cent had rules rigidly forbidding smoking—about 8 institutions have bothered to take so elementary a precaution on behalf of their patients!

How Cigarettes and Ulcers Are Related

Will a cigarette help bring on an ulcer? Consulting *The Practitioner* (March, 1952) we find that the general medical opinion is that tobacco smoking is harmful to the inflamed or ulcerated stomach and intestines, and should, therefore, be prohibited in such cases. New York University research has shown that patients who continued to smoke during ulcer treatment had more relapses than those who did not or had not smoked before. Ochsner Clinic in New Orleans which specializes in treating ulcer cases refuses even to undertake the treatment of any ulcer patient who will not stop smoking.

An article in *The West Virginia Medical Journal* (September, 1951) is the most definite of all. The authors insist that in cases of peptic ulcer a definite attempt should be made to break the patient of the tobacco habit. The article lists the following reasons: (1) Nicotine depresses the sympathetic nerve endings, allowing the vagus nerve to have greater effect, which results in increased gastric secretion and activity; (2) tars dissolved in sputum act as irritants when swallowed; (3) appetite is decreased.

Surgery

The smoker's troubles won't end with his ulcer. If he needs an operation, as ulcer patients often do, tobacco again multiples his woes. *The Lancet* for January, 1944, tells of a study of 257 cases with all types of abdominal operations which showed that the morbidity rate for smokers taking more than 10 cigarettes per day is about 6 times that of non-smoking operative patients. Many anesthesiologists believe that smokers are more difficult to anesthetize than non-smokers, says a piece in the *British Medical Journal* (November 6, 1954). Then, too, these patients are likely to develop laryngeal spasms during the administration of such anesthetics as ether. Such constriction could easily lead to death, as in the case reported in the article of a healthy young adult male smoker who was about to undergo a simple appendectomy. He developed a laryngeal spasm and died when it could not be relieved. The writers advise that any person contemplating surgery should stop smoking a long time in advance of the operation, and that a smoker should be sure to inform his surgeon of any observed effect he has noticed in himself as a result of smoking.

So you say none of these things bother you—you have no ulcers, no tuberculosis, no surgery impending? You're willing to take your chances if that's all smoking can do. Well, my friend, a poison so insidious as nicotine and its tars will not let you off so easily.

The Problem of Sterility

Perhaps the thousands of childless couples, one or both of whom are smokers, can trace a parallel to their cases in the one reported in the *Hawaii Medical Journal* (May-June, 1943). A young couple, wife 27, husband 33, had been married five years. The wife had been unable to conceive, although examination showed her to be healthy in every way, with no history of disease and a diet considered adequate by her physician. The husband showed up equally well in his report; however it was noted that he smoked 20 to 30 cigarettes per day. A sample of the husband's semen was analyzed and showed a large number of well-formed sperm—but they were all dead. It was suggested that the husband stop smoking. He did so on November 1, and on December 1 an analysis of his semen showed a large number of sperm, well developed and perfectly alive! Sometime in January the wife conceived and a healthy male child was born to them in October.

As a follow-up to this remarkable case, it is noted that the husband took up smoking once more, and on examination the semen again showed sperm in large numbers, but again all dead. Once more he left off smoking and, sure enough, a semen analysis a month later showed healthy, live sperm in more than adequate numbers. These observations were considered as proof that smoking and reproductive function were definitely connected in this case.

The Practitioner article on smoking quoted above

mentions, in this connection, an experiment carried on with rats to test any relationship between nicotine and reproductive processes. Dosing rats with nicotine resulted in increased number of nonfertile pairs and fewer litters. Descendants of chronically poisoned pairs also proved less fertile than control pairs. Translated into human terms, this, of course, could mean that parents who smoke stand less of a chance of becoming grandparents than those who do not.

The *Reader's Digest* for December, 1953, says that many doctors agree that tobacco causes toxic changes in the blood which impede the formation of sexual hormones. The article tells of a German study of 5,000 women which indicates that there may be a greater incidence of frigidity, sterility, menstrual disturbance and miscarriage among smokers than non-smokers.

Smoking During Pregnancy

What of women who smoke during pregnancy? How much nicotine does the fetus get from a smoking mother? This question is almost impossible to answer directly. However, the *Journal of the American Medical Association* offers a few indications in its January 9, 1954 number. We are told of experiments which show an actual rise in fetal heartbeat noted during maternal smoking. This change was taken to show that toxic products of smoke do pass through the placenta and enter fetal circulation. The effect on animals exposed to cigarette smoke equivalent to 20 cigarettes a day showed a stillbirth rate 10 times as great as those not exposed.

Postnatal Effects

As we have mentioned in Chapter 64, smoking can make things tough for a baby in his first few months of life, too. In the *American Medical Association Journal* for October 21, 1950, an interesting case is catalogued in which a baby was brought to a doctor, at the age of one year. The child was having an attack of asthma and had been having similar attacks from the age of 6 months. The cause was found to be in the mother who admitted to being a constant smoker for many years. She even smoked when nursing the baby, as well as when feeding and diapering him. At the doctor's direction, all smoking in the house was eliminated and within a few days all of the baby's symptoms cleared completely. For 18 months the baby was fine, so the mother commenced smoking once more. A dry cough developed in the child almost at once. The cough stopped as soon as the mother's smoking did.

Smoking Disturbs Kidneys and Pancreas

The deleterious effects of smoking, where the genito-urinary tract is concerned, do not stop with the reproductive problems just discussed. An enlightening experiment recorded in the *British Medical Journal* (March 24, 1945) shows quite definitely that the kidney function is also impaired. After setting up a schedule of the average voiding times and the volume of urine excreted by a group of 9 healthy persons, these subjects were required to smoke at intervals to see what effect, if any, smoking would have on their regular voiding habits. In seven of the subjects voiding was delayed from 1¾ hours to 3½ hours, while two experienced no change. The *Journal* concluded from this that "It would seem that those with impaired kidney function should not be allowed to smoke." A conservative conclusion, to be sure.

Pancreas disturbances are often traced to smoking when a thorough investigation is made. Both of the most common pancreatic diseases, hypoglycemia (a condition in which too much insulin is manufactured by the pancreas, thus cutting down on the body's sugar to below optimum amounts) and hyperglycemia or diabetes (a disease in which not enough insulin is manufactured by the pancreas, leaving the blood stream awash with vast amounts of sugar that it can't use) have been successfully controlled with an injunction against smoking. The *Journal of the American Medical Association* (May 10, 1946) found a "significantly higher incidence of thrombosed peripheral arteries" (the first step toward gangrene and amputation in diabetics) in the smokers among 301 male diabetics than in those who did not smoke, regardless of other illness factors.

Symptoms of Hypoglycemia

The symptoms of hypoglycemia (low blood sugar) are certainly frightening to experience. The victim gets the feeling that consciousness is about to be lost, and this is accompanied by blind staggers and dizziness. But look at the easy therapy:

The Practitioner for February, 1954, tells of 38 patients suffering from this disease of whom 36 were heavy smokers. Within one month after giving up tobacco the 36 smokers were completely free from the symptoms. Those who returned to smoking found that a recurrence of the symptoms was lurking in their first package of cigarettes. *The International Medical Digest* (March, 1954) relates the history of a hypoglycemia victim who had ingrained in himself the habit of consuming one-half to three-fourths pound of sugar each day to maintain the level of sugar in his blood, for he was so victimized by symptoms that even in crossing a street he could not be sure he would retain consciousness until he reached the other side. He admitted that he had, for 40 years, smoked 2 to 3 packs of cigarettes each day. Even in this extreme case, as soon as the man stopped smoking, all symptoms disappeared within a month!

How About a Smoke for the Nerves?

Well, one thing, says the smoker, there's nothing like a cigarette when your nerves are jumpy. This fallacy is the product of advertising that has pictures of people engaged in nerve-wracking endeavors reaching greedily for a cigarette before or just after they make their champion effort. The 500 mile racer needs one, the man going over Niagara in a barrel wouldn't make the trip without first calming himself with a cigarette, a ballerina about to do a hundred consecutive turns lets it be known that she wouldn't even attempt First Position without the aid of a cigarette to make her steady. Referring again to *The Practitioner,* we are told that the nervous system suffers seriously from heavy smoking." Chronic tabagism may lead to profound depression, stupor, melancholia and psychoneurotic states." One might find these attributes helpful for the trip over Niagara, but hardly for some of the other feats for which one is supposed to need a smoke.

Smoking Impairs Muscle Control

A more visual illustration of the cigarette's effect on the nerves was an experiment written up in *Time* (June, 1948). Dr. Austin Edwards of The University of Georgia wanted to prove the thesis that smoking has a harmful effect on the nerves, and he wanted to measure the results of smoking by noting changes in the steadiness of the fingers. Dr. Edwards invented a measuring device for the tests and called it a "tronometer." The finger tremors were measured before and after smoking. The tremor of regular smokers increased 39 per cent on one cigarette. In non-smokers who did not inhale there was no change. In non-smokers who did inhale the finger tremor increased 82 per cent.

As for endurance, factors were not considered controllable enough to obtain exact results, but Kapovich and Hale whose effort is included in *The Journal of Applied Psychology* felt impelled to conclude that "there are tobacco-sensitive people whose performance is impaired by smoking" and that the usual no-smoking rule for training athletes is a wise one. One of the greatest of all coaches, Knute Rockne, was quoted on the subject in these words, "Tobacco slows the reflexes and any advertising that says it helps an athlete is a falsehood and a fraud."

Smoking Affects Mouth Area

Etiquette has stepped in to frown on smoking at the table, perhaps because the satisfaction of fine cookery is sure to be dissipated by a cloud of smoke blown from across the table into one's face. And surely no true gourmet would consider numbing his taste buds with the harsh flavor of tobacco. More dangerously, smokers are prone to the ulcerative problems of lips and tongue that are associated with incipient skin cancer.

While we're in the area, what about the teeth and gums? Can smoking possibly have an adverse effect here? You bet! *The Journal of Dental Research* (June, 1947) tells of observation studies on 1,433 Danish Marines which showed that while 1.5 per cent of these men who were non-smokers had ulcermembraneous gingivitis, the count among regular smokers was 10 times that.

Smoking and the Senses

If you enjoy the smell of a roast or a whiff of your favorite perfume, the fleeting pleasure of a cigarette might permanently rob you of these delights. *The Journal of the American Medical Association* for May 19, 1951, states unequivocally that a loss of the sense of smell (anosmia) may result from excessive smoking.

The precious asset of good eyesight is in jeopardy when

one is a smoker. *The Virginia Medical Monthly* carries a piece in its December, 1955, issue which tells us that tobacco poisoning will cause a dimness of vision. After one or two cigarettes, opthalmoscope examination shows that the whole area of the optic nerve which carries the fibres of accurate vision shows a dull grayish outline and that gradually the entire disk comes to appear paralyzed.

Dr. Charles Sheard of the Mayo Clinic asserts that smoking cigarettes definitely interferes with best night vision possible. Dr. L. Tuendenhall in *Tobacco* (Harvard University Press) agrees and adds that optic neuritis plus dilated pupils and inability to focus are smoking consequences.

The effect of smoking on eyesight probably explains the statement of Dr. Robert Koons, Assistant Commissoner of the New York State Health Department, carried in the *New York Times* (March 26, 1957) in which he said that cigarette smokers seem to have more auto accidents than non-smokers. The Assistant Commissioner referred to studies that indicate a rise in an individual's auto accident rate as smoking increases.

Figures Help to Show Error of Smoking

As a parting barrage, let us quote the figures in Harry Dingman's book, *Risk Appraisal,* published by the National Underwriter Company. Note the added percentage of physical problems invited by the smoker. Habitual smokers have 62 per cent higher incidence of gas on the stomach. Habitual smokers have a 76 per cent higher incidence of nervousness. They have 100 per cent higher incidence of heartburn. The percentage of those who breathe in a labored way after exertion is 140 per cent greater in smokers than non-smokers. Habitual smokers have 167 per cent higher incidence of nose and throat irritation and, finally, a 300 per cent higher incidence of cough.

We have referred to cigarette smoking often throughout this chapter, but only because that is the commonest form of tobacco use. These disorders can arise from any type of smoking, so that pipes and cigars are equally dangerous.

Somewhere a doctor we read about gave his patients this advice: "If you're feeling under par in any way, and you are a smoker, give it up for a month's trial. Chances are that you will be a new person as a result, without a single other treatment."

We think it is excellent advice, and we are sure that the increase in vigor and the feeling of well-being a month free of smoking can bring will convince all but the most determined smoker against resuming the habit.

SECTION 19

ALCOHOL

Recent researches have proven that it is a fallacy to believe that a small amount of alcohol every day is good for older persons, that it opens up the arteries. It opens them up only temporarily, but its aftereffect is harmful. Alcohol uses up vitamin B in the body and is harmful to the nervous system. While some people seem to get along on a small amount of liquor every day, they would get along much better without it.

CHAPTER **68**

Is Alcoholism a Disease of Starvation?

Within the past 30 years perhaps no change in thinking in this country has been so great as the change in our thinking about alcoholism. In the last century the "drunk" was a figure of fun, abuse or contempt. Popular songs spoke righteously of the disgrace he brought on his family, the poverty, broken homes, deaths, illness and misery. Ministers railed in their pulpits against the evils of the demon rum. Temperance workers steadied the steps of confirmed alcoholics as they tottered forward to take the pledge. Wives nagged, children wept, doctors scolded, saloon keepers got rich, and through it all the agonized and helpless alcoholic suffered more shame, pain and bewilderment than anyone involved.

In those days apparently no one suspected that an alcoholic was ill, just as ill as respectable people who contracted tuberculosis, scarlet fever or diabetes. In those days it was believed that the alcoholic was the result of pure cussedness, and that he could give up drinking if he would just pull himself together. Somewhat the same theories had prevailed earlier about mental disease. Mental patients were beaten, chained and exposed to all kinds of outrages in the belief that this would cast out the devils that possessed them.

Modern Thinking

Today we know that mental disease and alcoholism are illnesses. There no longer remains a shred of doubt on which an uncharitable lecture can be hung. The true alcoholic is just as helpless in the grip of his illness as is the diabetic or the sufferer from heart disease. It is only within the last 25 or 30 years that science has gotten busy on the problem of alcoholism and has come up with some astounding discoveries. And high time it is, too, for if things go on at their present rate we can soon expect that today's alarming statistics will go completely out of bounds. As it is, there are an estimated 600,000 chronic alcoholic addicts in this country today. There are about two million "heavy" drinkers and 40 million "social" drinkers. As another statistician puts it, about 4 million Americans today drink to excess. About 750,000 have severely damaged their health through alcohol. In 1949 this nation spent 8 billion, 8 hundred million dollars for alcoholic beverages. By 1948 the per capita consumption of alcohol had risen to 1.98 gallons per year. The potential wage losses incurred as a result of drinking came to an estimated one billion dollars. Between 1941 and 1947 drinking by high school students rose 30.2 per cent, 58 per cent of which took place in the homes of the students, not in bars.

Who Is the Alcoholic?

What kind of people are alcoholics? Do personality and physical make-up give us any clue as to which people can "take it or leave it alone" and which people have a compulsive need to drink to excess? Many studies have been done on this aspect of the problem. Dr. James T. Smith of Bellevue Hospital in New York in a General Electric Science Forum radio program on January 9, 1952, said that an alcoholic is a person who becomes socially or financially irresponsible because of drinking, the person who gets an excessive effect from alcohol. . . . If he takes alcohol, he has lit a fuse which will inevitably lead on to the explosion of acute intoxication. In a detailed study of over 2,000 male alcoholics, it was found that they show physical characteristics differing from the average healthy male. Baldness is rare among alcoholics; they usually have a full head of hair, often prematurely gray. Acne, so common in adolescent boys, occurs seldom in history of alcoholics. Such physical characteristics are dependent on the chemical functioning of the body.

Another investigator, Jackson T. Smith, M.D., of Houston, Texas, has this to say in an article in the *American Practitioner and Digest of Treatment* for July, 1953: "More often than not the alcoholic is from a 'broken home,' either there has been a separation or divorce by the time he reached his teens or else one or both parents will have died. The alcoholic

may be very labile emotionally, tending to express his moods
without average restraint. There may be a continuously vacil-
lating attitude toward whatever authority he is faced with;
at one time he is openly defiant (particularly when drinking)
and at another totally dependent. It would appear that the
individual's confidence in himself varies from time to time, but
is always increased by his taking a drink. . . . Intellectually he
may be above average, but may have repeatedly failed to utilize his innate abilities to achieve any particular goal . . . he
is apt to be more self-conscious than average. . . ."

The Two Groups of Alcoholics

Harold W. Lovell, M.D. and John W. Tintera, M.D.,
of New York, writing in *Modern Medicine,* for May 15, 1951,
say, "Two distinct groups of alcoholics are recognized. One
group comprises the constitutionally hypoadrenocortic (suffering from diminished activity of the adrenal glands). Such individuals are tall, asthenic (inclined to be weak physically) men
who usually report low tolerance for alcohol from the outset.
These men are predisposed to alcoholism from an early age.

"In the second group are those with acquired adrenocor-
tical insufficiency. Initially, these individuals have good tolerance for alcohol, but prolonged overindulgence damages the
adrenal cortex and reduces cortical function. Consequently
alcohol tolerance is lowered and addiction results."

Genetic Determination

In an earlier issue of *Modern Medicine,* Dr. Tintera had
this to say: "For many years we have maintained that an adreno-
cortical deficiency is as much of a genetic factor as the well-
established diabetic hereditary factor. Individuals manifesting
this genetic influence . . . usually show a decreased metabolism,
marked hypotension (low blood pressure) and orthostatic
(caused by standing upright) changes in blood pressure, a characteristic hair distribution and a fondness or even a real craving
for salt and carbohydrates. . . . It is so often found that the
offspring of alcoholic parents either become alcoholics themselves or teetotalers because they realize their inability to handle
or tolerate alcohol. These same individuals are the ones who
retain their leanness and asthenia throughout life since they are
not able to metabolize carbohydrates properly. Like their teetotaler forbears they may expect to have longevity much beyond

the average with the assurance that senility due to arteriosclerotic changes will not usually ensue."

What do all these statements and big words boil down to? Well, the typical alcoholic seems to be a thin, not-very-energetic person, who is insecure and self-conscious. He may be above average in intelligence; he probably thinks of himself as a failure whether or not he is. His body seems to have a chronic inability to handle carbohydrates properly, and this is the reason why alcohol spells his downfall. This is what is involved in hypoadrenocortical function. And we will explain later on just how this mechanism for regulating the digestion of carbohydrates seems to work.

What Alcohol Does in the Body

First let us investigate how alcohol behaves in the body—what it does and what it does not do. Alcohol is a carbohydrate—that is, it is made of carbon, hydrogen and oxygen with a certain proportion and arrangement of molecules that differentiate it from other carbohydrates. Says John J. O'Neill in the *New York Herald-Tribune* for June 10, 1951, "alcohol acts in the body the way gasoline acts in an automobile engine. The gasoline is burned to provide heat and power but it contributes nothing to the maintenance and growth of the engine. Alcohol acts as a fuel, not as a food." Dr. Lovell in his book, *Hope and Help for the Alcoholic* (Doubleday and Company, 1951), says that alcohol is a depressant. The impression of a stimulating effect after a few drinks is the result of the temporary lift in blood sugar. But this is followed by a sharp decline if drinking is continued. A drink dilates the tiny blood vessels at the surface of the skin, bringing with the increased amount of blood a sensation of warmth. But if the skin is exposed to cold while these vessels are dilated, body heat is lost and the whole body temperature goes down. "Alcohol is not directly responsible for any disease except alcoholism," says Dr. Lovell, "alcoholics and other excessive drinkers may impair their resistance to many diseases by allowing themselves to become undernourished, but it is the bad nutrition and not the alcohol which is the direct cause."

Perhaps one reason why we keep coming back to the comparison of alcoholism with diabetes is this—diabetes is also a disease of those who cannot properly metabolize carbo-

hydrates. In the case of diabetics not enough insulin is produced by the pancreatic gland which has this function, so the
patient suffers from high blood sugar. This is why he must be
given insulin to reduce his blood sugar. In the case of alcoholics, there is *too much insulin* rather than too little, with
the result that the alcoholic has low blood sugar. Now the
answer would be simple if it were possible just to drain off this
extra insulin, but we find it is much more complicated than
that. What causes the extra insulin that causes the low blood
sugar? Apparently the function of at least two glands is
involved—the *adrenals* (and it is the *cortex* or covering of these
glands that is involved) and the *pituitary* (which regulates the
adrenals).

Says E. M. Abrahamson, M.D., in his book, *Body, Mind
and Sugar* (Henry Holt and Company, 1951), "Alcoholism is
caused by a deficiency in the adrenal cortical hormones—those
hormones whose action is antithetical to insulin. The trouble
may not be in the adrenal cortical itself, however, but in the
master gland, the pituitary, which for some reason fails to
stimulate the adrenal cortical glands as it does in normal operation of the endocrine system. It is believed, moreover, that this
disability of the pituitary is not caused by the alcoholism itself
but antedates its development." Dr. Abrahamson goes on to
tell us that physicians have achieved almost miraculous results
by giving injections of ACTH and cortisone to alcoholics in
their very worst condition of delirium tremens or hangovers.
ACTH and cortisone are the gland extracts of the adrenal
glands, in which the alcoholic is deficient. "These spectacular
'cures' are a great step forward," says Dr. Abrahamson, "and
they provide evidence in reverse for the theory which the
medical and the lay members of this collaboration arrived at
independently; that hyperinsulinism, with its chronic partial
blood sugar starvation, is an essential underlying condition of
alcoholism."

Diet Is the Answer

It all sounds almost impossibly complicated, doesn't it?
And yet the answer, as Dr. Abrahamson gives it, is so remarkably simple that we feel it should be blasted from loud speakers
in every metropolis in the country and headlined in newspapers
and magazines. The answer is a diet which regulates the blood
sugar so that it does not fall below safe levels. This is a diet

high in fat and protein and low in carbohydrates which will result—and *has* resulted in many cases treated by Dr. Abrahamson—in a complete lack of desire for alcohol. The alcohol was needed to raise the low blood sugar level which is responsible for the "jitters," the uneasiness, the lack of confidence, the restlessness of the alcoholic, which caused him to crave alcohol.

We then arrive at the question—did the alcoholic become an alcoholic because of his low blood sugar, or did the use of alcohol bring about the low blood sugar to begin with? The answer seems, at present, to be that both these suppositions are correct. That is, the individual who has a tendency (perhaps inherited) toward an improper functioning of the glands that regulate blood sugar may take to alcohol because it raises his blood sugar and thus relieves his jitters and nervousness. On the other hand, an individual who begins to drink early in life simply because of the exhilarating effect of liquor, may so damage the functioning of these glands (by drinking to excess) that he eventually gets a bad case of low blood sugar in which case, of course, he feels an overpowering compulsion to go on drinking to keep his blood sugar high.

Vitamins and Alcoholism

Another important aspect of the question, it seems to us, is the part that vitamins, especially the B vitamins, may play in the whole story. Dr. Roger J. Williams, of the University of Texas, is our authority for most of the work that has been done along these lines. Dr. Williams believes, according to *Time* for June 11, 1951, that "While all men need the same vitamins and minerals, they do not need them in the same amounts or the same proportions. Many human disorders, he thinks, arise because some people (partly because of heredity) need some life-essential substances in far greater quantities than normal diets supply." The craving for alcohol is one such disorder, he believes. In his experiments with rats he found that those animals whose diet was deficient in vitamins developed a craving for alcohol, while rats fed on a diet which supplied the necessary vitamins developed a dislike for alcohol.

Vitamin Therapy

Dr. Williams treated one human alcoholic patient with massive doses of vitamins A, C, D and E and all of the B vitamins. The patient went without alcohol without any dif-

ficulty and even, finally, demonstrated that he could take one
or two beers and then quit. "This individual," says Williams,
"probably constitutes the first case on record in which an
alcoholic has become a moderate drinker." Up to this time
there has been unanimous agreement that the true alcoholic
could never become a moderate drinker, no matter what the
"cure"—he would always have to be a teetotaler. But Dr. Williams has apparently proved otherwise. "Since then," says
Time, "doctors at Boston's Peter Bent Brigham Hospital have
tested the method with 85 alcoholics, giving some of them
dummy capsules to rule out the psychological factor, and report
at least one-third better results in the vitamin treated cases."

Our Diet, Lack of Vitamins and Alcohol

It seems to us that this discovery ties in well with Dr.
Abrahamson's plea for a diet containing little or no carbohydrate. White sugar and white flour that constitute more than
50 per cent of the average American diet are carbohydrates,
but they are also carbohydrates from which all the vitamins have
been removed by processing. Carbohydrates must be accompanied by B vitamins or the body cannot handle them, so to
digest white sugar and white flour foods, the body is robbed of
B vitamins until a deficiency is produced. Most drinkers also
smoke, which practically guarantees them a shortage of
vitamin C. Vitamin A deficiencies are extremely common, as
military doctors discovered among men in service.

Now, let us imagine an individual—man or woman—
whose body naturally requires far more vitamins than the
average. Perhaps this might be because of unusual gland activity of some kind—who knows? Right from the start this individual is getting less vitamins than he needs. As he grows up, on a
diet 50 per cent of which is de-vitaminized white flour and
sugar, his vitamin deficiency grows worse. In addition, if he is
predisposed to the adrenal disorders Dr. Abrahamson mentioned, his blood sugar level is bound to fall to dangerous
depths. Not knowing any better, he continues to eat a diet high
in carbohydrates, because they raise his blood sugar level giving him some comfort for an hour or so. If alcohol is at hand—
and where in this country is it not at hand?—he soon finds that
alcohol gives him release from jitters and self-consciousness.
From then on he is a gone gosling, for his body cannot handle

alcohol any better than it can handle other carbohydrates. As he drinks more, he eats less and less. What food he does eat certainly does not supply the necessary protein and vitamins, so he must drink more—not because he is depraved or lacks will power, but because his body is starving for food which he does not give it.

Stress and the Alcoholic

One other factor enters in, to which many researchers have devoted a lot of time. Says George N. Thompson, M.D., of the University of Southern California, writing in *Industrial Medicine and Surgery* for June, 1951, "The alcoholic is a person who, because he cannot stand the strain and tension of life without developing strong anxieties, escapes from responsibilities into oblivion . . . we are quick to state that the human organism can tolerate just so much stress. *But in spite of this knowledge, and in spite of the realization that our mental hospitals are filled with those who have fallen under the stress of their environments, under working situations intolerable to them . . . we continue to place workers in jobs for which they are unsuited, to enforce factors of stress to which we would not subject a mechanical contrivance and to expect performance beyond the capacity of the emotionally handicapped person."*

Such a statement arouses another question in our minds—is the alcoholic a person who cannot stand stress because of his glandular make-up, or does his constant anxiety and nervousness disorder his glands? And if so, what causes the original anxiety? Could it not be lack of those vitamins whose chief function is to safeguard the health of the nervous system? One of the chief treatments for alcoholism is, and for some time has been, psychotherapy and drugs which will make alcohol repugnant to him. The question in our minds is: is it possible to rehabilitate an alcoholic by removing the frustrations and stresses in his life, without at the same time repairing the functions of his glands that affect and are affected by these emotions? Quite apart from this, of course, is the question of how many of us can afford psychotherapy, even if it is available in our home town. And how many of us can afford hospitalization which the taking of Antabuse and other drugs necessitates?

It is noteworthy that practically all writers on alcoholism mention Alcoholics Anonymous. It appears to be one organization to which unanimous approval and support is given. But it has been pointed out that the word *Alcoholic* is always used by a member when he introduces himself. He does not qualify himself as a "cured alcoholic." For he knows that, unless and until he corrects the body disorder that creates his craving for alcohol, he must remain a teetotaler—at whatever cost to his peace of mind—and can never again touch alcohol. We are in agreement that, for the confirmed alcoholic, this organization offers much in the way of psychotherapy. Socializing with people who are in the same boat and who are dedicated with fanatic fervor to helping other alcoholics appears to us to be a healthful and sound step to take.

Try a High Protein Diet

We are convinced, moreover, that an alcoholic can be returned to health by diet and vitamin and mineral supplements, administered at home without expense and without upsetting the family's way of life. The diet we outline at the end of this article is the one Dr. Abrahamson publishes in his book which, incidentally, you can buy at your local bookstore or direct from the publishers—*Body, Mind and Sugar,* published by Henry Holt and Company, 383 Madison Avenue, New York City. Two other books on alcoholism we want to recommend are *Hope and Help for the Alcoholic* by Harold W. Lovell, published by Doubleday and Company, Garden City, New York and *Nutrition and Alcohol* by Roger J. Williams, published by the University of Oklahoma Press, Norman, Oklahoma.

For those of you who may have had alcoholics in the family or who, for some other reason, fear that some member of the family may have inclinations this way, we would say don't try to prevent alcoholism by scolding, lecturing and forbidding alcohol in the house. Liquor is easily available at almost any corner of the street these days. Instead, try putting the whole family on a high protein diet with as few sweet and starchy foods as possible. This means meat, fish, eggs, nuts, cheese, fresh vegetables and fruits, supplemented by brewer's yeast or desiccated liver for vitamin B, rose hips or some other natural food supplement for vitamin C, fish liver oil for vitamins A and D, bone meal for calcium and other minerals and wheat germ for vitamin E.

This is the diet for curing or preventing low blood sugar, as outlined by Dr. Abrahamson:

On arising—Medium orange, half grapefruit or 4 ounces of fruit juice.

Breakfast—Fruit or 4 ounces of juice, 1 egg with or without 2 slices of ham or bacon; only 1 slice of bread or toast with plenty of butter; beverage.

2 hours after breakfast—4 ounces of juice.

Lunch—Meat, fish, cheese or eggs; salad (large serving of lettuce, tomato or Waldorf salad with mayonnaise or French dressing); vegetables if desired; only 1 slice of bread or toast with plenty of butter; dessert; beverage.

3 hours after lunch—8 ounces of milk.

1 hour before dinner—4 ounces of juice.

Dinner—Soup if desired (not thickened with flour); vegetables; liberal portion of meat, fish or poultry; only 1 slice of bread if desired; dessert; beverage.

2-3 hours after dinner—8 ounces of milk.

Every 2 hours until bedtime—4 ounces of milk or a small handful of nuts.

Allowable vegetables: Asparagus, avocado, beets, broccoli, Brussels sprouts, cabbage, cauliflower, carrots, celery, cucumbers, corn, eggplant, lima beans, onions, peas, radishes, sauerkraut, squash, string beans, tomatoes, turnips.

Allowable fruits: Apples, apricots, berries, grapefruit, pears, melons, oranges, peaches, pineapple, tangerines. May be cooked or raw with or without cream but without sugar. Canned fruits should be packed in water, not syrup.

Lettuce, mushrooms and nuts may be taken as freely as desired.

Juice: Any unsweetened fruit or vegetable juice except grape juice or prune juice.

Beverages: Weak tea (tea ball not brewed); decaffeinated coffee, coffee substitutes.

Desserts: Fruits, unsweetened gelatin, junket (made from tablets, not mix).

Alcoholic and soft drinks: Club soda, dry ginger ale, whiskey and other distilled liquors.

Avoid Absolutely

Sugar, candy and other sweets, such as cake, pie, pastries, sweet custards, puddings, and ice cream.

Caffeine: Ordinary coffee, strong brewed tea, beverages

containing caffeine.   (Your doctor will tell you what these are.)

Potatoes, rice, grapes, raisins, plums, figs, dates and bananas.

Spaghetti, macaroni and noodles.   (We add crackers, pretzels, biscuits, etc.)

Wines, cordials, cocktails and beer.

(We have included bacon, ham, soft drinks and distilled liquors in this list, as Dr. Abrahamson does, but we assume that you will automatically have crossed these off as you read the list.   Of course, alcoholic beverages do not belong on a diet list for an alcoholic, *but we contend that he will soon not want them*.   Also note that we do not recommend using citrus fruits as freely as Dr. Abrahamson suggests, and we do not approve of drinking citrus fruit juice or milk.   Any lack of vitamin C can be made up by taking rose hips.)

SECTION 20

COFFEE AND TEA

Both are very harmful, but usually do not show their effects until in later years. The tottering gait of a senile old person is due greatly to drinking coffee or tea. The caffeine in coffee and the theobromine of tea destroy nerve cells, and in later years play havoc with the memory. They also lower the blood sugar. There is rose hip tea, peppermint, and many herb teas that make excellent drinks, including—Postum. We do not recommend the decaffeinated coffees, as they still contain some of the caffeine. Some people find their sleep interfered with even when drinking decaffeinated coffee.

CHAPTER **69**

Evidence Against Coffee

We made a very significant observation in our research on the scientific proof of the harmfulness of coffee-drinking. From 1900 to 1915 medical and scientific journals were full of articles on experiments done. From 1915 to 1925 there were far fewer articles. From 1925 to 1945 the number declined still more. And from 1945 on there has been, practically speaking, little or no investigation of the effect of coffee on human health. We do not know what this may mean. Does it mean, perhaps, that medical men are discounting the facts discovered earlier and hence do not think it worth while to pursue the investigation further? Does it mean that new drugs, chemicals and poisons now demand so much time that we cannot spare time to investigate older substances? Or does it mean simply that physicians and researchers alike have decided that the fragrant brown beverage most of them drink all day long can't possibly need any further investigation?

A History of Harmfulness

As far back as 1746, a treatise was published on *Tobacco, Tea and Coffee* by Simon Pauli, an Italian writer. Pauli appears to be a writer of some substance, for his works were accepted widely among the learned of his day. We know there were many misconceptions about physiology in those days, and, of course, present-day methods of investigation were not available. Yet it is startling that Pauli believes "it (coffee) is esteemed a great cooler (thirst quencher) for which reason it is drank by most, but if it is used to excess, it extinguishes the inclination to venery and induces sterility." He tells us further that in ancient times women of the East used coffee brewed extra strong as a purgative to prevent conception. Perhaps this is the reason why its use was forbidden to woman for many centuries by the early caliphs. He advances the theory that coffee induces sterility because it gradually dries up the body's procreative powers on account of the large amount of sulfur it contains.

Later in our own country a writer on health, Dr. William Alexander Alcott, wrote that coffee is essentially and properly a medicine—a narcotic. He quotes authorities of that day (his book was published in 1844) as saying that coffee possesses nervine and astringent qualities, is suspected of producing palsies, has a powerful effect on the nervous system, a pernicious effect on the stomach and bowels, exhausts the sensibilities of the part on which it acts, induces weakness, produces debility, alters the gastric juice, disorders digestion and often produces convulsions and vertigo, feverish heat, anxiety, palpitations, tremblings, weakness of sight, and predisposition to apoplexy.

He quotes Dr. Hahnemann, founder of homeopathic medicine, as saying that "coffee is strictly a medicinal substance. All medicines in strong doses have a disagreeable effect on the feelings of a healthy person." He also quotes Hahnemann as saying that coffee drinking produces the following diseases: nervous or sick headaches, toothache, darting pains in the body, spasms in the chest, stomach and abdomen, costiveness (constipation), erysipelas, disease of the liver, uterus and bones, inflammation of the eyes, difficulty in breathing and bowel affections. He compares the action of caffeine to that of arsenic, lead or prussic acid, asking "will anyone attempt to say that these substances are not poisonous because they poison slowly?"

Dr. Alcott is a cousin and associate of Amos Bronson Alcott, who was a famous educator and the father of Louisa May Alcott of *Little Women* fame.

Caffeine Is a Poison

Now perhaps these older writers may have jumped to conclusions when they laid down the unqualified statement that coffee was responsible for all the ills mentioned. Undoubtedly they did not use present-day laboratory methods to prove their statements. But they must have questioned their patients as to whether or not they used coffee and based conclusions on the answers. So while it does not follow that coffee-drinking was the sole and only cause of the symptoms their patients described, it does seem quite possible that coffee-drinking may have played a part in them. And it does seem significant that so much was written in times past about the possible harm of coffee-drinking. We do not find treatises attacking the use of apples, potatoes, carrots, bread or cheese. So we know, that, from way back, physicians have been concerned with the medicinal and narcotic aspects of coffee. And we cannot discount this concern as an old wives' tale.

We know that caffeine, the substance in coffee which apparently is responsible for its effects on the human body, is a powerful poison. A drop of caffeine injected into the skin of an animal will produce death within a few minutes. An infinitely small amount injected into the brain will bring convulsions. The amount of caffeine in a cup of coffee is quite small. Yet we drink coffee because of the effect of the caffeine, just as we smoke because of the effect of the nicotine. Both are drugs, both are habit-forming. We uncovered some interesting accounts of headaches produced as "withdrawal symptoms" when coffee-drinking was abruptly stopped. We also know that efficiency of work performance decreases when a confirmed coffee-drinker stops taking his daily dose of coffee. These are symptoms typical of addiction. When any drug is taken away from a drug addict, he suffers "withdrawal symptoms."

Habitual Coffee-Drinking and Stomach Ulcers

What do some of the modern researchers have to say about the effect of coffee on the human body? There are two modern disorders that the general public usually associates with coffee drinking—ulcers and heart trouble. This may be mostly because physicians frequently forbid coffee to their heart and ulcer patients. There seems to be no doubt that coffee is bad for the ulcer patient, although we do not find any researcher who has proved that coffee actually produces ulcers in human beings. J. A. Roth and A. C. Ivy whose animal experiments on coffee are famous, tell us in *Gastroenterology* for November, 1948, that 1. Caffeine produces gastro-duodenal ulcers in animals to whom the drug is given in a beeswax container so that their stomachs are absorbing caffeine continually. 2. Caffeine moderately stimulates the flow of gastric juices. 3. Caffeine produces very definite changes in the blood vessels of animals which are similar to changes produced by prolonged resentment, hostility and anxiety. 4. As we know one difficulty involved in ulcers is an excessive flow of hydrochloric acid into the stomach. Most peptic ulcer patients, say Drs. Roth and Ivy, respond to caffeine with a prolonged and sustained stimulation of the output of free hydrochloric acid. In other words, coffee causes more and more hydrochloric acid to pour into the stomach of the ulcer patient for quite a long time after the coffee has been taken. So, say these authors, although they cannot prove that caffeine causes ulcers, still it does seem that taking fairly large amounts of coffee may contribute to the development of ulcers and may aggravate the condition of an ulcer that exists already.

An investigation carried on at the University of Oklahoma by Vern H. Musick, M.D., Howard C. Hopps, M.D., Harry Avey, M.D. and Arthur A. Hellbaum, M.D., and reported in the *Southern Medical Journal* for August, 1946 involved a total of 39 patients—10 of them with no symptoms of digestive tract trouble of any kind, 25 of them patients with duodenal ulcers and 4 patients with gastric ulcers. The researchers found that the flow of digestive juice is considerably increased in the normal person when caffeine comes into contact with the lining of the stomach. In the patient with duodenal ulcer the flow of digestive juice is "prolonged and excessive." Dr. Musick, in discussing the subject before a meeting of the Southern Medical Association concluded, "I think it is all right for the normal person to drink caffeine-containing beverages but an ulcer patient or a patient who has a high secretory curve (that is, someone with a generally high level of hydrochloric acid in the stomach, which might predispose him to ulcers) should not drink coffee. He should not drink alcohol and by all means he should not drink black coffee the next morning after alcohol."

Sum Total May Kill

Now you will notice that, in all of these researches, caffeine was used—not coffee. This might lead someone to say, "Well, of course, straight caffeine is bad for you, but there is so little caffeine in coffee that surely coffee can't hurt me." On the same basis one could say there is so little nicotine in cigarettes, so little preservative in processed foods, so little arsenic on the outside of a sprayed apple, so little fluorine in fluoridated water, that there is no harm in taking any of these either. Once you begin to add up all these "small doses of poison" that you are taking every day, the sum total gets to be quite frightening.

Dr. R. Wood, M.A., B.M., B.Ch., B.Sc., writing in the *British Medical Journal* for August 7, 1948, tells us of experiments with cats in which he found that caffeine in the stomach has a powerful action on histamine, a substance which regulates gastric secretion. He also found that theobromine and theophylline (substances that occur in cocoa and tea) also have a similar action in some animals. "Our results support the Roth and Ivy conclusions," he says "that ulcer patients should restrict their intake of beverages containing caffeine and also that it is desirable to limit their consumption of foods and drinks containing theobromine and theophylline."

Coffee, Heart Disorders and Blood Pressure

Concerning heart trouble and coffee-drinking, most nutritionists and books on health state that coffee has a definite effect on the heart and blood pressure. According to James S. McLester, M.D., in his book, *Nutrition and Diet in Health and Disease* (W. B. Saunders, 1927), coffee raises the blood pressure slightly, slows and strengthens the heart, stimulates renal activity and prevents fatigue and depression. It also gives mild brain stimulation. He goes on to say that its excessive use is harmful, for stimulation and irritation are closely related. In cases of insomnia, cardiac irritability and rapid heart beat, even one cup a day will cause trouble when the heart is already irritated. More than one cup is especially harmful.

H. M. Marvin, M.D., in his book, *You and Your Heart* (Random House, 1950), states that the effect of alcohol, tobacco and coffee all vary among different individuals. Some find that their heart beats faster after a few drinks of alcohol or cups of coffee. Others find that their hearts beat just a little faster, or not at all faster. He says that no one knows why this should be so. Perhaps some people develop a "tolerance" for coffee and others do not.

That word "tolerance" keeps recurring in all the literature about coffee. Our medical dictionary defines "tolerance" as "the ability of enduring the influence of a drug or poison, particularly when acquired by a continued use of the substance." It seems peculiar that the word should be used in speaking of coffee, if indeed coffee has no harmful effects on the body. And is it possible that those of us who suffer no apparent ill effects from coffee have simply accustomed ourselves to it over a period of time, so that we can throw off the ill effects?

Kathryn Horst, Rex E. Burton and Wm. Dodd Robinson, writing in *The Journal of Pharmacology and Experimental Therapeutics,* Vol. 52, 1934, tell of an experience involving a number of young men whose blood pressure was tested before and after they began to drink coffee habitually. The maximum rise in blood pressure occurred during the first week they were drinking coffee. Later on, the article explains, a "tolerance" was developed, and the blood pressure remained at the same level.

When the coffee was withdrawn, the blood pressure returned to "normal." We don't know how you interpret this experiment, but to us it seems to show definitely that some substance in the coffee does have an unhealthful effect on the blood pressure. For those who can, after a time, build up a "tolerance" to this effect, the blood pressure does not go higher. But what of those who do not build up this tolerance? Might not coffee be a very important factor in continued high blood pressure which, of course, is one of the most widespread disorders in our country today?

Leafing on through our notes on coffee and heart ailments, we find that Jean Bogert in *Nutrition and Physical Fitness* (W. B. Saunders, 1949) states that coffee quickens the respiration (that is, makes you breathe faster), strengthens the pulse, raises the blood pressure, stimulates the kidneys, excites the functions of the brain and temporarily relieves fatigue or depression. Max M. Rosenberg, M.D., in *Encyclopedia of Medical Self Help* (Scholastic Book Press, 1950) tells us that coffee should be avoided by individuals who have heart disease, angina, high blood pressure, stomach trouble, skin affections, arthritis, liver trouble. Garfield G. Duncan, M.D., in *Diseases of Metabolism* (W. B. Saunders, 1952) tells us that caffeine causes an increase of 3 to 10 per cent in the basal metabolic rate within the first hour after the coffee is taken. (So, incidentally, does the smoking of one cigarette!) Basal metabolism is the rate at which your body makes use of the food you eat.

We want to elaborate a little on the whole business of coffee stimulating the heart. For someone whose heart needs a momentary stimulation, you might use coffee as you would use a hypodermic injection—for that occasion only. But what happens, do you suppose, when the heart, sick or well, is constantly stimulated, day after day, while all the time it is protesting that it is tired and wants to rest? One writer on the subject compares coffee to a whip used on a tired horse. Of course, the horse will move faster when he is whipped, but how long can you keep up this form of stimulation before the horse drops from exhaustion? The main danger, it seems to us, in the use of coffee by people who may have heart trouble (as well as the rest of us) is that instead of resting as they should when they are tired, they whip themselves to more effort by a cup of coffee and eventually—sooner or later—they are going to have to pay for the rest they are not getting.

Many people use the excuse that they drink coffee only in the morning, so it doesn't matter if they overstimulate their bodies. They are not trying to go to sleep! Instead they have to gird themselves to meet the day's problems, responsibilities and hard work, so they need to be stimulated. There is a serious fallacy in this kind of reasoning. If they are indeed so tired and run-down that each morning they cannot face the day without a cup of stimulation, then certainly there is something wrong somewhere. Either they do not get the right food, enough sleep, enough relaxation or enough freedom from worry. Over-stimulation even at breakfast time, means that an already tired body is "hopped up" to carry on when it should be resting.

Coffee Tars and Cancer

Does the use of coffee have any relation to cancer incidence? There is at least one researcher who believes that it does. We know well that certain kinds of tar produce cancer. Coal tar is cancer-producing. The tar from tobacco products produces cancer in laboratory animals. A. H. Roffo in an article published in *Boletin del Instituto de Medicina Experimental*, Vol. 15, 1939, describes the process of obtaining tar from coffee. He found that this tar has the same physical characteristics as that obtained from tobacco. He treated laboratory animals with this tar and 73 per cent of them developed tumors which ended as cancerous growths. In a later experiment he fed coffee tar to rats in non-toxic doses—that is, they did not receive enough of the tar to make them ill at any one time, for he was trying to discover what the long-continued effect of the tar would be. Definite sores in the stomachs and digestive tracts soon became ulcers which eventually developed into cancers.

Roffo believes that it is the roasting of coffee that produces these tars. He also says that they are not soluble in water, so perhaps they are not present in coffee as we drink it. Still, in chemical tests such as spectography and fluorescence, the coffee tars show the same characteristic as coal tar. This is the only scientific evidence we could find of a possible relationship between coffee-drinking and cancer. It seems strange that no one has done any further investigating to find out, for instance, how much, if any, of the offending tar we drink in a cup of coffee. Or, perhaps, is the tar that ugly black scum that settles on the bottom of the coffee pot and is so hard to wash off if the coffee has been standing for any length of time? Come to think of it, that black scum looks and acts very much like the black deposit on the bottom of a very dirty ash tray.

Should Pregnant Women Drink Coffee?

A German scientist, Heinz Fischer, has done research on the effect of caffeine on the placenta and embryo of pregnant rabbits. The rabbits were given caffeine daily in water solution. In an article in the German medical publication, *Zeitschrift fur Mikro-Anatomischer Forschungen,* Vol. 47, 1940, Dr. Fischer describes the results.

The growth and development of the embryo were slowed down. In the liver and kidneys of the embryo as well as in the blood vessels, there was obstruction of the passage of blood, resulting in edema or unhealthful swelling. The skin of the embryo was damaged and the cells of its liver showed definite disease. When all of these harmful symptoms became serious enough, the embryo died and was re-absorbed, becoming just a crumbled mass in the mother's womb. The placenta (the sac covering the unborn child) became swollen and diseased.

It is interesting to note that these results were reported for rabbits to whom caffeine was given first when they became pregnant. Other rabbits were given small amounts of caffeine over a period of time until they established a tolerance to it. (There's that word "tolerance" again!) Then, when they became pregnant, the placenta and embryo suffered no damage.

Once again, we remind you that caffeine (the concentrated poison that exists in coffee) was given to these animals—not coffee. But, even so, does it sound like such a good idea for an expectant mother in these days to drink coffee, taking into account the already considerable amount of various poisons she is getting in food, in air pollution, in chemicalized water and perhaps in cigarettes?

Does Coffee Affect Brain and Nerve Tissue?

The Department of Agriculture published a booklet in 1917 called *The Toxicity of Caffeine*. Their experiments involved animals. They tell us that the reaction of human beings and animals to caffeine may be quite different. Yet most scientific research these days (on chemicals, insecticides, cosmetics and so forth) is done with animals and it is taken for granted that any substance that shows up as poisonous to animals is quite likely to be not very good for men.

The authors tell us, too, that the effect of caffeine on individual animals is different in its intensity, and the effect varies with the dose. On the same basis, undoubtedly some human beings are less resistant to poisons than others. William Salant and J. B. Rieger, authors of the booklet, tell us that only one rabbit in 10 survived injected doses of caffeine. Those that survived generally succumbed to a second or third dose. The effect of caffeine on guinea pigs was even more drastic, although dogs and cats reacted differently. All showed symptoms of poisoning, which resembled poisoning from strychnine. In relation to its harmful action on tissues (chiefly brain and nerve tissue), caffeine is far more destructive than morphine. They conclude that the continued use of caffeine-containing beverages over a long period of time seems bound to be harmful.

Well, would you consider giving your family—children and old folks included—ever so small a dose of morphine every morning as part of breakfast, no matter how much they might like the taste? Keep in mind that caffeine showed up as being far more destructive than morphine.

Doesn't Contribute to Nutrition

This is the bulk of our evidence on the possible harm that may result from habitual, prolonged and excessive coffee drinking. It does not seem to us that someone who drinks one cup of coffee a day should go to a lot of trouble to give it up. But probably he will be the person who could give it up most easily. The person who is in danger from coffee, we believe, is the person who simply can't get along without it and who, if he stops and soberly counts up how many cups of coffee he has in any one day, may find that coffee is indeed a drug to him and that the habit of throwing off weariness and worry with a cup of coffee has brought him nothing but sorrow and ill health. These are the people who should be persuaded to give up coffee entirely.

If this should prove to be impossible, we have one last suggestion. According to our standards, we should eat and drink nothing that does not contribute in some way to nutrition. Any food or drink that contains neither vitamins, minerals, enzymes or protein should automatically be crossed off the list, for it is crowding out in our diets those beneficial protective foods we all need so desperately. If you must continue to drink coffee, then at least make certain that the rest of your diet is as healthful as possible. This means plenty of fresh raw fruits and vegetables every day along with plenty of good meat, eggs, fish and nuts. This means only completely whole grain cereals. This means no food at all that contains white flour or white sugar in any form, even including chewing gum and soft drinks. This means taking food supplements: fish liver oil for vitamins A and D, brewer's yeast or desiccated liver for the B vitamins, rose hips for vitamin C and wheat germ oil for vitamin E.

CHAPTER **70**

Coffee—A Cup of Trouble

Here are some more documented facts to make you aware that coffee is anything but "good to the last drop." It is well to remember, too, that these facts apply in almost the same way to tea-drinking, since tea also contains caffeine and, in addition, contains tannins.

There is an oft-told story of a young wife who tearfully asked a trusted family counsellor how to save her faltering marriage, and the counsellor, after deliberating only a few minutes, is said to have replied, "Learn to make a good cup of coffee." It has been rumored that this tale was born in a publicity office and the rumor is easier to believe than the story.

But who is to say that a coffee-loving husband couldn't be driven to that last, intolerable remark by a cup of gray-looking coffee? Well-made coffee means a lot to the average American.

And how did we come to be such connoisseurs? Simple enough—by experience. We drink more coffee than anybody else in the entire world! The American digestive system is practically awash with it. Half of every handful of coffee beans picked anywhere eventually ends up in an American coffee pot, and 92 per cent of our homes keep a coffee pot busy every day to supply the average dose of two and a half cups per person. No wonder we can spot a tasty cup of coffee as soon as we come within sniffing distance of it.

A Weak Heart Can't Take Coffee

Most coffee drinkers are vaguely aware of the fact that coffee keeps them up somehow. Some keep awake by having a cup in the evening, some can barely make it to the kitchen for the first cup of the day, and others need that mid-morning coffee break to keep them going till noon. But such artificial stimulation forces the body to use its emergency reserves that should be replenished by rest. Getting used to that added push will make one painfully short on reserves, in case a really serious need of extra energy should arise.

The culprit that hides behind the deceptively inviting aroma of freshly-brewed coffee is caffeine. It is this property that classifies coffee as a drug. *The New York Times* (August 29, 1954) quotes *New England Journal of Medicine* as saying that coffee-drinking can be classified with other drug habits such as opiates, alcohol, barbiturates and nicotine. The pure caffeine to be found in a cup of coffee isn't much to look at; about two full pinches of salt would illustrate the dose. Yet the amount of caffeine that occurs in three cups of coffee is equal to the therapeutic dose given by doctors as a heart stimulant! Suppose a coffee drinker whose heart, unknown to him, can't stand any more stimulation, were to drink 3 cups of coffee at a sitting? Couldn't it lead to serious consequences? Do you think that every coffee drinker is aware of the exact state of his heart? An article in *Reader's Digest* for August, 1950, confirms the general awareness that doctors often forbid coffee to patients with high blood pressure or hardening of the arteries. What could be more logical? What sense would there be to adding a blood pressure "raiser" to a system in which the pressure is already too high?

Soviet Medicine (Vol. 13, 1949) describes the effects of injected caffeine as used by a doctor to treat typhus cases, in which a sharp drop in circulation occurs. It produced initial increase of heartbeat lasting 10 minutes, then caused a decrease; also, a higher blood pressure lasting two hours resulted. Can even a healthy heart respond to caffeine with such gymnastics, on a regular basis, with no damage? A regular coffee drinker is asking much the same thing of his heart every day.

Ulcers Can Result

The *Reader's Digest* article, mentioned before, talks of a burning in the stomach as another of the symptoms many coffee drinkers suffer. Perhaps these experimental results recounted in the *Proceedings of the Institute of Medicine* in Chicago (July, 1945, Vol. 15) will explain why. It was reported that black coffee causes greater stimulation of gastric secretions than any other beverage. Caffeine-containing beverages were found to provoke prolonged and sustained increase in the total output of acid by the stomach, in patients with peptic ulcers. Seventy per cent of the ulcer patients studied complained that ingestion of coffee either initiated or aggravated symptomatic distress.

Along the same lines is a piece carried in *Gastroenterology* (the official journal of the Gastroenterology Association), November, 1946, which says that peptic ulcers may be produced in cats or guinea pigs, in relatively short periods of time, by the prolonged and continuous administration of caffeine alkaloid in beeswax. (The beeswax container is used so that the animal's stomach might absorb the caffeine continually.)

That information should give you a fair idea of why the burning stomach sensation is a close follower of coffee-drinking in many people. It's a pretty good indication that there is an excess secretion of stomach acids that can cause an ulcer. Don't wait for your doctor to tell you to stop drinking coffee because of an ulcer. Do it on your own before one develops.

A Biography of the Brew

It is strange that a beverage which is so foreign to our country should have become such a passion with us. Our climate will not permit the growing of even a single coffee bean of our own, so that we must import virtually every grain. Coffee's origin is much more remote than the Latin American countries that grow it in such abundance today. Legend says that the goats belonging to a Mohammedan monastery led to its discovery in Arabia. The goats would nibble the berries of the Kaffa tree and become so keyed-up that they ran and played all night instead of sleeping. Before the monks noticed a connection between the sleeplessness of the goats and their eating the berries, it was assumed that the goats were bewitched.

Eventually the monks brewed a hot water extract from the berries and spent a few sleepless nights of their own. They became addicted to the drink, and its use began to spread across the world. The Turks introduced it to Europe during their siege of Vienna, and the city has since made a great attraction of its quaint and special coffee houses. Johann Sebastian Bach, the great classical composer, was even moved to write a tribute to the brew which he called "The Coffee Cantata."

A phrase which has crept into American usage in recent years is "coffee break." Manufacturers and office executives were somehow sold on the idea that a mid-morning cup of coffee would greatly increase the efficiency of the staff resulting in more output at less cost. At direct odds with this supposition is an experiment described in the *Journal of Pharmacology and Experimental Therapeutics* (1934). It was found here that coffee exerted a marked influence upon man's performance of an acquired motor skill. When coffee was drunk, all performances suffered and there was a sustained deleterious influence on the subject. A statement of a more general nature, carried by *Chemical Abstracts* (1948, Vol. 42), further demolishes the idea that coffee improves performance. It says, "Maximum performance of hea'thy, rested subjects cannot be improved by alcohol or drugs (caffeine, etc)."

It can be safely assumed that any increased efficiency brought on by artificial stimulation will be temporary and will be followed by a reversal that will drag efficiency to a point far below the norm. Doctors maintain that the body must repay by rest added hours of stimulation by any source.

Cancer Lurks in the Background

One of the most serious indictments made against coffee is its possible link with cancer. *Chemical Abstracts* (1944, Vol. 38) says that tar extracted from coffee beans has strong carcinogenic properties. An experiment was conducted with 100 rats that were fed a stock diet of bread, milk and grain, plus coffee tar, added in *nontoxic* doses. Pathologic changes in the rats' digestive systems developed in 30 to 795 days. These consisted of sores that began with simple ulceration and terminated in cancer. The authors added that coffee tar resembles tobacco tar in the carcinogenic properties of its hydrocarbons.

An earlier experiment reported in *Chemical Abstracts* (1939, Vol. 33) used tar obtained from coffee by distillation and condensation. This tar again had the same physical characteristics as that obtained from tobacco. A group of rabbits were treated with this tar for from 7 to 20 months. Seventy per cent of the rabbits developed papillomas which ended as cancerous tumors.

The latest report in this connection is one which appeared in *The New York World Telegram and Sun* for April 12, 1957: "A potent cancer-causing chemical known as 3,4-ben-zypyrene has been found in coffee root obtained from coffee-roasting plants." Are these the first murmurings that will one day swell into a roar like the close association between cigarettes and cancer?

Getting Rid of the Habit

Once you've got the coffee habit, it's no cinch to get rid of it. The withdrawal symptoms as described in the *Journal of Laboratory and Clinical Medicine* for 1943 sound almost as bad as those for narcotics such as marijuana or heroin. In over half of 38 trials on a group of 22 coffee drinkers, very severe headaches were produced by sudden withdrawal of caffeine. Also, the headaches were often accompanied by nausea and vomiting.

And what about that steaming cupful that many people just have to have to finish a meal? *The Journal of the South Carolina Medical Association* (1924) speaks: "Strong coffee, taken after a full meal, retards the digestive process and should be avoided by dyspeptics."

Admittedly caffeine is the source of most coffee troubles. There are several brands on the market now which eliminate most of the caffeine. If one must drink coffee, these would certainly be less harmful. But no one claims to have eliminated caffeine from the coffee completely, and even a little of the stuff is not compatible with healthy body function. Switch to natural herb teas for your hot drink or Postum. They're healthful and delicious.

CHAPTER **71**

Thyroid Trouble or Too Much Coffee?

An illustration of how just taking too much coffee can bring on symptoms so serious that they can be misdiagnosed as a wrongly functioning thyroid condition.

A recent book (*Kathy,* by Katharine Homer Fryer, published by Dutton) tells the story of a young girl who was near death because of a wrong diagnosis of thyroid disorder, or rather, no diagnosis at all. From a normal healthy child, Kathy changed very gradually into a shadow of her former self. She lost weight steadily and lost all her good spirits and energy along with it. Day after day she drooped and weakened.

Doctors could find nothing wrong, and she was finally taken to psychiatrists who declared she was suffering from a psychosis. They recommended that she be sent to a mental hospital. Almost by accident she happened to be in the office of an M.D. who decided to test the functioning of her thyroid gland. He found it dangerously deficient. She was given a thyroid preparation—to supply the substance her own thyroid gland was not supplying—and improved within a matter of hours. In a few weeks she was back to normal.

Importance of Thyroid Gland

It seems to be extremely difficult to diagnose thyroid disorders, possibly because the thyroid is such an important gland that it takes part in many body processes. Any or all of these can go awry when something goes wrong with the thyroid. But, of course, they may be disordered from other causes than thyroid trouble, too.

The thyroid, through its hormone, thyroxine, regulates the way the body uses its food—the rate of metabolism or the rate at which food is broken down and built into cells. It has to do with the way the body uses calcium and other minerals. It influences the growth and the weight, determines personality and emotional behavior, is related in some important ways to reproductive function. The pituitary gland, the sex glands and the parathyroid glands are all closely related in function to the thyroid. So the jobs of all these, too, are influenced by the thyroid. If it is disordered, they are disordered, too.

The heartbeat, the body's reaction to heat and cold, the function of memory, the making of red blood corpuscles—all these are influenced by the thyroid gland. The interaction of the thyroid and the adrenal glands has something to do with blood pressure. It seems as if everything you do or are is determined at least in part by the working of your thyroid gland. So we can't possibly emphasize enough the vast importance of this gland to you, from the point of health, personality, happiness, mentality, appearance.

New Evidence of Wrong Diagnosis

A late issue of the *Journal of the American Medical Association* (November 23, 1957) tells us of misdiagnosis of a different kind in relation to thyroid trouble. The author of this article, Arnold S. Jackson, M.D., has discovered that many people are diagnosed as having thyroid trouble when they don't at all! And, since the handiest treatment for thyroid trouble is to take the gland out, many many people have thyroid operations when there is nothing or perhaps very little wrong with their thyroid glands.

Dr. Jackson says in 1937 he went to a meeting of the American Association for the Study of Goiter where 100 cases were presented. All of these patients had been advised to "have it out." Dr. Jackson found that in no instance was there any evidence of hyperthyroidism. At another meeting he and Dr. Elexious T. Bell, then Professor of Pathology at the University of Minnesota Medical School, presented the cases of 200 patients, all advised to have thyroid operations, in all of whom the thyroid gland was either completely normal or just slightly abnormal.

Unnecessary Thyroid Removal

In the *Journal* article Dr. Jackson tells us about 228 patients whose physicians had recommended thyroid operations, and all of the patients were suffering from something else—

nervous tension and exhaustion in 112 cases, menopause in 30, physical exhaustion in 27; 11 were normal; 11 had colloid goiters; 3 had rheumatic endocarditis; 8 had psychoneurosis; 6 had hypothyroidism (too little thyroid activity instead of too much) and 20 had assorted other ailments.

None of these patients should have had his thyroid gland removed, of course. But one of them, away from home and in a highly agitated condition, was rushed off to a hospital, and a large section of his perfectly normal thyroid gland was cut out. Dr. Jackson goes on to tell us what symptoms indicate hyperthyroidism (too much activity of the thyroid gland, for which operations are commonly performed). These are: steady weight loss although the appetite is good, progressive weakness, increased pulse rate, shaking, insomnia, sweating, palpitation of the heart and pulse pressure. A rise in the basal metabolism rate is another symptom.

The Causative Factor—Stimulants

However, in the case of the 228 patients we are discussing here, although certain of these symptoms were present, there was nothing wrong with most of the thyroid glands involved. In the 167 patients of the first three groups, what do you suppose was causing these frightening symptoms—serious enough to result in 167 recommendations to have healthy thyroid glands removed? Says Dr. Jackson, *"The most important single factor responsible was the overindulgence in the use of stimulants— coffee, tea and nicotine."*

Many of the patients smoked from 2 to 3 packs of cigarettes a day. Many drank from 5 to 30 cups of coffee every 24 hours. An average cup of black coffee contains 2½ grains of caffeine, so anyone who drinks 10 cups daily is getting about 3 medicinal doses of this drug, which doctors give with great caution. Anyone drinking 30 cups of coffee is getting about 10 such doses.

In addition, since the stimulants made them jittery, irritable and nervous, most of our patients were taking large doses of barbiturates, tranquilizers and other drugs, trying to combat the nervousness. Listen to some of the case histories. Do they sound like anyone you know?

The first case was a young woman who had come from a farm to get a job in the big city. Under the strain of city life she took more and more coffee, nicotine and soft drinks to keep going. One day she had an accident, and her doctor diagnosed her case as goiter resulting from the accident. It was decided to operate. Through the insurance company's insistence, she was examined by Dr. Jackson who took her off all stimulants and sent her home to rest. She recovered rapidly—with no operation.

Another woman, middle-aged, was brought from another state to have the thyroid removed by surgery. Dr. Jackson's examination revealed that her thyroid was normal. She needed rest from too much work and overstimulation.

A patient from New York City came expecting an operation. Instead, a few months' rest in the country, without stimulants, sent him back to work in good health.

Is an Operation Really Needed?

There are two lessons to be learned from this story. First of all (and Dr. Jackson says this in just so many words) if in doubt as to the diagnosis of hyperthyroidism, *don't rush into surgery or any other type of therapy.* First, make certain of the diagnosis. This, of course, is advice for a doctor. It's advice for you, too. Don't decide on operations—any kind of operations— while there is the vaguest chance the diagnosis might be wrong.

Our files are full of information about useless surgery— for gall bladders, for hysterectomies, for appendices, for tonsils, for prostate glands. Prominent surgeons themselves have made strong statements about the prevalence of unnecessary surgery. You need the various parts of your body with which you were born! It's senseless to have them cut out unless you have exhausted every possible chance of attaining good health by other means. And certainly, considering its importance in body function, the thyroid is the last item that should ever be removed without exhausting every other possibility.

Don't Overindulge

The second lesson to be learned is the tragic fact that symptoms so serious as to be almost fatal can result from the use of such harmless-appearing substances as coffee, soft drinks, tea and nicotine. Who knows what proportion of all the ills being treated in all the doctors' offices in this country are the result simply of overindulgence in these everyday drugs!

We said "overindulgence," and there are bound to be some people you talk to who will say, "But I never overindulge!

Thirty cups of coffee a day? Three packs of cigarettes! Not me. I'm temperate." Ask them if they've ever kept strict account of the amount of coffee, tea and soft drinks they drink over a period of a week. Ask them exactly how many cigarettes they smoke in a week, by actual count.

And even if they don't "overindulge," the story we have told illustrates the terrible harm that can come from these drugs. Isn't it logical to assume that if one uses a little less than these amounts, he is doing his body just a little less harm—it's still harm! Many readers, we are sure, have long since discovered that the best precaution to take with drugs is to avoid them entirely whether they come as medicines or in the attractive form of a hot cup of coffee or tea, or a sociable cigarette.

SECTION 21

HERBS

Excellent for use in cooking, for they add much delight to a low-salt diet. Herb teas are good beverages to drink. We rather doubt that any herb is a specific for any disease. But they do contain vitamins and minerals.

CHAPTER 72

Herb Teas for Health and Enjoyment

Books on herbs, used both medicinally and for meal-time beverages, take us back many centuries to those times when tea, coffee and chocolate were unheard of or were known only to the wealthy. Of course, before modern medicine brought us the dubious blessing of drugs, the only medications known were those made of herbs. Every home had its herb garden and every housewife was a specialist in the knowledge of just which herbs combined best as a cure for cough, fever, rheumatism, hives, tuberculosis or any other ailment that was bothering you.

The Modern Approach

We need not be patronizing about these old remedies. Many of our modern drugs, such as digitalis, are made from plants. And there is every reason to believe that the vitamin content of the wild and garden herbs was responsible for near miracles of healing among people who knew nothing of vitamins and did not have access to fresh fruits and vegetables the year 'round, as we have.

The whole subject of herbs in cookery has lately come into the limelight. These days it is smart to know how to use herbs in the kitchen. It is sophisticated to have a pot of basil and a pot of chives growing on the kitchen window sill. Modern women's magazines are including more and more recipes calling for herbs. So it's about time we catch up with these advances and get acquainted with the wealth of pleasure and good health to be found in herb cookery. Your local public library contains books on herbs. Ours yielded 3 entrancing books, giving recipes, cures and folklore background for all the common herbs.

Says M. Grieve, F.R.H.S., in his book, *Culinary Herbs and Condiments* (Harcourt, Brace and Company, 1934), "The study of herbs has been neglected—except by a few people—for many years, but now there are signs that it is being slowly revived. It is not at all an unusual thing to find a portion set aside for herbs in country gardens, cultivated by those who really understand something of their properties.

"Many things which we dislike at first, we afterwards acquire a taste for, and there is no doubt that Herb Teas are an acquired taste. They have a strange smell and a strange flavor, and that is the reason why they are not popular, for many people do not try to get used to them. Yet if the taste for them is cultivated, they certainly improve on acquaintance."

He then gives directions for making tea of balm, camomile, ground ivy, sage, peppermint and a whole list of mixed herbs, combining in one tea, for instance, rose leaves, rosemary and balm; in another aniseed, fennel, caraway and coriander; in another meadowsweet, agrimony, betony and raspberry. In each of these the procedure is about the same as for making our regular tea—boiling water is poured over the leaves. If you have your own herb garden, you can make teas with fresh leaves. And, of course, you can dry and store all manner of leaves every fall to last you through the winter.

Herb Teas You Can Make

Rosetta E. Clarkson in her book, *Herbs, Their Culture and Use* (the Macmillan Company, 1942), tells us that there are some 75 or more herbal teas taken for various ailments, even in these days of antibiotics and antihistamines! She goes on to say, "The aroma will remind you of the past summer days when you pressed these same fragrant herbs in your hot moist hand as you strolled down the garden paths. You will also enjoy these refreshing teas when you feel exhausted fro n the summer's heat. They will be drunk gratefully when you feel shivery with a cold coming on, or when you are ready to scream from frayed nerves.

"For afternoon tea a few leafy tips or a small handful of herbs may be added to a brew of ordinary tea—herbs such as lemon thyme, lemon balm, peppermint, spearmint, apple mint, lemon verbena, costmary, camomile, wintergreen or any one of these brewed by itself makes a deliciously different tea. The

French make a fragrant tea of the leaves and flowers of agrimony
to be served with meals. Speedwell tastes similar to Chinese
green tea and is commonly used on the Continent under the
name of *Thé de l'Europe.*" (European tea.)

Herbs for Cures

She suggests equal parts of peppermint and elder flowers,
equal parts of costmary and orange mint, two parts of rosemary
leaves and one part lavender flowers. For asthma sufferers mul-
lein or sweet marjoram make a good tea. For nervous headache
you might try camomile, or catnip, peppermint, aniseed, lemon
balm, rosemary, mugwort, sage, sweet marjoram, lemon verbena. For indigestion try beebalm, boneset, sage, aniseed, fennel seed, peppermint or basil. Wintergreen leaves, boneset or
celery are well-known among herb doctors as remedies for
rheumatism. Many readers have reported relief from the symptoms of arthritis after drinking tea made from alfalfa seed (the
untreated kind sold for human consumption, not the kind
bought by farmers for planting). A tea made of coltsfoot is a
good spring tonic, says Miss Clarkson, sage, red clover and elder-
blossoms, celandine, ground ivy and camomile are blood puri-
fiers.

Folklore Surrounding Herb Usages

Garden of Herbs by Eleanour Sinclair Rohde (Hale,
Cushman and Flint, 1936), takes us back for almost 400
years with recipes for herb dishes served in England, when
no dish was a dish worthy to set on the table if it did not contain herbs. She mentions plantain tea, feverfew tea, dandelion
tea, chickweed tea, eyebright tea—this latter was named by
the Greeks and has the reputation of restoring lost eyesight.
How would you like to sit down to dinner with a steaming cup
of lavender tea, or tansy tea or violet tea?

A garden of your own is the answer, if you are one for
experimenting in the kitchen, for the list of possible combinations of herbs for tea-making is practically endless. We cannot
give you the evidence of scientific experiments performed in
laboratories to indicate that herb teas have the wonderful healing qualities ascribed to them in the old herbals. But we do not
discount these tales. The marvelous and age-old folklore that
has grown up around the properties of the various berries, seeds
and leaves in the sickroom was not invented out of whole cloth.

Undoubtedly there are many healthful benefits to be gained from drinking herb teas.

If you do not have a garden (and once again we urge you to have one, even if it means digging up the back lawn), you will have to buy your herb teas. Don't expect to like them the first time you drink them. You had to learn to like tea and coffee, too. And each herb has its own pungent, unmistakable fragrance—a fragrance which is always fresh, clean smelling, refreshing. Buy small quantities at first until you decide which flavor is your favorite. Then surprise your friends the next time you have them over for dinner with a healthful cup of your own brewing. It's new, it's different and — these days — it's fashionable!

CHAPTER **73**

Some Herb and Seed Recipes to Try

In learning to get along without salt, you will find it helpful to use herbs for flavor. Here are some recipes which will make you forget that you ever liked the taste of salt.

When recipes are concocted with your good health in mind and when they come from a cook in a famous eating place, we are glad to pass them along to readers.

Take beet tops, for instance. We know these are one of our best foods, nutritionally speaking—richer in vitamin A than almost any other food, chock full of the B vitamins and vitamin C, to say nothing of iron, calcium and phosphorus. But don't you get discouraged sometimes, wishing there were some new ways to serve them so that your family will relish them and ask for seconds? Try this. Steam the beet tops and while they are still hot mix them with diced raw calves liver, "fine herbs," avocado bits, garlic (chopped fine), chopped parsley, steamed brown rice and two raw eggs. Toss the whole works in a skillet with chicken fat for just a few minutes so that the liver is barely cooked. Serve with real homemade whole wheat bread and a tossed salad.

Recipe for "Fine Herbs"

To make the "fine herbs" mentioned above, our professional cook gives the following recipe. (This will make about two quarts which he tells us will keep in the refrigerator for about two weeks.) Three hearts of celery with leaves, 4 large bunches of parsley, 3 leeks (split so they can be washed), five bunches of green onions or scallions (use the tops only or very little of the white). Wash all these ingredients and drain well to be certain there are no drops of water on them. Chop all ingredients fine and add 3 large cloves of garlic chopped and mashed. Melt enough fat to cover the chopped mixture (one-third fat and two-thirds herbs is about right). Use butter,* bacon fat* and chicken fat. Place this in a heavy iron skillet or stainless steel pot and add the following, rubbed and chopped fine:

1 tablespoon powdered ginger
1 teaspoon powdered mint
1 teaspoon thyme seed
1 teaspoon powdered sweet basil
1 teaspoon comino seed
1 teaspoon rubbed sage
1 teaspoon powdered savory
1 teaspoon caraway seed
½ teaspoon oregano, whole
½ teaspoon aniseed
½ teaspoon powdered marjoram
1 large leaf of bay
2 cardamom seeds (shelled out. Do not use the hull.)
½ teaspoon dried rosemary

Cook slowly and stir constantly so that the onions and parsley will not burn—for about 10 minutes or until it appears that all excess water is cooked out. Pour into flat dishes, cool and refrigerate. Use flat dishes so that when you take out some of the mixture to use, you will get plenty of herbs mixed with the fat.

---

* We frown on these.

Our expert suggests that you use this herb mixture with any or all of the following: cooked carrots, string beans, steamed cabbage, tomatoes, mayonnaise, cottage cheese, stuffed baked potatoes. To these latter you can add avocado scraps and additional fresh chopped parsley for extra vitamins.

If you are using the "fine herbs" in some food where you do not want the herbs themselves, melt the mixture in butter and strain out the herbs. The flavor will remain. This makes a delicious sauce for steaks, liver, fish, and is wonderful added to gravies and soups. We'd suggest that you make up only about a fourth of the recipe to begin with, until you're sure the mixture is exactly as you'll enjoy it most. If you don't like the taste of any of the herbs or spices, just leave them out. That's the nice thing about herbs. You can add or subtract as you wish, and the result will always be tasty. You can get most of these herbs in any large market these days. Buy the rest from an herb house, or grow them yourself if you have a garden. No bought herbs compare in flavor with home-grown ones that you dry yourself.

A Tasty Rice Dish

Here's a fine rice dish that can be the main or only dish of a meal. Use brown rice, of course. Fry it, add chicken or other stock and cook until the rice is done. Drain and keep hot. Prepare fresh or canned tomatoes; diced bell peppers; pimentos; pine nuts; diced, cooked meat (mutton or beef, etc.) sautéd with raisins. Add rice and "fine herbs." Toss on a hot stove until mixed well and hot. Serve with sour cream* on the side.

Potato and Carrot Preparations

Here's a tasty way to prepare creamed potatoes. Cook or steam the potatoes in their jackets, peel and dice. Make a cream sauce of "roux" and half cream, half milk. Add "fine herbs" and nutmeg. Mix and serve. A "roux" (pronounced "rue") is made by cooking butter or a mixture of butter and chicken fat with whole wheat flour until the flour is done—that is, it does not taste raw. Stir constantly to avoid burning. Use buckwheat, rye or other flours to vary the taste. For cream sauces you can use milk, cream, meat broths or vegetable juices.

* We suggest no dairy products.

We suggest not using any dairy products. Always keep the liquid in which vegetables have been cooked. Keep it tightly covered in the refrigerator and use it always in place of water in soups, sauces or gravies.

Try this for carrots, if you ever eat them cooked. They're more nutritious raw, of course. When the carrots are two-thirds cooked, drain them and use the juice to make a "roux." Add fresh chopped parsley, nutmeg, "fine herbs," whatever seasoning you wish and a dash of honey and cooking sherry, if desired.

Let Taste Be Your Guide

We haven't given measurements, for actually a really proficient cook who uses herbs decides for himself or herself by taste alone how much or how little to add. Begin with less than you think you might need, for herbs have a definite flavor to which you may have to become accustomed. Add a little more of the herbs as your taste and appreciation for them grow. Once you've begun to cook with herbs, you'll find you can't get along without them. And they're a manifold blessing for someone trying to cut down on salt. Any good modern cookbook will give you further suggestions for using herbs with various dishes such as fish, salads, eggs, meats and vegetables.

"Bouquet garni" is a French cookery trick that will add zest to all kinds of soups and stews. Make little cheesecloth bags in which you place dried basil, thyme, marjoram, savory, celery leaves, parsley, or any other herb you like. Tie the bags shut and keep them in a covered jar until you need them. Pop the "bouquet" into soups or stews and remove it just before serving.

SECTION 22

VEGETARIANISM VERSUS MEAT-EATING

We are not vegetarians, for our research indicates that a high protein diet is the best diet. We believe we should include animal protein because it contains all of the amino acids, or forms of protein that are essential to good health. Vegetable protein (with the exception of a very few foods such as soybeans) does not contain all these amino acids in the right amounts.

CHAPTER 74

Should We Eat Meat?

The question of vegetarian-eating versus meat-eating arises often among health-conscious people. Where does *Prevention* stand in this controversy?

We stand with the meat-eaters, and here are some of the reasons why.

Any vegetarian can rightfully point with horror to the condition of meat animals today—stuffed with antibiotics, hormones and tranquilizers. But surely that same vegetarian cannot claim that, beside meat, today's vegetables, cereals and fruits are natural and unspoiled by any tampering! What of the systemic insecticides that are shot into the plant to render it so poisonous no insect can bite it and live? What of the other hundreds of deadly bug-killers with which every edible thing from the garden, the field or the orchard is liberally drenched? What of the antibiotics sprayed on, to preserve fruits and vegetables? What of the dyes, the preservatives, the waxes?

Eskimos Live Healthfully on Meat

All the literature we have about the Eskimo shows that, in general, he has abundant good health so long as he stays far away from the "civilized" foods that white settlers take to the North.

Tooth decay, cancer, arthritis, diabetes and other degenerative diseases are practically unknown among the primitive Eskimos. They have almost incredible powers of endurance—". . . most explorers will agree that an Eskimo laughs as much in a month as the average white man does in a year. One reason why the Eskimo is happy is that in the uncivilized state he usually has enough wholesome food to keep him in perfect health. And if there is any royal road to happiness it is through health . . . When we realize that the Eskimos secure their living with little labor as compared with the rest of us, and that they are healthy and happy, it dawns on us that they are really inhabiting a desirable country."

These are the words of Vilhjalmur Stefansson, the explorer, in his book, *The Friendly Arctic* (Macmillan, 1943). Stefansson is generally accepted as an authority on Eskimo life. He is also an authority on living on nothing but meat, and tests have shown that his health has not suffered.

We have in our file a recent (September 27, 1958) report on the cholesterol content of the blood of 842 Eskimo men, which appeared in *The Lancet* for that date. The authors tell us that earlier researchers seemed to find that cholesterol levels in Eskimos were lower than those of other Americans. But Scott, Griffith, Hoskins and Whaley, who wrote this article, tell us that they found nothing unusual about the cholesterol level, although there is considerable variation from place to place.

CHAPTER 75

High Protein Diet Essential

It has been shown by modern researchers that we need a diet high in "complete protein" to be really healthy. We cannot manufacture all the amino acids which go to make up a complete protein. Some animals can, but not man. We must get them in our food. The amino acids that are called the "essential" amino acids are called that precisely because we cannot manufacture them—they must be obtained in food. Soybeans and sesame seed provide these amino acids in fairly good proportion, so these two foods can largely substitute for the amino acids of meat and eggs. But these are the only two vegetable foods of which we can say that.

Bridges' Dietetics for the Clinician (published by Lea and Febiger) explains what is meant by "physiological efficiency." "Proteins from animal sources readily provide a suitable selection of amino acids for building human tissue. Plant sources are considerably less efficient. The coefficient of digestibility for protein concerns itself with the percentage of the nitrogen intake which is absorbed. This has nothing to do with the popular concept of digestibility as measured by freedom from undesirable symptoms. Animal proteins have the highest coefficient of digestibility, rating 95-100 per cent. In general the cereals tend to give values around 85 per cent but when the coarser material is removed the coefficient will be 90-100 per cent. Fruits and vegetables may rate 80-85 per cent but can be lower. Proteins in nuts show a low coefficient—around 70 per cent.

"The biological value of a protein is concerned with the percentage of the absorbed nitrogen which is retained by the body. This has a quantitative aspect as well as qualitative. It takes a large amount of an inferior protein to equal a small amount of a superior protein."

Even if we accept the fact that the protein of potatoes is more "efficient" than that of meat, one serving of potatoes contains two grams of protein. A serving of meat contains about 20 grams of protein. You would therefore have to eat 10 potatoes to get the protein you get in one slice of meat.

Lack of enough good protein in the diet is mentioned often in connection with diseases of various sorts. It is the direct and only cause of a disease which is as common in certain parts of Africa, as cancer and heart disease are in our country. This disease can be cured within a matter of days with a diet rich in protein; it is a disease that can easily be fatal. It is caused by eating a diet high in starch because that is all that is available to the people in this part of the world. A diet naturally high in starch is bound to be naturally low in protein.

High Protein

The protein deficiency disease to which we referred above is called *Kwashiorkor*. It is common in tropical countries, especially those where the standards of living are low and starchy foods are eaten almost exclusively. The results, especially in children, are terrible and in many cases fatal. The cure is simple. Milk, eggs and meat bring almost immediate cure. Even one of these alone is effective.

Now, it is perfectly true that a vegetable food has been developed which cures kwashiorkor. A Department of Agriculture scientist, recognizing on a field trip that the diets of these children were inferior to those fed to his chickens at home, developed a high-protein food from corn, cotton-seed meal, sesame oil meal, kikuya grass and yeast which contains the complete proteins necessary to reverse the degenerative process in these protein-starved children.

The food is now being made for distribution in Central America. Nine years of intensive work went into planning the formula. It provides not only a high level of protein but, more important, the proper balance of the amino acids which make it possible for the body to make use of all its food.

Can We Satisfy Our Protein Need?

We believe that vegetable products can be used to provide complete nutrition so far as the various amino acids, or forms of protein, are concerned. But if it takes a learned researcher, working with all the facilities of a great modern laboratory, 9 years to develop such a food, does it seem likely that many of us are capable of guiding our eating habits and menu planning so skillfully that we can, every day, year after year, feed our families tasty and attractive meals which contain all the protein nourishment necessary—especially considering the fact that it is well nigh impossible to buy foods that have not been spoiled by chemicalization and processing!

Uric Acid and Meat-Eating

Uric acid is the substance looked on with horror by vegetarians as a symptom of the wrongness of meat-eating, a poison derived from the purines of food of animal origin, which man is unable to destroy. *Diseases of Metabolism* by Garfield G. Duncan, M.D. (W. B. Saunders Company) contains a statement about an experiment in which subjects kept on a diet practically free of purine remained in good health *and continued to excrete constant amounts of uric acid.* The body itself apparently manufactures purines; they take part in a number of extremely complex chemical reactions, all necessary to good health, and are then excreted. Gout is the disease which is commonly referred to as the example of the harm done by purine-rich foods.

This monumental volume, *Diseases of Metabolism*, which contains a thorough study of gout, goes on to say that there is no evidence that omitting foods rich in purine has any bearing at all on the course of the disease and, in fact, depriving the patient of meat at such a time is likely to be more harmful than beneficial.

Excretion of Uric Acid Varies Considerably

And while we are on the subject of purines and uric acid, let us review what is said in *Bridges' Dietetics for the Clinician* (Lea and Febiger): "The amount of uric acid which is excreted through the kidneys varies considerably. It depends upon the purine content of the diet, the nature of the non-protein foods ingested, physical activity of the subject, the destruction of uric acid in the body and renal efficiency."

In *Clinical Nutrition* by Jolliffe, Tisdall and Cannon (Hoeber), the following *vegetable* foods are forbidden to the patient suffering an acute attack of gout: whole grain products such as whole wheat bread, shredded wheat, oatmeal, asparagus, beans, cauliflower, peas, soups—because of their high purine content. The only meats forbidden are organ meats which are extremely high in purine.

So the arguments against the use of meat because of uric acid formation boil down to these facts: 1. Uric acid is also manufactured in the body and is not just the result of the amount of purines in the food.

2. Purines which form uric acid in the body occur in vegetable as well as animal food, so the argument that uric acid is harmful cannot be used to defend vegetarianism against meat-eating.

3. The disease which manifests most symptoms of the misuse of uric acid—gout—is caused by a number of different things—including some deficiency in the body which limits its ability to deal with uric acid. But one cannot say that eating food that contains purine is the cause of uric acid deposits any more than one can say that eating food that contains calcium is the cause of calcium deposits. It is a disorder in the body's metabolism which is responsible for the distress, in each case.

It is possible to devise vegetarian diets in which the nutritionally proper amino acids, or forms of protein, will be in a balanced proportion. This does not by any manner of means suggest that the average housewife, faced with preparing daily meals for the average family that will stay within the average budget, can accomplish such a feat even once, let alone 3 times a day every day. We say she cannot. And we say that she should not be asked to, especially considering that she must, usually, buy food that has been processed and chemicalized so that it hardly resembles food at all. When the happy day arrives to which we are looking forward—that day when all food will be fresh, unchemicalized, unprocessed, organically raised—on that day perhaps the average meal-planner will know enough about nutrition to guide her family's eating healthfully the vegetarian way.

One Man's Meat Is Another Man's Poison

Finally, here is a quote from an article in the *Medical Journal of the Royal Navy* (England), spring, 1956, by Surgeon Captain T. L. Cleave, of the Naval Medical Service: "At the North Pole the Eskimos are almost pure meat-eaters, rarely eating any plant foods at all. Per contra at the equator many races are almost pure plant-eaters living chiefly on roots such as the yam, cassava or sweet potato; or on cereals such as maize; or on a very wide range of fruits. . . . All meat-eating animals are accustomed to isolated big meals following a kill, whereas plant-eating creatures are usually eating something or other all day. This difference in meals is dictated by the plant food being so much more diluted than the meat foods, which necessitates a much longer time spent in consuming them.

"In these islands (England) we have descendants from northern races, such as the Vikings, and also descendants from southern races, such as the Romans. It is not surprising, therefore, that some, especially perhaps the fair ones, will be predominantly meat-eaters and will lack the so-called sweet tooth; whereas others, especially perhaps the dark ones, will be predominantly plant-eaters and will have the sweet tooth highly developed. The former will tend to prefer an infrequent big meal; the latter, frequent little meals.

"With all these differences, it is easy to see the very great importance of following the appetite; that one man's meat truly is another man's poison; and that the size and frequency of meals will vary greatly from one individual to another. It is also easy to see how heedless of the natural law must be the conception that the plant foods are better than the meat foods, as vegetarians are liable to postulate—for some people, especially perhaps the blond ones—the exact opposite is true."

SECTION 23

EXERCISE

A most important function of your body which cannot be neglected if you would be healthy is exercise. For those who work at sedentary occupations especially, it is essential that you exercise in the open air every day. Walking is especially good for you, bringing all the muscles into play and providing oxygen for the tissues at a rapid rate. One should walk at least an hour a day, unless one can do some regular exercise equivalent to it each day, not only at weekends.

Walking regulates the glands, reduces a high pulse and is extremely valuable in heart conditions. The average heart case should gradually get used to walking at least an hour a day.

Posture is important for health. Good nutrition helps you to preserve good posture by strengthening muscles. Exercise helps, too. And remember to pull in your stomach muscles, so that back and shoulders are in line.

CHAPTER **76**

Exercise

by J. I. RODALE

The subject of exercise is so important to a heart case and to people who would like to prevent heart disease that I will go into the subject quite extensively. I have not only learned from my own experience how one can save one's life through daily exercise, but have found a terrific amount of information in the medical literature regarding the value of taking daily exercise.

There was a time when I used to pooh-pooh its value, and used to tell the story of Chauncey Depew, the famous financier of the last century, who lived to be way over 90, and who always deprecated the importance of taking exercise. "The only exercise I get," he used to say, "is to act as pallbearer for friends who used to take exercise."

We All Need Some Form of Exercise

Perhaps he didn't take exercise as such, but I'll wager he was a big walker, for those were the days before the auto was known. He was a stockholder in many corporations and was known to attend many board meetings, going from one to another, sometimes merely to show his face and to collect the director's fee. But there is a reason why some persons live to 90 without exercise, and why others die at 50. It is a matter of the vitality endowment at birth, the condition of the glands, chest expansion, width of arteries, etc. If a man has chosen the right ancestors and received a good share of their physical perfection through the accident of birth, then he can break many health rules and still live to a ripe old age.

Mark Twain was another exercise scoffer. He used to say,

"Whenever I feel like exercising, I lie down until the feeling passes." But Mark Twain became very sick and died before his time. He no doubt did not have the physical endowment of Chauncey Depew.

One need not spend hours in daily calisthenics. Walking furnishes a very interesting form of exercise, although at least 10 minutes of daily setting-up exercises can be very valuable. I strongly recommend a walk of at least an hour a day. Some people seem to forget that they have feet. They forget that there is such a thing as walking. The other day in visiting a hospital I walked down two flights of stairs, and a nurse remarked, in amazement, "Are you *walking* down?"

Exercise for Heart Conditions

A doctor in a medical journal says, "The popular picture of the coronary heart disease victim is that of a burly business or professional man, fat and soft from overeating and lack of exercise." Another expresses it this way, "Motion is the essence of life. Like all things pertaining to life, we know little concerning it. It is an inherent characteristic of all animate things to move through space with ease and power, not only for protection but for the pleasure of doing so." I have learned to love my daily hour's walk, and wouldn't miss it for anything except rain or snow. In fact, I'm arranging to spend my winters in Florida so that I can walk all year round.

Dr. Paul D. White, the President's heart specialist, told a House Appropriations Subcommittee, "Coronary thrombosis is an epidemic . . . Wise exercise is one remedy."

As Elbert Hubbard said, "The mintage of wisdom is to know that rest is rust, and that real life is in love, laughter and work." But today the sleeping pill is the symbol of our sedentary age. People can't sleep because they do not tire themselves out by enough movement during the day. They spend hours slumped in front of their television sets. The man who created the internal combustion chamber that furnished the activating power for the automobile killed millions of people before their time. How can we undo the auto? The instinct of the bear in his cage tells him that he must walk up and back. But man in his cage has a blunted instinct. Even doctors who should know better violate this important rule. That is why doctors have 12 times as high a death rate from angina pectoris as farm workers.

As far as I'm concerned, I'm conscious of the fact that I have to move about as much as possible, in order to keep the fat out of my heart muscle. I have my telephone at another desk. Every time it rings I have to walk 15 feet to it and 15 feet back. My office is on the third floor, and every day I walk up and down, to and from it at least 4 or 5 times—sometimes more, because I purposely do not have a buzzer system. When I want to talk to one of my people, I go to them. I do not make them come to me.

A World of "Sitters"

There is too much sitting in this civilized world of ours. Cotton Mather in his book, *Angel of Bethesda*, 1724, said, "Scriveners, Tailors, and others sitt still, with little Motion of their Bodies, in the Work of their Hands, must think of frequent Exercise, to stir their Limbs. Be sure, Students and Men that lead sedentary lives, will do well to be on Horse-back, as much as they can."

John Homans, M.D., in *The New England Journal of Medicine*, January 28, 1954, said, "The prolonged sitting position occasions a degree of dependency stasis that may result in the rapid development of a quiet type of thrombosis in the deep veins of the calf. From this, a propagation of clot and pulmonary embolism may immediately follow. . . . Such matters are important enough to suggest the advisability of making movements of the toes, feet and lower legs when one is sitting for long periods and of getting up and exercising when opportunity offers. The right leg seems more susceptible than the left. There is evidence that persons over 50 years of age should have this particularly in mind and that physicians should be alert to recognize the significance of lameness after airplane flights, automobile trips and other occasions of a prolonged seated position."

At the theatre always take a walk during intermission.

Too Much Rest for Heart Cases

I would like to present a letter that Dr. Bernard E. Myers of London sent to the *British Medical Journal*, which was published in its July 31, 1954, issue:

"Sir,—Recently I went on a cruise to the Mediterranean and was appalled that two people died from heart complaints, one of whom was buried at sea. Another heart case had to be put ashore at Naples for hospital treatment. In addition, at least 5 other patients spent most of the cruise in the ship's hospital, of whom 4 were heart cases and one had a lung condition. Obviously, patients so severely ill are a great worry and anxiety to the ship's doctor, and depressing to other passengers. The doctor informed me that investigation has shown in many such instances that heart cases have been advised by their doctors to go on a cruise for the benefit of their health, but what of the danger and the sorrowing relatives on board?— I am, etc."

This doctor overlooks the fact that there is so much sitting about on these cruises.

If you have to do a lot of sitting at home, a good way to do it is in a rocking chair. This counteracts all the disadvantages of ordinary sitting and is a pleasant activity. It also stirs up the liquid in the spine and is an aid in the prevention of the petrification of the back. But don't look at television in a rocker, unless you can make the television set move in the same rhythm as the rocker. I tried it and after several months began to experience trouble with my eyes.

The Body Was Built for Movement

Dr. Laurence E. Morehouse, Professor of Physical Education at the University of California, said that the human body was built for the rigors of the hunt, and when the body's connective tissue is not exercised, it shortens and thickens, causing pressure on nerves, producing sensitivity and pain and upsetting the endocrine balance. "Movements of skeletal muscles in man," he says, "not only performed his external work in primitive days, but also acted as supplemental heart muscles in moving fluids through the body.

"The modern sitting man relies on his heart muscles alone to pump the fluids which support the internal environment of the body. The heart cannot do the job of circulation without the aid of other muscle pumps and sitting man soon begins to suffer."

Dr. Edward P. Luongo of Los Angeles in a report to an American Medical Association convention described a study of 100 heart cases in the 40-to-50-year-old age group, and stated that 70 of them showed no regular exercise patterns either at work or away from their jobs. Dr. Charles H. Bradford, at an

Eastern regional meeting of the International College of Surgeons in 1957 said that "Nature did not intend the intricate cardiac mechanism to serve a sedentary body. Certainly, the stimulus of natural exercise plays a wholesome part in regulating metabolic disorders."

Dr. E. R. Tretheave, of the Department of Physiology, University of Melbourne, writing in the May 12, 1956, issue of *The Medical Journal of Australia* says, "The cardiac patient, if he does not exercise himself within the limits of his heart's performance, finds his cardiac muscle is not favored thereby. It is also becoming recognized by some medical observers that the sedentary life in itself may be a contributory factor to certain cardiac illnesses."

Place the Blame on Inactivity—Not Insecurity

Dr. N. E. Chadwick, health officer of the city of Hove, England, claims that the increasing speed and strain of modern life is wrongly blamed for illnesses and early death. Insecurity, in some form, he says, has been present with every generation, but today's killer is inactivity.

Dr. Burgess L. Gordon of Philadelphia dogtrots each morning to his train and walks briskly to his appointments. "It's the habit of taking things easy most of the time and then placing a sudden strain on the body in an emergency that is dangerous."

Dr. Roy M. Keller, *Journal of Medical Physical Research* (September, 1953), says, "Inactivity does not utilize energy, and causes a damming back to the liver and a lowering of differentials (electric) and impaired function. Utilization of energy in the body is one situation in which one can eat his cake and keep it too." We must use or lose.

Dr. W. Pinnington Jenson in *The Lancet* of June 19, 1954: "Cardiovascular wear and tear is associated with the 7 fat years rather than the 7 lean ones, and the 7 fat years do not mean merely increased fat percentage of total calories, but increased percentage of mechanical transport, sedentary occupation, and nervous as opposed to physical exertion."

Dr. Joseph W. Still of George Washington University School of Medicine: "In our advice to the aged I believe we should generally emphasize activity, rather than rest. My observation is that older people tend to be too sedentary and I think this tendency must be combatted."

Many physicians advise their patients against climbing stairs. Except in rare cases, according to the best opinion today, this is a great blunder. In a recent issue of Bernarr Macfadden's *Joyous Life* (December, 1954) Macfadden says, "When President Harding was serving as a Senator, he signed a testimonial which we published in *Physical Culture Magazine*, in which he stated that he cured his heart trouble by climbing stairs."

I am a heart case and as I have said a few moments ago, I climb two flights of stairs 4 or 5 times every day, and have hardened myself because of it. I can now accomplish it without becoming winded. So many of my visitors come up to my office puffing terribly. It is a sign that they don't exercise every day.

Some years ago I visited a man who wanted to show me some paintings that were on the second floor of his home. He crept up the stairs on his hands and knees. I was informed that he was a heart case. I met him recently and commented about it, and he replied that he no longer did it. Evidently someone had put a scare into him.

Frederick Othman in his column in *The N. Y. World Telegram* (July 17, 1956) mentions a bill in the Senate to appropriate almost two billion dollars, part of which, or 50,000 dollars, was for the purpose of building an elevator in the federal courthouse at Anderson, South Carolina, which is a two story building. Senator Paul H. Douglas, Democrat of Illinois, demanded, "Am I to understand that the judges in South Carolina are so infirm that they can't climb a flight and a half of stairs?"

Quoting Mr. Othman: "The gentleman from South Carolina said he meant that the judges' doctors had recommended that they go easy on stair-climbing. This is hard on the judicial heart beat. 'Some new judges might be cheaper than a 50,000 dollar elevator,' snapped Senator Douglas."

As you see, some doctors are still suggesting no stair-climbing. And in New York they are clamoring for electrical escalators for all subway stations, which is part of a growing movement for reducing our daily quota of exercise and which is going to shorten our lives. Dr. Richard T. Smith, director of the Department of Rheumatology, of the Pennsylvania Hospital, recently said that human life may well be shortened below its potential by lack of both physical and mental activity. He said, "The heart is a muscle and must have maintenance of tone. It is not the athletic heart that kills us, but lack of it."

Exercise Means Longer Life

The fact that life can be prolonged by exercise is described by Dr. Raymond Pearl, the famous Johns Hopkins researcher, in his book, *The Biology of Death* (page 212). An experiment was performed with rats. The group that exercised lived longer than the one that led a sedentary existence.

In spite of all this evidence that our national inactivity is very harmful, little is being done to remedy it. But articles are beginning to appear with titles such as "Lack of Physical Fitness in U. S. Blasted by Government Official," "Muscular State of the Union," "Nation of Softies," "Nutrition Expert Bemoans Our Horror of Exercise," "N.Y.U. Head Decries Lack of Exercise," etc., etc., etc.

Fears Loss of Essential Vitality

Shane McCarthy, executive director of President Eisenhower's Council on Youth Fitness, said recently, "The tremendous aptitude for inactivity among Americans might end in a human erosion that could strip the nation of its strength within the next generation." Speaking at the Eastern College Athletic Conference, on December 13, 1956, he said that over 34 per cent of the draftees examined in October were rejected because they lacked physical fitness. Talking about his own sons, he said, "They all share one ambition. That is to become 16 so they can sit behind the wheel of an automobile."

In a test of the physical condition of American children as against those in Italy and Austria, 78 per cent of the Americans failed, whereas only $8\frac{1}{2}$ per cent of the Europeans could not pass. College freshmen have been becoming taller, but more lacking in endurance. This tendency in our youth to move less is bound to result in more heart disease when they grow up.

Is this enough? I can give you much more on the dangers of a sedentary life, but there are more aspects of the general subject of exercise which will have to be covered. So, whether you have heart disease or not, get out and move. Walk, do setting-up exercise, go window-shopping—any kind of movement will suffice. You will never regret it.

CHAPTER 77

Exercise–What It Does

by J. I. RODALE

Exercise is a powerful force for good, so far as health is concerned.

The most important thing that exercise does is to oxygenate the body, which is most desirable to a heart case, for it is lack of oxygen which is an important element in inducing a heart attack. Oxygenation of the body may be compared to the draft of a boiler which burns up the refuse and slag in the body.

Dr. Wm. B. Kountz, Professor of Clinical Medicine at Washington University, at a public meeting recently said that the medical profession has long been aware that a decline in the body's oxygen consumption causes such ailments as hardening of the arteries, heart disease, body-wasting and other typical manifestations of old age. This is important, he said, in the maintaining of the burning or oxidative process of the body. *The Journal of the American Medical Association* of September 15, 1956, states that when the oxygen supply to the tissues goes down, the number and size of the cells also decreases. This causes tissue atrophy, or aging. Thus, by taking exercise, and insuring the oxygenation of the body, one ages gracefully.

Another effect of oxygen was demonstrated by Dı. D. B. Hill of Harvard, who proved that the man who takes regular exercise requires "less oxygen to perform the same amount of work, mental or physical, than the man who does not" (*Time,* February 4, 1957). In other words, the person who takes daily exercise can turn out more work. Exercise also burns up sugar.

Angina pectoris, a disease marked by a sudden or periodic chest pain, sometimes with a feeling of suffocation and impending death, is due most often to lack of oxygen in the muscular substance of the heart; that is, the heart muscle.

Muscular Tone Improved

Another effect of exercise is to maintain the general muscular tone throughout the body. This includes the heart muscle, the importance of whose tone can well be realized. An important muscle is the diaphragm which, if its muscular tone improves, will enable a person to breathe more efficiently. This means healthier lungs. The diaphragm is like the piston of a pump in its action, and if it has good tone, it can more efficiently cause the suction of blood into the heart via the great veins. Exercise breaks up congestion in the lungs. Breathing becomes easier.

Exercise Aids Circulation

The effect of exercise is to quicken the circulation. *Science News Letter* of November 3, 1951, says in this respect:

"In a man at rest about a gallon of blood is circulated every minute . . . approximately the entire blood supply visits the tissues once every minute. With vigorous exercise these visits may be 8 or 9 times as frequent. The blood, instead of traveling at a rate of 55 feet a minute in the large arteries may move 450 feet a minute. This makes possible a more rapid and complete removal of waste from all parts of the body, and increases the amount of oxygen in parts of the body depending on it. Exercise taken simply and regularly tends to keep the arteries soft, warding off arteriosclerosis or other old age conditions."

The aorta, one of the blood vessels that convey blood to and from the heart, will maintain a more even flow of blood if it becomes more elastic through exercise. It is through the compression of the veins that blood is pumped into the heart. Good muscular tone causes them to do this job better. Good muscular structure will also prevent a blood clot.

The veins have valves which are there to stop the blood from going the wrong way. If the muscular structure is good, the veins have good compression and are thus able to pump the blood to the heart more easily. If not, stasis, or a slackening of the blood flow, can occur.

Dr. Paul D. White, the President's heart specialist, in a medical article (*Journal of the American Medical Association,* September 7, 1957) stated that exercise improves bowel function and digestion. It also helps to induce sleep, more "than any medicine, highball or television show." It controls obesity, and, most important, takes the fat out of the walls of the coronary and other important arteries. This is one of the most important rewards of exercise. It reduces the cholesterol level of the blood.

Three doctors at the Sinai Hospital in Detroit proved this in experiments with rabbits. "The amount of atherosclerosis present in the exercise group at the end of that time appeared to be distinctly less than that in the sedentary group, and chemical tests (cholesterol) showed the same thing." This was written up in the *Proceedings of the Society for Experimental Biology and Medicine* (December, 1957). The same thing was shown in 20 men who were hard physical laborers and who also took a high caloric diet rich in fats. Their cholesterol level was lower than average (*Journal of the American Medical Association,* September 22, 1956, p. 423).

According to the *British Medical Journal* (October 22, 1955), the low cholesterol levels found in Guatemalans and Africans are not attributed to their limited diets but to the muscular activity and energy expenditure required in these cultures. "Reflection will show that such an explanation is at least as compatible with the available observations as is the dietary fat explanation which has been so widely advocated. When this effect of exercise was examined experimentally in human subjects, it was found that doubling the calorie intake of young men who were consuming a very high fat diet did not increase the serum cholesterol or lipoprotein levels so long as the excess energy was expended in physical activity."

Higher Specific Gravity

Besides lowering the cholesterol level of the blood, exercise increases the specific gravity of the body, making the tissues more compact. This is highly desirable in connection with the body's general economy, but especially in regard to the functioning of the heart.

Dr. William Brady, in the *Chicago Daily News* of January 2, 1958, says that daily exercise—a brisk walk of several miles—causes the body to store up calcium. In other words, walking or other exercise promotes calcium metabolism. The reverse, says Dr. Brady, is also true. Prolonged confinement to bed or too much resting depletes the calcium reserve. That is why in so many cases a hip is broken after a bed-fast patient begins to move about. Many very old persons fall down, and it is thought that as a result they break their hip. Now it is believed that the hip is broken first, which then causes the fall.

The Effect of Exercise on Glandular Activity

Exercise causes added vitamins to be absorbed by the body, especially vitamin A (*Journal of Nutrition,* April 10, 1958). This is probably due to better oxygenation and through improved digestion.

Exercise causes all the glands to secrete their hormones, digestive acids, enzymes and other substances. For example, after a few moments of walking, the adrenal cortex gland begins to secrete cortisone. Is it possible that lack of exercise, and the failure to secrete sufficient cortisone, is one of the causes of arthritis? Then artificial cortisone is given, but it is nothing like the original natural product produced by the adrenal cortex, and in many cases caused dangerous side effects. The substances secreted by the adrenal cortex feed the brain. Thus, walking or other exercise could well be a valuable stimulation to better mental activity.

According to the *Journal of the American Medical Association* (October 5, 1957), "The greatest value (of exercise) lies in its stimulating effect on endocrine (glands) activity, perhaps the thyroid in particular, and in overcoming the tendency to sleep and snooze, too much a counterpart of obesity." When the endocrine glands are reduced in efficiency, a common occurrence with old people, it contributes to the fatigue of old age, which shows the importance of regular exercise for older persons.

Exercise Affects Every Part of the Body

Soviet doctor Vladimir Filatov in *My Path in Science,* in speaking about glaucoma, where the main symptom is increased tension inside the eyeball, said, "Another useful auxiliary treatment is increased muscular activity. I pointed out the value of this method for the regulation of intra-ocular tension as early as 1937. Observations on a number of patients showed lowering of the intra-ocular tension after long walks."

Dr. Paul Dudley White, the President's heart physician, in the *New York Times Magazine,* June 23, 1957, said: "Another part of the circulatory apparatus helped by exercise is that of the smallest blood vessels, arterioles, capillaries and venules, which are rendered more active in their function by their response to regular exercise. The peripheral vessels of the hands, the feet and the ears react beneficially with less likelihood of sluggishness and stasis (a stopping of the circulation.)"

There isn't a part of the body that doesn't seem to be aided by exercise and muscular activity.

Dr. William T. Foley of the New York Hospital, Cornell Medical Center, has worked out a "walking cure" for gangrene of the feet and legs. Says the *Science News Letter* of June 1, 1957, "Amputations were avoided and the gangrenous condition healed in 21 out of 22 cases when the patients got out of bed and walked around in spite of the ailment. . . . The gangrene was a complication of various circulatory diseases that had cut down the flow of the blood to the feet or legs. The customary practice is to keep such patients in bed and off their feet, but then the blood flow decreases even further and muscles begin to shrivel up.

"Along with the rest of the medical profession," Dr. Foley says, "we were hesitant to allow patients with gangrenous limbs to walk. The success of our surgical colleagues, however, in the treatment of fractures by exercise suggested that we might profit by their experience." So—even fractures are helped by exercise. Dr. Foley prohibits smoking in gangrene, since it constricts blood vessels and may cause the gangrene to return.

Pulse Lowered Through Exercise

Another very desirable effect of exercise is the reduction of the pulse if it is too high. (This will be covered in the several chapters on the pulse.) A high pulse is an invitation to a heart attack, and should not be tolerated by a heart case. With a little effort you can control your pulse.

An important consequence of exercise is the enlargement of the coronary arteries. *The Lancet,* December 12, 1953, p. 1261, says, "The more you exercise, the bigger your coronary arteries; the more you exercise, the faster the blood flows through them and the more difficult it is for an obstruction to develop on the walls." This authority says further, "I have for some time been considering various exercises with a view to providing the optimum coronary protection. I think skipping is the best, but people are intolerant of it, and for the ordinary person, dancing of the Scottish country type is the most practicable proposition."

Earl Ubell, science editor of the *New York Herald Tribune* (July 7, 1957) said, "It is possible that exercise can increase the number of branches of the coronary artery going into the heart and provide additional channels for blood flow in case one of the vessels becomes blocked with the fatty substances like cholesterol." Dr. C. F. Wilkinson of the New York University Post Graduate School of Medicine, in the Allentown, Pennsylvania, *Evening Chronicle* (February 19, 1958) stated, "The arteries which feed the heart do not connect with each other, so if one of these vessels is blocked quickly, the muscle which feeds it receives no blood. If, however, the blockage is slow, the heart changes its blood vessel pattern by forming connections between the narrow vessel and another one. These connections cannot be formed rapidly.

"If an individual has been taking a relatively constant amount of exercise over a period of years, and has had a slow narrowing of the coronary arteries, it is quite likely that he has formed these connecting vessels."

Common Sense Says Exercise

Dr. Richard W. Eckstein of Western Reserve University, Cleveland, Ohio, working with a group of animals, showed that "when the artery which winds around the top of the heart is narrowed in dogs, collateral growth is improved by exercise." *The Medical Journal of Australia* (May 17, 1958) states, "The capillary network of athletes' hearts is unusually richly developed." The article says also, "It has been said that man's first mistake was the wheel . . . while it would undoubtedly be better for the general health if everybody used their muscles—cardiac and skeletal—to a much greater extent than is usual in the wealthier countries, it is doubtful whether this will happen on any large scale, and modern medicine must develop some other means of compensating for the disturbed central nervous and peripheral neurovegetative equilibrium if we want to escape further degeneration. Meanwhile, common sense says: 'Exercise.' " In fact, the data in this article would certainly indicate that, if you are a heart case, the height of common sense would be to be sure to exercise every day.

CHAPTER 78

The Importance of Exercise

Here are some suggested exercises to try. You will notice almost at once the beneficial effect on your health in general.

A friend of ours decided to mow his big lawn one hot Saturday afternoon and went at it with vigor and determination. He wouldn't stop until he had finished slicing off the last tuft of crabgrass. That night he went to the hospital with a heart attack. He had overestimated his own capacity for violent exercise. Every fall the newspapers carry stories of businessmen who have heart attacks while they are out scouring the hills on all-day hunting trips.

Medical authorities are pretty well agreed on the fact that exercise, especially in competitive games, can be quite dangerous after you've reached middle age. *The Journal of the American Medical Association* for June 21, 1952, carried an editorial headed "Exercise Is Good—For What?" They call it a medieval therapy and comment: "Abundant medical evidence shows that with few exceptions strenuous exercise does not give increased resistance to disease, does not promote longer life, does not improve 'health'; rather it may damage the heart, cause temporary anemia and avitaminosis, produce strains, sprains and fractures and make a person better able to do only one thing—exercise."

It is known that harm can come from competitive athletics; we have heard of cases of heart attack and other serious disorders brought on by unaccustomed vigorous exercise which seems to become more hazardous if there is competition involved, which make the panting, exhausted participant struggle on in spite of his fatigue, so that the "team" will come out ahead. Such exercise is harmful. It is harmful, also, to overdo exercise that comes under the heading of work. An office worker who spends Saturday in the unaccustomed pastime of mowing a large lawn or getting an overdose of gardening or carpentering in the hot sun is courting trouble.

Mild Exercise Is Beneficial

However, we believe that mild exercise has a place in the annals of good health, especially for those of us who lead a completely sedentary life, and get our only exercise swinging from the strap of a bus or subway, or pressing our feet to accelerator pedals or brakes. Exercise does increase the body's intake of oxygen which is especially important for someone who works inside all day. It does stimulate the circulation of blood. It brings about healthful changes in the bone marrow. It rests certain parts of the body that have been in positions of strain or tension, and, most important of all, the correct exercises improve posture.

Exercise Systems and Their Value

There are almost as many systems of exercise for good posture as there are people who teach exercising, for everyone has developed his own system which, he claims, is better than any other. But if you study these exercises carefully you will find that they all aid in doing one job—strengthening those muscles which support the body in an upright, well-balanced position. Your body has a set of muscles which hold it upright, carefully matched, so that the muscles which pull you forward are teamed with those which pull you back. When one or another of these muscles becomes weakened, the pull is stronger from the opposing muscle, and bad posture results.

There are few of us that can boast of perfect posture. Among younger folks there is a tendency for shoulders to droop and chests to become flat and hollow. Among older people a tendency toward sway-back complicates things still further. As the muscles of your abdomen are weakened, there is more of a drag on the back muscles, pulling the spine down into an ugly, exaggerated curve. The pelvic structure tilts forward. If the stomach muscles are allowed to sag, the buttocks are bound to protrude, to keep your center of balance undisturbed. So you find more and more older people developing into a peculiar S shape (Fig. 1). In the body's effort to preserve good balance, the knees turn in, the feet turn out, and gradually, the curve in the back becomes more pronounced.

Exercise For Good Posture

Fig. 1   Most posture exercises are designed to correct these faults. And most of us need these exercises. They should be done slowly, as slowly as possible. Lie on the floor (or, if you prefer, on a bed), and put a hand behind the small of your back. You will probably find that although your shoulders and buttocks touch the floor, there is a hollow large enough for your fist right beneath the small of your back. Bend your knees, keeping your feet on the floor. This should enable you to flatten your entire spine along the floor, so that there is no hollow place left (Fig. 2). Now, lower your feet gradually, trying to keep your

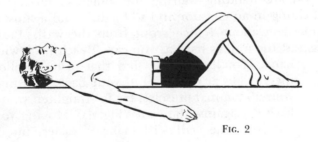

Fig. 2

back flat on the floor. This will strengthen the back and abdominal muscles. A very few minutes of this exercise every day for several months should enable you to hold your abdominal muscles in when you stand erect, so that the "sway-back" will gradually disappear.

Here is a more difficult exercise. Lie flat on the floor—the bed is too soft for this one. Raise your feet a little off the floor and you will feel a strong pull on your abdominal muscles

(Fig. 3). Lower your feet, and the next time try to raise them a

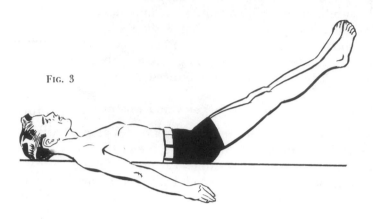

FIG. 3

little farther. Don't hurry. You must exercise slowly if you want it to be effective.

If you don't have time to go through these muscle-strengtheners every day, you can accomplish the same thing while you are standing waiting for someone, talking on the phone, riding in an elevator and so forth. Stand against a wall, with your feet about 4 inches out from the wall. Push your back against the wall as hard as you can. Reach back with your hand. You'll probably find that ornery hollow still there, right at the small of your back. Pulling in on your abdominal muscles, try to straighten your whole back flat against the wall (Fig. 4). Moving your feet out from the wall will make it easier, but as you become more expert you should slide your feet closer to the wall.

Now, after you have managed to strengthen the abdominal muscles enough that the hollow in your back disappears when you stand against the wall, try your best to remember to pull those muscles in all day long wherever you are, whatever you are doing. You will find it is almost impossible to pull in your stomach muscles while your chest droops. So while you are pulling in below, watch how your chest rises. Soon you will be standing straight and well-balanced.

FIG. 4

If your main trouble is drooping shoulders and hollow chest, it is necessary to strengthen the shoulder and chest muscles. Sit on the floor, with your legs straight in front of you, or, if it is more comfortable, cross your legs, or put your feet on the floor and bend your knees. Rest your fingers on your shoulders, lift your arms up, forward, backward and down again (Fig. 5). Can you feel the pull on those shoulder and chest muscles?

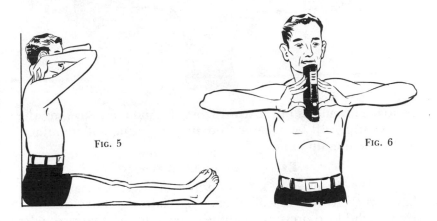

Fig. 5   Fig. 6

Here is one very simple exercise for strengthening chest muscles—and this means a more attractive bustline for the ladies. Stand up straight and tall, pulling in your abdominal muscles. Pick up a quite heavy book. A telephone directory or a desk dictionary will do nicely. Bend your arms and raise your elbows up level with your chin. This will bring your hands directly in front of your face. Hold the book between the fingertips of both hands and press as hard as you can (with your fingers and thumbs) as if you were trying to push right through the book on both sides. Do not use the flat part of your hand— only your fingers (Fig. 6). And don't overdo this exercise the first day or you'll have sore muscles.

Early Morning Exercises

Most of us could do with some toning up when we get out of bed in the morning. Editor Rodale suggests one exercise which he performs every morning, first thing, to wake him up, get his blood to circulating freely, and dispose of the lazy feeling

across arms, shoulders, neck and head. He stands straight and
tall, and raises his arms at the sides to shoulder height. Then,
keeping his elbows stiff, he rotates his arms in small circles, first
clockwise, then counterclockwise (Fig. 7). In fact, any firm,

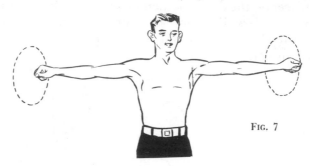

FIG. 7

regular movements of the arms from the shouders, keeping the
elbows stiff, will be a handy aid in preventing stiff shoulders
and loosening up joints.

Exercising Under Water

We recently ran across a series of exercises that we feel
have much to recommend them, especially for folks suffering
from high blood pressure or some other disorder that precludes
strenuous exercise. They are based on the fact that the body
weighs less under water! A 140-pound person weighs only about
10 pounds when he is submerged in water. So doing exercises
under water is much easier. With a very small amount of exertion, the muscles can get a good workout and all the benefits of
exercise can be had without any strain on the heart. It just
involves filling up your bathtub with water at body temperature
and exercising in the bathtub.

The 76-year-old Englishman who invented this method
of exercise became quite famous in the pages of the conservative
British Medical Journal and *The Lancet,* when a number of
British physicians began to realize what a boon such exercises
would be to their heart patients and patients who were partially
bedfast. T. R. Togna, the inventor of the exercises, did careful
experiments to prove how blood pressure, plus rate of oxygen
intake varied during the process of exercising in a bathtub full
of water.

He found that the pulse rate increased only slightly
above normal during 15 or 20 minutes of bathtub exercise,

whereas a similar amount of regular exercise might increase it a great deal. He found that blood pressure is generally reduced. There is no increase when the blood pressure is normal. If it is high, the exercise reduces it. If it is low, it is raised toward normal. He also found that the amount of oxygen intake for each pulse beat is high, with, of course, excellent results from a health standpoint, because plenty of oxygen is an essential for health.

Bathtub Exercises

He suggests massaging the body while you are exercising so that the by-products of metabolism will be swept away rapidly in the blood stream. Here are some of Mr. Togna's exercises you might want to try tomorrow morning when you are bathing. Water in the bathtub should be about 6 inches from the top after you are in the tub. Lie down with your head resting on the end of the tub. Stretch your legs out full length. Double your right hand into a fist in front of your chest while you bend your right knee and bring it up out of the water (Fig. 8). Then

Fig. 8

lower the right leg and stretch the right arm out on top of the water, while you bring up the left leg, and so forth. It is pretty much like bicycling, with your arms moving in unison with your legs except, of course, that your body has little weight, so there is very little exertion.

Then for a second exercise, as you bend your knees, massage them and your thighs just before you lower them into the water again. Another excellent bathtub exercise involves lying with your hands below you, bracing the buttocks. Raise the trunk so that it is suspended in the water. Then, do the exercise once again with the hands resting on the abdomen. Massage the abdomen while you are raising and lowering the trunk in the water.

Waist twisting is done in the same position by pivoting on the toes and swinging the body from side to side while the head and feet remain stationary (Fig. 9). As you become more

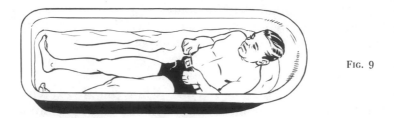

FIG. 9

adept at twisting from side to side, vary the exercise by bending one knee at a time and crossing it over the other knee (Fig. 10).

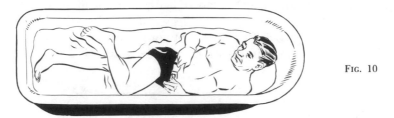

FIG. 10

If you find the twisting exercises too difficult, lay a straight rod across the bathtub and support yourself with it as you twist and turn.

Principle of Exercise—Gentle, Slow Movement

Finally, let us remind you of perhaps the most elementary principle of exercise, which is that almost any form of gentle and slow movement will rest muscles that are tired from being in one position too long. If you bend over your work all day, whether your work be reading, writing, typing, drawing, cooking or what not—stop frequently and turn your head from side to side, slowly and gently. Or stand up and bend over from the waist. Let your whole upper body hang as limp as possible. Let your arms dangle as though they belonged to a rag doll. When you straighten up, you will be surprised at the relaxed feeling in those tired muscles.

In general, keep in mind that violent rapid exercise which makes you puff and pant and get red in the face, not only brings you no benefit, but can actually do you harm.

Simple, slow, stretching exercises are beneficial, especially if they rest some tired, cramped muscle, or if they improve posture. And improving posture nearly always boils down to pulling in on abdominal muscles, tucking your buttocks underneath you and raising your chest, until you have achieved really superb posture.

Fig. 11

CHAPTER **79**

Everybody Needs Some Exercise

The official nod is given by the Journal of the American Medical Association *on the subject of exercise. They're for it—and so are we! Here are some more reasons why.*

Most persons think of exercise only as a means of losing weight, and if they are satisfied with their weight level, they simply leave exercise out of their health picture. That this attitude is unwise is stressed by the recommendations in an article on exercise carried in the *Journal of the American Medical Association,* April 5, 1958.

The need for some form of regular exercise, says the article, is based upon the fact that the body becomes more efficient when rigors of regular exercises are imposed upon it. For example, the normal heart and circulatory system respond to exercise by improved and more economical pumping action of the heart. The demand for increased circulation due to extended exercise results in a physiological readjustment which makes this new facility second nature. The body gets so used to supplying the added needs that it, so to speak, "forgets" to return to its sluggish performance of before. This same phenomenon occurs with every other faculty of the body. With added demands through regular exercise, the organs and muscles get stronger, can do more and tire less easily.

How Much Exercise?

When beginning a regular series of exercises, people first want to know how much they should do. They don't want to hurt themselves by making physical demands that their bodies are incapable of meeting. Doctors say the chances of healthy persons overdoing exercises are not very great. Usually the individual stops or reduces his exercise long before his actual physical limits are reached. Fatigue or the natural fear of doing too much are the safety valves that save one from any real danger. We suggest that those new to exercise start easily and carefully. Stop when fatigue sets in, rest and begin again, or wait until the next scheduled exercise period. Remember that exhaustion is not the aim of exercise. Overexercising is not necessary, for you will notice that even the slightest increases in exercise effort, as you feel ready for them, will soon become automatic and increase your endurance almost without your being aware of the effort involved.

Who Should Exercise?

Is exercise good for everybody? Yes, if the person is in good health and aware of his limitations. It is a physiological fact that muscle power is on the increase in most individuals into early adulthood—around the early twenties. The exercise natural to growing youngsters accounts for this in large measure. At age 30 or 40 there is a gradual decline in muscle strength. There is no unchangeable law of nature that forces this to occur, but people of this age bracket are likely to avoid exercise like the plague. They never walk when they can ride; they never lift something that can be wheeled; they never do anything by hand that can be done with a power tool. Is it any wonder that they decline in muscle strength? This is the age that demands a conscious effort to get needed exercise. Children don't need any encouragement to run, play, swim, etc., but a middle-ager needs determination to stretch his muscles and do so regularly.

Regularity is an important word in exercise planning. There are two reasons for this: one, it helps remind you to do it, if a time of day is set aside for exercise, a sort of appointment with oneself; two, without regularity, the progress one makes in a conditioning session one day might be completely lost if the advantage is not followed up by a bolstering workout the following day. It doesn't matter *when* you decide to have your daily period of exercise—morning, evening, any time—but do decide on a specific time of day.

What Kind of Exercise? Try Walking

Now what kind of exercise should one have? The answer to that depends largely on the individual. Do you like sports? Do you have children who will give you a workout in playing with them? Does the occasion for games that require physical effort arise regularly enough so that you can depend on them for exercise? Can you afford an electric exercise machine? Are you the type of person who can work with dumbbells and pulleys, or will you soon decide that it's too much trouble to assemble the necessary paraphernalia for each session?

We have come to the conclusion that walking is the perfect solution to a form of regular exercise. It requires no equipment, can be done alone or in a group at any time and is easily fitted into the schedule of just about anybody as a functional part of one's day. If you make a walk part of the trip to and from the office each day, it takes little time out of your day and accomplishes much for you. (Editor Rodale recommends an hour or two per day, if possible.)

Walking brings many of our vital muscles into play, muscles too seldom exercised since we ride so much. It brings us out into the fresh air, something else we get too little of, and brings plenty of health-giving oxygen into the blood stream. Another advantage of walking as an exercise lies in the fact that it is not too strenuous an activity, and, therefore, just about anybody of any age can indulge. If you get tired, fatigue comes gradually; you can turn around and go home long before any form of physical exhaustion can set in. There is no need to exert yourself, no need to finish the game, run one more yard, finish one last inning or set. When you walk and get tired, you can stop and sit down—even on a curb if you must, or in the grass under a shady tree. There's a lot to be said for walking as an exercise.

In the *Journal's* summary of the article, these points are

stressed: Start young with some form of regular exercise and continue at a good pace determined by experience; persons over 30 should not indulge in hard, fast, sustained games unless they have been maintaining an appropriate state of fitness; watch your ability to recuperate from an exercise session—if your heart is pounding for more than 10 minutes and the feeling of weakness persists, you'd better slow down.

We're happy to see recommendations for exercise in the *Journal* as an indication that orthodox medicine approves, as we do, of this natural measure for maintaining good health. We regard good diet as the most important way of insuring good health, but don't sell exercise short. Your body needs some every day. Make sure you get it!

CHAPTER **80**

Posture Is Important

If you have been exercising for years chances are your posture is everything it should be right now. If you haven't started a regular exercise program, better look to your posture which is ever so important for good health!

Stand on a street corner and watch the people pass. The vast majority of them have attractive faces, nice clothes, pleasant smiles. What then is it that gives this parade of human beings such a sorry woebegone look? Their posture! You may find one person in a hundred—man, woman or child—who holds his body correctly and walks as if he were glad he's alive. And that one in a hundred will probably turn out to be a model or a dancer or a gym instructor. The people whose livelihood necessitates a good figure and good posture have no choice. But how about the rest of us? How does it happen that we can go along, year after year, slumping, sagging, slouching as if we were made from rags instead of flesh and bones?

All of us know, or should know, what good posture is. If you don't, stand in front of a full length mirror, look at yourself in profile and imagine a plumb line dropped from the lobe of your ear to your foot. Half of you should be on each side of that line. Or have someone take a snapshot of you full length in profile, standing as you normally do. Then take a ruler and draw a line on the print. How does your posture look compared with the immutable straightness of that line?

The Result of Bad Posture

What happens when your posture is not good? If one part of your body slackens and slumps, other parts must, too, for otherwise, you could not keep your balance. The abdominal muscles are the part that is most likely to sag, especially in women who have had children. When these muscles sag, they pull on the small of the back so that a certain amount of sway-back becomes almost inevitable.

It is part of the function of the abdominal muscles and those of the lower back to keep the pelvic bones held in the proper position. When these muscles sag, the pelvis tilts forward. Organs that should be held in perfect position for functioning are thrown out of place. How can the stomach or intestines function properly when, because of bad posture, they are thrown together in a heap, rather than keeping to their separate, well-balanced locations?

If the abdominal muscles are slack and the lower back muscles reflect this slackness, then the shoulder and chest muscles are affected, too. The upper part of the back protrudes to balance the lower part which has caved in. So shoulders drop, chests flatten, chins jut out and round lumps of flesh begin to accumulate between the shoulder blades. Sound familiar?

Why Do We Have Bad Posture?

How do we permit ourselves to get into such terrible shape? How does it happen that primitive peoples everywhere still untouched by "civilization" walk proud and tall and even in middle and old age do not ever develop the paunches, stoop-shoulders and protruding buttocks that characterize just about everybody in our country? Food is important to good posture, of course. Lots of protein and calcium are absolute essentials for strong muscles. Boys and girls in their teens, using up what calcium and protein they get in their foods to add inches to their height, are likely to become round-shouldered. No amount of scolding will make them improve their posture—their muscles are probably not strong enough to hold their tall frames upright. Eating refined carbohydrates is responsible to a large extent for our bad posture. It puts on fat which makes a bigger load for our muscles, and it contributes nothing to the strength or health of those muscles. B vitamins are important for muscle health, and refined carbohydrates rob your body of B vitamins, too.

Another reason for our bad posture is, of course, the way we live. We are sedentary; we never walk when we can ride; we watch the dancing instead of participating ourselves; we walk on hard floors and hard sidewalks; we wear badly fitting and improper shoes. Primitive people walk barefoot. They carry loads, so they must learn to balance their bodies perfectly or the loads will spill. Shoes, sidewalks, floors, high heels—these attributes of civilization are unknown to the gracefully, perfectly poised men and women of primitive nations.

Exercise For Poor Posture

Once you have corrected your diet (and we hope all readers will), is there anything else you can do about poor posture? Yes, of course, there is. Almost any good book on the subject from your local library will give you exercises that you can do for 5 or 10 minutes a day or longer. As soon as we said the word "exercise," you probably lost interest, for it seems that the prospect of actually going through a set of exercises every day of your life is simply too much for most people to face. So, what about some exercises you can do while you are working, while you are reading the paper, traveling on the bus, riding in an elevator, washing the dishes?

The main object, remember, is to strengthen those abdominal muscles so that they will do their job of supporting the lower part of the body. The way to exercise them is to pull them in tautly and tightly. This may be impossible at first, if you have let them sag for years, but constant practice will help. Here's how to exercise those muscles. If you are standing—no matter what else you are doing—flex your knees slightly, tuck your lower back in as far as you can get it and pull in on your abdominal muscles. You will find that you automatically straighten your shoulders and lift your chest—can't help yourself.

A dozen times a day, back up against the wall of the room, place your feet about 6 inches out from the wall, bend your knees just a little, then press your back against the wall, tight as you can, all the way down. You will probably find that, right in the middle of your back there is a hollow place between you and the wall. Press back, trying your best to flatten that, too, against the wall. While you are doing this exercise, your abdominal muscles will be strengthened, and gradually—ever so gradually—your posture will improve.

You can do the same thing sitting in a chair. Sit straight, feet flat on the floor. Press your spine against the back of the chair trying to flatten it completely so that there is no space between you and the chair back. You can practice this exercise while you are working, watching TV, riding in the car, bus, or trolley.

Specialists in Adjusting Posture

The kind of mattress you use has a lot to do with posture, too. Soft beds are not beneficial. Your mattress should be firm, or, better yet, you should sleep with a bed board. One final word on posture. A friend of ours who is taking chiropractic treatments showed us X-ray pictures of his spine before and after a series of treatments. The very definite curvature in the "before" picture had been almost completely corrected in the "after" picture. It is well to remember that these members of the healing profession, chiropractors and osteopaths, specialize in adjusting posture, if you want to express it that way. They know better than anyone else what good posture is and they are better equipped to handle posture problems than anyone else.

CHAPTER **81**

General Principles of Posture

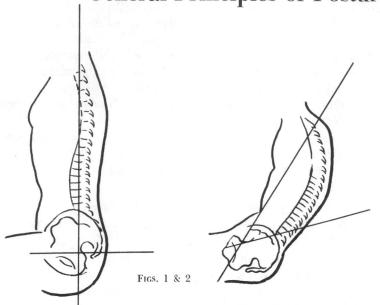

FIGS. 1 & 2

Here you can see what poor posture does to your spine.

Said Plato, "The most beautiful motion is that which accomplishes the greatest result with the least amount of effort." Leonardo da Vinci, one of the greatest anatomists that ever lived, believed that the center of gravity of the body was the most important single factor in good posture and graceful movement. Said he, "A man, in going upstairs, involuntarily throws so much weight forward and on the side of the upper foot as to be a counterpoise to the lower leg, so that the labor of his lower leg is limited to raising itself." He also pointed out that a man always throws the greatest amount of weight in the direction in which he is moving. So he is, in one sense, always pursuing his center of gravity. The faster he runs, the farther forward he leans, so that he throws more and more weight before him and then must catch up with it to keep from falling forward.

Later anatomists and physiotherapists decided that Leonardo was wrong—that movement in men was decided not by their center of gravity, but by the interplay of one muscle with another. If you want to step to the right, they said, the muscles of your right leg pull you in that direction, then the muscles of the left leg are activated to take the second step. Recently, however, we are beginning to return to Leonardo's theories concerning the importance of the center of gravity to movement and to posture.

Your center of gravity is, of course, the very center of your body if you were to draw imaginary lines horizontally and vertically through the middle of your silhouette. Your body is composed of certain masses grouped around your spinal column. So long as you keep these masses in alinement, so that your center of gravity remains actually *in the center of you,* you will have good posture. You will be able to move gracefully and efficiently, and you will not be bothered with all the many disorders that can result from bad posture. But as soon as you let one section of your anatomy get out of line, you must automatically adjust other sections so that you can remain upright. This means that another part of you must go out of line to balance that part already out of alinement.

High Heels Affect Your Center of Gravity

For example, consider for a moment the wearing of high heels. According to David H. Tribe, of the University of Queensland, writing in the *Medical Journal of Australia* for February 6, 1954, women who wear high heels spend the walking and standing part of their existence on an incline of about 30 degrees. To understand this, get yourself a board, prop it up at an angle of 30 degrees and stand on it barefoot. You will see at once that your whole body is thrown forward and you have to make certain adjustments in order to stay erect. You lock your knees, rather than keeping them slightly flexed or bent, which is the proper and healthful way to stand. Your hips are thrown back, and at once you develop a sway back—an ugly hollow in your lower back. To compensate for this exaggerated curve in your spine, your stomach protrudes and your chest flattens and sinks.

During the moment you stood on that board, you did yourself no harm, for your bones and muscles slipped back to normal as soon as you stepped off the board. But women who wear high heels force their bodies to assume this unnatural position all the time they are standing or walking. The harm that may be done can, of course, never be estimated, for who will ever be able to discover what drastic changes are brought about in internal organs when the bony cage that supports them is tilted at such an angle for 4, 6 or 8 hours a day?

How Do You Walk?

Take the matter of walking. During the past century it was considered polite to turn the toes out. As one anatomist of the 18th century, Peter Camper, put it, "The toes of gentlemen should always be turned out, those of peasants and particularly of boatmen, are always turned in." In the days when gentlemen wore knee breeches, it was mandatory to show off a well-turned calf. This could be done only in profile, so "toeing out" became fashionable. And it is only quite recently that we have seen the fallacy of such distortion and begun to teach our children in gym classes that the feet should be parallel when one walks. But the damage done to millions of older feet by "toeing out" has already been demonstrated on our older generation.

We used to believe that the toe should touch the ground first in walking—a thoroughly illogical idea, according to Dr. Tribe—for why, he asks, should we try to proceed with the weight bearing area advancing from front to back, when we wish to go forward! The mass of the body, which is to be supported, should, of course, be placed first on the heel, which is equipped to bear it, then should be gradually transferred to the toes as the forward step is taken. Is this the way you walk? Sometime when you are walking in light snow or sand, check your footprints to see whether you toe out and whether your weight is borne first on your heel when you take a step. You may be surprised at what the footprints reveal. The best way to correct "toeing out" is to set yourself with great deliberation and care to walking "pigeon-toed" for a while. You can easily do this while you are walking around the house or in the country where no one can see you. When you are going about your work, do your best to plant your feet parallel to one another, pointing directly in front of you.

How you walk is but one indication of the state of your posture. How do you sit? Dr. Tribe gives an interesting diagram showing how the various bones are arranged when you are sitting correctly (Figure 1) and when you are slumped (Figure 2). Notice how the center of gravity is thrown completely out of line when you slump, and all the bony structure must adjust itself to this condition. See how the whole pelvic basin is tilted backward. Obviously such a position affects more than bones.

Dr. Tribe tells us that slumping in a chair eliminates the normal curves of the back, forces the intestines down on the bladder and genital organs. The ribs are in a state of collapse so that breathing is hindered. The kidneys and liver are no longer supported by the curve of the spine and you may stretch too far the tissues that hold them in place resulting in a "floating" kidney or liver. Not breathing correctly may result in too little oxygen, tenseness, fatigue and so forth. Reading in this slouched position may cause you to hold the book too close to your eyes, bringing strain to the muscles that regulate the way your eyes focus.

The kind of chair you sit in is important for good posture, too. It should permit you to sit erect, without strain, and the bone on which you sit should have more cause to slide back in the chair rather than forward. The back of the chair should not come below the hips, as this may interfere with the lower curve of the back. You should be able to sit comfortably with both feet on the floor. And that is the way you should sit.

Dr. Tribe tells us that an investigation carried out by The National Health and Medical Research Council revealed that of 421 children examined, 66.5 per cent had postural deficiences and 46.3 per cent needed expert attention. We suppose that children in this country are not a bit better equipped so far as posture is concerned. "Yet the vast majority of people continue to sport postural defects unabashed and undismayed," says Dr. Tribe. "They suffer from the anatomical and physiological defects I have mentioned previously. Their vitality is poor, their appearance worse." Among the conditions they may be inviting are: flat feet, knock knees, bowlegs, sway-back, lateral curvature of the spine, protruding shoulder blades, humpback and osteoarthritis. He also tells us that a recent study has indicated that posture is related to personality. People with good posture have more self-reliance and self-respect than their slouching friends.

CHAPTER 82

Don't Let Poor Posture
Give You a Backache

Poor posture brings many a wrong alignment to body muscles and bones. Perhaps it may be a cause of backache. The health of your spinal column is definitely related to how you stand, sit and walk.

If the people of this country who suffer from back complaints of one kind or another ever form a club, they are sure to outnumber the D.A.R., Rotary International and the American Legion combined. That is why an article appearing in *The Canadian Medical Association Journal* of August, 1957, caught our attention. Written by Norman C. Delarue, B.A., M.D., M.S. (Tor.) F.R.C.S. [C], Toronto, the discussion not only suggests several possible reasons for the back pains that plague so many people, but it outlines several preventive exercises which can be done by the layman.

Dr. Delarue offers some very convincing evidence to show that backache is usually traceable to bad posture habits. Once these habits are formed, the body adjusts itself as best it can, but the spinal column cannot function well when it is tilted to an unnatural degree. Edges that were meant to be cushioned from one another by cartilage, meet and scrape, and, in time, pain makes standing erect almost unbearable.

Poor Posture Habits Start in Youth

Most of our poor posture habits are formed in our youth. In school and while working at homework in the evening, the child sits at a flat-topped desk, hunched over and leaning close to his work, deep in concentrated study. No wonder this position becomes second nature to him. In the interests of better posture, Dr. Delarue suggests desks with a tilted writing area and a flat margin above for reference books, pencils, etc. The seats should have contour backs and foot pedestals. These innovations would create in the student a tendency toward good posture as he works, because it would be more difficult to slump while using such facilities.

By the time one reaches his late teens his posture habits have been pretty well molded. The male who is by nature less conscious of his appearance than the female, tends to slump at work or when standing, without being aware that he is doing so. The female, on the other hand, is painfully conscious of her developing figure in adolescence. She squares her shoulders with almost military determination to avoid the look of flat-chestedness. At the same time she insists on kow-towing to fashion by wearing high heels. That she doesn't fall flat on her face thus extended, defies every principle of engineering known to man. (Fig. 1). Now if she holds her shoulders back, and chest forward, it means that milady must have her torso (and her spinal column) bent like a bow when the high heels are worn, with the rump extended quite beyond reason to act as ballast.

We Force Bad Posture Upon Ourselves

A few years of walking and working in this position would soon have a lady off the high heels and down to earth out of sheer discomfort. However, the tired tummies and protruding posteriors found means of support and disguise in the girdle and corset. So the American lady marches with all determination toward backache.

The male doesn't fare much better. His slumping round-shoulderedness leaves him with prominent thyroid cartilage, a particularly unattractive "Adam's apple," and sagging jowls from the necessity of burying the head lower in the shoulders to allow one to look straight ahead and below, instead of looking to the sky as the forced position of the head would dictate. (Fig. 2).

FIG. 1

But of even more consequence is the fact that the sternum (chest bone) is depressed in the round-shouldered individual, and this interferes with the normal expansion of the thoracic cage. The respiratory bellows are affected, resulting in shortness of breath and inability to sustain any kind of muscular activity.

Exactly How Were We Meant to Stand?

The entire basis for proper posture is the fact that the spinal column is designed to stand in a straight line, with segmented curvatures to provide flexibility and absorb stress from the base of the skull to the pelvis. To maintain this healthful position, the body has several main sets of tools: the abdominal muscles, the gluteal muscles of the buttock and the hamstring muscles of the back of the thigh. All of these serve to keep the pelvis at its proper level, allowing no permanent tilt either forward or backward, and thus offering a steady and level support for the spinal column. (Fig. 3).

FIG.

Dr. Delarue gives several rules and exercises for correcting dangerous posture habits before too much damage has been done. These are most effective when used by young people whose muscles and bones are still developing.

Posture Rules

For general back hygiene, one should observe proper methods of standing, sitting and lifting. When standing or sitting for any length of time, it is wise to flex the thighs comfortably to straighten the pelvic tilt by pulling the rear rim of the pelvis downward. When sitting for a long period, both legs should be supported on something. For standing for long periods without changing position, a leg rest, like the old brass rail in the swinging door bars of the nineties or a step of some kind should be handy.

FIG. 3

The rule for lifting heavy objects from a level lower than the hips should be carefully followed: one goes down on his haunches in a squat, the back is kept straight and the knees are flexed in the lifting. This simple precaution can save one from many other physiological complications not even related to posture and backache.

To maintain the efficiency of the thoracic bellows, avoid a hollow chest and keep the sternum elevated, the following exercise is suggested by Dr. Delarue:

Stand as tall as possible, with the head erect, chin in, chest out, tummy in and buttocks flat. Now square the shoulders, elevating and lowering them while breathing deeply. You can feel those lazy chest muscles working.

Do you have a sag in your sacroiliac? You shouldn't. But here's how you can check for yourself. Stand with your back against a wall with thighs, calves, buttocks, shoulders flat against it. Now see if you can fit your hand between the wall and the small of your back, just above the buttocks. If you can, your posture needs work. Bend slightly forward until the space between your back and the wall is eliminated, then try to straighten up without allowing the space to form. This will take plenty of muscle power in your abdominal region as well as the backs of your thighs and buttocks. If you don't seem to be getting anywhere at first, don't be discouraged. You can work on those muscles till they're strong enough to maintain such a position without your consciously trying.

Exercises to Do

For the abdominals try this: lie flat on your back and hold your legs straight, lifting them slowly to about 60° (or about the number two on a watch dial if the subject is lying at number 6), then lower them slowly. Repeat this with one leg, then the other. You should do it as many times as possible until you get tired—not exhausted, just tired. Keep count of the number you do, and try to increase the number at regular intervals, say one or two more per week. In no time you will feel new strength in your abdominal region, and find that standing and walking erectly comes much more naturally.

The exercises to strengthen the back muscles of the thighs (hamstrings) and the buttocks (gluteal) are much the same, except that the leg raising is done while lying face down.

Remember to keep the legs straight, as in the preceding exercise. Flexing the knees against resistance, such as your bedroom wall, will also act to strengthen these muscles.

Both of these exercises will give you the muscle power you need to keep the pelvis from tilting too far forward or backward. With the pelvis on an even keel, the rest of the torso will stay that way, too.

We think that there is no better exercise for posture, and for just plain all-around increase in health and well-being than walking in the open air. Editor Rodale arranges his busy schedule to fit in a daily two-hour constitutional, and considers the physical and mental benefits derived from this practice well worth the sacrifice of his valuable time. Do as much walking as you can, and try to practice the tips on good posture offered by Dr. Delarue while you walk. Skip the high heels and the girdles. Give your body a chance to work without such hindrances.

Good Posture Through Proper Diet

Make sure, too, that your bad posture isn't the result of bad diet. Get plenty of bone-building calcium from supplements such as bone meal and homogenized bone, so that your spinal column is made up of firm, hard bones. For the muscles, vitamin E and wheat germ for strength, and vitamin C from rose hips and fresh vegetables and fruits for healthy muscular tissue. Plenty of protein in the diet is important, too, for this is the very stuff of which muscles are made.

Good posture is not possible without good nourishment, and lack of good posture is almost sure to lead to backache at some later time in life.

CHAPTER 83

Good Posture Prevents Rheumatism

If your body is in perfect alignment you can avoid many aches and pains that might otherwise result in rheumatism.

What is the importance of posture in the prevention of rheumatism? Good posture is essential for good health, and it is especially important in any disorder in which bones, joints, and muscles are involved, for these are the parts of the body which suffer most from bad posture.

Dr. Ben T. Bell of Abington Memorial Hospital, writing on "The Diagnosis and Treatment of Low Back Pain" in *The Medical Clinics of North America* for November, 1940, says that the assumption of upright posture by man, with the resulting angulation, the systems of balance and leverage necessary to hold this upright posture, is one of the main reasons why the lower back is so susceptible to strain. The muscles of the lower back also seem to be insufficient to perform their work in the anatomy of mankind.

Back Strain

Says Dr. Bell, "Sedentary occupations or manual occupations in which the worker re-

Fig 1. Perfect posture . . . head, shoulders and feet in perfect alignment. Plumb line divides boy in half indicating body is in balance.

Fig. 2. Good posture . . . even though body is not quite in perfect balance. Pelvic structure has slight forward tilt as indicated by arrow.

Fig. 3. Posture becomes poorer as the forward tilt of the pelvic structure increases. Curve in boy's back starts to deepen and other adjustments follow.

Fig. 4. Bad posture . . . pelvic structure tilted completely out of line, curve in back deepens . . . chest hollows out . . . head thrusts forward at ugly angle.

mains seated all day together with poor habits of posture, result in a back which is barely compensating. A strain of lifting, or a fall, an excessive increase in weight or even increased weight-bearing will increase the load so that the symptoms of strain or more serious injury result. An illness resulting in further loss of muscle power may be the cause of insufficiency in the muscles and strain. In the back subjected to continued mild strain, chronic irritation increases the changes which appear as osteoarthritis in later life. . . . Often the patient with postural defects of flat feet, lumbar lordosis (swayback), sagging abdomen and obesity is symptom-free until some trauma (injury) is literally the last straw on the camel's back."

What Is Perfect Posture?

Doctors agree on the importance of good posture. They also agree that the individual determination to achieve good posture can work wonders, even though there are some postural handicaps that cannot be overcome without the aid of professional therapy. Perfect posture is so simple that there can be no disagreement as to what it means. It means keeping one's body in balance so that there is as little strain as possible on muscles, bones and nerves, when one stands, walks, sits or works.

The base of support for one's body is the pelvic structure —that is, the bony basin to which one's legs are attached, and which contains the abdominal organs. The first picture in the chart shows perfect posture, with the head, shoulders, knees and feet in perfect alignment with pelvic structure. A plumb line dropped from this boy's ear to his ankle would be straight and would divide him in half—that is, half of his body weight would be found to be on each side of the line.

What Is Bad Posture?

In the next picture, something has happened. Perhaps fatigue, perhaps injury, perhaps just carelessness and lack of exercise have thrown him a little off balance. His pelvic structure has been tilted forward slightly, with the result that the rest of his body must adjust itself somehow so that it can remain upright. By the time the fourth sketch was made, his pelvic structure had tilted completely out of line, the curve in his back had deepened, pushing his stomach out. Since the upper part of his body must compensate for this bad balance in the lower part, his chest is hollow, his shoulders rounded and his head thrust forward at an ugly angle. The sagging muscles of his abdomen must still support his abdominal organs. Since these muscles are attached to his spine, the added strain on them deepens the curve in his back and weakens it still further.

The next time you are standing on a street corner waiting for someone, look at the people who pass. You will be amazed to find that most of them have posture like picture number four. You will notice that bad posture can completely ruin an otherwise attractive appearance; you will see that tasteful and expensive clothes look like rags when the framework beneath them is sagging and out of balance. If you wait on your corner long enough, perhaps someone may come along who has good posture. He will look relaxed, rested, healthy. There will be a spring to his step and a buoyancy in his appearance that will make you feel good just to look at him.

You Can Regain Good Posture

When you get home, take a look at yourself in a full-length mirror. Just stand naturally, as you usually stand. How do you look? Like figure four—or perhaps figure three? Be honest with yourself. Then decide to do something to improve your posture. It won't be easy. If your body has accustomed itself to the frightfully bad posture of figure four, you will have to do a lot of coaxing to regain good posture, for by this time bones, muscles and nerves have gotten "set" in this bad pattern. Incidentally, looking at picture four, do you agree with us that there is a perfect setting for rheumatism, or, for that matter, any other bone, muscle or joint affliction that might be around? Every bone, small or large, is out of place in this body. Every muscle is strained. Every nerve is pinched and crowded.

Correcting Bad Posture

The first, and, yes, we might say, the only exercise necessary to begin correcting this sad off-balance posture, is to pull in on the muscles of your abdomen. It's just as simple as that. Look at figure four and imagine (if you could change it all at once) what would be the result of pulling in those stomach muscles. The curve in the back would straighten out, which in turn would correct the flat chest and rounded shoulders. As these fall into line, the legs and feet would assume their rightful positions, and posture number one would be a reality again!

However, if your posture is really like figure number four, you'll find that it's not easy to pull in your stomach muscles. They're flabby and soft from disuse. Try again the second day and the third. It may take weeks before you notice the slightest improvement in the trimness of your figure. You don't have to set aside any time for exercise if you want to have good posture. Just fit it into your daily regime. You can practice good posture while you are waiting for a trolley, standing in an elevator, talking on the telephone.

Posture in Terms of Housework

Housework involves a large percentage of us, so let's discuss posture in terms of housework. While you're getting breakfast in the morning, waiting for the eggs to boil, check on your posture. Pull in your tummy and tuck your lower back under where it belongs. Now see how you can improve posture and ward off fatigue while you're working. When you bend to pick something up, to reach something, or to do some particular kind of work, bend at your knees or hips—don't bend your back. No matter how you manage to do it, see that your sink, stove, laundry tubs and other working spaces are at exactly the right height for you—not so high that you must stretch to reach them, not so low that you must bend or stoop. Sitting is better than standing at any job where it can possibly be managed. Until you've tried sitting while you iron, you won't

Use leg and shoulder muscles to lift. Back-bending is back-breaking and can cause unnecessary posture-wrecking fatigue.

Sitting saves energy . . . sit at your job whenever possible. Use comfortable chair and keep back straight, stomach muscles in.

Height of table affects posture. Stand erect, have working surface at correct height. Make sure you do not have to stoop or bend over your work.

realize how much energy you can save this way. Sit down in the kitchen while you're preparing vegetables, sit down to wash the dishes. Make sure your chair is comfortable and that you are sitting with your back straight, your stomach muscles pulled in. Be certain you have support for your feet, check from time to time to make sure your shoulders are back, but relaxed, so that you are not "humped" tensely over your work.

You can exercise for good posture while you are making a bed, sweeping a floor, setting a table, running a sewing machine. If you remember only one basic commandment—keep your stomach muscles pulled in—the rest of your body will align itself properly. Have you ever estimated how much time you spend each week walking to and from stores carrying packages? Have you ever stopped to think how important to your posture is the way in which you carry those packages? At your dressing table mirror you can check on your shoulders. When you are standing as you normally do, one is probably higher than the other, for no other reason but that, since you were in school, you have become accustomed to carrying books, purse, umbrella, packages always in the same arm. In most people this practice results in carrying the shoulder of that arm as much as several inches higher than the other shoulder—bad posture. This throws the whole upper part of your body out of line, and somewhere your bones and muscles must compensate, resulting in a lot of wear and tear which you might easily avoid by simply remembering to carry equal weights in both arms, as in the picture, or by shifting the weight from side to side.

A Posture Reminder

Actually, the only hard thing about regaining good posture is reminding yourself of it. Once the muscles have been strengthened, you'll have good posture without giving it another thought. But meanwhile, make a habit of studying your reflection in shop windows when you're walking on the street. One glance will remind you to pull those stomach muscles in. At home or at work decide on some one object—a calendar, a window, a piece of furniture that will be your constant reminder every time you look at it to correct your posture. You may be saving yourself years of agonizing pain with arthritis later on in life.

SECTION 24

THE NECESSITY FOR TAKING
VITAMIN AND
MINERAL SUPPLEMENTS

Even if you eat the best possible diet, you do not obtain enough vitamins and minerals for robust health from today's refined and chemically fertilized foods. Much of the fresh food you eat has lost most of its vitamin content during the long shipping process before it reaches your grocery. We advise you to supplement your diet with vitamins and minerals from natural sources. Take them with your meals. They are food.

CHAPTER 84

The Vitamin Story

We are presenting here a study of all the known vitamins, the reason why we need each for good health and a list of foods and food supplements in which each is most plentiful. We hope it will help you as a quick reference in planning menus, buying foods and food supplements.

Vitamin A

Vitamin A is a fat soluble vitamin, that is, it dissolves in fat and it can be stored in the body, so you do not need to eat vitamin A every day. But if you happen to have gotten little vitamin A recently, it may take a long time for you to build up your body store of it again. People who have had serious illnesses or infections are almost certain to be short of vitamin A; anyone who suffers from any stomach, liver or intestinal disorder probably lacks vitamin A; the continual taking of mineral oil destroys vitamin A and the other fat soluble vitamins in the body.

In a recent survey in New York schools it was found that a slight vitamin A shortage is the most common diet deficiency. Experiments at Columbia University showed that animals who receive far more than the recommended daily requirement of vitamin A live longer and are freer from the symptoms of old age.

Why You Need Vitamin A for Good Health

A lack of the vitamin causes: night blindness, sensitivity to glare, difficulty reading in dim light, inability to store fat. It is necessary for skin health, fighting colds and infections, preventing kidney stones, good growth and dental health in children. The official recommendation is that we get a minimum of 5000 International Units of vitamin A every day.

Experiments indicate that far more than this is the ideal amount. There is no danger of getting too much in natural foods unless one should take enormous amounts of fish liver oil over a long period of time. We do not recommend taking any form of synthetic vitamin A. Fish liver oil, which we recommend as a food supplement for everyone, young and old, is a natural food taken from the livers of halibut, cod, etc. In the form of perles it is odorless and tasteless.

Foods in Which Vitamin A is Most Plentiful: Apricots, carrots, collards, dandelion greens, beef liver, mustard greens, sweet potatoes, turnip greens, watercress, butter, egg yolk and fish liver oil. Carotene appears in foods that are yellow or green and carotene is the substance which changes to vitamin A in your body. If your liver is not functioning well, this vegetable form of carotene may be wasted, so we advise again—make certain by taking fish liver oils in capsule form.

Vitamin B

There are a lot of B vitamins, including some which scientists know are present in certain foods, but have not succeeded in isolating and identifying yet. All the B vitamins are of great importance to Americans because more than half our national diet consists of foods made of white sugar or white flour. These two carbohydrate foods (from which all the B vitamins have been removed during the refining process) must be accompanied by B vitamins or our bodies cannot use them properly. So the more refined foods you eat the more B vitamins you need.

"Enriched" flour contains only 3 of the many B vitamins removed during refining. Don't depend on it for B vitamins. Smoking, drinking or eating sweets robs you of B vitamins. Many of the new drugs (the sulfas are one example) as well as sleeping pills, estrogen, insecticides and so forth create a condition in your digestive tract that is destructive of B vitamins. It may take years to overcome deficiencies caused by such substances.

B vitamins are soluble in water. They are lost when you throw away water in which meats or vegetables have cooked. They are harmed, too, by light and heat. Most of the riboflavin (one of the B vitamins) is destroyed in a bottle of milk left on the doorstep in the sunlight for an hour or so. Baking soda or baking powder destroy B vitamins.

The most important thing to remember about the B vitamins is that they should be taken all together and may do serious harm if they are taken separately in massive doses. Synthetic vitamin B preparations cannot supply you with the same effective vitamin B "complex" you get from foods which are rich in all these vitamins. Brewer's yeast and desiccated liver, which we recommend as food supplements for everyone, are natural products. The yeast plant, storing B vitamins for its own use, is dried so that the B vitamins become available to us. Desiccated liver is made from fresh liver with the fat removed, carefully dried at low heat to conserve all the B vitamins. These two food supplements have been found, in experiments, to protect laboratory animals from cancer and many other diseases. Liver has been found to be protective against poisons to which we are exposed today, such as DDT.

The names of the B vitamins are: thiamin, riboflavin, niacin, pantothenic acid, pyridoxine, choline, inositol, vitamin B_{12}, biotin, para-aminobenzoic acid. Do not try to take them separately. Take them all together in foods and natural food supplements.

Why You Need the B Vitamins for Good Health

Among them the B vitamins are chiefly responsible for the health of: the digestive tract, the skin, the mouth and the tongue, the eyes, the nerves, the arteries, the liver. They have been found to: prevent constipation, berberi and pellagra, prevent burning feet, burning and dryness of the eyes, tender gums, feelings of depression, nausea, indigestion, lack of appetite, fatigue, skin disorders, cracks at the corners of the mouth, certain kinds of anemia, fatty liver and so forth.

There are official recommendations for daily minimum requirement of only 3 of the B vitamins: thiamin—1.0 to 1.2 milligrams a day; riboflavin—1.5 to 3.0 milligrams a day; and niacin—10.0 to 18.0 milligrams a day. Even though no official minimum requirement has been set for the other B vitamins, they are needed every day, too.

Foods in Which Vitamin B is Most Plentiful: legumes, organ meats (heart, liver, kidneys) wheat germ, whey, chicken, peanuts, egg yolk, whole grains, soybeans, milk, fresh raw fruits and vegetables. Brewer's yeast and desiccated liver are the two richest sources.

Vitamin C

This is also a water soluble vitamin, the most perishable of all. Fruits and vegetables left unrefrigerated for several days may lose most of their vitamin C. Home canning destroys vitamin C, for it is sensitive to air and heat. Soaking foods or discarding the cooking water destroys vitamin C. Cutting, slicing, grating or chopping fruits or vegetables should be done just before they are eaten, for every cut surface exposed to air releases vitamin C. All fruits and vegetables should be refrigerated at all times until they are eaten. Fresh ones are, of course, preferable—eat them as soon as possible after they are picked. Frozen foods contain more vitamin C generally than canned ones. Baking soda or copper utensils in contact with fresh food destroy vitamin C.

There are physicians today who cure polio, pneumonia, influenza, the common cold, and many other diseases with massive doses of vitamin C. It is not apparently possible to get too much of the natural vitamin C, and it is believed that most of us are deficient in it. Smoking, stress, and exposure to poisons use up vitamin C and it must be replaced every day— it cannot be stored.

The official recommendation is for 75 milligrams to 150 milligrams of vitamin C a day.

Why You Need Vitamin C for Good Health

Vitamin C prevents scurvy, protects the health of all body tissues, including teeth, gums, bones, blood vessels, eyes, etc. It is necessary for the body to manufacture the cement that holds cells together—all cells. It protects against infections and colds. It causes wounds to heal quickly. Sure signs that you are deficient in vitamin C are easy bruising, bleeding gums or loose teeth.

Foods in Which Vitamin C is Most Plentiful: Green peppers, broccoli, cauliflower, watercress, kohlrabi, raw cabbage, strawberries, collards, cantaloupe, turnip greens, tomatoes, fresh peas and citrus fruit. It must be remembered that citrus fruit also contains citric acid which some people are extremely sensitive to. For this reason we advise eating citrus fruit in moderation, and always eating it, never juicing it, as the action of the citric acid is much stronger in the juice.

The richest source of vitamin C is rose hips—the fruit of the rose tree left after the flowers fade. These can be made into puree for winter use.

Vitamin D

This is a fat soluble vitamin which is absolutely necessary for body health, since it must be present for us to use calcium and phosphorus properly. It appears only in foods of animal origin. It is also available from the sun's rays. A substance in the bare skin manufactures vitamin D from the ultraviolet light.

Fish liver oil, which we recommend to everyone as a food supplement, is the richest source of vitamin D. We believe that children and adults alike should take fresh fish liver oil the year round, for vitamin A and D. It can be had in capsules. The official recommendation is 400 International Units of vitamin D per day for infants and young people up to the age of 20.

Why You Need Vitamin D for Good Health

Vitamin D protects the thyroid gland, prevents some kinds of arthritis, is necessary for strong bones and teeth, helps normal heart action and clotting of blood, may prevent nearsightedness in children, is active in every body function involving calcium and phosphorus—two most important minerals.

Foods in Which Vitamin D is Most Plentiful: Butter, eggs, herring, liver, mackerel, milk, salmon, tuna fish, fish liver oil.

Vitamin E

This fat soluble vitamin is removed from wheat when flour is milled. When flour is bleached, any vitamin E that might be left in the flour is destroyed by the bleach. Vitamin E protects the body's store of two other vitamins—A and C, so you will need less of these two vitamins if you are getting enough vitamin E. It has been used extensively in therapy for reproductive disorders, including sterility, miscarriage, menopause disorders and so forth. Many physicians are at present using it in the treatment of heart and blood vessel diseases. It has also produced some spectacular results in cases of diabetes. It has been used successfully in treating muscular dystrophy.

Vitamin E is destroyed in the presence of rancid fats or oils. Mineral oil also destroys it. Medicines that contain ferric chloride or other ferric salts inactivate vitamin E in the body. Our chief sources of vitamin E today are vegetable and cereal oils and whole grain cereals.

Wheat germ and wheat germ oil which we recommend to everyone as food supplements are made from that part of the wheat that is discarded when the grain is milled. We recommend taking both a wheat germ product and vitamin E.

Why You Need Vitamin E for Good Health

It protects the health of the heart, blood vessels, muscles and reproductive system; a lack of it may be a cause of muscular dystrophy; it is a natural anti-coagulant, thus preventing the possibility of a stroke.

Foods in Which Vitamin E is Most Plentiful: Corn oil, cottonseed oil, peanut oil, soybean oil, wheat germ, wheat germ oil, sunflower seed oil.

Vitamin K

This is a newly discovered vitamin so we do not know a great deal about it as yet. However, we do know that it protects against hemorrhaging, that it appears to prevent abortions, that it protects the body against some cancer-producing substances.

Taking aspirin, mineral oil or sulfa drugs destroys vitamin K in the body. A liver or intestinal disorder or a lack of bile prevents absorption of vitamin K and may result in a deficiency. Alfalfa or some other food supplement made from green leafy vegetables rich in this vitamin should be taken if you suspect a deficiency.

Why You Need Vitamin K for Good Health

It helps blood to clot, cures high blood pressure in animals, may help prevent miscarriages, protects against cancer-causing substances.

Foods in Which Vitamin K is Most Plentiful: Alfalfa, spinach, kale, carrot tops, all green leafy vegetables.

Vitamin P

Vitamin P has recently made the headlines as a traveling companion to vitamin C. They occur together in foods, and it has been found that both of them together work far, far better than either works separately. Rutin and bioflavonoids are two other names for vitamin P.

Why Your Body Needs Vitamin P for Good Health

It has been used in the treatment of bleeding gums, eczema, glaucoma, cirrhosis of the liver and psoriasis. It prevents hemorrhaging, lessens the possibility of "stroke" in high blood pressure cases and is useful in protecting against the harmful effects of X-ray.

Foods in Which Vitamin P is Most Plentiful: Green peppers, citrus fruit (it is in the white segments—another good reason for not juicing and straining citrus—you lose all the vitamin P), grapes, prunes, plums and black currants, rose hips.

Vitamin F

We mention this vitamin last because it has not been officially designated as a vitamin yet. It is the term used for the essential unsaturated fatty acids—essential because your body cannot manufacture them as it does other fatty acids. They must be taken in foods. These substances are contained chiefly in vegetable, cereal and fish oils. Animal fats are deficient in them. They are almost completely absent from hydrogenated fats—the solid ones, like margarine.

Why You Need Vitamin F for Good Health

In animals lack of this vitamin results in retarded growth, scaliness of feet and tail, kidney damage, fatty kidney, impaired functions of reproduction and excessive water consumption. Eczema in children has been found to be the result of lack of vitamin F. We have found medical evidence showing that vitamin F is useful in preventing prostate trouble, many skin diseases, mongolism, asthma, psoriasis, arthritis and many other diseases. It is also credited with rendering cholesterol harmless, thus reducing the danger from this fatty substance.

Foods in Which Vitamin F is Most Plentiful: Vegetable and cereal oils, such as salad oils, sunflower seeds and other unprocessed seeds like peanuts, whole grains and so forth. Fish liver oils are a rich source.

Minerals are actual constituents of body tissue. They also take part in many important processes, along with vitamins and enzymes. Some minerals like calcium and phosphorus we need in fairly large amounts. Others, called "trace minerals," we need in extremely small amounts but, nevertheless, we need them every day. This includes such minerals as zinc, cobalt, iodine and so forth.

Food as it is raised today is likely to be short in minerals, especially the trace minerals which are not present in commercial fertilizer. For this reason we feel that any health-conscious person should take food supplements for additional minerals. Bone meal (the powdered bones of young cattle) contains large amounts of calcium and phosphorus, along with all the trace minerals in exactly the proportions in which they occur in nature. Kelp, made from dried seaweed, is especially rich in iodine, along with all the other ocean minerals which are valuable for good health.

Finally, then, our recommendations for getting plenty of the vitamins and minerals are: eat a diet high in protein (fish, meat, eggs, poultry), nuts, seeds and fresh raw fruits and vegetables. These foods are richest in all the vitamins and minerals. Shun the refined and processed foods, like those made from white sugar and white flour. They dilute your diet to such an extent that eating them is bound to result in deficiencies. Take the following food supplements every day, regardless of how good your diet may be: fish liver oil in capsules for vitamins A, D and F, brewer's yeast and/or desiccated liver for the B vitamins, rose hips for vitamin C and vitamin P, wheat germ oil, vitamin E, bone meal and kelp for minerals.

CHAPTER **85**

Have You a Vitamin Deficiency?

Here are some symptoms that you can check, in yourself and in your family which indicate the possibility of a vitamin deficiency. The symptoms are not hard to recognize.

How can you tell if you have a vitamin deficiency? Are there any easy-to-recognize signs or symptoms? Is there any reason why one should suspect that skin disorders, dry hair, poor eyesight, bruises or sore mouths signify more than just a temporary or chronic condition that "runs in the family?"

Deficient in One = Deficient in All

There are many easily recognizable signs of vitamin deficiency—either slight or very, very serious. You yourself can tell whether or not you need more of one vitamin or another by simply observing yourself and your own health. We want to make one correction on that last sentence. It is doubtful if anyone was ever deficient in one or two vitamins. If you have even one symptom of deficiency in one vitamin, then it is almost certain that you are deficient in all others as well.

Why is this? Because, generally speaking, all the vitamins occur in the same foods. If you eat a diet that consists largely of these good foods, then you will be much less likely to be very deficient in vitamins. But if you consistently eat foods that are short in vitamin A, for instance, then you will almost surely be short on B vitamins, too, and vitamin C, perhaps vitamin E and vitamin K as well. So when you are reading the facts below, don't decide that you need just one vitamin. No one does. You need them all.

Vitamin A Deficiencies

Vitamin A deficiency results in one unmistakable symptom which, if you have not noticed it in yourself, you undoubtedly have seen in your family or friends—night blindness. This is chiefly an inability to adapt to bright lights or to darkness. If you can't see for quite a while when you come into a bright light from darkness, or when you are exposed to a sudden glare (such as headlights from an oncoming car at night), then you certainly have a deficiency in vitamin A.

If you find it uncomfortable to go outside in bright sunshine without dark glasses, then you are short on vitamin A. Notice how many of your friends squint when they are outside on a sunny day. Do you know anyone who doesn't? Folks who are getting plenty of vitamin A have no difficulty keeping their eyes wide open in bright sunlight.

Part of the job of vitamin A is to protect what the doctors call the "specialized epithelial surfaces" of the body—the mouth tissues, and those of the respiratory system; the salivary glands and those of the digestive tract; and the organs of the reproductive system, and the skin. So lack of vitamin A can cause disorders of any of these or, perhaps more important, a slight deficiency in vitamin A can weaken one or all of these parts of you so seriously that they are likely candidates for any infection that comes along.

We know definitely, for instance, that the throat and lungs of a person deficient in vitamin A invite cold germs, for the cells there, lacking this all-important vitamin, simply don't have the stamina to withstand the germs which are, of course, ever-present. Skin that is rough with the appearance of "goose pimples" especially on the elbows, above the knees, on buttocks and upper arms; hair that is dry, brittle and often full of dandruff—these are sure signs of vitamin A deficiency. Perhaps you are taking vitamin supplements. Did you know that if there is anything wrong with your liver, your body may not be able to use vitamin A? This suggests that you take larger doses and make certain that all the other vitamins necessary for liver health are abundant in your diet.

B Vitamin Deficiencies

We would like to consider each of the B vitamins separately and give you the list of symptoms produced by the deficiency of each. But every time we talk about separate B vitamins, we get letters from readers who have decided to take the one B vitamin we have talked about. Where can they get it, they ask. Sorry, folks, but you cannot get B vitamins separately unless you take them in a synthetic form, which is likely to do you more harm than good. You must take them all together in good healthful foods on your table every day and in completely natural food supplements like brewer's yeast, desiccated liver, wheat germ, and so forth. There is no such thing as a synthetic preparation containing all the B vitamins. They have not all been discovered yet. But we know they all occur together in foods rich in the other B vitamins.

So we will talk about symptoms of B vitamin deficiency—all the B vitamins—thiamin, riboflavin, niacin, pyridoxine, pantothenic acid, folic acid, biotin, choline, para-amino-benzoic acid, inositol, etc. Have you ever had a sore tongue, sore lips, with perhaps cracks that don't heal at the corners of your mouth; a burning sensation on the inside of your mouth? Is your tongue ever bright red and glossy, or slightly purple, with, perhaps, deep crevices in it? Does your tongue ever feel swollen? All these are symptoms of vitamin B deficiency—so definite and certain that they can be cured almost overnight by massive amounts of B vitamins.

General Symptoms of Vitamin B Deficiency

Here are other more general symptoms of B vitamins deficiency, in animals and in man: seborrhea (a greasy scaling about the ears, nose and eyes), breathlessness, nervousness, neuritis, serious defects in memory, spots before the eyes, diarrhea, colitis, insomnia, dizziness, headache, lack of appetite, weakness in legs, lassitude, burning sensations in the feet. This does not mean that every headache or every case of colitis is due to vitamin B deficiency alone. Other causes may be present. But in cases of severe depletion, where patients have been hospitalized because of vitamin lack, all these symptoms were present. So how are you going to know whether or not your symptoms are caused partly by vitamin B deficiency unless you get enough of it in your diet for once in your life and see how you feel then?

Remember, please, you cannot get vitamin B in natural form unless it is in the form of food—brewer's yeast, desiccated liver and so forth.

Most of Us Lack Vitamin C

One reason for the widespread deficiency in vitamin C these days is the fact that all of us are exposed to hundreds of various poisons every day of our lives—carbon monoxide gas,

LIMITED WARRANTY

This product is guaranteed against defects in workmanship and materials for one full year from the date of purchase. Should replacement or repair be necessary, please contact:

SPORTLINE
3300 West Franklin Boulevard
Chicago, Illinois 60624

insecticides in our food, tobacco smoke, drugs and so forth. It is the job of vitamin C to neutralize poisons in the body, *and the vitamin is destroyed in this process*. So the more poisonous our environment becomes year by year, the more vitamin C we need. And the more canned and processed foods we eat year by year, the less vitamin C we are getting.

The one surest sign of vitamin C deficiency is bruising. We mean by this that if you are getting enough vitamin C, you will never bruise, unless, of course, you are subjected to some violent accident. However, the average healthy person getting the average number of bumps and knocks day by day should never have a bruise. A bruise means that certain small blood vessels have been destroyed, and the blood has rushed out of them into the surrounding tissue. If you are getting enough vitamin C, your blood vessels are strong enough that they do not break at the slightest bump. When you take your bath tomorrow, look yourself over and note how many bruises you have. Even if you're been gardening, carpentering, sawing wood, moving furniture, you should not have bruises.

As you know, scurvy is the disease people get who have not had nearly enough vitamin C. Here are the symptoms of scurvy: weakness, easy fatigue, listlessness, shortness of breath, aching bones and muscles, rough, dry skin, bruises on legs, gradually spreading to the upper part of the body, swollen bleeding gums that are spongy to the touch, loose teeth, old ulcers and scars that open again, new wounds that fail to heal.

We are told that few people in our country today get scurvy. But we are also told that many of us have a deficiency in vitamin C that is not enough to put us to bed, but is certainly enough to cause many different kinds of symptoms like those above. For instance, readers have written us that their gums have stopped bleeding within days after they began to take vitamin C supplements. Do your gums bleed? Have you tried vitamin C for it?

Other Vitamins Less Likely to be Lacking

Vitamin D is, as we all know, especially necessary for children, for it must be present for their bones to grow straight. But it is also necessary for adults, for you must have vitamin D for your body to use calcium and phosphorus—two important minerals. Osteoporosis and osteomalacia are diseases of folks past middle age whose bones become soft and brittle. Part of the reason is undoubtedly too little calcium in the diet at mealtime. Could not part of it be that there is too little vitamin D for the body to use in connection with whatever calcium is available?

Vitamin E is essential for the proper working of the muscles and the reproductive tract. In animals such disorders as miscarriages, infertility, menstrual disorders and so forth are common when the animals' diet does not contain enough vitamin E. In animals, too, muscular dystrophy can be produced by depriving the animals of vitamin E. The vitamin E which we and our children should be getting has been removed from foods during the refining process.

Vitamin K is, as the nutrition books say, "widely distributed" in foods. It is necessary for the blood to coagulate properly, so any tendency toward hemorrhaging or excessive bleeding may indicate too little vitamin K in the diet.

Vitamin P (sometimes called bioflavonoids)—occurs with vitamin C in fresh foods and works in conjunction with vitamin C.

CHAPTER **86**

Synthetic versus Natural– What Does It Mean?

Here is our interpretation of the controversy over synthetic versus natural food supplements. Are they the same thing?

Not so long ago, premature babies were developing a condition called "retrolental fibroplasia" which resulted in many cases in blindness. Medical authorities were baffled. Why only premature babies? Why only some of them? Was it lack of a vitamin? How could it be prevented? By 1949 this disorder had become the leading cause of blindness in children under 5 years of age in one state at least.

Intensive work on the part of physicians and hospital staffs finally uncovered the cause of retrolental fibroplasia. What do you think it was? *Pure oxygen* given to the tiny prematures to keep them alive! Now oxygen is the lifesaving element in the air which we need every second of our mortal lives. How could oxygen have caused blindness? Look again. We said "pure" oxygen. In other words, oxygen given in a concentration in which it is not found in nature, without all the other elements that go along with it in the air we breathe. The order went out straightway that oxygen therapy for premature babies should be used only when necessary and then only in concentrations below 40 volumes per cent.

Natural Environment Best

What does this story have to do with the controversy over natural versus synthetic vitamins? Everything. It is another in the long series of exhibits we have collected as evidence that the human body cannot flourish and be at its best in manufactured environments. Pure oxygen does not naturally exist anywhere on the earth for purposes of breathing. Man has isolated it and uses it for his own designs. Sodium fluoride does not exist naturally anywhere in food or water, which is a pretty clear indication that man and animals were not meant to imbibe it. Fluorine in nature is accompanied by calcium, never by sodium. The B vitamins, such as thiamin, riboflavin, niacin, pyridoxine and so forth do not exist anywhere in nature in the "pure" state, unallied to all the other B vitamins that occur in plant and animal tissue.

Is this not evidence enough that taking in every day a little of such unnatural substances—cut off from the elements that accompany them in nature—may result in serious bodily harm?

Since there is no such thing in nature as thiamin, unaccompanied by other B vitamins, how can one believe that taking thiamin, alone and separate, can be anything but harmful?

Remember, there was nothing harmful to the premature infants in oxygen itself. Oxygen was harmful *only* when it was taken in the "pure" state, separated from everything that occurs naturally with it.

Nature Has the Only Formula

We have argued against water fluoridation many times on the basis of the fact that it is artificial, that it condemns the water-drinker to take in a substance that does not exist in nature. Yet proponents of fluoridation will still argue that "the fluoride ion is the fluoride ion, no matter where or how it appears." They apparently learned nothing from the story of retrolental fibroplasia, if indeed they know about it.

We have a file crammed with letters and articles from scientists and pseudo-scientists declaring that a vitamin is a vitamin no matter how or where it appears. Therefore, they say, thiamin or any other B vitamin, made according to a chemical formula, in a laboratory, is exactly the same as the thiamin which occurs in brewer's yeast or wheat germ or liver. The chemical formula is the same; therefore, they are identical. But, gentlemen, the oxygen was the same, too. And the oxygen which was given in a pure state blinded the premature babies. Oxygen given in a diluted state, combined with other things that accompany it in natural air, does not blind babies. How can you explain such a thing, gentlemen, since oxygen is oxygen and the chemical symbol is the same?

What do we mean by a natural vitamin as different from a synthetic one? Mainly the difference lies in this matter of "purity." We do not advise readers to take "pure" vitamins. By separating out all the so-called "impurities," biochemists have discovered what the actual ingredients of many of the vitamins are. Vitamin C, for instance, consists of 6 atoms of carbon, 8 of hydrogen and 6 of oxygen, arranged in a certain pattern. Chemists can make this in a laboratory. Is this the same vitamin C that occurs in an orange, a green pepper, a rose hip? Technically, yes. But it is only the carbon, the hydrogen and the oxygen, nothing more.

Bioflavonoids in the Vitamin C Complex

Not so long ago there was a lot of hullabaloo about the bioflavonoids—a substance occurring in fresh foods which was found to be valuable for treating and preventing many different kinds of disorders. Colds, rheumatic fever, tendency to miscarriages, hemorrhaging, capillary fragility, infections—these are some of them. Researchers told us that the bioflavonoids are part of the vitamin C "complex." But do they appear in the carbon-hydrogen-oxygen formula given above for vitamin C? Of course not.

So anyone taking synthetic vitamin C never got any bioflavonoids. But those who take natural vitamin C food supplements made from rose hips, green peppers and so forth have been getting the bioflavonoids for as long as they have been taking the food supplements. Furthermore, people who are taking natural food supplements are getting all the other *as yet undiscovered* parts of the vitamin C complex! Doesn't just this fact indicate the vast superiority of natural vitamins over synthetic ones?

Synthetic Vitamin B

Another example. Several members of the B complex of vitamins have been discovered quite recently—folic acid and vitamin B_{12} for instance. Before they were discovered, they could not, of course, be included in synthetic B complex vitamin pills because their formulas were unknown. Chemists did not know how to make them in laboratories, even though they suspected their presence in food. But Nature knows how to make them, and she did make them and included them along with all the other B vitamins in those foods in which they are plentiful. So, once again, readers who were taking brewer's yeast and desiccated liver were getting these vitamins, even though they had not as yet been isolated and synthesized. They are getting, too, all those other members of the B vitamin complex *which have not as yet been discovered.*

Why Not Take Synthetic Vitamins?

So much for the reasons for taking natural vitamins. Are there reasons for not taking synthetic ones? Plenty of them. Listen!

Shock From "Pure" Thiamin

The Journal of the American Medical Association for May 3, 1952, tells of a physician who received a daily massive dose of thiamin, one of the B vitamins. After the fifth injection, he went into shock and was saved from death only by the measures of his colleagues. The thiamin was "pure," isolated, synthetic.

"Pure" Folic Acid Dangerous

The Journal of the Indian Medical Association for August, 1951, in discussing folic acid, states that giving whole liver or the whole vitamin B complex has advantages over giving folic acid by itself, because "deficiency diseases are multiple in character and the imbalance of vitamins is thus avoided."

Synthetic "C" Only Half Effective

Dr. C. W. Jungblut, writing in the *Journal of the American Medical Association* for November 20, 1937, reported that, in his extensive experiments with monkeys, he found that administration of a factor from citrus fruit, identified as vitamin C, prevented the graver effects caused by polio. Synthetic vitamin C proved appproximately half as effective as the natural substance. Recent developments seem to indicate that the bioflavonoids may be the curative agents.

More on the Dangers of Thiamin

Another incidence of sensitivity to an individual (synthetic) B vitamin is reported in the *Annals of Allergy*, May-June, 1952. Thiamin, given in large doses by itself, caused the trouble. *The Journal of Immunology* for August, 1942, reveals that guinea pigs, given a diet deficient in vitamin C, could not be entirely cured of the resulting scurvy by synthetic vitamin C. But the feeding of fresh cabbage (rich in vitamin C and the things which accompany it in nature) brought them back to normal.

Vitamin D Poisoning

The Finnish Journal, *Annales Paediatrae Fenniae* (Vol. 2, part 2, 1956), tells of two children dying from overdoses of calciferol—synthetic vitamin D. The children had been receiving 500,000 units of the synthetic vitamin over a period of several years. Calciferol (not taken from fish liver oil, mind you, but manufactured according to chemical formula in a laboratory) is said to be 400,000 times as active as cod liver oil. It is inconceivable that such a thing could happen if you are getting vitamin D from fish liver oils, unless, of course, you disregard all instructions for dosage.

The "Rightness" of Natural Substances

Vitamin A poisoning has occurred, too, from taking incredibly large doses of the synthetic product. *The British Medical Journal* for March 8, 1952, tells of 17 recorded cases in children. Most of them received about 250,000 units of vitamin A daily for many months. It is possible, of course, for one to get that much vitamin A from a natural food supplement like fish liver oil. But you would have to take a whole handful of pills and you would have to ignore all instructions on the label.

Wheat Germ for Muscular Dystrophy

Recently we wrote about the researches of Dr. Ira Manville of the University of Oregon Medical School and the results he is getting by giving wheat germ oil to muscular dystrophy patients. According to the Associated Press dispatch for June 13, 1956, Dr. Manville used a "particular brand of wheat germ oil which supposedly retains natural vitamins and minerals in its make-up." We are not saying that you or I can cure a case of muscular dystrophy by giving wheat germ oil. Undoubtedly, there was more to Dr. Manville's treatment than that. We are saying that the chief ingredient in the cure was a wholly natural substance which has long since disappeared from most people's dining tables—the rich, precious interior of the germ of cereals, removed from flour for the convenience and greater profit of the millers.

The Effects of Synthetic Vitamins A and D

The American Review of Tuberculosis, Vol. 72, p. 218, 1955, describes a study of failures of vitamin A metabolism in TB patients. Synthetic vitamin A and cod liver oil were given. "The response was much better with the cod liver oil concentrate than with synthetic vitamin A," say the authors.

One final story about synthetic vitamin D. Vitamin D was used in feed for chicks as reported in *Food and Nutrition,* by E. W. H. Cruickshank, M.D. (Williams and Wilkins, 1951). Three groups were fed the same diet. The first group received no vitamin D at all. The second group received synthetic vitamin D. The third was given natural vitamin D in cod liver oil. The chicks receiving no vitamins gained 259 grams of weight. The synthetic vitamin D group gained 346 grams. And those which had the benefit of the natural vitamin D gained 399 grams. But the most important part of the experiment is that in the no-vitamin group, 60 per cent of the chicks died. In the group fed synthetic vitamins, 5 per cent died. In the group fed natural vitamin D, there were no deaths!

Synthetic and Natural Vitamins Not the Same

But the "experts" will tell you there is absolutely no difference between synthetic and natural vitamins! No, sir. They have the same chemical formula, therefore, they are identical! How do you explain these results, gentlemen, if synthetic and natural vitamins are indeed identical?

Get natural vitamins from your daily meals—as many as you can get by eating fresh foods, untampered with by processors. And, because there are not nearly enough vitamins and minerals in the food you can buy at today's markets, supplement your diet with natural food supplements. How can you tell natural vitamins from synthetic ones? There is no way to tell except your own confidence in the producer of the product and his guarantee that his product is not synthetic.

CHAPTER **87**

Natural Vitamins Are Shown To Be Best

Synthetic vitamins are the kind you buy at the drug store. We recommend another kind—the purely natural ones, present in food, as they exist in food—not isolated and chemicalized. This chapter tells you why.

Large amounts of time and money are spent yearly by scientific researchers in trying to isolate and manufacture synthetically undiscovered vitamin factors that occur naturally in food. Their efforts up to now have succeeded in proving one thing: no combination of known synthetic vitamins satisfies the nutritional requirements of animals or humans. It is in view of this admission that we have consistently recommended that our readers get their vitamins and minerals from natural sources. It is here that these nutrients occur with whatever elements are necessary to their proper assimilation by the body. No scientific observations or experiments have yet been able to untangle all of the intricacies of these natural combinations.

Even with evidence to the contrary from the most highly respected scientists, many physicians refuse to prescribe natural food supplements, making their patients rely instead on synthetic preparations which simply will not do the job.

The B vitamins are especially abused in this connection. This group of vitamins has been shown to multiply its effectiveness many times over when used as it occurs in brewer's yeast, liver, wheat germ and rice polishings, rather than single synthetic components. The importance of the B complex to proper nutrition cannot be overestimated, for without the minimum amounts, life cannot be maintained. It has been found, too, that even massive amounts of synthetic B vitamins will not support life unless natural sources of B vitamins are included in the diet.

Some Animal Experiments

An example of this truth is to be found in *Scandinavian Veterinary*, Vol. 30, pp. 1121-43, 1940, where we find an experiment in which silver foxes were fed a synthetic diet, so that each component of the diet could be known. The foxes were fed all of the known synthetic B vitamins as part of their rations, but the animals failed to grow; the quality of their fur deteriorated and the animals died. This condition was completely reversed with only one change in the diet fed to the foxes—B complex foods, yeast and liver were added. The animals grew normally, and the quality of the fur was greatly improved. The results achieved with the fur in this experiment should be of special interest to those of our readers with hair problems. Though no one seems to be able to pinpoint the exact reason for baldness, graying or generally unhealthy hair, it is likely that a lack of natural B vitamins in the diet could result in difficulties with the hair, just as the foxes' fur was affected.

Another case in which a lack of natural B vitamins affected the hair is noted in the *Journal of Nutrition,* Vol. 21, p. 609, 1941). Here a group of mice was placed on a synthetic diet, again including all known nutrients deemed necessary. They grew for a few days, then became stationary in weight. After 20 or 30 days they began to lose their hair and developed hunched backs. A similar group on the same diet, with whole yeast added was completely protected against these symptoms.

Human Diseases Respond to Natural B Vitamins

In humans, attempts to treat various disorders with synthetic vitamin B have often proven unsuccessful, while responses to vitamin B from natural sources have been gratifying in the very same cases. One such clinical experience was related in the *Canadian Medical Association Journal* (Vol. 44, p. 20, 1941). Fifteen cases of skin disease were treated with injections of synthetic vitamin B. There was no improvement noted from these treatments until yeast or liver extract was given. Observing physicians noted that a general beneficial effect was obtained.

The American Journal of Digestive Diseases (January, 1940) remarks that B complex therapy offers more help to many cases of digestive disturbances than careful dieting or drugs. In an experiment patients with digestive disorders were treated with brewer's yeast extract and had an excellent response in the loss of distressing symptoms. The patients were then taken off the yeast extract and given synthetic thiamin and riboflavin (both B vitamins). The symptoms returned. The test was tried in reverse by giving thiamin and riboflavin to patients as the first treatment, and the results were not beneficial. The yeast was then tried, and the symptoms simply disappeared. The B vitamins have long been known as important aids to digestion, and a good supply of them would doubtless erase the digestive disturbances experienced by many.

Vitamin Shortage Not Always Obvious to Victim

As with many cases of vitamin deficiency, a shortage of B vitamins does not always show itself so forcefully that the victim is willing to do anything about it. The deficiency is shown only in a feeling of laziness, or a lack of ambition; the patient seeks to describe it as "not being himself."

A rather classic experiment illustrating the need for, and efficiency of, foods rich in vitamin B is described in the *Journal of Nutrition* (December, 1942). Ten healthy men, between the ages of 23 and 40, were given a diet list to choose from that was inadequate in thiamin and the other known B complex vitamins. The foods consisted of white bread, soda crackers, macaroni, butter, egg white, ice cream, puffed rice, coffee, etc. Twice a week small portions of fish, meat or poultry were allowed.

The men were now divided into two groups, half of whom received two grams of thiamin a day with their lunch, and the other half received a placebo—that is, a pill containing nothing of any value. All were required to do hard physical work each day.

By the end of the first week, the men receiving the placebo had developed the following symptoms: a general feeling of lassitude, inefficiency and depression; they were easily fatigued; muscle and joint pains were noticed unlike those which usually follow exercise; general poor appetite; irregular bowel habits and constipation; irritability.

Those receiving synthetic thiamin had fewer and milder symptoms, but also complained of easy fatigue.

In the second week a daily dose of yeast was added to the

diet of all the men. After a lag of 48 hours, the subjects began to feel better. The improvement was sudden and dramatic, and by the end of 5 days all complaints had disappeared, although the same basic diet was being eaten.

Evidence Shows Natural B Vitamins Best

These results tended to prove that an adequate intake of natural and complete B complex is vital to a person doing physical labor. Also, a daily intake of thiamin alone is not enough, and physical deterioration will occur in spite of it. And, finally, when a complete B complex addition to the diet is indicated, a natural product such as yeast would seem to be a sure source of all the necessary components.

This is just a partial catalogue of the available evidence showing that natural B vitamins are far superior to those made synthetically. This fact has been thoroughly demonstrated in connection with all other food supplements as well as B complex.

It is difficult to imagine why anyone interested enough in his health to take food supplements at all would risk inadequacies by taking synthetics. Be sure that the vitamins and minerals you take do everything for you that you have a right to expect. Stay with the natural vitamins—they have been proven to be best for you.

Brewer's yeast, desiccated liver, wheat germ (the flakes, not the oil) and rice polishings are all good rich sources of the B vitamins. Take some of these every day.

CHAPTER 88

Good Nutrition Is Even More Essential If You Are Ill

Here is some light from an expert on the question of whether you should take food supplements when you are sick, or only when you are well. It appears that the sick person needs them even more than the healthy one.

A highly significant contribution to our thinking about health in relation to diet is made by Dr. Tom Spies of Birmingham, Alabama, in the June 7, 1958, issue of *The Journal of the American Medical Association.* Dr. Spies is one of our country's outstanding authorities on nutrition, a man who works tirelessly, patiently and understandingly with patients who come to his clinic.

Good Nutrition the Best Preventive Measure

He believes that good nutrition is the best preventive of disease. He believes that, while there are few "classic" cases of malnutrition walking around in America today, "the so-called typical or mild case is the usual one." His aim is to help these patients back to good health, and he accomplishes wonders by giving them vitamin and mineral supplements. But he also knows that vitamins and minerals by themselves do not constitute a good diet, and he spends a great deal of time talking to his patients about their diets and helping them to plan meals, so that they will form good food habits and will not, as soon as his treatment is over, slip right back into the same mistakes that originally made them sick.

Chain Reaction of Deficiencies in the Body

"In a series of 914 consecutive patients admitted to the Nutrition Clinic of the Hillman Hospital, Birmingham, the presenting symptom in 329 of these patients was soreness of the mouth and tongue," he tells us. Although this symptom would seem to indicate vitamin deficiency, it is not possible, he says, simply to prescribe a vitamin and let it go at that. He says, "Working many years in direct contact with the problem has taught us that dietary deficiency disorders arising from a lack of the vitamin B complex do not occur singly but as mixed deficiency diseases. The pattern of these disorders is different from person to person and even among individual members of the same family who may eat at the same table." Nothing will succeed in curing these patients unless the damaged tissues receive the essential nutrients needed to restore them.

Dr. Spies says that for 20 years he has been studying the effect of "hidden hunger," or substandard nutrition, on the growth of infants and children. He believes that what happens to an individual during this period may determine to a considerable extent his health later in life.

The things that go on in one's body are so integrated and so dependent upon an adequate supply of food essentials, he says, that an absence or a deficiency in any one food factor may impair the efficiency of a whole chain of reactions, each of which affects the health of a child.

Diet and Mental Health

As an example, he relates the case history of a young girl who was brought to the clinic at the age of 7 because she was nervous, had little appetite, didn't play with other children. She was given the prescription of the usual good diet and food supplements as well. Researchers at the clinic were meanwhile studying her growth with various tests, including X-ray. A year later the child had typhoid fever from which she recovered without much difficulty. During her illness she continued to take a good diet and all her food supplements. However, so great apparently were the demands made on her metabolism by her illness that an interruption of the whole nutritional process could be seen in X-rays of her bones. A defect appeared in the bone showing clearly just when the illness began and how seriously it affected the little girl.

After a number of years of good nutrition and supplements, another X-ray showed that the defect had healed completely. Would it have healed had the good nutrition been lacking? Obviously not. And who knows what dread disease, acute or chronic, might have attacked this patient much later in life as an indirect result of the typhoid fever incident! You could not say that the typhoid fever had caused the disease directly. But the interruption of normal bodily processes which occurs during disease can apparently lead to much more serious disorders later in life, especially if the quality of nutrition is not sustained at a high level.

So, according to these findings, the person who is sick should pay far more attention to diet and diet supplements than the well person, for the drain on the patient's body, the stress and strain of fighting the disease and finally pulling through apparently create the demand for far more in the way of nutrients.

Aches and Pains Yield to Nutrition

"The study of minor aches and pains is a difficult task," says Dr. Spies. "The breadth of the field, the lack of clearly defined disease manifestations and mechanisms, the almost complete lack of leads makes the medical approach difficult. We find that many persons with minor aches and pains sum up their problem by saying that they have not had any fun in years and that they can barely drag themselves around. They have vague pains, and perhaps even more difficult to endure is their great fatigue. Because of the vague nature of their complaints, such as 'nervousness,' 'forgetfulness,' 'I'm all worn out,' 'aching in my joints and muscles,' they often are called neurotics and usually considered nuisances."

How many of us does that sentence describe! And how much of this unhappiness and ill health would respond to good nutrition!

Mental Health and Good Nutrition

Dr. Spies is particularly concerned with mental health and its relation to nutrition. Bizarre mental disorders are sometimes symptoms of pellagra, which is a disease of vitamin B deficiency. Dr. Spies tells us how he and his colleagues have treated the mental symptoms of pellagra patients. Then they began to wonder about patients who had similar symptoms but did not have fully-developed cases of pellagra. These patients suffered from things like hysteria, anxiety, nervousness, depression. They disliked bright lights, bright colors, noise, odors and foods they had once liked. They were jittery, restless, tense.

They constantly expected something terrible to happen. Do you know people like that?

"I could not accept the concept that their brains were irreparably damaged; it seemed that the cells were waiting listlessly and would function again at full efficiency when we gave them the required nutrients," says Dr. Spies. He discovered that there was an alteration in the content of lactose and lactic acid in the blood leaving and entering the brains of these patients. He discovered that in patients who lacked B vitamins there was a *60 per cent decrease in the metabolism of the brain* —that is, the rate at which the brain could build foods into cells and energy.

Good Nutrition Helps Older People

Dr. Spies tells us that his group of researchers learned long ago that the emotional disorders of older persons can sometimes be overcome or relieved through good nutrition. He is talking about such troubles as these: Older people come to feel useless; they resist changes and their habits become fixed. Their personalities may become disorganized and their judgment poor. They may develop insomnia and may become disoriented as to time and place. A diagnosis of hardening of the arteries of the brain is not much help to patients like these, for this implies that little can be done to improve their condition. Proper nutrition can help, says Dr. Spies.

Among young and old alike, symptoms arise from damaged tissues, he continues. Protecting or repairing tissues will be held up if the tissues are not properly nourished. "Give them what they need and they will muster strength and come back. We do not have enough information, of course, to know all they need. The science of nutrition has only scratched the surface, but it has made some progress toward a real solution of mental illnesses."

His Stand on the Tranquilizers

Speaking of the tranquilizer drugs, he says that he feels they have helped greatly in the treatment of mental illness. But, he says, we must realize that there is, under certain conditions, a loss of nutrients in a patient who is being given tranquilizers. The best way to use them is to make sure there is a sound pattern of adequate nutrition present at the same time to protect the nervous system of the patient. Vitamin therapy does not replace tranquilizers and tranquilizers should not replace vitamin therapy, he goes on. They should always be used together when there seems to be a need for tranquilizers.

Everyone Can't Have a Good Diet

One final point which Dr. Spies makes seems to us important because it throws light on the knotty problem of when one can justify the taking of medicine. Dr. Spies tells us that many times the sufferer from chronic diseases is in such a condition that he cannot eat a good diet. The arthritis patient, for example, may be in such pain that he has lost his appetite completely. He may be so incapacitated by stiffness that he cannot earn money to buy food. He may be so depressed by the long years of suffering that he may not care whether he eats. He may not be able to eat because of stiff jaws. He may have nausea and vomiting and hence be unable to eat.

In cases like these certainly it seems to be wise to take drugs which will give temporary relief—even drugs like aspirin and cortisone. But just as soon as the patient is able to eat, every effort should be made to give him a highly nourishing diet and an abundance of food supplements. Otherwise, as soon as he stops taking the drugs, he will be right back where he started. But if he steadily builds his body tissues with nourishment *while he is taking the drugs,* he has a good chance to improve steadily and to need less and less of the drugs to control the disease.

In his summary Dr. Spies says, ". . . that excellent nutrition is basic, that disease is chemical in its origin, that the body cells can fight back to an amazing degree, and that our tissues when properly replenished, can come into their own again." An encouraging word for us all.

SECTION 25

VITAMINS A AND D

Most plentiful in fish liver oil. Make certain the product you buy is natural, not synthetic.

Chapter **89**

Vitamin A

The fountain of youth! Since time immemorial man has been seeking it. And today the birthday of anyone over 80 rates a newspaper notice with the inevitable question, "To what do you owe your long life?" How varied are the answers! For every 10 people who declare, "I lived this long because I never touched liquor or tobacco" there are bound to be 10 more who attribute their longevity to "a daily glass of beer and pipeful of tobacco." For every 90-year-old farmer who states he lived so long by keeping busy, there seems to be a 95-year-old watchman who knows that the only way to live to a ripe old age is to "take it easy."

And no doubt all of the answers are partly right, for surely each of us has his own peculiar make-up and, up to a certain point, what is one man's meat may be another man's poison.

But it seems to us that by now we should know more than we do about growing old healthfully and happily, especially since our population is showing a steady increase in individuals over the age of 65.

It should not be too difficult, it seems to us, to determine by experiments with rats which elements in food lead to longevity and which do not seem to be related to long life. We are fairly certain of one thing—longevity appears to have some relation to heredity. In a volume entitled *Vitamins and Hormones,* published by Academic Press, appears an article by Dr. Clive M. McCay of the Laboratory of Animal Nutrition at Cornell University.

What Affects Longevity?

Dr. McCay tells us he believes that heredity influences longevity. He tells us of one experiment at Cornell in which the careful records kept of each litter of rats indicated that a small number of the mother rats were responsible for a large per cent of the long-lived rats, and a small group of mother rats was responsible for the short-lived ones. In human experience it appears, too, that children and grandchildren may expect to live long if their ancestors did. Since there is absolutely nothing we can do about heredity, it would seem best for those of us who descend from short-lived parents to take special care with diet and other aspects of living so that we may bequeath to our children a longer expectation of life.

Dr. Henry Sherman of Columbia University has done a most intensive study on diet and longevity. His experiments were originally reported in *The Proceedings of the National Academy of Science,* Vol. 31, p. 107, and Vol. 35, p. 90, and *The Journal of Nutrition,* Vol. 37, p. 467. Of course, the experiments have also been discussed as the classical experiments in this field by almost every writer on nutrition since that time. As you know, the life span of a laboratory rat is only a few years, so that many generations of them can be studied in one man's lifetime. The rats used for these experiments were a community of the Osborne-Mendel strain. Their history showed that they were very normal, happy rats. There was nothing unusual at all about them. They had been living and thriving on diet A (whole wheat and milk) for 67 generations. So there can't be any question in anybody's mind about whether or not this diet was adequate. Hadn't it kept hundreds of rats healthful and fertile over 67 generations? (Remember, please, that rats make their own vitamin C, so they do not need the assortment of fresh fruits and vegetables we human beings need.)

Adding Twice the Usual Vitamin A

Now suppose, said Dr. Sherman and his associates in this experiment, we should increase this adequate diet with considerably more of one of the vitamins, then we might get some idea of how longevity might be increased. So they took one group of the rat family and doubled their allowance of vitamin A. The gentleman rats survived for a 5 per cent longer time and their wives lived 10 per cent longer than any of their relatives on the "adequate" diet they had been eating over the years.

Then for one group of rats the amount of vitamin A in the diet was once again doubled without making any other change in the diet. Rats getting this quadruple quantity of vita-

min A every day lived (for the males) 10 per cent longer and
(for the females) 12 per cent longer than the other rats.

But, you may ask, of what use would these extra years
be if you lived them in a state of senility, being a burden to
those around you and not able to enjoy yourself? *The added
years were not senile years.* It's difficult with rats to decide on
a criterion of "useful life." With these rats it was observed that
the reproductive life of the females was increased in even larger
proportion than the length of life.

Meaning in Terms of Human Beings

In terms of human beings this means that double or
quadruple amounts of vitamin A might bring about a 15 to
20 per cent increase in years of life, and an even greater increase
than that in active and useful life. Roughly estimated it seems
that we might expect to live to the age of 110 or 120 without
any difficulty, and to be "in the prime of life" up to the age of
70 or even older. Incidentally, when Dr. Sherman and his associates doubled the vitamin A ration once again, they found there
was no further improvement. So it seems that you cannot go
on and on adding vitamin A to the diet and increasing the
benefit. There is, it appears, a level beyond which your body
cannot use extra amounts of vitamin A. But it seems certain
that this level is far, far higher than we have been led to believe
up to now.

Can We Get Too Much Vitamin A?

How much should you take of the various food supplements? Go according to the instructions on the label. These
suggested doses are based on recommendations of the Committee on Foods and Nutrition of the National Research Council. They indicate the amount that apparently will keep an
individual in good health, or at any rate will prevent symptoms
of vitamin deficiency. In other words, the amount listed in the
official daily minimum recommendations is the amount the
rats were getting over the first 67 generations of their lives. We
have seen that quadrupling this amount of vitamin A resulted
in a very significant increase in length of useful life.

Many researchers feel that the daily minimum requirements have been set far too low. But here we have definite
proof of how much too low they are—at any rate in the case
of laboratory rats. And there is no reason to believe that the

same would not be true of human beings. The recommended minimum of vitamin A is 5,000 International Units daily for an adult man or woman. Is it possible that 20,000 units daily would result in much better health and much greater length of useful lives? Until experiments with human beings have demonstrated this, we cannot say for sure. And this means we will never be able to know, for certainly human beings cannot be as rigidly controlled in their diet as rats and we doubt if there is any human being who would consent to be the subject of a nutritional experiment all his life. However, there seems to be no reason for not taking 20,000 units of vitamin A per day if you want to, and perhaps your own lengthened life will give you the answer.

Why Vitamin A Food Supplements Are Essential

We must point out several other angles involved in the vitamin A story. If you are depending on your meals alone for vitamin A, keep in mind that vitamin A itself does not occur in foods. Carotene, which does occur in foods (yellow and green foods chiefly) is made into vitamin A by the body. If, through any disorder, you are not able to convert carotene into vitamin A, and you are not taking any food supplement that contains vitamin A itself, then you will surely suffer from a deficiency.

It was recently discovered and reported by two New York physicians that diabetics are unable to transform carotene into vitamin A. This experiment, too, was performed with laboratory rats. All the rats were fed carotene rather than vitamin A. Then studies were done which showed that the diabetic rats had only one-fourth as much true vitamin A in their bodies as the non-diabetic ones. But when true vitamin A, as in fish liver oil, was fed, both the diabetic rats and their healthy controls showed an equal amount of vitamin A. Dr. Albert E. Sobel and Abraham Rosenberg of the Polytechnic Institute of Brooklyn, who made the announcement of these experiments, said, "these studies carry the clear indication that the diabetic rat must receive some source of preformed vitamin A, such as fish liver oils, rather than the usual carotene source, such as vegetables. The discovery that the conversion of carotene to vitamin A is impaired in experimental diabetes can be regarded as the first step toward the discovery of an agent to control the premature aging of the arteries found in individuals suffering from diabetes mellitus."

Once again we have a link between vitamin A deficiency and aging! Now surely anyone who suffers from diabetes should be taking a fish liver oil supplement to prevent night blindness, skin disorders and the other symptoms of vitamin A deficiency, and those of us who suspect there is anything wrong with the function of our livers should also be taking fish liver oils, for liver disorders, too, interfere with conversion of carotene (in food) into vitamin A in the body.

Start Taking Vitamin A Early in Life

Note, please, that the rats in Dr. Sherman's experiment were not kept on the just adequate vitamin A diet until they began to approach middle age, and were then given the double and quadruple doses. No. They were fed from birth on the bigger doses. And the lesson here is plain for us to see. Most of us are not even conscious of our health, or of how we are taking care of it, until middle age or perhaps a little earlier when we contract some annoying disease, or begin to notice lines in our faces, or gray hairs, or bad teeth. All of a sudden, then, we scramble desperately around trying to make up for all the years we have ignored our health. Dr. Sherman's experiment does not show what will happen to rats whose diet is enriched with vitamin A late in life. But it does show that those which grow up with it reap worth-while benefits. So our suggestion would be, if you have children, give those youngsters the best possible start towards a long and happy life by increasing their vitamin A, either in meals or supplements or both. And for those of us who are middle-aged or older, who knows? Perhaps increased vitamin A will postpone those wrinkles, gray hairs, and other signs of aging for another 10, 15 or even 20 years! At least there's no reason not to give it a try!

CHAPTER **90**

More About Vitamin A

The official facts about vitamin A—symptoms of deficiency, how much you need, and what foods can supply it best.

One of the easiest vitamins to obtain in a well-rounded diet, not lost to any great extent in cooking or storing, vitamin A is generally present in the average American diet in sufficient quantity to prevent serious deficiency diseases. But, on the other hand, nutritionists suspect that a borderline deficiency of vitamin A is quite common in America. That is, most people seem to get enough to protect them from serious consequences, but never enough to be free from complaints of "not being up to par." In a survey done recently in the schools of New York City, it was found that a slight vitamin A deficiency was the most common diet deficiency found among the children.

Vitamin A can be secured from both animal and plant sources. The animal sources are better in general, for there the vitamin appears as a substance in itself, whereas in plants we eat "carotene" which is then changed into vitamin A in the body. However, considering all angles of a well-rounded diet, many of the plant sources of vitamin A are excellent food, because they also provide other vitamins as well.

Symptoms of Vitamin A Deficiency

Vitamin A can be stored in the body (in the liver, chiefly) so there may be considerable depletion of it before symptoms of deficiency occur. The first obvious symptom, which you might easily begin to notice in yourself quite gradually, is called "night blindness." By this is meant the inability to adjust to sudden changes of light. Perhaps when you go into a darkened movie from the lighted foyer, you cannot see where you are going or where the empty seats are. It may take several minutes for you to get your bearings and feel comfortable. Perhaps when you are driving a car at night, the glare from an oncoming headlight blinds you so that you can see practically nothing for the next quarter mile or so. These are symptoms of vitamin A deficiency. Not being able to read or work in a medium-dim light is another symptom. Or there may be itching and burning or slight redness of the eyelids.

A skin disease, especially in children, is another symptom of vitamin A deficiency. In adults a serious deficiency in vitamin A leads to a horny condition of the mucous membrane of the mouth, the respiratory system and the genito-urinary system. Bladder stones are produced in rats by vitamin A deficiency, also diseases of the nerves somewhat akin to sclerosis in human beings. It has been found in many cases that abundant vitamin A in the diet helps greatly the condition of people with hyperthyroidism or goiter. Inability to store fat is a symptom of not enough vitamin A.

It has long been debated whether vitamin A helps to fight infection. Is it powerful against colds, against sinus trouble, against pneumonia? Apparently no positive proof has been found. But scientists have observed that, especially in children, symptoms of very serious vitamin A deficiency are always preceded by colds and other respiratory troubles.

Perhaps most important of all its functions, vitamin A contributes enormously to growth and dental health in growing children. It is essential for the child to have vitamin A while his teeth are being formed, and he is growing to his full stature. Way back when our grandmothers were raising their children, they knew how beneficial a daily dose of cod liver oil was, even though they may not have known why.

Daily Requirements of Vitamin A

Taking vitamin A in sufficient quantity relieves all symptoms of deficiency very quickly. However, there are several conditions that prohibit the body from absorbing this vitamin. Gastro-intestinal or liver diseases or infections of any kind limit our capacity to use vitamin A. The continued taking of mineral oil dissolves the store of vitamin A in the body and carries it away before it can be absorbed. (One of the many good reasons for not taking mineral oil!)

Since vitamin A is stored in your body, it is not absolutely necessary to eat some of it every day. However, since there is no way of checking how much reserve store you have left, you may find that all your vitamin A has been exhausted, and you are suddenly showing symptoms of deficiency, unless you're pretty faithful about getting enough of the vitamin over a period of time. The daily minimum requirements of vitamin A have been set as follows:

Moderately active adults . . . .   4,000 International Units a day
Children up to 12 years old . . . . . .   1,500 to 4,000 Units a day

Many nutritionists believe that this minimum is too low and that actually everyone should have more vitamin A than these figures indicate. The easiest way to obtain it without much attention to diet is to take fish liver oil. Halibut liver oil contains about a hundred times as much as cod liver oil. These oils are now sold with the number of units of vitamins A and D that they contain specified on the label. These are standardized, so that you cannot make a mistake in dosage. Buy the oil in the most economical form for the amount you want to take. (Do not take more than the recommended dose, as overdoses of vitamin A may be toxic.)

Of course, it is best if you also include in your diet regularly other foods that contain vitamin A. These are listed below along with an estimate of the amount of vitamin A in each. Here are some suggestions on cooking and storing foods that contain the vitamin: the food value is lost if the fat in which it is contained becomes rancid. Always refrigerate butter and milk and keep your fish liver oil in the refrigerator, too. Vegetables containing vitamin A do not lose it when they are cooked, for it is not soluble in water. Milk does not lose vitamin A when it is boiled. It is better, however, to bring milk to a quick boil, rather than to keep it warm for any length of time in an open kettle. Butter loses very little of its vitamin A when it is stored in air-tight containers. Some of its vitamin content is lost when butter is cooked; all of it is lost in frying. Margarine, incidentally, does not contain vitamin A unless it has been added by the manufacturer, in which case the carton will state that vitamin A (synthetic) has been added.

Foods Containing the Largest Amounts of Vitamin A

Foods	*International Units of Vitamin A*
Alfalfa leaf meal, dry	8,000 in 100 grams
Apricots, fresh	2,790 in 3 medium apricots
Apricots, dried	2,230 in 4-6 halves
Apricot nectar	1,086 in ½ cup
Asparagus, fresh	1,000 in 12 stalks
Beans, snap	630 to 2,000 in 1 cup, cooked
Beet greens	6,700 in ½ cup, cooked
Broccoli	3,500 in 1 cup, cooked
Butter	3,300 in about 8 tablespoons
Carrots, fresh	12,000 in 1 cup, cooked
Carrots, dehydrated	117,000 in 1 cup, cooked
Cantaloupe	3,420 in ½ cup of cantaloupe balls
Celery Cabbage	9,000 in 1 cup
Chard	2,800 in ½ cup, cooked
Cheese, cheddar	2,000 in a 5-inch cube
Cheese, cream	2,000 to 2,210 in 6 tablespoons
Cheese, roquefort	2,500 to 4,000 in 2 sectors
Cheese, swiss	1,970 to 2,700 in 4 slices
Cod liver oil	85,000 in 100 grams
Collards	6,870 in 1 cup, cooked
Cream	1,640 in 6 tablespoons
Dandelion greens	13,650 in 1 cup, cooked
Eel	660 to 13,650 in 1 serving
Eggs, whole, fresh	1,140 in 2 eggs
Endive (escarole)	10,000 to 15,000 in 1 head
Kale	7,540 in ½ cup, cooked
Kidney, beef	1,150 in ½ cup cooked, cubed kidney
Lettuce, green	4,000 to 5,000 in 6 large leaves
Liver, fresh beef	19,200 in 1 piece, cooked
Liver, fresh calf	20,500 in 2 slices, cooked
Liver sausage	5,750 in 3 slices
Mango	1,000 to 1,500 in 1 mango
Milk, dry, whole	1,400 in 1 cup
Mustard greens	6,460 in 1 cup, cooked
Nectarines	2,800 in 2 nectarines
Olives, green	1,500 per pound
Papaya	2,500 to 3,000 in 1 papaya
Parsley	5,000 to 30,000 in 100 sprigs of parsley
Peaches, yellow	880 to 2,000 in every medium peach
Peaches, yellow, dried ...	3,000 to 3,250 in every medium peach
Peas, split	1,680 to 1 pound
Peppers, green	3,000 in 2 peppers

(Table continued on page 587)

Foods	*International Units of Vitamin A*
Peppers, red	2,000 in 2 peppers
Persimmons	2,600 in 1 persimmon
Prunes, dried	1,600 to 2,500 in 12 medium prunes
Pumpkin	1,200 to 3,400 in 1 cup, cooked
Sardines, canned in oil ...	1,080 per can
Spinach, fresh	9,420 in ½ cup, cooked
Spinach, canned	5,500 to ½ cup
Squash, winter	4,950 in ½ cup, cooked
Sword fish	1,595 in 1 serving
Sweet potatoes	7,700 in 1 medium potato, baked
Tomatoes, fresh	1,100 in 1 medium tomato
Tomato juice	4,770 in 1 pound
Tomato puree	8,540 in 1 pound
Turnip greens	9,540 in ½ cup, cooked
Watercress	4,000 in 1 bunch cress

CHAPTER 91

Vitamin D

Vitamin D is another fat soluble vitamin which occurs in the same concentrated form in the food supplement we recommend as a source for vitamins A and B. It is essential to good health, especially for children.

Most of us have known about the health-giving qualities of cod liver oil since we were very young. Many of us took it when we were children. Most of us have a vague idea that cod liver oil is good because it contains a vitamin; we know, too, that there is supposed to be something in sunshine that is good for us if we get just enough and not too much. The good fairy in cod liver oil and sunshine is vitamin D—or perhaps we should say the vitamin D's, for there are two which are important for human nutrition—vitamin D_2 and D_3.

The chemical names for these substances are sometimes used rather than the letters. The vegetable substance which later becomes vitamin D_2 is called ergosterol. When it is irradiated by sunlight or by ultraviolet light, it is called calciferol. When this product has been diluted and is sold commercially, it is called viosterol. Chemists seem to delight in complicated names, but whenever you see one of the above jawbreakers, just remember that it stands for vitamin D_2. Practically all the vitamin D that we obtain in food comes from animal sources and is called dehydrocholesterol, or vitamin D_3. There is no vitamin D_1. The substance that was first discovered and called by that name was later found to be part of D_2.

Perhaps we can understand the human importance of vitamin D better if we know first how necessary this vitamin is to animals. Feather and fur-bearing creatures get their vitamin D from the sun. Apparently there is a substance in fur and feathers which is converted to vitamin D in sunlight. In the case of animals whose hair is quite thick and long, as some kinds of dogs and cats, it is believed that these animals get their vitamin D by licking their coats. So Tabby's bath is perhaps not so much a matter of cleanliness as of good health. Rats which have rickets from lack of vitamin D can be cured of the disease by exposure to sunlight, but they must be allowed to lick their fur or the sunshine does no good. Many animals hibernate during the winter months when there is little benefit to be derived from the sun's rays. If they are given daily doses of vitamin D, they will not hibernate, for there is then no need for it.

Manufacturing Vitamin D from Sunlight

Human beings, too, manufacture vitamin D in the presence of sunlight. Summer sun is most effective. In fact, winter sun has few of the ultraviolet rays necessary, so that a very long exposure to winter sun is necessary to produce the same good effect as a short exposure during the summer. At the seashore the concentration of ultraviolet light is intense, for it comes from the sky and is also reflected from the water. Clouds, fog and dirt in the air prevent the sun's rays from reaching us, which is one reason why a summer vacation in a city, no matter how good a time you have, will not bring you the health benefits of a vacation at the shore, in the country or in the mountains.

The oil glands of the skin secrete the substance that becomes vitamin D in the presence of sunlight. In human beings this vitamin D is then absorbed through the skin and passes into the blood stream. Anything that removes the oily secretion from the skin will also remove the vitamin D. So suppose you take a sun bath and fill your skin with healthful vitamin D, then come inside and immediately take a shower with lots of soap. All of the vitamin D disappears, and you might just as well have saved yourself the time and trouble of the sun bath. This seems to be an excellent reason why primitive people in the tropics seldom suffer from lack of vitamin D. They got lots of sunshine, they wear scanty clothes, they bathe infrequently and they never use soap. No one knows how long it takes for all the vitamin D to be absorbed from the skin, but it seems wisest to bathe at night rather than in the morning, when you plan to be in the sunshine during the day.

You Can Get Too Much Sunlight

Who has not experienced the miseries of a bad case of sunburn? The intolerable pain and later the itching and peeling for which no medicines can bring relief testify to the fact that we must use sunlight wisely. Sunburn thus warns us that we've had too much sun. But suppose we "tan" carefully and bring home from the shore a dark brown leathery skin which makes us look so healthy to all the stay-at-homes. Actually such a procedure is probably even more unhealthy than a sunburn. Tan is nature's provision against too much ultraviolet light.

As the summer progresses and your tan grows deeper, you absorb less and less ultraviolet light, hence your body manufactures less and less vitamin D. A farmer or a lifeguard, for instance, may be outside every daylight hour from May to October, and, if he has a handsome tan by June, you may be certain he will absorb no more vitamin D that summer. Now what happens when winter comes? No vitamin D has been stored away, winter sunshine does not provide any ultraviolet light and our farmer or lifeguard is quite likely to suffer from a serious shortage of vitamin D throughout the winter. Probably he will not consider taking fish liver oil (what, a healthy, tanned, outdoor guy like him?). But, as we will see, a vitamin D deficiency can have serious consequences.

Clothing and window glass shut out ultraviolet rays, so

your sunning should be done outside with a minimum of clothing. Any part of your body that is exposed to the sun will absorb ultraviolet, and the vitamin D manufactured will be carried to all parts of your body. And you need not sit in direct sunlight, for on a bright summer day ultraviolet rays are reflected, so you can sunbathe in the shade, too. Dark complexioned people absorb less utraviolet than their fair-skinned cousins, so they need a longer exposure to sunlight to produce the same amount of vitamin D. Incidentally, a new kind of window glass is available which permits ultraviolet rays to enter. This is inexpensive and very beneficial, although in time its effectiveness will disappear. Your local hardware store can undoubtedly give you more details.

A Good Team—Sunshine and Cod Liver Oil

The unwashed Polynesian child, playing all day in the sunlight summer and winter has no need for cod liver oil. But what about children in northern hemispheres who get their sunshine for perhaps 3 months in the summer and live the rest of the year in cities where little of the sun's ultraviolet light penetrates? These children are bound to contract rickets if their diet is not supplemented with a good, assimilable source of vitamin D. Until quite recently most children in our country had rickets to a greater or lesser degree, evidenced by bowlegs, knock-knees, bad teeth, poor posture and faulty bone development, for rickets is a disease of teeth and bones.

It is not known exactly how vitamin D works in the body to prevent rickets, but it is believed that the vitamin assists the body to assimilate phosphorus, the mineral which combines with calcium in the body. A lack of vitamin D, then, means almost certainly a lack of phosphorus and calcium, even in a diet in which there is plenty of both these minerals. On the other hand, of course, no one can live on sunshine and cod liver oil alone. So for the vitamin D to do you any good, there must be plenty of calcium and phosphorus in your diet.

Vitamin D Is the Beauty Vitamin

Vitamin D, therefore, is of utmost importance to children, for they are growing and their bones and teeth must be made from minerals which they can secure only from their diet and which their bodies will be able to use only if they have sufficient vitamin D. Country children who are outdoors all summer and take cod liver oil in the winter seldom have rickets. But city slum children who see little of the sun and whose mothers know nothing of nutrition may grow up deformed, small in stature, with little chance for beauty, for their faces are narrow, their legs bowed, their jaws under- or over-developed, their teeth crowded into dental arches too small to contain them, their foreheads bulging. So vitamin D is the beauty vitamin, too, for how can a child attain the wide chest and hip structure, the normal mouth structure, straight legs, strong back and good posture that go with beauty, unless the proper minerals are present, along with vitamin D to create this handsome bone structure? In one sense vitamin D is the most important of all vitamins, for with all the others, the conditions caused by a deficiency can be corrected. But once a bone has stopped growing, nothing will make it grow again, once a leg bone has been bowed, no diet will straighten it out and once a jaw structure has grown small and misshapen, no vitamin can transform it.

Fish Liver Oil for Vitamin D

So modern mothers give their children fish liver oil, which is richer in vitamin D than any other substance. It goes without saying these days that any doctor delivering a baby advises fish liver oil right from the beginning of the baby's life. And most babies in our country these days reach the age of 4 or 5 without contracting rickets. But all too often the dose of fish liver oil is discontinued too soon. Remember that children keep on growing until they are fully mature. And for good growth, sound teeth, long straight limbs and strong backs, fish liver oil should be part of their diet until full growth has been achieved. Aside from the matter of beauty, vitamin D is important for health in later life. If the body structure of a chest is narrow, diseases of the chest are likely to be more easily contracted. A woman with a narrow pelvic structure (caused by lack of vitamin D in childhood) is almost certain to have a difficult time in childbirth.

Vitamin D Deficiency in Adults

Osteomalacia is the disease of adults that corresponds to rickets in children. It is a condition in which the bones become soft and weak because they have been robbed of their mineral content in earlier years. Lack of vitamin D in the diet can bring about such a condition. But plenty of vitamin D is of no use unless there is plenty of calcium and phosphorus, too. And a diet rich in minerals will be of no benefit without vitamin D.

How Much Vitamin D Do You Need?

Daily requirements of vitamin D are hard to establish, for, of course, the amount one needs depends not only on the kind and quantity of food he eats, but also on the amount of summer sunshine he is exposed to. Children in large cities who do not have the opportunity to play outside in bright sunlight the year 'round need much more vitamin D than those who can be outdoors part of the day all year. Then, too, the amount and kind of milk the child drinks is important, too.

Vitamin D is measured in International Units. It is believed that 135 units daily will protect an infant from rickets, if he also has a quart of milk a day or some other reliable source of calcium and phosphorus such as bone meal. A daily intake of 300 to 600 units will produce the best effects on growth, development and health for children. Some older children may be able to assimilate calcium easily. They will have healthy teeth and bones. Taking vitamin D appears to benefit them little. But the vast majority of children in our country have difficulty absorbing calcium, and additional vitamin D will aid greatly in helping them to use this important mineral.

The National Research Council which studies and recommends minimum daily requirements has this to say about adults: need for supplemental vitamin D by vigorous adults leading normal lives seems to be minimum. People who work at night, nuns (because of their heavy garments) and older people appear to need vitamin D. Of course, we believe that no adult in the northern part of our country gets enough sunshine the year 'round that he can afford to do without a vitamin D supplement in his diet. True, his bones and teeth are no longer growing, but calcium is important for many other functions, and if his body does not assimilate calcium, all these functions suffer.

Vitamin D Is Important for Adults, Too

For instance, it has been discovered that there is some relationship between thyroid function and vitamin D, for a deficiency in the vitamin causes an increase in the metabolic rate—the rate at which food is burned. Since this is determined by the thyroid gland, it seems that the amount of vitamin D taken is of extreme importance to the good health of this gland. Some types of arthritis have been improved or cured by the administration of vitamin D. Some eye diseases improve when vitamin D is given. Children who suffer from myopia (near-sightedness) have shown a lack of either calcium or phosphorus in their blood, indicating that a well-rounded diet, including lots of minerals and vitamin D, might prevent this disorder. Vitamin D is also valuable to maintain nervous stability, normal heart action and normal clotting of the blood, since all these functions are also related to the body's supply of calcium and phosphorus.

One final reason for both adults and children taking vitamin D is the fact that it also influences the body's ability to burn sugar. Whether it is natural sugar in fruits, vegetables, honey and so forth, or white refined sugar, it is carried by phosphorus through the intestinal wall and from the blood stream to be stored until it is necessary for energy. If there is little vitamin D present, there is also a shortage of phosphorus, so the sugar will not be burned efficiently. This means that sugar will be lost in the urine and the feces, and the energy that should be forthcoming will be sadly decreased.

Adelle Davis in her book, *Vitality Through Planned Nutrition* (The Macmillan Company, 1949), suggests that lack of vitamin D may be a reason why many people seem to have less energy in the winter. Perhaps this is why growing children crave sweets.

Miss Davis agrees with us that adults assuredly need vitamin D. She reminds us that very few adults pay enough attention to their diet, so they are apt to have very little calcium and phosphorus. The less they have of these two minerals, the greater is the necessity for them to take vitamin D to conserve as much as possible of these minerals. "The amount of vitamin D desirable for an adult is not known. Outstanding authorities have suggested 800 units per day."

Sources of Vitamin D in Daily Diet

Very few foods contain any considerable amount of vitamin D. Butter, eggs, herring, liver, mackerel, milk, salmon and tuna are the best sources and the amounts obtained in these foods are very small indeed. Butter, eggs and milk in the summer contain much more than in winter. But even so, 100 grams of egg yolk contain only about 200 units of vitamin D, whereas the same amount of halibut liver oil contains 60,000. There is practically no vitamin D in the green, leafy vegetables that are so rich in other vitamins.

Not so long ago it was discovered that foods could be irradiated with ultraviolet light to increase their vitamin D content. Milk is the food most often treated in this way. "Irradiated" milk is milk that has been exposed to ultraviolet light, so that it contains more of the vitamin. "Metabolized" milk is milk from cows that have been fed irradiated yeast. The vitamin D content of this milk varies with the amount of yeast fed daily to the cows. "Fortified" milk is milk to which a tasteless vitamin D concentrate has been added.

Since vitamin D is a fat soluble vitamin, it can be stored in the body, but not in as large quantities as vitamin A. As is true of all other fat-soluble vitamins, vitamin D is destroyed in the intestinal tract in the presence of mineral oil—another excellent reason for never taking this laxative.

Too Much Vitamin D Can Be Dangerous

Vitamin D in enormous doses is sometimes prescribed by physicians for certain diseases, but they must always be alert to the possibility of poisoning from too large a dose. It is hardly likely that anyone taking fish liver oil would give himself too large a dose if he pays any attention at all to the suggested dosage on the bottle. More than 400,000 units daily are considered toxic for adults. Taking 30,000 or more units daily over a period of time can easily produce symptoms of poisoning in babies, and 50,000 units are dangerous for children. So be sure to take your fish liver oil in the suggested dosage. And unless you live outdoors summer and winter, be sure that every member of your family takes fish liver oil for vitamin D. Cod liver oil contains less vitamin A than halibut liver oil. This means that if you take enough halibut liver oil to give you your daily requirement of vitamin A, you will not get so much D as if you were taking cod liver oil. Either is good.

A letter from a reader pointed out to us recently that he had been using a certain brand of fish liver oil for many years. Recently he happened to look at the label and found to his amazement that this product now contained large amounts of synthetic vitamin D and was no longer just natural fish liver oil. The label stated that this change had been made to avoid any possibility of a "fishy" taste. It is wise to check on every bottle you buy, to make certain that you are getting a wholly natural vitamin product, with no synthetic substances added. Of course, the finest possible companion for fish liver oils in your daily food supplements is bone meal, which supplies the calcium, phosphorus and other minerals which the vitamin D will make certain you assimilate.

CHAPTER **92**

Fish Liver Oils Are Food

Fish liver oils are not medicine. They are pleasant and easy to take in today's dependable preparations.

In the eighteenth century the physicians of England discovered that fish liver oil could cure rickets. Fish liver oil had been eaten in Iceland and Norway for centuries before that. In those days this is how they made oil, because there was no other method known for extracting it from the fish livers. The livers were allowed to putrefy, to rot, until the oil came to the surface and could be skimmed off. The imagination is staggered at the thought of the aroma that must have clung to the walls of the buildings in which this process took place, the clothes worn by the fishermen, the containers in which the fish liver oil was collected.

Its Value Known in Past Centuries

And yet, hundreds and hundreds of years ago, human beings knew so much about the potency of fish liver oils that determined mothers in northern countries pinned down their squalling youngsters and poured into their protesting gullets

quantities of this putrid, offensive oil—and watched them grow
tall and straight and healthy as a result. It was not suspected
until quite recently why fish liver oil is so important to growth
and good health. From the Manchester, England, Infirmary,
Dr. Robert Darbey wrote to a friend in 1782: "For several
years after I came to the infirmary I observed that many poor
patients, who were received into the infirmary for the chronic
rheumatism, after several weeks trial of a variety of remedies,
were discharged with little or no relief. . . . About ten years
since, an accidental circumstance discovered to us a remedy,
which has been used with the greatest success, for the above
complaint, but is very little known, in any county, except
Lancashire; it is the cod, or ling liver oil." Drummond and
Wilbraham go on to tell in *The Englishman's Food* that the
infirmary doctors were so pleased with the results they obtained
that no less than 50 or 60 gallons were prescribed annually
in spite of the fact that the smell and taste were so repulsive
that many patients could not stomach it.

Fish Liver Oils Contain Vitamins A and D

In those days almost any disorder of the bones or joints
was called "rheumatism" so, of course, rickets, tuberculous joint
diseases and so forth were among those cases of "rheumatism"
cured by the new remedy. About the middle of the nineteenth
century, an incident in the London Zoo confirmed the potency
of the new medicine. The curators had always been unable to
raise lion and bear cubs, for they developed rickets easily and
early and soon died. The animals were fed on a raw meat diet.
On the advice of a prominent British physician of the time,
crushed bone, milk and cod liver oil were added to the meat.
From then on, there were no further casualties among the 200
animals. Looking for the reason for such wonderful properties,
one investigator of the early nineteenth century decided it was
the iodine in the fish liver oil that performed the miracles. And
indeed up until the time of Sir Edward Mellanby and his
famous experiments with rachitic puppies, only about 30 years
ago, no one knew that the precious ingredients of fish liver oils
are the concentrated vitamin A and D they contain. Nor
does anyone know up to the present time why these vitamins
occur in such abundance in fish livers. Presumably they are
stored there by the fish, but why in such quantity?

"It is not surprising," says Drummond and Wilbraham, "that the possibility of other fish liver oil possessing therapeutic value aroused interest after cod liver oil re-established its reputation in England. *The Lancet* drew attention to the possibilities of using shark liver oil in 1855, but the extraordinary potency of the liver oils of such fish as the halibut and tunny was unsuspected until quite recently. Perhaps this is understandable. Cod liver is exceedingly rich in fat (30-50 per cent) whereas most of the livers which yield the very potent oils contain a much smaller proportion (2.8 per cent). When substitutes for cod liver oil were sought it was natural to turn to those like the shark, which also have a large amount of oil stored in the liver."

H. C. Sherman, Columbia University's world-famous nutritionist, in his book, *Food Products* (The Macmillan Company, 1941), has this to say about fish liver oils as food: "Hitherto in this country, the fish liver oils have been commonly considered as medicines rather than food. But cod liver oil has been a stable article of food in some fishing communities; moreover its clinical value seems to lie in its contribution of two dietary essentials, vitamin A and vitamin D. For these reasons, there is justification in thinking of these fish liver oils as vitamin-rich foods."

Why Fish Liver Oils Are Important

Let us briefly consider some information on these two important vitamins. Vitamin A can be obtained from animal and vegetable food. Vitamin D is available only in animal products and in the ultraviolet rays of the sun, that is, some substance in your skin can manufacture vitamin D from sunlight. And the amount of vitamin D in animal products (cream and butter, for example) is infinitesimal compared with the wealth of vitamin D in fish liver oil.

The Importance of Vitamin A

Vitamin A is necessary for a healthy skin. It is important, too, for the eyes. Its deficiency results in "night blindness," which means inability to adapt to light after darkness, or darkness after light. Research has indicated that vitamin A is important for the prevention of infections, such as colds. It has been found that plenty of vitamin A in the diet helps the condition of people with goiter or other thyroid trouble. Vitamin

A deficiency results in inability to store fat. For children, the vitamin is an absolute essential if bones and teeth are to be healthy and if the child is to grow strong and tall. Bladder stones are caused in laboratory animals by lack of vitamin A.

Vitamin D Prevents Rickets

Vitamin D is essential for the proper use by the body of calcium and phosphorus—perhaps the two minerals most important for good health. No matter how much of these two minerals you get in your diet, you cannot use them unless you also have plenty of vitamin D. So rickets, a deforming bone disease, can be caused in children by lack of any one or more of these 3—calcium, phosphorus or vitamin D. Animals manufacture their vitamin D from sunlight. And it has been found that hibernating animals do not hibernate when they have been given enough vitamin D. They know, you see, that the sun's rays in winter time are not strong enough to provide the amount of vitamin D they need. Osteomalacia is the adult disease corresponding to rickets in children, when the bones become decalcified from lack of one of the two important minerals, or vitamin D.

Vitamin D for Adults, Too

For many years it has been accepted practice to give babies in this country fish liver oil to prevent rickets. And the incidence of rickets has greatly decreased as a result. But why should we stop giving this vitamin-rich food when children reach adolescence? At that time they are growing very rapidly and need all the calcium and phosphorus they can get for making bones and permanent teeth. Calcium is one mineral that, all nutritionists agree, is deficient in the American diet. We do not eat enough leafy green vegetables, eggs and cheese to supply anything like the amount of calcium we need. Why not, then, just to be on the safe side, get plenty of vitamin D so that we can use effectively all the calcium we get?

We believe that everyone, children and adults alike, should take fish liver oils to be assured of getting plenty of both vitamin A and vitamin D. In case you live in the South and spend a lot of time out in the sunshine, take one of those oils which is richer in vitamin A and has less vitamin D. If you live in the North, you are well aware how puny and how brief the rays of the winter sun are, especially when they are filtered through the smog and smoke of a large city. Do you think you can afford to take a chance on too little of either of these necessary vitamins?

How to Take Fish Liver Oils

Here is a table taken from *The Englishman's Food* showing the variety of vitamin D content of the different fish liver oils:

	International Units of Vitamin D per gram
Cod	50-200
Halibut	1,000-4,000
Sea Bass	4,000-5,000
Swordfish	4,000-10,000
Yellow Fin Tunny	13,000-45,000
Striped Tunny	220,000-250,000

Compare this, please, with the vitamin D contained in butter (1 unit per gram) or egg yolk (1.5 to 5 units per gram). Halibut liver oil has largely displaced cod liver oil as a food supplement today because it is also extremely rich in vitamin A, so that a small amount of it provides much more vitamin A than cod liver oil does.

Too Much May Be Dangerous

Because of the high concentration of vitamins in fish liver oil, don't make the mistake of deciding that, if a little is good, a lot will be better, for fish liver oil taken in enormous quantities is dangerous. Read the directions on the container in which you get your oil. The minimum daily requirement of vitamin A is 5,000 units per day for adults and from 1,500 to 6,000 units per day for children according to age. The vitamin D requirements are 400-800 units for children. The National Research Council, which sets these minimums, does not suggest any minimum requirements of vitamin D for adults. More than 400,000 units of vitamin D daily is considered toxic for adults, and more than 30,000 units daily is toxic for children. This is easily understandable when you think of the vitamins in terms of food. Eating five times as much as you should have of almost any food would be bound to make you sick, no matter how healthful the food may be. So be guided by the suggested daily dose on the container.

One word more. There are food supplement manufacturers who do all kinds of things to vitamin preparations. They may use synthetic vitamins—that is, they make up the vitamins in a chemical laboratory, putting together the chemical elements (oxygen, hydrogen, nitrogen and so forth) as they occur in the natural vitamin. These are not for you, if you would be healthy. Then some processors take natural fish liver oil and add different substances to it, to increase the potency. These are also not for you. When you buy fish liver oils, for yourself or your children, make certain that they contain nothing—but nothing— except the fish liver oil. The label will tell you what the contents are, and the potency. That is, the label will indicate that one perle contains 5,000 units of vitamin A and 200 units of vitamin D or whatever it may happen to be. Take the fish liver oil according to the suggested dosage.

And—lucky you—to be alive today when fish liver oils have been shorn of their taste and smell!

SECTION 26

VITAMIN B

Take brewer's yeast and/or desiccated liver for all the vitamins of the B complex. Wheat germ is also very rich in vitamin B, as are sunflower seeds. It is much better for you to get your B vitamins from a natural source like this than to take just one or several in a synthetic vitamin preparation.

CHAPTER 93

Vitamin B

Our own bodies contain marvelous defenses against germs and disease if we but furnish the right ammunition in sufficient quantity. As one doctor put it: "There is no such thing as disease, there is only an unhealthy body." It has been found that we have tuberculosis, pneumonia and polio germs and viruses always with us. Yet, only those persons whose resistance is low become diseased. Now we are finding more and more that cancer and other degenerative ailments can attack our bodies only when they lack some vital substances. An article in the *New York Times* of April 4, 1952, tells how the vitamin B complex helps the body build antibodies to fight disease.

At the annual scientific meeting of the National Vitamin Foundation, Incorporated, Dr. Elaine P. Ralli, Associate Professor of Medicine at the New York University College of Medicine reported on an experiment in physical stress endured by normal young men, in which B vitamins were found to "cushion" the unfavorable effects.

These young men when on an ordinary diet, were immersed in cold water for 8 minutes, and this stress, although brief, produced chemical changes in the blood and urine, as well as in the temperature, blood pressure and heart rate. There was a significant increase in the ratio of certain waste products of the body and a decrease in two substances in the blood—the granular red blood cells and the circulating white blood cells which are the disease-germ fighters of the body.

Then for 6 weeks the men were "built up" with large doses of a member of the vitamin B group (calcium pantothenate) and again given the cold-water immersion experience. Tests identical with the former showed that the changes in the blood and urinary components were less than before, and that this occurred because the vitamins had strengthened the effectiveness with which the adrenal glands produced various hormones, possibly including cortisone. These adrenal outpourings help the body to overcome physical strains, and thus the B vitamins increase the body's capacity for resistance.

Effects of Vitamin B Are Long-Lasting

These cushioning effects persisted in some patients for 4 months, but all had worn off after 5 months. This persistence is the more surprising since we know that most of the B vitamins are not stored in the body, being soluble in water, and any excess of daily intake is thrown off in the urine.

Another proof of the vital importance for health of the vitamin B group was given at the same meeting, by Dr. A. E. Axelrod of Western Reserve University at Cleveland. He had deprived rats of 3 of the B vitamins: pantothenic acid, pyridoxine and pteryloglutamic acid, and found the animals severely impaired in their ability to build up antibodies with which to fight disease.

Thus we have two more links in the chain of proof which we have been forging: that plenty of vitamins are absolutely necessary for health, and health means, among other things, the power to withstand disease. Medical science is approaching it another way: its search for specific remedies for specific diseases has brought it at last to the vital elements in foods; and using these as drugs, *after the disease has invaded a body,* it is performing miraculous cures. In effect, these doctors are supplying in massive doses, and in fragmentary particles, elements which the poor bodies have been deprived of through years of deficient nutrition or faulty assimilation.

The relation of the vitamin B complex to infantile paralysis is discussed in articles reproduced in this book. Quotations from writings of Dr. W. J. McCormick of Toronto, Canada (in *Good Health,* July, 1938) and of Drs. Spies, Chinn and McLester (in the *Journal of the Amercan Academy of Applied Nutrition,* autumn, 1948) state the same hypothesis: that polio may be one of a group of diseases having similar symptoms, which arise from a deficiency of the B vitamins. Beriberi, pellagra, encephalitis and other nervous diseases have been found to be greatly improved by the administration of vitamin B, and

Dr. McCormick relates some dramatic cures from this therapy in his articles in the *Medical Record* for November 1 and 15, 1939, and June 4, 1941.

Vitamin B Strengthens Endurance

Important for an understanding of vitamin B is the splendid work done at the Sloan-Kettering Institute for Cancer Research, described in detail in the *Journal of Nutrition* by Kanematsu Sugiura. Rats in whose livers cancer had been induced by the feeding of an artificial coloring matter named Butter Yellow (details of experiment in next chapter), were put on diets containing varying amounts of vitamin B complex-containing foods such as dried milk, brewer's yeast, dried beef liver and others. It was found that cancer was prevented in proportion to the concentration of vitamin B contained in the foodstuff, and that a certain daily minimum was necessary for complete protection. That is, when brewer's yeast constituted 15 per cent of the diet none of the rats developed cancer, while 10 per cent of dried beef liver protected them from the disease on a cancer-producing diet.

In view of the fact that the B vitamins are only meagerly supplied in the foods most commonly eaten, and the further fact that soil impoverishment renders the vitamin content of all foods uncertain, except those grown on soil organically fertilized, it seems imperative that we should add a good quantity of the vitamin B group to our menus daily. The two richest sources are desiccated (dried) liver and brewer's yeast; while wheat germ, whole grains, soybeans and the organ meats such as liver and heart are also rich. The remarkable effect of desiccated liver in strengthening the endurance of swimming rats is discussed in this book, as reported in the *Proceedings of the Society of Experimental Biology and Medicine* for July, 1951, along with an extended discussion of the wonderful values it carries in addition to the greatest concentration of the B vitamins of any known food.

What person, knowing that the B vitamins are necessary to build up his body's power to combat physical stress, to create antibodies against disease and to protect him against cancer, would neglect to include an adequate quantity in his daily diet? What woman, knowing that a sufficiency of the vitamin B group might be one of the factors to enable her children to avoid infection from the polio virus, would fail to work out some way of including these precious elements in her menus, so that her family would not only eat them and like them, but also enjoy robust health?

Vitamin B and Paralysis

Several years ago an astounding testimony to the effect of vitamin B_1 and vitamin C therapy was reported in the *Medical Record* for November 19, 1941. A young man whose spine had been fractured in an accident was a patient in a general hospital in Toronto. The fracture had resulted in complete paralysis and loss of sensation of all the lower half of his body, including the muscles that control the functions of urination and excretion. Lying in bed for almost a year, the patient had contracted bedsores. In patients confined to bed continuously, where they lie without moving, this condition is brought about by the pressure of the mattress against bony parts of the body which have the least flesh covering to protect them. This patient had 14 bedsores, some of them deep enough to expose the muscle to a depth of two inches. The sores were inflamed and filled with pus. The patient was emaciated, feverish with a weak and rapid pulse. He had no appetite.

W. J. McCormick, M.D., who wrote the article, had studied the effects of vitamin B_1 and vitamin C in curing open skin sores, so he directed that the patient be given vitamins B_1 and C, in addition to a diet that stressed wheat germ, brewer's yeast, fresh fruits, green vegetables, milk and egg yolks.

Within a week there was an amazing change for the better in the bedsores. The discharge gradually became less, the diseased tissue disappeared and healthy new tissue began to fill these ugly craters. Within about 3 months, the largest sores had decreased to half their original size and one had closed entirely. In addition, the general improvement in the patient's condition was almost incredible. His temperature and pulse rate rapidly became normal. There was a great improvement in the condition of his urine. His appetite increased until he was eating heartily and soon put on 25 pounds, which padded the bony parts of his body, thus helping to prevent more bedsores.

Most unbelievable of all are the other changes that occurred. Within a week from the beginning of vitamin therapy, the patient was able to move his toes for the first time in 6 months. Gradually he recovered the use of other muscles. Within less than two months the muscles controlling urination and bowel function were almost completely normal. The patient's paralyzed sensory nerves were so improved that for the first time since his accident he could feel the pressure of a hand or a bandage.

Drugs, Sedatives Increase Vitamin Demands

It is difficult to analyze exactly how vitamins B_1 and C brought about these improvements, says Dr. McCormick. Vitamin B_1 deficiency makes one susceptible to an unhealthy tone in the blood vessels, which could result in the rapid formation of bedsores, because of a lessened supply of oxygen in the tissues. A lack of vitamin C would impede the formation of new tissue necessary to heal and close wounds. Dr. McCormick believes the patient may have been suffering from a deficiency of vitamins B_1 and C when he met with his accident. The drugs and sedatives he was given had greatly increased the demand of his body for these vitamins. It has been shown, says Dr. McCormick, that *even moderate doses of barbiturates and narcotics may increase the bodily requirement of vitamin B_1 by as much as 40 per cent. Hospital diets are notoriously lacking in these vitamins.*

We have shown over and over again the results of vitamin B deficiency and the almost overnight improvement when vitamin B is included in the diet. We have insisted on the fact that a large segment of our population suffers from this deficiency due to the devitalizing and refining of our foods. Everyone who smokes or drinks increases his body's demand for vitamin B. Everyone who takes sleeping pills containing barbiturates must suffer from a tragic vitamin B deficiency. The B deficiency will naturally make such a person more nervous and jittery; he will have to take more sleeping pills, which will decrease his supply of vitamin B even more, in a vicious cycle.

The way out of this dilemma is not very complicated really. Eat foods that are rich in vitamin B—all the B vitamins. You can find them in any book on nutrition. Don't take synthetic vitamin preparations. Take the natural food supplements which contain all of the vitamins in the B complex—namely, brewer's yeast and desiccated liver.

We speak often of the necessity for taking vitamins in their natural form—that is, in food products rather than as they are synthesized in laboratories. All members of the B complex of vitamins should be taken together, rather than just two or three. These vitamins occur together in the same foods for a very good natural reason—they work together in the physiological processes of human beings, and one cannot function properly without the other.

Two experiments that came to our attention recently bring us further proof of the validity of our views. In *Science* for March 14, 1941, we found an article by Agnes Fay Morgan, a famous nutrition researcher from the University of California. Dr. Morgan reports on experiments in which the diets of animals were carefully controlled to include or exclude certain members of the B complex of vitamins. The results were startling. Three animals all of whom received the full diet along with adequate amounts of all the vitamins were alive and well at the end of the experiment.

Two animals received the full diet except for niacin, pantothenic acid and the "filtrate factor." Niacin and pantothenic acid are two of the B vitamins. The "filtrate factor" is that part of the B complex which has not as yet been thoroughly investigated. Researchers know that it consists of B vitamins and that it occurs in food along with other B vitamins, but they have not as yet broken it down into different vitamins and shown what part each of these vitamins plays. The animals on this diet were alive and well but developed gray hair, became inactive, with elderly sedate behavior and impaired digestion.

Four animals received ample diet in every respect except pantothenic acid and the "filtrate factor." Three of these died from paralysis. The fourth who was near death from paralysis was given the "filtrate factor" and a year later was alive and well. Her graying hair had turned dark once again.

Four animals were given all the vitamins except niacin. Two of them died of paralysis, the third was showing signs of paralysis when the experiment was reported on and the fourth who was given pantothenic acid, rather than the "filtrate factor" was alive and well. The last two animals received pantothenic acid and niacin but no "filtrate factor." After 6 months on this diet, both animals showed evidence of progressive paralysis and hair that was not gray, but was dull and powdery instead of glistening black.

Large Amounts Dangerous

The author concludes that for good health all these B vitamins are necessary, including the ones not yet discovered but known to be present in the filtrate factor. She emphasizes that concern must be given to the possible danger of administering large amounts of certain vitamins which are available in great quantities to people having multiple deficiencies. Adding isolated concentrations such as thiamin and nicotinic acid (niacin) may bring on more serious conditions than the mild deficiency coming from a poor yet balanced diet. Equal improvement in all directions is needed, the research expert stresses.

The second experiment was reported in the *Journal of Experimental Chemistry* for August, 1952. Rats which were normal and rats which were deficient in pantothenic acid were fed varying amounts of cholesterol. The normally fed rats developed fatty livers as a result of a very high cholesterol diet. But the rats who were deficient in pantothenic acid did not develop fatty livers. And when the pantothenic acid (a B vitamin, remember) was removed from the diet of the normally fed rats, the fatty livers returned to normal. The authors of this article, R. R. Guehring, L. S. Hurley and A. F. Morgan, do not comment except to point out that there seems to be a definite relationship between pantothenic acid in the diet and the use the body makes of cholesterol-rich foods.

What does all this indicate? That a diet deficient in niacin may result in gray hair and premature aging? Not exactly. That lack of niacin alone will cause paralysis? Not necessarily. That cholesterol begins to accumulate in the liver because pantothenic acid is in the diet? Certainly not. Actually what both the experiments show is simply that members of the B complex of vitamins should be taken together—all of them—or there is danger of serious upsets in nutrition and, consequently, in health.

In planning our everyday diets and especially in deciding on food supplements to take, it is most important to keep in mind what Dr. Morgan says about the possibility of making things much worse than the vitamin deficiency state, by taking large amounts of only one or several of the B vitamins. If you are going to a doctor and, for some unusual condition of ill health he should prescribe large amounts of, let's say, niacin or thiamin, then he is using this particular B vitamin as a medicine for a limited time only.

But when you are considering a food supplement that you will take regularly in order to prevent illness, then it is not only unwise, but positively dangerous to take only one or only several of the B vitamins. Many readers send us labels from various vitamin and mineral preparations they are taking and ask our opinion of them. Our opinion is always the same: if the supplement is made from natural food substance, then the combination and the proportion of vitamins are correct and healthful, for this is the way they occur in natural foods. If you inquire from the manufacturer, you will discover that such a substance is made from liver or yeast—two foods in which all the B vitamins are concentrated. A reliable manufacturer should not hesitate to tell you whether his product is natural or synthetic.

If the product has been made synthetically, you will probably find that some of the various B vitamins are listed, such as thiamin, niacin, pyridoxine and so forth, but not all of them. If a chemist has merely put these vitamins together in a laboratory and then combined them into a food supplement, it would be positively dangerous to take this supplement. It cannot possibly contain all the other members of the B complex. All of them have not as yet been discovered. But we do know that they exist in foods in which other B vitamins are plentiful.

Then, too, by our "enrichment" program for breads, flours and cereals we are laying the groundwork for certain disaster. *All* the vitamins are removed from the grain in processing these cereals. *Only a few are replaced synthetically.* No one has ever studied the result, over a period of years, of getting these few synthetic vitamins without the others that should go with them in natural foods. However, the experiments above show plainly that taking one B vitamin without the rest is inviting trouble. Our recommendation would be to avoid "enriched" food like the plague. Eat only completely whole grain cereals and flours. And take food supplements made from natural foods only—no synthetics!

CHAPTER **94**

Desiccated Liver

by J. I. RODALE

*Some astonishing facts about the powerfulness of desic-
cated liver are brought to light in this chapter.*

On reading a medical journal the other day, I came
across a piece of research which seemed unbelievable. It was the
kind of thing that I am continually seeking for, and praying
that I shall find. I am glad that this time it is not in the *Thou
shalt not* category. It is something positive.

In the medical publication called *Proceedings of the
Society of Experimental Biology and Medicine,* for the month
of July, 1951, B. H. Ershoff, M.D., describes a fantastic experiment he performed with rats in order to test an anti-fatigue diet.
He had an idea that there is something in liver that might
produce energy. He used 3 groups of rats, feeding them for 12
weeks as much as they wanted of 3 different diets. The first
group ate a basic diet, fortified with 9 synthetic and two natural
vitamins. The second group ate this same diet, vitamins and
all, with a plentiful supply of vitamin B complex added. The
third group ate the original fortified diet, but instead of vitamin
B complex, 10 per cent desiccated liver was added to their
ration.

Desiccated liver must not be confused with *extract* of liver
which is used in the treatment of anemia. Desiccated liver is
the *entire* liver of selected, healthy cattle-liver that has been
freed of external connective tissue and fat, and dried in a
vacuum at a temperature far below the boiling point so as to
conserve as much of the nutritional content as possible. The
final, powdered or tableted product is about one-fourth by
weight of the fresh raw liver.

The first group of rats, which were given the ordinary

diet, showed the least amount of growth in 12 weeks. The second group that received the extra B vitamins, experienced a little higher rate of growth in that period. But the third set which, instead of the additional B complex, were given the desiccated liver, grew about 15 per cent more than group one.

A Test for Fatigue

Then Dr. Ershoff tested his rat subjects for fatigue. They were placed one by one into a drum of water from which they could not climb out. They had to keep swimming or drown.

The rats on the original diet, which was well fortified with vitamins, swam for an average of 13.3 minutes before they gave up. The second group of rats, who had the added fortification of the ample B vitamins of brewer's yeast, swam for 13.4 minutes before giving up. Of the last group of rats, 3 swam for 63, 83, and 87 minutes. The other 9 rats of this group, the ones that had the desiccated liver, were still swimming vigorously at the end of 2 hours when the test was terminated. In other words, the rats that had received desiccated liver could swim almost 10 times as long as the others, without becoming tired.

Here was something to get excited about. Ever since I was a little boy, about every year some enterprising publisher ventured forth with a book on how never to get tired, or how to conserve energy. I read them, and not only did the reading make me tired, but when I ended, I was where I started. In my opinion they rarely offered anything real. They were just *books* as far as I was concerned.

Gelatine for More Energy

The first real development in the field of the conservation of human energy came about 7 or 8 years ago when the Knox Gelatine Company advertised that taking their gelatine would prevent fatigue. It was not the sugared jello that was meant, but the concentrated gelatine powder which came in small envelopes. You were supposed to take 3 packets a day in milk or juice, and brother, it *did* give you energy. I started taking it, and within a few days began to feel like Tarzan. But at the end of a 30-day period a dull feeling set in my head which persisted for days, and I dropped the gelatine regimen like a hot potato. As far as gelatine is concerned I know that Knox's is the best, and it may have special temporary medical uses, but

I still feel that there is something about its continuous taking that says, "caution."

A few years later, forgetting my previous experience, I began taking the gelatine again, and again the same thing happened. It enabled me to stay up later, but in a few weeks the tell-tale dull feeling came in the head to warn me that I was getting extra energy at the expense of harming some other bodily function. I recall also that I caught a cold at the time. Perhaps it might be safe to take only one packet of gelatine a day, but I cannot guarantee it, as I never tried it. I recall also about 8 or 9 years ago, taking regularly acidophilus milk, and I discontinued it because it gave me a similar dull feeling in the head.

Sodium May Be Cause of Trouble

In checking up, I find that gelatine is very high in sodium, and we know that, from studying the effect of table-salt (sodium chloride) on the body, it is the sodium that does the most harm. I find also in the *Journal of the American Medical Association* of November 17, 1951, the mention by a physician that the treating of a patient with the amino acid glycine caused the blood pressure to shoot up from 130 to 230. Over 20 per cent or one-fifth of gelatine consists of glycine.

I have before me 3 medical references. One says that "rats are quite unable to grow when given gelatine as their sole source of protein." Another says that "animals fed gelatine-supplement diets could not maintain blood glucose levels." The third one stated that the feeding of 6 per cent gelatine created an amino acid imbalance in rats.

The trouble with gelatine is that it does not contain 2 of the 20 amino acids of which protein is composed and is defective in two others. Besides, it contains too much glycine and sodium. It is interesting to note that in the Knox Company experiments, women did not experience an increase in energy from taking gelatine. It affected only the men.

We Should Rely on Liver

So let us rule out gelatine and go back to that cruel experiment in which innocent rats gave up their lives so that the diets of human beings could be improved. Although I feel sorry for the rats, yet even men by the millions spill their blood on battlefields so that our homes can be protected from some marauder-like Hitler, whose thinking may be defective, just like gelatine. It may seem cruel to drown rats, although many a kindly-disposed householder has often drowned a surplus or superannuated cat without the least compunction, knowing it was for the best interest of man and cat.

With regards to liver, its protein contains all of the amino acids, and it helped male as well as female rats to keep on swimming for two hours. Liver seems to be the thing, to be sure, that we should have in our diets in adequate amounts, in order to prevent certain nutritional deficiencies. We know that extract of liver cures anemia. No one can question the value of taking liver. There is nothing harmful about it.

Liver and Cancer

Over a period of years a remarkable series of experiments took place at the Sloan-Kettering Institute for Cancer Research in New York City. They were described in detail in the *Journal of Nutrition* (July 10, 1951) by Kanematsu Suguira who contributed a major share in the researches. The experiments mentioned in the previous chapter found that an artificial coloring substance, a dye known as butter yellow, could produce liver cancer in rats within 5 months. This poisonous chemical is no longer permitted to be used in the food industry.

Brewer's Yeast Tested

To test the effect of brewer's yeast in a cancer-encouraging diet, 3 groups of rats were put on a diet of rice and butter yellow. In addition, one group was given 3 per cent brewer's yeast, the second, 6 per cent and the third, 15 per cent, while a control group of 50 animals were fed only rice and butter yellow. Reported on in 1941, this test successfully demonstrated that brewer's yeast prevents liver cancer. All 50 animals in the control group receiving no yeast had cancerous livers within 150 days. All of the rats receiving yeast had smooth and practically normal livers. But it was found that the 15 per cent ration of yeast was necessary to offset the disease. Thirty per cent of those who received 3 per cent of brewer's yeast had completely healthy livers, but 70 per cent had livers with numerous cancer nodules. Of the animals who received 6 per cent brewer's yeast, 40 per cent of them still had normal livers at the end of the same 150 days, but 30 per cent of them had developed cirrhosis, while another 30 per cent had a few cancer nodules. To summarize: this experiment proved that the inclusion of 15 per cent brewer's yeast in the diet will prevent liver cancer in rats.

Dried Beef Liver Tried

In a second experiment dried beef liver was substituted for yeast with similar results. Ten per cent of this food saved animals on the cancer-producing diet. When this protection was cut to 2 per cent, cancer appeared in the livers of the test animals. It seems certain, therefore, that both yeast and dried beef liver contain substances which, when included in the diet in sufficient quantity, prevent cancer.

In another experiment it was found that whole beef liver was not as effective as dried beef liver in holding down the cancer. This would seem to indicate that desiccated liver is better than whole liver for this purpose.

Although the experiments described were done with rats, Dr. Suguira says in the *Journal of Nutrition* article that, "These dietary influences may prove to play a very large part in the causation, prevention and treatment of human cancer."

Tuberculosis and Liver

In the latter part of February, 1953, a new drug made the headlines in reference to a tuberculosis cure. The New York Department of Hospitals confirmed the fact that "very encouraging results," had been obtained in connection with two new drugs which were administered by mouth to 200 tuberculosis cases which would not respond to the regular medical procedures. The results were hailed as being highly dramatic, temperatures from 100 to 105 dropping down to normal within a few weeks. Within a week, patients who had been emaciated and refused food, were eating ravenously and gaining pounds so rapidly that they were soon back to their normal weights.

The drugs are niacin derivatives, and niacin is one of the B complex vitamins. In other words, here is a nutritional approach to the cure of one of our most baffling diseases. Liver contains an abundance of the vitamins of the B complex, including niacin, a vitamin which is known to prevent pellagra and the deficiency symptoms of depression, nervousness, confusion and fatigue. It afforded protection against one of the most dreaded diseases. Liver and brewer's yeast are the two richest sources of niacin. We cannot at this point tell you that taking liver will cure tuberculosis; but on the basis of this recent medical discovery, it looks as if liver would be a good food to take to insure good all-around health.

Is Liver a Gray-Hair Preventive?

As we investigated the subject of liver a little farther, we ran across something so startling and so promising that it brought us up short in our tracks. Perhaps the combination of food elements in liver might add up to the magic preventive of graying hair!

Experiments performed in 1931 by Keil and Nelson and reported in *The Newer Knowledge of Nutrition* by McCollum, Orent, Keiles and Day (published by Macmillan) reveal that the hair of anemic black rats turns gray, just as human hair does. Iron was added to the diet of the rats, and their hair remained gray. But when copper was added along with the iron, the rats' hair soon returned to its glossy black color. It is well known that there is more copper in the skin of black rats than in that of albinos. The relation of these findings to the color of human hair and skin had never (by 1947) been determined. Can it be that copper combined with iron is the nutritional answer to the problem of graying hair? Liver contains considerably more copper than its closest copper-containing competitors—nuts, wheat bran, molasses, dried peas and broccoli. It is thought that there is more in calves' liver, because it has been stored there, as the iron has, to provide the young animal with enough to last for some time.

Here is a list of the food items that contain the most copper:

Almonds	1.21	milligrams per 100 grams
Brazil nuts	1.39	milligrams per 100 grams
Hickory nuts	2.38	milligrams per 100 grams
Wheat bran	1.17	milligrams per 100 grams
Broccoli	1.37	milligrams per 100 grams
Dried currants	1.12	milligrams per 100 grams
Molasses	1.93	milligrams per 100 grams
Dried peas	1.40	milligrams per 100 grams
Whole milk	.02	milligrams per 100 grams
Dried whole milk	.15	milligrams per 100 grams
Yeast	none	that we can find
Beef liver, raw	2.15	milligrams per 100 grams
Calves' liver, raw	4.41	milligrams per 100 grams

Turning over a few more stones in our investigation, we found that two other ingredients of liver have also been credited with anti-gray hair virtues in animal experiments.

As reported in Rose's *Foundations of Nutrition* (published by Macmillan) and Proudfit and Robinson's *Nutrition and Diet* (published by Macmillan), when rats were fed a diet low in pantothenic acid (one of the B vitamins in liver) their hair became gray. Put back the vitamin, hair returned to its original color.

Gray Hair May Be Nutritional Problem

Apparently all human beings who are being treated with para-amino-benzoic acid do not react in the same way, according to observations made over a period of 6 months, on a group of patients. However, in the *Journal of Investigative Dermatology* for December, 1950, C. J. D. Zarafonetis, M.D., reports on 20 patients of his who were being given para-amino-benzoic acid for various skin troubles. Among these, 5 patients whose hair had been white or gray turned dark again in the course of the treatment. Also, where their hair had been thin before, it now grew thickly. Para-amino-benzoic acid, one of the newest of the B vitamins to be discovered, is not found in many foods. Among those which contain it are: liver, yeast, wheat germ, rice polishings, and also several other foods in which B complex vitamins are plentiful.

Perhaps, say some investigators of the subject, the darkening of the hair depends on not just one of these B vitamins (para-amino-benzoic acid and pantothenic acid), but on the ratio of the two in any given food. All the writers seem to feel that more experimenting must be done with human beings and animals before any scientific conclusions can be drawn.

We plan to search further through medical literature of the past 20 years, to see if we can uncover more facts about this pesky problem of graying hair, which probably causes more distress to people's vanity than any other one thing. We're convinced that it is a nutritional problem, related to a diet deficiency of one kind or another. We rather suspect it may involve two or three food elements rather than just one.

I am nothing less than thrilled with the four aspects of taking liver which reveal themselves in these researches. The taking of liver may be a factor in contributing to the prevention of fatigue, the prevention of tuberculosis and cancer and the retention of the original color of the hair. I say "may," because not enough work has been done on each one of these subjects to clinch it scientifically. But the thread that holds the 4 together is a powerful one. We do know that liver has been used for over 20 years in the treatment of anemia. What I like about it is that it is a food, and not a drug. How can you go wrong by eating liver, unless you are a vegetarian? And we must respect *their* viewpoint. However, in the case of bone meal and desiccated liver tablets the vegetarian might take the attitude of George Bernard Shaw, the world's most famous vegetarian.

A friend of his seeing him swallowing some liver tablets said to him, "I thought you were a vegetarian." Shaw replied, "I am. This is medicine." My advice to vegetarians is to consider bone meal and liver tablets as a medicine.

I strongly recommend the taking of bone meal, liver tablets and brewer's yeast. The liver may have something that the yeast lacks and vice versa. To these could very well be added vitamin D and A perles made from fish liver oils, and vitamin E from vegetable matter. Always check to see that your vitamins are all natural . . . not synthetic, coal tar products.

Natural Vitamins Best

Incidentally, I understand that the niacin compound that was used to cure tuberculosis was made from coal tar. It did the work, but it produced toxic side effects such as nausea and dizziness. Evidently some chemical was used with the niacin to make it more active. Had those people been taking brewer's yeast and desiccated liver since childhood, it would have worked more slowly and prevented the tubercular condition from setting in. I am sure that it is healthiest for us if we would take vitamins made from food products rather than from coal tar. In an emergency, of course, the synthetic product can be used, because it takes a long time and continuous use for such synthetics to develop trouble in the human body, which fortunately is a rugged instrument and will withstand abuse.

Now don't you think it would be a good idea to get yourself some desiccated liver tablets?

CHAPTER **95**

More Facts on Desiccated Liver

Here is some further exciting evidence on just what desiccated liver can do for health.

Investigation into the needs of human nutrition is generally made by experimenting with animal diet. Certain animals seem to require the same food elements as man, so their reaction to various foods gives researchers an insight into the probable effects of these foods in human nutrition. Mice and rats are favorite subjects for study. Colonies of these animals have been bred to have certain characteristics, so that their entire family history for generations is recorded, as it may predispose them to one condition or another.

Animal Food Versus Vegetable Food

A certain colony of mice was helpful in furthering two kinds of research recently—research into the value of animal food versus vegetable food, which led into research involving desiccated liver. These experiments were reported in *The Journal of Nutrition* for January, 1949. They were conducted by D. K. Bosshardt, Winifred J. Paul, Kathleen O'Doherty, J. W. Huff and R. H. Barnes of the Department of Biochemistry of Sharp and Dohme, Incorporated, Glenolden, Pennsylvania.

The colony of mice had been fed on a diet of vegetables and cereal grains during the war. Brewer's yeast, a plant, was included in the diet as well as some synthetic B vitamins. After many generations had been fed on this purely vegetarian diet, it was noted that the addition of liver to the diet of some of the mice increased their rate of growth considerably over that of the mice who did not receive liver.

After the war was over, meat scraps and dry skim milk were included in the diet. After some time on this diet, which included animal proteins, liver was fed again, and it was discovered that there was then no difference in rate of growth between those mice who had received liver and those who had not. So it was assumed that the mice could store for a certain period of time the "animal protein factor" contained in the meat and milk, and not in the vegetables and yeast.

Results of a Diet Lacking in Animal Protein

In a second experiment, 35 mice who were about to have litters were placed on a diet in which there was no animal protein whatsoever. Of the first litters produced on this diet, an average of 7.1 mice were raised to weaning age. In the second litter with the mothers still on an animal-protein-free diet, 6.8 mice per litter were weaned. Of the third litter, only 4.2 lived to weaning age. Of all the mice from the fourth litters, not a single mouse lived to the age of weaning. These two experiments show significant facts about the importance of animal protein in the diet. They also show that liver contributes a vitally necessary factor, especially when animal protein is lacking or scanty in a diet.

In a third experiment mice from some of the first 3 of these litters (whose mothers had been living on vegetarian diets, remember) were also placed on a vegetarian diet. Then one group of them was given a supplement of desiccated liver. Those offspring from the first litter after this experiment began showed an average gain in weight of 6.05 grams in the mice who had no liver in their diet. Those who had the liver gained 10.98 grams in the same time. In the second and third litters there was a weight gain of 2.20 grams and .90 grams for those who did not have liver and 10.43 and 10.40 grams for those receiving liver.

The authors indicate that this experiment shows a definite relationship between lack of animal protein in the diet of the mothers and the very disappointing gain in weight of their offspring. It also shows that some substance in liver corrects this "animal protein" deficiency.

Other Research on the Importance of Liver

In drawing their conclusions, the authors review other work which has been done on the importance of liver in the diet. As early as 1932 and 1933, L. W. Mapson showed in the *Journal of Bio-Chemistry* Vol. 26 and 27, that an apparently adequate diet can be improved by the addition of liver. His work demonstrated that liver contains a substance not present in yeast that has a stimulating effect on the growth and lactation of rats. Neither yeast nor wheat germ added to the diet produced this particular result.

Two experiments of B. H. Ershoff and H. B. McWilliams in 1947 and 1948 proved that feeding liver would completely counteract the retardation of growth in rats which had been fed a diet containing toxic amounts of thyroid, which would ordinarily stunt their growth. Wheat germ had no effect; yeast produced a slight effect, but liver supplied some factor which permitted these rats to grow normally even though they were being fed daily a substance which retards growth.

Our authors conclude: "The evidence appears to indicate that liver contains a multiplicity of unidentified growth factors. At least one of these factors is present in wheat and another, or the same factor, is present in yeast. Liver may contain at least two factors not present in yeast." These "factors" are not identical with any known vitamin.

Good Effects of Liver on Reproductive System

A surprising development in research on the potency of liver is announced in an editorial in the British medical publication, *The Lancet,* for February 16, 1952. Reviewing the history of sex hormone research, the editorial states that the human liver has been found to be an important controlling organ in the function of the sex hormones of both men and women.

Sex hormones are the chemical substances produced by the endocrine glands. These circulate in the body and cause the various activities of the reproductive organs: for instance, menstruation, pregnancy and lactation in women, and potency and sperm production in men. Apparently the human liver plays a large part in regulating the production of these extremely important sex hormones. In a series of 450 cases studied by M. S. Biskind and reported in *Vitamins and Hormones,* Vol. 4, 1946, a striking correlation was found between nutritional deficiency and an unbalance of sex hormones. In women these manifestations included various menstrual disturbances, painful breast changes and acne; in men the disturbance of the sex hormones resulted in enlargement of the breasts, softening of the testes, loss of hair in the armpits and decreased sexual drive. In both sexes infertility threatened.

"Treatment with vitamin B complex, especially in the form of desiccated whole liver produced in addition to the healing of the vitamin-deficiency (symptoms) rapid and dramatic improvement in the endocrine disturbances"—that is, in the changes mentioned above.

In another article in the *Archives of Internal Medicine,* Vol. 88, 1951, R. S. Long and E. E. Simmons report on a series of women patients who had apparently no liver disorder, but complained of painful menstruation and tenderness of the breasts. A high-protein, low-fat diet, *richly supplemented with B vitamins and liver* brought good or excellent recovery in all cases.

The Riddle of Human Life

We are sure you feel as we do—a great humility as we contemplate this further proof of the incredible complexity of the human body. But every new bit of information we find encourages us more and more. It seems as though every day true scientists get closer to a final answer of this complicated riddle of human life. And we feel certain that the time is not far off when scientific research will have proved beyond a shadow of a doubt that good nutrition—natural, wholesome food—is worth more for human health than all the drugs and chemicalized nostrums in the world.

As indicated in the two articles we have reviewed, desiccated liver contains some vitally important unidentified substance that is not in brewer's yeast or wheat germ. Desiccated liver has a powerful effect in regulating at least some of the functions of the reproductive system.

CHAPTER **96**

Brewer's Yeast

Brewer's yeast, inexpensive, easy to take and loaded with B vitamins, is also a good source of protein and minerals.

Over the centuries since the days of the early Egyptians, yeast has been used by men for baking and brewing. As more and more information has been accumulated about the nature of yeast plants, the cultivation of them has developed into a major industry.

Yeast is the smallest of all plants—about 1/4000th of an inch in diameter or about the size of a human blood corpuscle. Today the cultivation and harvesting of the plant is carried on under conditions in which the seed bed and the temperature are controlled. The production of present-day brewer's yeast can be guided, very much as plant specialists can guide the production of fruits and vegetables, so that only the best breeds will be used to produce plants rich in vitamins, proteins and minerals.

So carefully grown are the yeast plants that we eat in brewer's yeast that the manufacturer can foretell very accurately what the content of the final product will be in terms of protein and vitamins. The yeast plants are grown in large vats until they have produced the maximum number of yeast cells possible. They are then separated from the waste products of this growing process and dried at such a temperature that none of the nutritional value is lost. Then the yeast is pulverized and made into powder or is tableted.

Baker's Yeast Compared with Brewer's Yeast

Baker's yeast—the kind you use to raise bread—contains yeast plants that are still alive. As the tiny plants multiply, your bread increases in size. Housewives are well aware that they must treat live yeast plants with care. They require a temperature of about 80 degrees in order to flourish. When your bread

is risen and you put it into the oven, the yeast plants are killed
by the heat. In the same way the yeast plants in brewer's yeast
are destroyed when the yeast is dried. It is not advisable to eat
live yeast—baker's yeast, that is. The yeast plant needs a large
amount of B vitamins to grow. Once inside your digestive
tract and still alive, the yeast plant steals B vitamins from you.
But, in the case of brewer's yeast, the yeast plant is no longer
alive, and you are able to eat all the B vitamins the plant
stored up for itself.

Brewer's Yeast and Other Foods

Brewer's yeast contains all the elements of the vitamin B
complex. It is also a rich source of complex proteins—that is,
protein containing all the essential amino acids or building
blocks of protein. Other foods containing complete proteins are
meat, fish, eggs. Altogether 16 of the 20 amino acids are contained in brewer's yeast.

In comparison with several other foods high in B vitamins, here is how brewer's yeast stands:

Food	*Parts of Vitamin B_1 Per 100 Grams*
Brewer's yeast	5,000 to 8,000
Lean pork	300 to 750
Dried lima beans	450 to 600
Liver	300 to 420

Food	*Parts of Vitamin B_2 Per 100 Grams*
Brewer's yeast	2,500 to 4,700
Lean pork	200
Kidney	1,700 to 2,200
Dried lima beans	790
Liver	1,800 to 2,200

Of course, one does not eat as much brewer's yeast as
one might eat of liver or beans. But it is a highly concentrated
food, and three tablespoons of brewer's yeast a day will weigh
about as much as a serving of liver and will give you almost 10
times as much thiamin and about the same amount of riboflavin
as liver. So you can use brewer's yeast as a bonus food—a supplement to be taken with meals or between meals to add enormously to your store of B vitamins.

In present-day America there is a widespread deficiency in the B vitamins, due partly to our over-refined food, also to the fact that refined sugar and alcohol steal B vitamins very rapidly from the body. As our national consumption of both of these has increased enormously in the last fifty years, our national vitamin B deficiency has probably increased in proportion.

A lack of thiamin (B_1) results in personality changes—irritability, depression, "nerves," skin disease, muscular weakness, hives. A lack of riboflavin (another B vitamin) produces an extreme sensitivity to light, eye fatigue, sores around the mouth, nostrils, ears. An extreme deficiency in niacin produces the disease called pellagra—with sore tongue, skin trouble, painful mouth, dementia or possibly insanity, and diarrhea. When the deficiency is a little less, these symptoms may exist to a lesser extent. Choline and inositol are two B vitamins that combat hardening of the arteries and diseases associated with it. Four other members of the B complex of vitamins are also very important for good health, although not so much is at present known of exactly what functions they perform in the body.

All these vitamins exist abundantly in brewer's yeast—in the natural proportions which are most important for good results. A diet poor in one vitamin is usually poor in others, too. And a dose of just one or just a few of the B vitamins without the others may bring you grief. This is the main reason why brewer's yeast is so much better as a food supplement than synthetic vitamin B preparations. Another reason is the goodly supply of protein and minerals in yeast.

Brewer's yeast is available in tablet or powder form. They are equally good, although one must take a large number of tablets to equal the amount of powdered brewer's yeast one gets in a tablespoon. So if you want to be sure you are getting enough B vitamins, take 2 or 3 heaping tablespoons of brewer's yeast daily. Sprinkle it over food or beat it into drinks.

SECTION 27

VITAMIN C

Rose hips contain more vitamin C per gram than any other food. You must have vitamin C every day. Your body cannot store it. Take a rose hip preparation for vitamin C.

In case of the first sniffle of a cold, take large doses of vitamin C . . . 200 or 300 milligrams every 15 or 20 minutes until the effect is obtained. There is no harm in taking 50 or even 100 times the regular dose, because vitamin C is water-soluble, is not stored by the body and any excess is excreted in the urine.

CHAPTER **97**

Vitamin C

As long ago as 460 B.C. physicians knew about scurvy. Hippocrates wrote of it in that year. In the time since then soldiers in isolated camps, sailors on long voyages and family groups during time of famine or crop failure have been victims of scurvy. Until quite recently there were epidemics of scurvy throughout northern Europe. There were 30,000 cases of scurvy among the soldiers in our own Civil War. During the first World War there were more than 11,000 cases of scurvy and 7,500 fatalities from it among Allied soldiers fighting in the Near East. More sailors have died of scurvy than have been killed in all the naval battles ever fought.

Evolution of Scurvy

At some date in history, someone decided that scurvy must be caused by something people ate or didn't eat. For instance, a group of sailors desperately ill from scurvy were put ashore on the New England coast to die, during the early days of colonization. Indians who found them gave them a tea made from evergreen needles, and the men recovered almost immediately. Captain Cook, the famous sailor, took his ship on a 3-year voyage around the world and not a sailor got sick, for Captain Cook carried a large supply of barley on board, which was sprouted and made into a drink. He cleverly gave the drink only to officers at first, so that the sailors got the idea it must be something very special. Thereafter they insisted on having a daily dose of the barley-sprout liquid.

By the beginning of the 19th century it was well known that lemon juice protected against scurvy, and it became a mandatory daily drink for all British seamen. By 1932 researchers had discovered in lemon juice a crystalline substance which

protected guinea pigs from scurvy. Now we know this substance as vitamin C or ascorbic acid, as it is called in chemistry.
Incidentally, guinea pigs, the ape family and human beings are
the only animals that do not make vitamin C in their bodies,
and so must have it in their food. This is one reason why guinea
pigs rather than other animals are used in laboratory experiments on vitamin C.

Vitamin C Deficiency Widespread

Vitamin C is the one vitamin most people seem to have
heard something about. In other words, they have a vague idea
that they ought to drink orange juice and from time to time eat
some salad. Beyond that, their knowledge is quite incomplete.
"But after all," you may say, "we surely don't have scurvy
today. Nobody I know has died of scurvy!" True, in the
United States the deficiency disease of scurvy has been largely
conquered, due to the splendid publicity given to the healthfulness of fruits and vegetables, and also to the fact that most fruits
and vegetables are available here the year 'round.

But, in this country we have a condition that is perhaps
almost as distressing as scurvy: a large part of our population
gets just enough vitamin C to prevent symptoms of scurvy, but
not nearly enough to prevent other harmful results on their
body economy. These folks have, as doctors put it, a "sub-
clinical" case of scurvy, which is difficult to detect without doing
careful laboratory tests to determine the amount of vitamin C
in the blood.

American Diets Lack Vitamin C

So we have millions of Americans who swig down their
fruit juice at breakfast, feeling righteous about it, and give not
another thought to vitamin C for the rest of the day. As a result we are a nation that suffers continually from minor ailments such as colds, sinus trouble, bleeding gums, pyorrhea,
mineral deficiency, cataract, loose teeth and so forth. Not
scurvy, no, but certainly not good health. Tests have shown
that people in the West get more vitamin C than Easterners.
Two-thirds of the college students tested in a western college
got sufficient vitamin C in their daily diet, while only one-fourth
of the students in Massachusetts and Rhode Island colleges got
enough. In summer and fall people generally get more vitamin
C because they are eating fresh fruits and vegetables in quan-

tity. In winter and spring they do not usually eat so much of these foods and what they do get have been so long in storage or in transport that most of the vitamin C is gone.

Vitamin C Performs Many Functions

What is the function of vitamin C in the body? As the red blood cells carry oxygen to each individual cell of the body, so vitamin C carries hydrogen, another substance necessary for the proper burning of our foodstuff. In addition, vitamin C is necessary for the health of our connective tissues—that is, the substance which binds all the individual cells together, composes cartilages, veins, ligaments and so forth. If this substance is not in good repair, many disastrous consequences may result.

For instance, in a child who does not get vitamin C, the bones do not grow at the proper rate or perhaps do not grow at all. The joints may swell. "Growing pains" so-called may be caused by deficiency of vitamin C. Suppose there is not enough of the vitamin to keep the walls of blood vessels in good repair? The tiniest vessels, the capillaries, break and a slight hemorrhage follows. This is actually what happens when one suffers a bruise. Have you noticed that some people, particularly older people, seem to bruise very easily, while others can get a hard knock and show no bruise at all? Bruising indicates lack of vitamin C, for the discoloration that follows is nothing but the hemorrhaging of the tiny capillaries.

Hemorrhaging and Tooth Decay

Vitamin C is so important for the prevention of hemorrhaging that it is often given before and after surgical operations or tooth extractions. Lack of vitamin C also affects the dentine of the teeth, causing it to wear away, resulting in damage to the enamel and finally decay. Our "sub-clinical" deficiency of ascorbic acid is undoubtedly one good reason for the widespread amount of tooth decay in America. Vitamin C is also necessary for the proper absorption of iron in the body, so it becomes extremely necessary in anemia, which may be caused by lack of the vitamin even though ample iron is present in the diet.

The precious minerals such as calcium and phosphorus which our body needs for so many functions are stored in our bones until they are needed. If not enough vitamin C is present, the tissues of this storage place will not retain the minerals, and they are lost to us. Finally, vitamin C is a powerful agent against the infections that plague us. An individual who gets over and above his daily quota of the vitamin will not be subject to these many infections. There are almost unbelievable stories of the effectiveness of vitamin C in the treatment of diseases we have come to think of as mysterious and incurable. Some of these are: polio, diabetes, muscular fatigue, radiation sickness, hay fever, rheumatic fever, drug sensitivity, metal poisoning (such as lead poisoning), pernicious anemia and arthritis.

How to Preserve Vitamin C in Foods

Storage and preparation of food is more important to the preservation of vitamin C than of any other vitamin. This means simply that *vitamin C is the most highly perishable vitamin there is.* It is soluble in water. If you bring home from market a head of cabbage or lettuce and soak them in water to "crisp" them, all their vitamin C content immediately disappears into the water. Since cabbage is one of the foods richest in this vitamin, make certain you do not ever waste it by soaking cabbage. Wash all vegetables as rapidly as possible in cold water and place immediately in your refrigerator, preferably in a "crisper" or air-tight container, for contact with air also destroys vitamin C.

To get the most value from vitamin C foods, it is best to eat them raw, just as soon as possible after they are picked. If you must cook them, follow these simple rules. Have the water boiling briskly before you put the vegetables in, for the boiling water destroys an enzyme which helps to cause loss of vitamin C. Boil them for a minute or so, then turn down the heat and let them cook more slowly for the briefest possible time—just until they are tender. Even with this amount of care, perhaps a fourth of the vitamin C will have passed into the cooking water, along with other water soluble vitamins, such as the B vitamins. So save all water in which you have cooked vegetables! Keep it in the refrigerator, tightly covered, and use it for soups, gravies or other recipes that call for water.

Eat Immediately After Preparing

When you are preparing vegetables to eat either raw or cooked, do the whole job just before they are served or cooked. Let's say you're shredding cabbage for cole slaw, dicing carrots or slicing string beans. Every cut surface of the vegetables means loss of vitamin C, so do not ever let prepared or shelled vegetables stand before using them. Steaming, stewing, baking and frying are all destructive to vitamin C because of the long periods of cooking time or the high temperatures required. If you are making a meat stew or soup which requires long, slow cooking, do not add the vegetables until a few minutes before serving—just long enough to tenderize them. Open-kettle canning destroys practically all vitamin C, in home-canned tomatoes, for instance. From this point of view, commercially canned tomatoes are much richer in this vitamin, as they have been canned by vacuum pack, so that no air enters to destroy this vitamin. Frozen vegetables kept at very low temperatures retain vitamin C reasonably well.

Cautions to Remember

We scarcely need to remind you that baking soda added to cooking water destroys not only all the vitamin C but vitamin B as well in the vegetables you are cooking. So if you drop a pinch of soda into green beans or peas, to give them a nice green color, you might just as well look at them and not bother to eat them at all, for there will be little food value left. One final caution—contact with copper destroys vitamin C. If you have beautiful and expensive copper cooking utensils, hang them on the wall for decoration, but never, never use them to cook in. Beware, too, of chipped enamelware pans, for the base of enamelware is copper. And do not use plated spoons, knives or forks whose plating has worn off, for the substance exposed may well be copper.

How Much Vitamin C Do You Need?

Here are the minimum daily requirements for vitamin C, as determined by the Food and Nutrition Board of the National Research Council:

	Milligrams of Vitamin C
Children under 1 year	10
Children 1- 5 years	20
Children 6-11 years	20
Children 12 years and over	30
Adults	30

Very little vitamin C is stored in the body, so it must be taken every day. The minimum daily requirements, as suggested, is the amount that will prevent the symptoms of scurvy. In our opinion and the opinion of many nutritionists, everyone should get far more vitamin C than this. There is no danger of getting too much, especially if it is taken in natural foods. In treating various illnesses, physicians sometimes prescribe several thousand milligrams of the vitamin per day, with no unpleasant symptoms.

Foods That Contain Most Vitamin C

In the chart below we give you the names of foods high in vitamin C. When you are planning how to include enough vitamin C in the family menus, keep in mind the facts we have told you above about its perishability. And, for safety's sake— because this vitamin is so perishable and because none of us gets enough of it especially in the winter, do add rose hips to your food supplements. They contain, gram for gram, more vitamin C than any of the foods listed below. And they are the outstanding natural food supplement containing this most elusive and necessary vitamin. You can take them as powder or in capsule or tablet form, or you can gather your own rose hips and make them into purée.

Food	*Milligrams of Vitamin C*
Asparagus, fresh green	20 in 8 stalks
Beans, green lima	42 in ½ cup
Beet greens, cooked	50 in ½ cup
Broccoli, flower	65 in ¾ cup
Broccoli, leaf	90 in ¾ cup
Brussels sprouts	130 in ¾ cup
Cabbage, inside leaves, raw	50 in 1 cup
Cabbage, Chinese, raw	50 in 1 cup
Cabbage, green, raw	50 in 1 cup
Cantaloupe	50 in ½ small cantaloupe
Chard, Swiss, cooked	37 in ½ cup
Collards, cooked	70 in ½ cup
Currants, red	40 in 1 cup
Dandelion greens, cooked	100 in 1 cup
Grapefruit, fresh	45 in ½ grapefruit
Grapefruit juice, fresh	108 in 1 cup
Grapefruit juice, canned	72 in 1 cup
Guavas	125 in 1 guava
Honeydew Melon	90 in ¼ medium honeydew
Kale, cooked	96 in ¾ cup
Kohlrabi	50 in ½ cup

(*Table continued on page 632*)

Food	*Milligrams of Vitamin C*
Leeks	25 in ½ cup
Lemon juice	25 in 1 tablespoon
Lime juice	18 in ¼ cup
Liver, beef	30 in 1 slice
Liver, calves	25 in 1 slice
Liver, chicken	25 in ½ cup
Liver, lamb	20 in 1 slice
Loganberries	35 in 1 cup
Mandarin orange	46 in 2 small oranges
	(A small orange weighs about 100 grams)
Mustard greens, cooked	125 in ½ cup
Orange	50 in 1 medium orange
Orange juice, fresh	120 in 1 cup
Orange juice, canned	80 in 1 cup
Parsley	70 in ½ cup
Parsnips	40 in ½ cup
Peas, fresh, cooked	20 in 1 cup
Peppers, green	125 in 1 medium pepper
Peppers, pimiento	200 in 2 medium peppers
Persimmon, Japanese	40 in 1 large persimmon
Pineapple, fresh	38 in ⅔ cup
Pineapple juice, canned	25 in 1 cup
Potatoes, sweet	25 in 1 medium potato
Potatoes, white, baked	20 in 1 medium potato
Potatoes, white, raw	33 in 1 medium potato
Radishes	25 in 15 large radishes
Raspberries, black	66 in 1 cup
Raspberries, red	23 in 1 cup
Rose hips	500 to 6,000 in 100 grams
Rutabagas	26 in ¾ cup
Spinach, cooked	30 in ½ cup
Strawberries, fresh	50 in ½ cup
Tangerines	48 in 2 medium tangerines
Tomatoes, canned	20 in ½ cup
Tomatoes, fresh	25 in 1 medium tomato
Tomato juice, canned	48 in 1 cup
Turnips, cooked	22 in ½ cup
Turnips, raw	30 in 1 medium turnip
Turnip tops, cooked	130 in ½ cup
Watercress	54 in 1 average bunch

CHAPTER **98**

You ARE Vitamin C

In this chapter we present more facts about the great importance of vitamin C for body health. You need it every day in considerable quantity.

Since the first sample of vitamin C (or ascorbic acid) was extracted from a laboratory beaker of lemon juice in the days of the mid-twenties, constant experimentation with this vitamin has given us ever-increasing proof of man's dependence upon a good supply of vitamin C. It is almost impossible to keep up with the research in this field for the powerful influence of vitamin C on the body is always challenging scientists to see what else this magic substance can do to keep us healthy or if it can be used to treat an illness that seems to have no cure.

Book Describes Uses for Vitamin C

In a book, *Vitamin C,* published by Merck and Company, Incorporated, Rahway, New Jersey, we came across many interesting facts about vitamin C and its use, both as a preventive medicine and a treatment in the relief of many symptoms. Incidentally, so far as we know, this book is available to those in the fields of biology, nutrition or the healing professions. Write to Merck and Company to inquire about price.

Though we have always been convinced of the body's need for vitamin C, we were astounded at the many ways in which experimentation has shown it to be effective, and dramatically so.

The Vitamin C in Your Body

It is not too great an exaggeration to say that we *are* vitamin C! It is the vital ingredient which welds the cells together and these are, after all, the very stuff of flesh, bones,

blood and organs. Without vitamin C these things cannot maintain themselves—and without these things we cannot exist.

We know that the body does not manufacture ascorbic
acid, nor can it be stored. It must come to the body in a steady
and undiminished supply by way of the foods we eat—fresh
vegetables, fresh fruits, rose hips, etc. (Fresh liver is also a rich
source of vitamin C.)

Once in the body, ascorbic acid is absorbed by the walls
of the small intestine. However, since the food passes through
the small intestine quickly, there is a limited amount of time
for this absorption to take place. *The American Journal of
Physiology* quotes an experiment which indicates that only
small amounts of vitamin C can be absorbed at a single time,
and the rest is wasted when it has once passed through the small
intestine. It is therefore obvious that the dosage of ascorbic
acid must be spread across the day, allowing for small amounts
to be taken which can be quickly assimilated. The body will
expel in the urine any surplus or unabsorbed vitamin C.

How Vitamin C Leaves the Body

The ease with which vitamin C leaves the body is
emphasized by several experiments which have shown:

(1) Ascorbic acid is drained by prolonged treatment
with ACTH or Cortisone, used for arthritis cases. Patients
showed symptoms of scurvy which were relieved only by the
administration of large doses of vitamin C. (*American Medical
Association Archives of Internal Medicine,* December, 1951.)

(2) Sulfa drugs stimulate the urinary excretion of vitamin C to 2 or 3 times the normal amount. The author of
a piece in *Southern Medicine and Surgery,* September, 1943,
suggests the administration of 100 milligrams of ascorbic acid
per day to replenish the lost stock during sulfa therapy. We are
opposed to the use of sulfa drugs, and we consider 100 milligrams of ascorbic acid a very minute therapeutic dose when the
body is subjected to such stress as sulfa treatment.

(3) Prolonged administration of antibiotics may result
in deficiencies of vitamin C and vitamins of the B complex, too.
(*Annals of Internal Medicine,* December, 1952.) The German
journal, *Klin. Wchnschr,* March 15, 1955, goes further by saying

that blood and urine levels of almost all vitamins fell during antibiotic therapy.

(4) Deficiencies of vitamin A are sure to lead to depletion of vitamin C resources. Vitamin B and vitamin E work more efficiently in the body when enough vitamin C is present. (*Journal of Nutrition,* May 10, 1948.)

(5) The blood level of ascorbic acid is lowered by smoking. Nicotine added to a sample of whole human blood of known ascorbic acid content decreased the ascorbic acid content of the blood by 24 to 31 per cent. . . . *American Journal of Digestive Diseases,* March, 1953.

Those are just some of the ways vitamin C supplies can be depleted in the body. Now for a few instances of the uses this workhorse vitamin C is put to:

In Formation of Teeth and Bones

(1) Its use as a bone maker is demonstrated by an experiment which is detailed in the *Journal of Physiology* for November 30, 1942. It was found by experiments that two milligrams of vitamin C per day are needed to insure adequate regeneration of an injured bone of a small laboratory animal, and less than one milligram would seriously retard regeneration. In humans the same results would be produced by 40 and 20 milligrams of vitamin C.

(2) It is presumed that the teeth of infants are affected in a way similar to the way the teeth of experimental guinea pigs were affected in a report carried in the *Journal of Dentistry for Children,* Third Quarter, 1943.

In vitamin C-deficient guinea pigs the dentine in the developing teeth ceased to form and the pulp became separated from the dentine by liquid. There was either a cessation of dentine manufacture, or the dentine manufactured was of inferior quality. The pulp itself was shrunken and, free from the dentine, was apparently floating in a liquid. Rapid repair followed the administration of vitamin C in natural form. Obviously infants whose teeth are forming must receive sufficient vitamin C.

(1) Experimental human scurvy was induced by reducing ascorbic acid to zero for 13 weeks. With total vitamin C deficiency, failure of wound healing occurred—the tissues, under

microscope showed a lack of intercellular substance. Vitamin C dosage brought about good healing and considerable intercellular substance appeared within 10 days. . . . *New England Journal of Medicine,* September 5, 1940.

(2) A 50 per cent diminution of tensile strength in healing incisions was one result of freely induced vitamin C deficiency for experimental purposes. Unfavorable conditions such as decreased blood supply or excessive wound tension prevent primary wound healing in the absence of vitamin C. . . . *Surgery, Gynecology and Obstetrics,* January, 1947.

(3) *The Journal of the American Medical Association* for May 28, 1955, states that in the evaluation of vitamin needs for surgical patients, ascorbic acid is the only nutrient, lack of which has been proved to delay or prevent wounds healing in man.

(4) In 62 burn cases the *New York State Journal of Medicine,* October 5, 1951, reports that use of ascorbic acid shortened the interval before skin grafts could be performed and antibiotic therapy was seldom required. Also, it stated that the use of ascorbic acid hastens the healing period and lessens the need for other therapy.

Pregnant women need much Vitamin C

(1) Latent scurvy may be present in the infant at birth, according to the *Proceedings of the Society for Experimental Biology and Medicine,* November, 1942. It was shown that the umbilical cord carries vitamin C to the infant from the mother. Therefore, a major deficiency in the mother would certainly be reflected in the child, as she is the only source of vitamin C supply for her baby.

(2) *The Canadian Medical Association Journal,* January, 1942, reported that the percentage of successful pregnancies among poor women was increased by giving them ample foods containing vitamin C, thiamin and riboflavin (two B vitamins). Infants born to the women in the test were rated good, fair and poor. The percentages of "good" babies born to the mothers in relation to their diets were: 62.3 per cent to those on poor diets; 72.3 per cent to those on good diets; 92.5 per cent to those on supplemented diets. The course of preg-

nancy was good on 66 per cent of the women on poor diets, 85 per cent of those on good diets and 94 per cent of those on supplemented diets.

(3) Mothers' milk analyses showed a high content of vitamin C, which points to the baby's need for this element since it is included in this most natural of diets. . . .*American Journal of Diseases of Children,* September, 1945.

(4) In cases of habitual spontaneous abortion the *Journal of the American Medical Association* for July 28, 1951, suggests the administration of ascorbic acid and vitamin D to all pregnant patients who have essential hypertension. It is thought that these vitamins in high enough dosage will reduce fragility of the blood vessels and tendency to premature separation of the placenta.

Vitamin C and the Aging Process

The important role of vitamin C in the aging process is stressed by the results of a study of 569 supposedly healthy men and women more than 50 years old (*Journal of Nutrition,* March, 1955). The women at all ages had higher blood ascorbic acid levels than the men. In both sexes a maximum ascorbic level was shown at 60-64 years. There was a relation between the ascorbic acid levels and the income group. Thirty-nine per cent of the group had no teeth, and 17 per cent had gingivitis. A great proportion of those without teeth and with gingivitis were found to be among those who showed low ascorbic levels. It is difficult to eat fresh raw foods if teeth are missing and difficult to buy them on low incomes.

In another study of people over 50, diseases of the circulatory and digestive systems were associated with low intake of ascorbic acid. (*Journal of the American Medical Association,* 1953.)

Vitamin C for Gastrointestinal Disorders

(1) In the treatment of peptic ulcers by supplementing an antacid with ascorbic acid. The addition of vitamin C was followed by longer remissions and fewer relapses when compared with control groups who received antacid treatment without ascorbic acid. It is recommended that more consideration be given to ascorbic acid supplementation in the therapy of peptic ulcers (*American Practitioner,* February, 1952).

(2) *The British Medical Journal* for May 17, 1947, details a case in which the patient was hemorrhaging from the digestive tract. His intake of vitamin C had been low in recent years due to symptoms of peptic ulcer. Within half an hour after the intravenous injection of 1,000 milligrams of ascorbic acid, the patient who had appeared near death, became alert and cheerful. It took 3 weeks for the urine tests to show a saturation of the body with vitamin C. Vitamin P was also administered. No more blood vomiting occurred. Blood gradually disappeared from the stool.

(3) *American Journal of Digestive Disease,* October, 1948, suggests that when a patient continues to bleed uncontrollably in spite of repeated transfusions, the possibility of a vitamin C deficiency must be considered. Two such patients were given injections of 100 milligrams of ascorbic acid every two hours and a cessation of the hemorrhage was brought about. Recovery followed. The article states that the diet of an ulcer patient should be fortified with ascorbic acid because of its favorable effect in case of hemorrhage.

Infection Therapy

The value of vitamin C therapy in cases of infection is common knowledge; however, its use in cases such as the following is less well known:

(1) In cases of rheumatic infections, scarlet fever and diphtheria, it was illustrated by a group of patients that fever accompanied by infection may increase vitamin C utilization and thus create a shortage in the body's supply. . . . *American Journal of the Diseases of Children,* September, 1942.

(2) *Journal of the American Medical Association,* July 17, 1948, cites several references to support the contention that adequate doses of vitamin C are essential in the diet of patients with rheumatic fever.

(3) In cases of whooping cough an experiment with 90 children proved ascorbic acid to be effective. The children were given ascorbic acid orally or by injection in a daily dosage of 500 milligrams for the first 7 days, gradually reduced until 100 milligrams daily was reached. This last dose was continued until recovery was complete. The results of the experiment: duration of disease in children receiving ascorbic acid,

15-20 days, average duration for children receiving vaccine, 34 days. When ascorbic acid therapy was started during the catarrhal stage, the spasmodic stage was prevented in 75 per cent of the cases. (*Journal of American Medical Association*, November 4, 1950.)

Older folks treated successfully with vitamin C

(1) Severe ulcers of the cornea of the eye have been treated with good results by intravenous injections of ascorbic acid. Large amounts of ascorbic acid have been suggested to aid the dwindling metabolism of the lens when cataract is present. . . . *American Journal of Ophthalmology*, June, 1951.

(2) In *Geriatrics*, August, 1954, painful arthritis shows response to vitamin C treatment. High vitamin C intake resulted in a significant decrease in pain and some improvement in appetite and well being, though there was no improvement in mobility or swelling of joints.

In multiple sclerosis, with large doses of ascorbic acid, objective and subjective improvement was noted in the majority of cases.

Let's Get All the Vitamin C We Can

These cases do not, by any means, comprise our total evidence for the effectiveness of vitamin C. We could continue indefinitely. However, we feel that, with the list you have just read, our aim has been accomplished. The wide range of uses for vitamin C has been demonstrated satisfactorily, we think. No person, knowing these things and having an interest in good health, would allow himself to risk the danger of a deficiency of this absolutely essential nutrient.

Remember, vitamin C comes chiefly in fresh, raw fruits and vegetables—especially the green, leafy ones. The richest source is rose hips, and we recommend that everyone take natural vitamin C supplements, made of rose hips, green peppers, etc., every day.

CHAPTER 99

A Rose by Any Other Name Is Vitamin C

A delicacy, long popular in Europe, turns out to be one of the best and least expensive sources of vitamin C.

That troublesome problem of how to get enough vitamin C keeps cropping up every time we outline a model diet or suggest ideal food supplements everyone should have. Citrus fruits contain vitamin C, but we already know that the consumption of too much citrus juice, especially from commercially-grown citrus, is not healthy. Green peppers contain vitamin C in abundance. So do watercress and parsley. But, after all, you can't carry around a quart or so of watercress and peppers for all-day nibbling, just to be sure you're getting enough vitamin C. Synthetic vitamin C has been available for a long time, but nutritionists admit that synthetic vitamin C (ascorbic acid) does not have the same healthful effects as the natural vitamin. Other factors are present in natural vitamin C. Food supplements made of natural vitamin C are available, but they're a little more expensive, because they're so difficult to make. Of course, it would be best, too, to get vitamin C in food that contains at least a smattering of other vitamins, as well.

Rose Hips the Answer

We believe we've found the answer in a fruit you've probably never thought of eating before. It's well known as nourishing food in Europe. It's well known as favorite food among the bird population in our country. It goes by the name of rose hips. For those of you who may not know, rose hips are the fruit of the rose, which mature after the petals of the flower have fallen. Looking back over human history, you might well wonder how mankind decided on which plants to eat and which not to eat. Suppose that for generations back, apples were admired only for their blossoms. Perhaps no one would ever have thought of eating the fruit, and today we'd be planting ornamental apple trees, developing larger, more fragrant flowers and having spring shows of apple blossoms in greenhouses. Probably, too, there would be a few "food faddists" who would insist on eating the fruit. Instead of that, we eat the fruit of apples and grow roses as ornamental flowers, with hardly a thought of the possible food value of their fruit.

But all along, the birds have known what delicious food rose hips are. Today many people are growing multiflora rose hedges, to provide food for countless birds next winter. Birds like sunflower seeds and whole grains, too. Perhaps we could do no better than to follow the sensible example of our cardinal, wren and chickadee friends and give ourselves a nutrition treat —rose hips.

Rose Hips Contain Vitamin A, Also Vitamin C

Olaf E. Stamberg of the Department of Agricultural Chemistry of the University of Idaho has written in detail about the vitamin content of rose hips in *Food Research* for September-October, 1945. Mr. Stamberg tells us that garden varieties of rose hips are low in vitamin C, but that some varieties of wild roses contain astonishing amounts not only of vitamin C but also of vitamin A. Rosa Rugosa, for instance, contain from 2275 to 6977 milligrams of vitamin C per hundred grams. Oranges contain only 49 milligrams per hundred grams. Rosa Laxa displays a vitamin C content of 3000 to 4000 milligrams to every 100 grams, compared to 150 milligrams per hundred grams of green peppers.

In preparing the rose fruit for eating, Mr. Stamberg experimented with different methods of preservation. Rose hips packed in sealed mason jars and placed in a freezing locker at a temperature of about 5 degrees below zero were analyzed over a period of 6 months, and showed little loss of vitamin C in that time. Rose hip jam, made very much as any fruit jam is made, showed a high vitamin C content, of which very little was lost over 6 months. But dehydrating the hips caused an 80 per cent loss of the vitamin in his experiments. Juice and purée of rose hips, kept in a refrigerator for eight days lost only a small percentage of its vitamin C content.

"The juice of rose hips in various foods, such as fruit soups, juices, jams and jellies should be valuable," says Mr. Stamberg, "owing to their high vitamin C and carotene (vitamin A) content. Investigations into the culinary aspects of preparing rose hips should lead to many new and interesting ways of utilizing them."

Preparing Rose Hips to Eat

Writing in the *Canadian Journal of Research* for December 1943, J. Tuba, G. Hunter, M. J. Hutchinson and L. L. Kennedy have lots to say about utensils and methods which will help to save the precious vitamin C in preparing rose hips in the kitchen. Care should be taken that they do not come into contact with any copper utensils, as copper destroys vitamin C on contact. Aluminum utensils also cause a considerable loss. Glass or enamelware vessels preserve the most vitamin C, but be sure that the enamel kettles are not cracked, so that the metal underneath shows through. Wooden spoons and stainless steel knives should be used, lest somewhere an edge of copper might touch the hips. These researchers had good luck with drying rose hips at a temperature of 175 degrees Fahrenheit, retaining 80 per cent of the original vitamin C in their dried rose hips. Storing the dried powder, however, resulted in considerable loss.

They also found that the best time to gather the hips is when they are fully ripe, but not overripe. Rose hips are bright scarlet in color when they are ripe, orange when they are unripe and dark red when they are overripe. Altitude and latitude make a difference in vitamin C content, too, with roses farther north showing more vitamin C than those grown farther south . . . perhaps a kindly provision by nature for people and birds whose vitamin C is used up during long winters and not sufficiently replenished during short growing seasons.

The Taste of Rose Hip Products

There's one writer who objects to the taste of rose hip products. H. S. Redgrove tells us in *The Gardener's Chronicle* for October 25, 1941, that he made some rose hip purée according to directions and found that it tasted like vanilla. There's nothing wrong in this, we guess, except that he had been told it would taste like tomatoes or peaches. He complained of the taste in print and was sent a sample purée prepared by an expert. He admitted that this purée had an aroma and flavor reminiscent of tomatoes, but made into a juice cocktail, it lost its flavor and was decidedly unpleasant. Of course, some people who live on drugstore lunches and sundaes object to the taste of sunflower seeds! However, Mr. Redgrove agrees that the nutritive value of rose hips should not be wasted and suggests that they be made into food supplements rather than beverages or preserves.

Foreign Countries Enjoy Rose Hips

Rose hips have long been a popular delicacy in northern European countries, according to Ivan B. O'Lane writing in the January, 1949, issue of *The Journal of Home Economics*. In Sweden rose hips are carefully gathered and used for soups, tea and puddings. Mr. O'Lane says, "for a soup, the hips are ground and boiled for about 10 minutes, then strained and again brought to a boil, sugared to taste and thickened with four level teaspoons of potato flour which has been prepared with 2 cups of cold water. This *nyponsoppa* (soup) is then served hot or cold with cream and almond cookies or oven-toasted bread. Puddings are prepared by adding a greater amount of potato flour. A few almonds added during the boiling enhance the taste."

Vitamin and Mineral Content of Rose Hips

Here are some figures from Sweden showing vitamin and mineral value of rose hips compared to oranges available in Sweden:

	Rose hips	*Oranges*
Calories	750 per kilogram	480 per kilogram
Protein	1.2%	0.9%
Carbohydrate	17%	11.2%
Phosphorus	.03%	.02%
Calcium	28% more in rose hips	
Iron	25% more in rose hips	
Vitamin A	5000 International units	200 International units
Vitamin C	2000 International units	50 International units

The authors of an article on Rose Hips in the German medical magazine, *Hippokrates,* No. 6, 1942, have as their theme the supreme importance of the relationship of one vitamin to another. For this reason Von Dr. A. Kuhn and Dr. H. Gerhard find that rose hips are superior, for they contain a wide assortment of vitamins in the natural proportions in which they are found in nature. In speaking of vitamin C requirements, our researchers remind us that what they mean is natural vitamin C the chemical biocatalyst, in its "nature-given harmony with all other biocatalysts and principal nutrients as nature offers it in plant tissue. The effect of each individual vitamin in nutrition is related to the presence of all other vitamins." (A biocatalyst is a substance that brings about chemical reactions in other substances.)

Drs. Kuhn and Gerhard found in rose hips considerable amounts of other vitamins as well as A and C. Their experiments showed the following vitamin content for rose hips, which we have compared to that of oranges and black currants, two other well-known vitamin C foods.

Vitamin Content of 100 Grams of Rose Hips

	Rose hips	Oranges	Black currants
Vitamin A	5 milligrams	.1140 milligrams	.24 milligrams
Vitamin E	47 milligrams (in kernel oil)	——	——
Vitamin K	100 units	——	—
Vitamin C	*500 milligrams	49 milligrams	200 milligrams
Vitamin B_1	.10 milligrams	.80 milligrams	.30 milligrams
Vitamin B_2	.007 milligrams	.30 milligrams	1.4 milligrams
Niacin	.4 milligrams	.2 milligrams	——
Vitamin P	240 to 680 units	490 units	75 units

* Other species have as high as 6000 milligrams of vitamin C per 100 grams.

Recipe for Rose Hip Extract

In one of our favorite cookbooks, *Let's Cook It Right,* by Adelle Davis (published by Harcourt, Brace and Company), Mrs. Davis, ever practical, advises collecting all the rose hips you can find from wild roses, your own rosebushes or your neighbors'. Can rose hip extract, she says,—enough so that each member of your family can have at least one teaspoonful daily. Add it to fruit juice, salads, appetizers, sauces and soups. This is how she advises preserving the extract in your own kitchen: Gather rose hips; chill. (This is to inactivate the enzymes which might otherwise cause a loss of vitamin C.) Remove blossom ends, stems and leaves; wash quickly. For each cup of rose hips, bring to a rolling boil one and one half cups of water. Add one cup rose hips. Cover utensil and simmer 15 minutes. Let stand in a pottery utensil for 24 hours. Strain off the extract, bring to a rolling boil, add 2 tablespoons lemon juice for each pint, pour into jars and seal. (Remember, don't make the mistake of using copper or aluminum utensils when you are cooking rose hips.)

Roses and Their Vitamin C Content

Here is a list of roses, along with the approximate vitamin C content of their hips. In general, they are not the showy, expensive roses sold by nurseries. A botany book may help you to identify wild roses in your neighborhood. You probably know the names of those in your garden.

Milligrams of Vitamin C per hundred grams of rose hips

Rosa Laxa	3000-4000	R. mollis	1260
R. acicularis	1800-3500	R. Sherardi	1260
R. cinnamomea	3000	R. nipponensis	1180
R. rugosa	3000	R. megalantha	694-1124
R. Eddieii	2780	R. spaldingii	694-1124
R. Moyesii	2383	R. coriifolia	1080
R. arkansana	1300-2000	R. Afzeliana	1000
R. woodsii	1300-2000	R. tomentosa	690
R. nutkana	1200-1370	R. dumetorum	590
R. canina	711-1338	R. multiflora	250

SECTION 28

THE FLAVONOIDS

The flavonoids, substances that occur along with vitamin C in many foods, have recently been found to be powerful against many disorders, including the common cold. They occur chiefly in the pulpy part of fruits, and some of the names for them are hesperidin, rutin, citrin and so forth. They occur in natural food supplements like those made of rose hips or green pepper.

CHAPTER **100**

Vitamin P (the Bioflavonoids)

The story of vitamin P is the best example we know of illustrating the superior value of natural vitamins over synthetic ones. Vitamin P is a substance that occurs along with vitamin C in foods. So when you take synthetic vitamin C made in a laboratory, you don't get any vitamin P, of course. But when you eat foods rich in vitamin C or take vitamin supplements made from natural foods such as rose hips or green peppers, the vitamin P comes right along with the vitamin C. And we have discovered that in countless situations where vitamin C alone is not effective, the combination of the two will work wonders.

In February of 1955 a meeting was held in New York to honor Nobel Prize winner Albert Szent-Gyorgyi who has done such outstanding work on vitamin C and vitamin P. At the meeting researchers spoke on their experiences with vitamin P, or, as they called it, "the bioflavonoids." Actually we should not speak of the bioflavonoids as a vitamin until their status has been clarified. The official scientific body which determines terminology like that has decided that the bioflavonoids are not a vitamin. Until we discover that they occur in the human body, we should not speak of them in terms of being a vitamin.

The Meaning and Use of the Bioflavonoids

What are the bioflavonoids? They are brightly colored substances that appear in fruits, along with vitamin C. They have also been called citrin, hesperidin, rutin, vitamin C-2, vitamin P, flavones, flavonols, flavonones and so forth. These names are important to biochemists but do not have to concern us. It's up to the researchers to separate and sort, study and test these various substances. We need only to be grateful for the work they are doing, and make the most we can of their discoveries.

At the meeting in February Charles E. Brambel of Mercy Hospital, Baltimore, spoke on the use of the bioflavonoids in anti-coagulant therapy. Because of the tendency of blood to coagulate too easily in certain heart and vascular diseases, doctors give medicines that they call "anti-coagulants" designed to prevent blood clots or thromboses. Coumarin is one of these. Coumarin keeps the patient's blood in such a state that it cannot clot and stop up a blood vessel. But you can see that such a medicine might cause some difficulty. What if it keeps the blood in such a free-flowing condition that the patient has hemorrhages instead? Dr. Brambel has studied 2000 patients using anti-coagulant medicines. Five per cent of them developed bleeding complications. One hundred milligrams each of hesperidin (bioflavonoids) and vitamin C were given four times daily. The areas where the hemorrhages had been, cleared rapidly. Dr. Brambel tells us that hesperidin and vitamin C together accomplish this, whereas neither of them alone will do the job.

Treating Rheumatic Fever and Miscarriages

Dr. James F. Rhinehart of the University of California spoke at the meeting on the subject of rheumatic fever. It is his belief that vitamin C and the bioflavonoids have considerable value in the treatment of rheumatic fever. Dr. Carl T. Javert of Cornell University spoke of using vitamin C and flavonoids to prevent miscarriages. In a study of 1334 patients he found that 45 per cent of three groups tested were deficient in vitamin C. This is in contrast, he says, with normal nonpregnant women, *only one-third of whom are deficient in vitamin C.* (Note that last statement. Our nutrition "experts" keep on telling us that we get enough of all the vitamins in a well-balanced diet, and yet figures like this, for "normal" women, keep cropping up.) Giving large doses of vitamin C and the bioflavonoids to 100 pregnant women with histories of habitual abortion, he achieved a successful pregnancy in 91 per cent. These patients took a diet rich in vitamin C (350 milligrams) plus a supplement containing vitamin C and the flavonoids—making a total of 500 milligrams of vitamin C per day. The vitamin C or the bioflavonoids

alone did not do the job. But the combination of the two
worked the miracle.

Dr. Robert Greenblatt of the Medical College of Georgia
also reported on using vitamin C and the bioflavonoids for
habitual abortion. A group of women who had never been able
to carry their children and bring them into the world alive were
examined to determine the state of their capillaries—that is, the
tiny blood vessels that spread through every inch of our bodies.
It was found that they suffered from capillary fragility—that is,
the walls of these tiny vessels burst easily, causing bruised areas.
Vitamin C and the bioflavonoids were given to them with excellent results. Eleven of thirteen patients with two previous abortions delivered live infants.

Dr. George J. Boines of Wilmington, Delaware, spoke
on using these two food substances for curing polio. He said
that tests indicated that all 400 patients with acute polio were
found to have abnormal capillary fragility, indicating that they
need vitamin C and the bioflavonoids. They were given 600
milligrams of vitamin C and 600 milligrams of hesperidin daily
until the state of their capillaries improved. Eight per cent
responded in the first 5 weeks. Appetites improved within the
first week, and by the second week there was increased warmth
to touch in the involved arm or leg.

Relation of Bioflavonoids to the Capillaries

What are the capillaries and why are they so important?
We have some rather startling information on this. The capillaries—those tiny, fragile blood vessels—exist in such profusion
in the human body that if the capillaries of one man were
stretched out in a single line, they would reach two and a half
times around the globe! According to one expert, "This vast
ocean of capillaries provides the working barrier separating the
blood from the cellular elements and tissues. Across the walls of
the capillary must pass all life-giving ingredients found in the
blood whether they are in the form of gas or solids."

The most important part of the capillaries is the layer in
their walls which contains the intercellular cement. Any change
in the composition of this cement is bound to have a tremendous
effect on how substances pass through the capillary wall into and
out of the blood. The composition of the cement is influenced
largely by vitamin C and the flavonoids. So you see why the

vitamins are so important and why the capillaries are so important.

According to researchers who have experimented with these two food stubstances, there is no diseased state in which the capillaries are not harmed. And, too, there is no diseased state that will not be improved by improving the state of the capillaries. Habitual abortion, rheumatic fever, rheumatoid arthritis, diabetes and diabetic retinopathy, hypertension—in all of these there is one common symptom—the capillaries are failing. So in all of these vitamin C and the bioflavonoids should be used.

While none of our researchers declare that other methods of therapy for these various diseases should be abandoned, they do claim that *"the combination of vitamin C and the bioflavonoids benefits every condition in which it has been tried and should be considered by physicians as 'supplemental therapy' of value in virtually all diseased states and specific in action with respect to some."*

Those are strong words—"of value in virtually all diseased states," but actually why should they not be used? We are talking of two substances which, when used together, keep the walls of the blood vessels healthy. Every cell in your body depends, every second of the time, on the materials that are brought to it through the blood vessels. So what could be more important?

Bioflavonoids and Infections

Vitamin C and the bioflavonoids have been used successfully in the treatment of colds. A group of nurses at Creighton University School of Medicine was given tablets containing the two substances and then checked for a year against another group which got nothing. The treated nurses had fewer colds by about 55 per cent, and their colds lasted only an average of 3.9 days compared with 6.7 days in the untreated group. In the *American Journal of Digestive Disease* for July, 1954, Morton S. Biskind and W. C. Martin reported on 22 patients who had respiratory infections varying from a simple cold to influenza. Twenty of them recovered in a 8 to 48 hour period after treatment with the bioflavonoids and vitamin C. The patients got 600 milligrams of each of the two substances every day. Vitamin C alone or the flavonoids alone did not produce results. But together they did.

A bibliography of the medical articles on the subject of bioflavonoids and vitamin C, compiled by the Sunkist Growers, lists 511 separate pieces of information on this subject—an imposing list, which shows the immense interest that has been aroused in the subject within the past 15 years or so.

How Can You Get Bioflavonoids in Your Diet?

Where are you going to look in food for the bioflavonoids? The substance used by many researchers comes from citrus fruits—it is contained in the white skin and segment part of the fruit—not in the juice. We are told that the edible part of the orange contains a tenfold concentration of bioflavonoids, compared to the quantity in strained juice. In the fresh peeled orange there are 1,000 milligrams of bioflavonoids and about 60 milligrams of vitamin C. In the strained orange juice there are only about 100 milligrams of bioflavonoids. Here we have one excellent reason for not juicing citrus fruit; eat it instead. And when you eat it, don't do as the cookbooks tell you to do and remove all the white layers under the skin and around each segment of fruit. That's where the bioflavonoids are. Lemons, grapes, plums and black currants, grapefruit, apricots, cherries and blackberries also contain flavonoids. You will get probably enough to maintain health if you eat lots and lots of fresh raw fruit, especially if you can eat it fresh from the tree or vine.

But how are you going to get bioflavonoids in your food supplements? Natural vitamin C food supplements made from rose hips or green peppers contain the bioflavonoids, for, of course, they occur along with the vitamin C right in the foods from which these supplements were made. Or you may find natural food supplements with added bioflavonoids. The flavonoids may be called rutin, hesperidin, vitamin P.

CHAPTER **101**

Vitamin C and Bioflavonoids

The relationship of bioflavonoids to vitamin C, in foods and in the way they work together in the body, shows perfectly the importance of taking a natural food supplement containing these vitamins.

Early in 1955 at a meeting in New York City certain scientific researchers got together to talk about the merits of a certain element called "bioflavonoids." This is a substance that appears in many fresh foods along with vitamin C. It is closely related to rutin which has recently gained fame in the treatment of high blood pressure. At the meeting it was brought out that the bioflavonoids, given with vitamin C, help the body to use the vitamin C properly. It was also announced that the two together had been found to be powerful against the common cold.

We were delighted with this news because, as you know, we believe that natural vitamins are far superior to synthetic ones. In natural vitamin preparations the bioflavonoids naturally accompany vitamin C, since they occur along with the vitamin in foods—fruits, rose hips, etc.

Vitamin C-Bioflavonoid Combination for Colds

And, of course, we believe that colds can be prevented if, at the first sign of a sniffle, you begin to take massive doses of natural vitamin C. We also think that colds are shortened and made much less serious and troublesome if you take natural vitamin C preparations straight through the course of the cold. But we firmly believe that you should make every effort to prevent colds rather than trying to cure them after they get started. And preventing colds is easy—with plenty of vitamin C in natural form, which means that it will be accompanied by the bioflavonoids. So much for bioflavonoids and colds, then.

In the November 24, 1956, issue of *The Journal of the American Medical Association* appeared two articles written by medical researchers declaring that all the hullabaloo over the usefulness of the bioflavonoids in treating colds is nothing but hullabaloo. These gentlemen say, in essence, that the bioflavonoids have no effect at all on the incidence of colds or the course they may take in the body. And they produce an astonishing array of evidence to back up their claims. A total of almost 2000 persons were involved in one of the studies. "The overwhelming impression gained," says the *Journal,* "is that there is a singular lack of effect in altering the course of the common cold, by either the bioflavonoids or vitamin C."

A Feud Between Drug Companies

These articles set off a veritable furor of claims and counter claims in the magazines of the drug industry. *Advertizing Age* put it this way: "Grove Laboratories, Inc., leading maker of bioflavonoid cold tablets and the American Medical Association aimed squarely for the whites of each other's bleary eyes today" when the article was published. Grove declared that the research was paid for by a competitor of theirs who, we presume, didn't want to see the bioflavonoids cutting in on his profits from another cold remedy. The competitor, who manufactures Anahist, answered with a blast, and the battle was on.

Should We Become Concerned?

Our advice would be, relax, folks, and let the drug companies fight it out. If or when they come to any conclusions not arrived at by counting dollar signs, there may be reason to look further into the matter. But not until then. What are our reasons for this point of view?

First of all, the battle is drawn between two opposing drug companies. We have nothing but suspicion for drugs, no matter what kind of drugs. Synthetic vitamin C and bioflavonoids extracted from their natural base and put into tablets are certainly not what *we* are talking about when we advise taking natural vitamin C to prevent colds. Furthermore, the tests were not tests of anything, to our way of thinking, for the amounts of vitamin C and flavonoids used were certainly not large enough to signify anything at all.

And, since no check was made on daily habits of the people who took the pills, we have no way of knowing how much of the small amount of vitamin C they took could actually be used by the body to ward off colds. Did they take sleeping pills? Did they smoke or were they exposed to lots of tobacco smoke? Were they exposed to any of the other common industrial substances which destroy vitamin C in the body? Did they make any effort to get fresh, living raw foods in which natural vitamin C is present? All these questions were not considered important enough by the investigators to necessitate any consideration at all in the tests. So far as we are concerned they are the most important factors of all.

How Much Vitamin C for Colds?

The several thousands subjects tested were given 200 milligrams of synthetic vitamin C every day during the test, with or without bioflavonoids. To our way of thinking, this amount of vitamin C (if it were natural vitamin C) might conceivably be enough for reasonably good health if one were exposed to none of the possible destroyers of vitamin C that are ever-present in our modern civilized life. But it is the function of vitamin C to be destroyed, to be oxidized or burned up in the performance of its task which is, to a large extent, the neutralizing of poisons. The numbers and extent of poisonous substances to which you are subjected each day determine largely how much vitamin C you need for good health.

But in the case of a cold, or for that matter, any other illness of an infectious nature, vitamin C and bioflavonoids in massive doses will nip the infective process in the bud and the cold will be a thing of the past before it ever gets started. How much vitamin C and bioflavonoids do we mean when we say "massive doses?" To a certain extent this depends on you and your need for this particular vitamin. But, in general, it means far, far more than you take every day for good health, and it means taking the vitamin in large amounts at frequent intervals during the day—at least every 4 hours, for it takes the body just about 4 hours to use up whatever vitamin C is there and excrete the surplus.

W. J. McCormick, M.D. of Toronto who uses vitamin

C regularly in his practice gives doses as large as 3 or 4 thousand milligrams per day, with great success when he is treating infections. We would not advise taking less than several hundred milligrams at 4 hour intervals if you are preventing a cold. And many people need much more than this. Remember, please, that you must start the vitamin C at the very first symptom—the first sniffle, the first sneeze, the first feeling of rawness in the throat.

Bioflavonoids for Gum Disease

In the thick of the battle over bioflavonoids for colds, we were glad to find in our files an article in *Dental Digest* for August, 1956, on the subject of bioflavonoids for periodontal disease. Joseph D. Lieberman, D.D.S., of New York tells us in this article that diseases of the gums (such as pyorrhea) cause the loss of far more teeth than all other dental diseases combined. Soft, swollen, tender, reddened gums that ooze blood or bleed profusely at the slightest touch of a toothbrush—these are symptoms of periodontal disease.

Says Dr. Lieberman, "Among the nutritional disturbances prominent in relation to nutrition and gingival (gum) health are those associated with ascorbic acid (vitamin C) deficiency. This may be demonstrated by the frequent occurrences of a low-grade infectious gingivitis among school children which McCall points out may be the result of, or at least associated with, subclinical vitamin C deficiency."

Gums Benefit from Vitamin C

For his investigation, Dr. Lieberman gave a bioflavonoid-vitamin C-vitamin K preparation to 101 patients, ranging in age from 22 to 84 years, for whom the "usual conventional methods of treatment" had been unsuccessful. The patients were given 8 tablets daily for the first 10 days (2 tablets 4 times a day). For the next 3 weeks the dose was reduced to 4 tablets daily (1 tablet 4 times a day). No other treatment was given.

Analyzing 11 typical cases, Dr. Lieberman finds that the treatment resulted in controlling the bleeding and restoring the gums to an "essentially normal healthy condition," in about 90 per cent of the cases within 10 to 30 days! The tablets which Dr. Lieberman used in this experiment contained 50 milligrams of (synthetic) vitamin C, two milligrams of (synthetic) vitamin K and a total of 72 milligrams of the various parts of the bioflavonoid complex of substances. As you can see, such a preparation would give only 400 milligrams of vitamin C per day and a similarly small amount of the bioflavonoids. But even these doses were effective against an ailment that affects almost everyone in our land over middle age!

Natural Vitamins Best

Note, too, that the tablets contained synthetic vitamins. We are convinced that far more impressive results can be obtained using natural vitamin preparations. Why? The story of the bioflavonoids is the best answer to this question. For many years we have known that vitamin C is necessary for good health and powerful against many human disorders. But our scientists did not even know of such a substance as bioflavonoids until recently.

But health-conscious people who were taking natural vitamin preparations all along got the bioflavonoids along with their vitamin C, so actually they had the benefit of this scientific discovery long before it was made, for the simple reason that they believed that nature knows best and that taking food in natural forms is best. What other food elements are there that naturally go along with vitamin C and the flavonoids? Scientists do not know as yet, but you will be getting them all in natural food supplements such as rose hips, of course, in your daily meals, chiefly in fresh raw fruits.

SECTION 29

VITAMIN E

This occurs in whole grain foods, chiefly. If you have been eating refined cereals, you are undoubtedly deficient in vitamin E. We believe that everyone should take vitamin E as a daily food supplement. Use the supplement from a natural vegetable source, not the synthetic.

Vitamin E is a most important vitamin which has been almost entirely removed from our foods by processing. Children as well as grownups should take vitamin E. It is present in wheat germ in small quantities. We believe you should take both vitamin E and wheat germ daily.

Vitamin E is a preventive for heart disease and should be taken in large doses by heart cases.

CHAPTER 102

Vitamin E

The chemical name for vitamin E is tocopherol which comes from 3 Greek words—*tokos* meaning "child," *pherein* meaning "to bear" and *ol,* "alcohol." The name explains why vitamin E was first studied in connection with fertility. One of the authorities, who has studied vitamin E for many years, K. E. Mason, says in his book, *Vitamins and Hormones* (Academic Press, New York City): "Its chemical nature is known, its laboratory synthesis accomplished, its wide distribution in the plant and animal world recognized and the effects of its absence extensively studied in a large series of laboratory animals. *Its physiological role in the animal body is still a matter of conjecture.*"

There are several different kinds of vitamin E. The most important are alpha, beta, gamma, and delta. These are the Greek letters corresponding to our a, b, c, d. So alphatocopherol is A-tocopherol, beta-copherol is B-tocopherol and so forth. Alphatocopherol is the most active biologically.

Vitamin E and the Birth Process

A number of years ago it was discovered that female rats on a diet of milk, yeast and iron were incapable of raising young. This aroused interest in what substance might be missing in such a diet. The result of this investigation was the discovery of vitamin E. Female rats conceive on a vitamin-E deficient diet, but the embryo dies and is re-absorbed into the body rather than developing and being born. Researcher Mason tells us that the cause of this misfortune is abnormality in the system of blood vessels, leading to thrombosis (the formation of blood clots). As the blood vessels contract, there is anemia and, finally, hemorrhaging which causes the death of the fetus. Even though the anti-hemorrhage vitamins K and C are administered, the embryo dies. Vitamin E supplies the missing substance in the diet, and conception and development of the embryo proceed normally if the diet contains ample vitamin E. In male rats permanent sterility results from a diet that does not include vitamin E. Male chicks and guinea pigs also suffer degeneration of the testicles when they are deprived of vitamin E.

In the case of rats on diets that are low in vitamin E, litters can be born, but the young rats often develop paralysis of the hind legs shortly after birth. This paralysis (much the same as muscular dystrophy in human beings) spreads rapidly to other muscles of the body. No one knows what exact chemical process is involved, but there seems to be ample evidence that vitamin E is closely related to healthy muscles. And, don't forget, the heart is a muscle!

Vitamin E Protects Vitamins A and C

A third indication of the necessity for vitamin E in the diet came with the discovery that ample vitamin E protects the body's store of two other vitamins—A and C. Both these vitamins are very sensitive to the presence of oxygen and may lose much of their value over a period of time. But the presence of vitamin E in the digestive tract protects them from oxidation. From this we might assume that, all other things being equal, you would need to take less vitamin A and C if you were taking vitamin E at the same time.

Experiments With Vitamin E

So far as human nutrition is concerned, experiments on vitamin E have been conflicting. How is it possible, you might ask, that one group of researchers can perform an experiment in which vitamin E added to the diet produces a certain effect while another group of researchers might obtain exactly the opposite effect or no effect at all? The answer lies in the great complexity of all the chemical aspects of testing a new vitamin. Scientist A, working over a period of many years, might be able to discover just one important scientific fact about vitamin E. Scientist B, working in another laboratory, might meanwhile be investigating some other aspect of vitamin E in human physiology. But all his work might be in vain if he performs it before scientist A has proved his one fact. And when Scientist

C uses A's method, he may get one result. If he uses B's method, he may get quite a different result, and so forth.

Dr. Walter Eddy in his very valuable book, *Vitaminology* (published by the Williams and Wilkins Company, Baltimore), says of vitamin E and muscular dystrophy: "Some positive results have been claimed for vitamin E therapy in muscular dystrophy of certain types. Two are of particular interest in suggesting combination with other vitamin material for effective action.

"In 1940 a researcher reported treatment of 5 patients with muscular dystrophy; one with muscular atrophy following anterior poliomyelitis; one with muscle atrophy after an attack of multiple neuritis. He found that improvement took place in all cases and the addition of vitamin B to vitamin E appeared to give even better results."

All Vitamins Must Be in the Diet

Now this statement alone might very well answer our question about conflicting results in the use of vitamin E for human nutrition. One doctor giving vitamin E to patients might pay no attention to their diet, might make no effort to see that they are also getting all the other vitamins so necessary for good nutrition. This doctor might not get any results from his vitamin E therapy. But another physician, aware of the great importance of one vitamin in relation to another, might check carefully to see that his patient is getting all the vitamins in abundance. And in this case the addition of vitamin E to the diet might work wonders!

Vitamin E for Circulatory and Reproductive Disorders

We print elsewhere in this book a great deal of information about the Shute Clinic in Canada where the Shute brothers use vitamin E in curing heart disease. The Shute brothers are medical doctors, M.D.'s, who carry on general practice as well as their work at the heart clinic. They use vitamin E as a medicine for sick hearts, that is, they study each individual case and prescribe exactly the dosage they feel will be most beneficial, then watch the patient carefully, changing the prescription if necessary, just as any physician does in treating a disease. We are told that other scientists have experimented with vitamin E for heart disease without results. What does this prove? That vitamin E has no effect on the sick heart? It may. Or it may prove only that the other researchers were not using the same methods the Shutes use.

Elsewhere we have reported on vitamin E in its relation to reproductive system disorders. We have told of sterile marriages to which children were born after vitamin E therapy. We described cases of habitual abortion cured by administration of vitamin E. These facts were taken from reputable scientific and medical journals, and they were simply reports on actual experiments made. Now if some other experimenter does not obtain these same results, perhaps this means that vitamin E has really nothing to do with reproductive disorders in the human being. Or perhaps it means that the vitamin has everything to do with a healthy reproductive system, and the researchers who got the good results knew exactly what combinations would bring about those good results.

Are the Results Always the Same?

Vitamin E has been used in the treatment of rheumatism and related disorders. Some physicians have had good results; others report no results at all. Was it the fault of the vitamin E or the fault of the method used? We do not know.

A report in the *Texas State Journal of Medicine* for January, 1952, reveals that alphatocopherol was used for a group of surgical patients to prevent thrombosis or embolism (formation of a blood clot) after the operation. It was found to be very effective. Does this mean that vitamin E will always, under any circumstances, prevent thrombosis? Or does it mean simply that we have one more piece of valuable evidence as to the place of vitamin E in human nutrition?

Vitamin E for Buerger's Disease

The *International Record of Medicine* for July, 1951, reports on the use of vitamin E in cases of Buerger's Disease. This is a disease of the blood vessels which may result in gangrene. Of 18 patients treated with vitamin E 17 were cured, only one was not. It was found that the medication must be continued indefinitely. Now in this case, too, vitamin E was used as a medicine, as an emergency measure in, we assume, very large doses, for that is the way one must take a medicine. But, if large doses of vitamin E cure the disease, does it not seem at least partly reasonable that ample vitamin E in the diet would have prevented the disease in the first place?

In an article in *Science* for October 4, 1946, we are told that cattle on a diet deficient in vitamin E throughout their entire lives drop dead suddenly for no apparent cause. Does that not sound exactly like the reports of heart attacks that appear in such numbers every day in our newspapers? Can ample vitamin E in the diet of human beings prevent this kind of sudden death, as it does in the case of cattle?

An article in *Coronet* for October, 1948, called "For Heart Disease Vitamin E," by J. D. Ratcliff, is a sample of the kind of publicity that has been given to the Shute brothers and their clinic. We do not know whether *Coronet* has reprints of this article available. You might write them and inquire.

How Vitamin E Is Destroyed

Vitamin E is inactivated by rancid oil or fat. So if there is rancid fat in the diet, all the vitamin E in the world will do no good. We know, too, that some of the inorganic iron compounds destroy vitamin E activity. Let's say a patient is being treated for anemia and is taking some kind of iron supplement containing ferric chloride. No amount of vitamin E in the diet will do this patient any good, because this particular form of iron will destroy vitamin E which thus will never get a chance to function inside the patient's body. In the same way mineral oil used as a laxative destroys vitamin E along with the other fat-soluble vitamins in the digestive tract.

Wheat Germ—The Best Source of Vitamin E

As you can imagine, with all this controversy over the rightful place of vitamin E in human nutrition, no one has decided as yet what the recommended daily requirement of this vitamin is. Nutrition books tell us that it is present in many, many foods. Yet, actually, the food richest in vitamin E is wheat germ—that part of the wheat we threw away when we introduced white, highly milled flour. Is it just a coincidence that heart disease mortality figures have climbed steadily during the past 50 years—that is, since we have been eating bread from which the vitamin E is removed? Is it just a coincidence that vitamin E works best in association with the B vitamins. Vitamin E and the B vitamins are both plentiful in the germ of grains. Does there not seem to be ample evidence that our refining of foods has worked this fatal mischief on our hearts, our joints, our muscles?

Processing Destroys Vitamin E

Dr. Henry C. Sherman of Columbia University says in his *Essentials of Nutrition* (published by The Macmillan Company, New York) that vitamin E is plentiful in foods, "doubtless occurring very widely among food materials of both plant and animal origin *which have not been artificially refined.*" How many of us ever get any food these days that is not artificially refined, except, of course, for our fresh green vegetables and fruits? Glance at the chart at the end of this article which gives the vitamin E content of various foods. Corn oil, cottonseed oil, peanut oil, soybean oil, and wheat germ oil contain the largest amounts. How much of any of these do you or your family eat in one day? Of course, vitamin E appears, too, in small amounts in various fruits and vegetables. But, having destroyed our best source of vitamin E in the germ of the grain which we throw away in the milling, how can we be sure that any one of us is actually getting enough vitamin E to keep us healthy from day to day?

As our readers know, we do not prescribe cures for diseases. We are not skilled mechanics who can piece together the shattered parts of human machines and make them run again. We are trying to prevent the bad management and the poor care that causes this machine to break down. We do not believe that any sensible person deliberately does things that harm his health. *Our human machines break down because we do not know what we are doing that is unhealthful.*

Should You Take a Vitamin Food Supplement?

We believe that the average American diet does not contain enough vitamin E for good health. All the evidence points in that direction. We believe that we should include in our daily fare as many foods as possible that are rich in vitamin E as prevention against those disorders that may result from a lack of vitamin E. This means, among other things, that, if you are going to eat bread or other products made from any

grain flour, never, never use white flour! Use whole grain flour
and, if at all possible, use flour that has been organically grown
and freshly stone-ground just for you.

In addition, we believe you should supplement your
diet with wheat germ oil and a natural vitamin E preparation.
What is the difference? Wheat germ contains other substances
than vitamin E. So you will not get as much vitamin E in wheat
germ as in a pure vitamin E preparation, but you will get the
other food elements present in wheat germ. These elements
are extremely important, too. You need them as well as the
vitamin E.

When vitamin E is taken from wheat germ oil and put
into a separate preparation, you are, of course, getting nothing
but vitamin E—in much greater strength than you get it in
wheat germ oil. Now different kinds of wheat may have different amounts of vitamin E. This we call "potency." In addition,
there are, remember, several different kinds of vitamin E—alpha,
beta, and so forth. The most potent of these is alphatocopherol.

How Much Should You Take?

We cannot tell you how much vitamin E or wheat germ
oil you should take. As we stated above, minimum daily
requirements have not been set. Besides, if you are eating a
a diet rich in natural wheat germ (your own homemade bread
and whole grain cereals), if you use a lot of vegetable oils and
eat a lot of salads, you obviously need less vitamin E in a food
supplement than somebody else might. If you buy a wheat
germ oil or vitamin E product whose label says, "The need for
vitamin E in human nutrition has not been established," this
means just what we have told you above—that there is still a
great deal of controversy about vitamin E and human nutrition, and standards have not as yet been set.

If you are already suffering from heart disease and want
to use vitamin E you should certainly consult one of the medical authorities, for this involves using very potent and very
large vitamin E doses, just like a medicine. He may be able
to recommend a physician in your locality who uses the Shute
methods. Your own physician may agree to write to Dr. Shute
about your case and learn how to treat you with vitamin E.
You may wish to arrange a trip to Canada to consult personally with Dr. Shute.

Foods Containing Large Amounts of Vitamin E

Food	Milligrams of vitamin E
Apples	.74 in 1 medium apple
Bacon	.53 in about 10 slices broiled
Bananas	.40 in 1 medium banana
Beans, dry navy	3.60 in ½ cup steamed
Beef steak	.63 in 1 piece steak
Beef liver	1.40 in 1 piece liver
Butter	2.40 in 6 tablespoons
Carrots	.45 in 1 cup
Celery	.48 in 1 cup
Chicken	.25 in 3 slices
Coconut oil	8.30 in about 6 tablespoons
Cornmeal, yellow	1.70 in about ½ cup
Corn oil	87.00 in about 6 tablespoons
Cottonseed oil	90.00 in about 6 tablespoons
Eggs, whole	2.00 in 2 whole eggs
Grapefruit	.26 in about ¼ grapefruit
Haddock	.39 in 1 piece haddock
Lamb chops	.77 in 2 rib chops
Lettuce	.50 in 6 large lettuce leaves
*Margarine	54.00 in 6 tablespoons
Oatmeal	2.10 in about ½ cup cooked oatmeal
Onions	.26 in 2 medium raw onions
Oranges	.24 in 1 small orange
Peanut oil	22.00 in 6 tablespoons
Peas, green	2.10 in 1 cup peas
Potatoes, white	.06 in 1 medium potato
Potatoes, sweet	4.0 in 1 small potato
Pork chops	.71 in 2 chops
Rice, brown	2.40 in about ¾ cup cooked rice
Soybean oil	140.00 in 6 tablespoons
Tomatoes	.36 in 1 small tomato
Turnip greens	2.30 in ½ cup steamed
Wheat germ oil crude	150-420.00 in 6 tablespoons
Wheat germ oil medicinal	320.00 in 6 tablespoons

* We do not recommend eating margarine in spite of its high vitamin E content. It contains too many synthetics.

CHAPTER **103**

A Doctor's Experience With Vitamin E

by NELSON GEORGE, M.D., *London, Canada*

The effectiveness of vitamin E in treating diabetes is clearly shown in this chapter written by the doctor who used it on himself.

In the spring of 1930 I discovered that I had diabetes. I commenced using insulin, at times taking up to 26 units daily and continued it for 20 years, eating a diet ranging around 2000 calories per day. My blood sugar, however, was up to as high as 360 mgm. per cent before my cerebral thrombosis, causing a left- sided hemiplegia (stroke). I recovered gradually, even doing a little practice, finally. On an admission to Victoria Hospital, London, in December, 1948, my blood pressure was 164/80 and my blood sugar was 217. Early in 1950 my right foot (on the non-paralyzed side) became badly ulcerated, the circulatory impairment extending almost to the knee. This caused an extremely painful and inflammatory condition. On re-admission to Victoria Hospital on March 13th of that year my blood sugar was 229 and I was given 10 regular and 15 units of P. Z. insulin, going home March 29th on 8 and 10 respectively. In the next few months the pain in the leg became steadily worse and I was confined to bed most of the time. By June 1, 1950, eating and sleeping were practically impossible. Indeed, I ate so little that 8 units of insulin controlled the blood sugar readily. Realizing that the foot had to be amputated, I called in a leading local surgeon, who concurred in my diagnosis and prognosis. When admitted to the hospital my blood sugar was 116 mgm. per cent. I was operated on June 10th, 1950, and lost the right leg 9 or 10 inches above the knee. I had taken about 75 mgm. of alphatocopherol (Vitamin E) daily since May 22, 1950, but had had no benefit from so small a dose. On the day of the amputation my blood pressure was 205/80. The pathological findings were "atherosclerosis and Monckeberg medical sclerosis of arteries, with chronic indolent ulcers of amputated foot overhead first metatarsal and under four toenail—pipestem vessels."

While the wound was healing, the left foot became ulcerated, and by September 1, 1950, was discharging from several toes and the heel. The pain was severe. Soon a large ulcer about 4 cm. in diameter developed on the heel. I had been confined to bed since the amputation, of course.

Higher Dosage the Answer

On October 5, 1950, I called in Dr. Wilfrid Shute, who prescribed a daily dose of 400 i. u. of alphatocopherol. In about one week the pain had subsided and I was able to sleep without sedatives, something I had not done for many months. The result achieved with a larger dosage of Vitamin E was such that one would think a different drug had been used. This matter of dosage is one the Shute brothers have long stressed, but is often ignored.

The healing process was gradual but definite, and by March, 1951, my foot was completely healed. There has been no return of pain. Incidentally, the changes in the heel ulcer have been photographed. Considering the pathological changes reported in my amputated extremity this healing seems quite remarkable.

At the present time (October, 1951) it is difficult to find even the smallest scar on my foot. I have a full set of new toenails! I can stand on my remaining (paralyzed) leg and have considerable use of my left (paralyzed) arm and hand.

General Health Improved Also

My general health has improved in every way. My blood pressure which was formerly over 200, is now normal (150/86).

My blood sugar, which at one time was as high as 360 mgm. per cent, is now normal at 110 mgm. per cent, and I have used no insulin since commencing to take alphatocopherol in high dosage. I am now on a normal diet with the exception that I abstain from sweets.

I cannot speak too highly of the wonderful efficacy of vitamin E. Surely my case history speaks for itself, and I hope that recounting it will help others.

NOTE: To readers who may be suffering from diabetes:
Dr. George's treatment was under the supervision of the Shute
brothers of Canada, who specialize in vitamin E therapy.
Under no circumstances do we or they advise self-treatment
of diabetes. If you wish to take vitamin E, show this article
to your physician and ask him to write to the Vitamin E Society
for further information.

This information is reprinted from *The Vitamin E
Bulletin,* October, 1952.

CHAPTER **104**

Vitamin E Used for Heart Disease

*Heart and circulatory disorders are those most frequently
and successfully treated with vitamin E, suggesting that we all
suffer from a shortage of the vitamin, which makes us susceptible to these ailments.*

Heart disease is today's number one killer, and any one
of us has very good reason to fear it. Formerly thought of as a
degencrative disease attacking only those well past middle age,
heart disease now claims for its victims many persons in their
30's and 40's, as well as a frightening number of teenagers and
persons in their 20's.

The bulletin from the Vitamin E Society of Canada
brings us news of cures worked by the powerful alphatocopherol
(vitamin E) in other countries. It is an impressive story, well
worth carrying with you to show to dubious friends, who may
doubt the potency of vitamin E because it sounds too easy.
"What," they may say, "a mere vitamin given in its natural
form, can cure phlebitis, Buerger's disease, heart disease, thrombosis? Impossible. You are being taken in."

Well, folks, here is the record. And at the risk of clutter-
ing up our pages with a series of long, academic-looking words

and foreign words, we are giving you the full names of authors, periodicals, volume numbers, dates and countries from which this information comes. If your own physician should tell you he doubts that vitamin E can really be of any benefit in heart and vascular conditions, perhaps he is sincerely unaware that so much research has been done. Perhaps he does not really know what wonders have been worked in recent years with vitamin E. Physicians are busy men with little time to study. But they are receptive to new ideas if they come from dependable sources. If he is doubtful, show your physician these references. Ask him to write to the Shute brothers in Canada (pioneers in vitamin E therapy) and obtain even more information.

Its Action on the Blood

In the *American Journal of Physiology,* Vol. 153, p. 127, 1948, K. L. Zierler, D. Grob and J. L. Lilienthal describe laboratory experiments in which they discovered that vitamin E has a profound effect on the blood, especially the clotting of the blood. It has a strong anti-clotting effect both in laboratory experiments and in the veins and arteries of human beings. Now there is a special natural substance in the blood called heparin which is made in the liver, whose job it is to prevent the coagulation of blood. In their tests these scientists found that the action of vitamin E on the blood takes place regardless of how much or how little heparin is present in the blood stream of the patients. So there can be no doubt but that the anti-coagulating action is the result of the vitamin E and nothing else.

In an Italian journal, *Bollettino Societa Chirurgia,* Vol. 18, p. 155 (1948) R. Castagna and G. Impallomeni report on 7 patients with phlebitis (inflammation of a vein) and one 71 year old woman who had had an ulcer measuring 5 by 3 inches on her lower leg. The phlebitis responded dramatically to the use of vitamin E alone. The woman patient's ulcer healed in 26 days. The authors have also used vitamin E in treatment of vascular disease (any disease of the blood vessels) and for "strokes." They tell us that in thrombophlebitis (inflammation of the vein in which a blood clot is involved) the improvement by using vitamin E is extremely rapid. In addition, they say, treatment with vitamin E does not require a rigid blood control as do other medications.

From Brazil (Publication of the O Hospital for July,
1949) D. de Olivera describes two cases of phlebitis, one during
a pregnancy and one following childbirth. In both cases fever
fell rapidly, and there was no recurrence of the disease when
the first patient had her child. The conservative British medical
publication, *The Lancet,* Vol. 2, p. 132, 1949, carries an article
by A. M. Boyd, A H. James, G. W. H. and R. P. Jepson saying
that clinical results with vitamin E are far better than any
obtained with any other treatment in cases of obliterative diseases of the blood vessels. It can be used most successfully for
the relief of cramps in the calves of the legs. "May we repeat,"
say these authors, "that it is our considered opinion that the
clinical observations so far made warrant the continued use of
vitamin E therapy."

Phlebitis and Thrombosis Healed

O. Mantero, B. Rindi, and L. Trozzi, writing in the
Italian magazine, *Attivita Congresso degli Cardiologia,* Stresa,
May, 1948, discuss 5 cases of acute and subacute phlebitis which
were rapidly healed by vitamin E therapy. J. H. Kay, S. B.
Weiss, G. H. and A. Ochsner mention in *Surgery,* Vol. 28,
p. 124, 1950, 4 cases of phlebitis treated only with vitamin E
given orally in which "inflammation subsided and the swelling
disappeared."

A Norwegian physician, H. Sturup, writing in *Nordisk
Medicin,* Vol. 43, p. 721, 1950 tells us he has seen a number of
cases of thrombosis helped by vitamin E therapy. He discusses
in detail the case of a 33-year old patient who had chronic
phlebitis of the left leg, 5 years after an operation. This patient was not even confined to bed, but took vitamin E daily,
and within 6 days the pain and swelling disappeared.

The Annals of Surgery, Vol. 131, p. 652, 1950, reports
that vitamin E and calcium appear to be helpful in the treatment of vascular diseases. Dr. A. W. Allen of Boston, commenting on this article, tells us that he has used vitamin E on a
number of patients and can report that 50 of these who were
"vulnerable"—that is susceptible—to thrombosis escaped this
serious condition. This seems to us particularly important, for
in these cases vitamin E was used to prevent rather than to cure,
and 50 lucky patients continued in good health. Dr. J. C.
Owings of Baltimore comments that he has treated many leg

ulcers due to phlebitis with a combination of rutin and vitamin E, all of which stayed healed, so long as the patient continued to take the medication.

Vitamin E and Blood Clots

Postgraduate Medicine, Vol. 10, p. 794, 1951, carries a report by A. Ochsner who believes that vitamin E is the best preventive of a blood clot, because it is a natural substance, so there is no hazard involved in its use. The use of other anti-coagulants is dangerous, and tying off veins should not be practiced because it will not protect against the detachment of clots. He states that he does not know whether vitamin E combined with calcium is the final answer, but adds that it seems to be best, because it is perfectly safe and does not bring any danger of producing bleeding.

Medical Thesis, published in Paris, No. 471, 1951, quotes a physician as saying he has found vitamin E and calcium useful for preventing blood clots after surgery. R. Bauer, writing in *Wiene Klinisch Wochenschrift,* a German publication, Vol. 31, p. 552, 1951, says Dr. Ochsner's method can be used successfully in reducing one-tenth of the usual incidence of thrombosis and should perhaps be used to decrease the danger of clot in coronary thrombosis. M. Reifferscheid and P. Matis writing in *Medizinische Welt,* Germany, Vol. 20, p. 1168, 1951, announce they have found vitamin E to be definitely protective against vascular clotting. They found that large daily doses were necessary. They describe 5 cases of diabetic gangrene, 9 cases of Raynaud's disease (a gangrenous condition), 7 cases of Dupuytren's contracture (contraction of tissues under the skin of the palm) and 14 cases of hemorrhagic (bleeding) diseases all yielded to treatment with vitamin E.

Dr. W. E. Crump and E. F. Heiskell, writing in the *Texas State Journal of Medicine,* Vol. 11, 1952, agree that the use of the regular anti-coagulants for routine prevention of clotting diseases in patients after operations is too dangerous for general use. In most cases where these medicines are used, as many patients die of hemorrhage as might have died of clots, and 16 per cent of other cases develop non-fatal bleeding complications. When vitamin E was used as treatment by these physicians, no bleeding occurred and only minor side reactions were noticed. When cases of phlebitis occurred during treatment, they were mild and had no complications. There were no lung clots, fatal or non-fatal, in patients being treated with vitamin E. Dr. Terrel Speed, commenting on these statements, says "considerable evidence is accumulating to substantiate the value of this therapy. However, I have gradually expanded its use and now it is used routinely in essentially the same group of cases mentioned by the authors. If the promising preliminary results are borne out, relative protection against one of the most feared complications of surgery will have been obtained."

SECTION 30

GARLIC

Garlic has been successfully used in treating high blood pressure. It is available in capsules. It is a blood-purifier.

CHAPTER **105**

Garlic

Headlines make history in the health field:

1922—Paris: "Blood pressure fall of 10 to 40 mm. after two days dosage with garlic."

1923—China: "Garlic possesses valuable antiseptic properties."

1925—Germany: "Garlic effective in treating intestinal disease."

1926—Germany: "In treating human hypertension garlic helps 19 of 20 cases tested in advanced arterial disease."

1930—Japan: "Rabbit tests show garlic reduces blood pressure."

1931—South America: "In 10 cases drop of blood pressure 30 to 50 mm. by garlic injections."

1932—England: "25 uniformly successful experiments in relieving hypertension with garlic."

1938—Sweden: "Garlic used to prevent polio."

1948—Brazil: "Garlic effects 100 per cent cures of 300 patients with intestinal infections ranging from enterocolitis to amebic dysentery."

None of these modern headlines would have surprised a physician of 2,000 years ago. He would merely have nodded his head and said, "Yes, of course, we've known right along that garlic could do all these things." And research shows just that— for more than 5,000 years physicians have been working cures with the smooth, odoriferous little bulb that anyone can grow easily in a garden plot. The Babylonians 3,000 years B.C., knew of the curative powers of garlic. In the days of the Egyptian empire a Pharoah spent the equivalent of nearly two million dollars buying garlic to feed the workers who built the great Cheops pyramid. The Vikings and the Phoenicians, intrepid adventurers, packed garlic in their sea chests when they started on their lengthy sea voyages. The Greek physicians, fathers of present-day medicine, used garlic regularly in their practice and wrote treatises on its effectiveness.

An almost miraculous healing power seems to exist in the garlic bulb. Throughout all these thousands of years it has been used to cure many of the conditions of ill health that are being studied today in our super-scientific laboratories. Garlic, said the Egyptians, the Chinese, the Greeks, the Babylonians, is a cure for the following: intestinal disorders, flatulence, infections of the respiratory system, worms, lice and nits, skin diseases and ulcers, and the symptoms of aging. Up until recently the reasons why garlic was potent against these infirmities were not known. In the last 10 or 15 years an enormous new interest in the subject of garlic has resulted in laboratory experiments which almost, but not quite, explain why the evil-smelling little bulb is powerful against so many different disorders. A Russian investigator who concentrated on the healing powers of various plant oils made garlic oil so famous among the medical profession that it is sometimes spoken of as "Russian Penicillin."

Antibiotic Power of Garlic

And, indeed, its action is comparable to that of penicillin, except that with garlic there are no bad aftereffects, no limit to the dosage and no dangers of disrupting the delicate relationships among the various bacteria that exist in our bodies, for it is believed that garlic inhibits these bacteria rather than killing them outright. Not so long ago it was customary to use the garlic bulb itself in the treatment of various diseases. In diphtheria, for instance, the patient held the bulb in his mouth and scored it with his teeth from time to time, to release the garlic oil. Within a matter of hours he felt better, his temperature went down and the dread symptoms of diphtheria present in his throat disappeared. Garlic juice mixed with oil or lard was customarily used as a plaster or ointment for external relief of respiratory infections, boils, carbuncles and all manner of suppurating sores. We are told that during the great plagues that swept Europe in the Middle Ages those who ate garlic were immune, and garlic was used successfully to disinfect the crowded burial grounds and prevent the plague from spreading.

No doubt the ancients used either the garlic bulb itself or oil extracted by compressing or pounding the bulb. Perhaps in those days there was no social feeling against the smell of garlic. Or perhaps the general lack of sanitary measures resulted in so many assorted smells that the garlic aroma went unnoticed.

Today, however, most of us have a definite prejudice against that individual who may sit next to us in the movies, and who had obviously just come from a meal in which garlic was undoubtedly an emphatic item. So, partly because of this social disapproval of the smell and partly because many very ill patients are nauseated by the odor of garlic, ways and means have been discovered to remove the offensive odor by dehydrating the garlic and packing it in neat little capsules, sometimes with a mite of charcoal which absorbs the odor, or a bit of some other substance which prevents the capsule from disintegrating until it is safely inside the intestine.

The Garlic Cure for Tuberculosis

Down through the years physicians have been experimenting with garlic. One of the earliest of our modern researchers was Dr. W. C. Minchin, an English physician practicing in Ireland, who, at the beginning of this century, caused an enormous stir in medical circles in England with his letters and articles about garlic to the *Lancet* and other conservative British publications. Dr. Minchin was in charge of a large tuberculosis ward in Kells Hospital, Dublin. Most of his patients were sent to him as hopeless cases, doomed to die of this disease which was at that time the number one killer. Dr. Minchin invited several physicians to send some of their patients to his hospital. While they were undergoing cure, their own physicians visited them, noticed the great improvement and marveled at the new method of treatment Dr. Minchin was using. He did not tell them what it was and they did not once suspect it. Dr. Minchin used garlic as an internal medicine, as an inhalant and also as ointment and compresses for tuberculous joints and skin.

Country People Use Garlic

In answer to his published letters and articles, letters poured in from physicians all over the world who were intensely interested in the subject and reported their own experiences with garlic medication as well as the way garlic was used by individuals to cure illnesses in their own homes. In general, the tone of the correspondence went like this: "The peasants and farmers hereabouts have always used garlic as a cure for coughs, colds, tuberculosis, intestinal and digestive disorders, boils, poisoning and so forth. Perhaps this is not just superstition. Perhaps they are wiser than they know." Indeed the instinct of the country people was sound, for it has now been established that garlic is a powerful warrior against germs, which can be used in almost any quantity with perfect safety.

Case Histories Prove Effectiveness of Garlic

The numerous case histories which illustrate Dr. Minchin's writings are startling proof of the effectiveness of garlic in the treatment of tuberculosis. Here are some samples. A boy 10 years old with tuberculosis of the hand, in which all the bones of the hand were involved, was admitted to the hospital to have his hand amputated. Dr. Minchin undertook to treat him with garlic compresses and within 6 weeks the hand was completely cured. A girl of 15 suffered from tuberculosis of the cervical glands. All her glands from ear to ear in the neck and beneath the jaw were involved. It took 6 months of treatment with garlic until the young woman was completely healed.

In treating pulmonary tuberculosis, Dr. Minchin allowed his less serious cases to go about their work, while they took garlic internally and used garlic compresses and inhalations only at night. Here, too, his record of complete cures is astounding. He also treated tuberculosis of the skin and larynx.

An American Tries Garlic

At almost the same time Dr. Minchin's papers were being published in England, Dr. M. W. McDuffie of the Metropolitan Hospital in New York was experimenting with tuberculosis cures. His ward was the hopeless ward where in his own words "practically every case is a stretcher case and the majority die within a few days or weeks after admittance." Dr. McDuffie's article called "Tuberculosis Treatment" appeared in the *North American Journal of Homoeopathy* for May, 1914. In it he describes work with 1,082 patients using 56 different kinds of treatment, all the way from hydrochloric acid to chest surgery, to garlic. Of the 56 treatments used, he says in his summary, "Garlic is the best individual treatment found to get rid of germs and we believe same to be a specific for the tubercle baccilus and for tubercular processes no matter what part of the body is affected, whether skin, bones, glands, lungs or special parts. . . . Thus nature by diet, rest, and exercise, baths, climate and garlic, furnishes sufficient and specific treatment for the medical aspects of this disease."

How Does Garlic Act on Germs?

Although physicians 50 years ago did not have access to the laboratory methods that can be used today for determining how and why a certain treatment brings about results, yet they were on the right track with garlic, for experiments in modern laboratories show exactly how garlic works in the presence of germs. *The Medical Record* for June 4, 1941, carries a story by Emil Weiss, M.D., of Chicago, on a series of experiments on 22 subjects all with a known history of intestinal disorders. These were observed for several weeks before the experiment began and careful notes taken of everything relating to their digestive processes. Daily specimens of urine and feces were collected. Garlic was then administered to part of the group, while the other part took no medication. Headaches, mild diarrhea and other symptoms of intestinal disorder disappeared during the garlic treatment. But, more significant yet, there was a complete change in the intestinal flora of all the subjects who took garlic. Intestinal flora are the bacteria living in the digestive tract. Some of these are beneficial, helping with the digestion of food. Others are harmful, resulting in conditions of putrefaction and ill health. By the end of the garlic treatment, the beneficial bacteria were increasing in all of the cases and the harmful bacteria were decreasing.

An article by T. D. Yanovitch in the *Comptes Rendus de l'Academie des Sciences de l'USSR*, 1945, Vol. XLVIII, No. 7, describes experiments using garlic juice on actual colonies of bacteria. Introducing the bacteria directly into the juice caused the complete cessation of all movement of the bacteria within 3 minutes. When garlic juice was added to a culture of bacteria, the bacteria were dispersed to the edge of the culture. After two minutes, immobile bacteria began to appear and within 10 minutes all activity had ceased. This author notes that dilution of the garlic juice reduced its efficiency, and freshly prepared juice was much more effective than juice which had been preserved for several months.

So much research has been done on the subject of garlic and the treatment for hypertension (high blood pressure) that current articles do not present much actual information on the facts involved, with documentation of how many patients were cured. Rather these authorities are now disputing exactly how it is that garlic cures hypertension. In an article in a European publication, *Praxis,* for July 1, 1948, G. Piotrowski, ·visiting lecturer and member of the faculty of medicine at the University of Geneva writes of his experiences with the use of garlic on "about a hundred patients." It is generally agreed by the medical profession that the administration of garlic reduces high blood pressure, but there are two schools of thought as to just how it brings about this result. One group of researchers contends that since garlic is such an effective germ killer, its antiseptic action on the intestines purifies them of all the poisonous substances and putrefaction, and this results in lowered blood pressure.

Dr. Piotrowski, however, contends that garlic lowers blood pressure by dilating the blood vessels. Although he does not deny the valuable work done by garlic in cleansing products of putrefaction from the intestines, he claims that this is not productive of a fall in blood pressure. He indicates, too, that it is difficult to conduct experiments with hypertensive patients and equally difficult to interpret the results, for it is generally accepted that hypertension is the result of a wide variety of causes.

Verified Results Are Quite Favorable

This researcher eliminated from his study any patients whose conditions might further confuse the results—that is, patients whose blood pressure dropped when other medicines were administered, those who had kidney trouble and so forth. He tells us that Schlesinger, another investigator, secured a drop in pressure after 15 days of treatment with garlic. Pouillard claimed a decided drop in pressure within an hour after the first administration of garlic. Dr. Piotrowski has no such sensational reports to make and he declares that he believes that intermittent dosage with garlic just for the purpose of obtaining a decided drop in blood pressure is not advisable. He prefers to administer oil of garlic for 3 weeks. He reports that he has obtained a drop of at least two centimeters in blood pressure in 40 per cent of the cases—these were all cases in which he knew that the drop was due to the garlic and could not have been caused by anything else. Incidentally, all of his patients were going about their daily work as usual during the treatment, so lack of fatigue or rest in bed did not have a chance to influence the results.

He tells us that apparently neither age nor blood pressure reading of any individual patient enables one to predict results, for it seems that good results do not occur just because the patient is young or because his blood pressure is not especially high. The expected drop of two centimeters in blood pressure generally takes place after about a week of treatment. Dr. Piotrowski begins his hypertensive patients with fairly large doses of garlic and gradually decreases the doses over a period of 3 weeks. Then he gives smaller doses during the rest of the treatment. He does not say how long "the rest of the treatment" is, but we assume he means until the patient's blood pressure is normal, and he has none of the symptoms of the disease remaining.

Symptoms of Hypertension Disappear

Doctors generally discuss two kinds of symptoms—the ones the physician can discover (in this case, the actual blood pressure reading) and the "subjective symptoms"—that is, the things that are wrong with him that only the patient can know and describe. The subjective symptoms of hypertension vary with the individual, but most such patients have one or more of the following: headaches, dizziness, angina-like pains and ringing in the ears. Some of these patients also complained of pains in their backs between their shoulder blades. In 80 per cent of the patients dizziness disappeared with the garlic treatment. Headaches also vanished. The pains, which seemed to occur in proportion to the degree of hypertension, were relieved in some cases. The only subjective symptom that was not relieved by the garlic treatment was ringing in the ears. Dr. Piotrowski does not give any reason for this, but it seems to us quite possible that this condition may not have been related to the hypertension, for certainly many people complain of head and ear noises who do not have high blood pressure.

Dr. Piotrowski tells us that the subjective symptoms of his patients began to disappear in 3 to 5 days after they began the garlic treatment. They also found that they could think much more clearly and concentrate better on their jobs. His conclusions are that garlic certainly has useful properties in the treatment of high blood pressure. It usually causes a drop in pressure and, even in cases where it does not, its use is justified by the relief it brings for the uncomfortable symptoms the patient has had. He ends by recommending that many more M.D.'s begin immediately to take advantage of garlic therapy in treating their hypertensive patients.

Garlic Therapy By Two American Doctors

It would appear from what we have said so far that Europeans are far ahead of Americans in gathering information about garlic. Garlic has always been a plant more typical of the rest of the world than of America. It is only within the past 20 years or so that garlic has come to have any place even in American diet, whereas Europeans, especially those in south and central Europe, have used it for centuries. An article in *The New York Physician* for September, 1937, gives the experience of two New York doctors using garlic products in their practice. David Stein, M.D., and Edward H. Kotin, M.D., tell us that because of its therapeutic value, they believe that garlic must contain vitamins A, B and C and its C content is probably quite high. The mineral content of garlic, they say, indicates the presence of aluminum, manganese, copper, zinc, sulfur, iron, calcium and chlorine.

Researchers Discover Scores of Benefits

Before describing their own experience, the authors review the findings of other researchers on garlic and tell us that garlic has been found useful for the following purposes in therapeutics: as an aid to feeble digestion, because it stimulates gastric juices. It is a fine carminative, which means that it relieves flatulence, dyspepsia and colic, it is an intestinal antiseptic, stimulating the growth of healthful bacteria in the intestine. "Diarrhea from infectious diseases such as diphtheria, scarlet fever and tuberculosis respond favorably to garlic therapy." It is a harmless but potent preventive of pneumonia, diphtheria, typhus and tuberculosis; it is an expectorant, useful in all respiratory infections, but particularly those characterized by a dry, hacking cough—in bronchitis, colds and asthma. It is an excellent nerve tonic, effective in cases of neurasthenia and nervous insufficiency. It is an anthelmintic—a destroyer of round and thread worms. It is a rubefacient and counterirritant which may be applied in compress form for intercostal neuralgia, pleurisy, tuberculosis of the larynx and catarrhal pneumonia.

Then these two authors give case histories of 12 cases treated by them with garlic. The diagnoses of these patients range from tuberculosis to bronchitis, pharyngitis, shortness of breath, asthma, constipation, flatulence, heartburn, nervousness, diarrhea, cramps, nausea, vomiting, chills and fever—chest and abdominal cases, they call them. In every case they treated there was relief, sometimes within a week, always within a month. "In conclusion," say these authors, "we feel that garlic is an excellent medicament, for employment in a diversity of conditions. We believe that the vitamin and mineral factors do much to cause this to be a drug of noteworthy usage."

What We Recommend

In garlic we have yet another example of the kind of food we love to discover and tell our readers about—a food known for thousands of years to the plain, everyday people of the earth who have had to keep themselves strong and healthy in spite of hard work, poverty, ignorance and bad sanitation. Now at last we sophisticated folks of the twentieth century have "discovered" it. And it looks as though the unassuming little bulb may be the answer to many of our problems.

Garlic is a food, a very necessary and important food which should be eaten every day by all of us. Used as an herb in almost any vegetable, meat or cheese dish, cooked or raw, employed as an essential part of every salad, it will probably still not appear in our diet in anything like the quantity we should have.

Besides, there is still the social hazard connected with eating it. There can be no doubt of it—the volatile and highly flavored essence of garlic does infect one's breath. Even though you may educate all your family and friends to the healthful joys of garlic-eating, so that they won't ever notice your breath, you must also have consideration for the strangers you meet— or the people you sit next to in movies. The answer to this problem, of course, is to take garlic perles. They have been treated so that they do not dissolve until they are safely assimilated far down in your digestive system, so, unless you take enormous quantities, there's no chance of garlic perles tainting your breath.

We urgently suggest that you add garlic perles to your daily food supplements. Whether or not you are suffering from any of the disorders discussed above, there's no need to wait until you are ill, when you can so easily prevent symptoms by including as much fresh garlic as possible in your meals and adding garlic perles to your regular food supplements.

CHAPTER **106**

Experiments With Garlic and Cancer

Garlic has been found to be powerful against a surprising list of man's enemies in the field of disease. Is it possible that it may some day be used to control cancer?

Research on the effectiveness of garlic against disease has not been so popular of late as it has been during the past 50 years or so. This is one reason why we were especially pleased to find in *Science,* Vol. 126, November 29, 1957, p. 1112, an account of research that seems to show that garlic is powerful against tumor-formation. And that means, of course, cancer, too.

Garlic Preparation and Cancer Growth

Working with laboratory mice, Austin S. Weisberger and Jack Pensky of Western Reserve University found that by injecting cancerous cells into mice they could produce rapid growth of cancer and death within 16 days. They could produce the same result even when they treated the cancerous cells with an enzyme they had isolated from garlic. The enzyme by itself did not protect from cancer. But when they treated the cancerous cells with an equal amount of the garlic enzyme and the substrate which is also present in garlic (that is, the substance with which the enzyme is naturally associated in foods), and then injected mice with the treated cells, no cancer grew and there was no mortality among the animals for a period of six months (equal to about a fourth of a lifetime in a human being).

Thus we see that the cancer cells were prevented from doing any damage by treating them with the preparation from garlic. But our researchers went further than that. They inoculated mice with the virulent cancer cells and then gave them injections of the garlic preparation. The garlic delayed the onset of the malignant tumor and in some instances completely prevented its formation and saved the lives of the mice. However, in all cases it was necessary to keep giving the garlic preparation, for tumors developed very rapidly if it was discontinued.

Enzyme and Substrate Must Work Together

Such findings, which link the humble, smelly garlic bulb with the prevention of cancer, the greatest modern plague, are spectacular. But, in addition note some of the details of this experiment. Scientists have known for a long time that there is a certain enzyme in garlic that is powerful against disease bacteria. But when they used just this enzyme, you will notice the Western Reserve scientists got no results. They had to use both the enzyme and the substrate from garlic to attain success in preventing cancer. The word *substrate* refers to the substance which works with the enzyme to bring about chemical changes. Every enzyme has its substrate; indeed, every enzyme takes its name from its substrate. Thus the enzyme named *lipase* reacts chemically with fats or lipids. Proteinases react chemically with proteins, and so forth.

In the case of garlic the enzyme alliinase is liberated when the garlic bulb is crushed. It immediately reacts with its substrate to form a new chemical compound which is the powerful anti-bacterial compound for which garlic is noted.

Using the enzyme alone or using the substrate alone produces no effect. The researchers found that they must use them together. They do not, of course, know why they obtained these results, and they suggest in the article several possible ways in which the garlic enzyme and substrate may bring about the desired result. So we learn two lessons from such an article—first, that the simple garlic bulb is indeed a powerful agent against disease and secondly, that wholeness is best where health is concerned. The less we separate, divide and fragmentize where food is involved, the better off we are. Whole foods, containing everything that occurs naturally in them, are best.

CHAPTER **107**

Garlic for Intestinal Disorders

Dyspepsia, especially that arising from a lack of the beneficial intestinal bacteria, yields easily to treatment with garlic preparations, as we show in this chapter.

"Lack of time and space prevents me from going into more detail on the interesting history of this plant (garlic) as a medical and popular remedy. Its use is age-old. It was used by Hippocrates and Paracelsus and is frequently mentioned in the herbals of the middle ages as a remedy. Its range of uses was extremely varied. In recent times garlic has been highly recommended in France particularly as a remedy in the case of lung diseases attended by copious and ill-smelling expectoration as well as a remedy against hypertension."

We are quoting Professor E. Roos of St. Joseph's Hospital, Freiburg, Germany. These words form the introduction to an article of his telling how he has used a garlic preparation in his own practice, treating patients who suffered from a variety of intestinal disorders, most of them involving diarrheal conditions. We found this article in an old (September 25, 1925) copy of *Munchener Medizinische Wochenschrift,* a medical magazine which is, of course, published in Germany.

Harmful Intestinal Bacteria

Dr. Roos speaks mostly in this article of cases of intestinal complaint arising from the presence of disease-causing bacteria in the intestine. Generally speaking, the more serious forms of

diarrheal diseases seem to result from the presence of some such
bacteria. At any rate, large numbers of one or more of such
bacteria are found in the stool of these sufferers. As our readers
know, an overabundance of the harmful bacteria in the intestine
can completely crowd out the helpful ones which normally live
there, and unpleasant consequences may result. One of these
may well be diarrhea—acute or chronic. And you may be sure
that, if the helpful bacteria are not soon re-established, the
diarrhea will continue.

Garlic Goes to Work

Dr. Roos tells us in the 1925 article that he had, at the
time he wrote it, treated 96 patients with a garlic preparation
which he made himself. We imagine it must be very like those
sold in this country. It contains the essence of garlic, but it is
without its possibly unpleasant aftereffects in the way of taste
and odor, because it is prepared so that it does not dissolve and
go to work until it is far down in the intestine. So there is
little danger of the anti-social qualities of the raw bulb being
noticeable.

He gave his patients garlic in dosages of one gram or
more and one of his tablets which weighed a gram contained
the same amount of raw garlic—one gram. He tells us that he
feels garlic is effective against 3 different kinds of digestive or
intestinal upsets which could conceivably occur all at the same
time in the same patient. "There is in garlic," he says, "a
special intestine-soothing and diarrhea-allaying effect which
occurs in various colonic affections." There is an effect, also,
that cleanses the intestinal flora (the bacteria that live in the
intestines) of disease-causing bacteria or at least abnormal mixtures of bacteria. Then, too, there is an anti-dyspepsia effect in
the taking of garlic. "Probably," he says, "the same healing
influence on the intestinal mucous membrane lies at the basis
of all 3."

Diarrhea Stopped—and No Constipation

The first effect which soothes the intestine is almost, he
says, like the effect of a narcotic. So far as the diarrhea is
concerned, it is frequently stopped within a very short time and
at the same time the pains, the stomach ache or other difficulties
disappear too. If you give narcotics for diarrhea (and this seems

to have been the standard treatment at that time), constipation is likely to follow. It seldom does when garlic is taken.

"Quite to the contrary," he says, "we have even observed, following week-long use on the part of patients who do not have diarrhea, regular daily stool, though sometimes in these cases a mildly inhibitory influence makes itself noticeable. It makes little difference what kind of diarrhea you are dealing with or where it principally has its origin. A favorable result has been obtained in the great majority of cases treated, even in stubbornly chronic cases with recurrence." He reminds us that good results cannot be hoped for if the diarrhea is the symptom of some serious organic disorder—cancer or tuberculosis.

Garlic Helps Tuberculosis Patient

Then, almost as if to contradict the statement he has just made, Dr. Roos goes on to describe the case of a young woman who did have tuberculosis and was suffering from a severe diarrhea. In addition, she was subject to spells of vomiting, severe body swelling and pain on pressure. He prescribed his garlic preparation. "The patient takes the remedy in the same dose for 6 weeks. Appetite quickly becomes very good, the general condition improved, the temperature after 6 weeks still showed only occasional light rises. After four weeks the stool is practically normal, for the most part once a day."

The lung inflammation subsided and the swelling disappeared. Says Dr. Roos, "Even if the probable tuberculosis was not cured by garlic, still one receives the distinct impression that the patient has been relatively quickly tided over the serious stage through the rapid improvements in the intestine and the appetite."

Dysentery Improved

In other cases of serious organic trouble the garlic preparation helped. Dr. Roos tells us of a 41-year-old farmer who had had a case of dysentery for many years complicated by rectal polyps. This unfortunate man also suffered from what Dr. Roos describes as a "constant restlessness of body," abdominal rumblings and colic-like pains. For 3 months he took two grams of the garlic preparation 3 times a day, and, finally, two grams twice daily. For as long as he remained under the influence of the remedy, his trouble was much improved. His stools became for the·most part much more solid and less frequent. He became happier and was able to work. He took a long trip each week to obtain the garlic remedy. Four months after completion of treatment he told Dr. Roos that his condition was still more supportable and his body quieter than before, even though the diarrhea and slimy evacuations reappeared from time to time.

More Case Histories

A scholar who was troubled with abdominal pains, stomach trouble, hyperacidity and diarrhea found that he apparently had appendicitis and prepared for an operation. By chance the surgeon was not available and meantime the patient took some of the garlic preparation, two grams, twice daily. After a few days he declared that he was perfectly well and didn't want to hear any more about an operation. A couple of months later he wrote for more of the prescribed medicine, and Dr. Roos suggested that he have the operation. He says, "I record this not for the purpose of recommending substitution of garlic medication for an indicated appendectomy, but in order to show its soothing influence even in organically conditioned troubles."

Another Dysentery Case

One final case history. This was a laboratory assistant who had by accident infected herself with a bacteria which causes dysentery. Her symptoms were alarming. Loss of appetite, vomiting and diarrhea were followed by bloody stools. The girl was pain-racked and weak. She was given the garlic preparation, two grams, 5 times daily for 6 days. The vomiting stopped almost at once, and she began to take food. It was not until the nineteenth day of illness that the illness began to subside, but quite some time before this, the patient was out of bed cheerful and feeling like herself.

"I could not maintain," says Dr. Roos, "that the length of time of actual illness was considerably shortened, only that convalescence transpired in a surprisingly rapid manner. To everyone experienced with cases of dysentery the contrast must be extremely surprising between the obviously very severe form of the disease and the extremely light discomfort following introduction of treatment, along with only a mildly exhausted condition."

In the second part of his article, Dr. Roos goes on to give case histories of other patients suffering from different conditions who improved when they used garlic.

Some of Them

1. A churchman, 33 years old, who suffered from chronic colitis which manifested itself in frequent diarrhea, along with pain and other unpleasant sensations. In the beginning he took two grams of garlic twice daily for 14 days, then once daily. Within the first few days, he felt better. Three weeks after treatment began he had two normal stools daily.

2. Acute enterocolitis. A 24 year old woman who suddenly experienced terrific body pains, nausea, chills and fever combined with persistent diarrhea. She took two grams of garlic 3 times a day and by the fifth day her condition was perfectly normal.

3. Subacute colitis. A doctor of 35 years. Fell sick with diarrhea and colic pains. He took two grams of garlic 3 times a day and soon became normal.

4. Acute enterocolitis. A 28-year old doctor whose diarrhea occurred every time she took food. A dose of garlic—two grams 3 times a day for 3 days—brought her back to normal.

5. A case of nervous diarrhea. A patient who suffered from this complaint when he became excited. The diarrhea was improved from time to time by the use of garlic. Dr. Roos notes that the patient came for the remedy quite often.

Disorders from Harmful Intestinal Bacteria

The second group of patients discussed by Dr. Roos are those whose intestinal contents showed evidence of large numbers of harmful bacteria. For 17 years the first patient, a professor, had suffered from gas, dyspepsia and colitis. At times his diarrhea alternated with spells of constipation. Two grams of the garlic preparation taken two to three times daily were prescribed. In two and a half months this patient was fully satisfied that his troubles were over.

The second patient was an eccentric who had been starving himself. Examination of the stool showed copious infiltration of harmful bacteria. It took 4 weeks of treatment with garlic to bring this patient back to normal.

Another patient was a woman of 59 who had always been

delicate and had formerly been constipated. She had suffered
from diarrhea for about 9 months. When she began to take
garlic, there was at first only a slight improvement, but by the
end of 6 weeks she was in good health and her stools were
normal. Her appearance was better and she had gained weight.
When she came for treatment, examination showed rather
copious infiltration of harmful bacteria in her stools. After
treatment these had disappeared.

Garlic Aids Dyspepsia Cases

Patients who suffered from "dyspepsia" are next described by Dr. Roos. The first was a 23-year-old student who
complained of excessive gas, restlessness, loss of weight, general
feeling of ill health and diarrhea. After taking garlic he returned to normal with only one brief relapse.

A master baker of 48 suffered from intense pressure pains
in the upper abdomen. This pain had bothered him for more
than a year, and sometimes it was present for the entire day.
He did not suffer from gas. Taking two tablets of garlic 3 times
a day he found that he experienced great improvement within
a matter of days, and within 6 weeks he declared himself in
perfect health.

An inspector of 31 suffered from diarrhea, poor appetite,
gas. He had taken many drugs with no relief. By the end of
the fourth week on garlic, he was satisfied that he was cured.

Two school teachers—one 35 and the other 47, both
suffered from diarrhea, gas, frequent bloating and belching, also
headache and heart palpitations. Six weeks on garlic sufficed to
do away with these symptoms.

Therefore, says Dr. Roos, we see that garlic preparations
show special anti-dyspeptic effects, no matter whether they cause
any great change in the consistency of the stools. "Often, after a
very short time, the difficulties improve, the patients feel relieved and look better. One has the impression of a complete
alteration in the intestine and of its complete transformation.
So far as our patients could later tell, the effect also seems to
last."

The How and Why of Garlic Treatment

How does garlic achieve its effects? We do not know
exactly, he says, but it appears to have a purifying effect on the
bacteria of the intestine, brought about probably by some bio-

logical healing of the intestinal wall and its glands. But, he adds, in cases where there is no evidence of any unfavorable or abnormal concentration of harmful bacteria in the intestine—that is, for instance, in cases of "nervous" diarrhea, garlic is also helpful, apparently because of this same healing effect on the mucous membrane.

Naturally, he says, treatment with garlic, as with every other kind of treatment, has as well its unsatisfactory results, its failures and its limitations. He recommends as the best possible daily dose for intestinal complaints two tablets 3 times daily. In severe cases one should take two tablets 5 times daily; in lighter ones two tablets once to twice daily—without any fear of disagreeable side effects.

We have tried without success to get a sample of the actual tablet used by Dr. Roos. Its name is Allisatin and apparently it is no longer being manufactured. However, from what we know of it any garlic preparation would produce the same results.

SECTION 31

KELP

Kelp provides abundant iodine, especially necessary for those who live inland in "goiter" regions and for those who do not eat sea fish. It is seaweed and is extremely rich in minerals.

CHAPTER **108**

Kelp

In the Chinese *Book of Poetry* written in the time of Confucius (between 800 and 600 B.C.) there is a poem about a housewife cooking seaweed. During this period in Chinese history seaweed was considered a delicacy, worthy of being offered to the gods as a sacrificial food. Several kinds of seaweed were used in ancient China. And seaweed still forms an important part of the diet in eastern countries.

In Japan, we are told, seaweed is used to a far greater extent than in any other country and provides about 25 per cent of the daily diet! The brown seaweeds are incorporated into flour and are used in almost every household as noodles, toasted and served with rice or in soup. Two other kinds of seaweed are used for sweetening and flavoring. Relishes, beverages and cakes are made from them.

In western countries seaweeds have never been generally accepted as part of daily meals, although in Ireland, Iceland, Denmark, Wales, Scotland and the Faroe Islands, seaweeds have been eaten extensively. The national dish of South Wales is laverbread, which contains seaweed. The Irish eat dulse, a seaweed that is called "sea lettuce" because it is tender, crisp and tasty like the land variety. W. A. P. Black, writing in the *Proceedings of the Nutrition Society* of England, Vol. 12, p. 32, 1953, says that a certain seaweed, porphyra, is eaten in Scotland, grilled on toast. He tells us it looks like spinach and tastes like oysters.

Intestinal Bacteria Digest Seaweed

Dr. Black also tells us that there may be present in the intestinal tracts of the Japanese people a specialized bacterial flora, giving the seaweeds a greater nutritional value. The bacterial flora are the beneficial bacteria which live in the intestines and manufacture certain vitamins there, as well as helping in the digestion of food. Dr. Black says that in digestibility tests with cattle it has been found that when seaweed is first introduced into the diet, it is completely undigested and appears unaltered in the feces. After a few days, however, no seaweed as such is found in the feces. So it seems that the bacteria in the intestines have an important part in the digestion of seaweed. In Japan it appears that children develop the proper intestinal bacteria, since they are fed seaweed products from infancy on.

Seaweed—A Valuable Food

Back in 1920, according to *Popular Mechanics,* for July, 1952, a man named Philip Park who was touring England was startled to see cattle passing over rich, lush grass so that they could feed on kelp or seaweed. He investigated the food content of this seaweed and went into business to produce it for animal food and human consumption as well. At his non-profit research organization, experiments are carried on to find out even more about this remarkable plant.

Kelp is harvested by special boats equipped with a great hook which pulls the plant up out of the sea. Special cutters then mow off the tops of the kelp plants which are carried back to the boat on a conveyor belt arrangement. At the processing plant, the kelp is chopped fine, dried, sterilized and shredded. There is no boiling or draining off of water. Everything in the way of minerals remains that was in the original plant. We are told that kelp plants are so vigorous in growth that plants cut to a depth of 4 feet will reach the surface of the sea again within 48 to 60 hours.

We are well acquainted, all of us, with the fact that plants growing on the land form, or should form, a large part of the diet of the healthy individual. What of the plants that grow in the sea? Is there any indication that they may be good for us, too?

Something About Seaweeds

Sea plants go under the collective name of "algae." There are 3 kinds, depending on color—the green, the brown and the red. In some ways they are like land plants, but in other ways many of them have little in common with what we are accustomed to thinking of as plants. They have no roots. They cling to stones, wharves or pilings with "holdfasts." They do not have stalks and branches in the same sense that land plants do. In many seaweeds there are no special parts of the plant either for support (like the stems of land flowers or the trunks of land trees) or for conducting nourishment from one part of the plant to another. Many seaweeds have structures that look like leaves, but they are not leaves in the same sense that we use for leaves of land plants. They do not manufacture food for the rest of the plant to eat. In seaweeds almost every part of the plant can make its own food. Seaweeds have nothing that looks like flowers, fruit or seeds.

They grow tall, some of the largest kelps stretching up for a hundred feet or more from the floor of the ocean. Because of their simple structure and the fossils in which they have been found, paleontologists (scientists who decide about the age of earthly things) have said that algae probably represent the first form of life that appeared on our planet. The seaweeds you find today have developed considerably since those first primitive times, of course, but even so, they still retain many of the primitive characteristics of early life. They are not nearly so complicated as the land plants which came much later in history.

The Brown Seaweeds

The brown seaweeds are the ones we are going to talk about, for they are the commonest and the ones used most widely for food. Many of them are thick and leathery. Kelp comes in this category. Just as people in far corners of the world have eaten seeds, bones, insects and other foods that seem peculiar to us, just so have many peoples of the world eaten seaweed. And now it seems likely that kelp will become an important part of American diets.

Content of Seaweeds

What do seaweeds contain that might make them valuable as food? First of all, of course, just like other plants, they contain carbohydrates—that is, starches and sugars. The sugar of seaweed is called mannitol. It is not very sweet, has a mild laxative effect in large doses and does not increase the sugar content of the blood. This would be an important factor to diabetics if the seaweed-sugar should ever be used to a wide extent. Fats and proteins also exist in seaweed, the proteins

about as useful to human bodies as the protein of land plants—
that is, not as useful as protein that comes from animal sources,
such as meat and eggs. Seaweed is not a very fatty plant, but it
does contain at least one of the unsaturated fatty acids necessary
to human health.

In the way of vitamins there seems to be some vitamin
A and a certain amount of the B vitamins. Dr. Black of the
British Nutrition Society tells us that the vitamin C content
of seaweed is comparable with that of many vegetables and
fruits. With some Eskimo nations seaweed was at one time used
as their chief source of vitamin C. One test showed a vitamin
C content of 5 to 140 milligrams of vitamin C per 100 grams of
wet seaweed. Oranges contain about 50 milligrams per 100
grams.

The Minerals in Seaweeds

However, our main interest in seaweed or kelp as food
is not in its protein, carbohydrates or vitamins—although it is
good to know the status of any new food in these categories.
What interests us mainly about kelp is its mineral content. It
seems reasonable, does it not, to expect sea foods to be rich in
minerals? Aside from the fact that sea water as such is a
veritable treasure trove of minerals, land minerals are constantly washing into the sea, enriching it still further. Every
river in the world carrying silt and soil that has washed away
or eroded from the land runs eventually to the sea, giving up its
minerals into the salty depths.

Plants that grow on land take up minerals from the soil.
By testing the amount of minerals in any given plant, we can
get a good idea of how many minerals were in the soil in which
it grew, for vegetables and fruits from mineral-rich land will
also be rich in these so-important food elements. The same is
true of sea plants. So we can expect seaweed or kelp to be a
good source of minerals. How good it is surprised even us.
Dr. Black tells us that the ash of seaweed may be from 10 per
cent to as high as 50 per cent. This means that if you burn
seaweed, you may have half the volume of the seaweed left as
minerals! Compare this to some other foods. Carrots leave an
ash of 1 per cent as minerals. Apples have a mineral ash of .3 per
cent, almonds 3.0 per cent, beets 1.1 per cent.

Dr. Black says further, "It can be said that seaweed contains all the elements that have so far been shown to play an

important part in the physiological processes of man. In a balanced diet, therefore, they would appear to be an excellent mineral supplement." We know that, of the minerals which are needed in relatively large amounts like calcium, iron, phosphorus, potassium and so forth, the average fruit or vegetable contains an amount approximate to the amounts listed on the tables and charts in nutrition books.

They Supply Trace Minerals

But, as important as these minerals are, perhaps even more important are the trace minerals—iodine, copper, manganese, boron, zinc and so forth. These minerals appear in minute quantities in food. Our bodies need only microscopically small amounts of them. Yet if that tiny amount is not there, the consequences may be fatal. Our land is becoming trace-mineral-poor. Floods and poor farming practices are causing our soil to be washed away. And with it go the trace minerals. Applying commercial fertilizer to the soil does not improve the situation, for this does not, cannot, contain the trace minerals. Only by organic farming—that is, returning to the soil everything that has been taken from it—can we be certain that our food contains all of the precious trace minerals necessary for health. What happens to the trace minerals that wash away from our farmlands? They wash into the ocean and are taken up into seaweeds. So the worse-off we become so far as trace minerals in foods are concerned, the more do we need a substance like kelp as a food supplement. Those of us who farm organically probably need it less than those of us who must buy all our food from a store.

Iodine in Kelp

From the point of view of nutrition, the most important single trace mineral in kelp or seaweed is iodine. Why do we say this? How can one be more important than the others? It isn't that iodine is more important, exactly. It's simply that there are whole sections of the world where iodine *is completely lacking* in the soil. No food grown there contains any iodine at all. Many parts of the middle inland section of our country are deficient in iodine so far as soil is concerned. These localities are called "The Goiter Belt." We know that iodine is an absolute essential for the body, for it is the main ingredient of the product of one of our most important glands—the thyroid gland. Goiters are just one of the possible unhealthful results of too little iodine in the diet. There are many others.

Iodine from Iodized Salt

For a long time public health authorities have promoted the use of iodized salt to prevent goiter. This is plain table salt to which potassium iodide has been added by chemists. Our objection to this is our objection to all medicated foods. Table salt (sodium chloride) is a drug—a pure substance denuded of everything that accompanies sodium chloride in nature. To this we add another drug—potassium iodide. Such a product still has no relation to nature, so far as we are concerned. Besides we believe that most of us get far too much salt. So we recommend not using table salt either in cooking or at the table. Where then can someone who lives in the "goiter belt" get the iodine that is so essential for his well-being? Why not from kelp?

In Borden's *Review of Nutrition Research* for July-August, 1955, we are told that to get 100 micrograms of iodine (estimated as the normal daily requirement for human beings) one would have to eat

10 pounds of fresh vegetables and fruits, or
8 pounds of cereal, grains and nuts, or
6 pounds of meat, freshwater fish, fowl, or
2 pounds of eggs, or
.3 pounds of marine fish, or
.2 pounds of shellfish

They go on to state: "The problem of obtaining sufficient iodine from food of non-marine origin may be seen from values shown in this table. Iodine-rich seaweed is an abundant source on a limited scale for some peoples. Kelp contains about 200,000 micrograms per kilogram (about 2 pounds) and the dried kelp meal nearly 10 times as much or .1 per cent to .2 per cent of iodine. Used as a condiment this would provide 10 times as much iodine as American iodized salt."

Best Source of Iodine and Minerals

Kelp, then, it seems to us is the perfect answer for a mineral supplement for health-conscious folks. It is practically the only reliable food source of iodine, aside from sea food. It is rich in potassium and magnesium. It contains, in addition, all of the trace minerals that have been shown to be important for human nutrition and many more whose purposes we have not yet discovered.

It does contain sodium chloride, true. So does almost everything else that you eat. It contains more sodium chloride than vegetables and meats because it comes from the salty sea. But its content of sodium chloride is not high compared to table salt which is, of course, 100 per cent sodium chloride. We do not believe that the salt in kelp is harmful, because it occurs along with the other minerals as a natural part of the food. We do believe that the other minerals, especially the iodine in kelp, make it one of our most valuable food supplements.

Here is an analysis of an average sample of kelp, neither especially high nor low in minerals: In some cases we have compared the mineral content of kelp with that of some other food especially rich in this same mineral: You will note in every instance how much higher is the mineral content of the kelp.

	Kelp	*Other Food*
Iodine	.18%	Clams ... 1900 parts per billion
Calcium	1.05%	Milk .... .001%
Phosphorus	.339%	Wheat Germ ..... .01%
Iron	.37%	Eggs .... .0005%
Copper	.0008%	Eggs .... .0000023%
Potassium	11.15%	Almonds 7%
Magnesium	.740%	
Sodium	3.98%	
Chlorine	13.07%	
Manganese	.0015%	
Sulphur	1.%	

Trace minerals in kelp, not listed above are: barium, boron, chromium, lithium, nickel, silicon, silver, strontium, titanium, vanadium and zinc.

CHAPTER **109**

The Value of Seaweed in Nutrition

*Here are some further scientific facts about the value of
sea products in nutrition.*

The effectiveness of seaweed as a food for animals should
give us some better idea of the worth of this food for human
beings. Has seaweed been used to feed animals? If so, with
what results? Dr. W. A. P. Black, who seems to be a world
authority on the subject, has a lot to say about seaweed in
animal nutrition in an article in the British magazine *Agriculture,* Vol. 62 pp. 12-15 and 57-62, 1955.

Says Dr. Black, feeding trials with animals must be carried out for a considerable length of time, because it apparently
takes some time for the intestines to accustom themselves to
this diet, so that the seaweed can be completely digested.

Mineral Content of Seaweed

"Seaweeds have the advantage over land crops in that
they grow in an ideal environment, in which the nutrients in
sea water are being constantly renewed by nature," says Dr.
Black, "whereas on the land modern methods of intensive cultivation lead to complete exhaustion of the soil unless, with a
knowledge of the nutritional and other growth requirements
of the crops, the deficiencies are replaced by man. Seaweeds,
therefore, contain all the elements found in sea water, as well
as a rich bacterial microflora which contributes to their composition."

The brown seaweeds (of which kelp is one) contain all
the elements present in sea water, says Dr. Black, and can
accumulate some of them to *several thousand times* their concentration in the surrounding water. So they must contain all
the elements shown to play an important part in animal nutri-

tion. We know full well, Dr. Black goes on, that several of the
well-known animal diseases result from not having in the diet
enough of one or another of the "trace" minerals—that is, minerals which occur in food in such small amounts that one can
say there is only a "trace." One cannot use kelp as the only
mineral supplement, he believes, because its calcium and phosphorus content is too low. But if you use also some mineral
supplement (such as bone meal, we suggest) which is rich in
calcium and phosphorus, seaweed can provide everything else
that is needed in the way of mineral supplement.

The Value of Iodine in Seaweed

The iodine in seaweed is in the form of iodine amino
acids—in other words it occurs in kelp in just the same form in
which it occurs in the thyroid gland. Possibly this is the reason
that kelp is so effective. There can be no question about how
well the kelp's iodine is used by the body—it is in the same form
in which iodine occurs in the thyroid gland, where most of the
body's supply exists.

Dr. Black tells us that these iodine amino acids make
kelp a valuable food supplement for animals, "increasing the
milk and butterfat production of dairy cows, for egg production, fattening swine and reviving spermatogenesis in bulls and
rams." We are especially interested in the last part of that
sentence, for it seems to indicate that trace minerals (is it the
iodine or something else?) have a noteworthy effect on fertility.

Doesn't it seem possible that human infertility, too, may
result from lack of the important trace minerals which are
found so abundantly in kelp? It would seem that just the evidence alone, which is presented here by Dr. Black, should be
enough to send medical researchers scurrying to use kelp in
treatment of their patients who are trying to overcome
infertility.

Vitamins in Seaweed

Seaweeds are interesting for their vitamins, too, says Dr.
Black, most particularly because they contain vitamins like B_{12}
which, he thinks, exists in seaweed because of its attached bacteria. The vitamin B_{12} content varies with the kind of seaweed,
but several of the green varieties, he says, contain as much
vitamin B_{12} as is found in liver—the richest source.

Vitamin E, not so plentiful in present-day foodstuffs, is

present in kelp in a rather large quantity. Vitamin K is there, too. It is believed by scientists that vitamin D does not occur in vegetable matter. We need vitamin D in order to use calcium properly. Children need it so that they will not get rickets. Fish liver oil and sunlight are the two best sources for vitamin D. No one has ever been able to find vitamin D, as such, in any vegetable product. But now we hear that scientists have kept young chicks from getting rickets by feeding them seaweed. Up to the age of 16 weeks these chicks had seaweed as their only possible source of vitamin D—and they thrived. So there must be vitamin D in seaweed.

Seaweed in Animal Food

As early as 1812, Englishmen were feeding seaweed to their cows in wintertime. It improved their health and increased their milk yield. Since the First World War, many feeding experiments have shown that kelp can take its place among other fodder as a valuable nutritional aid. In one experiment in Ireland it was shown that seaweed meal of one kind has a food value about two and a half times that of potatoes and is about halfway between hay and oats. In addition, because it exerts a very favorable effect on the digestive tract of the animal, it enhances the nutritional value of the original ration fed, for the animal can profit nutritionally from other food much more when seaweed is also fed. Fed to hens, seaweed increases the iodine content of their eggs.

It was found, in feeding seaweed to hens, that one per cent seaweed meal given to the hen each day was enough to supply all the iodine requirement of an adult man eating one of this hen's eggs each day! In many cases studies were made of how much seaweed could profitably be added to the ration. And it was found, in general, that 10 per cent was about the right amount that might be fed with good results.

In many of the trials, says Dr. Black, no beneficial effects have resulted from adding seaweed to the ration. But it must be remembered that in these cases the seaweed has merely replaced an equal amount of a carefully balanced diet which could not possibly be improved by any supplement. (Human beings don't live on diets nearly that good!)

In Eire seaweed meal is added in quantity to many animal foodstuffs. In New Zealand seaweed meal has benefited cattle grazing on mineral-deficient land, by replacing the minerals missing from the soil. In this country great improvement has been noted in the health of cattle and chickens when seaweed was fed. In France, 10,000 tons of seaweed meal go annually into cattle foods. In the British Isles the seaweed industry, still in its infancy, sells 7,000 tons per year.

We have a newspaper clipping from Saint John, New Brunswick, Canada (no date available) telling us that dulse, another kind of seaweed, is being processed there. Pills and capsules are being made. Dulse is being added to flour, too, which can be used to enrich biscuits, bread, cake and so forth. Dulse is said to contain 300 times more iodine than whole wheat and 50 times as much iron. In New Brunswick, the clipping tells us, dulse sells for 10 cents a bag in grocery stores.

A Medicinal Use of Seaweed

An unusual comment on a medicinal use of seaweed comes from the *Journal of the Philippine Medical Association* for June, 1946. Several investigators there used a kind of seaweed called *Digenia simplex* as an antihelmintic—that is, to kill intestinal worms. During the war they were unable to get their usual drugs (which was just as well, we'd say, for they were probably highly toxic preparations), so they tried the powdered seaweed, made into tea. Their conclusions were that the drug, as they call it, is 73 per cent effective; it is non-toxic, can be administered under any conditions without preparing the patient prior to giving it to him. They suggest that further study be given to the matter. We have not been able to find in medical literature any indication that any further research has been done.

Seaweed for Sausage Casings

The *New York Times* for October 23, 1955, published an article about a new sausage casing made of seaweed which is being promoted by the Visking Corporation, largest producers of sausage casings. Up to now, cellulose casings have been used. They have no food value whatsoever. Of course, the seaweed does.

SECTION 32

WHEAT GERM

Wheat germ (oil or flakes, or both) is excellent as a source of vitamin B and some vitamin E, although the vitamin E it contains is so limited that one should also take vitamin E as such. It has been proven to increase one's endurance.

CHAPTER **110**

Wheat Germ: A Wonderfully Good Food

Why all the enthusiasm for wheat germ? Why should we, while cautioning readers against getting too much of cereal foods, recommend wheat germ in the highest possible terms? Here are some of the reasons. We're sure they will make you agree that you should add wheat germ to your daily menus.

What Is Wheat Germ?

Wheat germ is that part of the wheat which is responsible for sprouting and making the new plant. This means that it is very much alive, carrying, as it does, the spark of the new life. In addition, it must provide everything the new plant needs to sustain itself—chiefly protein, vitamins and minerals.

Look at the sketch. Notice how the valuable parts of the kernel are concentrated in the bran and in the germ. The endosperm, the large, light-colored section, is mostly starch. Yet, believe it or not, when wheat is milled into white flour, the bran and the germ are discarded, and the starchy endosperm is all that is used.

Nutritional Value of Wheat Germ

A half cup of wheat germ contains 24 grams of protein— as much as one-fourth pound of turkey, more than one-fourth pound of beef, 4 times as much as an egg and 8 times as much as a slice of white bread. A pound of wheat germ supplies about 200 grams of protein and may cost as little as a quarter, whereas an amount of steak yielding that much protein would cost in the neighborhood of 10 dollars.

Only a few foods (liver, parsley and greens of various kinds) are richer in iron than wheat germ. Iron-deficiency anemia is common in America and many a child and woman

is condemned to a lifetime of swallowing iron-containing medicines, just because they eat white flour products and thus avoid
the very best food we have for supplying an abundance of iron.

There is not a great deal of calcium in wheat germ.
Cereal products are noted for their lack of calcium. And
wheat germ is extremely rich in phosphorus. Here we must caution our readers. Lots of phosphorus demands lots of calcium.
The two work together. Large amounts of phosphorus will be
excreted if your diet is high in it, and calcium will be carried
along with the phosphorus. So be sure to get enough calcium
from another source if you are eating foods like brewer's yeast,
wheat germ and other cereal products rich in phosphorus. Bone
meal is your best natural source.

Wheat germ is also rich in many other minerals that
are essential for good health—manganese, magnesium, copper,
potassium.

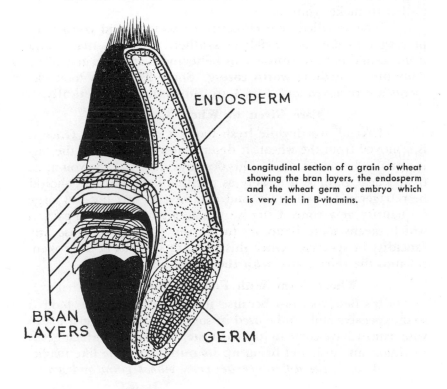

ENDOSPERM

Longitudinal section of a grain of wheat
showing the bran layers, the endosperm
and the wheat germ or embryo which
is very rich in B-vitamins.

BRAN
LAYERS   GERM

Perhaps most important of all are the B vitamins—important because there are so few foods rich in the B vitamins and because wheat germ is abundantly endowed with all of them. That half-cup of wheat germ gives us far more vitamin B_1—thiamin—than any other food except brewer's yeast—about two and one-half milligrams. Riboflavin, perhaps the B vitamin most difficult to get enough of, is plentiful in wheat germ, too. Only 4 foods—yeast, liver, kidneys and milk—contain more riboflavin than wheat germ. About the same is true of niacin. Pyridoxine, pantothenic acid and inositol, other B vitamins, are all present in goodly quantity in wheat germ.

One reason why these B vitamins are so important (apart from their own worth) is that they take part in the processes our bodies use involving other important substances, the unsaturated fatty acids, for example. These, too, are present in wheat germ, along with vitamin E, so necessary for the health of all muscle tissue, especially the heart. As you know, not a single one of all these vitamins remains after wheat has been milled to make white flour.

The so-called "enrichment" of white bread consists of putting into the flour a dab of synthetic thiamin, niacin and iron. Don't make the mistake of believing that this remakes the flour into something worth eating. Some 25 known food elements are removed and 2 or 3 are substituted, synthetically.

Care Given to Wheat Germ

Like all worthwhile fresh foods it spoils easily. Once it is removed from the wheat, it deteriorates rapidly, and the fats it contains become rancid. This destroys vitamin E. So you must treat wheat germ as if it were as perishable as meat. It should be refrigerated at all times, and it is best to buy not too large a quantity at a time. Usually, wheat germ is vacuum-packed which means there is no air inside the package to cause any rancidity or spoilage. Once this vacuum seal has been broken, it's into the refrigerator with the wheat germ!

Wheat Germ With Food Supplements?

It's best, too, just because this superlatively fine food is so inexpensive and can be used in so many ways. Once you and your family have come to like the taste, you can add wheat germ to almost any dish and bring up its nutritive value like magic. *What is the difference between wheat germ and wheat germ oil?* Just the same difference there is between peanuts and peanut oil, or corn and corn oil. Wheat germ oil is pressed out of the germ. It contains all the fat-soluble vitamins that are in the germ. But not the protein or the water-soluble vitamins like the B vitamins. Of course, wheat germ flakes like the kind you buy have not had the oil removed from them. It is still there for your benefit.

By the same token, of course, wheat germ oil is far richer in the fat soluble vitamins than wheat germ flakes could be, for these are concentrated in the oil. So you will get more vitamin E and the unsaturated fatty acids in the oil.

Toasted or Raw Wheat Germ?

Most people prefer the taste of the toasted germ. Raw germ has more in the way of vitamins, for some of the very sensitive B vitamins are destroyed by heat. However, if you buy raw germ and then don't like the taste of it, you can toast it yourself in a very slow oven, spread out on a large pan. You will lose very little vitamin content. If your family will eat more of it willingly if it is toasted, then toast it.

It goes well with almost anything. It is particularly useful as a substitute for bread or cracker crumbs—in meat loaves, casseroles, cutlets, things of that kind. Many people use it in salads as well or sprinkled over fruits or berries for dessert. It is perfectly acceptable as a breakfast cereal all by itself or with fruit or yogurt. And, of course, you can add it to any kind of bread you are making, with no change in the recipe except that you may need more liquid.

Are Vitamins Lost During Cooking?

Yes, and for this reason we advise eating it as it is, and not cooking it. But if you want to enrich cooked foods, then the wheat germ must be cooked, too. And you do not lose any more vitamins out of wheat germ in cooking than you lose out of liver or eggs when you cook them.

CHAPTER **111**

Wheat Germ Oil and Endurance

by Ed Gorman

The role that wheat germ plays in maintaining endurance during athletic tests is the subject of this chapter. A carefully controlled experiment, performed in a university laboratory, brought to light these facts.

A teaspoonful of wheat germ oil, taken daily in conjunction with exercise, has been shown to increase men's physical capacity and endurance by as much as 51.5 per cent.

That and many other findings which point to wheat germ oil as a "valuable nutrient supplement" are being reported scientifically for the first time by Dr. T. K. Cureton, head of the University of Illinois Physical Fitness Laboratory.

The reports are based on experiments carried on at the University for more than 4 years on more than 200 men, including varsity wrestlers, swimmers, youths selected at random from a fraternity house and middle-aged men who were in poor physical "shape" when they began a training program.

The studies were conducted under grants from VioBin Corporation in Monticello. Heretofore, they have been kept under wraps because, Dr. Cureton said: "We wanted to make sure."

Now, he disclosed, 10 scientific consultants have recommended publication of the results in scientific journals.

Cureton reported the findings with this assertion:

Valuable in Diet

"Wheat germ oil is a valuable dietary supplement to men doing hard exercise, and it has possible application to competitive sports. We have tried it sufficiently to believe that this is true. It provides something that enables men to bear hard stress and continue to do hard labor without deteriorating. It particularly affects physical endurance and heart response."

Wheat germ oil, he explained, was tested in a continuing search for something that will give men extra drive and energy. Alcohol, benzedrine, caffeine, cocaine, digitalis, gelatine, fruit juices and hormones have been tried in the past and discarded as ineffective, Cureton said.

Until the wheat germ oil tests were run, vitamin B complex offered the most encouraging results but, Cureton declared, the evidence in behalf of it was "contradictory at best."

Wheat germ oil, however, has proved "consistently effective" in all the experiments run in the UI laboratory, where men run on a treadmill until they drop and undergo other tests of physical capacity while doctors measure heart action, oxygen consumption, blood pressure and other body functions.

Other Tests Used

The treadmill is only one of many tests in which men's performance was measured in the experiments. It, however, well illustrates the credit given by Cureton to wheat germ oil.

Eight middle-aged professors who combined wheat germ oil with physical training gained 51.5 per cent in the time they could run on the treadmill before they were exhausted. They had no opportunity to practice on the treadmill in between tests. They were tested for a first time, given 12 weeks of other types of exercise along with wheat germ oil, and then tested again. They did not go near the treadmill during the interim.

At the same time, a matched group of men—matched in age and in run-time after the initial test—gained only 19.4 per cent after receiving the same physical training without the wheat germ oil.

These, Cureton emphasized, were sedentary professors, unaccustomed to great physical exertion before they began training in the laboratory.

Works on Athletes

Equally convincing evidence, according to Cureton, was obtained in tests with athletes already at the peak of training—such as the varsity wrestlers and swimmers.

Cureton said it has been well established that men cannot be kept at a peak of physical condition indefinitely—that most of them reach a "plateau" after about 12 weeks of hard training and begin to slump.

However, when the athletes were given wheat germ oil after they began their slump, the scientific measurements of their performance jumped up to new peaks. At the same time, a "control group" which did not receive the wheat germ oil continued their slump.

Results were particularly noticeable in the increased strength of "T waves" measured in electrocardiogram tests of their hearts, Cureton said. He explained that the "T waves" measure the electrical energy of the heart's contraction.

"Never before in any experiment," said Cureton, "have I seen a subject train hard for 12 weeks, reach the plateau, and then go on to a higher peak."

Exercise Needed

Dr. Cureton emphasized, however, that few if any of these results can be obtained unless the wheat germ oil is coupled with physical training. On the other hand, wheat germ oil and exercise together produce results not obtained by physical training alone.

His explanation is that exercise opens up the tiny blood vessels (capillaries) of muscles and heart tissues, increases the blood flow of arteries, and allows the nutrient to reach the muscle and tissue where it is needed.

"The exact nature of this mechanism in wheat germ oil has not been determined, but we have established that it is significantly effective as a dietary supplement," Cureton said.

Editor's Note:

In all previous experiments with vitamins, researchers have been forced to use as subjects persons who either were ill or who were kept on a controlled diet to induce vitamin deficiencies. This is necessary because a natural diet includes at least some of all known vitamins. Processors of wheat germ oil have known for many years that it is a good source of natural vitamin E. They have also known that wheat germ oil is one of the richest natural sources of essential fatty acids. Yet these values are relatively insignificant in the light of our new knowledge of wheat germ oil. Wheat germ oil is an unrefined vegetable oil, derived from wheat. The average diet contains very little, if any, unrefined vegetable oil. The values in wheat germ, which also may be present in other vegetable oils, are denied to the average American.

For a number of years it was thought by scientists that vitamin E was the distinguishing and important feature of wheat germ oil. However, when vitamin E was crystallized in pure form (that is, made synthetically) it was found that vitamin E and wheat germ oil do not produce the same clinical results. An earlier University of Illinois study, published in 1951, showed that wheat germ oil contains also a "survival factor" which aids young animals to survive.

Other Studies

The Montreal Neurological Institute has published the results of 10 years of study on the use of wheat germ oil in the treatment of certain forms of muscular dystrophy. Positive results were obtained. Dr. Wayne Silbernagel of Columbus, Ohio, reported that a concentrate of wheat germ oil reduced miscarriages in pregnancy from 14 per cent to 3 per cent. A report published in the scientific journal, *Endocrinology*, credited wheat germ oil with hormonal effects—that is, having the same effects as the hormones produced by the body's glands.

Some experimenters are now making an effort to show that wheat germ oil contains a factor that influences glycogen metabolism. The theory is that all these effects may be explained by a new discovery that the sugar chemistry of the body is involved. Glycogen is a form of sugar in blood which provides energy of muscles. Such a discovery would indeed revolutionize many of our ideas of blood chemistry and its proper maintenance!

Reprinted from the Urbana (Illinois) *News Gazette* for March 14, 1954, by permission of the editors and the author.

CHAPTER **112**

Wheat Germ: The Food of Champions

It's power-packed—that little flake of wheat—the living part of the grain that present-day refining so casually removes in order to make white bread.

Evidence continues to mount on the effect of wheat germ oil on human endurance and physical performance. The latest clipping from the *Philadelphia Evening Bulletin* carries these headlines, "Wheat Germ Diet Helped Aussies Smash Olympic Swimming Records, Doctor Says." The doctor was Thomas K. Cureton of the University of Illinois whose experiments with wheat germ we have described in the previous chapter.

Dr. Cureton announced that Australian swimmers made "chumps" out of their Olympic opponents partly because they trained on a scientific "power-packed" diet, the main ingredient of which was wheat germ.

Six months before they were to compete in the games, the Australian team was put on a supervised program of physical training, in which heavy emphasis was placed on scientific feeding. The athletes were fed an allotment of wheat germ oil and wheat germ cereal every day, and their diet was heavily fortified with vitamins and minerals. This was in addition to their regular meals at which they might eat anything they wanted except fried foods.

American athletes, who got an allotment of wheat germ just before they took off on the Olympic trip, got too late a start to do them much good, according to Dr. Cureton. The 3 American swimmers who had been taking wheat germ for a long time before made the best showing of all the American team in the games.

Director of Cortland State Teachers College confirmed

these findings of Dr. Cureton's, stating that Cortland track stars showed improved endurance when wheat germ oil was given to them. A swimming star at Springfield College, Massachusetts, broke the world's record for the 200-meter race after he took wheat germ oil. A woman swimming champion set a new A.A.U. record for the women's 100 meter free style at Indianapolis in 1955. We are told that when she came out of the pool her first remark was, "Wheat germ oil! I don't get tired at the end of a race any more!"

Vitamin E Improves Their Game

Some time ago we published the story of the Canadian Maple Leaf baseball team. According to the *Toronto Daily Star* for September 6, 1956, "a vital factor in the overall picture has been the use of vitamin E by the Toronto team this season." Before the season began each player received a bottle of vitamin E capsules and was instructed to begin taking them before training began. They started with 200 milligrams of vitamin E, and the dose was later increased. What happened to the batting averages of that ball team when the vitamin E began to take effect reads like a club manager's dream. And vitamin E gets all the credit!

Vitamin E occurs in wheat germ, of course. Wheat germ contains many other substances as well—unsaturated fatty acids and certain other fatty substances which doctors are now claiming prevent hardening of the arteries and accumulation of cholesterol. It is our belief that everyone should take both vitamin E and wheat germ.

Vitamin E Given to Race Horses

An interesting study of the effect of vitamin E on race horses appears in *The Summary* for December, 1956 (published by the Shute Foundation for Medical Research, London, Canada). At two racing stables, tests were made by giving certain horses vitamin E, increasing the dosage just before the race, "to increase muscular stamina and utilization of oxygen further."

Earnings of the horses were almost doubled, indicating, of course, many more wins. The percentage of wins per horse was 2.7 compared to 2.3 last year when a smaller dose of vitamin E was given and 1.8 the year before when no vitamin was given.

Horses taking vitamin E showed far less nervousness than those which did not, and the stamina of the vitamin E-fed horses was markedly increased. The owners of the horses warn that vitamin E is not a shot-in-the-arm which can make a Derby winner out of a mediocre horse overnight. The horses to which the vitamin was given were all in excellent condition at the beginning of the experiment. But vitamin E brought about a great improvement even in their former excellent performance.

Important for Human Beings, Too

The editor, commenting on this experiment, reminds us that the same conditions apply to human beings. "If there is such a thing as optimal health these athletes possessed it during the period of their competition. It is of genuine physiologic interest that one can improve the cardiac efficiency and skeletal muscle power of the superb 'normal' animals.

"This further emphasizes the importance of vitamin E for so-called normal men, or men who regard themselves as being in excellent health. Obviously it means even more to men in failing health, people who have less than normally efficient hearts and skeletal muscles. The whole study stresses the importance of improving tissue oxygenation."

Endurance Influenced by Desiccated Liver

We have only two other reminders—the experiments on endurance performed by Dr. Ershoff with desiccated liver, in which he found that animals given quite large doses of the liver showed many times the endurance of animals given no supplement. Desiccated liver is rich in B vitamins, vitamin A and many important minerals, as well as certain other factors which apparently exist only in liver, for results like this cannot be achieved using other foods rich in B vitamins, it seems.

Remember, too, that bone meal is important for the health of the sportsman. This is particularly evident in the case of the dangerous sports. How many skiers and hockey players could be spared broken bones if they went to the fray well fortified with bone meal—for years, of course, not just a few hours before the sporting event begins. Since bone meal is so important for good teeth, it should interest young sportsmen even more. For what would-be baseball player or trackman wants to miss practice because he's gone to the dentist?

Often mothers write us asking how they can interest their children in eating healthfully amid the ever-present lure of the candy-coke-ice-cream-parlor world in which they live. Surely experiments like those reported above can be used effectively to convince the young ones. What boy would not like to follow the example of Olympic champion swimmers and Maple Leaf baseball players? Wouldn't he be willing to take almost anything, if it might make him better at sports? Wouldn't stories like the ones above be likely to convince him that there *is* something to this nutrition business after all—it's not just a dull subject dealt with in laboratories—it's the real stuff of which champions are made!

Think of the amount of money spent by high schools, colleges and universities to produce winning teams in athletics —just for the glory of the old alma mater. But think of the rewards if a program of good nutrition, and especially a regular program of taking vitamin E and wheat germ were to be instituted. The glory of the old alma mater would grow brighter with every new victory. But, far more important than that—the team's improved stamina and good health would be reflected in better grades, better citizenship, finer personalities.

Professional athletes and the men who coach and manage them are interested in profits. Winning games means more money, and good nutrition (especially vitamin E and wheat germ) means winning more games. Couldn't we amateurs learn a lesson from the pros?

CHAPTER **113**

You Need Cereal Germs

That part of the cereal removed by modern processing is the only worthwhile part.

It should not surprise us that many diseases unknown to our forefathers should be related to the absence of the germ of whole grain in our diets. For thousands of years mankind has eaten whole grains. In many countries it is almost the only food; in many others it is the mainstay of the diet. Until we began to refine our grains, bread was the staff of life.

What Processing Has Done

But today our food processing companies have persuaded us that we want to eat white bread and refined cereals. Not because we really prefer them, mind you, but because this makes things easier for the processors. They no longer have to deal with the highly perishable germ of the cereal. They just remove it and—lo and behold—flour can be stored for years at any temperature, shipped in any kind of boxcar to all parts of the world with nary a rancid taste to spoil it and deplete the profits of the millers and the bakers. The germ—the live, nourishing part of the grain—is disposed of elsewhere. We feed it to our domestic animals, for any raiser of cattle or other animals knows full well that they cannot live or thrive on a diet such as their owners eat.

What do we remove when we remove this germ from wheat? We don't know. That sounds peculiar, considering all our modern scientific skill. But it's true. We know some of the things in cereal germs—the B vitamins, for instance. Cereal germ is one of our richest sources. Calcium and phosphorus are plentiful in cereal germ. Calcium is the mineral in which we modern Americans are most deficient. Cereal germ is a rich source of iron. Did you know that modern American women are in general so anemic that a large percentage of them have been rejected as blood donors by the Red Cross? Could the removal of iron from our cereals have anything to do with this? Finally, vitamin E is plentiful in cereal germ.

Wheat Germ Oil Put to the Test

Many times we are inclined to think of vitamin E as the only important food element we miss when we do not eat whole grains. But there seems to be no doubt—wheat germ oil contains something else that is a powerful force for good health.

Wheat germ oil was tested in the laboratories of a great university for its effect on physical endurance and heart response. The tests were conducted like this: all subjects ate what they usually did and as much as they wanted. They were brought up to the peak of condition by exercise. They were given various tests to measure their physical condition. Then one-half were given a teaspoon of wheat germ oil daily. The other half were given a teaspoon of another vegetable oil containing as much vitamin E as is found in wheat germ oil. Neither group knew who was getting the wheat germ oil. Both groups continued their exercise for several weeks, then they were tested again.

Everybody being tested improved 24.8 per cent during the 12 weeks of physical training. But those who were given wheat germ oil improved 47.4 per cent during the test. In other words, after they had reached their very best performance, without added supplements, they were given wheat germ oil and improved another 22.6 per cent!

Wheat Germ Proves Its Worth

The next year the experiment was repeated, most men on the wheat germ oil being given the other oil instead. The results were the same—those taking the wheat germ oil excelled in physical endurance. Said Dr. T. K. Cureton of the University of Illinois who gave the test: "We've tried vitamins, gelatin, fruit juices, hormones and other foods in the laboratory, but wheat germ oil has consistently shown the best results in enabling men to bear hard stress without deteriorating."

There is a definite relationship between wheat germ and the human reproductive system. This powerful substance may prevent sterility, tendency to miscarriage, menopausal flushes, and so forth. It seems that the germ of cereals is especially important in this field because of its own function as the tiny portion of seed from which the cereal reproduces itself. This is truly the "live" part of the grain.

Wheat Germ for Muscular Dystrophy

Bicknell and Prescott in their book, *Vitamins in Medicine* (Grune and Stratton, 1953), tell us that past research indicates that muscular dystrophy may be caused by the inability of the muscles to use vitamin E. They can produce muscular dystrophy in an animal at any time by simply removing all traces of vitamin E from its diet. However, giving wheat germ or vitamin E does not necessarily bring about a complete and certain cure in human beings. So these authors believe that the muscular dystrophy patients simply cannot use the vitamin E in their food.

However, an article in *Archives of Pediatrics*, Vol. 49, 1949, tells of 25 children with muscular dystrophy treated with fresh wheat germ oil every day, all of whom improved, and one of whom recovered completely. These children, incidentally, were given the B vitamins and vitamin C as well as the wheat germ oil. Doesn't this seem to indicate that wheat germ oil, *plus a good diet* may be the answer to the prevention of muscular dystrophy?

Drs. Bicknell and Prescott tell us that children who have improved on the wheat germ oil are, in general, children who have been given excellent, fresh diets including whole wheat and home-made bread. In general, children whose diets remain unchanged except for the wheat germ do not show improvement.

Contents of Wheat Germ

An article in the German publication, *Kinderartzl. Praxis*, for May, 1955, tells us that wheat germ contains the following in addition to the B vitamins: Vitamin E, unsaturated fatty acids, amino acids, calcium phosphate and magnesium phosphate, diastase, amylase, lipase, phosphatase and tyrosinase. These last items are enzymes, all of them important for the way the body uses various foods like carbohydrates, phosphorus and so forth.

In the German experiment, 71 prematurely-born infants were given ground wheat germ, another 71 were used as controls and did not receive the wheat germ. The wheat germ increased the weight of the infants and, while it had no effect on their resistance to infections or on anemia, it did seem to reduce the incidence of rickets in the prematurely-born infants. In rickets the body does not get enough calcium, phosphorus and/or vitamin D. Do the various enzymes in wheat germ have something to do with the way the body uses these precious minerals and vitamins?

Wheat Germ and Proper Oxygenation

A clipping from the *St. Louis Post* for September 29, 1955, tells of a lecture by Dr. William B. Kountz, Assistant Professor of Clinical Medicine at Washington University. Said Dr. Kountz, there is a decline in the body's consumption of oxygen as one grows older, leading to such ailments as hardening of the arteries, heart disease, body wasting and other typical manifestations of old age. He went on to say that the proper understanding of diet and the stimulation of body build-up by food is infinitely important for good health.

Vitamin E, contained in wheat germ, has a peculiar relationship to the body's oxygen. When vitamin E is present, the body can get along on less oxygen. So you are sparing yourself and, perhaps, postponing old age when you add vitamin E to your diet. Remember, the body is able to use less and less oxygen as it grows older. But, with vitamin E present in sufficient quantity, it doesn't need as much oxygen.

Neuromuscular Disorders Cured

One final review. In the *Journal of Neurology, Neurosurgery and Psychiatry,* London, for May, 1951, we learn of 151 patients with neuromuscular disorders who were given wheat germ oil, and whose cases were followed for 12 years. About 10 per cent showed definite improvement. These include two cases of a typical muscular atrophy. In 5 (3 children and two adults) out of 25 patients with progressive muscular dystrophy, symptoms were arrested, and moderate to marked improvement occurred. Three out of five patients with menopausal muscular dystrophy showed remarkable improvement.

Three cases of dermatomyositis (inflammation of both skin and muscles) responded favorably.

These patients were not placed on any particular diet. What excellent further results might there have been had they been given a diet rich in unprocessed and raw foods, vitamins and minerals!

CHAPTER **114**

Processed Cereals Are Not for You

No matter how attractive the package or the premium offered, don't be misled into counting on cold, processed cereals to add anything nutrition-wise to your diet.

An article that cheered us more than anything we have read in a long time appeared in the December, 1957, issue of *Pageant* magazine. Entitled "The Unappetizing Truth About Dry Cereals" the article, by Richard Carter, pulled no punches in revealing the sordid and shocking truth about a business which garners some $300,000,000 every year from the American people.

We disagree with some of Mr. Carter's point of view, and we only wish he would do a similar story on other refined cereal products like white bread and polished rice. But, considering the fact that most magazines get a handsome income from advertising the cereal products he is attacking, we must congratulate *Pageant* for its courage in publishing such an article, and Mr. Carter for his in writing it.

Some of his facts will astonish you. Did you know that roughly 800,000,000 pounds of cold, processed breakfast cereal are consumed in this country every year, in spite of the fact that the average serving of cold cereal weighs less than an ounce! Did you know that an estimated 15,000,000 Americans (almost a tenth of our entire population) eat nothing but cold cereal for breakfast! "A depressingly large number of children" are among these, according to Mr. Carter.

Kinds of Dry Cereal

Some of the forms of dry cereal which are most popular are flakes (bran, corn, wheat, rice, etc.), puffs (rice, wheat), shreds and nuts. Here is the process through which flakes are put before they get into the cardboard box with the enticing premium offer that is propped before so many children every morning at breakfast.

Grits (kernels of corn which have been soaked in lye) are cooked in live steam, mixed with a flavoring syrup (refined sugar, of course), dried until hard and then run through rollers which exert 75 tons of pressure. The end product is then toasted and packaged as corn flakes. What you started out with was a grain of corn, fairly rich in protein, phosphorus, vitamin A and the 3 most important B vitamins. What you take out of the attractive cardboard box contains no vitamin A, very little, if any, vitamin B (unless it has been added synthetically) and, what is perhaps most dangerous of all, the protein remaining in the poor, processed kernel has been changed irrevocably, perhaps into something that is definitely harmful to the body.

Why Do People Eat Prepared Cereals?

It's perfectly true, as Mr. Carter says, that the American public has been completely sold on the healthfulness of eating cold cereal for breakfast. "As they put this mixture into their mouths," he says, "many of the feeders actually glow with a sense of well-being. Decades of tradition and millions upon millions of dollars in advertising have trained them to regard their ready-to-eat breakfast cereal as the last word in morning nourishment. Any suspicion that the stuff is nutritionally inferior to other breakfast foods is bound to be dispelled by the sales literature printed on the brightly-colored boxes."

How many mothers do you know who actually insist that their children spoon down a bowlful of this woefully inadequate food every morning? And actually the kids don't object. One reason for the great popularity of cold cereals is that the advertising companies have turned the box tops, the premiums and the TV and radio programs into veritable treasure troves for the youngsters. At a cost of practically nothing to the food companies, millions of dollars worth of junk is sent out each year with a come-on that is so attractive to kids that you can't really blame them for putting up an awful squawk if Mom tries to get them to eat something else for breakfast. What difference do calories, food values, minerals and vitamins make to a youngster who is bent on getting a free treasure map, a ray gun, a spaceman's mask, a set of picture cards?

But, you may object, isn't it better for the children to eat cold cereal for breakfast than to eat nothing at all? Possibly. But the only reason we say this is that they may eat milk and fruit on the cereal—even if ever so little—and possibly the small amount of calcium, protein and B vitamins that comes in the milk and fruit is better than nothing.

Good Food Habits Are Important

But look at the harm that's being done. Probably the most important single good health heritage you can give your child is a set of good habits where food is concerned. One of the most important of these is the habit of eating a serviceable breakfast. By this we mean a breakfast high in protein, which "sticks to his ribs," a breakfast in which refined carbohydrates are ignored as if they did not exist.

For many people breakfast is the one meal in which they are completely bound by habit. Many people eat the same breakfast menu every day throughout their lives. Every day your child eats cold cereal for breakfast he is making stronger an eating habit that with every passing year becomes harder to break. And many children consume cold cereals not just for breakfast, but for lunch, too, sometimes for dinner and very often for a bedtime snack. What chance does such a child have to eat even a small portion of the nourishing food he must have if he is to grow up healthy, physically and mentally? The worthless refined starch of the cereal has stuffed him until he doesn't want anything more to eat!

But cold cereals are so cheap and so easy to fix! Of course, they're cheap. They're mostly air and starch. Why shouldn't they be cheap?

Should You Eat Breakfast Cereal?

What should be your attitude toward cold cereals? Are there any that are any good? Not so far as we are concerned. We think they should be ignored completely in planning meals.

Hardly a month goes by that a great new promotion campaign is not launched to sell you on some new cold cereal, praising its high protein content, its nourishing vitamins and so forth. Bunk. And please don't write us, sending in box tops to check on some favorite that you've been using. There are no exceptions, so far as we are concerned. None of the cold, processed, ready-to-eat cereals should be on your grocery shelf. None.

The only cereals that are worth eating are real whole grain cereals. So far as we know they cannot be purchased in grocery stores, with the exception of brown rice, which is now pretty widely available. You must make special arrangements with somebody to get real whole grain cereals. Your local health food store has them. Or you can buy whole cereals from farmers quite cheaply and grind your own. Of course, all of these must be cooked.

In some cases the most valuable part of the cereal is available as a separate food. The germ of the cereal contains practically all of the nutriment except starch. The rest of any cereal kernel consists mostly of starch. This makes wheat germ a peculiarly valuable food in which protein, minerals (especially iron), the B vitamins and vitamin E are concentrated. There are 24 grams of protein in one-half cup of wheat germ. There are only about 3 grams of protein in more than a cup of a processed cold cereal. Rice polishings (a little harder to find) contain the germ of the rice, so they, too, are crammed with vitamins and minerals and protein.

The Trend Away from Cold Cereal

What if your family absolutely refuses to relinquish their cold cereal? We suggest taking it away from them so gradually that they won't know what happened. Wheat germ is your best ally on an operation like this. Add a little to the bowl of cold cereal tomorrow morning. Nine chances out of 10 no one will notice. In a month or so begin adding a little more. And a little more. This will mean a little less of the cold cereal. In due time, suggest hot cereal for breakfast, and make the hot cereal whole grain. If the family is unenthusiastic, serve it with some special treat—real maple syrup, raisins, nuts or dates. Finally, you should be able to wean even the most stubborn of families away from cold cereal. Part of the battle will be won because they will discover for themselves that the right kind of breakfast sticks with you so you don't have to have a coffee break around 10, or 15 minutes for a snack around 3. Improved teeth, skin, nerves, hair and general good health will come gradually as you shift from phony breakfast food to real food.

We have addressed these suggestions to folks who have been confirmed users of cold cereal. Most of us eat too much cereal, you know. Fruit and eggs make the best breakfast by far—high in protein and the natural sugar that doesn't upset your blood sugar level and leave you hungry, inefficient and grumpy by 10 o'clock.

CHAPTER 115

The Chemistry of Seeds

Here is the how and why of the nutritive value of seed foods. They are rich in certain elements but poor in others.

How do seeds in general stack up against other foods from a nutritive point of view? They compose a very necessary and important part of the diet, but they should be combined with other foods, if they are to offer the best possible advantage. The reason for this is that seeds, in general, lack certain minerals and vitamins that exist in large quantities in other classes of food. So the other foods complement the seed foods in a most satisfactory way.

Leafy Foods Complement Seeds

McCollum, one of the country's outstanding experts on nutrition, has this to say about the way in which leafy foods complement seeds: "The leaf proves to be a very different thing from the seed from the dietary standpoint." The leaf contains from 3 to 5 times as much mineral content as the seed and is always rich in just those minerals in which the seed is poorest

—calcium, for instance. The leaf contains a wealth of vitamin A and vitamin C, neither of which is found to any great extent in the seed. The leaf contains protein amino acids, as the seed does. And it seems that those of the leaf complement those of the seed, so that leaves and seeds together result in a meal rich in all the various forms of protein or amino acids.

Phosphorus in Seeds

Phosphorus is the mineral which abounds in seeds. It is an important mineral from the standpoint of nutrition, and one should be careful to see that he gets enough phosphorus in his diet. But most of us do. The animals that live on grasses and leaves are the ones which are in danger of lacking phosphorus. This is one reason why proper feed for horses and cattle must be planned to include plenty of phosphorus. But human beings get phosphorus in cereals, legumes, nuts and foods of animal origin like meat and eggs. The animals that graze do not, of course, eat these, with the exception of cereals.

Foods high in vitamins (fresh fruits and salads) do not supply large amounts of phosphorus. We are told, for instance, that one would have to eat nearly a bushel of apples a day or half a bushel of oranges to obtain a liberal supply of phosphorus. Nine and a half pounds of carrots, or 11 pounds of beets would be required to provide as much phosphorus as you find in one pound of lentils or beans, wheat or oats. These last are all, of course, seeds.

Calcium-Phosphorus Balance of the Body

Phosphorus is important to body functions. It is present in all body cells. Calcium and phosphorus stand first and second respectively in the quantity of mineral elements in the body. The use of phosphorus in the body is closely interrelated to the use of calcium, so that when we are speaking of one, we must constantly refer to the other. The exact amount of phosphorus needed by the body is not so important as the relationship between the calcium and the phosphorus. This ratio is two and a half to one—there should be two and a half times as much calcium as phosphorus.

Nations that live chiefly on fruits and vegetables might suffer from a lack of phosphorus. Adding meat, cereals or nuts to their diets would improve them. People living chiefly on cereals are likely to get into much more serious trouble, for

they are almost bound to have a wrong balance between calcium and phosphorus. Cereals contain little calcium; refined
cereals none at all for all practical purposes. Furthermore,
cereals contain phosphorus in a peculiar chemical combination
called phytase which grabs off calcium wherever it can. So the
inveterate cereal-eater loses even more calcium, and his calcium-
phosphorus balance goes even farther off, unless he takes care
to eat plenty of calcium-rich foods—fruits and vegetables, leafy
green things. And so we come back to the fact that seeds need
other foods in the diet to complement them.

Phosphorus exists in bones and teeth along with calcium.
It is present in fluids and soft tissues, too. You need it for your
body to use fat properly. It also combines with protein, so that
the protein can be digested. You cannot digest several of the
important B vitamins unless phosphorus is present. Phosphorus
is an important ingredient of brain tissue.

To properly assimilate and use phosphorus, remember,
you must have plenty of calcium in the diet at the same time.
Vitamin D is important, too—the sunshine vitamin, which you
need in order to use either calcium or phosphorus. Furthermore—and this is perhaps the most important single thing to
remember about phosphorus in seeds—your body does not use
phosphorus unless there is plenty of calcium present at the same
time. So, if you are using lots of seed materials in your diet—
cereals, nuts, legumes—remember to check thoroughly on
the amount of calcium you are getting. Bone meal as a food
supplement is your best assurance that all will be well, for it
contains calcium and phosphorus, too, in just the right combination as they appear in healthy young bones.

Other Minerals in Seeds

Iron is another mineral in which seeds are rich. Most
American women and many adolescents are suffering from iron-
deficiency anemia to a greater or less extent. Probably the most
significant reason for this is the refining of flour and sugar, for
iron is removed from cereals when the germ is removed, and
the iron originally found in sugar cane is left in blackstrap
molasses after the sugar is refined.

Wheat germ is rich in iron. Other cereal seeds when
they are taken whole—that is, unrefined—are also rich in iron.
So the refinement of our cereals has deprived us not only of

our best source of B vitamins, but also of two of the most important of our minerals, for calcium is removed along with iron. So the iron and calcium deficiencies, already widespread in this country, grow worse as we continue to eat and to feed our children on refined cereals.

Our Body Needs Magnesium

Magnesium is another mineral substance that is abundant in seed foods. In fact, it is surprising to find that the foods listed as highest in magnesium are generally all seed foods. For instance, those that rate high (from 120 to 250 milligrams per hundred grams) are: almonds, barley, lima beans, brazil nuts, cashew nuts, corn, whole wheat flour, hazel nuts, oatmeal, peanuts, peas, pecans, brown rice, soy flour, walnuts. Apparently, magnesium is used for something very important by the seed as it grows into a mature plant.

It is important for the body, too. We have not made any studies of magnesium deficiency in human beings. But in animals on controlled diets a deficiency in magnesium adds up to dilation of blood vessels, kidney damage, loss of hair, rough, sticky coats, diarrhea and edema (unhealthy swelling).

Remember, please, that magnesium is removed, along with all the other minerals when foods are refined. The magnesium which we said above would be found in whole grain flour is not present in white flour. The magnesium in brown rice is not present in white rice. So be sure you get your seed foods unrefined.

Vitamins in Seeds

The most precious food element in seeds is probably their content of B vitamins and vitamin E. Apparently the plants need these vitamins just as we do, so the seeds must be well supplied if they are going to grow. Nuts, legumes and unrefined cereals are all rich in B vitamins. Soy beans and wheat germ provide the largest amounts of this vitamin in this group of foods. The B vitamins are important for the health of the nerves. A population whose supply of thiamin has been destroyed by the miller and baker will be a nervous population and will suffer from mental disorders. Their digestive tracts will not function properly, for the B vitamins are especially important for this function. Constipation, diarrhea and dyspepsia will be rampant. The B vitamins are important for the

health of the skin. Removing them from foods practically
guarantees many different kinds of skin disorders.

Seeds, nuts and legumes are relatively rich in pyridoxine
—another B vitamin, not so thoroughly studied as the others
up to now. Spies and Jolliffe, two of today's most noted nutrition specialists, have successfully treated *paralysis agitans*
(palsy) with massive doses of pyridoxine. This leads us to
believe that perhaps muscle and nerve disorders of this kind
may result from a life-long deficiency in this vitamin. Adding
unrefined seed foods to your diet will add to your store of
pyridoxine. Remember, this B vitamin has been removed, along
with all the others, from any refined food.

Vitamin E Aids Many Body Functions

Vitamin E, whose richest source is wheat germ, is an
absolute essential for the smooth functioning of all the reproductive processes. Its lack results in miscarriages, sterility and
difficult births. It is important for the welfare of every muscle
in the body, so lack of it can produce paralysis, heart disease
(for the heart is a muscle), dystrophy and the host of other cruel
twisting diseases to which the people of America are so peculiarly susceptible, due, largely, to the refining of their foods,
we believe.

Seeds Rich in Unsaturated Fatty Acids

The unsaturated fatty acids, called vitamin F by some
researchers, are plentiful in seeds, too. A wide variety of disorders may be caused by a lack of these important fats in the
diet—eczema, dry skin, dandruff, brittle nails, falling hair, kidney disease, disorders of the prostate gland. Fats are carried
in the diet by a substance called lecithin, which dissolves easily
in body fluids, so that the fat may be properly distributed to the
various places where it is needed.

Cholesterol, a fatty substance that exists in different
kinds of foods and is, in fact, manufactured in the body as well,
depends on lecithin to keep it in a state of emulsion so that
the body can use it. Cholesterol, without lecithin, is likely to
collect in the walls of blood vessels, or as "stones" in the gall
bladder. Where is this essential lecithin found? Chiefly in the
fatty portions of seeds. If you get no seeds in your diet or if you
eat only seed foods from which the lecithin has been removed
by processing, you are likely to run into serious trouble.

Dr. Francis Pottenger, M.D., a nationally known nutrition expert, tells us, "The effect of processing cereals with the accompanying loss of minerals and the vitamin B complex has received much attention. However, the loss of the important fats in the processing of our vegetable oils and our cereals has not received due consideration. The removal of the fats would appear to be as deleterious as the removal of the water soluble parts of the germ," by which he means the B vitamins.

Summary

To sum it all up—what are the most important elements in seeds as food? First, their mineral content—phosphorus and iron being the two most important of these. Keep in mind that both of these are practically destroyed by refining of cereals, so don't count on refined cereals (that is, processed breakfast cereals and white bread) to give you minerals. Remember, too, that if you eat large amounts of seed foods, rich in phosphorus, you should help to balance the phosphorus by eating plenty of calcium-rich foods, too. Green leafy vegetables and fruits supply calcium. Bone meal, too.

Secondly, the seed foods provide vitamins—the nerve-digestive tract-skin vitamin B complex and the ever-so-important vitamin E which prevents heart disease and other muscle trouble. Then the seed foods provide the fatty substances that are necessary for the proper use by the body of other vitamins and cholesterol—lecithin and the unsaturated fatty acids, sometimes called vitamin F. The seed foods also supply the body with valuable protein.

Seed foods are a veritable nutritional treasure chest packed full of precious vitamins and minerals. Do you think you can afford, nutritionally speaking, to do without a goodly supply of these foods, in their fresh, unrefined untampered-with state?

SECTION 33

LECITHIN

Lecithin is a fatty substance occurring with cholesterol in foods. It is believed that lecithin renders the cholesterol harmless. Anyone fearing hardening of the arteries or high blood pressure should get plenty of lecithin. You get it in natural foods, not in refined foods. Eggs and unprocessed vegetable oils are rich sources of lecithin. You can also get it in a food supplement.

CHAPTER **116**

Lecithin

Our interest in lecithin at this particular moment in history springs almost entirely from our interest in another fatty substance—cholesterol. Because of cholesterol we have come, during the past 10 years, to think of any fat in the diet as being dangerous, even possibly to the point of being actually poisonous to us.

As a result diets are being prescribed right and left in which fat has been reduced to a minimum. A recent issue of a women's magazine carried a reducing diet which had obviously been worked out with great care to include all the vitamins and minerals for which official daily minimum requirements have been set. We checked it closely and found indeed that vitamins A, B$_1$ and B$_2$, vitamin C, calcium and iron were all plentiful in this diet. But most of the other B vitamins, vitamin E and the essential unsaturated fatty acids, sometimes called vitamin F, were practically non-existent in the menus for the simple reason that the diet was low in fat. No salad dressings were used, foods were prepared without vegetable oils, and whole grain cereals (one of our best sources of vitamin-rich fats) were not recommended.

Why this furor over fats? The reason is simple. Not so long ago it was discovered that cholesterol, a fatty substance that occurs only in animal fats, is largely responsible for hardening of the arteries. Investigating the thick chunks of matter that clog hardened arteries, researchers found that it consisted mostly of cholesterol. So right away everybody became panicky about cholesterol. The popular magazines carried frightening articles about it. Fat-free diets became the rage. Fat—any and all kinds of fat—became anathema.

The *American Heart Journal,* Vol. 39, 1950, tells the

results of a survey of the cholesterol content of the coronary arteries and blood of a group of patients who died of coronary thrombosis (a blood clot in the coronary artery). It was about 4 times the average of that of normal patients. Since an overabundance of cholesterol was found in patients who died of coronary thrombosis, it seems reasonable to believe that for some reason the bodies of these individuals are not able to handle fatty substances properly.

Another article in *Archives of Pathology*, Vol. 47, 1949, states that cholesterol is constantly present in the disordered blood vessels of a patient with hardening of the arteries. And it seems to be true, too, that the amount of cholesterol in the blood vessels increases with age.

Low Fat Diet and Cholesterol

Suppose we delete all food that contains cholesterol. Will we then be free from any menace? No, we won't, because cholesterol is produced in the body at a much faster rate than we could eat it. Apparently it is necessary for many body functions, among them, the formation of vitamin D, the sex hormones and the adrenal hormones and the bile salts, so important for the proper digestion of all kinds of fats.

It has been shown that, by eating a high-fat diet, approximately 800 milligrams of cholesterol are obtained daily. But the perfectly normal human liver produces 3,000 milligrams of cholesterol or more per day, all by itself! So even though you cut out any and all foods containing cholesterol, your body will still continue to manufacture it—and probably will also continue to misuse it so that you will still get deposits of cholesterol where they are not wanted—in the walls of blood vessels and in gallstones.

You see, once you cut out all fatty foods, you also cut out all foods that contain lecithin, which is the substance that apparently can control cholesterol, keep it going its helpful way and prevent it from depositing where it is not wanted.

A Nutritionist Speaks Up for Lecithin

Adelle Davis, in her book, *Let's Eat Right to Keep Fit* (Harcourt Brace and Company, New York, New York), has this to say about lecithin. "Another cousin of the fat family, lecithin, is supplied by all natural oils and by the fat of egg yolk, liver and brains. Lecithin is an excellent source of the two B vita-

mins, choline and inositol; if health is to be maintained, the
more fat eaten, the larger must be the intake of these two vitamins. This substance can be made in the intestinal wall
provided choline, inositol and essential fatty acids are supplied.
Lecithin appears to be a homogenizing agent capable of breaking fat and probably cholesterol into tiny particles which can
pass readily into the tissues. There is evidence that the major
causes of death, coronary occlusion and coronary thrombosis
are associated with deficiencies of linoleic acids (essential unsaturated fatty acids) and the two B vitamins, choline and
inositol and perhaps with a lack of lecithin itself. Huge particles of cholesterol get stuck in the walls of the arteries; they
might be homogenized into tiny particles if sufficient nutrients
were available for the normal production of lecithin. When
oils are refined or hydrogenated, lecithin is discarded."

Where Is Lecithin Found?

Lecithin is pronounced *less-i-thin* with the accent on the
first syllable. The word comes from the Greek *Likithos,* meaning the yolk of an egg, for lecithin is abundant in egg yolk. This
is one reason why we have only recently begun to hear about
lecithin—egg yolk was too expensive a source of it to be very
plentiful for experimentation. Quite recently another less expensive source has been found—soybeans.

The Cholesterol Threat Is Man-Made

Doesn't it seem significant that lecithin should appear
in such quantities in egg yolk which is also rich in cholesterol?
Doesn't it seem like a most beneficial provision of Mother
Nature (who knows nothing about refining foods) to provide
two substances that the body needs together in one food so that
you could not possibly get harmful amounts of cholesterol without also getting enough lecithin to keep the cholesterol in a
proper fluid state?

According to Adelle Davis, a study at the Almeda County
Hospital involved patients who were given fat from egg yolks
equivalent to 36 eggs daily, and in no case did the blood cholesterol level rise above normal. The egg yolk, you see, contained
also the B vitamins, the lecithin, and the other natural substances necessary for the proper use of the cholesterol by the
body.

So we come back again to the only possible conclusion—

we ourselves have created the threat that cholesterol poses—
by our arrogant meddling with natural foods. Hardening of
the arteries, heart disorders, gallstones—these are the results
of our meddling.

Cholesterol appears in foods of animal origin—fat meats,
butter, oils from fish, eggs and so forth. So far our brilliant
food chemists have not found any way to meddle with these
fats. We cook them, and if we raise the temperature to an
excessive high degree, the fats are bound to be harmful to us.
Deep fat frying and browning butter are two cooking processes
that should be forbidden by law. But aside from this, fats of
animal origin have not been tampered with to any great extent.

What About Vegetable and Cereal Fats?

What about fats of vegetable and cereal origin, so rich
in lecithin, the B vitamins and the essential fatty acids sometimes called vitamin F? We have done everything possible to
destroy completely these vitally important fats, and not just
destroy them, but render what remains of the food positively
harmful to human cells.

We remove all the health-giving fats when we refine
grains. The germ of the cereal contains the lecithin, the B vitamins, the essential fatty acids and vitamin E. So we throw this
exceedingly important part of the grain away (because it spoils
easily!) and eat only the starchy remnant, practically vitamin-
free, which bakes into white, pasty bread with just about the
same nutritive value as laundry starch. Your baker will tell you
how they have "enriched" this pasty mass by adding some synthetic vitamin B_1 and iron. Ask him how much of the fatty
part of the cereal grain has been replaced! This part is used
instead for stock feed. Animals thrive on it.

Other Natural Sources Are Destroyed

And what of other natural sources of lecithin and all its
accompanying vitamins? Seeds are rich sources. What seeds
does the average American ever eat that have not been tampered with? Nuts are the only ones we can think of at the
moment, and even these he seems unable to eat unless they have
been roasted almost to nothingness. Primitive peoples eat seeds
of all kinds—melon seeds, sunflower seeds, cereal seeds, corn
kernels, acorns, millet, whole rice and so forth. We smart
Americans take the perfectly good seeds and other healthful

foods Mother Nature gives and press out the oil. So far so good.
If we stopped there (cold-pressed olive oil for instance), all
would be well. Such oils are rich in lecithin, vitamin E, the
unsaturated fatty acids and the B vitamins. And research seems
to prove that in lands where cold-pressed oils are the basic fatty
foods, hardening of the arteries, heart disease, gallstones and
other diseases involving cholesterol deposits are not common.

What Does "Improve" Mean?

But our food technologists have developed ways of
"improving" our vegetable oils. And you can be certain when
that word "improve" comes in the front door, Mother Nature
goes out the back. We "improve" oils by hydrogenating them.
What does this give us? Hydrogenated shortenings—those lifeless
(and, we are firmly convinced, deadly) solid white shortenings
you buy in a can and use for making pastry, frying, cake baking,
deep-fat frying and so forth. They don't spoil; they're so
economical; they're so much more convenient than messy
liquid shortenings. You have all the arguments for them on
your television commercials.

But unfortunately for you and me, all the lecithin, the
B vitamins, vitamin E and the essential fatty acids have been
destroyed in the process of hydrogenation. How is your body
going to handle fats such as these without the natural substances
that accompany fats in nature? It's an obvious impossibility.
And all of the other food substances that depend on fats for
their proper absorption—calcium, phosphorus, vitamin A and
so forth—all these are going to be used improperly, too.

Consider for a moment all the conscientious mothers
who "bake" for their families. To worthless white flour, completely denuded of all its nutritional value, they add white
sugar (a drug with no food value but calories). Then, adding
insult to injury, they cream into their cake hydrogenated
shortening. The women's magazines, supported by advertising
for these very products, devote themselves to dreaming up new
horrors in the way of cake making, to persuade the completely
unaware housewife and mother that she is not "doing her
duty" to her family if she doesn't whip up one of these mon-
strous pieces of nutritional rubbish this very day.

Is it any wonder we as a nation shudder at the word
"cholesterol" and bring children into the world afflicted with

heart disease? What can we do to avoid cholesterol deposits? Stop eating eggs, fish and meat? No, of course not. Stop eating any fat that has been tampered with by food technologists. Read labels looking for the word "hydrogenated" and don't buy any product so labelled. Incidentally, margarine is of course, hydrogenated vegetable oils. And any packaged foods you buy like crackers are probably made with hydrogenated shortenings. Get completely natural oils from plant sources. Olive oil is often available from Italian importers in large cities.

And what's the matter with getting most of our quota of healthful untampered-with vegetable oil from sunflower seeds anyway? They're delicious to eat, a wonderful between-meals snack because they "stick to your ribs," being high in protein. And they contain the finest oil you can imagine, untouched by any human hand but yours.

CHAPTER **117**

Unsaturated Fatty Acids Are Essential

Have we been neglecting all these years one vitally important food factor that may one day be designated as a vitamin—the unsaturated fatty acids?

In determining what food factors constitute a vitamin, certain general principles have been laid down by researchers. If the food factor is essential to good health and if a deficiency in this factor causes a deficiency disease, then the factor is a vitamin. This, in general, is the criterion by which we designate or do not designate certain substances as vitamins.

When a new substance is discovered which seems to have the properties of a vitamin, much research is done with animals. The animals are put on carefully prepared diets which include all necessary elements except the one being tested. If some disorder results, the substance in question is then administered to see whether it will cure the disorder. If it does, then we are fairly sure that such-and-such a food element is necessary for health—at least in the case of animals. With some substances, it seems that animal tests do not prove out in the case of human beings. We then assume that such-and-such an animal needs such-and-such a substance, but human beings do not. This has always seemed to us like a most unsatisfactory way of doing things. Animal physiology is very much like our own. If it were not, there would be no reason at all for using animals in diet experiments.

It has always seemed to us that the very strict controls employed in animal experimentation may be the reason why some of these experiments do not prove out in regard to human beings. When a diet is decided upon for an animal experiment, nothing can be left to chance. There is no possibility for this rat or guinea pig to get out of his cage and go on a binge of eating forbidden foods. Temperature, rest, bedding, possible psychological irritants, family life, emotions, water, air, light— all these factors are most rigorously controlled, so that the animals' health cannot possibly be influenced either negatively or positively by any of these things. In planning diets for the experiments, the utmost care is taken to feed only those foods which have been shown to produce the ultimate in good health; vitamins and minerals, proteins and enzymes are supplied in ample quantities. Only the substance being tested is left out of the food for the first part of the experiment, then put back into the food for the latter part. And it is perfectly true that we know a lot more about what constitutes a healthful diet for a laboratory animal than for a human being. So, safe to say, these animals get the very best of everything that can be had.

Human Life Is Not a Controlled Experiment

Human beings do not live this way. No single human being lives this way. On this troubled planet, it is impossible to conceive of a human being who can live in the safe, unhurried, unstressful, relaxed, healthful atmosphere of one of these animals. Our human diets are full of all kinds of errors, no matter how careful we may be. The air we breathe is full of pollution from industry. Our water is loaded with chemicals. Our lives are subject to stress, insecurity, frustrations, hurry, lack of proper rest, lack of exercise or possibly work that is too heavy and exacting. We try to keep up with the Joneses. Early in life we are endowed with a set of ideals that glimmers before us constantly from then on, inspiring us to try to achieve many things that may be far beyond our reach. Surely we need much more of the important food elements to carry us through this kind of life than a laboratory rat needs to live healthfully in his hygienically controlled environment.

Unsaturated Fatty Acids—Vitamin or Not?

The subject of this chapter is a set of food factors that were once spoken of as a vitamin. Animal experiments show that they are essential to the good health of animals. But we still do not classify them as vitamins in speaking of human nutrition. We want our readers to know of these food factors so that they can decide for themselves whether or not they should be included in a healthful diet for human beings. These food factors are the unsaturated fatty acids, once called vitamin F. Specifically, they are linolenic acid, linoleic acid and arachidonic acid. The names need not frighten you. The chemical names of most of our familiar vitamins are equally long and unpronounceable.

Unsaturated Fatty Acids in Animal Health

There is a disease which occurs in laboratory rats called "fat deficiency disease." By breaking down the different fatty elements of the diet, researchers have found that the disease does not occur from lack of fat—any kind of fat. It results only from lack of the unsaturated fatty acids. The rats show arrested or retarded growth, a raised metabolic rate (that is, they burn their food up very rapidly), changes in skin and hair, kidney disorders and impairment of reproductive function. Rats who received no unsaturated fatty acids in their food ate just as much as the control rats, but they did not grow or put on weight, so apparently the food was simply burning rapidly without contributing anything to building the body. First over the paws, then over the face and gradually over the rest of the body a dryness and scurfiness (dandruff) spread. Cold weather— the kind that chaps hands—accentuated this condition. The rats developed kidney stones and many difficulties in reproducing.

In the case of the female rats there was disturbance of the whole reproductive cycle. In many cases litters were not born but were re-absorbed. Or, if the mother rat finally had the litter, she had prolonged labor and hemorrhage, and the litters were underweight and sickly. Male rats deprived of unsaturated fatty acids refused to mate and were sterile. It was found, too, that there was some relationship between deficiency of unsaturated fatty acids and pyridoxine and pantothenic acid, two of the B vitamins. A deficiency of any two of these factors caused a much worse condition than a deficiency of just one.

. . . In Human Health

Now in regard to human beings, there are two extremely important aspects to this problem. First of all, human milk is rich in unsaturated fatty acids—far, far richer than cow's milk. If these acids are not vitally important to human nutrition, how could Mother Nature have made the mistake of including them in such quantity in mother's milk, where every drop must count towards the nourishment of the child? Furthermore, it has been found that stores of fatty acids are built up in the heart, liver, kidney, brain, blood and muscle, and the body holds on to them tenaciously. In rats who were deprived of fatty acids for a long time, it was found that there was still some remaining when 76 per cent of the body fat of the rat had been used up. As soon as the unsaturated fatty acids were completely gone, the animal became very seriously ill. The body stores food factors it will need. And in cases of deficiency or starvation, it relinquishes first those factors which are not so important, and until the very end, hangs on to those things that are essential to life. So on this basis, too, we believe we are justified in assuming that the unsaturated fatty acids are important enough to be called a vitamin.

We are told that nothing is known about human requirements for the unsaturated fatty acids. Yet the National Research Council which sets the standards and makes the decisions on matters of this kind in this country says, "in spite of the paucity of information . . . it is desirable that the fat intake include essential unsaturated fatty acids to the extent of at least one per cent of the total calories." Bickell and Prescott, writing in *Vitamins in Medicine* (Grune and Stratton, 1953), tell us that only about one-half this amount has been available in

England since 1945. In this country there is no shortage of foods that contain unsaturated fatty acids, but do we realize how important they are, and do we make every effort to include them in every day's menu?

Diseases That May Be Related to Deficiency

A number of human disorders appear to be related to a deficiency of unsaturated fatty acids. Medical literature contains many instances of infant eczema that has been cured by including the unsaturated fatty acids in the infants' food. As a matter of fact, we recently found an ad in *The Practitioner,* a British medical publication, for a substance called F99 to be used in the treatment of eczema. It consists of unsaturated fatty acids to be used, says the ad, "in cases of infantile eczema, adult eczema, furunculosis (boils) and other skin disorders associated with a deficiency of essential fatty acids. It is also successful in cases of varicose leg ulcers of long standing." So the physicians are already using these food elements to cure disease.

Bicknell and Prescott (in *Vitamins in Medicine*) suggest that the acids may be very important in any disease where fat absorption is impaired. This includes diarrheal conditions of many kinds. It may include many cases of underweight. Much of the research we did some time ago on acne seemed to show that acne patients are unable to use fat properly. Could a deficiency of unsaturated fatty acids be one of the causes of acne? Could it be one cause of the dandruff that appears almost universally on American scalps? Bicknell and Prescott tell us that the fact that the unsaturated fatty acids are so carefully stored and husbanded by the body may be why symptoms of deficiency are not more marked and severe. In other words, many of us may be suffering from a sub-clinical deficiency—not enough to make us definitely ill, but enough to prevent our being completely healthy.

Other Deficiency Disorders

The Lee Foundation for Nutritional Research, 2023 West Wisconsin Avenue, Milwaukee 3, Wisconsin, has contributed perhaps the most to the study of unsaturated fatty acids in this country. They have booklets available on the subject: *A Survey of Vitamin F and Vitamin F in the Treatment of Prostatic Hypertrophy* which present startling evidence of the importance of these substances in human nutrition. Harold H.

Perlenfein, who wrote the first booklet, tells us that the unsaturated fatty acids reduce the incidence and duration of colds. He says that deficiency may be responsible for dry skin, brittle, lustreless, falling hair; dandruff, brittle nails and kidney disease. He states that the acids function in the body by cooperating with vitamin D in making calcium available to the tissues, assist in assimilation of organic phosphorus, aid in the reproductive process, nourish the skin and appear to be related to the proper functioning of the thyroid gland.

Unsaturated Fatty Acids and the Prostate

James Pirie Hart and William DeGrande Cooper, writing on prostate treatment (Lee Report No. 1), describe 19 cases of prostate gland disorder which were treated with unsaturated fatty acids. In all cases there was a lessening of the residual urine—that is, the urine which cannot be released from the bladder due to pressure from the enlarged prostate gland. In 12 of the cases there was no residual urine at the end of the treatment. There was a decrease in leg pains, fatigue, kidney disorders and nocturia (excessive urination at night). In all cases the size of the prostate rapidly decreased. Chemical blood tests which were made showed a great improvement in mineral content of the blood at the end of the treatment. We have been able to find no further work that has been done along these lines, but we believe that these findings are significant.

Processed Foods Cause the Deficiency

Why should any of us be deficient in the unsaturated fatty acids? For the same reason we are deficient in so many other necessary food elements—food processing. Bicknell and Prescott tell us that in processed and stale foods, these acids have deliberately been destroyed to improve the keeping qualities of the food. Unsaturated fatty acids occur in vegetable and seed fats—such as corn oil, cottonseed oil, wheat germ oil, peanut oil and so forth. They may occur in animal fats, such as butter, depending on what the animal has been fed. They are destroyed very easily by exposure to air, and they then become rancid. This rancidity can be responsible for destroying other vitamins as well—vitamins A, D and K are destroyed in the presence of rancid fat. When fats are hydrogenated, much of the unsaturated fatty acid is changed into saturated fatty acids. This means that certain chemical actions take place which completely change the character of the fat and render it almost useless for the various conditions we have described. Hydrogenizing gives the fat a solid form, rather than a liquid form.

At present, much of the fat we use has been hydrogenized. Shortening such as we use for making pastry or for frying has been hydrogenized, margarine has been hydrogenized—little or no unsaturated fatty acids are left. In a family where the meal-planner depends on fried foods and pastries for fats and where margarine is consistently used in place of butter, there is every possibility that such a family will be deficient in unsaturated fatty acids, unless a lot of salad oil is used, unheated, in salads. This is one reason why we feel certain that Americans in general may have a serious sub-clinical deficiency along these lines.

Unsaturated Fatty Acid in Common Fats

	Per cent of essential unsaturated fatty acids		
Butter	4.0	to	6.0
Beef fat	1.1	to	5.0
Lard	5.0	to	11.1
Mutton fat	3.0	to	5.0
Liver fat	3.0	to	7.0
Milk	.15	to	.23
Fish oils	Traces		
Margarine	2.0	to	5.0
Barley germ oil	63		
Cocoa butter	2.0		
Coconut oil	6.0	to	9.2
Corn salad oil	70		
Cottonseed oil	35	to	50
Linseed oil	72	to	83
Maize germ oil	42		
Oat germ oil	31		
Olive oil	4.0	to	13.7
Palm oil	2.0	to	11.3
Peanut oil	20	to	25
Rice bran oil	29	to	42
Rye germ oil	48		
Soybean oil	56	to	63
Sunflower seed oil	52	to	64
Wheat germ oil	44	to	52

Some of these foods sound exotic to us and, so far as we know, are not at present available to American consumers—such as oat germ oil, barley germ oil and so forth. But surely we have all heard enough about wheat germ oil during past years to realize anew that this extremely important substance (rich in vitamin E as well) should be a part of our diet. Corn oil, cottonseed oil, peanut oil, soya bean oil are sold as salad oils in every grocery. So far as we can determine, nothing has been done to these oils in preparing them for the market that would destroy their content of unsaturated fatty acids. If we should uncover some evidence that their processing *does* have this effect, you may be sure we will let you know, so that you will not continue to depend on them as good sources. But for the present, we would advise crossing off your shopping list all hydrogenated fats, such as the shortening that comes in a can, and margarine.

See to it that your family eats plenty of vegetable or seed oils—in salads, as that is by far the best way of taking them. If you must fry something—and we take a dim view of frying anything—use vegetable oils for the process. But keep in mind that the less heat you apply to any oils or fats, the better they are for you. In addition, we firmly believe that all present day Americans should take wheat germ oil or flakes as a daily food supplement. These contain not only the unsaturated fatty acids we have been talking about, but vitamin E as well and all the other fractions and elements of the wheat germ that may be vitally important for health, even though researchers have not as yet gotten around to isolating and defining them.

SECTION 34

BONE MEAL

Lack of calcium, phosphorus and other minerals is one of our most serious diet deficiencies, resulting in tooth decay and scores of other ailments. We need minerals that are easily assimilated. Bone meal provides them in completely natural form. Take bone meal every day—either in tablets or powdered. Bone meal aids the digestion and, as with all the vitamins, should be taken with meals.

749

CHAPTER **118**

Bone Meal

by J. I. RODALE

What is bone meal? It is the bones of selected cattle ground as fine as flour and sprinkled over food or taken in tablets. Let me tell you what aroused my interest in this subject.

In the latter part of 1941, an amazing situation in Deaf Smith County, Texas, was brought to the attention of the American public. It was discovered that inhabitants of that county, living mainly in and around Hereford, had remarkably healthy teeth with the almost complete absence of dental caries. Authorities who investigated found that the Deaf Smith Countians had teeth superior to anything known anywhere in the world. Even the horses, dogs and cats in that region of Texas had perfect teeth. When strangers moved into this section their dental troubles vanished. New cavities did not form.

A study of the locality revealed the fact that underlying the soil was a rich deposit of lime (calcium) and phosphorus with a trace of fluorine. Since all soils have been formed from their underlying rock structure in a weathering process extending over eons of time, it was found that the soil in and around Hereford was rich in lime and phosphorus and contained some fluorine. These 3 elements are extremely important in connection with the formation of tooth and bone, and since the food raised in Deaf Smith County soil absorbs sizable amounts of these substances, it gives the residents of this county healthy tooth and bone structure. Farmers of this section bring in spindly cows and steers from across the border in Mexico and after pasturing and feeding them with local produce build them up into fine big-boned animals.

A New England dentist avidly read the reports about the teeth in this celebrated county and his imagination ran completely away from the daily grind of drills, forceps and bicuspids. He cleverly reasoned that if he could find some food that was plentiful and which contained those 3 elements, namely calcium, phosphorus and fluorine in sufficient quantities, he might be able to accomplish the same purpose without causing a gold rush on Deaf Smith County. That man is Dr. S. G. Harootian, connected with the Worcester State Hospital, in Massachusetts.

He found such a food—the bones of beef cattle ground as fine as flour. In an astounding 9-month experiment with 9 mental patients at his hospital, he absolutely arrested the formation of cavities. Only one new cavity was formed in all that time. These patients were chosen because of their notoriously poor dental history. They were fed a capsule consisting of 5 grains of bone flour 3 times daily, along with their regular diet.

In the case of one of the patients, a filling was removed so as to expose the cavity to the ravages of the elements. It was continually packed with food debris, naturally. This would have been suicide for that particular tooth under ordinary conditions, but this wasn't an ordinary condition. Under the bone flour regimen that tooth did not decay. This experiment received a great deal of publicity and was written up in many journals.

My Own Experiments

When I read about all this, I decided to experiment upon myself. I had a tooth that was extremely sensitive to cold. When I drank cold water it would act up. After two weeks of taking 3 capsules of bone meal a day, this condition miraculously cleared up. I could drink the coldest water without experiencing pain in that tooth. I had a friend who I knew suffered from the same condition. I gave him some of the bone meal capsules and the same thing happened to him. No more pain on drinking cold water. At this writing my family has been taking bone meal for about 5 years without noticeable harm to our system, and we believe it is a factor in the reduction of our cavities in the teeth. Some of the family forgot to take it from time to time and suffer more from cavities than the others.

The attitude of the dental profession has been that bone

meal is not a factor in reducing caries (cavities in teeth). Many dentists have told me that once the tooth is formed the fluorine that we take in cannot become a part of it. But the evidence that I have assembled seems to indicate that it can—both in children and adults. The dentists prefer to paint the fluorine on the outside of the teeth. But I am sure that after you read the material herein presented you will be convinced that the best way to get fluorine is through bone meal.

Bone Meal for Minerals

In order to understand what you are getting when you take bone meal, let us review broadly a few simple facts of nutrition. In the constitution and functioning of the human body, proteins, carbohydrates, minerals and fats take part. Let us express it in a different manner. Our foods consist of two groups—organic and inorganic. The inorganic is water and mineral matter. The organic is proteins, fats and carbohydrates.

The proteins build the tissue of the body. The carbohydrates are mainly for the purpose of furnishing energy. Naturally we must have both of these, although the latest medical researchers indicate that a high protein diet is best for optimum health. But an exceedingly important part of the diet is the mineral group, and often there are serious deficiencies in this classification. Minerals are needed to carry out the physiological processes of the body. The rigidity of our skeleton depends on them. A lack can produce nervous irritability. They take part in digestion and are needed in the metabolic processes of the body. For example, iron is so important to the oxygen-carrying function of the blood. A lack of it causes one to fear and worry about things. Iodine is needed to prevent goiter. A lack of potassium will cause painful menstruation, and a shortage of magnesium will induce a lack of sex control. If there is too little sulphur, there may be intestinal stasis, that is, a reducing of the peristaltic contractions of the stomach that are so important to good digestion.

We are supposed to get our minerals in our food—in the vegetables, fruits and meats that we eat. But with the modern methods of farming and the use of chemical fertilizers there is a progressive depletion in the mineral content of our foods and we must take it in the form of mineral supplements. Bone meal is ideally suited for this purpose. In the book, *Nutrition and*

Physical Fitness, by L. Jean Bogert, M.D. (published by Saunders) there appears the statement: "The bulk of the mineral substances in the body is concentrated in the skeleton or bony framework." In the case of calcium, 99 per cent is found in the skeletal framework, which includes the teeth. In the case of phosphorus, 70 per cent is in the bone structure.

Dr. Henry C. Sherman of Columbia University expressed the same fact as follows in his book, *The Nutritional Improvement of Life* (Columbia University Press, 1950): "The body's framework or skeletal system of bones and teeth owes its strength and normal form to the fact of its being well mineralized. Smaller amounts of much more soluble mineral salts are constantly present in the soft tissues and fluids of the body." He refers to the minerals as "putting life into" the proteins of the body tissues and fluids.

Here is a statement from another source, *Dietary of Health and Disease,* by Gertrude I. Thomas, Assistant Professor of Dietetics, University of Minnesota (Lea and Febiger): "From 4 to 5 per cent of the body weight is mineral matter. It is found in all tissues and fluids, but especially in the bones, teeth and cartilage."

Analysis of Raw Bone Meal

Here is a typical analysis of raw bone meal as furnished in a letter from the United States Department of Agriculture dated September 1, 1950. This is an average figure from a number of samples:

	Per Cent		Per Cent
Sodium oxide (Na_2O)	0.46	Chlorine (Cl)	0.22
Potassium oxide (K_2O)	0.20	Carbon dioxide (CO_2)	1.59
Calcium oxide (CaO)	30.52	Phosphoric oxide	
Magnesium oxide (MgO)	0.73	(P_2O_5)	22.52
Barium oxide (BaO)	0.001	Boron oxide (B_2O_3)	Trace
Copper oxide (CuO)	0.0005	Fluorine (F)	0.043
Iron oxide (Fe_2O_3)	0.004	Iodine (I)	0.00002
Manganese oxide (MnO)	0.0014	Sulfur (S)	0.25
Lead oxide (PbO)	0.005	Organic matter	34.88
Zinc oxide (ZnO)	0.018	Moisture	6.76

Note the fact that it contains iodine. We see, therefore, that bone meal is not only important for good teeth, but also as an insurance of general bodily health. In our typical modern diet there is no bone. Here is a wonderful way to include it. And we must remember that bone meal is not a medicine. It is a food.

There are ways of taking mineral supplements that you can purchase in a drug store, but bone meal is safer because the minerals in bone are diffused in more natural proportions. There is no danger of an overdose.

More Minerals From Natural Foods

In connection with the proper mineralization of the skeleton, much medical data exists which asserts that vitamin D promotes better absorption of minerals. This vitamin seems to exert some sort of controlling action, especially so in the process of calcification at the ends of growing bones and in the healing of bone fractures. Vitamin D is obtained by being out in the sun, but it should not be overdone in this form. Too much tanning is dangerous. Cod liver oil gives vitamin D. I recommend the combination of D and A made from fish liver oils. This and bone meal are blood-brothers.

In parting on this subject, bear in mind that you will get more minerals if you will consume food that is closest to its natural state. Avoid processed foods as much as possible. Eat your vegetables raw as much as is possible. Do not cook peas, for example. Cooking destroys minerals. Nature has created a delicate balance of minerals in plants and the less you change it the better, with a few exceptions, of course. To cook carrots is a crime against nature. Much of the mineral matter goes down the drain in the cooking waters that are thrown away, and then sugar is substituted to restore the taste. In the raw carrot, the minerals contributed their share toward the taste. Look to your minerals and they will look after you.

CHAPTER **119**

Bone Meal and Tooth Decay

Certain proof of the effectiveness of bone meal against the almost-universal scourge of tooth decay is presented in this chapter.

Conclusive proof that supplementation of the average American diet with bone meal capsules will bring tooth decay to a virtual standstill is to be found in the testimony of S. G. Harootian, D.M.D., visiting oral surgeon of the Worcester City Hospital, Worcester, Massachusetts. In March of 1943 he read before the Dental Society of that city a paper on "The Influence of Administration of Bone Flour on Dental Caries" (published in the *Journal of the American Dental Association* in September of that same year). The results achieved in Dr. Harootian's experiments are so important as to merit noting the plea contained in the end of his report. He points out that if so simple a means as adding bone flour to the diet can bring a significant increase in the resistance to dental caries, that benefit should be withheld from the general public no longer than necessary.

Why Not Give Bone Meal a Try?

"How long is necessary?" is a logical question to ask at this time. For Dr. Harootian's charitable and humane words were spoken as long ago as 1943 and still the epoch-making success of his work has brought no "boon" to caries-riddled American mouths. We consequently feel that, whether further intervening experimentation has convinced the experts of the efficacy of bone meal in the prevention of tooth decay or has failed to do so, prescription of it is at least worth the try in the attainment of such a bright goal. Readers cannot fail to be convinced by the remarkable results affected by Dr. Harootian's simple approach to the problem.

Dazzled by Dr. Edward Taylor's account of the extraordinary dental health of residents of Deaf Smith County, Texas (discussed elsewhere in this book), he pondered over the possibility of supplementing the diet of Americans less favored geographically with the wonder-working ingredients responsible for the miraculous state of affairs there. After learning that meal from the bones of beef animals is rich in the Texas-prescribed calcium, phosphorus and fluorine, and that this readily procurable product exists in unlimited supply, he needed only to be assured that its fluorine content was not too high, in order to embark on his simple test.

Tests Made on Mental Patients

Nine patients were chosen from the Research Service of the Worcester State Hospital to be the beneficiaries of his project. All of them suffering major mental disorders of a psychotic type, the resultant slovenliness in personal hygiene, listless psychological torpor and dietary indifference that characterizes patients of this sort might have been expected to take a heavy toll in their general health records including teeth. This was indeed the case, for all had a higher-than-average rate of tooth decay. According to the authoritative work of C. F. Bodecker, "Modified Dental Caries Index" (*Journal of the American Dental Association,* September, 1939), which tabulates the caries incidence of the American people by means of actual statistics taken from the dental records, arranges them in age-brackets and secures from them the expectancy or likelihood of future decay for each group from the extensiveness of the caries noted in the records, these Worcester patients, averaging 34 years of age, should have exhibited approximately the caries average of 41.32 cited by Bodecker for the age-group of 30 to 34. A staggering total, this estimate of normal American dental health underlines the stark fact that, to judge from this sample, and as Dr. Harootian observes, our populace is far beyond normal in being subject to dental caries."

But in the case of his patients he found an even grimmer picture of dental disease and a sad commentary on the state of American knowledge of dental nutrition. All of them displaying a frightful amount of missing teeth, fillings and new carious surfaces, their decay-average had climbed to the ominously altitudinous peak of 54! And whereas dental statistics compiled by Bodecker estimate average future decay susceptibility at this age to be 9.01, theirs—without Dr. Harootian's proposed preventive treatment—would surely have soared to even more astronomical heights, had they continued untreated in their higher-than-average tempo.

Commencing with January 29, 1942, and extending over a period of 9 months, each patient was given 3 daily 5-grain capsules of bone meal with an individual content of about 320 milligrams, 89 milligrams of which were composed of calcium, 45 of phosphorus, and 0.31 of fluorine. No other change or vitamin supplementation was made in the normal hospital diet served throughout the study period, so that if any improvement were to be noted, it could not be ascribed to any factor other than the bone meal capsules. The dental condition of all 9 patients was carefully watched and meticulous notes were taken in each case once every month, in order to record the appearance of any new cavities or alterations in the state of existing ones since administration of the bone meal to their diets had been begun.

The Nine Months' Results

At the termination of the test period 9 months later, Dr. Harootian tabulated results which he calls "gratifying," a very mild word indeed with which to describe them. In all 9 cases there had occurred no progress in caries deterioration at all, a fact which the experimenting dentist believes necessary to explain on the basis of a complete cessation of all decay that must have started practically as soon as the first bone meal capsules made their effects felt on the patients' systems. Treatment with them had reduced the index of susceptibility to future caries from Bodecker's 9.01 plus to an absolute zero in the cases of 8 patients and to a possibility of only one more cavity in the case of the ninth. As another piece of incontrovertible evidence in support of the prodigious efficacy of bone meal, Dr. Harootian cites the case of a gum cavity in one of the patients. This had been drilled to be fitted with a filling but then had been left in a dangerously exposed condition by never being protected with one. Though at each of the 8 monthly check-ups accumulated food debris had to be excavated from it, those deposits that would have given encouraging hospitality to bacterial microbes in even a healthy mouth had in no way at all undermined the dentine or enamel enclosing the hole in the tooth. Both had grown strong and impervious to any further action of decay, and this incredible regeneration of health in the sick tooth could be assigned to only one cause—feeding of that tooth with the vitalizing ingredients found in bone meal.

Should Fluorine Get All the Credit?

In accounting for the miracle he and the bone meal had wrought, Dr. Harootian inclines to attribute it not so much to the slight additional supplements of calcium and phosphorus contributed to his patients' total diet (already containing enough of these elements to have made their beneficial effects felt to some degree), but rather to the fluorine present in the bone meal. In support of this now idly debated contention as to whether fluorine does any real dietary benefit to a tooth that is already erupted and mature, he cites the work with dogs by F. J. McClure ("Fluorides Acquired by Mature Dogs' Teeth," *Science,* March 6, 1942), who was also successful in increasing the fluorine content of enamel and dentine in his subjects by adding sodium fluoride to their daily digestive intakes, despite the fact that other experts queried on the subjects were emphatic in saying—without putting the matter to a test, however —that a fully grown tooth cannot be fed fluorine through dietary channels. Putting them to the right about, McClure produced dog enamel that contained 0.011 per cent of fluorine as contrasted with the 0.006 per cent content of the enamel in control dogs he had not fed fluoride. This ratio corresponds to and is compatible with the 0.0069 content of fluorine found in the enamel of carious human teeth as versus the 0.0111 per cent in healthy noncarious ones.

Against other expert opinion that fluorine exists in an insoluble form in bone, Dr. Harootian counters logically with the reply that its form when found in water is equally insoluble, in spite of which drinking of such water has provenly improved tooth enamel. Actually, whether taken in the diet as solid or liquid, in the course of its path through our bodies it finally reaches the tissues also in an insoluble form, since it is the blood, a calcium-containing agent, that takes it there.

Though Dr. Harootian envisages the possibility that the most important share of the credit for caries-prevention should be ascribed to neither the calcium, the phosphorus or the fluorine as found individually or in combination in the bone meal, but to "some (other) unidentified and unrecognized constituent," to the layman it is surely not important to haggle over the particular ingredient on which to pin the medal. Suffice it to recall that McClure's experiments with dogs and Dr. Harootian's treatment of 9 seemingly hopeless cases of pernicious advanced caries were both eminently successful by reason of one or more of the constituents. Consequently, if bone meal does the job (and it does!), it is better prevention to take it internally than to take it apart analytically.

CHAPTER 120

Report on the Clinical Use of Bone Meal

by ELIZABETH M. MARTIN, M.D.

How an enterprising M.D. used bone meal to bring her patients back to good health and discovered in the process many cases where it did the job where nothing else would.

Because of the recent popular and professional interest in bone meal as a therapeutic agent we have considered that the records of our past 4 years' experience with it may be of interest and value to the profession.

The case for which this agent was first used extensively was that of the 6-year-old son of one of our nurses. The child had a cleft palate and hare lip, both of which had been repaired before the age of two years. There was, however, a grave defect in his dentition, his primary teeth being very poor and having almost no covering enamel. He had gained only two pounds in the previous year. In consultation with our dentist, Dr. Wm. J. Siebert, we decided to have these poor upper teeth removed. There was considerable question as to how sound the secondary teeth would be, but it was felt this would give them a better chance.

There were no further physical defects in the child, excepting his undernutrition. He complained bitterly of pains in his legs—the so-called "growing pains" of children. He was given a brand of dicalcium phosphate with vitamin D in 10-grain doses twice a day with some improvement in his symptoms but no weight gain, and he had much restlessness with night terrors. His mother noticed that the little chamber he used at night was becoming encrusted with calcium deposit. We supposed from this that he was getting very little absorption of the calcium which he took.

It occurred to us that if we gave bone meal to calves and young pigs and puppies to promote proper growth, why should not nature's own combination of bone minerals be completely utilized by any animal body? Accordingly, we sifted and pulverized the available bone meal and filled 10-grain capsules by hand. In one week the child was playing as hard as any of his schoolmates. There was no more excess calcium deposit, although he was getting three 10-grain capsules daily. He began to grow and gain weight, until he caught up to the normal average for his age. His teeth were very slow to appear, it being about a year before his central incisors came through, but they were sound when they did arrive. He then made steady progress in the 3 years in which we had him under observation.

The results in this case were so striking and so immediate that we decided to run a series of cases. Any child complaining of "growing pains" or whose parents stated that he or she kicked and screamed in the night was put on calcium gr. xx daily, and alternate patients, on bone meal capsules gr. xx daily, with the minimum requirement of A and D as a supplement in each case. Records kept over a two-year period on 113 children showed complete remission of symptoms in all children on bone meal (57) and of 22 on dicalcium phosphate; with some complaints still, though not so marked, in the remaining 34 children. Just as a matter of curiosity these 34 were changed to bone meal and in all cases the symptoms disappeared.

We also had a small group of pregnant women who were very much interested in preserving their teeth during pregnancy, and in some cases the multiparae dreaded the dental neuralgia they had had to endure during previous pregnancies.

All of these women agreed to have their teeth checked and all cavities repaired at 3 months' gestation, with a final checkup at the 6 weeks' examination. Dr. Wm. J. Seibert, our dentist, kindly did all the dental work and kept dental charts for us.

Twenty-five women were given 10-grain bone meal capsules 3 times a day (two of the women who would have been on dicalcium phosphate, thought it gave them heartburn, so they were changed over in the first week) and 20 women were given 15-grain dicalcium phosphate wafers twice daily during the last 6 months of pregnancy and the first 6 weeks of lactation. None of the women had dental neuralgia. Those who had suffered from this previously had never had supplementary medication during their former pregnancies. Each one of these women also received A and D; 7,500 units "A" and 750 "D" daily to ensure proper mineral metabolism. None of the women had aching legs or cramps in the legs at night nor cramps in the legs on delivery. All of the babies were healthy at birth, but those whose mothers had been given bone meal had such long silky hair and such long nails that the phenomenon was remarked upon by the nurses.

At the 6 weeks' examination all of the babies were doing very well and the mothers were healthy. About one-quarter of the babies were still breast-fed. The dental checkup revealed that not one woman on bone meal had a new dental cavity and the cavities for the other women averaged one and two-tenths per patient. The dentists stated that even this was well below the expected number following an unprotected pregnancy.

Bone Meal the Best Source of Calcium

We use bone meal in place of any other form of calcium for all evidences of calcium deficiency in our patients, including muscular pains and cramps in the legs in both sedentary workers and laborers. The condition exists very widely because of the habit of most Canadians in ingesting a diet very low in calcium. All of these symptoms clear up promptly on 10 to 15 grains of bone meal daily. This is now supplied to us in a soft gelatin capsule containing finely pulverized meal from selected bones, combined with sufficient A and D to ensure absorption.

If vitamin D is to be effective as an aid to calcium metabolism, the calcium ingested must be at least the minimum requirement and must be available for absorption. The availability appears to be greatly enhanced by using natural bone minerals without trying to make any alteration in nature's formula.

Reprinted from *The Canadian Medical Association Journal,* June, 1944.

CHAPTER **121**

Bone Meal After Middle Age

Calcium and other minerals seem to be even more important for the elderly than for children. How and why to use bone meal as you get along in years is the subject of this chapter.

When we were babies, our mothers carefully measured every spoonful of food and followed the pediatrician's orders in respect to cod liver oil, orange juice, milk, cereal and so forth. One of the most important food elements is calcium—our mothers knew that. So most of us grew up with straight bones and fairly good teeth, regardless of what happened to those teeth later in life. But as we grow older, how many of us pay any attention at all to this extremely important matter of getting enough calcium? And, if there are older people living in the house with us, how much attention do we pay to the amount of calcium they are getting?

Why Do Older People Need Calcium?

Of course, older people don't need calcium for growing bones and teeth, as children do. But calcium has many, many uses in the body aside from healthy growth. And for all of these it must be supplied in food which, in the case of older people, is usually woefully lacking in this important mineral. We take for granted these days that a fall means a certain broken bone for an older person. Why? Their bones are brittle, we say. But must they be brittle? If proper attention is paid to diet, why is it not possible to keep the calcium level high in older people as well as in children, so that they need not suffer from broken bones that will not knit, as well as all the other distressing symptoms, such as nervousness, that lack of calcium brings about.

Their Calcium Intake Insufficient

A recent study reported in *Nutrition Reviews,* June, 1953, showed the actual calcium intake of a group of 33 women and 5 men between the ages of 68 and 96 who were living in an institution. Most of them were suffering from heart disease, senility, central nervous system disorders or blood vessel diseases. Their daily calcium intake was between .2 and 1.1 grams, and their phosphorus intake between .45 to 1.7 grams. Of those subjects who took .5 grams or less, 74 per cent revealed X-ray evidence of loss of bone calcium, which, of course, would lead to "brittle bones." Among those who took every day over .5 grams of calcium the incidence of soft, brittle bones was only 14 per cent. About the same results were found when the phosphorus content of bone was investigated.

Dr. Clive McCay of the Laboratory of Animal Nutrition at Cornell University tells us in *Vitamins and Hormones,* Vol. VII, published by Academic Press, that it appears that women from the ages of 52 to 74 years need a gram of calcium per day if they are to maintain their body stores of the mineral—that is, if they want to keep their bones hard, their nerves healthy. He says that another investigation reported in the *Journal of the American Dietetic Association,* Vol. 24, p. 292, indicates that a group of elderly women living in an institution were getting only .4 to .7 grams of calcium daily—or only four tenths to seven tenths of the amount required. Another woman who lived alone and ate a diet which was rich in starch and sugar was losing regularly more than 100 milligrams of calcium a day. Another who was often emotionally upset lost calcium during her periods of depression and regained it again when she began to feel more cheerful.

Older People Are Less Likely to Assimilate Calcium

In Dr. McCay's experiments with animals the oldsters were compared with the youngsters in their ability to absorb dietary calcium. Young animals could store about 78 to 88 per cent of the calcium they ate, he found. But animals old enough to compare with human beings of 50 could not generally even maintain what calcium they had in their bodies, let alone store any more. In other words, they were constantly losing calcium.

A lot of fat in the diet of the older animals appeared to make them lose more calcium and at a faster rate. Then, too, the older animals did not seem to be able to select the proper diet when they were left to their own choice. Young rats will be very careful about their diet and will be certain they have had enough food containing the necessary vitamins and minerals before they will touch such worthless foods as sugar. But older rats appear to lose their power of discrimination and will turn greedily to a sugar solution, neglecting the healthful food put before them. They will continue to do this even while they die of malnutrition, says Dr. McCay.

The Two Necessities of Older People

From these observations it would appear there are two absolute necessities in the care of older people—and these are just as essential, if not more so, than in the care of infants. They need large amounts of calcium in their diets, for they have just as much need of it as children have and they lose it at a faster rate. Then, too, if they have lost the ability to choose foods that are good for them, their diets must be supervised as closely as infants' diets, to make certain they are not trying to stay alive on starch and sugar.

Many researchers have found that older people tend to have less hydrochloric acid in their stomachs than younger people. This digestive juice is necessary for the assimilation of calcium, and perhaps a lack of it explains why older animals lose calcium so rapidly. A diet rich in all the vitamins, especially the B vitamins, appears to be the best guarantee of ample hydrochloric acid in the stomach. It has been found, for instance, that lack of thiamin or of niacin in the diet results in lessening the hydrochloric acid or gastric juice available for the digestion of food.

Dr. McCay then takes up the question of whether or not hardening of the arteries and calcium deposits in the kidneys can be caused by too much calcium in the diet. We are glad to repeat here exactly what Dr. McCay has to say on this subject (and remember, please, that Dr. McCay is one of the country's outstanding authorities on nutrition, with many books and articles to his credit): "In the course of two decades of research with rats we have seen groups at the time of death with heavily calcified arteries and kidneys while parallel groups were relatively free. This calcification of soft tissues was due to unknown variables in the diet and could never be related to dietary calcium."

Lack of vitamin C may be largely responsible for kidney stones and other misuses of calcium by the body. But we have never been able to find a shred of evidence to show that too much calcium could be the cause. On the contrary, all the experiments and the surveys show beyond the possibility of a doubt that our diets today are grossly deficient in calcium and that it would take many times what we receive in food or food supplements to approximate even an optimum amount!

Two Inexpensive Ways of Getting Calcium

Dr. McCay tells us that one of the most serious aspects of the diet of older people in institutions is the great quantity of bread they consume. This is partly because we have been led to believe that bread is the staff of life, partly because bread is cheap and partly because older people who lack teeth or dentures can eat soft white bread more easily than most other solid foods. White bread is a mockery of good food. What then can older people eat that will be rich in calcium, easy to chew and not expensive?

We nominate marrow bone soup as the answer to the problem. Any butcher will give you a marrow bone absolutely free, especially if you tell him you want it for the dog. Beyond this you need nothing but free water (or juices in which vegetables have been cooked) and a stove to manufacture one of the most nutritious foods imaginable. Have the bone sawed or split if you can, for the more cut areas available, the more calcium will be poured out of your soup bone into the soup. Add just a dash of vinegar when you put the bone on to boil. This acid will cause more calcium to be deposited from the bone into the liquid. You can let the bone boil as long or as short a time as you wish. The calcium and other minerals from the bone will stay right there in the soup until you are ready to eat it. If you add vegetables, cut them up rapidly and let them cook just long enough to become tender. Wouldn't you say this is a remarkably cheap way of obtaining calcium?

To make certain of an ample supply of calcium every single day, whether there is marrow bone soup for dinner or not, older people should take bone meal. We wish it were possible to convince every reader thoroughly on one point—bone meal is not a medicine. It is a food. Our ancestors regarded bone as an important food. In many parts of the world today bones are eaten as regularly as any other food. Bone meal is simply whole bone ground up so that we do not have to chew it. It contains nothing more.

Now surely no one would be afraid to eat marrow bone soup every day because it might turn him into a stiff calcium deposit. So why should anyone hesitate to take bone meal for fear he might get too much calcium? In 3 bone meal tablets a day he gets, we suppose, just about the same amount of calcium and other minerals he would get from a two-day supply of marrow bone soup.

In the case of old people, especially, we think bone meal is the ideal answer to sufficient calcium. For they *are* fussy about what they eat. Their eating habits have been established for many years, and it may take a great deal of skill and persuasion to change them. An infant can eat only what we give them, but grandma has access to the refrigerator and the candy store. So if she complains about eating foods rich in calcium, or if she really cannot properly digest raw vegetables, let the marrow bone soup and bone meal tablets every day keep her calcium store up to the level where you will not have to worry about broken bones.

CHAPTER **122**

Bone Meal and Minerals

The many minerals in bone meal, occurring in the same natural proportions as they occur in food, make this supplement the most valuable source of minerals available.

Bones were used in the diet of man earlier in history than milk was used. Primitive man hunted and fished long before he domesticated any animals from which he might obtain milk. Undoubtedly he ate the fish bones and as much of the animal bones as he could chew. Then he pounded the larger bones into powder so that they could be eaten easily. In many countries today, bones are eaten right along with meat or fish and bone meal is a valued food, especially for pregnant or nursing mothers who, of course, have a great demand for lots of minerals.

We have published many articles on bone meal, as well as a booklet, *Bone Meal for Good Teeth* (Rodale Books, Emmaus, Pennsylvania, price $1.00). And every time we look back through our files we find even more information on the subject of just how much good bone meal can do in human diets. We think it is in order right here, to point out that bone meal, taken instead of milk, will supply all the minerals in a form that is just as easily assimilated by the body.

Here is an analysis of minerals in a typical sample of bone meal as furnished by the United States Department of Agriculture:

	Per Cent		Per Cent
Sodium oxide	.46	Lead oxide	.005
Potassium oxide	.20	Zinc oxide	.018
Calcium oxide	30.52	Chlorine	.22
Magnesium oxide	.73	Phosphoric oxide	22.52
Barium oxide	.001	Boron oxide	trace
Copper oxide	.0005	Fluorine	.043
Iron oxide	.004	Iodine	.00002
Manganese oxide	.0014	Sulfur	.25

It is almost impossible to compare the mineral content of milk with that of bone meal since the bone is more than half mineral while only .7 per cent of milk is mineral, due to the large amount of water, fat, carbohydrate, protein and so forth in milk.

Experiments with Bone Meal

In the *Journal of Nutrition* for February 10, 1953, two researchers from the Department of Animal Husbandry at Cornell University report on their experiments with fresh bone. They say, "Drake and others made studies on foods containing fresh bone prepared for us in Europe and, using balance trials on human subjects, compared the availability of bone calcium with that of milk and found them nearly equal under the conditions of their experiment." This research was reported in *The Journal of Nutrition,* Vol. 37, p. 397.

Drs. McCay and Udall from Cornell go on to report that the animals fed with fresh bone in their experiments absorbed about 56 per cent of the calcium of the ground bone and about 49 per cent of the phosphorus. These are the two basic minerals, most important from the nutritional standpoint. Of course, all the trace minerals (boron, zinc, copper, etc.) were also present in the bone and, we presume, were absorbed.

The 4 researchers mentioned by Dr. McCay and Dr. Udall have this to say about bones in the diet: "Present human dietaries are largely dependent on milk and milk products to supply the bulk of this calcium. This, however, was obviously not the case centuries ago, as man in the past, in common with other carnivora, was dependent on animal and fish bones for a large portion of his calcium intake. Today many aboriginal people still depend on bone as their chief source of calcium. Bone also supplies many other minerals essential for normal nutrition.

"In many areas of the world the supply of milk and milk products is not sufficient to provide the recommended dietary allowances for calcium. During and immediately after the last war a large proportion of the canned meat products prepared in Canada for U. N. R. R. A. contained 15 per cent of cooked ground bone; this resulted in the final canned meat containing approximately .8 grams of calcium per 100 grams. Today all flour sold in Newfoundland, where the consumption of milk is small, contains ½ of 1 per cent bone meal. For many years bone meal has been an ingredient of certain infant cereal products."

In the light of the present hullabaloo over water fluoridation, it is interesting to go back and read an article that appeared in the *Journal of the American Dental Association* for February 1, 1947. This article discusses the opinion of the Council on Dental Therapeutics of the ADA so far as bone meal is concerned. These gentlemen say that the "basis for their use (bone meal preparations) is the assumption that active tooth decay is, to a significant extent, a manifestation of individual or combined deficiencies of calcium, phosphorus, fluorine and vitamin D. Although it may be conceded that these dietary factors, with the possible exception of fluorine, are essential during the development of the teeth available evidence does not indicate whether they are important after tooth formation is completed. Despite the array of reports attributing to fluorine a caries-inhibiting role, analysis of the literature on the subject discloses a lack of conclusive information. This lack renders largely presumptive any course of treatment in which fluorides, natural or synthetic, are ingested to influence the incidence and severity of the disease."

Fluorine in the Form of Calcium Fluoride

Yet only a few years later, the American Dental Association was officially on record in favor of water fluoridation as the greatest find of the century for preventing tooth decay! Anyone who says a word against fluoridated water is a crackpot, according to them. Yet they themselves announced, in 1947, that fluorine probably didn't have anything to do with preventing tooth decay. They were talking of the fluorine in bone meal, of course. Now if the fluorine in fluoridated water can do such a remarkable job of preventing tooth decay as the officials of the Dental Association now feel it does, why not admit officially that the fluorine in bone meal may possibly perform the same function?

It has been shown experimentally that calcium, taken along with fluorine, protects against the poisonous action of the fluorine. Drinking fluoridated water does not guarantee any calcium supply at all. But in bone meal the calcium comes right along with the fluorine. Fluorine in bone meal is in the form of calcium fluoride. The fluorine compound used for fluoridating water is sodium fluoride, which does not appear anywhere

in nature. Sodium fluoride is used because it is more soluble
in water. This means that your body undoubtedly assimilates
more of the fluorine in this form than it could if the fluorine
were in the form of calcium fluoride, which is less soluble.

Most of the foods you eat contain fluorine. Two and a
half quarts of milk contain about the same amount of fluorine
you would get from a day's recommended ration of bone meal,
which, incidentally, is far, far less than you will get by drinking the average amount of fluoridated water per day and which
is also in the form of calcium fluoride, not nearly so soluble—
meaning that your body takes up far less of it.

Bone Meal for Diseases

Bone meal is recommended for canker sores in the
standard reference book, *Dietetics for the Clinician,* edited by
Harry J. Johnson, M.D. (published by Lea and Febiger).
The editor tells us that you can generally get rid of a canker
sore within 48 hours with a 15-grain dose of bone phosphate
twice a day. Do you suppose that the national incidence of
canker sores is nothing more or less than a symptom of our
national deficiency in minerals which bone meal supplies in
such abundance?   '

We have published in this book and in our booklet on
bone meal, much evidence of the healthfulness of taking bone
meal. Physicians have used it—not to prevent but to cure long-
standing and critical cases of bone diseases; one physician used
it at her hospital for new mothers and their children, to prevent
cramps, growing pains, pregnancy complications and tooth
decay. A dentist gave it to patients at a mental hospital, with
the result that tooth decay stopped overnight in these patients,
without any other treatment at all. We believe that far more
research of this kind should be done with bone meal. But
meanwhile those of us who know about bone meal should certainly be taking it, for we cannot get in any other food the
concentration of minerals—natural, well-balanced minerals—
that we get in bone meal. All the minerals that are in milk
are in bone meal, just as easily assimilated and just as well used
by the body.

SECTION 35

SLEEP

Never sleep with your head pressing on your arms. It can cause neuritis in the arms. Make sure that you do not cross limbs or head over other parts of your body. It stops the circulation. One should sleep on a very hard mattress, or place a board under a soft one. If one has pains in the neck, try sleeping without a pillow.

CHAPTER **123**

Sleep and Rheumatism

by J. I. RODALE

I would like to tell you the story of how I stumbled upon an interesting fact about neuritis.

Around 1940 I began to experience neuritic pains in the hands, arms and shoulders. There would be dull twinges and pains, and I found it extremely difficult to don my overcoat. If I raised my arms above a certain level, the pain would increase. I couldn't turn my head without experiencing pain in the neck and shoulders. I would get up in the morning with a feeling in the shoulders and neck as if someone had sat on me all night, and my fingers had a numbness which made it difficult for me to tie my shoelaces.

The doctor diagnosed it as neuritis, but its cause had him baffled, and in spite of months of medical treatments of all kinds, including osteopathy, the painful condition persisted. As I look back now I can see that in this doctor's practice, he specialized in finding cures, but never spent any time in seeking causes. He asked me no questions about my daily life and habits in order to come upon some clue that might lead to the answer. I just kept coming and he kept treating it, mainly with diathermy, but nothing happened.

A friend of mine had about the same symptoms that I did and every time we would meet we would swap talk about our condition.

The Cause Discovered

One night I discovered the cause of my trouble. It was about 3:00 a.m. when I suddenly awoke from a disturbed sleep. My entire arm was numb from shoulder to finger tips. In fact, it was practically paralyzed. I tried to think quickly, and noticed that I had been sleeping with my head on the paralyzed arm. I became convinced that this habit was at the bottom of all my trouble. My own hard head had been digging down on my arm for hours.

I stayed awake for a long time, thinking, and observing the actions of my arms and head. I would catch my arm attempting to move upward so that it could be a pillow to my head, but I fought against it. It took about a week to win complete control over them, and after that the habit was completely mastered. Never again did I sleep with my head on my arms, and miracle of miracles, the neuritis in my arms completely vanished.

I then went to see my friend who had the same condition I did, and when I related my experience to him, a light came into his eyes. He did not sleep with his head on his arms. In his case it was a way he had of folding back his left arm in a v-shape and sleeping with his body pressing on it. He now cured himself of this habit, sleeping with his arm spread out in a relaxed way, and within a week his neuritic pains completely disappeared.

When I saw how simple it was to cure these two cases, I began to think of the hundreds of thousands of people who must be suffering from the same thing, and since in questioning people I found that a majority of them did sleep with their head pressing on *their* arms, I figured that I had a job to do. I had to share my knowledge with as many persons as possible. So I wrote a book on the subject in 1940, as well as several articles which appeared at that time in *Fact Digest* and *True Health Stories,* two magazines which I edited and owned. As a result, hundreds of people have been cured of what I call pressure neuritis.

Medical Recognition of the Idea

I was surprised when in 1944, Dr. Robert Wartenberg sent me a reprint of an article he wrote in *The Journal of Nervous and Mental Disease* (May, 1944) in which he mentioned my work in this field. I was surprised that a physician would mention the work of a layman.

A doctor friend of mine, a phlebitis specialist in New York, was incensed when he received a copy of my book, and said to me at our next meeting, "Why do you meddle in such things? You are not a doctor."

To give you another reaction from a doctor, may I quote from a letter received from Mrs. Susan Snyder, 135 Eastern Parkway, Brooklyn, New York (October 29, 1953):

"The doctor tells me that I have osteoarthritis. The pains I complained about—terrific headaches and pains from the back of the neck up and down to lower back as well as between shoulders completely disappeared after I arose and walked about for about a half hour. I asked my doctor (an M.D.) if it wasn't pressure pains. I suspected what your book confirmed. The doctor gave me some 'double talk' and said that the pain was due to adhesions, and he suggested 'radar' treatments. I went 3 times a week, until your book opened my eyes. I was mad clean through. Why wasn't my doctor honest enough to tell me the pains were due to pressure exerted in sleep?

"I sent him your book and told him 'I know and so does Mr. Rodale that osteoarthritis is incurable (degenerated bones cannot be restored) but I am glad to have been corroborated in my suspicion that my pains were pressure pains and I didn't need a doctor for that.' "

Mrs. Snyder turned over to me the answer from her physician. He said, "Proper sleeping habits are helpful in these conditions—but by no means curative—since they do not remove the, as yet, unknown cause or causes. Mr. Rodale over-simplifies the entire matter, principally through ignorance of the basic sciences relating to the human body. Improvement by any method of treatment may be only apparent, concurrent and coincident with a period of natural remission of symptoms— which usually recur in spite of the continuance of the temporarily 'miraculous cure.' "

Others Experience the "Miraculous Cure"

I make no comment except to say that my own cure has so far been in effect for over 16 years. Many others have had similar experiences. I have had hundreds of letters testifying to my method's efficaciousness in completely clearing up pressure neuritis.

Here is a typical case: One day I was in a broker's office and overheard the bookkeeper complaining to a customer's man that she had been having terrible pains in her arms and shoulders. "I have to go to my doctor this afternoon for vitamin B injections and dread going," she said, "and tomorrow I am supposed to go to my dentist to have my teeth X-rayed. The doctor thinks that it might be infected teeth, and I might have to have all of them extracted."

I walked over to her and related my own experience. When I explained that possibly head pressure could be the cause of her own trouble, she was delighted to find an excuse for not going to the doctor or dentist. She at once admitted that she slept with her head on her arms. In about a week that girl was as free of pain as a new-born baby, without the benefit of any vitamin B injections. Of course, not everyone who has pains in the arms and shoulders get them from sleep pressures, but it is surprising how many cases do arise from this cause.

Some Letters

Here are a few letters received from readers who have benefited from my book on the subject. They are only a few chosen from hundreds:

Here is one from Bernard Singer, 16 Shanley Avenue, Newark, New Jersey:

"I had been experiencing sharp pains across the back occasionally. After reading your pamphlet I became aware of two faulty sleeping habits. I was resting my head on my right arm and my wife frequently threw one leg over my back as I slept. By avoiding these two faulty habits, I have found that my backaches disappeared."

James M. Moore, Route 4, Greenville, Ohio, writes:

"I had found my two big toes were becoming numb, with almost no feeling in them. By breaking myself of lying so that one leg was under the other, this situation has cleared up also. Now these toes have a normal feeling."

Mrs. C. C. Wacker, Wilton Junction, Iowa, writes:

"I used to wake up more tired than when I went to bed, and so full of aches and pains that I was miserable—until I read your book *Sleep and Rheumatism*. Now I wake up refreshed. It's almost like a miracle. Others have been helped by your method through my telling them, including my husband who has been greatly benefited. So we decided to give 4 of these books as Christmas presents."

John H. Stevenson, 26 Southbridge Street, Worcester, Massachusetts, writes:

"Your book *Sleep and Rheumatism* has taught me how to get more rest in my sleeping hours. Now I get up in the morning without that swollen feeling in my hands, which our family doctor says is a sign of arthritis. We are hearing too much about that dreadful trouble, and I believe you have told me how to stop it."

Hugo Mayerhoefer, Salem, Oregon:

"My dear Mr. Rodale: Your book *Sleep and Rheumatism* told me exactly where 90 per cent of my rheumatism came from. However, none of the positions you illustrated fit my case and so it did me no good for about a year or so until I finally discovered that my collarbone, in sleeping on my side, pressed against some nerve and choked off the 'supply line' and a few weeks after noticed a change for the better. Twenty years suffering because my doctors didn't find the cause of my trouble. A million thanks to you."

Some Additional Facts

The sleep neuritis comes from pressure on nerves which damages them, and also from blood congestions caused by pressure on veins, but the amazing thing is how quickly the condition clears up when the sleep pressures are eliminated. You might ask, but how can I prevent myself from doing these things during sleep? The answer is that you begin by trying, and pretty soon your subconscious mind has learned a new set of sleeping habits. All you need do is to draw an imaginary line along your shoulders, and in sleep never let your arms go above that line, keeping your arms down at the sides, and as relaxed as possible.

In Germany a survey made a few years ago showed that practically 100 per cent of the population aged between 40 and 50 were afflicted with some form of arthritis or neuritis, but this, of course, included very mild cases. Ask any person over 60 and you will find that they are suffering from vague bodily pains and twinges. Many of these cases are due to pressures exerted in sleep, although I have also found that some of it is due to sleeping on soft mattresses, which cause the spine to curve downward. Most of those people continue to suffer because cures are usually attempted with medication, whereas the cause is purely a mechanical one.

Dr. Emanuel Josephson of New York City, who wrote a

commentary on my book, said that pressures on the arm and shoulder during sleep can lead to bursitis. The cause is injury to the lubricating system of the shoulder. There is a delicate sac in the shoulder joint which is moistened by an oily fluid. Pressure on the shoulder muscle during sleep can in some cases cause a breakdown of its lubricating system, giving rise to a case of subdeltoid bursitis and so many of these cases are usually operated on.

Drunkard's Neuritis

Many a drunkard has fallen asleep in a hallway and because there are no pillows handy, used his arm for that purpose. But when one is drunk, the circulation and forces of the body are at even a lower ebb than in ordinary sleep, so that when the man is suddenly awakened his arm is so paralyzed that he can hardly move it. Such cases sometimes have to be hospitalized, and in the big cities so many of them are brought into hospitals that this condition has been called Drunkard's Neuritis. It has also been called Saturday Night Neuritis, from the fact that so many workers are paid at the end of the week, indulging in wild bouts of drinking and sleeping it off under tables, etc.

Yet, though the doctors have handled so many of these drunkards, and knew that it came from sleeping on their arms, they did not think to associate it with other cases of arm neuritis. You can search high and low in the medical profession and nary a word will you find that the head pressing on the arm in sleep is the cause of these thousands of cases of pressure neuritis. Patients come to doctors with symptoms of waking up in sleep with arms paralyzed, and the doctors call it *Brachialgia Statica Paresthetica,* which means numbness in the arm during sleep, but always in their writing about it they state that it comes upon the person suddenly and that the cause is not known. I am wondering if what I have discovered is really *Brachialgia Statica Paresthetica.*

Idiopathic Nocturnal Paresthesia?

In the November 5, 1955, issue of the *Journal of the American Medical Association,* a physician asks a question of the editor. A patient of his, a 30 year old plumber, complains of his hands becoming numb every night during sleep. Upon awakening he has to shake his hands vigorously to do away with the numbness. There seems to be no evidence of disease that could be at the bottom of it. What could be the cause?

The editor replies. It is possible that this could be a scalenus anticus syndrome, the background for which could be a cervical rib and enlarged transverse process of the cervical spine, or even a hypertrophy of the scalenus anticus muscle. The editor advises an X-ray, and an injection of procaine solution into the affected muscles. The trouble could also be in the thyroid, says the editor, and advises quite a complicated and expensive procedure, including complete studies of the spine.

Then he says that sometimes such a condition has been vaguely diagnosed as *idiopathic nocturnal paresthesia*. This means a night-time numbness of spontaneous origin, which I will discuss in a little while. Sometimes patients with this condition have what is called arteriospasm and for this, priscoline is given 3 or 4 times a day, as well as barbiturates. Also treat-

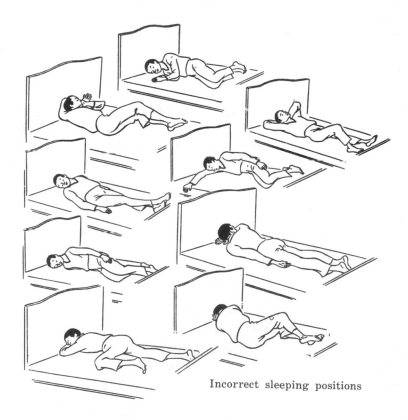

Incorrect sleeping positions

ments with mecholyl every second day, 10 times in all, have helped.

Now with all due respect to this editor's medical gobbledegook, which I have attempted to simplify, all that is probably the matter with this plumber is that he is sleeping with his head on his arms, causing pressures on nerves and the circulatory system. Sometimes people sleep with their arms curled up in positions which also cause stagnation in the circulation. All that is needed is about 3 nights of relaxed sleeping, with the arms down at the sides, and presto, no more *nocturnal paresthesia*. (Now he's got *me* talking that way.)

My little booklet, *Sleep and Rheumatism* (35 cents) explains it all, and I have sent a free copy to the doctor who asked the question. We have dozens of letters from people who have read it and who have cured themselves in no time at all. In my work and in my travels in the last 25 years I have encountered at least 20 cases of people who had vague pains in their arms and shoulders, and in practically every case I later found that after they followed my simple instructions there was a complete cure—or as the doctors would say, a complete remission of symptoms.

Its Meaning to Me

Now what is this *idiopathic nocturnal paresthesia* that the editor mentioned? Years ago when I was doing a thorough research of the medical literature, I made it my business to read as many articles on the subject as possible. It seems that *idiopathic nocturnal paresthesia* is a form of numbness in the arms which comes on during the night for no reason at all. It just as suddenly disappears and nobody seems to die from it. But the medical profession seems to be baffled as to its cause. The medical profession is so easily baffled, and then goes on to create elaborate, expensive cure procedures which pay them handsome premiums for their lack of desire, or energy, or what-have-you, in looking for causes. But from the experience that I had had in this field, my opinion is that there is no such thing as spontaneous paresthesia. The numbness must be caused by a pressure of one part of the body on the other. It can't be otherwise.

Just about that time I was invited to speak to a health group in Cincinnati, and part of my talk was to be devoted to pressure neuritis in the arms. In going over my papers the night before at the hotel, I found an article that had appeared in the May, 1944, *Journal of Nervous and Mental Diseases*, entitled *"Brachialgia Statica Paresthetica."* *Brachialgia* means pain in the arms, *statica*, at rest, and *paresthetica*, an abnormal sensation, as burning, prickling, etc. This article was practically a complete review of what was known in this field. The author, Robert Wartenberg, M.D., even said in it, "Under the titles: 'Sleep and Rheumatism,' 'How I Cured Neuritis,' and 'Pain in the Finger,' etc., a layman, J. I. Rodale, wrote a book and magazine articles on this subject."

Again it was stressed that arm numbness could come about during the night spontaneously, without pressure being applied, and again I questioned it. Evidently my subconscious mind was reading the article along with me and differed with me, for during that night I had the most beautiful case of *idiopathic nocturnal paresthesia* you would ever want to see, and I am sure that it was my subconscious which did it, purely to teach me a lesson.

Now, I must tell you that a few years before, I had cured myself of a severe case of *pressure neuritis* in my arms by learning not to sleep with my head on them. I had learned this so thoroughly that it had become automatic. I suppose that that little imp which was my subconscious, stood watch for me while I was asleep to see that my arms did not go above my shoulder line. Thus my head would not be able to reach them.

But on this night of which I speak I know that I had a case of arm numbness brought about without any pressure. It was purely psychosomatic. It did not last very long, but there it was. The next morning I took my subconscious to task and spoke to it in no uncertain terms. "Subconscious," I said, "you and I are going to go through life together. We are going to read many medical journals and articles. We are going to have lots of fun but don't take it personally or be too serious about it. Be objective! Remember what I tell you, now, because I don't want to have any more trouble with you. I don't want to insult you by telling you who is the master, but let us each know our place and function. I need you to remember things for me. Remember them well, but don't try any more experiments on my body."

That was about 10 years ago, and I have not had any similar trouble since. My subconscious and I have been the best of friends.

CHAPTER 124

Sleeping on the Floor

by J. I. RODALE

Sleeping on the floor may be the best answer to the problem of getting a comfortable bed that is hard enough to permit one to relax in a good position which will not cause backache.

Many years ago I read somewhere that the late Bernarr McFadden, the well-known physical culturist, slept on the floor. He did it, of course, to prevent his spine from sagging downward in sleep. He knew that spinal abnormalities—curvatures and distortions—can produce disease, and that a strong, straight back is insurance that the nerves radiating outward from the spine will function efficiently, for the spine is the nerve switchboard that controls the health of man.

As a young man I dismissed this quirk of McFadden's as one of the things that only rabid physical culturists do, but as I went through life I heard more and more of people who were being advised by their physicians to sleep with a board under the mattress to prevent it from sagging. This was because of their back troubles, and I could see that Bernarr was not far off the track. In fact, at the age of 40 I had to have my own board under the mattress because of rheumatic back pains.

It is amazing how many people are attacked with this affliction. In Germany a survey was made some years ago which

showed that practically 100 per cent of the people over 50
had some form of rheumatism, although some were only mild
cases. So many of the traveling public are suffering from back
troubles that the Hotel Vier Jahrzeiten in Frankfort, Germany,
will make your bed up on order—either soft, medium or hard.

The mattress makers were quick to cash in on the need
for a harder sleeping surface, and you will find dozens of orthopedic mattresses on the market. I have a typical advertisement
in front of me. It says: "Throw that backache out of your life—
designed to give you healthful sleep and ache-free days." This
is true. These mattresses help. So does the board. But I found
a better answer than either of these two devices.

An Experiment in Floor-Sleeping

I recalled old Bernarr McFadden sleeping on the floor,
and living to be way over 80, and parachuting off bridges. There
must be something to this floor-sleeping business, I figured. So
one evening I lay down on our living room rug and experienced
a delightful half hour of soothing repose. I was surprised to
find it so restful. I did it again on other nights and became
convinced that sleeping on a hard surface was not as difficult
as one would imagine. We know that half the world sleeps
on the floor, or its equivalent. People in the vast regions of
Asia, Africa, South America and other so-called uncivilized
areas, have never even seen a bed. A G.I. friend of mine now
stationed in Japan writes about a Japanese carpenter employed
in the barracks, expressing great surprise when he saw his first
bed there, which reminds me of the old Chinese lady who
visited a family that slept on beds. She kept falling out of hers.
Her subconscious mind had not learned the task of standing
guard for her during sleep. The edge of the bed is a mental
hazard which is unconsciously kept track of by the inner mind.
Almost every child has fallen out of bed a few times until its
subconscious mind became disciplined to the task of standing
guard. In the same way one can learn to adopt non-pressuring
postures during sleep, for the subconscious soon becomes
habituated to the new "rule."

But there was something about sleeping on the floor that
did not appeal to me. It was all right for Asia and Africa and

for physical culturists, but I visualized one of my friends whispering to another, "Rodale sleeps on the floor"—not to mention what the good wife would say out loud.

The idea of sleeping on a real hard surface would not leave my mind. I kept thinking about orthopedic mattresses and under-boards, going over their advantages and disadvantages. There was still too much "give" to them. In either case the springs were somewhat compressed by the weight of the body and, since they had nowhere to go, especially in the case of the board, their increased tension kept pushing upward against the sleeper.

The Floor Is Taken to the Bed

One day, an idea began to percolate. Why not put the board on top of the mattress instead of under it? I smiled. If I could do that, in effect, I would be taking the floor and putting it on top of the bed, thus sleeping on the "floor" but saving face—a sort of eating one's cake and having it too (although I never eat cake). This idea I liked, except that I did not relish sleeping on a plain board. I therefore figured that I would put a few blankets over it and sleep on the blankets.

I was weaving this idea in and out of my mind when one day I ran into Donald Goodman, of the Bethlehem Furniture Company, manufacturers of mattresses. By this time I had added something to my idea. "Donald," I said, "can you make a board, the size of my bed, with about three-fourths of an inch of soft material over it, and cover both board and material with something to hold them together?" When I explained the purpose of the idea he entered into the spirit of adventure of the thing with enthusiasm and agreed to make it. In a few days I was called to see the contraption. But when I beheld it I was both amazed and delighted. The plant superintendent, Ted Collins, fortunately was a perfectionist and was not satisfied with a mere board. He had made it more functional, at the same time creating an article of commerce that had selling appeal. What he showed me looked in all respects like a real mattress. Had he just made a board, he said, it would have jiggled around on top of the bed during sleep. What he did was to mount the board on top of a wooden frame, placing the three-fourths inch of soft material over the top of the thin board and encasing the whole device in an attractive, colorful mattress-covering material as shown in the illustration.

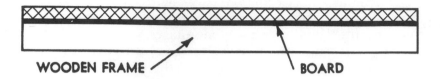

WOODEN FRAME   **BOARD**

For all practical purposes it looked like a regular type of mattress, although it was an inch or two lower. But it did not have a single spring in it. The under-inside merely contained reinforcing struts of wood, to prevent the top board from belly-ing downward.

I tried it out right in the factory. In fact we all took turns lying on it, and unanimously agreed that it wasn't any-where near as hard as we thought it would be. That night I slept upon it and must say that it gave me a fine night of rest. It seemed like the answer I had been seeking. It was as near perfection as I could ever hope to attain in a mattress. I tried it for a week, and when I was sure that I still was in love with it, I went to see Donald and told him that we had something we must share with the rest of the world.

A New Type Bed Is Born

Again Mr. Goodman entered into the proper spirit. He agreed to manufacture the new mattress, and asked me for my proposition. Personally, I told him, I did not wish to share monetarily in its manufacture. I gave the idea to him, lock, stock and barrel. I did not wish to be a sharer in a commercial project that had anything to do with health, vitamins, etc., as I did not want to become prejudiced in my writings. However, as a gentleman's agreement, there was a promise on his part to make occasional contributions out of his profits to the Soil and Health Foundation, of which I am president. This founda-tion, 99 per cent of whose income has been going as grants to universities, and whose charter prevents any officer from draw-ing a salary, is doing the spadework in research to show the dangers to human nutrition of using chemical fertilizers in growing our food crops. Its activities will soon be extended to take in general health research projects.

A patent is being taken out on the new mattress and an intensive sales campaign will be conducted on it all over the country. I am terrifically excited about this new development in sleeping. It could do a lot of good, and I would like to see the idea widely adopted.

Its Advantages

A few words more about the new mattress. I observed one marvelous hidden advantage in it. It is soft enough to prevent stagnation of the blood circulation, yet hard enough to offer a certain unlooked for benefit. The average person turns many times in sleep, sometimes 50 to 100 times or more in a night. A softer mattress takes much more energy to make each turn than a harder one, because the elbow digs down deeper, and it requires an effort to pull it out. It is like the difference between walking on a hard pavement or in very soft sand on an ocean beach. The hard surface of the new mattress provides a leverage which makes the turn easier. In this respect it causes a more restful sleep, because the turn can be made in a condition of semiconsciousness, whereas on a very soft mattress and especially in the case of a susceptible individual, the turns can cause complete awakenings in every instance. A friend with whom I discussed this idea mentioned the fact that his wife had recently undergone surgery performed on her heart and had been advised by her doctor, until it healed properly, to sleep on the hardest mattress she could obtain, for the very reason that it would be easier to make the turns without straining her heart. Our new type of mattress would be perfect for such cases.

Another unexpected advantage, a wonderful feature, is the eliminations of the little knots and indentations above each spring of the ordinary mattress. It has an absolutely straight, smooth top. There are no lumpy spots to bite into you, because there are no springs that require anchoring. You must sleep on such a surface to appreciate it. This top smoothness is the balancing feature that compensates for the loss of the springiness.

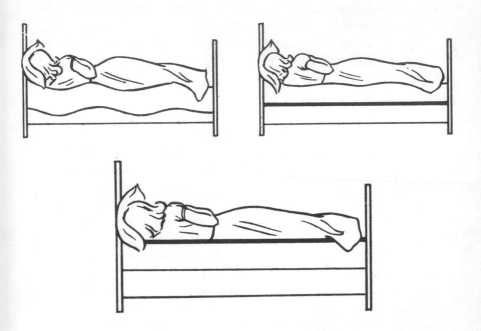

Life is a matter of habit. Sleeping on such a mattress takes a bit of doing, I will admit, but with a little perseverance you will master it, and gain a feeling that you are gradually rebuilding your back to what it was during your youth. The framework that God gave us should be carefully preserved. Wasn't it Thomas Edison who said, "The doctor of the future will give no medicine but will interest his patients in the care of the human frame?"

However, I wish to report one very serious drawback about this new mattress and it *is* serious. In a whole month of sleeping on it, it still holds good. You cannot *jump* into bed. I miss that. On the new mattress, I jumped into bed the first night, but never repeated the performance afterwards.

SECTION 36

TOOTHBRUSHING

We are against the use of toothpastes, as they contain harsh chemicals that are absorbed into the blood stream through the pores of the gums. Brush the teeth with plain water, 3 or 4 times a day, being sure to use a downward movement, starting from the gums for the upper teeth, and an upward movement for the lower teeth. It is desirable to stimulate the gums by the friction of the brush to prevent pyorrhea.

CHAPTER **125**

Daily Habits and Toothbrushing

Why do we get what dentists call "periodontal disease"— or disease of the gums? How does it happen that more teeth are lost from gum disease than from all other reasons combined? In recent years, the science of periodontistry has achieved ever greater importance. For many Americans, especially those who are past middle age, are faced with the prospect of losing all their teeth, not because of diseases of the teeth but because of unhealthful gums!

Dr. Sidney Sorrin, D.D.S., Associate Professor of Periodontia at the New York University College of Dentistry, has done excellent work in discovering and presenting to the dental profession many highly significant facts about the how and why of gum disease.

A List of Gum Disorder Causes

In an article in *The Journal of Dental Medicine* for January, 1955, Dr. Sorrin and his associate Dr. Marvin Simring list the possible causes of gum disorders. They may come under the heading of (1) functional—that is, how one's teeth perform their functions of biting and chewing. Teeth that are too big or too small for their supporting gum structure, teeth that do not meet properly in a "bite" so that much of the force of the bite is lost, teeth that are clenched or ground because of nervous habits are likely to be responsible for lots of gum trouble.

In addition, (2) irritants on the inside of the mouth may help to bring on gum disorders. Impaction of food, tartar on the teeth, mechanical irritants such as dentures that don't fit and hence rub against the gums, chemical irritants, atmospheric irritants (mouth breathing), improper toothbrushing—all these may help to bring on trouble with gums. Then, too, there are the possible systemic reasons—having to do solely with bodily health—faulty nutrition which may mean that the body is too acid or too alkaline, that there is vitamin or mineral deficiency or both; chronic diseases; gland disorders; anemias; allergies or sensitivity to drugs; pregnancy; psychological causes.

Vitamin C is the single most important food factor for gum health, vitamin A and vitamin B being almost as important, as well as calcium and the other minerals that are so necessary for bone health. (Much of our trouble with gums arises from the fact that jawbones disintegrate and wear away so that the whole mouth and tooth structure are thrown out of alignment. American diets are notoriously short on calcium, so necessary for healthy bone structure.)

A Case History

Here is one of Dr. Sorrin's case histories—a woman patient, aged 39, who came to him with an extremely bad case of gum disease. Her gums had receded and eroded, they bled at the slightest touch, and they were filled with pus. He tells us that this patient had always used an upward, downward and circular method of toothbrushing. She had the following abnormal habits: pencil biting, bobby-pin biting, bone chewing, hangnail biting, biting on nuts. Her diet was unbalanced, with large quantities of cake, pies, pastries and candies being eaten. She also told Dr. Sorrin that she had pains in her elbows and knees, slight heart trouble and used laxatives constantly. Furthermore, she had high blood sugar, low blood pressure and anemia. So it seems that her gum disorder sprang from completely inadequate diet, poor mouth hygiene, especially so far as toothbrushing was concerned and bad habits of which she was probably unaware but which apparently had a lot to do with the poor condition of her gums.

Toothbrushing and Malocclusion

In another chapter in this book we discuss toothbrushing, giving Dr. Sorrin's ideas as to exactly how the teeth should be brushed, if you want to avoid gum trouble. For cases of malocclusion—that is, where the "bite" is not right, your periodontist should be consulted. And incidentally, this is a job for a specialist, not your regular dentist. He can adjust dentures or plates, or he can grind certain teeth down so that your two jaws will be able to work efficiently together again.

As for the habits that can be so harmful to teeth, here is a list of the commonest ones. Check over it carefully. And better check with your family, too! Perhaps you actually do some of these things without being aware of it.

Habits That May Do Serious Damage

First of all, Dr. Sorrin cautions against the use of dental floss, saying that you may do far more harm than good by using it. You may defeat your own purpose by injuring the gums further. Dental floss should be used only by dentists, says Dr. Sorrin. Now check your score on these:

1. *Neurotic habits:* Lip-biting, cheek-biting, toothpick-biting, tongue pressure against teeth (that is, pressing or thrusting your tongue against your teeth), fingernail-biting, pencil- or pen-biting, biting on ear parts of eyeglasses, playing with bridges or dentures (slipping them nervously in and out of place) clenching teeth for control of emotions, biting on straws, matches, etc.

2. *Occupational habits:* Thread-biting, keeping pins or needles in the mouth, holding nails between teeth, cigar-biting (cigar workers may do this), using a reed in playing a musical instrument, any occupation in which the patient grinds his teeth in rhythm with the work at hand, package-wrappers who constantly keep cord between their teeth while packing parcels, stone-cutters, bricklayers, plasterers (dusts erode their teeth), bending wire with teeth while making artificial flowers, etc., etc., etc. Probably every manual occupation carries some risks if at any time you hold anything in your teeth while you are working.

3. *Miscellaneous habits* (and these are the ones most of us are guilty of): Pipe-smoking, biting on various objects such as safety pins and hair pins, biting or chewing a cigarette holder, opening tops of bottles with the teeth (yes, aparently there are some people who do!), cracking nuts or bones with teeth, chewing of cigars and/or tobacco, abnormal sleeping or reading habits (with the fingers pressed against the teeth), mouth breathing which dries out the mucus membrane in the front part of the mouth, pressure on the teeth from the hand when the head rests on the hand (how often do all of us do this, when we are sitting at a table!), thumb-sucking, chewing on one side of the mouth only (a very common habit), wedging of toothpicks between teeth, opening bobby pins with the teeth, biting the

end of a tobacco pouch string (where the individual closes the pouch by holding one end of the string in his mouth while he is rolling or filling his pipe).

How to Avoid These Habits

It seems surprising, doesn't it, that a learned dental researcher should have to take the time to point out in the pages of a learned dental magazine that such habits are harmful and very destructive to teeth and gums alike! Yet how often are any of us conscious of doing any of these things? How many of us had any idea of the harm they might do?

Dr. Sorrin says, to the dentists to whom he is addressing his remarks: "The eradication of an established habit is easier if the patient becomes conscious of the involuntary habit, realizes its harm and cooperates in its elimination by the exercise of will power or by the adoption of a harmless substitute. After the habit is discovered, the means of correction must then be determined. In some instances, for example, the teeth can be ground so that it will be impossible for the patient to resume the abnormal position of the teeth."

A word to the wise is sufficient. We are sure that readers will make every effort to correct habits such as these and will watch their children and other members of the family to make sure that such habits do not develop.

CHAPTER **126**

How to Brush Your Teeth

What is the best way to perform the daily ritual of brushing the teeth? Here are some ideas from an expert on the subject.

Fashions in toothbrushing come and go. We used to be told that we should brush our teeth straight across horizontally. We don't know who invented this method, but it seems apparent that it couldn't work, using the average toothbrush, because the brush would not be able to penetrate between the teeth where most of the food debris lodges.

Then came the advice to brush teeth up and down, vertically, so that the brush would get to all the cracks and crevices between the teeth. Then someone suggested brushing with a circular movement.

Dr. Sorrin, of whom we spoke earlier, has utmost confidence in a completely different method of toothbrushing, which at the same time massages the gums. Here is a complete review of the method which Dr. Sorrin advocates, along with pictures illustrating exactly how it is done:

First, the toothbrush should have a short working head, long stiff bristles and a long handle. See figure 1.

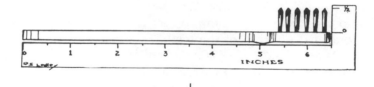

1

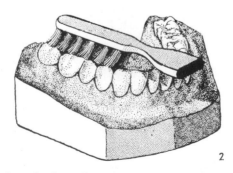

2

How to Brush the Chewing Surfaces. Before massaging the gums, clean the chewing surfaces of the teeth by scrubbing or pressing the points of the bristles into the grooves. This also serves to prepare the brush for gum massage. See figure 2. If you are using a plastic-bristle brush, the chewing surfaces should be cleaned after the gums are massaged.

Placing the Brush. Place the bristles of the brush flat against the teeth, the bristles being parallel to the teeth and pointing toward the gums. See figure 3. The bristles should cover the teeth and one-eighth inch of the gums. Point the bristles upward on the upper teeth and downward on the lowers. If the bristles are placed flat against the teeth with the flat of the brush handle and the base of the bristles against the chewing surfaces and the bristles pointed toward the gums, the brush will be in the correct position.

Pressing the brush. Turn the brush to an angle of 45 degrees by twisting the handle until the outer row of bristles touches the gums, producing just enough pressure to bend the bristles. See figure 4. Your gums should blanch slightly (that is, turn a little pale) at the pressure, for the blood is driven out of them.

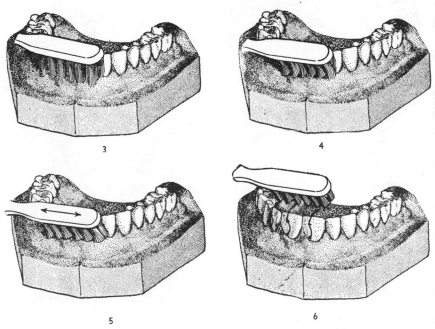

3

4

5

6

Pumping the brush. The handle of the brush is moved from side to side causing the bristles to bend, *but not to move from their original position.* The movement is taken up by the sway in the bristles only. See figure 5.

Pulling the brush. Continuing this movement, gradually draw the brush toward the chewing surfaces of the teeth. Repeat 4 times in the same area. Then move to a new area until all the teeth have been brushed. Overlap some teeth in each area. See figure 6.

In figures 7, 8, 9 and 10 you will see how these movements of the brush are carried out in brushing the inner side of the upper teeth.

In figures 11, 12, 13 and 14 you will see how to brush the outer surfaces of the lower teeth and in figures 15, 16, 17 and 18 the inner surfaces of the lower teeth.

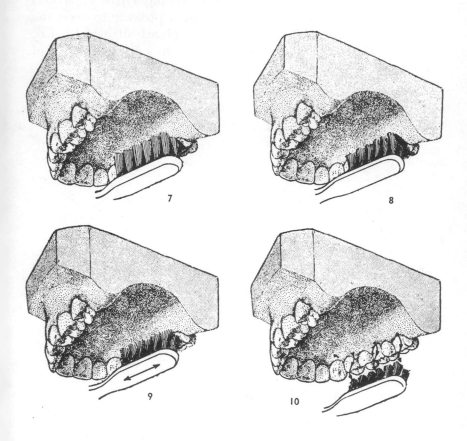

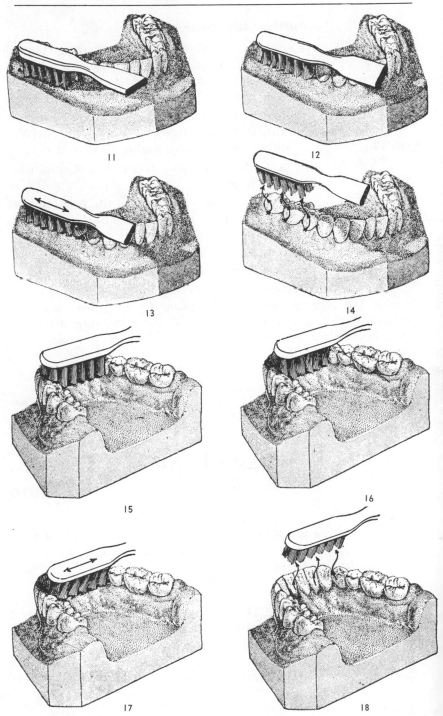

Further Directions to Observe

1. Always start with a thoroughly dry brush. Have 3 brushes in use at all times. Allow each to dry 24 hours before using it again. Hang the toothbrush where it can dry. Do not keep it in a closed container.

2. Discard the brush when the bristles become too soft (usually 2 to 3 months). Rinse brushes carefully. The bristles will harbor germs unless they are thoroughly clean and dry.

3. When you are brushing your teeth, do not start with the brush too high on the gums.

4. Do not scrub the gums. The ends of the bristles must not move from their original position when the brush is pumped.

5. When you brush the front of the lower front teeth, hold your lip away to prevent injury to it.

6. Should any sore spots develop, you are brushing incorrectly. Go over the instructions again. If your gums have been bleeding, they may continue to do so for a few days after you first begin your brushing program.

CHAPTER **127**

Toothpaste Is Nothing But . . . Ballyhoo

Why waste money on toothpaste? Everyone who knows anything about the subject agrees that it does no good and may do considerable harm.

The American Dental Association has finally asked Congress for a law which would forbid toothpaste advertising which is misleading and detrimental to the public. At hearings before the House Committee on Legal and Monetary Affairs, a member of the ADA council on legislation said that there is no reason why toothpaste manufacturers should not be required to prove the statements they make about their products.

Chief targets of attack were these 3 claims: stopping tooth decay, ending "bad breath" and once-a-day brushing. Said the ADA spokesman, there is no toothpaste that stops decay or bad breath and the latter may be the symptom of some serious disorder which should be cared for before it gets worse. As for once-a-day brushing, dental hygienists for years have been trying to persuade people to brush their teeth after every meal. The current advertising is undoing most of the good work that has been done in this campaign.

Many readers don't need to be told that toothpastes do nothing beneficial for your teeth and, in fact, can do them harm. But we still get letters from new readers asking what kind of toothpaste they should use and insisting that they must use one or another, because, they say, no one can even feel clean unless he uses lots of toothpaste.

Why the Toothpaste Industry Has Grown

Since the nineteen twenties, the toothpaste industry has been built into a near-two-hundred-million dollar business (in 1954). This has been accomplished with ballyhoo and nothing else. A long succession of "miracle ingredients" have been foisted on the American public, advertising with all the power of TV shows, movie-star endorsements and finally, of course, pictures of the heroic man in white, standing (in the ads) beside his dental chair and drill, pleading with the public to use Glossydent brand of toothpaste and prevent decay.

The fact seems to have escaped this noble fellow that, if the public believes his words, buys his toothpaste and really does prevent decay, he and all his colleagues will be out of jobs. Of course, the white-coated dentist in the ads is a photographer's model and, of course, nobody believes what he says about preventing decay or curing bad breath. Yet, such is the hypnotic power of advertising, that almost everybody goes right on buying toothpaste.

In the 1920's you were urged to prevent "detoxification," whatever that is! A few years later they were selling toothpaste composed of synthetic saliva! Honest! During the 30's you could buy toothpaste to remove stain, to prevent pink toothbrush, to neutralize acidity by "releasing lime and water."

In the 40's the hullaballo got noisier. Ammonia was discovered to be the final cure-all and almost everybody started to use ammoniated toothpaste. In 1951 we discovered chlorophyll—that excellent green coloring matter which exists in most living plants. There's nothing wrong with chlorophyll, surely, and the effectiveness of many green-colored foods is undoubtedly due in part to this natural dye. But there is little evidence anywhere that chlorophyll is going to stop tooth decay or do any of the other fantastic jobs promised for it, in the ads. Yet before the chlorophyll boom was over, one-third of all toothpaste customers were buying chlorophyll products.

Anti-Enzyme and Fluoride Toothpastes

The next miracle ingredient was the anti-enzyme. Nobody, including the ad writers, was very sure just what an enzyme was, but it must be something bad, because somebody had decided that an anti-enzyme was just what was needed to prevent decay. And off we went on another buying spree which, in this case, is still with us. Except that fluoride toothpaste may soon crowd out the anti-enzymes, because, as everybody knows by now, the United States Public Health Service itself in its grand push for water fluoridation has decided that fluorides are absolutely necessary for tooth health. And it is only a hop, skip and jump from there to a fluoride-containing toothpaste, guaranteed to stop decay in its tracks. Featured in ads for this wonder-working dentifrice are boys and girls drinking water and the subtle suggestion is that fluorides in toothpaste are as effective as fluorides in drinking water for decay prevention.

And maybe they are, for there are serious doubts in the minds of many medical men and statisticians as well, as to whether water fluoridation does anything but postpone decay for a few years if, indeed, it does even that. Suffice it to say that there is little or no research showing that fluorides in toothpaste can be anything but the deadly poison they are.

Miracle Ingredients Boost Sales

Newest in the picture are the antibiotic toothpastes. These must be obtained by prescription, and we cannot imagine why anybody would take the chance that is involved in using one of these. Pick up any of the trade magazines and you will easily see at a glance why the boom in toothpastes goes on. There's money in it! So long as people can be persuaded to buy one or another of the miracle-ingredient pastes, in spite of everything they read which assures them toothpaste cannot possibly help their teeth, just so long will the drug companies and the soap companies go on raking in their millions.

In 1953, *Chemical Week* published a letter from a reader who accused its editors of being a bit less than enthusiastic about anti-enzyme toothpaste . . . "If additives and formulations can be developed to boost sales it is good for everyone . . . Let's forget about whether any particular toothpaste is good or bad . . . You, in some stuffy and unprogressive fashion, seem to prefer that everyone should stick to eating apples."

So you see the people who make toothpastes know as well as everybody else that nothing they say in their ads is true. But they think they are perfectly justified in going right on collecting money from the public for a worthless product.

Do Any Toothpastes Help?

What is the true story about the tooth-decay-preventing properties of toothpaste—any toothpaste? In 3 words, there aren't any. And every test that's been made shows conclusively that people who brush their teeth every time they eat tend to have less decay than people who don't. And it doesn't matter whether your toothbrush is covered with stripes or mint-tasting goo or just plain water. Brushing your teeth helps to remove particles of food that cling to them. If you eat refined carbohydrates—sticky, gummy foods that tend to cling to teeth— then brushing after every meal becomes even more important. Eating an apple after every meal will get the same results as brushing.

They Can Do Harm

Granted that no toothpaste can do your mouth one whit of good, is it possible that they might do harm? It is indeed, and there are plenty of instances of harm related in the medical journals. For instance, cinnamon oil in one toothpaste caused canker sores about the mouth of a patient who had been using a certain toothpaste. And in case you're wondering what a perfectly natural product like cinnamon oil was doing in a toothpaste, apparently it was flavoring it. The other ingredients in this particular toothpaste were as follows: calcium phosphate, urea, glycerin, sorbitol, dichlorodihydroxydiphenylmethane (the technical name for hexachlorophene), a detergent solution, diammonium phosphate, carboxymethylcellulose, anise oil, peppermint oil and methyl salicylate. Doesn't it sound inviting? Why should any health-conscious person fill his mouth several times a day with such a welter of chemicals?

Anti-enzyme toothpastes have caused difficulties among several readers who have written to us about them. An article in *The Armed Forces Medical Journal* for July, 1955, tells us, "Physicians and dentists are encountering a new oral lesion since anti-enzymes have been added to dentifrices . . . irritating, painful mouth and a tingling tongue." It is possible, the article goes on to say, that neutralizing naturally occurring enzymes is just about the worst thing you can do, for you destroy at the same time enzymes absolutely necessary for mouth health and produce a condition which causes a degeneration of the cells of the lining of the mouth.

Incidentally, it is well known that fluorides destroy enzymes. Your children may be interested in the new striped toothpaste which sends colors ribboning down their toothbrushes when they squeeze the tube. Let us remind you that dyes are mentioned more often than any other chemical in connection with cancer and other harmful aftereffects.

Toothpaste Can Cause Tooth Decay

Finally, we have an article from the *New York Dental Journal* for April, 1956, in which Albert Schatz, Joseph J. Martin, Karl E. Karlson and Vivian Schatz show that dentifrices *can lead to tooth decay*. Experiments performed by these researchers showed that water soluble contents of toothpastes can be used by organisms which digest keratin, one of the substances in teeth. The value of alkalinity, ammonia and urea in dentifrices is questioned, say these authors, because these very factors have been shown to make the enamel organic matrix more susceptible to attack by oral bacteria.

Finally, doesn't it seem reasonable that fair amounts of chemicals from toothpastes penetrate the gum tissue and enter the blood? Do, by all means, stop using toothpastes, if you still do. You'll be surprised at how much cleaner and fresher your mouth feels.

SECTION 37

PULSE

You can test by taking your pulse which foods are good for you and which you may be allergic to. Eat each food individually, taking your pulse one-half hour before eating and every one-half hour thereafter for several hours. If your pulse goes up, this is an indication that the food is not good for you. Test other foods in the same way, finally making up your meals of only those foods that do not raise your pulse. The method is described in The Pulse Test, *by Arthur Coca, M.D., available from Lyle Stuart, 241 Sixth Avenue, New York, New York.*

CHAPTER **128**

Pulse

by J. I. RODALE

My 64 page book called *This Pace Is Not Killing Us* is based on a series of articles by the same title that appeared in PREVENTION, but with much additional data. The main contention of the book is that not only are we *not* traveling at a faster pace, but that it is not the pace that kills. In fact, I showed that the reverse was true. Most heart cases die because of a killing inactivity. Their hearts cannot take such indolence.

When the book was completed, I realized that I was the worst offender in regard to what I had written. I was the most typical example of the sedentary businessman that I had been so loudly censuring. Being over 50 and a heart case, I can now see from what I have learned about the evils of inactivity, that unless I change my way of life I am in for consequences. Only 10 months ago I was turned down for life insurance. When I walk upgrade, there comes a feeling of pressure in the chest region. It is difficult to pin down the exact nature of my condition. The doctors seem to be vague about it. One of them called it coronary sclerosis.

So there I was, the author of a book proclaiming that lack of movement is a cause of heart disease while I kept sitting in cushioned comfort. This will never do, I said. After all, even in the irresponsibilities and impracticalities of authorship there is a limit! To regain my self-esteem, I would have to take a dose of my own medicine.

Effect of Walking on My Pulse

So I began to walk—10 minutes the first few days, then 15 and in about a week I was doing a full hour every morning, covering about 2 or 3 miles—briskly. One day, as I heard my heart pounding, I decided to stop and take my pulse. To my surprise I found it to be 112. At rest it was usually between 76 and 80. Walking, therefore, had upped it about 35 beats a minute.

Thinking that danger might be concealed somewhere in this fact, I decided from this point on to keep a record of my pulse during these walks. I did it scientifically, that is, I took it 11 times each day, at exact predetermined spots, so that the comparative daily record would mean something. Each day I added up the 11 figures and divided by 11. Here are the average daily pulse results for the 7 weeks of record keeping:

July 12 ..... 95.6	July 29 ..... 87.0	Aug. 15 ..... 86.0
July 13 .....101.0	July 30 ..... 89.8	Aug. 16 ..... 86.3
July 14 ..... 97.5	July 31 ..... 92.3	Aug. 17 ..... 84.8
July 15 ..... 98.5	Aug. 1 ..... 95.5	Aug. 18 ..... 91.4
July 16 ..... 94.1	Aug. 2 ..... 95.1	Aug. 19 ..... 90.7
July 17 ..... 94.8	Aug. 3	Aug. 20 ..... 96.7
July 18 ..... 96.1	Aug. 4 ..... 95.2	Aug. 21 ..... 90.0
July 19 ..... 96.7	Aug. 5 ..... 94.5	Aug. 22 ..... 85.4
July 20 ..... 97.7	Aug. 6 ..... 93.1	Aug. 23 ..... 83.6
July 21 ..... 96.1	Aug. 7 ..... 90.9	Aug. 24 ..... 85.1
July 22 ..... 96.3	Aug. 8 ..... 87.4	Aug. 25 ....
July 23 ..... 93.3	Aug. 9	Aug. 26 ..... 83.4
July 24 ..... 93.6	Aug. 10 ..... 87.3	Aug. 27 ..... 84.7
July 25 ..... 94.4	Aug. 11 ..... 86.7	Aug. 28 ..... 82.7
July 26	Aug. 12 ..... 87.5	Aug. 29 ..... 81.3
July 27 ..... 93.8	Aug. 13	Aug. 30 ..... 80.7
July 28 ..... 94.4	Aug. 14 ..... 86.6	

For those who do not like to analyze figures, I have made a chart. Note the remarkable reduction in the last few readings. To me this is nothing short of miraculous. After only 6 weeks, I can walk an hour with my pulse about 10 beats per minute less than its high at the beginning of this period. I am also certain that as more time elapses, there will be much more improvement. I will be able to subject my heart to this hour of exercise with a much lower rise in its pulse action.

I can also say that after the second week I began to finish off the walk with a wonderful feeling of euphoria, with no pounding of the heart. I would feel thoroughly relaxed with no suffering of fatigue or exhaustion.

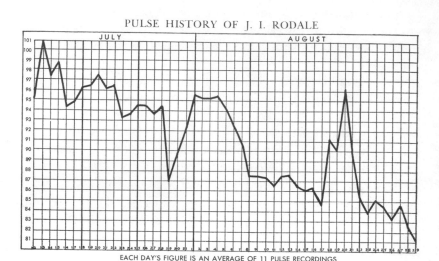

PULSE HISTORY OF J. I. RODALE

EACH DAY'S FIGURE IS AN AVERAGE OF 11 PULSE RECORDINGS

How to Take Pulse

A word about the method of taking my pulse. When I stop, I wait about 20 seconds, and then count the beats of my heart as I note the ticking off of 30 seconds by the watch. I then take the count of the next 30 seconds and that is the one I record. This, of course, is then multiplied by two. It is best to plan a walking course which has a few upgrades in it. I stop for a rest of about a half minute to a minute halfway between each pulse recording stop, thus making about 20 stops in all. However, if I experience any pressure symptoms, I will stop for a moment wherever necessary. Remember, I am still a heart case.

Symptoms Disappear

The most unusual thing of all is that in the last 6 days my chest pressure symptoms have all but disappeared. For the first 5 weeks or so I continued to experience these symptoms— more on some days, and less on others, but I felt them only in the first 15 minutes of walking, as this part of the walk contains several upgrades. After this first quarter of an hour, I could make the other hills with rarely a pressure pain. Evidently by this time the body had become thoroughly oxygenated, and the physical exercise had caused the blood to flow more vigorously through the coronary arteries.

But, in the last 6 days there have been practically no pressure symptoms even during the first 15 minutes, and you can imagine how I feel about it. It will be sensational if this keeps up. If I never again experience the pressure pains on movement of any kind, it would be stupendous! And, of course, it would add to my life. Is it possible that I will be absolutely cured? I cannot believe it, but will continue with this experiment. As long as I am physically able, and the elements permit, I will walk my brisk hour and more every day.

Chest Pains and Pulse

It is interesting to study the chart and to note the successive waves, each one going lower than its predecessor. With regard to the sudden leap upwards of August 18, 19, 20, I have a theory. In order to explain it, may I say that during all these walks I found no direct relationship between the experiencing of a chest pressure symptom and the pulse at that moment. I could have a low pulse when there was a chest pain, and a high pulse when there was none, or vice versa. Now, it was beginning with the morning of August 17, the start of the period of the banishment of heart pressure symptoms, that my pulse suddenly began to shoot upwards. For 3 days it kept leaping. This set me to wondering. What could be the reason for it? I have come up with a possible explanation, although I know that it is rank theory. But it is worth while talking about it.

As my walks progressed, from day to day, there occurred a reduction in the pulse, and a development gradually of a sense of well-being towards the end of each walk. This indicated possibly that the flabbiness of the heart was turning into muscle. But there was still something wrong either with the heart, or the arteries leading in and out of it, that gave me the pains during the first 15 minutes of walking each day. Then these practically disappeared, and at the same time there was a sizable increase in the pulse. Does this indicate a second step in the rebuilding process? Have the heart muscles become so strong that they can do some function that they could not do before? Have they been able to close some kind of gap? Have they engaged in some additional physical building of something in the heart, an action which required the help of the whole heart to pump more blood for its accomplishment? Such a project would definitely raise the pulse.

Then the thing is done. The heart goes back to its previous pace. It goes down as precipitately as it went up. Is this fantastic reasoning? Perhaps. But it will have to do until someone works out a better reason. Perhaps it was not the heart alone. Is it possible that my lungs were strengthening themselves, being able to perform more efficiently so as to give more oxygen to the heart with less physical action of taking breaths? Is it possible that on August 17 something physical happened with regard to my lungs, something that knitted together, something in which the heart had to take part by furnishing more blood for the building?

It is interesting to be aware that when a man-made machine has to be fixed, it must stop working and outside forces do the job. But the heart performs the job of reconstruction itself and at the same time it pumps blood to the rest of the organs of the body.

One more observation. Beginning a few days ago, I noticed that the pulse during the second half minute of its taking goes down more than it used to. Before this, the pulse in the second period would be almost as high as that of the first. It indicates a newly acquired ability of the heart to snap back to normal after exertion. Another thing. I note that I breathe better while working at my desk.

Vitamin E and Perspiration Aid Heart

I also wish to say that I can recommend the taking of vitamin E, based on a 4 year detailed study of conservative medical researches regarding it. If you are interested, read *Alpha Tocopherol (Vitamin E) in Cardiovascular Disease,* by Drs. W. E. Shute and E. V. Shute, Ryerson Press, Toronto, Canada, $7.00. This is a scientifically documented book of 236 pages which proves conclusively that vitamin E is a specific for practically all heart cases. Like exercise, it oxygenates the tissues, and I have taken this vitamin in big doses for over 10 years. The trouble with the average heart case no doubt is a stagnation within the body, a lack of circulating oxygen, due to a sedentary life.

During my daily walk, I perspire profusely. Perspiration is one means the body employs to get rid of toxins, or poisons. Is it possible that such poisons, remaining in the body because of a sedentary daily regimen, make the heart work harder to rid the body of them through other means and channels?

Is it also possible that these toxins by remaining in the body and distorting the blood chemistry on a permanent, continuing basis, further interfere with various internal processes, which throw additional strain onto the heart, thus forcing it to pump more rapidly in an attempt to reduce the condition?

There must be a reason why my pulse is going down, and I choose to think that a good sweat-out each day is part of it. By the sweat of thy brow shalt thou earn thy daily bread. Is this why farm workers are far less subject to heart disease than office-inhabiting men? Of course, they exercise more, but I think it is the combination of the two. Exercise breaks down old cells, causing new ones to form. It gives rise to an increase in the blood-flow. Breathing is extended, and body functions stimulated. Muscles are kept in good repair, and their "tone" improved. There is a great improvement in the coordination of muscles and nerves. The circulation and elimination processes of the body are stimulated.

Reduction of Pulse Rate Means Longer Life

The late Dr. Raymond Pearl of Johns Hopkins University, who studied the pulse records of thousands of individuals who died young, found that on the average their pulse rates were higher than normal. In the *Journal of the American Medical Association* of August 7, 1954 (Drs. Hammond and Horn) appears the following: "A Study Conducted by the Society of Actuaries revealed that, among persons with a high pulse rate, the number of deaths from cancer was about 60 per cent above the expected amount."

If you want to see an example of a heart shouting for help, examine my pulse readings for July 12, 13 and 14. A few weeks later I am able to do the same walk without the pulse once going over 100. It now looks as if it will be kept below 90 within a week or two. An hour a day of walking exercise must be a remarkable tonic to the body. I believe it is better than playing golf once or twice a week.

I was surprised, on August 1, 1954, to read in the Sunday *New York Times* magazine section that Roger Bannister, outstanding mile-runner who broke many records, was able to do so by a method he used of reducing his pulse. "By making his heart a more muscular pump, he was able to reduce his pulse beat from its original 72 in repose to below 50," says this magazine.

By making his heart a more muscular pump! That must be what I am doing to mine.

Incidentally, my doctor, who examines my heart action and blood pressure once and sometimes twice a week, is quite satisfied with what he observes. Action is definitely improved, and my heart murmur is all but eliminated. Blood pressure which, when I began was about 135/85, recently came down to 120/70, a figure which is well nigh perfect for any age, and which I never had before that I can remember.

Should All Heart Cases Follow My Example?

Not every heart case will be permitted to do what I have done. The physician must be the judge. Mine may be the ideal form of heart disease for this method of treatment. But there are more serious cases, and I would urge extreme caution. There are leaking hearts and oversized hearts. There are hearts damaged in various ways, and some that have had thrombosis, or blood clots. These people must depend on their physicians for guidance. I will say, however, that many individuals who have been suffering from a variety of heart ills and who have been immobilized, should have been set moving and walking as soon as possible. I further believe that vitamin E can be a great insurance against a heart attack during these walks, but within the medical profession this is a subject of violent controversy. Why? I cannot understand.

What I have thus far done for my heart has two implications—one, I have built up the heart muscle—that is, improved the heart itself. Two, I have induced a condition in which the body can exercise with less effort, with less pumping on the part of the heart. Eventually, this walking may greatly reduce my "at rest" pulse. The other day I ran after a bus and was able to do it with the greatest of ease. There was no aftermath of pounding, nor the feeling that I might get a heart attack.

Food and Exercise Affect the Pulse

One more thing about the pulse: What we eat affects it. Dr. Coca of Oradell, New Jersey has worked out a whole science about it, and a few years ago, following his ideas and checking the effect of each food individually on my pulse, I discovered

6 that were causing my heart to pump more whenever they entered my stomach. By eliminating them I was able to get my pulse at repose from about 86 to 76. By combining both methods, that is, diet as well as exercise, phenomenal reductions in the pulse rate could be brought about.

A few days ago I made a startling observation. My first heart symptoms had appeared in 1937, but it was in 1949 that they became really temperamental and troublesome. It was then that I increased my vitamin E dosage astronomically in order to relieve the chest pressure symptoms. I now know the reason why. A friend and I used to go on hikes, sometimes for 8 or 9 miles. It was in 1949 that he moved to Philadelphia, and from then on I fell into a most sedentary routine—no long walks; and my heart rebelled.

I was told recently of a man who for 40 years was a track-walker for a railroad. For 8 hours each day he walked the tracks to check for imperfections. A few years ago he retired and said, "Now I will rest." He then sat on his porch all day long. He was a healthy man, but within a year they laid him away to eternal rest. He had a heart attack. His heart could not stand the killing inactivity.

I look forward to these daily walking periods. It has become a time for thinking. One day when it rained and I could not walk, I felt depressed about it all day, so that on a later day of inclement weather I went for my walk with an umbrella. It was a little difficult taking my pulse and holding the umbrella at the same time, but the actual readings were lower than for the previous day.

CHAPTER **129**

Food and the Pulse

by J. I. RODALE

Did you know you can discover what your allergies are by taking your pulse? This chapter introduces you to this fascinating subject.

A book called *Familial Nonreaginic Food-Allergy* written by Arthur F. Coca, M.D., which was published by Charles C. Thomas Company of Springfield, Illinois, is an extremely technical piece of work and is not suggested for the average layman. It describes a method of reducing the pulse by eliminating foods to which a person is allergic. However, it does not do it by the usual needle-skin-scratch system. With the method outlined I was able to reduce my pulse from about 86 to about 76.

In following the system, you choose a time about an hour and a half after you have eaten and eat a small portion of one food that you wish to test, taking your pulse immediately before the test. You then take your pulse a half hour later, and again a half hour after that, recording the figures in a ruled blank book, with the date, time, etc., and leaving room for a list of the food eaten, and other comments. It will become a valuable record for later study. If the figures are kept on pieces of paper, it is easy for them to get lost.

It is best to take your pulse-reading at the wrist using the two fingers. Never use your thumb because it has its own pulse.

I found that the average food raised the pulse from 3 to 5 points per minute, although there were some that did not raise it at all, but that when a food caused the pulse to run up 8 or 9 points, it was one of the allergy-causing ones. In my own case I had a high pulse, but no apparent allergies. Through years of study and analysis of my condition, I was able to become so healthy that I no longer suffered from headaches or colds, and my blood pressure had gone down more or less to near normal, but it still was worth while to reduce my pulse.

How Some Foods Affect the Pulse

I discovered that figs, honeydew melon, whole wheat and fried foods of any kind were the basic trouble-makers. It was absolutely fascinating running them down. For example, at first the indication showed that chicken raised my pulse unduly. But after I had accumulated sufficient records, showing in each case whether the chicken had been fried or broiled, I found that my pulse went up only when I ate fried chicken. I could eat broiled chicken without any trouble at all.

In the case of wheat I made a rather thorough study. I found that whole wheat bread raised my pulse, but white bread did not. I could also eat wheat germ, which is present in whole wheat and not in white bread, without having the pulse go up. I therefore concluded that it was the bran that was difficult for my stomach to handle. This would indicate that, for me, the best kind of bread would be one with everything in it but the bran—a branless whole wheat bread. However, I found that I could eat raw wheat without raising the pulse.

French fried potatoes would send my pulse up, but not mashed or baked with the skins. It was the oil used in frying that I seemed to have a difficulty in handling. I could eat cantaloupe but not honeydew, and regarding figs, I used to eat them by the pound. No wonder my pulse had been around 85 and sometimes 95. (Note: A few weeks ago I checked my pulse again on figs and found that now I could eat them without raising it. It may indicate a gradual strengthening of the body.)

I found that coffee did not raise my pulse even a point, and was surprised. I am not a regular drinker of alcoholic beverages but, just to test, I drank some scotch and soda and beer, and was amazed to find that such drinks also kept the pulse down.

Regarding coffee, I discovered that the way we made it, in glass, it did not raise my pulse, but if boiled in an aluminum utensil, it *did* raise it unduly. In this respect, I would like to mention the fact that Dr. Coca, in the book which I have mentioned, cites the cases of 6 patients whose pulses were raised by eating foods cooked in aluminum pots. Coca says, "Vaughan in his *Practice of Allergy,* p. 831, mentions 'the cure of cases of long-standing refractory colitis following change from aluminum cooking utensils to enamel or glass vessels.' "

What About a Vegetarian Diet?

Since there seems to be such a strong vegetarian movement and at times I have been tempted to try a vegetarian diet, I made sure to observe carefully the effect of meats on my pulse. In no case were they unfavorable. In other words, in my stomach, meat is digested very easily. It is a known medical fact, incidentally, that meat does not have to be chewed much. It is the carbohydrates that need lots of work in the mouth. Bear in mind, however, that these idiosyncrasies with regard to food vary with different persons. I may have an allergy to honeydew, for example, while you might eat it with impunity. So it is important that you check your own case thoroughly.

What Does a Reduction of Pulse Mean?

It is terrific in its implications when one considers what a reduction of the pulse actually means. In my own case the pulse was reduced by 15 points per minute. This means that every hour my pulse beat 60 x 15 or 900 times less. And in a full 24 hour day my heart had to expand and contract 900 x 24 less times or 21,600 less times a day. Merely by eliminating a few foods that I can easily get along without, my heart saves 43,200 movements in only one day. This is 21,600 expansions and 21,600 contractions. The heart actually moves between one and two inches each time in such expansion and contraction. Can you visualize this? Try and open and close your fist 21,600 times, moving it each time from one to two inches.

This means a saving of 15,768,000 movements a year for my little old heart. Is it any wonder that Dr. Raymond Pearl found that people who die young on the average have high pulses?

It certainly will pay everyone who reads this to check his or her pulse immediately, and if it is above 75 to try to discover what is raising it. In Coca's work he is able to bring patients' pulses down to as low as 65.

If you do decide to study your pulse, my suggestion is to note down the record of your pulse before and after each meal (one-half hour and one hour after) for about one week so that you can have something to shoot at. After you have found the 5 or 6 offending foods that have been playing havoc with your pulse, you will note the effect of their elimination on the pulse recordings after full meals.

A Personal Experience

In my own case I had one extremely interesting experience which is worth telling. Several times, my pulse went up after a meal more than it should have according to what I ate, and after thinking about it, I discovered that at those meals I had forgotten to take my vitamins. I then proceeded to check on it by alternately taking my vitamins and leaving them out after meals, and it worked every time. It would indicate that the vitamins I was taking were aiding my digestion. This also shows that it was best for me to take my vitamins at my meals. I checked the effect of each vitamin separately. Some worked and others did not. But bone meal worked every time in keeping the pulse down. It would be interesting to have readers experiment on this phase of pulse checking.

In his book Coca describes symptoms which disappeared by lowering the pulse, in conditions of migraine, fatigue, nervousness, indigestion, dizziness, constipation, neuralgia, canker sores, chronic rhinitis, heartburn, urticaria, epileptic seizures, overweight, psychic depression, asthma and many others. It looks to me as if here we have a method that may revolutionize our entire conception of health and disease. Physicians should get a copy of Dr. Coca's work which is now in a new edition.

In Connection with the Heart

Shall we do away with labor-saving devices and the automobile? No! But let us keep moving as much as possible during our leisure hours. Let us form hiking groups for young and old.

Regarding vegetarians—many of them live long, and I believe it is because they are generally health-conscious. A great many vegetarians are physical culturists, and know the value of exercise and walking. Witness the fantastic activities of Bernarr MacFadden who lived to be way above 80.

I knew a vegetarian who lived to be 94. He would have lived to be 100 if he hadn't fallen out of a nut tree that he was pruning at the age of 92. He came to see me about 5 years ago and explained the value of his diet which was practically limited to fruits and nuts, but I believe it was his keeping on the move which was an important part of his formula for long living.

At the time of his visit to my farm he was 90 and spent most of his time prowling about the fields. He was more active than a barrel of monkeys, and if it had been pruning time, he would have "done" all our trees. I have to smile now when I recall him, but I was blind at the time, being an enemy to all forms of exercise. However, it is not too late.

Thus far I have stressed nutrition and physical movement. If we wish to live to be 90 or more, I believe there should be added one more plank in the platform—something spiritual. Without it, not only would it be difficult to attain to a nonagenarian state, but you wouldn't want to. It would be boring. There must be a belief in the idealistic way, a tolerance toward your fellow man, a lightness of spirit, a strong belief in God, and a sense of humor. Given nutrition, movement and spirit, there would be far less of disease and far more of life.

My final advice to all—keep moving, but stay out of trees after you are 90.

CHAPTER **130**

The Pulse Test

by ARTHUR F. COCA, M.D.

Some thoughts by Dr. Coca on the subject of his pulse test technique follow in this chapter.

Notwithstanding the opposition of the organized medical profession to the scientifically based principles and practice of the pulse-dietary method of examination, the practical use of that method under the convenient name of "The Pulse-Test" has gradually extended among the laity and physicians through the past 20 odd years.

After a number of scientific reports on the subject had been rejected by leading medical journals, I came reluctantly to the decision to risk my hard-earned reputation as a scientific investigator by offering a popular version of the new method to the "public."

Fortune (or Providence) favored my search for a publisher. In fact, I didn't have to search for him at all—he happened to me through the mere circumstance that his wife had attended my 4 lectures on the subject at The New School for Social Research in New York. And so in October, 1956, Lyle Stuart published the first printing of "The Pulse-Test."

I wish to devote the major part of the space allotted to this article to a consideration of the paramount importance of the preventive application of the pulse-test in children.

Illustrative Cases

First, I shall describe some illustrative cases.

Various behavioral abnormalities have been shown to be allergic by Dr. Susan Dees at Duke University and by Dr. Hal C. Davison, the distinguished Atlanta internist and allergist. I have seen two such cases, boys of 3 and 11 years, that were definitely "problem children." The younger boy was in some danger of losing his sight from chronic inflammation, and he also had an itching eczema. A mild nerve operation followed by the pulse-testing resulted in complete cure of the eczema and the inflammation and a disappearance of his intractable behavior. The older boy had the same treatment and immediately was relieved of his stammering with facial twitching and became an "honor" student in school.

Two boys of 9 years in different families were failing in their school work; both inattentive, sleepy. Both were completely normal and alert after the nerve-operation and pulse-testing.

Allergies May Cause Juvenile Delinquency

These experiences inevitably suggest that the most serious behavioral abnormality of the young—juvenile delinquency —may also be a manifestation of the newly defined allergy; and there seems to be no reasonable difficulty nor objection to the

study of that dangerous group with the pulse-dietary principles
and technics as described in *The Pulse Test*.

It would be a most gratifying outcome of this article if
some open-minded reader could and would persuade those in
institutional charge of juvenile delinquents to give those marked
youngsters the sporting chance of rehabilitation through this
new method.

Arthur P. Locke, long experienced in biological research,
has given us the, till now, almost entirely neglected means of
demonstrating the allergic nature of a particular manifestation.
In a large-scale inquiry concerning the common cold, Dr.
Locke had found that only about 5 per cent of unselected white
persons are free from the allergy that affects the pulse. That
is a small number but it can be sufficient for large-scale statis-
tical investigation. For example:

Shows Cause of Juvenile Delinquency

According to Locke's convincing figures, a simple examination of 500 unselected high school students will reveal
about 25 students who never have headaches, nor indigestion,
nor any of the many other allergic symptoms, who never have
colds and whose brothers and sisters and parents are similarly
unaffected.

If, then, 500 juvenile delinquents are similarly examined and if not a single one is found who is unaffected by
the "pulse-test allergy," then juvenile delinquency must be a
manifestation of that allergy.

Having in this way established the *cause* of juvenile
delinquency, we shall have next to apply the technic-of-preven-
tion with the pulse-dietary method which has been found so
brilliantly effective in all the other studied manifestations of
this newly discovered kind of allergy—excepting *dementia praecox,* a form of insanity. We may consider the possibility that
even dementia praecox can be prevented if the pulse-dietary
method is applied *before* the arrival of that hopeless manifestation; that is, in young school-age children.

One day the pulse-test will be made a part of the regular
public school curriculum, to the great benefit of the students'
average school-record and athletic abilities. And so, by this
preventive course, the tendency of some to delinquency will
most probably be forestalled.

Prevention of the manifestations of the pulse-affecting allergy through the pulse-test will add an average of more than 20 years to our fully functioning lives, which will be free from the common disabilities of "old-age."

The total neglect, not to mention the truly more reprehensible attitude, of the medical and public-health authorities with respect to the new science of disease-prevention is indirectly responsible for the incalculable loss of the sometimes unique service of our leaders in industry, in the arts and sciences and in national and local government.

Is Caution Advisable?

Caution has its place in the acceptance of new ideas, especially those of revolutionary dimensions; but listen to Dr. Anspacher's warning concerning "incredulity." (*Challenge of the Unknown,* p. 305; Louis K. Anspacher, 1947. Current Books: A. A. Wyn.)

"Of course, there are limits to our credulity; but there must also be limits to our incredulity, or else exact science is impossible." In the case of the pulse-test, the decision as to its credibility is relatively easy. One reads "The Pulse Test" to engender an interest; then chooses the most convenient and profitable "guinea pig"—one's self—and on a week end, carries out the simple, hourly food tests, finishing with the exciting game of interpreting the results, according to the "rules-of-interpretation" in the book, plus the exercise of "common sense."

SECTION 38

VACCINATION

Vaccination is a present-day evil. We believe that a time will come when we will be so healthy, vaccinations will be unnecessary. We urge our readers to live with this goal in mind. Meanwhile, if you or your children must be vaccinated, a good diet program will protect you from possible bad effects. Vitamins B and C are excellent antidotes for poisons of many kinds.

CHAPTER **131**

Vaccination

During the early part of the eighteenth century, Lady Mary Wortley Montagu, wife of the British ambassador to Turkey, wrote the following letter home:

"The smallpox, so general and so fatal among us, is here entirely harmless by the invention of ingrafting which they term inoculation. There is a set of old women who make it their business to perform the operation every Autumn . . . They make parties for this purpose and when they are met . . . the old woman comes with a nut-shell full of the matter of the best smallpox and asks what veins you are pleased to have opened.

"She immediately rips open that you offer to her with a large needle—and puts into the vein as much venom as can lie upon the head of her needle . . . The children or young patients then play around and keep in perfect health until the eighth day.

"Then the fever seizes them and they keep their beds two days—seldom 3. They have rarely more than 20 or 30 pustules on their faces, which leave no mark, and in 8 days they are as well as before their inoculation . . . I am very well satisfied with the safety of the experiment since I intend to try it on my own dear little son . . ."

Jenner Proposes Cow Pox Inoculation

Lady Mary brought the smallpox inoculation back to England with her and for a time this arm-to-arm inoculation became very popular. The Royal College of Physicians gave it their blessing. However, eventually they began to realize that this kind of inoculation was spreading smallpox and that diseases such as erysipelas, syphilis and tuberculosis were being transmitted as well. According to a statement in the *Journal of the Royal Sanitary Institute* (Vol. XLVIII, No. 4), 1927, "It has been calculated that from 1721 to 1758 smallpox inoculation was responsible for the deaths of not less than 22,700 persons from smallpox in London alone. It is not therefore surprising that when Jenner proposed that smallpox inoculation should be given up and cowpox substituted for it—thus covering the retreat of the profession from an untenable position, his ideas were accepted by all whose interests were not inseparably bound up with the older form of treatment."

Jenner is the founder of modern vaccination (from *vacca*, meaning "cow") in which the disease under consideration is cultured in an animal and then transferred into a human being. Edgar M. Crookshank, Professor of Comparative Pathology and Bacteriology at King's College, London, investigating Jenner and later writing a book about him, tells us that cowpox (the disease in cows which provided the vaccine for human beings) resembles human syphilis more nearly than any other illness. He further states, "We have no known test by which we can possibly distinguish between lymph (blood, that is) which is harmless and one which might be harmful to the extent of communicating syphilis."

What Happened After Jenner's Discovery?

Jenner, inoculating right and left, soon set his feet on the path of glory followed by inventors of vaccines in the times since then. He was awarded an income by Parliament, his vaccine was rapidly shipped to other countries which also heaped honors and rewards on him and by 1840 vaccination was made "free" in England to all who would accept it. The old method of arm-to-arm inoculation was declared illegal. In 1853 vaccination was made compulsory in England. Everyone had to be vaccinated, whether or not he wanted to. The results? Fourteen thousand, two hundred and forty-four deaths from smallpox in London from 1857-59. Twenty thousand, fifty-nine deaths in the 1863-65 outbreak. Annie Riley Hale in *The Medical Voodoo* (Gotham House, 1935) says: "In England and Wales 44,840 persons are said to have died of smallpox in the 1871-73 epidemic at a time when, according to official estimates, 97 per cent of the population had been vaccinated."

In Leicester, England, Vaccination Acts were burned

publicly. In Leicester the city government decided to try sanitation instead of vaccination. We are told that, in the 20 years from 1878 to 1898, the death rate from smallpox in Leicester was less than 13 per million, whereas in the much vaccinated and re-vaccinated British military services the rate was 3 times as high. As vaccination fell off and became less and less popular, smallpox incidence declined. When the laws for compulsory vaccination were repealed, vaccination fell to less than 40 per cent by 1921.

Re-Investigation of Vaccination

In the 1871 report of the New York City Health Department we find these words: "This extraordinary prevalence of smallpox over various parts of the globe, especially in countries where vaccination has long been efficiently practiced; its occurrence in its most fatal form in persons who gave evidence of having been well vaccinated; and the remarkable susceptibility of people of all ages to re-vaccination are new facts in the history of this pestilence which must lead to a re-investigation of the whole ubject of vaccination and its claims as a protecting agent."

Dr. Sydney Moncton Copeland in the eleventh edition of the *Encyclopedia Brittanica* says: "It is somewhat unfortunate that there exists no official definition of what constitutes a successful vaccination and it is open to any practitioner to use his own judgment in awarding certificates."

Miss Hale gives the following facts about smallpox in the Philippines. Since 1903 there has been compulsory vaccination there. In 1918 an epidemic of smallpox began which lasted for 3 years and caused 163,044 cases with 71,170 deaths.

In speaking of tuberculosis, Miss Hale quotes Dr. Raymond Pearl, head of Biological Research of Johns Hopkins as saying, "As a matter of scientific fact, extremely little is known about why the mortality from tuberculosis has declined." She also quotes Karl Pearson, highest authority on biometrics, who said that "mortality from tuberculosis has been declining since 1838, long before any special measures for prevention or control were instituted."

What evidence about vaccination have we in more recent years? Vaccination is now so commonly accepted as part of the medical arsenal that it seldom occurs to the general public to raise any questions about it, except, of course, in the cases of those individuals who have decided that they will not have their children vaccinated, when the state laws indicate that it is compulsory.

Medical journals contain, from time to time, descriptions of startlingly violent reactions from smallpox vaccine. In the *British Medical Journal* for January 1, 1955, A. Fry tells of a baby recently vaccinated from whom a young mother got a "vaccinia," a sore, resembling the sores of smallpox.

In the *British Medical Journal* for August 21, 1954, is the story of a boy who got fatal tetanus (lockjaw) after a tetanus injection. *The Journal of the American Medical Association* for September 5, 1953 describes the case of a youngster who got "vaccinia" 10 days after being vaccinated for smallpox. An antibiotic was used to clear up the disorder.

Vaccination Condemned

From *The Medical Press* for March 10, 1954 we get some interesting comments on vaccination. Says J. Pickford Marsden, M.D., of Kent, England, " 'Vaccination' like 'democracy' is a word which conveys different meanings to different people. Strictly speaking, vaccination merely means inoculation with vaccinia virus . . . We know that if the vaccination 'takes' the virus grows in the skin, where it has been implanted and, in consequence, specific antibodies appear in the serum of the patient who thus develops an immunity against (this) complex of diseases. On the other hand, if the virus does not live, the vaccination 'fails to take' and protection does not arise. Yet both such individuals have been 'vaccinated.' "

He goes on to say, "The disturbance caused by primary vaccination which may be considerable in the adult, is least in the young baby; and at that time the risk of encephalitis is slight." Encephalitis is, of course, inflammation of the brain. We find that it is not an uncommon sequence of vaccination. In 1928 there were 139 cases with 41 deaths in Holland from encephalitis following vaccination. The result was that that country repealed its compulsory vaccination laws in a hurry.

Miss Hale quotes a letter written by George Bernard Shaw in 1931, in answer to a question from an M.D. as to his opinion on vaccination. Said Shaw: "I was vaccinated in infancy and had 'good marks' of it. In the great epidemic of 1881 (I was born in 1856) I caught smallpox. During the last considerable epidemic at the turn of the century, I was a member of the Health Committee of London Borough Council, and I learned how the credit of vaccination is kept up statistically by diagnosing all the re-vaccinated cases as pustular eczema, varioloid or what-not—*except smallpox.*

"I discovered a suppressed report of the Metropolitan Asylums Board on a set of re-vaccinations which had produced extraordinary disastrous results. Meanwhile I had studied the literature and statistics of the subject. I even induced a celebrated bacteriologist to read Jenner. I have no doubt whatever that vaccination is an unscientific abomination and should be made a criminal practice."

Why Has Incidence of Smallpox Declined?

There is pretty general acceptance at present of the fact that smallpox results from unhygienic conditions. Recently we reprinted a most convincing article showing that smallpox is spread by bedbugs. In a house free from bedbugs no one will get smallpox. Miss Hale puts the argument against vaccination this way: "Seeing that the preponderance of evidence is on the side of those who affirm that filth and ignorance are the most fruitful causes of disease; and that the only prophylactic, as well as the only cure, is through hygienic living and optimistic thinking, Karl Pearson's statement that the decline in tuberculosis began in 1838 is very significant. For it was about that time that men's thoughts in Europe and America began to turn to sanitation, with the invention of plumbing and the appearance of the first bathtubs. Another 50 years went by before the superiority of sanitation over vaccination in the eradication of smallpox had been demonstrated, and then only in isolated areas whose inhabitants could be persuaded to try cleanliness instead of blood pollution as a means of disease-prevention. Nevertheless it is a fact upheld by the vital statistics of every country . . . that with the coming of sanitation . . . the general health of the people began to improve; and in the exact ratio that sanitation and personal hygiene have been practiced while inoculations have been neglected, all (infectious) diseases have notably declined."

The Layman Speaks is a monthly magazine published by the American Foundation for Homeopathy, Incorporated (1726

Eye Street, Northwest, Washington, D. C.) The position of homeopathy on immunization is interesting. The entire August, 1955 issue is devoted to this subject. Says the editorial, in part, "There is good reason to believe that improved sanitation and regulation governing the processing and handling of food and milk were the main factors in bringing them (the old epidemic diseases) under control, just as the modern uncontaminated water supply has given the *coup de grace* to typhoid fever. If it were not so, to what should we in the United States and similarly advanced countries ascribe our relative freedom from these scourges of earlier generations? In the case of smallpox, surely not to vaccination—homeopathic and effective as Dr. Jenner's cowpox inoculation proved to be. For, considering the undetermined duration of immunity—the most optimistic estimate is five years—how many of our 150 million people are 'protected' as of this moment? . . . There is sufficient evidence of smallpox and typhoid, or their indistinguishable counterparts, following vaccination—not only of individuals but of groups—to justify a lively skepticism in regard to the elimination-by-vaccination theory."

CHAPTER 132

Is There a Good Case Against Vaccination?

A look at the reasons advanced for eliminating the use of artificial immunizing agents against diphtheria. Do the same objections prevail in the case of other immunizations?

The rapid decline in diphtheria deaths over the past 25 years has been claimed as a major victory for those who advocate immunizing by vaccination. This claim is not easily proven either by statistics or time; nor is there undeniable proof by the opposing view which says that diphtheria would have declined just as quickly without vaccination. Everyone knows the case for vaccination. It is based on the theory that a mild injection of a germ into the blood stream will lead to the manufacture of a number of antibodies which will repulse any more serious attack by the germ in the future. There are also impressive figures which show that the incidence of diphtheria has indeed decreased in the era of vaccination.

A comprehensive article we came across in a British magazine, *Health for All,* gave the case for the opposition to artificial immunization against diphtheria, and we offer their views for the consideration of those readers who might appreciate knowing on exactly what grounds the argument against vaccination stands. The article, of course, used British figures, but the arguments apply for all so-called enlightened countries.

Why the Decline in Death Rate?

First, it is admitted by both sides that there has been a steady decline in the diphtheria death rate among those who have been immunized. However, there is the less publicized fact that there has been a parallel and almost equal lessening in the diphtheria death rate among those who have not been immunized by vaccination. It is further pointed out that, if immunization were responsible for eliminating diphtheria, the death rate among those vaccinated should not have dropped "steadily," the death rate should have disappeared. If those vaccinated were really immune, none of them could have contracted diphtheria, hence there should have been no deaths at all among them. Further, this decline in the diphtheria death rate has continued to take place among the unimmunized at the same rate, so says the Ministry of Health Report of 1953. This drop should certainly not have occurred in the unimmunized if vaccination were the only reason for the decline. Those not vaccinated should still be suffering from the high death rate of 50 years ago. As the Ministry stated: "A simultaneous decline in morbidity and mortality rates from diphtheria suggests that factors other than artificial immunization may be operative."

Better Sanitation Is the Answer

If immunization is not the cause of a lessened threat from diphtheria, what is? We live cleaner lives—it's that simple! Our personal hygiene is improved; we are more careful of our drinking water; the drainage and sewage problems are met more carefully. All of these, when neglected, offered ideal breeding conditions for diphtheria germs. Once they were eliminated the problem began to evaporate. A look at some figures would indicate the logic of this assumption. In the 10 year period, 1891 to 1900, the death rate per million, due to diphtheria, in England, was 873 for children under 15 years of age. In the 10 years, 1921-1930, the rate had decreased to 298— and this was *before* immunization was being used.

In arguments against vaccination it is emphasized that no objection would be made if it were true that artificial immunization is perfectly harmless or perhaps beneficial to even a few. But those who oppose do not believe this to be so. They cite cases of serious upsets suffered by vaccinated babies and even some deaths attributed to artificial immunization. It is affirmed that no responsible doctor will say that vaccination entails no risks whatsoever, but, rather, that the risks are negligible and the lesser of two evils. It is suggested that though the doctor thinks the risks are negligible, the parents might not be of that opinion. They should be told the facts and allowed to decide for themselves.

The Body's Own Vaccination

A basic element in the case against artificial immunization is this: just as outward sanitation has helped rid us of some basic causes of diphtheria, so internal cleanliness of the child's system would surely take care of the rest of the problem. A clean and healthy blood stream, achieved by a good diet of unrefined foods, healthful exercise and use of food supplements, has a high immunity of its own to all infections. There is no need then to inject a new immunizing factor to combat each contagious disease, for the body will manufacture its own as the need to defend itself arises.

And what are the side effects of this type of immunization? They are healthy teeth and well-developed dental arches, good complexion, vitality, joy in living and easy, efficient and natural functioning of the body's organs. This must indeed be labeled as ideal immunization.

The arguments on both sides of the question are hard for parents to ignore. What is one to do about diphtheria injections for one's children if one is not absolutely convinced one way or the other? It is a difficult decision. We take this view: if and when our national nutrition reaches the point of enlightenment at which food values are considered in the light of their true importance, if the popularity and lure of dangerous, lifeless processed foods should diminish and disappear, if the serious problems of spraying and the chemical treatment of food and soil should be solved—then one could feel free to ignore the problem of diphtheria, as well as other contagious diseases. A healthy, well-nourished body is a poor breeding ground for disease. Of course, such a time is yet to come. Few present-day parents can feel secure in the knowledge that their children eat only foods that are good for them, or that even the good foods they eat have been grown in good soil under ideal conditions. Unless you are one of these lucky few whose children have dietary habits that are above reproach, the anxiety of what *might* happen to your child if he does not have the injection could cause more physical damage, and be an even greater risk to your health and his than the injection itself. In such case we think the injection would be the wiser choice. To forestall any side effects, we urge parents to fortify their children with extra amounts of food supplements before the injection is given. This gives the body extra ammunition in the war against the toxic attack the injected germs wage in the blood stream. Extra nutrition is the best insurance we know against the dangers of artificial immunization.

SECTION 39

CHILDBIRTH

The nutrition of the prospective mother (and father, too, incidentally) has much to do with the health of the unborn child. Lack of certain food elements is bound to result in deficiencies in the child. We know, for instance, at what exact day the unborn child develops certain anatomical parts. And we know the vitamins and minerals that must be present for this development. If these are not there in sufficient quantity, we know that this particular part of the child's anatomy will be defective.

CHAPTER **133**

How the Mother's Life Influences Her Unborn Child

Years ago grandmothers, mothers, doctors and midwives used to terrify prospective mothers with dire predictions about what would happen to their offspring if they did or did not do certain things. The pregnant woman who was frightened by a mouse was told that her child's body would carry on it somewhere the mark of this experience. If a child was born with a flaming red birthmark, the mother was reminded of a fire she had seen sometime during her pregnancy. This must have caused the birthmark! If she wanted her child to be musical, the expectant mother was told to sing while she was carrying it. A literary child would certainly result if the prospective mother spent her time reading Browning and Tennyson.

Old-Time Suggestions Apply to Present Day

Today we know that many of these notions are just notions. But, on the other hand, today's scientists are continually being surprised at how right the old-timers were about some things relating to the embryo child carried within its mother. (Embryo is the term used for the unborn child up to the fourth month of pregnancy.) Until very recently we had little information about the life of that embryo and no explanation for many of the unfortunate children that were born with one or another irregularity in their physical or mental make-up.

New Discoveries

However, we have now discovered a number of most significant things about the relationship of the mother to her unborn infant. We know, for instance, that there are illnesses of the mother which may severely injure the child. Rubella, or

German measles, is one of these. In *The Archives of Pediatrics* for December, 1953, Edward E. Brown, M.D., F.A.A.P., discusses mongolism in its relation to maternal illness before birth.

Mongolism

Mongolism is a condition in which the child possesses the mentality of an idiot, along with certain definite physical traits such as a broad face, with a flat, stubby nose and eyes set obliquely (hence mongolism, for the appearance of the eyes resembles those of the Mongol group of people). The mouth of the mongol child hangs open, the skin is fat and soft, the muscles flabby.

Dr. Brown quotes other authorities for the statements that, in one series of 8 mongol idiots, the history of 4 revealed bad health in the mother before birth. Another authority who studied 379 cases of mongolism reported ill health in 179, or 47.2 per cent of the mothers. Bleeding during pregnancy, the continuation of menstruation during pregnancy and severe vomiting were common symptoms. "With increasing frequency mongolism is being noted after virus and streptococcal diseases attacking the mother usually in early pregnancy," says Dr. Brown, "Virus diseases include rubella, measles, mumps and influenza. Among the presumably streptococcal diseases are mastoiditis, pleurisy, otitis media (inflammation of the middle ear), sinusitis and nephritis."

Dr. Brown reports on 11 cases of mongols and "missed mongols" in which 10 of the 11 revealed some history of maternal illness during the (most critical) early months of pregnancy. Inquiring into the history of 11 normal babies, he found nothing more serious than nausea as a pregnancy complication.

Of the mothers whose children were mongols—or deficient in such a way as to be almost mongols—he found that several had suffered from severe constant colds, influenza, nephritis, asthma, rheumatic pains or violent vomiting throughout pregnancy. His conclusions are: "Viral and bacterial diseases during the first 3 months of pregnancy may be a more common cause of mongolism than has been recognized previously. Further studies of the health of mothers during the first trimester (3 months) of pregnancy are needed to verify this suspected relationship."

Another study in *The Lancet*, December 12, 1953, discusses congenital heart defects that are associated with illness of the mother during pregnancy. Seventy-eight children who had congenital cataract were studied. It was found that 44 of these children had heart disease. In all cases the mothers had contracted German measles early in pregnancy. In another series of cases there were 21 children with heart irregularities among 61 born to mothers who had had German measles. It is believed, says the editorial in *The Lancet,* that heart defects in children result from arrested development of the heart of the embryo during the early months of pregnancy.

Experiments Show Effect on Embryo

Now we come to the work of Josef Warkany of the University of Cincinnati which shows by means of scientifically controlled experiments in a laboratory what happens to embryo animals whose mothers are deprived of certain nutritional substances. In a report in *The American Journal of Anatomy,* July, 1949, Dr. Warkany and Dr. James G. Wilson of the University of Rochester describe their experiments with rats. They found definite irregularities in the heart and the aorta of rats born from mothers on deficient diets. The aorta is the large blood vessel that carries blood from the heart to all parts of the body. Dr. Warkany and Dr. Wilson fed female rats diets that were deficient in vitamin A prior to and during their pregnancy. The rats born from these mothers showed heart deformities in 75 per cent of the cases. In addition, there were serious irregularities in eyes and organs of the genital and urinary tracts. After describing the form these various irregularities took, the doctors tell us that it appears they were caused on or after the twelfth day of pregnancy.

In an address before the Academy of Pediatrics, reprinted in *Pediatrics,* May, 1951, Dr. Warkany summarizes the knowledge we have up to now regarding malformation in human children which may result from malnutrition of the mother. He says, "Adverse factors acting in prenatal life contribute appreciably to the mortality of infants and many children go through life deformed or crippled because of unfavorable intrauterine (prenatal) conditions." He tells us that congenital (existing at birth) deformities are at the root of many chronic and some incurable diseases of childhood.

Many diseases of the urinary tract, for instance, are now

recognized as proceeding from prenatal influences, that is, influences that were effective before birth. Intestinal disorders that were formerly just called "vomiting" or "malnutrition" are now known to spring from this same source. Heart disorders and disorders of the glands may result from maternal malnutrition. Nervous diseases and mental deficiency may be traced to the same cause. He tells us also that congenital deficiencies may be traced to heredity, to be sure, for these appear regularly in families. However, he says, "One can disturb the normal development of the embryo by depriving the pregnant female of certain essential nutritional elements. General starvation of the mother results in sterility, abortions or stillbirths. . . . However, under certain special experimental conditions, *when the pregnant animal is kept in a borderline state of depletion of a specific nutritional element, the embryo may be damaged without being killed.*"

Nutrition of Expectant Mothers

We have italicized this statement of Dr. Warkany's because we believe this "borderline state of depletion" is what we are dealing with in many of today's mothers. Dr. Warkany says that he does not believe that dietary deficiency of mothers in this country is a factor in producing congenital irregularities in children. However, he believes that in countries where food is scarce and knowledge of nutrition is lacking, conditions such as their laboratory animals endured may be prevalent.

In a book called *Ecology of Health*, edited by E. H. L. Corwin, Ph.D., from the proceedings of the New York Academy of Medicine, Institute on Public Health, 1947, published by the Commonwealth Fund, 1949, we find a chapter on maternal health and nutrition. This chapter describes 3 experiments in maternal nutrition conducted at the University of Toronto, the Philadelphia Lying-in Hospital and Harvard University School of Public Health. "That the dietary habits of the mother are related not only to her condition during pregnancy, labor and convalescence, but also to the condition of her baby has been demonstrated by these studies," says the account.

Dietary Experiment with Pregnant Women

In the experiment 90 women were left on their usual diets which were apparently quite inadequate. Ninety other women were given special dietary supplements in the form of eggs, milk, canned tomatoes, cheese, oranges, vitamin D and wheat germ. Reviewing the various complaints of the women of both groups, we find that those on the inadequate diet (by which we mean their usual diet at home) reported the following: Anemia—24 as against 14 in the group with the supplemented diet; toxemia 24 as against 15; hemorrhage 13 as against 9 in the second group; pyelitis (inflammation of the pelvis of the kidney) 5 against 3, numerous other complaints— 24 against 14 in the supplemented group. During childbirth the figures are equally revealing with 5 premature births in the first group compared to two in the second group, 4 miscarriages compared with one, 3 stillbirths compared with one in the supplemented group. The rate of deaths after birth was 15 per cent higher for infants whose mothers were in the first group.

Vitamin C Deficiency

In addition, it was found that the children from the group whose diets had been supplemented were taller and weighed more. But Dr. Warkany has said that he does not believe the American diet is deficient enough to cause irregularities in unborn children. Yet a study at the New York Lying-in Hospital reported in *Ecology of Health* shows that while non-pregnant patients have a level of about one milligram of vitamin C in their blood, the level in the blood of pregnant women at the time of childbirth is about .3 milligrams or about one-third of a milligram. "Since a level of .5 milligrams of vitamin C in the blood is . . . indicative of a deficiency, many so-called normal pregnant patients are in reality subnormal with respect to vitamin C." In the New York Hospital it has been found that patients who suffer from threatened abortions show no vitamin C at all in their blood! At the Philadelphia Lying-in Hospital it has been found that pregnant women with depression, fatigue, lassitude recover quickly when they are given vitamins of the B complex. So, either their diets were deficient in these vitamins, or they were not absorbing what vitamin B there was in their diets.

These facts, from the New York Academy of Medicine Institute on Public Health strengthen our point of view which is that many pregnant women in this country are suffering from slight vitamin deficiencies, or at any rate, their condition and that of their children could be greatly improved by supple-menting their diets.

Finally, to get back to the theories of doctors and mid-wives of past centuries, we want to review an article that appeared in the *Ladies' Home Journal* for February, 1954. Written by Ashley Montagu, Chairman of the Department of Anthropology at Rutgers, and Gertrude Schweitzer, this article is titled, "There is Prenatal Influence." Dr. Montagu tells us that modern science has shown that the old-timers were not so far wrong, after all. We have found, for instance, that some profound emotional shock occurring to the mother during preg-nancy can result in a nervous, perhaps neurotic child. We have found that the child in the womb can be trained to respond to external stimuli.

In this interesting experiment a doorbell with the gong removed was used. The unborn child of a woman 8 months pregnant did not respond when the doorbell was vibrated close to the mother's abdomen. When the gong was replaced, the baby jumped inside the womb. After repeating the experiment many times, it was found that the baby began to respond by jumping when the bell was vibrated, even when the gong (or sound) was not present.

We have also found that the pregnant woman's craving for certain kinds of food may result in definite damage to the child. Two cases are cited. In one the mother craved nuts and ate about a pound a day during her pregnancy. The baby was born normally and not until he was 4 years old did he develop any signs of allergy. Then he became allergic to—of course, nuts. A second mother ate a lot of wheat products when she was pregnant—a loaf of bread a day, cakes, pies, crackers and so forth. When the baby was 7 months old and began to eat cereals for the first time, she developed a violent allergy to all wheat products. The explanation of this phenomenon appears to be that proteins, such as are contained in wheat and nuts, can pass through the placenta to the unborn baby. We know that adults may produce an allergy in themselves by overeating one food. In these cases the allergy was produced in the children by the mothers' overeating.

Dr. Montagu covers the question of nutrition and, re-viewing Dr. Warkany's work which we discussed earlier, he reminds us that maternal nutrition is of the utmost importance to the welfare of the baby. Then, because he is not a nutritionist, he does not go into all the ramifications of this problem. He mentions smoking. It seems to be definitely established scientifically that even one cigarette smoked by the mother may produce a change in the heartbeat of the unborn child. Dr. Montagu thinks it is quite within the realm of possibility that smoking by modern mothers may be responsible for part of today's big increase in heart disease cases.

Height Affected

The child's height we have always believed is decided by the genes—those tiny substances that carry hereditary traits from one generation to the next. But Dr. Montagu tells us that the genes carry only the height "potential" of the new individual. Taking into account the height of both the mother and father we might say that Junior could be 6 feet tall—no taller. But whether or not he actually reaches the height of 6 feet is determined by his mother's nutrition and economic status, as well as whether the birth is normal. It is also dependent on the kind and amount of love the baby receives. Says Dr. Montagu, "There are cases on record of children whose growth was arrested during periods when, for one reason or another, they were deprived of affection, and who began to grow again at a normal rate when they once more came under the influence of love."

Is Love Enough?

Dr. Montagu believes there is nothing for prospective mothers to worry about in his findings. If the mother loves her baby from the moment of its conception and if the mother herself is loved, then the baby will be happy and well, or at any rate can grow into a happy and well individual. We go along with this theory up to a certain point. But what about all those mothers in the New York survey who, we assume, loved their babies, but simply did not know what foods they should have eaten during pregnancy? What about the patients nearing childbirth whose blood showed a complete lack of vitamin C, that most vital food element? No amount of love is going to provide the vitamin C unless the mother knows that the vitamin C is necessary. What about all the women who contracted virus diseases bringing heart disorders or mongolism to their babies? It seems to us that the prevention of virus diseases involves having a strong, healthy, resistant body. And the most important factor in perfect health is a good diet, well supplemented to prevent any possible deficiencies. After that, the love comes naturally, for people just naturally love healthy individuals, and healthy babies are the most beloved of all.

CHAPTER **134**

When Having Babies Was Part of a Busy Day

Primitive woman had a baby with only a short pause in the day's occupation. These are some of the reasons why she was able to do it.

Any mother will tell you that giving birth to a child is a gratifying experience. Most mothers will tell you, too, that it is a painful and exhausting experience. (This conclusion forms the basis for the famous Read Method of Natural Childbirth). In the plan of nature this misery was clearly not meant to be. The reproduction of one's own kind takes place in every animal, except for civilized man, with relative ease and speed. No wild animal tarries longer than a few hours to deliver herself of often not one, but several babies, after which she is soon up and about, searching for nourishment for herself so that she can properly nurse her young.

Childbirth—Indian Style

That this is the normal course of things, for the human animal as well, is evidenced by the many accounts of childbirth among the primitive natives of North America. Explorers, missionaries and hunters were astounded at the ease with which these native women gave birth. They contrasted the elaborate lying-in period of the European women with the matter-of-fact attitude of the Indian women who thought childbirth hardly worth a pause in the day's occupations. Indeed many of these women did no more than to pause, have their babies and proceed immediately to the next chore of the day. Illustrative of this custom is this account from the book, *New Voyages to North America,* written in 1905 by Baron de Lehontan: "If the women should be in labor in the night they deliver themselves upon their mats without crying out, or making a noise. The next morning they rise, and go about their ordinary duties within doors and without as though nothing had happened." And from Father Sagard's book, *Long Journey to the Country of the Hurons* (1824), we get this picture: "I have seen them (Huron women) come in from the woods laden with a big bundle of wood, and give birth to a child as soon as they arrive; then immediately they are on their feet in ordinary employment." Another writer tells of a group traveling on horseback; included in the party was an Indian woman whose time had come. She simply pulled to the side of the road while the rest rode on. She had her baby, wrapped him against the weather and caught up with the party within an hour.

The journals of the Europeans who explored North America after its discovery, and had a chance to observe the natives in their unspoiled environment are all full of similar accounts. Some say that the Indian woman would go alone from the village to a place in the woods when the baby was due. She would emerge a short time later with the child neatly wrapped and clean, and ready to resume her daily chores. All agree that the Indian woman would never cry out in childbirth, and while some writers say that custom forbade their crying out, others are of the opinion that the women didn't cry out simply because there was no great pain, hence no reason for doing so.

What Natural Nourishment Gave to the Indians

How these women arrived at this enviable state of nonchalance in childbirth is open to speculation. Most probably it was their reward for natural living. They ate the most primitive fare, but Dr. Weston Price says the diet of the Indians of the Far North provided 5.8 times as much calcium, 5.8 times as much phosphorus, 2.7 times the iron, 4.3 times the magnesium, 1.5 times the copper, 8.8 times the iodine and 10 times the fat-soluble activators of modern diet. Kaare Rodahl, M.D., in his book, *North—The Nature and Drama of the Polar World,* remarks that ". . . all internal organs and plants which have the highest vitamin content, especially vitamin C, are considered particular delicacies by the Eskimo and that though he knows nothing about vitamins, some of his methods of preparing stored foods offer the best possible preservation of vitamins." Similar statements could be made on the native diets of most primitive people, though further south the problems of preserving food became acute. These natives were trained by necessity to eat the whole animal as soon as it was killed, and it was not unusual for 6 or 8 Indians to eat an entire buffalo at a single sitting, without the slightest discomfort. Then, of course, there were many days of absolute starvation, when no animal food was to be found.

Reason for Ease of Labor Suggested

The theory is offered that the constant activity of the busy, hard-working Indian woman, even in the most advanced stages of pregnancy, serves to place the child in the most advantageous position for effortless passage through the birth canal. Though this might be true, it is more logical to assume that the proper position of the baby was only one of a number of factors. Not the least of these was the superb physical condition of the mothers. They had to be in excellent health to withstand the rigors of the life they led. They slept under the stars in temperatures of 40 degrees below zero, we're told; the women were required to do all of the heavy work, for the men were busy hunting; they were constantly on the move traveling to exhaustion just to keep up with migrating wildlife. These women got plenty of exercise. Their muscles were full of tone and developed to a fine degree. With such physical equipment, it is no wonder that child-bearing was, for them, almost as effortless as eating.

As soon as the child was born, it was washed in the snow until it began to cry from the shock. The mother would wash herself in the same way. Her couch was usually a few boughs of fir in a trough of snow, dug for protection against the cold winds. If there was no snow, the mother and child went for a dip in the coldest streams or in the ocean. Some of our North Pacific Coast Indians made a daily ocean bath, winter or summer, an unbreakable ritual from their earliest days till the day they died.

And what kind of children resulted from these easy births and rigorous conditions of early life? Quoting Baron de Lehontan once more: " 'Tis a great rarity to find any among them (the Indians) that are lame, hunchbacked, one-eyed, blind or dumb." For another impression of native children, listen to Captain F. W. Beechey in his book, *Narratives of a Voyage to the Pacific and Bering Strait,* ". . . children are reared to a healthier state than in other countries, and are free from fevers and other complaints peculiar to the greater portion of the world . . . nothing is more extraordinary in the history of the island than the uniform good health of the children; the teething is easily gotten over, they have no bowel complaints, and are exempt from those contagious diseases which affect children in large communities." These opinions are almost universal among those who write of any primitive peoples. There is virtually no congenital disease, and perfect development as the children mature is a foregone conclusion.

Sickness Brought About By Modern Living

Sad to say, this condition persists only so long as the people are permitted their proper environment. Once they deviate from the native diet and improve on native discomforts and hardships, their ruggedness and resistance to disease is no more. Dr. A. E. Marden, Surgeon to the United States Indian Service, summed up the situation in these words: "That the robust condition and easy mode of childbearing are rapidly disappearing from even the full-blooded Indian women there can be no doubt. The bed has taken the place of the blanket or the pallet or straw, and the 'puerperal state' (time of recovery) that of the ready condition for renewed toil immediatedly after childbirth. The daughters and granddaughters of these sturdy aboriginal matrons consult the pale-face doctor, and are rapidly acquiring the methods of pale-face women. . . . From an out-of-door life of activity with plenty of fresh game and wholesome food and clear water, with healthful tepees for homes, the change has been made to log cabins, with overheated close air. Poor food, with flour and salted meat of inferior quality, is mostly what is found in the modern Indian home. In exchange for an active life there is much of idleness and indoor confinement. . . . Partly on this account the naturally robust constitution is deteriorating, and miscarriages and diseases peculiar to women are noticeably increasing."

Should the Modern Woman Go "Primitive"?

To many of the women who read this, the "modern" conditions described in that paragraph would seem primitive still. The "overheated log cabins" would seem unbearably chilly and draughty, the "white flour and salted meats" would never compare to our supermarket foods in the fine degree of processing we are used to. In short, the women of our society have been living for several generations on this type of debilitating existence that is ruining the Indians—and with refinements that the Indians never dreamed of!

It is, of course, out of the question for our women to do an about-face and expose themselves to the rigors that were commonplace with primitive Indians. These people had been conditioned by centuries of custom and habit to live with the elements and to master them. But there is a lesson—and a clear one—that can be learned from all primitive peoples: eating unadulterated, unprocessed, natural foods is a strong factor in their resistance to disease, as well as the resistance to disease displayed by their offspring. When they are introduced to refined food, they are introduced to bad health, susceptibility to disease, difficulty in childbirth and serious contagion.

One Major Concern

For women who are pregnant or in the age of childbearing, a careful diet is a most valuable asset. Good food, coupled with moderate, regular exercise, will help to nourish the child developing in the womb, and to assemble all of the mother's resources that make for ease of delivery and quick renewal of strength. The modern woman should make every effort to fortify herself against the inroads that today's easy living impose on her natural vitality. She should walk in the air whenever she can, and do simple daily exercises that will give tone to the muscles she'll need when she has her child. She should eat fresh, organically-raised fruits and vegetables as well as properly prepared meats. Processed foods, artificial sweets, cigarettes, salt, coffee—all these should be taboo to her. Her only concern should be the baby she is carrying and she should eat nothing without first assuring herself that it will be of value to the health of the expected child or her own health. The primitive Indians didn't have such problems, for the only foods available to them were rich in the food elements they needed. The closer we can come to having that type of diet, the closer we, and our children, will come to the perfect health the primitive Indians enjoyed.

SECTION 40

ROYAL JELLY

Royal jelly, the food fed to queen bees, may or may not be important in human nutrition. While it has marvelous powers for bees, we have no proof that it works these same miracles for human beings in the amounts in which it can be consumed.

CHAPTER **135**

Royal Jelly

For thousands of years honeybees have occupied a unique niche among all the living creatures that have come to live with man. Because of their intricate and fascinating community life, we human beings have always known that there was something special about bees—something not quite comprehensible to mere man. In all parts of the world in times past, and in many agricultural countries even today, the bees share in family celebrations. At Christmas and Easter, for weddings and funerals, special ceremonies must be performed near the beehives. If a disaster or a blessing befalls the family, the bees must be told, first of all.

It is not surprising that men have such reverence for these furious and conscientious little insects. Bees not only organize their community life along the strictest lines, not only do they work at unbelievable speeds and collect incredible amounts of food in the way of nectar and pollen, but they communicate with one another. They have their own system of mathematics, geometry and geography so well worked out that the bee who discovers a cache of honey can describe to the other members of the hive exactly where the honey is located, how much there is and what is the shortest and best route to take to get there. All these facts have been verified by scientists.

Royal Jelly—Food for the Queen Bee

Recently another fabulous aspect of bee-life has been getting publicity—royal jelly, the food of the queen bee. *Look* for October 19, 1954, carried a feature story on it. The New York Sunday *Mirror* for June 27, 1954, carried a syndicated feature story. *The News* from Sarasota, Florida for October 21, 1954, carried a front page story on a beekeeper there who shipped in 20 million bees, in the hope that he can produce royal jelly commercially. We have received clippings on royal jelly from state after state. And many letters from readers asking where they can buy this miracle food.

Apparently the answer is not at the corner store, for there is a peculiar problem involved in producing royal jelly which will invariably limit its usefulness so far as human consumption is concerned. Royal jelly is the food produced by the worker bees to feed the queen bee. A queen bee is both mother and ruler of an entire hive. During one season she may become the mother of as many as a quarter of a million bees. A queen bee has been known to lay more than 2,000 eggs (more than her own weight) in a single day. Of the eggs she lays, the fertile ones may develop into either worker bees or queens. Their development depends entirely on their food. All the eggs are fed royal jelly for the first 2 or 3 days after hatching. But the egg destined to be a queen bee, and then the queen bee herself, receives royal jelly throughout her life. So it seems reasonable to assume that the food is solely responsible for the great difference between the queen bee and the workers, for no other circumstances of their growth are different, except for food.

Worker bees grow up in from 21 to 24 days. Queen bees mature in 16 days. Worker bees work furiously and live from 2 to 6 months. Queen bees, working just as hard at their egg laying, may live as long as 8 years. What a powerful force of longevity and fertility must be contained in royal jelly!

How to Get Natural Royal Jelly

But here is the catch to the whole thing. Worker bees feed royal jelly to create a queen only when they need a queen— that is when the old queen is dying or they have decided to get rid of her, or when, for some other mysterious reason of their own, they want a new queen. To produce royal jelly for experiments, scientists must first remove the reigning queen. The bees know at once that she is gone and they work desperately feeding royal jelly to several more larvae in order to produce a new queen. The experimenters again remove the royal jelly, and the bees must frantically produce more.

As more and more royal jelly is removed, it seems to us that the frenzy and frustration of the bee colony must become frightening. And which of us can predict what will be the final

effect on the well-ordered life of the bee colony after this process
has gone on for some time? Can we afford to endanger the whole
structure of bee society and possibly do serious damage to the
bees in order to procure for ourselves the marvelous royal jelly
that has such potency so far as bees are concerned?

What Does Royal Jelly Contain?

Well, then, you might say, let us study the royal jelly,
find out what it contains, and manufacture our own! Easier said
than done. For royal jelly has so intrigued scientists of recent
years that they have conducted extensive researches on it, without finding in it any substance that would explain its marvelous
power. They have taken royal jelly apart until they know what
all its ingredients are, they think. Then they put these ingredients together in the laboratory, and what they get is not royal
jelly at all! So apparently there are substances in the jelly with
which we are not only unfamiliar, but whose presence we cannot
even detect.

Melampy and Jones reported in the *Proceedings of the
Society of Experimental Biology and Medicine,* Vol. 41, p. 382,
1939, that they could detect no vitamin A in royal jelly. There
was some vitamin B_1 (thiamin). Pearson and Burgin in the
same magazine, Vol. 48, p. 415, 1941, reported that royal jelly
contains more pantothenic acid than any other known substance. Between $2\frac{1}{2}$ and 6 times as much as yeast and liver.
Pantothenic acid is another B vitamin.

Other investigators have reported little or no vitamin E
in royal jelly, and no detectable amount of vitamin C. Thomas
S. Gardner, writing in the *Journal of Gerontology* for January,
1948, tells of experiments involving fruit flies which were fed
royal jelly. According to him, the pantothenic acid in royal jelly
increased the life span of the flies. He goes on to say that no
one knows as yet how much of the valuable B vitamin is needed
by the average human being, but it has been estimated that we
need about 11 to 15 milligrams a day. In the average American
diet most of us obtain only about 5 milligrams a day. However,
no one has done any research apparently to find out whether
pantothenic acid, either in or out of royal jelly, will increase
the life span of human beings.

And so the story goes. When we first began to collect
clippings about royal jelly, we wrote to some 10 or 15 labora-

tories where, according to the clippings, research is in progress. None of them could give us any help. They referred us to the information we have given above, but without exception they told us that they know of no research involving human beings. We also wrote to all our advertisers who sell honey. More than anyone else, beekeepers are respectful when they speak of all the marvels of bee-life and community organization. And they are all sure that royal jelly must be a truly miraculous substance, for they see what happens in their beehives to those individual bees that feed on royal honey as compared with those which do not. But none of our beekeeper friends had heard of any research involving human beings. And most of them stated that royal jelly is not very tasty. It is a white, milky paste with an acid flavor.

Although there is some new information on royal jelly and tumors in laboratory animals, we have seen nothing that convinces us of the usefulness of royal jelly as a supplement for human beings.

SECTION 41

SOAP

We believe the average person has little need for soap in bathing. Washing with plain water is best. Soap, or detergents, turn the skin alkaline, whereas its natural healthy condition is acid. Men should not use shampoos or wash the hair, but should brush it vigorously several times a day.

CHAPTER **136**

Why Use Soap?

A recent inquiry from an attorney came as a result of an article on detergents. This gentleman was representing a client who believed she had contracted a dermatitis from using a detergent. So little has been written in magazines in general circulation about the possibility of skin injury from detergents that the attorney could not find medical or scientific background for presenting his case.

We searched for material on the subject and found two very enlightening articles dealing with detergents, soaps and other cleansers in their relation to skin health.

Joseph V. Klauder, M.D., of Philadelphia, writing in the *Archives of Dermatology and Syphilology*, Vol. 63, 1951, tells us that a total of 3,709 cases of skin diseases have been presented for claims for compensation under the Pennsylvania law since this law went into effect. Of these, 1,673 were occupational in origin; 2,036 were non-occupational. Of the occupational dermatoses, 13.1 per cent were the result of "wet work"— that is, working in water, water and soap or water and detergents.

Dr. Klauder reviews standard tests of the ability of the skin to withstand such substances. The normal pH, or acidity, of the skin on the hands ranges from 4.5 to 6.5, so normal skin is acid. When the skin is bathed in sweat, its acidity increases. Exposing the hands to alkali increases the alkalinity of their skin in proportion to the length of time they are exposed and the frequency, and the degree of alkalinity. The two persons in Dr. Klauder's article whose hands required the longest time to return to normal were two dishwashers whose hands, of course, were in soapy water most of their working time. It was discovered that not until 20 hours after their hands had been exposed to soap and water did the pH of their skin return to normal. This means that during their daily work their hands were constantly in an abnormal, alkaline condition, for the pH did not ever have time to return to normal on those days. On their days off they might expect a normal condition of the skin on their hands just as they were ready to go back to work!

Dr. Klauder studied the effects of many commercial detergents and reported on them: 7 nonsoap detergents advised for dermatitic hands, 103 hand cleaners for industrial workers and 19 nonsoap detergents for kitchen and household purposes. Of the 103 hand cleaners, 94 were alkaline and 57 were gritty powders which contained one or more alkaline salt detergents.

The Normal Skin Is Acid

A. L. Hudson, M.D., of Toronto, Canada, writing in the *Canadian Medical Association Journal* for January, 1951, tells us more about the effect of soaps and detergents as well as different drugs, shampoos and ointments on the skin. We have somehow come to think of alkalinity as something to be highly desired. But when speaking of the skin, it is well to remember that alkalinity is not normal. Dr. Hudson tells us that normal skin has a pH from 4 to 6, depending on the location of the skin and when it was last washed with an alkaline substance. In parts of the body where a great deal of perspiration is excreted, the acidity is greater. And, naturally, in hot weather this pH goes even lower, for then there is more perspiration. This normally acid condition of the skin is spoken of as "the acid mantle." If one can maintain a constantly acid condition of the skin, one can prevent the development of contact dermatitis, since the skin is much more susceptible to disease when alkaline.

Soap Increases Alkalinity

Tests have shown that a skin area with a normal pH of 4 shows a pH of 7 one minute after it is washed with soap and may require 70 minutes before the skin returns to its normal pH. When washing with some soaps, it has been shown that this increased alkalinity may be present for as long as $3\frac{1}{2}$ hours. We should keep in mind that when we talk of alkalinity in connection with soap, we mean all soap, because alkali is set free in water as soon as soap is put into it and the alkalinity of the solution may rise to as high as 10 or 11.

When there are certain kinds of disorder present in the

skin, this change to alkalinity is more marked and more prolonged in the diseased area and the skin directly around it. In
summer when the skin is normally more acid, it takes less time
to return to the normal pH after using the soap. This may be
the reason, says Dr. Hudson, why so many more people complain of dermatitis and eczema on their hands in winter. Variations in normal skin acidity occur according to: the character
and quantity of perspiration, the prevention of evaporation of
this perspiration, the amount of secretion of the oily glands of
the skin which becomes akaline as it is evaporating. So the
acidity of the skin and, to a certain extent, the health of the
skin, depend on the composition of sweat and how much of it
is left unevaporated on the skin. Other conditions aside from
washing with soap make the skin alkaline—dust, disintegrated
sweat glands, seborrhea, psoriasis, tuberculosis and several other
skin diseases.

It seems obvious that medicines, ointments or soaps
applied to any part of the body where the alkalinity is already
high, should, if possible, be acid, so that they may bring that
part back to normal acidity rather than increasing the alkalinity.
Especially in the case of fungus growths, such as cause athlete's
foot, any medication used should make the skin more, rather
than less, acid. Of course, soap on athlete's foot is bound to
increase the alkalinity still further and make the condition
worse.

The pH of Different Soaps

In testing soaps and shampoos, Dr. Hudson reports on
Canadian products with which we are not familiar, but mentions several American products as well: Ivory soap has a pH
of 7.5 which means that it is quite alkaline. French castile is
somewhat better with a pH of 6. Tide, the detergent, has a
pH of 9.5—extremely alkaline. Drene shampoo has a pH of 6.5
and Halo a pH of 4.0.

Soaps Produce Unhealthy Skin

Dr. Hudson summarizes by telling us that the pH of the
skin is the result of the physiological functions of the skin and
is changed by certain environmental conditions and/or agents
and by disease. Soaps increase the pH for relatively long periods
and thus may make the skin much more susceptible to irritants
or allergenic material. Once a dermatitis has been contracted,

the use of soap will prolong it by keeping the skin alkaline rather than allowing it to return to its normal pH. So using soap or alkaline detergents is the most harmful thing you can do under these conditions.

If you have one of the skin conditions mentioned, you are probably being treated by a physician, so there is no further precaution you should take except to avoid soaps and detergents like the very plague. If your hands, feet and legs suffer in cold weather (and what housewife can honestly say she never has trouble with rough, painful hands in winter?), you would do well to take every precaution against exposure to soaps and detergents. It's awkward to use gloves for every kind of household task, but it's worth it in the end. So when you are doing laundry, washing dishes, cleaning and especially if you are using water outside in the winter, make certain that you do wear gloves, for you will be protecting your hands against painful roughness and possible skin disease.

Too many of us are likely to dismiss rough winter hands as "a bad case of chapping" and rub on some lotion which we hope will make them smooth again. Alkaline soaps and detergents, as we have seen, produce a definite unhealthy state of skin by the chemical action of changing the pH of the skin. And many kinds of disorders may result. You can buy lined rubber gloves these days which are much easier to work in, as well as to put on and remove. You can buy gloves with ridged fingers so that wet, slippery dishes will not slip out of your hands.

Cut Down on the Use of Soap

Some time ago we printed the experience of an explorer in the tropical jungle who discovered that so long as he refrained from using soap, he, along with those natives who also did not use soap, was completely free from the many skin afflictions that tormented the others members of the party who used soap religiously. On the basis of this evidence, Editor Rodale began an experiment which he has continued up to the present—you guessed it, doing without soap. A daily shower or bath in clear water with the help of an efficient wash cloth has meant the elimination of any tendency to tender skin or skin disorders. Furthermore, he no longer uses soaps or shampoos on his hair, nor does he wash his hair, even with plain water. Every day he gives it a thorough, vigorous brushing. Dandruff has disappeared and his barber comments approvingly on the wonderfully healthy state of his scalp.

We would like to advise eliminating soap and detergent entirely, but in these days of coal, soot and smog, we know that no housewife can get through her work using just water. But use as little soap or detergent as you possibly can. As for bathing, it seems to us quite unlikely that the average person, unless he does very grimy work, gets dirty enough to use any soap in his bath or shower. Try washing in plain water and see if you can't get rid of any wintertime eczema or other skin complaint.

SECTION 42

EYEGLASSES

Do not wear rimless eyeglasses. They may cause a skin cancer to form under the eyes where the sun throws its hot rays right through the glass, as a magnifying glass that, by the sun's rays, causes paper to burn.

We are against the use of sunglasses, as they are a crutch. Eat sunflower seeds to give your eyes ability to withstand sun-glare.

CHAPTER **137**

Rimless Spectacles and the Skin

Rimless eyeglasses, once extremely popular, and still worn by many thousands of people, hold a danger to the skin of the wearer not generally known. *The Archives of Dermatology and Syphilology* (April, 1949) discusses findings made at Jefferson Medical College showing that a type of skin cancer, epithelioma, can be caused by rimless eyeglasses. It seems that the sun's rays, shining through the glass, are deflected to, and concentrated at, the edges of the lens, the part which is closest to the cheeks of the wearer. The concentration of light upon this area of the cheek causes the skin temperature to rise as much as 3 degrees Fahrenheit above the temperature of the adjacent skin area. The result is a "burning" of the skin directly under the rim of the lens, much as one would burn paper by concentrating the sun's rays through a magnifying glass. This "burning" occurs day after day on the cheeks of those who wear rimless glasses, and the constant irritation leads to skin cancer.

What Solution to this Problem?

The authors of the *Archives* article point out that masking the edges of the lens with black laquer or paint will effectively eliminate the hazard of the refracted light. Of course, the new dark plastic frames for spectacles are the more practical and more attractive solution to the problem.

Some Case Histories

The authors included 12 illustrative case histories, among which is that of an executive, aged 55, who had a small growth below the lower rim of his glasses. In certain positions the rimless spectacles caused a bright focus on several points of his cheeks. One of these was directly opposite the site of the current growth, and a scar there gave evidence of an active break in the skin at some previous time. The patient admitted that it was the result of a similar growth, diagnosed as skin cancer at an earlier date.

A woman, aged 52, had a sort of small pimple containing liquid on the left cheek just a fraction of an inch below the lower arc of her spectacles. It had been present for about two years before the patient was examined. The lady told the doctor that she had worn rimless bifocal lenses for the past 8 years. The growth proved to be cancerous, and was indeed at the seat of the focus of light through her lens.

A mechanic, who frequently worked bareheaded in the summer, showed two bright, concentrated points of light below the lower rims of his glasses, exactly where two pea-sized growths were located. A biopsy showed evidence of cancer. The patient had worn rimless glasses at one time and changed, on his own, to plastic frames, apparently too late.

Conclusion: Don't Wear Rimless Eyeglasses

The other cases are similar, and point out the frightening fact that health hazards are found in the most unlikely items. It is to our best interests to at least avoid those dangers which we can see and about which we have been warned.

If you know anyone who wears rimless eyeglasses, point out this very real danger to them. If you have been wearing them yourself, change to some other type at once.

SECTION 43

SUN BATHING

Be careful to avoid too much exposure to the sun. It can have disastrous effects.

CHAPTER **138**

Sun Bathing . . . Good or Bad?

Because there is so much confusion on this subject, we want to talk about it in some detail. In this chapter we will talk only about some of the diseases associated with too much sunshine. This should give you an idea of how serious the matter can be.

First of all, there is the condition known as "photosensitivity" which means, of course, sensitivity to light. We are told in an article by W. Harvey Cabaniss, Jr., M.D. in *Modern Medicine* for November 15, 1956, that the way photosensitivity comes about is not known. It seems that certain compounds in the skin absorb specific wave lengths of radiant energy which apparently alter them sufficiently to cause disease conditions in the skin.

Drugs Causing Photosensitivity

There are some drugs which make the person taking them photosensitive—sulfa drugs, barbiturates, some antihistamines, Thorazine (one of the tranquilizers) may cause a rash on areas exposed to sunlight. Stilbamidine, another drug, remains in the skin for a long time, and photosensitive reactions may occur months after the last injection.

Coal tar derivatives may lead to photosensitization. What do we mean by coal tar derivatives? Well, anything that contains coal tar comes under that heading, and that means just about everything we use these days in the way of drugs, cosmetics, lotions, perfumes, soaps and household preparations. Just about any of these could be the cause of a skin disorder in areas exposed to sunlight. Have you ever noticed that women who are excessively sunburned sometimes have their tan in unsightly streaks? The streaks may represent places where they had cosmetics or perfume on their skin when they went to sun-bathe.

Internal Medicine for Sunburn Protection

Extracts of a certain plant, *Ammi majus,* cause blistering and an excess of color when they are applied to the skin and then exposed to the sun. Doctors have used these extracts in treating the disease, *vitiligo,* in which white, unpigmented spots appear in the skin. The drug is given either orally or applied to the skin, and the skin is then exposed to the sun. It may take as long as 6 to 9 months for the pigment to reappear.

Because this drug produces pigment in the skin, it has been suggested for use as a "sunburn pill." It has been tested with fair success on numerous volunteers, but the official lay magazine of the American Medical Association, *Today's Health,* stated in its August, 1956, issue that the drug made from *Ammi majus* is a potent one, quite likely to cause serious side effects. "Approximately 3 years of testing in this country and centuries of use in Egypt in the crude form have not proved it either safe or useful for all." Their conclusion is that until more is known about its reliability and toxicity, it should remain an experimental drug.

Sensitivity to light is a symptom of several diseases: *porphyria* (a rather mysterious disease in which certain chemical substances are excreted in the urine), *lupus erythematosus* (a tuberculous disease of the skin), pellagra (a disease of vitamin B deficiency) and *xeroderma pigmentosum* (an often fatal disease of the skin characterized by dryness). In all of these diseases exposure to the sun's rays brings redness, itching and burning to the skin.

Sun and Tuberculosis

In the early days of sanitarium treatment of tuberculosis, it was believed that long, long hours of sunshine were necessary for a cure. The *British Medical Journal* for January 25, 1957, reviews an article that appeared as early as 1921 indicating that lengthy exposure to the sun might be the very worst possible thing for a tubercular patient. Prolonged sun bathing, especially for those who can indulge in it only occasionally, is exhausting, says the *Journal,* and exhaustion can open the door to the tuberculosis germ. In general, it is now conceded by experts that TB patients should not sun-bathe to the extent of getting any sunburn at all.

Everyday Conditions Caused By Too Much Sun

Long-continued exposure to the sun's rays produces symptoms in otherwise healthy people. "Farmer's" or "sailor's skin" is thickened, dry and tanned. *Senile keratoses* (horny spots) often appear on individuals with these skin changes and may turn into skin cancer. Scales, freckles, yellow discolorations of the skin may occur, and the lips may become whitened and dry and crack easily.

Says Otto C. Stegmaier, M.D., in the same issue of *Modern Medicine,* "Sunlight is one of the main causes of cancer of the skin. Cancers generally appear on parts of the body exposed to sunlight and are most common among farmers, laborers and others exposed to the sun almost continuously!" Skin cancer is more common in southern than in northern climates.

Other Diseases Caused By Sunlight

Dr. Stegmaier lists several other diseases influenced by sunlight: *vitiligo* (the disorder characterized by patches of completely white skin), *albinism* (persons who are born with no pigment in skin or hair are called albinos), *pityriasis rubra pilaris* (chronic inflammatory skin disease, often fatal) and *Keratosis follicularis* (a form of acne).

It seems peculiar, but there are whole families of individuals who suffer from these disorders who must avoid the sun at all costs. In the March 3, 1953, issue of *Life* appeared the picture of a Wyoming man who must wear a hooded mask whenever he goes out in the sunlight. This gentleman suffers from *lupus erythematosus.* A medical journal tells of an Illinois family, unable to go out in sunlight, who work in the mines all day and conduct their business and social life only after dark.

The Journal of the Florida Medical Association for October, 1952, describes the following as some of the hazards of too much sun: hives, especially about the mouth (somewhat like cold blisters), *folliculitis* (inflammation which may block the sweat glands and cause infection), *chloasma* (spots of pigment in the skin), showers of pigmented moles, and persistent, increased sensitivity to sunlight.

A report on the incidence of skin cancer according to the complexion of the patient is given in the *Archives of Dermatology and Syphilology* for April, 1950. It seems that fair-skinned persons are far more susceptible. Of 100 persons studied, only 13 had brown eyes while 87 had eyes of a lighter color. Only 46 per cent of the brown-eyed group were "burned," while 83 per cent of the blue-eyed group were. No patient with two brown-eyed parents gave a family history of skin cancer; four with one brown-eyed parent gave such a history, while 21 who gave a family history of skin cancer had two blue-eyed parents. It seems that the more brown-eyed inheritance a person has, the more protected he may be against skin cancer resulting from exposure to the sun.

Research on Sunlight Very Slight

An article in the science section of the *New York Herald Tribune* for July 30, 1950, mentions something which we believe is extremely significant in relation to sunburn. John J. O'Neill, author of the article, tells us that exposure to strong sunlight stimulates the pituitary gland in human beings. He expresses surprise that more research has not been done along these lines.

It seems that what research there is began with a study of the effect of strong light, either natural or artificial, on birds and animals. Changes in plumage and mating time of birds and equally extensive changes in habits of animals were noted. "Tanning of the skin is a photochemical reaction," says Mr. O'Neill, "if anyone whose skin tans sufficiently quickly cares to try the stunt, he or she would find it possible to have the sun print a photograph or an insignia directly on the skin by covering an area with a negative."

We Need the Sun

What are we trying to show with all this information? Is it that even a moment of sunshine is dangerous, and we should all take to living indoors all the time? Of course not. We need the sun, and we cannot be healthy without it. What we are trying to show is that sunshine is a powerful chemical force which must be treated with great respect if we do not want it to harm us.

Spending long uncomfortable hours in the sun "to get a good tan" is tempting fate. A force so powerful that it can be the single most important factor in ailments like those we have described above cannot be trifled with.

CHAPTER **139**

How Much of a Friend Is Mr. Sun?

Don't let those travel folders fool you. Lying in the sun is not the safest way to spend your vacation.

Convincing people of the advantage of good diet and the need to avoid unhealthful foods is difficult sometimes, but to convince them that there can be danger in too much sun is even harder. "What could be more natural than a sun bath?" they ask. "You're always preaching about the natural life, why do an about-face on this point?" A natural exposure to the sun is not objectionable, but there is nothing natural about the sun worship of many people who are content to suffer in the heat of it, no matter how intense and uncomfortable, frying first one side, then the other, in pursuit of a tan. Usually those with fair skin, who burn easily and painfully, are the only ones careful of how much sun they get.

Problem Not Trivial

There is more to the problem of too much sun than a sleepless night or a back that can't be slapped. Sunburn is the result of ultraviolet radiation. In big enough doses these rays could kill you, but usually the horny layer of the skin deflects or absorbs much of these rays. One's individual resistance to sunburn depends largely upon the thickness of this layer of skin. When the rays penetrate the skin, a reaction takes place in which the blood vessels of the skin become swollen, and this is what causes the redness of sunburn.

In tanning, the sun's rays cause increased production of a pigment called melanin. The rays cause the renewed supply of melanin to move to the surface of the skin, and that's how it gets a tanned appearance.

How Much Is Too Much?

The important question is, how much sun should one get? After all, it does give us vitamin D, and besides one couldn't avoid it entirely in any case. But too much sunlight, like too much of anything, is just too much! In *Pageant* magazine for August, 1958, sun bathing is discussed in some detail, and some interesting facts emerge. For example, did you know that some tuberculosis patients should not be exposed to the sun, lest it be fatal? At TB sanitariums there is a rigid rule that lung TB patients must lie in the shade and never in the sun. Some substances produced by the sun on the skin pass quickly into the blood stream, elevating the blood pressure and exciting the heart—particularly dangerous to the TB patient.

A little closer to home, consider this fact printed in the *Pageant* article: about 7,500,000 work days a year are lost to industry due to absenteeism because of sunburn, and about the same number is considered lost due to impaired efficiency because of sunburn.

Most Widespread Cases of Cancer

The chances of incurring skin cancer from overexposure to the sun seem to be pretty good. Dr. Charles S. Cameron, of the American Cancer Society, says, "Repeated sunburn is perhaps the most widespread of the known causes of cancer." In climates which feature the greatest amounts of sunlight, such as near-tropical Australia, skin cancer is 5 times more prevalent than in cloudy New England. And persons exposed to intense sunlight in their work are far more susceptible to skin cancer than others. For example, skin cancer in United States Navy men at sea is 8 times more frequent than it is among city people who work in offices.

Exposure to sunshine for those who wear rimless eyeglasses presents a special danger. The rays of the sun are concentrated as they pass through the glasses to the place on the skin at which they rest. This extra irritation of the skin has been shown many times to be a cause of skin cancer. Don't ever wear glasses without rims, for they can cause a serious problem.

While speaking of sunlight and the eyes, it should be mentioned that sunflower seeds can be important in this connection. Aside from their basic value in strengthening the eyes, sunflower seeds have been found by Editor Rodale to be tremendously effective in mitigating the effects of glare. The strain imposed on the eyes by glare is especially evident at the beach where white sand and rolling water reflect the sun brilliantly. If you find yourself exposed to the bright sun frequently, an extra handful of sunflower seeds added to your diet might be just the eye insurance you need.

It is the opinion of many dermatologists that constantly repeated exposure to the sun exhausts the skin's healing ability by weakening its pigment and its thickening powers. And who are those most likely to be affected with sunburn? A *New York Times* article (August 21, 1958) asserts that persons between the ages of 21 and 50 are particularly susceptible to sunburn. Pregnant women, up to their seventh month, are also likely candidates for a red skin. The change in hormone supplies in the body at this time is said to be responsible.

Favorable Conditions for a Bad Burn

It was stated in the *Times* article that high humidity, light clouds and a lack of wind are the ripest conditions for a bad case of sunburn. The humidity causes the body to perspire, and the perspiration makes the skin particularly sensitive to the sun's ultraviolet rays. Without the wind to help dry the skin, the danger of the situation is heightened. Finally, the light clouds act as reflectors for the sunshine and thereby intensify its effect.

The Protection to Expect From Lotions

Are the suntan lotions, being peddled from every drugstore counter and Five and Dime Store, effective? Well, since we spend $10½ million a year on them, it would be a shame to report that they do no good at all, but you'll never find a guarantee in the package you buy. These lotions are intended to screen out the shortwave ultraviolet radiation of the sun, while admitting the longer rays which are thought to produce the much-wanted tan. We think the main danger involved in using such preparations is that they give rise to a false security in those who use them. The customer thinks that because he has slathered himself with lotion, he can defy warnings about overexposure and exposure at the height of the sun's intensity. This is simply not true. Apparently no brand of lotion gives protection to everybody who tries it. Even those found by testing to be most effective work on only 70 per cent of those who use them. In the same tests 15 brands were found to offer protection to only one-third to two-thirds of those who used them, and 15 brands gave so little protection that they were of almost no value at all. If you must go into the sun for long periods, you might as well get whatever protection you can from a good suntan lotion, applied liberally and often, but don't expect it to take the place of caution and common sense in protecting you from the consequences of overexposure to strong sunshine.

What About a Pill for Sunburn Protection?

The question of a pill for protection against excessive sunburn and encouraging suntan comes up periodically. The side effects such as stomach upsets, nausea, nervousness, insomnia and moods of depressed feeling have made them highly suspect. A recent article in *The Medical Journal of Australia* (December, 1958) discussed the fact that the committee on cosmetics of the American Medical Association has concerned itself with the subject of these orally administered protectives. Basically, they all come from a pigment-stimulating agent derived from an ancient Egyptian plant. The Committee found that while improved tanning did occur in many cases, careful supervision of dosage is required as well as limited exposure to sunlight. If either is too large, the result may be just the opposite of that which is desired, that is, redness, swelling, blistering and pain. It was concluded that a dosage of 10 or 20 mg. of methoxsalen (meloxine or oxsoralen) for most adults was safe for 1 or 2 weeks, but an increase might have unknown deleterious effects on the skin. Who will supervise the sun-worshippers who might buy the drug and take it by the boxful for every day of a month's vacation? Who will time their exposure to the sun? The whole suggestion of approving any drug on such a basis is preposterous—especially when its main purpose is nothing more than a suntan for cosmetic reasons. Is there any sense to the use of such a preparation—whose other more lasting effects might not even be dreamed of—when comfort and common sense, as well as the warnings of serious scientists, tell us that we should avoid getting too much sun if we possibly can do so?

If one does get sunburned, and seriously enough, one might require a doctor's care and even hospitalization. Included in such extreme treatment can be pain killers, antibiotics, anti-fungus drugs and even transfusions. Why chance it?

Easing the Pain

For the more run-of-the-mill sunburn that just won't give you any peace, there are dozens of remedies, new and old. The least messy and easiest to prepare seems to be a compress of cool tea. Many persons simply soak a tea bag in some cool water to moisten it well, and gently sop it over the affected area. The tannic acid in the tea is said to be responsible for the cooling, soothing effect. Some other suggested treatments are oatmeal baths and a very diluted solution of vinegar—about one teaspoonful to a quart of water.

If you do find that you spend excessive time in the sun, perspiring profusely and giving rise to bouts with prickly heat, you will be interested in a letter printed in *The Journal of the American Medical Association* (March 10, 1951) written by Dr. Frederick Reiss. Dr. Reiss noted that one sequel to prickly heat is a depletion of vitamin C in the system, and he suggests dosages of 900 to 1,000 mg. per day to bring up the level. He also believes that a vitamin C shortage can be caused by excessive perspiration. Do you increase your dosage of this nutrient on hot, sticky summer days?

Sunstroke

A word should be said here about sunstroke. Use of alcoholic beverages in hot weather can be a predisposing factor to sunstroke. It is actually a serious illness and can be fatal. Sunstroke is caused by too long exposure to the hot sun, plus a humidity which interferes with the evaporation of perspiration, an important device the body has for keeping cool. The loss of large amounts of water and body salt through perspiration are other factors. The symptoms of sunstroke are frightening to the extreme. Usually they begin with a severe headache. Everything looks red to the victim, and he loses consciousness. He develops a fever which can make the thermometer shoot up to 110°. If the unconsciousness and high temperature last for any length of time, the danger is great. Sometimes the patient collapses and dies within a few minutes.

Make a friend of the sun, but don't presume on the friendship. Some sun in the early morning or late afternoon can be soothing and healthful. But don't be tempted to broil yourself in the hot rays of mid-day just to acquire a fashionable tan. The dangers to health which are involved far outweigh the fashion advantage offered by brown shoulders and tanned cheeks.

SECTION 44

OVERWEIGHT AND UNDERWEIGHT

Overweight and underweight can both be overcome, we believe, by following the diet outlined in these pages. Overweight is considered one of the leading illnesses in our country today. Associated often with high blood pressure, heart disease, diabetes, cancer and many other tragic diseases, obesity can and should be overcome.

CHAPTER **140**

Underweight

Being too fat is distressing both from the point of view of health and happiness. But being too thin is almost as great a problem, as those of us know who grew up to the derisive cat-call of "Hey, skinny!"

Excessive thinness is not attractive. And it may produce unusual fatigue, nervousness and a predisposition to many ills. It is considered quite healthy to be slightly underweight. Deaths from most of the degenerative diseases—heart and blood vessel disorders, diabetes, cancer and so forth—are much fewer in that group of people who consistently maintain their weight at a little below "normal." But some diseases such as tuberculosis claim most of their victims from among those who are very thin.

We put the word "normal" in quotes above, for we have the idea that many of us tend to measure our degree of over- or underweight by the tables that are put out by the insurance companies according to age and height. But what is underweight for one person may be normal for another, so it is not wise to go entirely by the standard tables when you are figuring out just where you stand. These tables are compiled not from any ideal weight, but from averages over the country as a whole. So if you happen to be 35 years old and 5 feet 6 inches tall, the table does not mean that 142 is the ideal weight for you. It means simply that this is the average or "normal" weight for others of your age and height all over the country.

So don't spend too much time worrying if you show up quite a bit underweight according to the tables. It seems that it is perfectly natural and healthy for many people to be thin. Doctors call these people "sthenic." They have good muscles and the average amount of endurance and stamina. They have good resistance to disease; they are poised and emotionally stable. They have a well-balanced nervous system, but their bodies somehow just don't deposit fat. If you are this kind of person, don't worry about your underweight. You will probably live to a healthy old age untroubled by the high blood pressure and diabetes that make your stout neighbors' lives unendurable.

The Asthenic Person

The other kind of thin person is called "asthenic." Such a person lacks endurance, is easy prey to fatigue and diseases, is nervous and physically weak. He is not able to meet the demands made on him by society either from a physical or personality standpoint. Usually such an individual has a narrow, shallow chest, poor posture, flabby muscles and a weak digestion. Subconsciously he fights the idea of taking more food, for he is convinced that food does not agree with him. So he continues to grow thinner. If you are an "asthenic" type of thin person, you would do well to increase your weight if you can, for obviously your body is badly nourished, and the outcome may not be a happy one.

Eating More Isn't the Answer

Medical literature and the books on library shelves are full of suggestions on losing weight. Almost every month a new book on reducing is published, a new reducing diet appears at regular intervals in monthly magazines, radio programs advertise countless diets and reducing medicines that line the shelves of drug stores. In fact, it seems that the plight of the overweight person gets much more attention that that of the thin one. One good reason for this is the large number of Americans who are overweight. Underweight is not nearly so general a problem. But there is another reason, too. It is pretty generally agreed that the overweight person can reduce by simply eating less. But it does not follow, apparently, that the thin person can gain weight by eating more. Throughout all the research we did in medical journals we found very, very little material on the subject of gaining weight. And what articles we found specified that there is no one formula for success. Serious underweight is a hard problem to lick.

There is general agreement on the fact that there are two kinds of underweight—exogenous and endogenous. Some people are thin simply because they don't eat enough of foods which will put on weight. This is exogenous underweight—coming from circumstances *outside* the body. But others are thin apparently from some reason that has nothing to do with how much food they eat, for they may have good appetites and (without gaining a single pound) may eat as much as others in their family who are overweight. This is the endogenous underweight—arising from something *inside* the body.

In the case of the first group the answer is simply to eat more food. Yet perhaps we had better not say "simply," for sometimes there are complex reasons why people do not eat enough, just as there are complex reasons why others eat too much. Faulty habits of eating are perhaps as responsible as anything else for inadequate intake of food. An example is the child who gets up too late to eat breakfast, wolfs down a few bites for lunch because he is eager to get back to playing, and hastens through dinner with one eye cocked toward the television set. In the case of children, of course, the parents must play the biggest part in correcting bad eating habits, for the child cannot possibly foresee what difficulties may result later from these habits. But how can he be taught good food habits by a father who habitually gulps a cup of coffee for breakfast, skips lunch or eats a sandwich while he stands up at a drug store counter and then finds himself too exhausted to do justice to dinner—or a mother who also skips breakfast and can't be bothered to make lunch because no one else is home at lunchtime?

Learn the Importance of Food and Appetite

Children and adults alike should be taught the importance of food and of mealtimes. Three times a day at least, all other activities should be dropped completely for meals. Meals should be eaten in a quiet, unhurried and unworried atmosphere, regardless of what television programs are at hand or what other activities are pending. Mealtime should above all things be a pleasant time—no scolding, no worrying, no arguing, no recitals of bad news should ever be permitted within 10 feet of a dinner table. Meals should be served at regular hours. If dinner is delayed an hour beyond the regular time, children and adults alike will be so hungry that they are bound to be grumpy and cranky. If they have taken the edge off their appetites with crackers or candy, the worthwhile food served at the meal may go uneaten.

Persistent worry, psychological upsets and a feeling of being unwanted or unloved can result in lack of appetite. In fact, the whole phenomenon of psychological disorders getting in the way of appetite has become so common that it has been given a medical name—*anorexia nervosa*—nervous lack of appetite. As the appetite dwindles, and the individual eats less, his stomach shrinks accordingly, he has a desire for less and less food. As his body loses nourishment, he may develop an extremely serious condition that can result in death—death from starvation actually, although there is plenty of food around him.

In the case of children one nutritionist, Jean Bogert, has put the matter quite directly in her book, *Nutrition and Physical Fitness* (Saunders, 1949)—we do not let our children decide on what clothes to buy, whether or not they wish to go to school or what time they go to bed, so why in the world should we leave it up to the children to decide what they will or will not eat? Obviously this is a matter needing mature judgment. And the child who is allowed to have as much candy, soft drinks, chewing gum and ice cream as he wants between meals will not have any appetite for the meats, vegetables and fruits which he should be eating at his meals.

Appetite Arousers

Bringing back appetite to adults is a little harder to accomplish. And sometimes it necessitates a firm hand and as much will power as the overweight person needs to refuse food. One element that should be kept constantly in mind is that a lack of vitamins—B vitamins particularly—results in loss of appetite. We have yet to see or hear of the thin person without appetite who can hold out against a whopping big dose of brewer's yeast or desiccated liver daily. He has no choice. Regardless of "nerves," stubbornness or a deep psychological hatred of food, 3 or 4 weeks of brewer's yeast or desiccated liver therapy *will* give him an appetite—it's bound to—unless there are conditions of ill health present that prevent him from absorbing the B vitamins.

Of course, we should not have to remind you that food should be attractively served to tempt the appetite of a thin person. A rest (yes, we mean lying down!) from 5 minutes to a half hour before and after meals will bring enough relaxation that food may appear attractive again. If appetite has been poor for some time, it will take a while to establish normal eating habits again. The stomach must be stretched so that no feeling of disagreeable fullness results. Snacks in mid-morning and mid-afternoon as well as something to eat before going to bed may be the answer, for it is hard to eat enough at only 3 meals if you have been accustomed to nibbling on meals.

What Should a Thin Person Eat?

Now throughout all this discussion of how to get thin persons to eat more, we have not touched on *what* they should eat. Not so many years ago the theory was that since sweet and starchy food make a fat person fatter, therefore a thin person should eat lots of them to gain weight. In fact, one medical article that we found, written only about 15 years ago, advised all kinds of starchy foods—spaghetti, macaroni, bread and butter—for gaining weight. But more recently the thinking has been that, just as high protein diets regulate metabolism so that the fat person loses weight, so high protein diets are valuable for gaining weight. True, the thin person need not watch calories on foods like potatoes, beans, butter and so forth. But he should certainly not try to put on weight by eating lots of refined cereals, foods like noodles, spaghetti, cake, pie, or foods that are high in refined sugars such as candy, ice cream and so forth. A diet high in protein and starchy vegetables (prepared to retain all their vitamin and mineral content) with a minimum of sweets and plenty of butter and vegetable oils should certainly result in weight-gaining.

Some Deterrents to Food Absorption

The second kind of thin person who wants to gain weight presents a much harder problem to solve. This is the individual who has a good appetite and eats as much as the average person, but who still remains scrawny and bony, in spite of everything he can do. In the book, *Diseases of Metabolism,* edited by Garfield G. Duncan, M.D. (W. B. Saunders Company, 1952), there is a full page list of factors which can produce undernutrition. Skipping those which have to do with lack of appetite, and purely mechanical causes such as bad teeth, diseases of the mouth and diseases such as peptic ulcers and so forth, we find quite an extended list of conditions that prevent absorption of food, which might be what is wrong with our thin person who cannot gain weight no matter how much he eats.

Here are some of them: 1. Those which increase destruction of food before the body has assimilated it—lack of hydrochloric acid in the stomach, or the taking of alkaline medicines such as bicarbonate of soda.

2. Those which interfere with absorption of food—absence of normal digestive secretions, dysentery, colitis and other diarrheal diseases, sprue, vitamin deficiencies, drugs which prevent absorption, such as mineral oil, cathartics and so forth.

3. Those which interfere with utilization or storage—impaired liver function, alcoholism, hypothyroidism, therapy with one or another of the sulfa drugs, or X-ray therapy.

Implications of These Deterrents

Now how does such information apply to those of us who are underweight? Well, have you had an illness during the past 10 years or so for which your doctor prescribed sulfa drugs? If so, it is quite possible that these drugs affected a very important part of your digestive tract—the intestinal flora—those friendly bacteria that dwell inside you and help in the digestion of food and the synthesis of some vitamins. This might be an excellent reason why you are short on B vitamins and why you are not assimilating your food as you should. Do you take mineral oil? If so, you're bound to be suffering from a shortage of all the fat-soluble vitamins—A, D, E and K, for these are dissolved and carried away in the presence of mineral oil. Do you suffer chronically from any condition involving diarrhea? If so, perhaps a great deal of your food is excreted without being assimilated, so that no matter how much you eat, your food is doing you little good.

Or perhaps you have not been eating correctly, and so you have a real deficiency of many vitamins. This will prevent you from making proper use of your food. People who are underweight should try as much as possible to eat concentrated foods.

Food supplements are a highly concentrated food. For instance, let's say you are underweight and have been taking mineral oil and so are short of vitamin A. Don't try to get all that vitamin A from carrots. Although carrots are good food for many reasons, you must eat more than one cup of diced carrots to get the amount of vitamin A that is contained in a few perles of a commercial vitamin A product. Carrots are quite low in calories, so they will not help much in your weight building program.

Most advice on gaining weight will tell you to avoid bulky foods that are low in calories, such as salad greens. Under no circumstances would we advise cutting out raw green leafy vegetables—you must have them. But you can cut down to, say one salad a day provided you get plenty of vitamins C, A and B in food supplements. That would mean taking rose hips, fish liver oil, and brewer's yeast or desiccated liver—highly concentrated sources of these 3 vitamins.

Do You Know How to Save Energy?

Finally, authorities are agreed that the most common reason for underweight among people whose appetites are good is a waste of nervous and muscular energy. If they are children, they are striving to be the best student in the class or the captain of the team. If they are adults, they are perfectionists in everything they do—driving themselves all day long, never relaxing, and too busy to waste much time sleeping. If this is your difficulty, the only way to solve it is to begin to take it easy. Don't rush. Do everything with the least possible expenditure of energy. Don't walk if you can ride. Don't stand if you can sit. Don't sit if you can lie down. The more energy you use up in everyday activities the more fat you are burning. And you need your fat. You need it to pad your bones. You need it to provide support for your abdominal organs so that they will not become displaced. And you need it against some possible future day when an illness may use up even more fat and energy than you expend when you are healthy.

Facts to Be Remembered

In general then, this would be our advice for those of you who are worried about being underweight.

1. Watch your diet. Don't try to gain weight by stuffing yourself on desserts and candy. A diet high in protein—meat, fish, nuts and eggs—is best for you, along with plenty of vegetables and fruits, fresh and dried.

2. Relax and stop burning up so many calories in your daily activity. Take naps. Rest before and after meals if possible. Be sure that you eat 3 good, big meals a day and have wholesome snacks between meals and at bedtime (if this does not spoil your appetite).

3. Eat concentrated natural foods high in calories. Remember, though, that refined foods—white breads, bakery goods, and refined cereals—will do you no good and may do you considerable harm. Make certain you are getting enough vitamins and minerals by taking food supplements—the most highly concentrated foods there are. Take fish liver oil for vitamin A, brewer's yeast or desiccated liver for vitamin B and rose hips for vitamin C.

The Metropolitan Life Insurance Company publishes a handy little book called *Overweight and Underweight* which contains calorie lists of foods. You can send for it at their New York office. Or you can send to the Superintendent of Documents in Washington, D. C., for a copy of the Department of Agriculture Handbook No. 8, *Composition of Foods,* which gives the protein, vitamin and mineral content of all foods, as well as the calories.

CHAPTER **141**

Overweight

Overweight predisposes one to many different diseases. It is far safer to keep your weight below average rather than above it. This chapter tells you why.

Although it is pretty generally known that overweight is unhealthy, it is not commonplace knowledge that underweight predisposes one to fewer diseases and infections. An article in the *Journal of the American Medical Association* of

November 24, 1951, describes an experiment showing "increased resistance to infectious disease due to undernourishment." This does not refer to a state of serious or long-continued undernourishment, but discusses a laboratory experiment of several days' duration in which 50 well-fed healthy rats were inoculated with staphylococcus germs; all of the animals were then fed well. For 36 hours thereafter some of the rats were given nothing to eat, while the others ate as usual. Then their intestinal condition was examined.

It was found that 38 per cent of the leukocytes of the hungry rats showed phagocytosis, compared with only 19 per cent in the well-fed ones. (Phagocytosis is the process by which the leukocytes, or white blood corpuscles, destroy disease germs.) In the hungry rats, 423 bacteria had been destroyed for every 100 white blood corpuscles, while in the well-fed ones only 129 germs per 100 leukocytes had been destroyed, indicating that while the clinical significance of these findings is not yet apparent, the article stressed the need for further studies suggested by the facts gathered so far. The experimenters report that not eating at all, as a health measure, does not continue to become progressively more effective. The leukocytes do their best fighting from 36 to 48 hours after fasting begins. After 5 or 6 days, this activity dwindled to almost nothing.

More About the Value of Under-Eating

Further evidence of the value of under-eating comes from Norway where, at a meeting of the Norwegian Public Health Association, it was shown that heart disease decreased decidedly in Norway during the German occupation of that country, when food (especially food rich in animal fats) was scanty. From 1917 to 1940 the mortality rate from circulatory and heart diseases had risen steadily. Then from 1941 it fell, reaching its lowest point in 1943-44. After the end of the war, as food again became plentiful, heart and circulatory diseases again began to increase.

Deaths from hardening of the arteries and heart inflammation decreased during the occupation much more in city areas where rationing was rigidly enforced than in the country where people raised and ate their own food. In a large Oslo hospital, too, deaths from thrombosis and blood clots declined during the war and rose again as conditions came back to normal. The only possible conclusion is that overweight and meals containing an abundance of animal fat are unhealthy, especially for heart and blood vessels. Vegetable fats contain no cholesterol, so they are regarded as less harmful.

Low Calorie Diets and Cancer

Perhaps more startling than either of these reports is an article in the *Annals of the New York Academy of Sciences* for September 7, 1947, on the effect of low calorie diets on the formation of tumors. In this experiment, a control group of mice was fed as much as they wanted to eat of a basic ration, plus cornstarch. A second group was fed limited quantities of the ration, without cornstarch. Throughout the experiment the underfed mice revealed fewer disorders of the heart, kidneys, liver and so forth than did the control mice. In addition, by the time the mice were 100 weeks of age, 26 animals in the group allowed to eat had developed tumors. No tumors had appeared in the underfed group.

In a second experiment the mice were injected with a substance known to produce cancer. Only 11 tumors grew in the group on the restricted diet, compared with 32 in the well-fed group. In addition to a decrease in the number of tumors in the underfed group, there was also a delay in the average time of appearance of tumors. In a further experiment the calorie content fed to several groups of mice was measured and, sure enough, it was found, after due time, that the less calories eaten, the fewer tumors.

Significance for Human Beings

What significance have these experiments for human beings? Surveys by life insurance companies show that middle-aged individuals who are overweight are more likely to die of cancer than those of average weight or less. Persons 25 per cent or more overweight have a cancer mortality of 143 per hundred thousand. Those who are 15 to 50 per cent underweight have a mortality of only 95 per hundred thousand. It seems, therefore, that the avoidance of overweight may result in the prevention of cancer or at least a delay in the cancer process.

Can the answer lie in the candies, pies, cakes, fried foods and bread which make up a large part of our diet? We cannot state positively which foods should and should not be eaten in a program of cancer- and disease-prevention. We do know from the above experiments that one of the surest ways of being healthy and able to withstand cancer and many other diseases and infections is simply to get up from the meal table just a little hungry and to eliminate with an iron will power between-meal and bedtime snacks.

CHAPTER **142**

Overweight Is a Mistake You Can Correct

Some suggestions for a sensible reducing program follow. Following the PREVENTION *system in full is perhaps your best guarantee against gaining unwanted weight.*

A clever man once summed up the reason for overweight thusly: "There are only two real causes of being overweight—chewing and swallowing." We would add, ". . . the wrong foods." The important thing about this statement, however, is that it gets to the heart of the weight problem: eating. Of course, there can be other factors involved in overweight, but careful selection of foods is really the source of healthy body weight, and all the pills and gadgets in the world won't help a bit if one's diet is ignored.

There Is No "Easy" Way

Millions of dollars are made every year by investors who plan a campaign to take advantage of the heavy person's desire to reduce the easy way. Though the customer is well aware that reducing by simply taking a pill or spending an hour with a masseur is impossible, he is still hopeful enough of some miracle to risk a dollar or a hundred dollars on a "painless" reducing plan. The "pain" involved is the rejection of sweets. the elimination from the diet of pastries, salt, fried foods and second helpings.

Is it possible somehow to lose weight healthfully without giving up these things? Any responsible doctor or layman who knows even the most elementary facts about human physiology will tell you it is not. These foods contain the very stuff overweight is made of, so that eating them and hoping to reduce permanently and healthfully is as foolish as heaping wood on a fire hoping at the same time that it will go out!

The Metropolitan Life Insurance Company issues a booklet entitled "Overweight and Underweight" which says this about the so-called miracle reducing preparations that are supposed to be a short cut to a normal weight. "Any drug which can increase the body's rate of burning calories enough to effect weight reduction without dieting is dangerous. One drug, released in the early 1930's without medical sanction, 'worked,' but it also caused deafness, blindness and paralysis before it was withdrawn from the market. Even if drugs are prescribed by a physician they will be used in addition to—not in place of—a diet."

The Reason Dieting Works

The theory behind dieting is quite simple. It is based upon the fact that food is the fuel that keeps the body working. One's body can use only so much fuel per day to perform its job, just as a furnace can burn only so much coal to perform its job of keeping a house warm. In the case of the furnace any extra coal piled into it will simply lie there, waiting to be used. In the body extra food that the body can't use will lie there, too—in the form of fat.

To avoid having any left-over fuel that will pile up uselessly and unhealthfully, one can introduce either of two effective dietary systems into his eating. He may either weigh his food exactly to the body's needs by counting calories, or he may use fuel that will not be stored at all, by eating high protein foods which will either be used by the body as they are eaten, or be thrown off as waste, should the body be so well nourished that it has no need for them. While either of these methods is worth while and sensible, the calorie-counting has its drawbacks. Many calorie-counters are of the opinion that they will lose weight and stay healthy on a 1,200 calories-a-day diet even if the 1,200 calories consist of two 600-calorie pieces of pie. This reasoning, of course, can only lead to a physical breakdown much more serious than overweight. The 1,200 calories must be carefully calculated to give your body the nutrients it needs to operate efficiently. The foods must be packed with protein and vitamins. Worthless foods on a low calorie diet are, for all practical purposes, suicidal.

Another objection offered against calorie-counting is the counting itself. The constant referring to a table of numbers, and the temptation to give oneself the benefit of the doubt in borderline cases, or in foods not mentioned in the list, can lead to discouragement and eventual impatience with the whole routine.

Our plan for reducing is simply to rid your diet forever of any foods which the body might not be able to use or throw off. Use only completely natural foods, unprocessed and untreated and prepared in the simplest way—minus salt. This leaves out all white flour and white flour products, all refined sugars and processed fats. On such a diet one can let his appetite rule him as it did early man, who ate what he wanted and could be sure his instincts would tell him when he'd had enough. There was no danger of getting fat, because one simply didn't want to eat enough of anything to do so.

With this scheme, there is no need to weigh foods or consult lists. You have only to limit your choice to natural foods —any kind—and you will soon revert to your proper, healthful weight.

Official Opinion on Patent Weight Reducers

If you're tempted to use an "easy way" to proper weight, and hope thereby to lose weight without dieting, remember this slogan from *Overweight and Underweight*—"No easy way is safe; no safe way is easy." Though this type of statement has received wide publicity, patent reducing preparations are still being bought everywhere. In August, 1957, a Congressional Committee under Representative John A. Blatnik (Democrat of Minnesota) heard doctors and federal officials blast product claims of weight-reducing-pill promoters. Their conclusion, according to *Chemical Week* of August 17, 1957, was this: ". . . the pills just don't do the job and overweight consumers are wasting the money they spend on them." Under existing laws, all that the Federal Trade Commission can do is to order an end to extravagant claims. And what claims they must be! According to an article on these same hearings printed in the

New York Times (August 8, 1957), a spot check in Washington, D. C., showed that over one million dollars a year is spent on reducing pills, candies and gums in that area alone!

Dr. Peter Farago, Deputy Medical Director for the Food and Drug Administration testified (according to the *New York Times* for August 9, 1957) that one drug, phenyl propanolamine, probably would have a mild effect on cutting the appetite if the dosage were doubled. But this might subject users to heart palpitations, high blood pressure and insomnia. In other words, the drug is useless except in dangerous doses.

Several years ago the thyroid was often blamed for overweight problems. Thyroid injections and pills have since been discontinued as utterly useless in reducing. One thyroid-containing patent medicine has even been banned by federal court order, according to the *Allentown Morning Call*, March 14, 1955, edition.

What About Exercise and Steam Baths?

We know that reducing preparations are not the only means we hear of for losing weight. Many persons have definite programs of exercise which they are convinced will keep their weight down. Well, the principle of exercising to burn up excess calories is a sound one, but it takes a tremendous amount of exercise to make a dent in an armour of fat that's been built up over the years through ruinous eating. Many pound-foolish people consume 3,500 calories at a single meal, yet, according to the *Handbook of Physiology and Chemistry* (McDowall), it would take a day of active outdoor life to burn that number of calories in a man. How many eating that kind of food could label their day as one of "outdoor activity?" Even a 6-day bicycle rider only uses 10,000 calories per day, and his is a grind of continual physical exertion over long, long periods of time. There are few of us indeed who have the stamina for the kind of exercise that will take weight off a person who won't combine regular and careful exercise with better dietary habits.

Another of the "easy ways" that doesn't do much good, and can cost a lot of money, is steam baths. After the prescribed period of "steaming," the patient rushes immediately to a scale and discovers, to his intense joy, that there is a weight loss! But he forgets to weigh himself again after he's thirstily drunk several glasses of water to relieve the dryness caused by the loss of water he sweated out, and which accounted for his temporary weight loss. It's all back on him before he's had time to pay his bill and get his clothes on.

Emotions and Overweight

As in many physiological problems, the blame can be traced, in some degree, to psychological sources. Overweight is such a problem (*Newsweek,* November 11, 1952). The article made the point that excess pounds are a sign that the personality is out of kilter. This opinion was the result of psychological tests on 130 overweight women volunteers. Their personalities were not nearly so well adjusted as those of normal weight who were tested. The main problems of these women were these: they were more tense, anxious and depressed than others; they were too preoccupied with themselves; they had a strong fear of failure; they did not seek out new friends; they did not enjoy social relationships. Any doctor will tell you that all of these things can lead to compulsive eating—a craving for food that is every bit as passionate and frenzied as the alcoholic's need for liquor—and just as dangerous.

Women Look Fatter, But Can Lose More Easily

Unfortunately, because their appearance means so much to them, it is sad to report that women look fatter than men, even when their weights are exactly the same. *Science News Letter* reported this in its June 15, 1957, edition, where it carried an article on the work of Dr. Stanley M. Garns, anthropologist of the Fels Institute, Antioch College, Yellow Springs, Ohio. Dr. Garns concluded that women carry more weight on the outside of their frames (where it shows) than men do. He made measurements on 107 healthy women and 81 healthy men by picking up and measuring rolls of fat, such as the "inner tube" around the waist, the upper arms, etc. Out of nine places measured, the women's rolls of fat were larger in all but two. At the same time the total body weight was not materially different for the two sexes.

If it is of any comfort to the women, the Oklahoma City *Times* of November 29, 1954, carried an article quoting the United Nations Food and Agriculture Organization which says a woman can diet and lose weight faster than a man can. A woman only needs 2,300 calories per day to keep going, while a man needs 3,200. Women also do not radiate heat from their bodies as men do, so they can get along on fewer calories. The average woman should eat 900 calories less than her husband, says the piece.

How Much Should One Weigh?

The question of just how much one should weigh is too individual a one for exact designations, but *Parade* magazine for November 3, 1957, carried a guidepost that makes sense. One should weigh 14 per cent less at age 50 than at age 35. Dr. Charles F. Wilkerson, Jr., of New York University Post Graduate Medical School, formulated this norm. He explains it in this way: From age 35, body muscle is likely to decrease due to lowered physical activity, and as it does, it is replaced by fat. Thus while the total body weight might stay the same, the percentage of fat is rising steadily. Nature accounts for these changes, says Dr. Wilkerson, by the fact that your body needs less food to operate smoothly after 35, and, as a result, you should want less to eat.

The Danger of Excess Poundage

There are hundreds of facts, experiments and theories on overweight and diet which we cannot go into here, but they all have one thing in common: they all agree that weighing too much is seriously dangerous. *The Practitioner* for July, 1955, gives a few of the reasons. The article warns that the mortality rate of fat persons is high compared with the standard or expected mortality rate. The causes of death in overweight people are mostly degenerative diseases of the heart, arteries and kidneys. The latter rate is one and one-half times the expected one. Diabetes causes death in four times more obese people than in the average. Cirrhosis of the liver and gall bladder problems occur one and one-half times as often, and childbirth is always open to complications when the mother is appreciably overweight.

Excess poundage is a danger and a disadvantage in every way. Insurance is harder to get and chances for a job lessened as well, when the applicant is beyond his best weight by many pounds. So do yourself a favor. Watch your weight carefully. Eat foods that will be used, not stored unnecessarily. Pay attention to sensible portions of food, and don't eat more than you're actually hungry for. Get enough exercise to help your body use its food effectively. Walking is the best possible exercise. Also when dieting, or any time, be sure that your body's needs are being met by taking plenty of supplemental foods, especially vitamin B and C.

If you're eating properly, weight won't be a problem for you. If you are not eating properly, it's a problem you can't avoid!

CHAPTER 143

Reducing Sensibly

Pounds of reducing candies and cases of reducing pills won't take off those extra pounds. The only answer is a sensible diet—high in protein and low in carbohydrates.

"Overweight is always curable, and there are no exceptions to this rule." We're quoting Dr. Max Millman from an article in *Today's Health* (April, 1957). We couldn't agree more. There are over thirty million Americans heavier than they should be. Fortunately, they are becoming more and more aware of the danger each unnecessary pound represents. Just about any periodical you would care to name has printed some type of diet within the past year. Some magazines have made diets a regular feature, so that a new plan for peeling off unwanted pounds appears as consistently as the table of contents or the letters to the editor.

There Is No Miraculous Way of Reducing

Of course, it would be impossible to comment on all of the diets that have come to our attention, but, as our readers know, we have remarked on several that reached more than average prominence. Often we were impelled to do what we could do to warn our readers against the dangers of the fad diets that swept the country. Sometimes we were able to add our recommendations to a diet which had appeal as well as sensible, natural method to its credit. The point is that there is no miraculous 4-day formula that can make a lily out of a dandelion, or a fair lady out of a fat one. You can eat appetite-killing candies by the boxful, swallow packets of reducing pills by the hundreds, you can ride an electric horse or strap yourself into reducing machines until your brains are a-jangle from the shaking, but unless the basis of your reducing is a simple diet, high in protein and low in carbohydrates, with sweets severely cut down or eliminated entirely, you're wasting your time. The type of food you eat, even more than the amount, is what governs your poundage. If you are eating foods the body can use efficiently, they will not show up in a month as an increase in waist measurement. Eating much of foods that the body can only use sparingly will force the body to store them in folds of fat which are the despair of so many women who can't zip up a skirt and men whose top button won't close.

Will Power and Common Sense to Reduce

An autobiographical article on diet appeared in *The Ladies' Home Journal* for January, 1957. The ideas and point of view seemed so sensible and realistic that we are calling it to your attention. It is entitled "The Diet That Turned Me Into A Model." The author tells the story of how she went from fatness to fitness when will power and common sense took over.

Her weight troubles began when she went to boarding school. Feeling insecure in the strange environment, our heroine took to tossing down the calories by the thousands. She gives the reader the impression that the only time she wasn't eating was during the walk from the dining room to her bedroom where veritable mountains of edibles were stored. Well-meant hints from her teachers about the state of her circumference aroused resentment or led her to short-lived reforms with the cooperation of her roommate. As an example of the latter, she tells of the time they both resolved to use a diet based on eating a special type of candy before going down to dinner. The experiment was a complete fiasco because before the girls knew it, they'd eaten the whole box of appetite-killers and were more than ready to go to dinner to fill in the gaps!

Embarrassment at being "left out" and a frank talk with her doctor finally made the author resolve to cut down and revise her eating habits, as the only way to health, slimness and popularity.

The diet this young lady allotted herself in a typical week is printed beside a picture which gives evidence of its efficacy. To us it sounds fine, with a few exceptions. For those of our readers who have read the *Journal* article, and might wish to see what our idea of dieting might be, we offer a flexible scheme for eating healthfully and attaining a healthful and attractive weight level.

Our Diet Compared With That of the *Journal*

The variations on the suggestions above are infinite. Your health menu is limited only by your imagination and by good sense. Change the menus in any way you like—but stay with foods high in protein and low in carbohydrates. Avoid the white flour products, the artificially sweetened foods, use no salt and let the processed foods stay in the grocery store.

This is a diet one can live with permanently. No need to count calories or weigh portions. An extra peach now and then will never make you fat, but an extra plate of ice cream certainly might.

In comparison, the foods we suggest and those suggested in the *Journal* piece are not too dissimilar. Both lists have been formulated with solid nutritional basics in mind as well as the possibility of maintaining such a diet indefinitely.

Of course, we differ with the *Journal's* suggestion of coffee or tea as beverages. Artificial sweeteners are mentioned once or twice and our readers know we abhor their use. We also advise against the milk products that are included, and the cooking of vegetables that are better served raw such as broiled tomatoes.

To Maintain a Healthy Body

Despite our changes we are pleased to see such a diet printed in a magazine with the circulation of *The Ladies' Home Journal*. It indicates to the public that a healthful diet is synonymous not with food faddism but with intelligence and good sense. We think that, on such a diet, a person will lose unnecessary weight while maintaining good health, due to both the nutritious foods suggested and the method of preparation. To insure against deficiencies we added food supplements to the outline. Wheat germ and brewer's yeast for vitamins E and B, plus a daily intake of vitamin C (rose hips) would be a minimal inclusion. Some extra source of unsaturated fatty acids should also be added in the form of fish liver oil perles which will also supply vitamins A and D.

Individual needs would dictate other changes, but at least the *Journal* has printed a diet that will get people off on the right foot. It doesn't suggest that one stop eating everything but dextrose and skimmed milk for a month, nor that one eat a pound of rice a day to the exclusion of all else. It says what we believe: Good food results in a healthy body, and a healthy body is one which maintains its proper weight.

Prevention's **Healthful Reducing Plan**

Give yourself a fighting chance by beginning the day with a breakfast that can work for you—plenty of protein, fortified with extra nutrients carried in food supplements, such as wheat germ or brewer's yeast.

> 1 large glass of fresh raw fruit or vegetable juice (not citrus).
> 1 cup fresh berries or other fresh fruit.
> 1 average portion (about 4 oz.) of broiled liver or fresh fish—or 2 eggs, boiled or poached.
> 1 cup herb tea or a glass of soybean milk.
> Your morning food supplements.

For the light meal of the day, you can try your own variation of this menu:

> 1 cup fresh fruit.
> 1 serving of lean meat, such as chicken or broiled, lean hamburger—or a fresh vegetable plate of, say, sliced tomatoes, cucumbers, carrots and asparagus.
> 1 serving of homemade apple sauce (no sugar).
> 1 glass fresh juice.
> Your normal food supplements.

For the large meal of the day, how about something like this:

A relish tray of iced fresh vegetables (whole small tomatoes, celery stalks, green peppers, etc.).

1 serving of lean meat (baked or broiled, such as steak, veal, or lambchops, liver, turkey, etc.).

1 medium-sized baked potato (white or sweet).

1 hot, fresh vegetable, simply prepared, such as spinach, broccoli, cauliflower, stringbeans, etc. (Emphasize the green and yellow ones.)

A large salad bowl, brimming with as many green leafy vegetables as you can find, tossed in a salad oil (olive oil, sunflower seed or corn oil), sprinkled with freshly-chopped herbs such as oregano, parsley, mint, chives, etc. (You need a fresh salad daily for the unsaturated fatty acids in the oil you use for a dressing, as well as the nutrients you get from raw vegetables.) Fresh pineapple wedges for dessert.

1 cup herb tea.

Food supplements.

INDEX